# Windows 2000 Quick Lau
# and Additional Window C

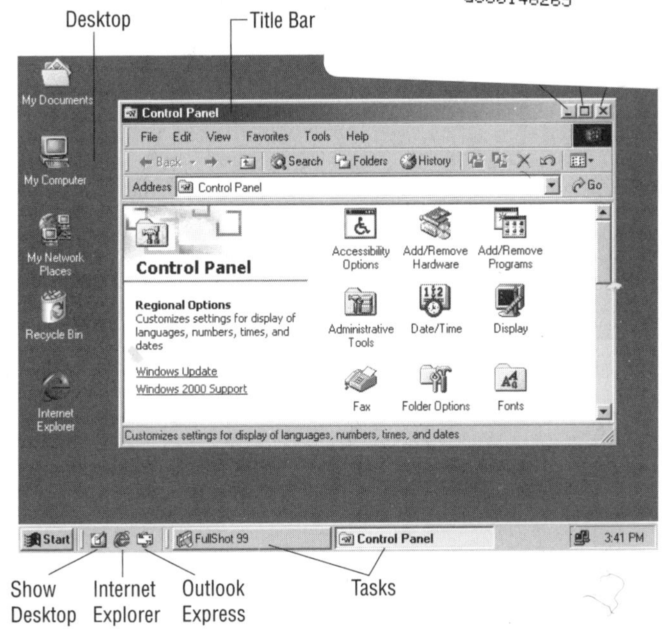


# Windows Explorer Components

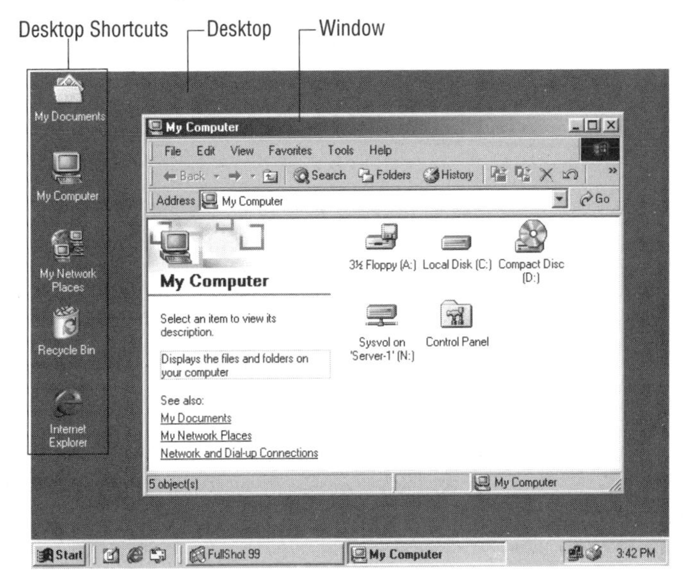

# Windows® 2000

## Instant Reference

Jutta VanStean

San Francisco • Paris • Düsseldorf • Soest • London

Associate Publisher: Roger Stewart
Contracts and Licensing Manager: Kristine O'Callaghan
Acquisitions & Developmental Editor: Ellen Dendy
Editor: Elizabeth Welch
Project Editor: Linda Good
Technical Editor: Dallas Releford
Book Designer: Seventh Street Studios
Graphic Illustrator: Tony Jonick
Electronic Publishing Specialist: Maureen Forys, Happenstance Type-O-Rama
Project Team Leader: Teresa Trego
Proofreaders: Dave Nash and Nancy Riddiough
Indexer: Nancy Guenther
Cover Designer: Design Site
Cover Illustrator/Photographer: Sergie Loobkoff, Design Site



Library of Congress Card Number: 99-68699
ISBN: 0-7821-2572-7

Manufactured in the United States of America

10 9 8 7 6 5 4 3 2 1

*Für meine Eltern, Dr. Rolf und Irene Galle.*

# Acknowledgments

As is true with any published material, many different people took part in the making of this book. I would like to take this opportunity to thank all of them for their contributions, direct or indirect, and would like to say up front that the process of writing this book has been a truly joyful experience.

I'd like to start with the people at Sybex, all of whom are wonderful people to work with. First, there's Tracy Brown, who was the first Developmental Editor on the project. Tracy, I very much appreciated your patience in answering my many questions at the outset of the project. During the course of this project, Tracy moved to Ireland, so from that point on I had the pleasure of working with Ellen Dendy, Acquisitions and Developmental Editor. Thank you, Ellen, for the expert guidance and project coordination you provided throughout this project. Later in the project, I met Linda Good, who worked as the Project Editor. My gratitude, Linda, for doing such a great job keeping all of the editing efforts flowing smoothly and making sure that everyone always had all of the information necessary to go through a successful editing process. I would also like to take this opportunity to thank all of the other people at Sybex who contributed to the making of this book, but whom I did not have a chance to meet directly. Specifically, I'd like to thank Teresa Trego, the Project Team Leader, who managed the book in Production; Maureen Forys, the Electronic Publishing Specialist, who molded the book into physical shape; and Dave Nash and Nancy Riddiough, the book's proofreaders.

As the editing process went into full swing, I was delighted to meet and work with my freelance editor, Liz Welch. Liz, my sincere thanks to you for thoroughly questioning any and all things unclear, and doing such a superb job editing the manuscript. It will make this book a joy for anyone to read. Thank you also to my freelance technical editor, Dallas Releford, for verifying all of the facts presented in this book.

Additionally, I would like to express my heartfelt gratitude to Todd Cameron, who couldn't have been more supportive. Todd, thank you so much for always being there, and for understanding when my writing at times kept me in front of the computer for hours. Thanks also go to all of my friends, for your support always.

Finally, I would like to say thank you to my parents, without whose unquestioning support I would not be here today writing these words. Danke, Mama und Papa, for always having been there for me, and for having taught me that I can accomplish whatever I choose. Danke also for having taught me to enjoy life in all that I do, as it is short. Nothing I have ever accomplished would I have been able to do without you.

# Introduction

Windows 2000 Professional and Server are built on Windows NT Workstation and Server technology and also incorporate features and functions of Windows 98. They provide you with many previously existing features and functionality, as well as several new and enhanced features and functionality in the areas of reliability, management, connectivity, security, and performance. Though enhanced, the GUI interface of Windows 2000 is very similar to that of earlier versions, so you can get started using Windows 2000 right away. Some of the functions available in earlier versions have been moved to different locations or have changed names; this book will tell you how to access any covered function. Additionally, you can check the Windows 2000 Help system for the entries New Ways to Do Familiar Tasks and If You've Used Windows Before.

# How This Book Is Organized

This book contains a detailed, alphabetical guide to the major features and commands found in Windows 2000 Professional and Server. Each entry in this guide provides you with a description of the feature or command, tells you how to access it, explains the interface (such as screens, menus, and toolbars), and, in many cases, provides step-by-step instructions to perform tasks related to the command or function. Most entries also contain one or more references to other entries so that you can easily find related information. Throughout this guide, you'll also find graphic images that illustrate topics or tasks that are being discussed.

# Who Should Read This Book and Why?

*Windows 2000 Instant Reference* was written for beginning, intermediate, and advanced users as well as technical personnel (such as administrators and technical support personnel) who will be using Windows 2000. In this book, you'll find information on anything from using the Start button and menu, to configuring your desktop environment, to creating and configuring objects in

Active Directory. No matter where on the learning curve you are, you'll find this book useful. Each entry in this guide covers the subject at hand thoroughly but doesn't get bogged down in details. And, because the book is organized alphabetically, you'll be able to quickly find entries regarding the subject you're interested in. Using this book, you'll be able to gain an understanding of a given topic and learn how to perform related tasks, thus making you more proficient.

## Setup Considerations

The setup used in the writing of this book was a Windows 2000 Server computer installed with default options, functioning as a domain controller with Active Directory installed, and a Windows 2000 Professional computer that is a member of the domain. Both computers were formatted with the NTFS file system as recommended for Windows 2000. If your setup is different, available commands and functions may vary. This guide indicates when a function or command is available only in Windows 2000 Professional or only in Windows 2000 Server, or only on a server computer that performs a certain role within a network (such as domain controller).

## Conventions Used in This Book

Throughout the book, you'll find consistently used conventions that make it easier to find information. You'll see graphic images of menu options and/or icons just below each entry title (where applicable) so that you can easily tell what topic is being discussed. You'll also often find graphic images or icons that are being discussed within a topic included as a visual reference. At the end of an entry, you may find *See also* references. These references point you to other entries in the book and may provide either information necessary to use the currently discussed feature, or information that is simply related and will provide you with greater understanding. For example, under the entry for Logical Drives you will see the following reference:

**See Also** Microsoft Management Console (MMC), Computer Management, WMI Control

You'll find additional information provided in the form of Notes, Tips, and Warnings, as described below:

**NOTE** Notes provide additional information about the current topic.

**TIP** Tips give you information on how to better use a function, alternative ways to perform a task/function, or shortcuts to a task/function.

**WARNING** Warnings alert you to potential problems when using a feature or performing a task.

# Terms Used in This Book

The following terms are used throughout the book to indicate specific actions:

**Click** Move the mouse pointer over an item and press and release the left mouse button. This action often selects an item.

**Double-click** Move the mouse pointer over an item and press and release the left mouse button twice in fast succession. This starts an action (such as running a program or opening a folder).

**Drag** Move the mouse pointer over an item, press the left mouse button to select it, then drag the item to a different location (or drag to resize an item, such as a window). Release the left mouse button at the desired destination.

**Right-click** Move the mouse pointer over an item, then press the right mouse button. This activates a pop-up menu that contains items appropriate to the item you right-clicked. The pop-up menu is sometimes also called the shortcut menu.

INSTANT REFERENCE

# Windows 2000

# Accessibility

Choose Start ➢ Programs ➢ Accessories ➢ Accessibility to access the Accessibility Wizard, Magnifier, Narrator, On-Screen Keyboard, and Utility Manager.

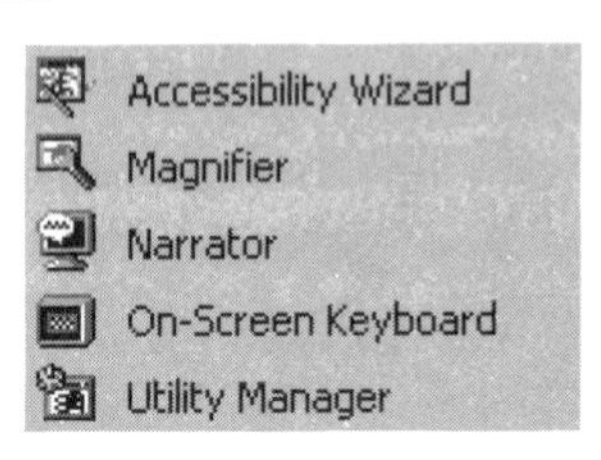


**See Also** Accessibility Wizard, Magnifier, Narrator, On-Screen Keyboard, Utility Manager, Accessibility Options

# Accessibility Options

Configures settings that make using the computer easier for users who have physical disabilities, such as hearing and vision impairments, as well as users who have difficulty using the keyboard and mouse.

Choose Start ➢ Settings ➢ Control Panel and double-click Accessibility Options to open the Accessibility Options dialog box.

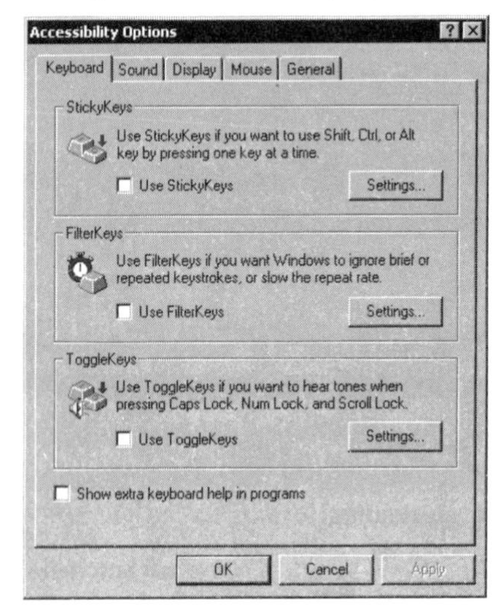

**TIP** Many of the Accessibility Options can be turned on and off with a keyboard shortcut to make them accessible to users who have trouble using a mouse. These shortcuts will be explained in this section. Shortcuts are enabled by default; you can turn them off by clicking the appropriate Settings button and deselecting the Use Shortcut check box.

The Accessibility Options dialog box contains five tabs: Keyboard, Sound, Display, Mouse, and General. Select the appropriate check box to turn on a feature, and click the Settings button to adjust the default settings.

**Keyboard** Contains the StickyKeys, FilterKeys, and ToggleKeys options. Useful for people who have trouble using the keyboard.

StickyKeys means that when you press the Shift, Ctrl, Alt, or Windows logo key, that key stays activated until you press a key other than the Shift, Ctrl, Alt, or Windows logo key. (A tone also sounds when you press a key with StickyKeys activated.) Therefore, users can press key combinations without physically having to hold down two or more keys. FilterKeys means that either repeated or short keystrokes are ignored and the repeat rate is slowed down. ToggleKeys is used to sound tones when you press the Caps Lock, Num Lock, or Scroll Lock key. You can also specify that programs display additional keyboard-related help.

**TIP** The shortcut for StickyKeys is pressing the Shift key five times. The shortcut for FilterKeys is holding down the right Shift key for eight seconds. The shortcut for ToggleKeys is holding down the Num Lock key for five seconds.

**Sound** Contains the SoundSentry and ShowSounds options. Useful for people with hearing impairments.

SoundSentry means that when the system generates a sound, part of the screen flashes to alert the user. ShowSounds means that when programs use speech or sounds, text or icons are displayed to represent/explain the speech or sound.

**Display** Contains the High Contrast option. Useful for individuals with vision impairments.

High Contrast means that the Windows display will use certain fonts and colors that make reading the screen easier.

**TIP** The shortcut for High Contrast is pressing Left Alt+Left Shift+Print Screen.

**Mouse** Contains the MouseKeys option. Useful for people who have trouble using the mouse.

MouseKeys means that you can use the keyboard's numeric keyboard to control the mouse pointer.

**TIP** The shortcut for MouseKeys is pressing Left Alt+Left Shift+Num Lock. For a complete explanation of how MouseKeys maps the numeric keypad to control mouse pointer movements, search the Help System Index for the keyword MouseKeys.

**General** Contains options for Automatic Reset, Notification, SerialKey Devices, and Administrative Options.

Automatic Reset means that options are turned off after a specified amount of time during which the computer is idle. Notification lets you specify warning messages or sounds when features are turned on or off by using shortcut keys. SerialKey Devices lets you enable support for an input device that is not a keyboard or mouse. Administrative Options lets you apply settings to the logon desktop and to defaults for new users.

**See Also** Accessibility Wizard, Magnifier, Narrator, On-Screen Keyboard, Utility Manager, Accessibility

# Accessibility Wizard

Wizard that helps you set up Accessibility Options to make the computer and Windows easier to use if you have difficulties with your vision, hearing, or mobility. Choose Start ➢ Programs ➢ Accessories ➢ Accessibility ➢ Accessibility Wizard to open the Welcome to the Accessibility Wizard dialog box.

Follow these steps:

1. In the Welcome to the Accessibility Wizard dialog box, click Next.
2. Select the size font you're comfortable reading, and then click Next.
3. Choose whether you want to change the font size to increase the text in some areas of the screen, such as title bars and menus, and whether to use Microsoft Magnifier, which enlarges part of the screen. You can also specify whether you want to use personalized menus (enabled by default). If the option is available, choose whether to switch to a lower screen resolution. Then click Next.
4. Check the appropriate check boxes that correspond to a disability or difficulty that applies to you. Click Restore Default Settings to restore default settings (this undoes any changes you made on previous screens). Click Next.
5. Depending on your choice in step 4, you are now prompted to adjust various Windows settings to fit your needs. Click Next after making each selection. You can choose to:
   - Adjust the size of scroll bars and window borders.
   - Change the size of icons.
   - Alter the contrast of text and colors on the screen.
   - Change the size and color of the mouse pointer.
   - Display visual warnings for Windows sounds and captions for other programs' speech and sounds.
   - Use StickyKeys to make pressing key combinations easier.
   - Use BounceKeys to ignore repeated keystrokes.
   - Use ToggleKeys to make a sound when Caps Lock, Num Lock, or Scroll Lock is pressed.

- Show extra keyboard help when applicable and available.
- Use MouseKeys to control the mouse pointer through the numeric keypad.
- Adjust MouseKeys' settings, such as when to activate MouseKeys and what pointer speed to use, and whether the mouse should be set up as right- or left-handed.
- Disable personalized menus.
- Specify whether to always enable accessibility features and whether to make these settings apply to the current user and all new users, or only the current user.

6. On the Save Settings to File screen, click Save Settings to save your settings to a file, which you can then take to another computer. Click Next.
7. On the Completing the Accessibility Wizard screen, review your choices. If you want to make changes, use the Back button to return to a choice and change it. Finally, click Finish.
8. If you made changes to the desktop display, you will notice these changes now. Any sound- or mouse-related changes will not be obvious until sounds are played and their corresponding captions displayed or you use the mouse through the keyboard.

**See Also** Accessibility, Magnifier, Narrator, On-Screen Keyboard, Utility Manager, Accessibility Options

# Accessories

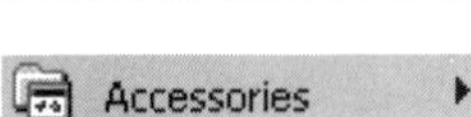


Windows 2000 predefined program group. Windows 2000 includes many programs you can use to configure your Windows 2000 computer and perform different functions. You can find many of these programs in the Accessories program group. To access options in this group, choose Start ➢ Programs ➢ Accessories. The programs and program groups available in Accessories depend on the choices you made during the Windows 2000 installation and when you installed other programs. If you selected defaults, they will include the following:

**Program groups** Accessibility, Communications, Entertainment, Games, System Tools. Windows 2000 Server also includes the Microsoft Script Debugger program group, which is installed if you didn't deselect the default installation option for Internet Information Server (IIS).

**Programs** Address Book, Calculator, Command Prompt, Imaging, Notepad, Paint, Synchronize, Windows Explorer, and WordPad.

**See Also** Accessibility, Communications, Entertainment, Games, System Tools, Microsoft Script Debugger, Address Book, Calculator, Command Prompt, Imaging, Notepad, Paint, Synchronize, Windows Explorer, WordPad

# Active Desktop

Windows 2000 lets you set up your desktop to look and function like a Web page. With Active Desktop turned on, you can display and update Web content on your desktop. An example of this is displaying a stock ticker on your desktop that automatically updates to show you the latest stock quotes. The fact that Web content can be automatically updated is why the desktop is called *active*.

You can enable the Active Desktop feature in several ways:

- Choose Start ➢ Settings ➢ Control Panel, then open Folder Options. On the General tab, under Active Desktop, select Enable Web Content on My Desktop.
- Right-click anywhere on the desktop and choose Active Desktop ➢ Show Web Content from the pop-up menu.
- Choose Start ➢ Settings ➢ Control Panel, then open Display. Select the Web tab, then check Show Web Content on My Active Desktop.

By default, when you enable the Active Desktop feature, your current home page displays on the desktop. If your current home page is located on the Internet, you must be connected to the Internet for the page to display. You can change which page you want to display on your desktop on the Web tab of Display Properties.

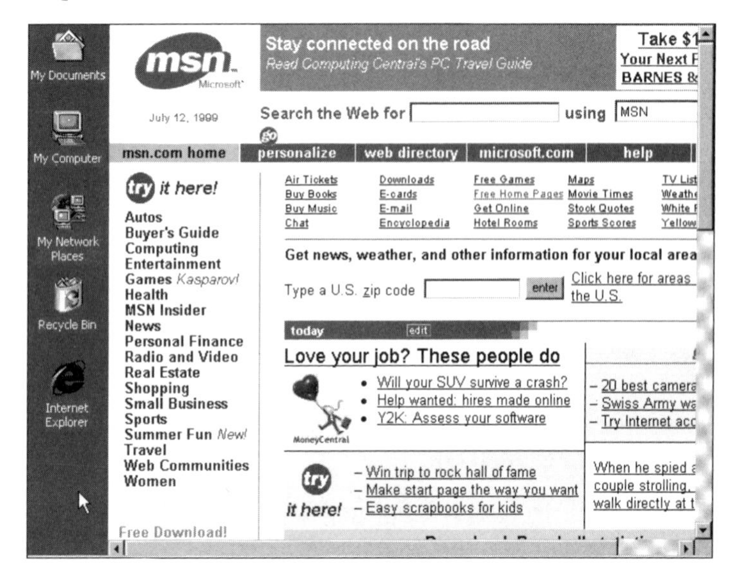


Once the Active Desktop is enabled, you have several other options available to configure your Active Desktop. To access these options, right-click anywhere in a blank area of the desktop and choose Active Desktop. The following options are now available:

**Show Web Content** Toggles the Active Desktop feature off and on.

**Show Desktop Items** Toggles the display of desktop icons off and on.

**Lock Desktop Items** Toggles the Lock Desktop Items feature off and on. Locking desktop items means that you cannot resize or move Active Desktop items.

**Synchronize** Updates Web content.

**My Current Homepage** Toggles the display of your current home page off and on.

See the subheading Web Tab under the heading Display in this book for more information on adding Web content to your Active Desktop.

**See Also** Display, Folder Options

# Active Directory

Scalable directory service new in Windows 2000 Server. Active Directory lets you identify resources, called *objects*, in the network, and makes those resources accessible to users via a single logon. Examples of resources are users, users data, groups, computers, servers, and printers. Active Directory has a component called the Directory, whose function is to store information about these resources, as well as store services that make that information available. Because all network resources are represented as objects in the Directory, Active Directory provides single-point administration.

Active Directory uses DNS (Domain Name System) for its naming system. It also supports other name formats, such as HTTP URL, UNC, RFC 822 (name @domain.extension), and LDAP URL. Active Directory supports LDAP (Lightweight Directory Access Protocol) versions 2 and 3 for accessing directory service information, and HTTP (Hypertext Transfer Protocol), which enables users of the network to display Active Directory objects as HTML pages.

**TIP** Because Active Directory supports LDAP versions 2 and 3, it can share information with other directory services that support those versions of LDAP, such as Novell's directory service, NDS.

Active Directory is installed on Windows 2000 domain controllers. Because in Windows 2000 all domain controllers in a domain are peers (multimaster model), each domain controller in the domain holds a copy of the Directory. When you install Active Directory on a domain controller, the Directory database and the shared system volume are created. The shared system volume is called SYSVOL, and its default location is SYSTEMROOT\SYSVOL. By default, it contains some of the domain's group policy objects as well as scripts.

**TIP** By default, SYSTEMROOT on the Windows 2000 Server computer is C:\WINNT\SYSVOL.

## Active Directory Structure

With Active Directory, you can create a Directory structure that will let you organize your network resources logically according to your company's internal structure, rather than based on the physical location of resources. The Active Directory structure consists of objects, such as user accounts, computers, printers, files, organizational units, and domains, as well as trees, forests, and sites.

### *Object*

An object represents a resource in the network. It has attributes whose values define the characteristics of the object. A user account, for example, might include the first name, last name, logon name, and other attributes. Examples of the attribute values would be Jutta, VanStean, and JVANSTEAN. Some objects are container objects, meaning they can contain other objects, such as organizational units and domains. Objects are grouped into object classes, such as users, groups, computers, and domains.

### *Organizational Unit*

An organizational unit (OU) is a container object that can hold other objects, such as users, groups, printers, other OUs, and computers. OUs are used within domains to organize objects into logical groupings for administrative purposes. An OU might represent a department or building, for example.

**TIP** Although there is no limit as to the depth of the OU structure, a too-deep structure will eventually negatively affect performance.

### *Domain*

Domains are container objects that are used to logically group all objects in the network. They can contain objects such as users, groups, computers, printers, files, and OUs. Active Directory can contain one or more domains to reflect your organization's structure. Each domain keeps information only about the objects stored in that domain. Active Directory controls access to objects in a domain through access control lists (ACLs). ACLs hold the information that specifies which users can access a domain object and what type of access is granted.

**TIP** You should not have more than 1 million objects per domain, although theoretically a domain can hold up to 10 million objects.

**Domain Controllers** Domain controllers are computers that run the Windows 2000 Server operating system and also contain a copy of the (Active Directory) Directory. They perform authentication for the domain, and they service Active Directory requests made by clients or other server computers on the network.

**Member Servers** Servers that do not contain a copy of the Directory are called member servers. An example of a member server might be an application server.

**TIP** Servers that have Windows 2000 Server installed but are not part of a domain are called stand-alone servers.

**Mixed Mode vs. Native Mode** Domains can be in either mixed or native mode. By default, Windows 2000 domain controllers are installed in mixed mode, which means that both Windows 2000 and Windows NT domain controllers can be part of the domain. Native mode means that only Windows 2000 domain controllers can be part of the domain. An administrator has to manually switch the mode from mixed to native to change the mode of a domain controller.

### *Tree*

An Active Directory tree is a grouping of one or more domains that use the same contiguous name space.

Note the following characteristics:

- A child domain's name is made up of the relative name of the child domain name with the name of the parent domain appended to it.

- Domains in a tree share the same global catalog. A global catalog holds information about all objects in the tree.
- Domains in a tree share the same schema. A schema defines the object types that can be stored in Active Directory.

### *Forest*

An Active Directory forest is a grouping of one or more trees. Each tree in the forest uses its own name space.

Note the following characteristics:

- Each tree in a forest has its own naming structure.
- Trees in a forest share the same schema.
- Domains in a forest share the same global catalog.
- Forests enable communication across the entire organization although domains in a forest operate independently of one another.

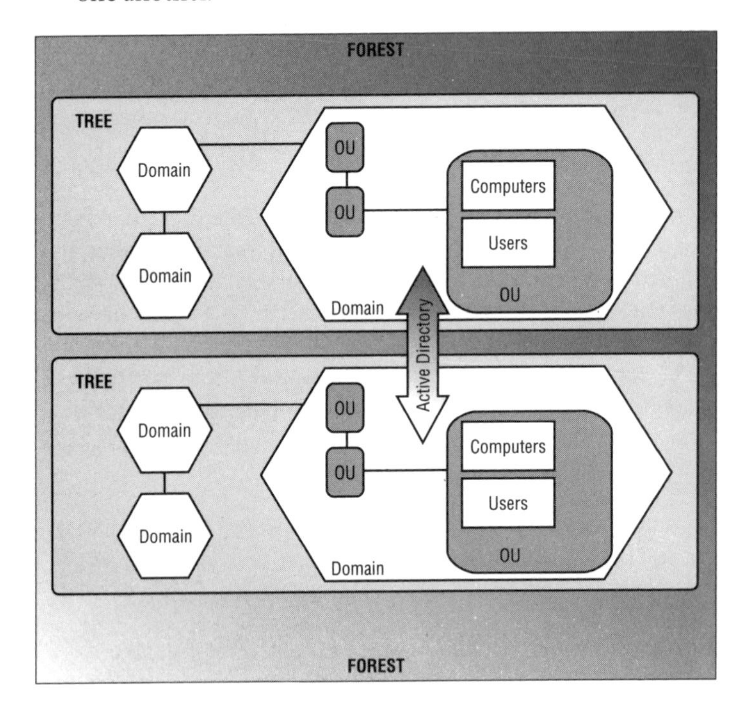

### *Sites*

Sites define the Active Directory physical structure. A site is composed of one or more IP subnets. The boundary of a site is usually the same as that of a LAN. Grouped subnets should be connected via fast connections (minimum speed 512Kbps). Sites contain computer and connection objects, which you use to configure inter-site replication.

## Trust Relationships

Trust relationships can exist between domains to enable user access from one domain to objects in another domain. Two types of trust relationships exist:

**Two-way transitive trust** Automatically established between parent and child domains in a tree. Enables access from all domains to all objects in all domains in a tree or forest. Also used between top-level domains in a forest.

**Explicit one-way trust** Used to establish trusts between domains in separate trees. Enables backward compatibility with Windows NT 4.*x*. Also enables trust relationships between domains in separate trees.

## Replication

Active Directory employs the multimaster replication model, whereby all domain controllers are peers to one another or, put a different way, no one domain controller is the master domain controller and each domain controller stores a copy of the Directory. Changes to the Directory can be made to any of the copies on any of the domain controllers in the domain, and are replicated to all other copies. This ensures fault tolerance. Should a domain controller become unavailable, another domain controller is still present to provide services and information to users.

**See Also** Active Directory Domains and Trusts, Active Directory Sites and Services, Active Directory Users and Computers, Configure Your Server

# Active Directory Domains and Trusts

Active Directory Domains and Trusts Microsoft Management Console (MMC) snap-in installed on Windows 2000 domain controllers that lets you manage Active Directory domains and trusts on a Windows 2000 domain controller. To access Active Directory Domains and Trusts, choose Start ➢ Programs ➢ Administrative Tools ➢ Active Directory Domains and Trusts. The console tree displays the available domains.

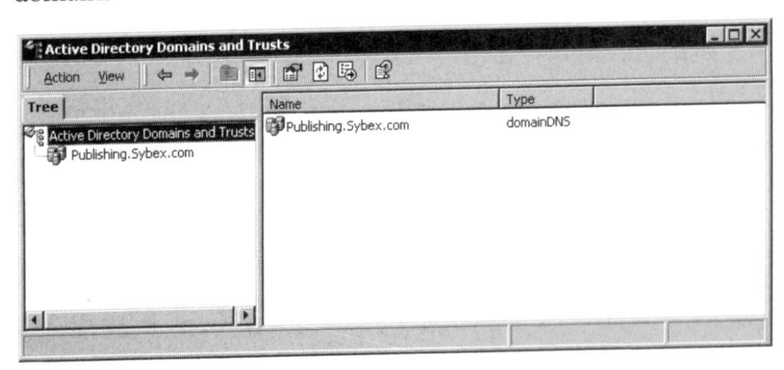


## Domain Properties

To access the domain's properties, select the domain object in the console tree and choose Action ➢ Properties. You'll see the following three tabs:

**General** Lets you view the domain's name, the domain's pre-Windows 2000 name, the description, and the current operation mode. You can click Change Mode to change the mode from mixed to native. Once the domain is in native mode, it cannot be changed back to mixed mode.

**WARNING** Do not change the domain mode unless all domain controllers in the domain are running Windows 2000. If you still have Windows NT 4.0 domain controllers in the domain, replication between Windows 2000 domain controllers and Windows NT 4.0 backup domain controllers stops.

**Trusts** Lets you view and edit existing trust relationships (both explicit and transitive), and add and remove explicit trust relationships between this domain and other domains. For an explicit trust relationship to be established, you must establish the applicable portion of the trust relationship in the properties of one domain and the other portion that completes the trust relationship in the properties of the other domain.

**Managed By** Lets you specify the name of an Active Directory user who will manage the domain.

### Managing the Domain

To manage the domain, right-click the domain object and choose Manage. This opens the Active Directory Users and Computers MMC snap-in, where you can perform many domain management functions.

**See Also** Active Directory Users and Computers, Microsoft Management Console (MMC)

## Active Directory Users and Computers

MMC snap-in installed by default on Windows 2000 domain controllers that lets you create, modify, delete, and organize Active Directory user and computer accounts, groups, OUs, contacts, printers, and shared folders in the Directory. To access Active Directory Users and Computers, choose Start ➢ Programs ➢ Administrative Tools ➢ Active Directory Users and Computers.

**TIP** Alternatively, you can choose Start ➢ Programs ➢ Administrative Tools ➢ Active Directory Domains and Trusts, then right-click the domain object and choose Manage.

### The Active Directory Users and Computers MMC Console Snap-in Window

Lets you manage Active Directory users, groups, computers, and other published resources through Action menu options. The options available on the Action menu vary depending on the item you have selected in the console tree pane. Some of the Action menu options are also available on the toolbar.

### Console Tree

The console tree contains the following items by default for the current domain:

**Domain** Contains folders for Active Directory user and computer management for that domain.

**Builtin Folder** Contains the domain local groups that are created by default, such as Administrators, Print Operators, and Users.

**Computers Folder** Contains the computer accounts created in this domain.

**Domain Controllers Folder** Contains the domain's domain controllers.

**ForeignSecurityPrincipals Folder** Contains foreign security principals. A security principal is a user or computer account, or group. Security principals are objects with an automatically assigned security identifier. The security identifier enables these objects to log into the network and access resources. A foreign security principal is a security principal from an external domain that has been given access to resources in this domain. An external domain is a domain in another forest with which a trust relationship has been established.

**Users Folder** Contains user and group accounts created in this domain. Includes both built-in and manually created user and group accounts.

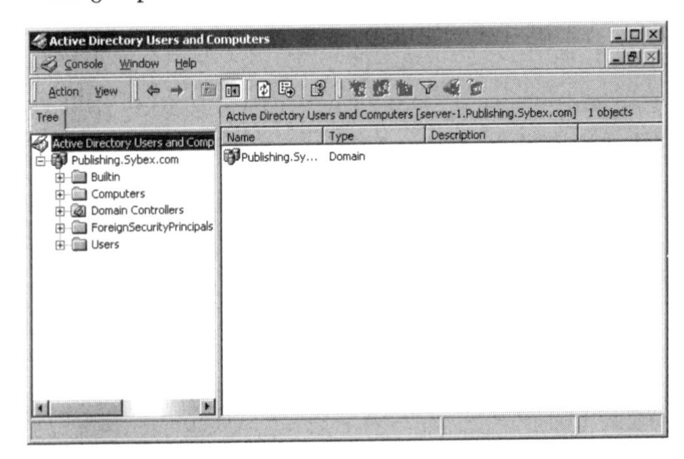

Additional folders are available by selecting the domain object and choosing View ➢ Advanced Features. This displays the folders LostAndFound and System. These folders are used for advanced configuration.

## Organizational Units

You can use organizational units (OUs) to organize objects according to your organization's structure. For example, you might want to create OUs to represent your company's departments and then add users and other resources to these OUs.

### *Creating an Organizational Unit*

To create an OU, follow these steps:

1. Right-click the domain object in the console tree pane, then select New ➢ Organizational Unit.
2. Type a name for the OU and click OK. The OU is created and a folder with the OU's name is added to the console tree pane below the domain object.

## User Accounts

Active Directory user accounts enable people to log onto the network and use network resources. Some user accounts are created by default, such as Administrator, Guest, and others, depending on the services installed. Two built-in user accounts are created by default: Administrator and Guest. Additional user accounts are also created automatically, depending on the services installed.

### *Creating User Accounts*

You can create a new user account in any folder; however, Microsoft recommends that you create them in OUs. To do so, follow these steps:

1. Right-click the folder in the console tree pane where you want to create the new user (for example, Users or a particular OU you created) and select New ➢ User.

**TIP** Alternatively, you can select the appropriate folder or object, and then click the Create a New User in the Current Container button on the toolbar.

2. In the New Object – User dialog box, type a first and last name for the user in the appropriate text boxes. As you do this, the Full Name text box is filled in automatically; however, you can change the full name to something different afterward.

3. Type a logon name for the user in the User Logon Name text box. If necessary, select the domain from the domain drop-down list. As you type the logon name, the pre-Windows 2000 logon name is filled in automatically (for backward compatibility). You can change the pre-Windows 2000 logon name if you wish.

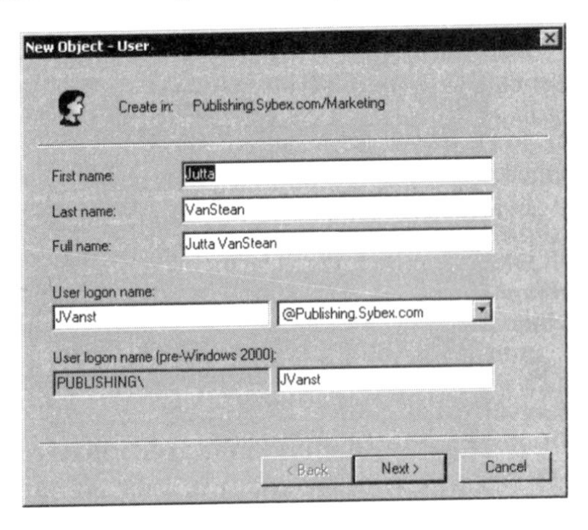


4. Click Next.

5. If you wish, type a password for the user in the Password text box and confirm the password by typing it again in the Confirm Password text box.

6. Check any password options you want to apply to the user. Choices include:

   **User Must Change Password at Next Logon** Requires that, to be able to log on the next time, the user must enter the current password and then specify (create) a new password at logon time.

   **User Cannot Change Password** Specifies that the user cannot change his or her password.

**Password Never Expires** Specifies that the password does not expire.

**Account Is Disabled** Deactivates the account.

7. Click Next.
8. Read the summary information. This includes where the account will be created, the user's full name and logon name, and any password options you chose. Use the Back button to make any necessary changes.
9. Click Finish to create the user.

### User Account Properties

You can configure user accounts by using the user account's property sheet. To access a user account's properties, right-click the account and select Properties, or select the account and choose Action ➢ Properties. The resulting property sheet contains many tabs; what tabs are available depends on the Windows 2000 Server installation and configuration. Use the right and left arrows to the right of the tabs to reveal hidden tabs. With a default installation, you'll see the following tabs: General, Address, Account, Profile, Telephones, Organization, Member Of, Dial-in, Environment, Sessions, Remote Control, and Terminal Services Profile.

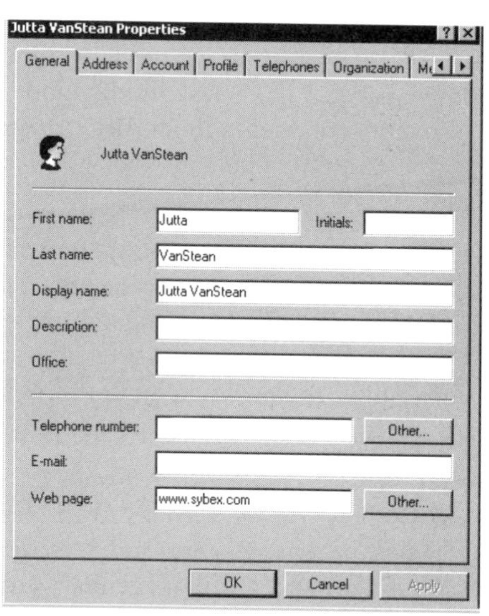

**General** Lets you configure items such as first name, last name, initials, display name, description, office, telephone numbers, e-mail, and Web page addresses. To configure and view additional telephone numbers or Web page addresses, click the appropriate Other button.

**Address** Lets you enter postal address information, such as street, P.O. box, city, state/province, zip/postal code, and country/region.

**Account** Lets you configure account information/options, such as Windows 2000 and pre-Windows 2000 logon name, logon hours (when the user is allowed to log on), which computers the user can log onto, password and other security options (encryption, delegation, and authentication related), and account expiration. This tab also allows you to see if an account has been locked out through too many unsuccessful logon attempts. If an account is locked out, you can unlock it by deselecting the Account Is Locked Out check box (available only after an account has been locked out).

**Profile** Lets you specify the path for the user's roaming or mandatory profile, the path to a logon script, and the path to a home folder.

**Telephones** Lets you enter various telephone numbers, such as home, pager, mobile, fax, and IP phone numbers. You can also enter comments about these phone numbers. Use the appropriate Other button to view and add telephone numbers.

**Organization** Lets you enter information about the user regarding his or her position within the organization, such as title, department, and company name. You can also select the user's manager from the list of Directory users. Any users on whose Organization tab this user is specified as the manager will appear in the Direct Reports list box.

**Member Of** Lets you view which groups the user is a member of. Also lets you add the user to and remove the user from groups by using the Add and Remove buttons, respectively. Also displays the user's primary group (Domain Users by default). If the user belongs to other global or universal security groups, you can set one of those groups as the primary group for the user by selecting the group and clicking Set Primary Group (primary groups are used by Macintosh clients and POSIX-compliant applications).

**Dial-in** Lets you configure dial-in or VPN options, such as whether to allow remote access or to control access through Remote Access Policy, whether to verify a Caller-ID (if yes, you can specify the Caller-ID to verify), and whether to use call-back (if yes, you can configure callback options). Also lets you configure whether a static IP address should be assigned (if yes, you can specify an IP address) and whether static routes should be assigned (if yes, you can define routes).

**Environment** Lets you configure the Terminal Services startup environment, which will take precedence over client settings. You can configure whether to run a program at startup, and if yes, which program; whether client devices and printers connect at logon; and whether to default to the main client printer.

**Sessions** Lets you configure Terminal Services timeout and reconnection settings, such as when to end a disconnected session, what action to take when a limit is reached, and how to allow reconnection. You can also set active and idle session limits.

**Remote Control** Lets you configure Terminal Services' remote control settings, such as enabling and disabling remote control. You can specify whether user permission is required for remote control, as well as the level of control (view or interact with the user's session).

**Terminal Services Profile** Lets you configure the Terminal Services profile for the user, including the path to the user's roaming or mandatory user profile (for logging on to terminal servers), and the path to the user's terminal services home folder. Also lets you specify whether to allow logon to a terminal server.

**TIP** If a profile path and home directory are specified on the user's Profile tab, those paths will also apply for Terminal Services, unless different information is specified on the Terminal Services Profile tab.

### *Working with User Accounts*

You can perform several actions regarding user accounts via the Action or pop-up menu. Select a user account and click Action or right-click a user account in the Details pane to bring up the pop-up menu. You'll see these options:

**Copy** Lets you create a new user using some of the property sheet information from the currently selected user (such as group membership). You'll be able to specify a new name and password for the user.

**Add Members to a Group** Lets you select a group or groups to which to add the selected user or users.

**Disable Account** Lets you disable the selected user account(s).

**Enable Account** Lets you enable the selected user account(s). Available when selecting a single disabled user account, or when selecting multiple user accounts (even if they are not disabled).

**Reset Password** Lets you change the selected user's password.

**Move** Lets you move the selected user account(s) to another folder or OU.

**Open Home Page** Opens the home page for the user in Microsoft Internet Explorer if a Web page is specified on the General tab of the user's property sheet.

**Send Mail** Lets you send e-mail to the selected user account(s) if an e-mail address has been specified on the General tab of the user's property sheet.

**All Tasks** Displays a submenu that contains all previously described tasks (Copy, Add Members to a Group, Disable Account, etc.).

**Delete** Deletes the currently selected user account(s).

**Rename** Lets you rename the currently selected user account.

**Refresh** Refreshes the currently selected user account.

**Properties** Displays the user account's property sheet.

**Help** Displays context-sensitive help.

**TIP** Some of the options are also available if you select more than one user account.

## Groups

Groups let you assign rights and permissions to more than one user at a time, which greatly reduces administrative effort. You can also use groups to send e-mail to all members of the group at once and to filter group policies.

Windows 2000 Server includes several built-in groups, such as the domain local groups Administrators and Users and the domain global groups Domain Admins, Domain Users, and Domain Guests. These built-in groups are security groups that provide various levels of default rights and permissions and often are designed to cover assigning the appropriate rights and permissions for typical user and administrative needs, minimizing the need to create additional groups. As you install additional services, other groups are automatically created to accommodate rights and permission needs for users and administrators of those services. You'll find default domain local groups in the Builtin and Users folders and default domain global groups in the Users folder below the domain object in the console tree.

Several group scopes and types are available.

### *Group Scopes*

**Domain Local** Members can be accounts (user or computer), contacts, or groups from any Windows 2000 or Windows NT domain. You can use domain local groups to assign permissions only to the domain in which the group exists.

**Global** Members can be accounts, contacts, or groups from the domain in which the group was created. You can use global groups to assign permissions in any domain in a tree or forest.

**Universal** Members can be accounts, contacts, or groups from any domain in a tree or forest, and you can use universal groups to assign permissions in any domain in a tree or forest. You can't create a security group (explained below) of universal scope in a mixed mode domain.

**WARNING** Exactly what groups can be what type and what membership is allowed also depends on whether the domain is in native or mixed mode. See Active Directory Users and Computers Help for more detailed information.

### *Group Types*

Two types of groups exist:

**Security** Listed in discretionary access control lists, (DACLs), which specify object and resource permissions. Can also be used as groups to which you can send e-mails, thus enabling you to send e-mails to all members of the group.

**Distribution** Not listed in DACLs; can be used only as groups to which you can send e-mails.

### *Creating a Group*

You can create new groups in any folder; however, Microsoft recommends adding them to OUs. To create a new group, follow these steps:

1. Right-click the folder or OU where you want to create the new group, then choose New ➢ Group.

**TIP** Alternatively, you can select the folder or OU and then click the Create a New Group in the Current Container button on the toolbar.

2. Type a name for the group in the Group Name text box. The pre-Windows 2000 group name is automatically filled in for backward compatibility. You can change this name if you wish.
3. Select the scope of the group and the group type.
4. Click OK to create the group.

### *Group Properties*

Use a group's properties to configure the group. The group's property sheet contains four tabs:

**General** Lets you view the group name and specify the pre-Windows 2000 name, description, e-mail address, type, and scope of the group. Also lets you record notes about the group.

**Members** Lets you view current members of the group and add and remove members.

**Member Of** Lets you view groups this group is currently a member of and add the group to (or remove it from) another group.

**Managed By** Lets you assign an Active Directory user account as the manager of the group. Information about the user, such as office, street, city, state/province, country/region, telephone, and fax number, is filled in automatically from the user account's property sheet. You can click the View button to see and modify the user account's properties.

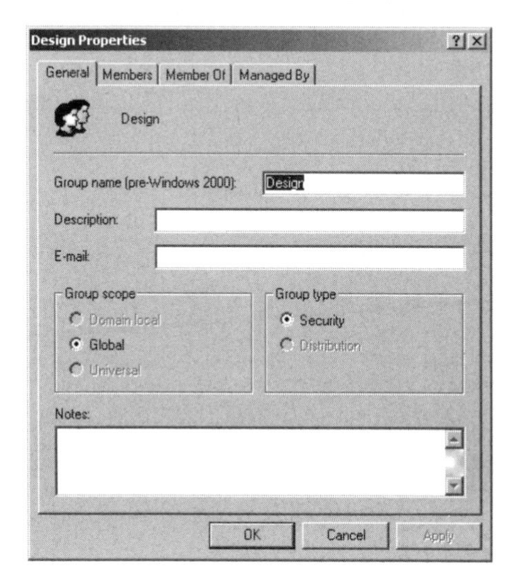


## Computers

Active Directory computer accounts are used to log on and authenticate to a Windows 2000 domain. When a computer joins a domain, a computer account must exist for that computer. The computer account can be created either through Active Directory Users and Computers or during the process of joining a domain. In the Computers folder below the domain object in the console tree of Active Directory Users and Computers, you'll find computer accounts created during the process of joining a domain. You'll find domain controller computer accounts in the OU called Domain Controllers.

### Creating a Computer Account

You can create computer accounts in any folder or OU. To create a new computer account, follow these steps:

1. Right-click the folder or OU where you want to create the new computer account and choose New ➢ Computer.
2. Type a name for the new computer account.
3. If you wish, change who can join the computer to the domain by clicking Change, selecting a user or group from the list, and clicking OK. By default, any member of the Domain Admins group can join the computer to the domain.
4. If applicable, select the Allow Pre-Windows 2000 Computers to Use This Account check box.
5. Click OK to create the account.

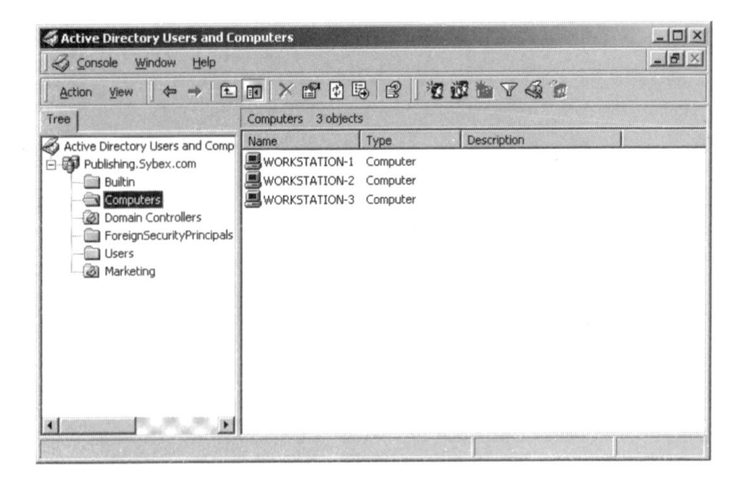

### *Computer Account Properties*

Each computer account has configurable properties. To access a computer account's property sheet, right-click the account and choose Properties from the pop-up menu. You'll see five tabs:

**General** Lets you view the computer account's name, pre-Windows 2000 name, DNS name, role (workstation or server), and description. You can also specify whether to trust the computer for delegation, meaning that services local to that computer can request services from other servers.

**Operating System** Lets you view the operating system name and version, and the service pack installed on that computer.

**Member Of** Lets you view the computer account's current group membership and add the computer to (or remove it from) other groups. Also lets you specify the computer's primary group (available only if the group you select is a global or universal security group).

**Location** Lets you specify the computer's physical location, such as an office name or building number.

**Managed By** Lets you assign an Active Directory user as the manager of this computer account.

## Printers, Shared Folders, and Contacts

In addition to creating users, groups, and computers, you can use Active Directory Users and Computers to create printers, contacts, and shared folders in Active Directory. To do so, right-click the folder or OU in which you want to create the object, then choose New and select Printer, Contact, or Shared Folder and provide the necessary information to create the object. You can add contacts to groups, but only for the purpose of sending e-mail to the contact via the group membership. You cannot assign security to contacts.

## Finding Resources

You can use Active Directory Users and Computers to find users, computers, contacts, groups, printers, shared folders, and OUs in Active Directory. Follow these steps:

1. Select any object or folder in the console tree.

2. Click the Find Objects in Active Directory button on the toolbar or choose Action ➢ Find.
3. Select what you want to find from the Find drop-down list, and choose where you want to search (current folder, domain, or Entire Directory) from the In drop-down list. To specify a different folder, click Browse.
4. Enter information about the object you want to find in the appropriate fields (they will change depending on the type of object you're searching for). Select the Advanced tab to further refine your search.
5. Click Find Now to start the search. The results of your search appear at the bottom of the Find window.

## Domains

Active Directory Users and Computers also lets you perform some tasks related to the domain and domain controller. Right-click the domain object in the console tree to access these unique options:

**Delegate Control** Starts the Delegation of Control Wizard, which lets you delegate control of Active Directory objects to other users.

**Connect to Domain** Lets you connect to another domain so that you can manage that domain.

**Connect to Domain Controller** Lets you connect to a specific domain controller in the current domain.

**Operations Master** Lets you transfer several operations' master roles to another domain controller. An operations master is a domain controller that has been assigned a particular function that cannot be executed in multimaster mode, such as schema changes and resource identifier allocation, meaning the change can take place on only one domain controller.

### *Domain Object Properties*

The domain object has configurable properties, which you can access by right-clicking the domain object in the console tree and choosing Properties. Details about Domain object properties are described under the entry Active Directory Domains and Trusts; however, one tab is available exclusively through Domain object properties in Active Directory Users and Computers:

**Group Policy** Lets you view current group policy object links, create new group policy objects, edit existing group policy objects and policies, configure link options, delete group policy object links and objects, and configure group policy object properties. Also lets you set the priority of group policy object links and block policy inheritance. You can find additional information about group policies under the entry Group Policy.

**See Also** Active Directory, Active Directory Domains and Trusts, Microsoft Management Console (MMC), Group Policy

# Active Directory Sites and Services

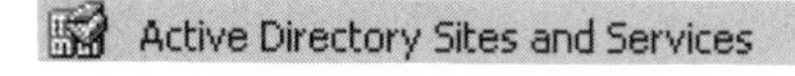


MMC console snap-in installed on Windows 2000 domain controllers that lets you manage Active Directory sites and services.

Sites are created to specify the boundaries of physical sites in the network so that replication and authentication is performed, ensuring greatest efficiency. When you publish a site to Active Directory, Active Directory can then determine how to best perform replication (data is replicated both within and between sites) and which domain controller (typically within the same site) should handle service requests. This minimizes network traffic and enables you to make the best use of available bandwidth. This is particularly important in a wide area network (WAN). It is also critical because Windows 2000 uses the multimaster replication model, which enables any domain controller to service any request. Otherwise, for example, it could easily happen that a user attempts to authenticate over a dial-up connection to a domain controller located thousands of miles away.

The Services feature is used to publish service information to Active Directory, which is then used by client applications and thus simplifies access to services. Examples are binding information (which allows Windows 2000 to automatically establish connections to services) and application configuration information. Several services are published by default.

To access Active Directory Sites and Services on a Windows 2000 domain controller, choose Start ➢ Programs ➢ Administrative Tools ➢ Active Directory Sites and Services. You'll see the Sites node in the console tree, which contains several folders.

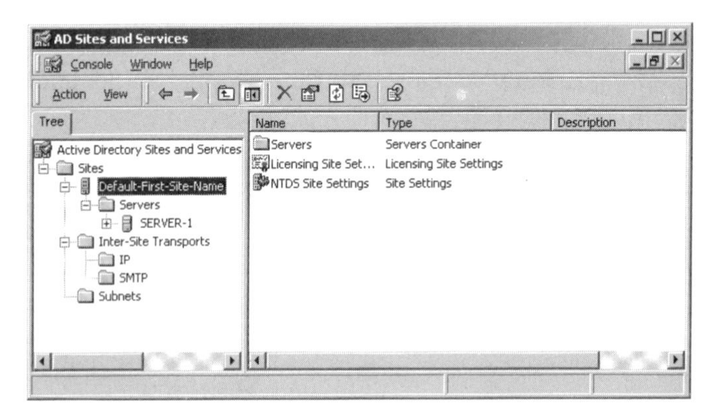


## Sites Node

The Sites node contains the Default First Site object, which is created automatically, as well as any other sites you create subsequently. The Sites node also contains the Inter-Site Transports folder and the Subnets folder.

### *Sites*

Site objects contain the Servers folder, which in turn contains the server(s) that are currently part of the site. In this folder, you can also add new servers, move servers, and change server properties (such as the transports available for inter-site data transfer). In the server's property sheet, you can also assign the server as a bridgehead server for specific transports. Bridgehead servers are dedicated to intra-site replication.

The site object also contains the Licensing Site Settings object and the NTDS (NT Directory Services) Settings object, both of which you can view and configure.

### *Inter-site Transports*

Use this folder to configure the properties for existing site links, to create new site links (a minimum of two sites must be part of a site link), and to create site link bridges between two or more site links. You can create either IP or SMTP site links and site link bridges and specify the cost of the connection between the site links and the replication interval you want to use. You can also set up a replication schedule, enabling you to specify the best setup for replication between sites.

### *Subnets*

Use the Subnets folder to create IP subnets that you can then associate with sites. Creating and associating IP subnets defines the physical boundaries of a site. Computers are added to sites by belonging to a subnet you specify as being part of the site.

## Creating a Site

To create a site, follow these steps:

1. Right-click the Sites node and choose New Site (or select New ➢ Site).
2. Type a name for the site in the Name text box.
3. Select a site link object from the list and click OK twice.
4. Right-click the Subnets folder and choose New Subnet (or select New ➢ Subnet).
5. Enter the subnet address and mask, then select the site object you just created from the list. Click OK.
6. Move an existing server from another site to this site or install a new server (domain controller).
7. Select the new site object and display the properties of the Licensing Site Settings object in the display pane. On the Licensing Settings tab, click Change and select a computer to be the licensing computer for the site. Click OK.

## Services Node

The Services node is hidden by default. To display it, choose View ➢ Show Services Node.

Below the Services node, you'll find the service information that is published to the Active Directory by default. It includes MsmqServices (Message Queuing Services), NetServices, Public Key Services, RRAS (Routing and Remote Access Service), and Windows NT.

**See Also** Microsoft Management Console (MMC)

# Add/Remove Hardware

Starts the Add/Remove Hardware Wizard, which helps you add, remove, and troubleshoot hardware on your system, such as network cards, modems, disk drives, and CD-ROM drives.

Choose Start ➢ Settings ➢ Control Panel ➢ Add/Remove Hardware to start the Add/Remove Hardware Wizard.

**TIP** An alternate way to access the Hardware Wizard is to double-click the System icon in Control Panel, select the Hardware tab, and click Hardware Wizard.

## Add/Remove Hardware Wizard

Guides you through the steps to add new hardware to a Windows 2000 computer after you've physically installed it, to prepare Windows 2000 to physically remove or unplug hardware from the computer, or to troubleshoot a device that is experiencing problems. The Hardware Wizard automatically makes the necessary changes, including changes to the Registry and configuration files, and installing, loading, removing, and unloading of drivers.

**NOTE** You must have administrative privileges to add, remove, or troubleshoot hardware with the Add/Remove Hardware Wizard.

**TIP** Devices added with the Add/Remove Hardware Wizard can be Plug and Play, non–Plug and Play, SCSI, and USB devices.

### *Adding New Hardware*

Before you start the Hardware Wizard, power off your computer and install the device or plug it into the appropriate port. Turn your computer back on. If Plug and Play detects the new hardware and has the appropriate drivers for it, the hardware is added automatically and no further action is required.

If Plug and Play did not detect your hardware, follow these steps:

1. Choose Start ➢ Settings ➢ Control Panel and double-click Add/Remove Hardware to start the Add/Remove Hardware Wizard. Click Next.
2. Choose Add/Troubleshoot a Device, then click Next.
3. Windows will search for Plug and Play hardware. If none is detected, you'll be presented with a list of devices installed on your computer and the opportunity to add a new device. Select Add a New Device and click Next.

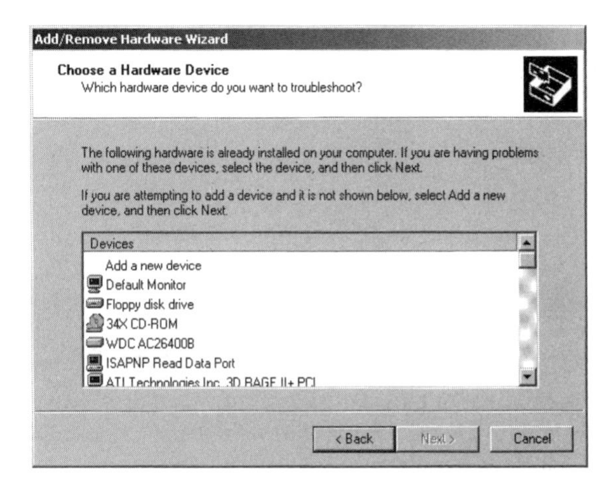


4. You can choose to have Windows search for the hardware. Even though Windows did not detect the hardware when you booted the computer, Windows may find it if you choose to search for it now. If you know the manufacturer and model of the hardware you want to install, choose to select the hardware from a list. Click Next.

**NOTE** If you choose to let Windows 2000 detect the hardware, you'll see a progress window as Windows 2000 is searching for the different categories of hardware devices. This may take some time, so be patient.

5. The remainder of the process will vary greatly, depending on the choice you made above as well as on the type of hardware you're installing. Follow the on-screen instructions.
6. When the process of finding or selecting hardware and configuring settings for the hardware is finished, a screen appears that tells you the installation is complete. Simply click Finish.

### *Removing/Unplugging Hardware*

When you use the Add/Remove Hardware Wizard to remove hardware, Windows 2000 gives you two choices: You can completely remove hardware from the computer (physically removing the hardware and permanently removing drivers), or you can temporarily disable a device so that the physical device can stay connected to the computer but its drivers are not loaded (Windows 2000 makes the appropriate Registry changes). If you want to use the device again, you can simply enable it. Follow these steps:

1. Choose Start ➢ Settings ➢ Control Panel and double-click the Add/Remove Hardware icon to start the Add/Remove Hardware Wizard. Click Next.
2. Choose Uninstall/Unplug a Device and click Next.
3. Choose Uninstall a Device to remove the driver and the device permanently from your computer. Choose Unplug/Eject a Device to disable the device so that you can unplug it or eject it safely.
4. Follow the on-screen instructions, which will vary depending on your choice in step 2 and the type of hardware you want to remove or unplug.

**TIP** If you don't see the device you want to uninstall in the list of devices, select the Show Hidden Devices check box to display the complete list of devices installed on your computer.

5. When the process is finished, the Completing the Add/Remove Hardware Wizard dialog box appears. Click Finish.

**TIP** If the device you want to remove is a Plug and Play device, it is not usually necessary to run the Add/Remove Hardware Wizard. After powering down the computer, you can just remove the device and restart the computer. (In some cases, you don't have to power down the computer to remove the device; however, I would recommend always powering down a computer before changing hardware.) Windows 2000 automatically recognizes that the hardware is no longer present and makes the necessary configuration changes.

### *Troubleshooting a Device*

You can use the Add/Remove Hardware Wizard to troubleshoot devices that are not working properly. Choose Start ➢ Settings ➢ Control Panel and double-click the Add/Remove Hardware icon to start the Add/Remove Hardware Wizard. Click Next, and then select Add/Troubleshoot a Device. Click Next, wait for the Add/Remove Hardware Wizard to search for new devices (which it should not find since you're not installing new hardware but troubleshooting a device), then select the device you're having problems with from the list. Click Next, then click Finish, and the appropriate troubleshooter in the Windows 2000 Help System starts automatically. Answer the question regarding the problem you're having, click Next, and follow the instructions.

**TIP** Using the Add/Remove Hardware Wizard to troubleshoot devices is an easy way to go to the appropriate Help system troubleshooter without having to search the Help system.

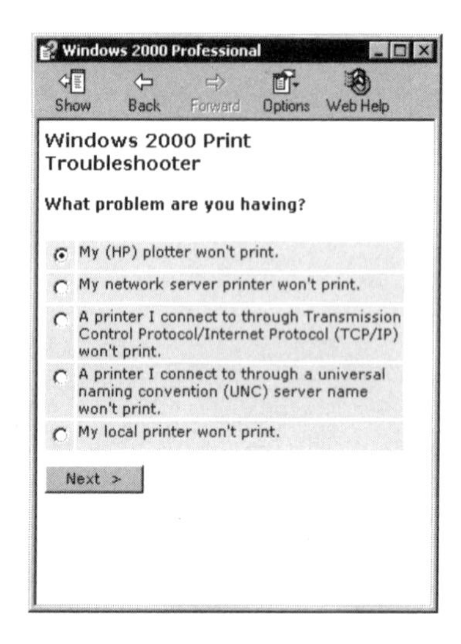


**See Also** Help, System, System Information

## Add/Remove Programs

Installs or removes programs and Windows 2000 components from your computer. Examples of programs are Microsoft Word or Microsoft FrontPage; examples of Windows 2000 components are Administrative Tools or networking options. You can also use Add/Remove Programs to install other operating systems on different partitions. Choose Start ➢ Settings ➢ Control Panel and double-click the Add/Remove Programs icon to open Add/Remove Programs. You'll see the Change or Remove Programs screen. The left pane of the window contains three buttons for changing, removing, or adding programs and for adding or removing Windows components. The information in the right pane changes depending on which option you've selected.

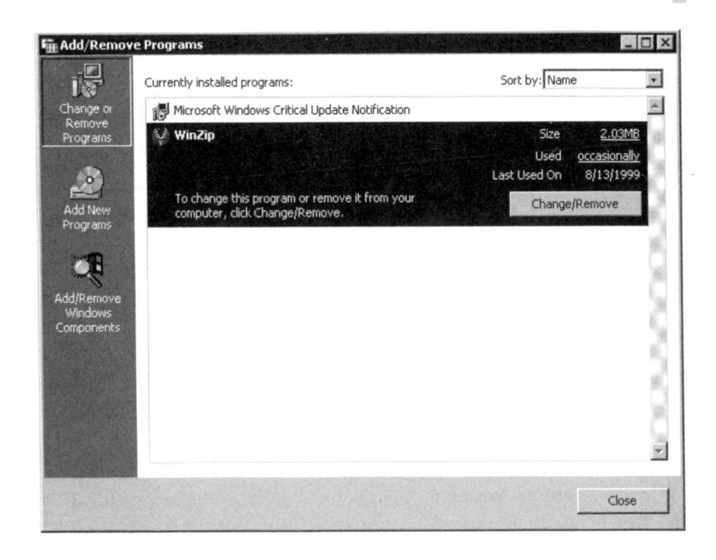


## Change or Remove Programs

Changes or removes programs installed on your Windows 2000 computer. The Currently Installed Programs list box shows you all of the programs that are currently installed on your computer. When you select a program in the list, you may see some or all of the following additional information:

**Size** Estimates the amount of space the program takes up on your hard drive.

**Used** Tells you how often the program is used, based on how many times you've run the program in the last 30 days. Possible values are Rarely (you never or hardly ever run the program), Occasionally (you sometimes run the program), or Frequently (you run the program often).

**Last Used On** Provides the date on which the program was last run.

The Sort By option lets you sort the list by name, size, frequency of use, and date last used.

You can change or remove any program by selecting it in the list box and then clicking the Change/Remove button or the

Change or Remove button, whichever button type displays. What happens next depends on the program you're trying to change or remove. A wizard may start that can guide you through changing (that is, reinstalling) or removing the program. If the program can only be removed but not changed, you may be prompted by several confirmation messages telling you the actions the Uninstall procedure will perform (such as removing program files, program groups, and Registry and configuration file entries) and verifying that you really want to remove the program. Just follow the prompts. When the program has been uninstalled, you may receive a message to that effect.

**WARNING** Some programs may be removed immediately after you click the Change/Remove (or Change or Remove) button without showing any of the warning messages described.

## Add New Programs

Adds new programs to your Windows 2000 computer. When you click the Add New Programs icon, the right pane changes to display several options for adding a new program to your computer. You can add programs from these sources: CD, floppy disk, Microsoft's Web site (through Windows Update), and the network.

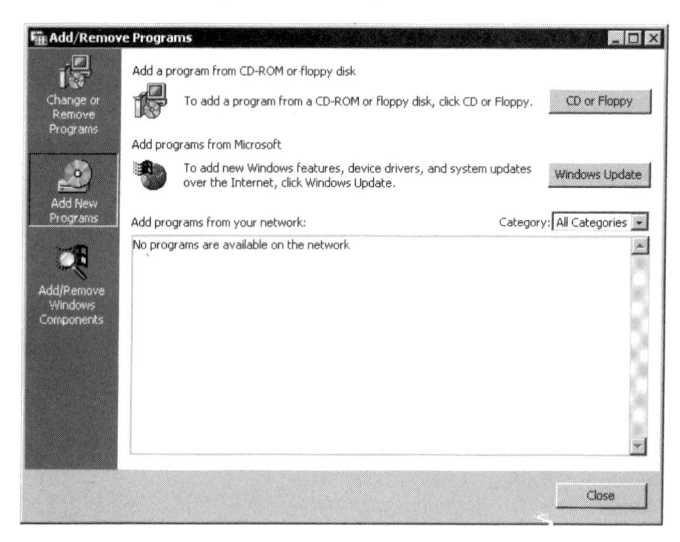

### *From CD or Floppy Disk*

To add a new program from CD or floppy disk, click the CD or Floppy button. A wizard then guides you through the individual steps.

### *From Microsoft*

You can add Windows 2000 system updates as well as new features and device drivers through the Windows Update feature.

**TIP** You can also access Windows Update by choosing Start ➢ Windows Update.

To begin, click Windows Update. Once you do, Internet Explorer opens to the Microsoft Windows Update home page, where you can obtain downloadable product updates and other support information. You must be connected to the Internet for this function to work.

### *From Your Network*

If you're connected to a network, any programs that have been published in the Active Directory and to which you've been given access will appear in the Add Programs from Your Network list box at the bottom of the screen. A network administrator may have placed programs into different categories; select different categories (if available) in the Category drop-down list to find the application you're looking for.

## Add/Remove Windows Components

Adds or removes Windows 2000 components. When you click the Add/Remove Windows Components icon, the Windows Component Wizard starts. This wizard walks you through installing, configuring, and removing Windows 2000 components. Follow these steps:

1. In the list of components, place a checkmark in the check box of a component you want to add, or remove the checkmark from a component you want to remove. To see a description of a component, how much total free disk space it requires if you want to add it, and how much

space is left on your hard disk, select the component. (You don't have to enter a checkmark to see the description, but you do have to enter one to see the required space and hard disk information.) This information is displayed below the list box. If a component has subcomponents, you can see details about these subcomponents by clicking the Details button. You can add or remove subcomponents by checking or unchecking subcomponents (by default, all subcomponents are checked when you check a component).

**TIP** If a component does not have subcomponents, the Details button will be inactive (grayed out). If you uncheck a subcomponent, the main component's check box becomes shaded in gray to inform you that only part of the component will be installed.

A description and disk space information is also available for each subcomponent, and subcomponents can have additional subcomponents. Make your selections (component and subcomponent). When you make subcomponent selection changes, click OK to accept them. To get back to the Windows Components screen, you may have to click OK several times. When you've finished, click Next.

2. Wait for the wizard to make component configuration changes (either installing or removing components). If you're adding a component, you may be prompted to insert your Windows 2000 CD or to provide an alternate path to Windows 2000 files. Follow any other prompts.
3. When the installation is finished, the Completing the Windows Components Wizard screen displays. Simply click Finish.

**TIP** Some Windows 2000 components must be configured before you can use them. If such a component is installed but not configured and you click Add/Remove Windows Components, you'll have two choices: Configure, to configure components, or Components, to add/remove components.

**See Also** Windows Update

# Address Book

Address Book

Lets you manage your contact information, such as postal and e-mail addresses, telephone numbers, business and personal information, and home page addresses. You can also use Address Book together with other programs, such as Internet Explorer, Outlook, and Outlook Express.

**TIP** To open Address Book from Internet Explorer, choose Go ➢ Address Book. To open Address Book from Outlook Express, click Address Book on the toolbar.

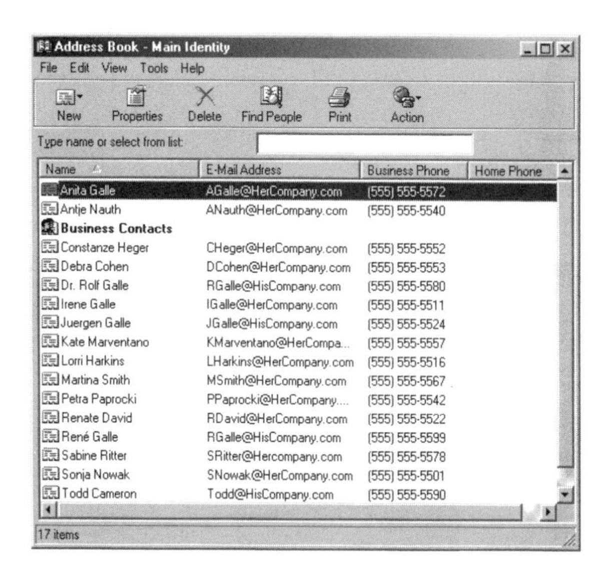


## Address Book Window

Choose Start ➢ Programs ➢ Accessories ➢ Address Book to open Address Book. The Address Book – Main Identity window appears. This window contains the list of address book entries, a toolbar, and a menu bar. The contacts visible in this screen are saved in the Main Identity's Contacts folder. You can create additional identities as well as additional folders for each identity to organize your address book. Identities are used for sharing address book information with other people.

The address book contact list shows information about each entry in your address book, including name, e-mail address, and business and home phone numbers. To see and specify additional items, double-click an entry, or select a contact or group and click Properties on the toolbar. You can sort the list by any of the column headings by clicking a column heading, and you can sort the list in ascending or descending order by clicking the column heading by which the list is currently ordered.

Entries in your address book can be contacts (individual persons) or groups (containing contacts). Contacts are represented by a business card icon. Groups are represented by a business card icon with two people's heads on the business card. Creating a group enables you to send e-mail to more than one person at the same time (to all group members).

You can go directly to an entry in the list by entering the name of a person in your address book in the Type Name or Select from List text box.

If you want to display folders, choose View ➢ Folders and Groups. This displays the Folders and Groups pane in the left portion of the Address Book window.

## Toolbar

The Address Book toolbar contains these buttons:

**New** Lets you create a new contact, group, or folder entry in your address book.

**Properties** Lets you access the properties of the selected contact or group.

**Delete** Lets you delete the currently selected contact, group, or folder. If a contact you delete is a member of a group, the contact is also removed from the group.

**TIP** You cannot delete the Shared Contacts or Main Identity's Contacts folders.

**TIP** Alternatively, you can select a contact or group in the contact list, or a folder in the Folders and Groups pane, and choose Delete to delete the selected contact, group, or folder.

**Find People** Lets you search for people in the address book or on the Internet.

**TIP** You can find detailed information on how to find people using Windows 2000 under the heading Search.

**Print** Lets you print the currently selected or all contact and group information in memo, business card, or phone list format.

**TIP** For more information on printing from the address book, see the subheading File Menu.

**Action** Lets you send e-mail, or place a regular or Internet call to the currently selected contact or group.

## Menus

Address Book has some familiar as well as some unique menu options.

### *File Menu*

The File menu contains the following unique menu options:

**New Contact** Lets you create a new contact.

**New Group** Lets you create a new group.

**New Folder** Lets you create a new folder.

**Properties** Opens the currently selected contact's or group's Properties dialog box.

**Delete** Deletes the currently selected contact or group.

**Import** Lets you import other Windows Address Books (WAB files), Business Cards (VCF files), or address books, such as Eudora's and Netscape's address books.

**Export** Lets you export your address book to a WAB file, a VCF file, or other address book file formats.

**Print** Lets you print the current contact, multiple contacts, or the entire address book in memo, business card, or phone list format. Memo format prints all information for each contact, business card format prints business information for each contact, and phone list format prints only phone numbers for each contact.

**Switch Identity** Lets you switch to a different identity (if multiple identities have been created).

**Show All Contents** Displays the contents of the address book for all identities in a separate Address Book window.

### *Edit Menu*

The Edit menu contains the following unique options:

**Copy** Lets you copy an address book contact or group.

**Paste** Lets you create another address book contact or group using existing information from the copied contact or group.

**Profile** Lets you create an address book entry to use as your Internet profile (profile identity). You can use it on Web sites where you can submit a profile identity instead of manually entering information about yourself.

**TIP** Profile identities are represented in the contact list by a business card icon with a single person's head.

**Find People** Opens the Find People dialog box, where you can search for addresses in the address book or on the Internet.

### *View Menu*

The View menu contains the following unique options:

**Folders and Groups** Toggles the display of the Folders and Groups view.

**Sort By** Lets you choose how you want to sort the contact list by making choices from the submenu. Choices include Name, E-Mail Address, Business Phone, Home Phone, First Name, Last Name, Ascending, and Descending.

### *Tools Menu*

The Tools menu contains the following unique options:

**Accounts** Lets you view, add, remove, import, and export directory services, such as Active Directory and Internet Directory Services. You can also configure the properties of each directory service, designate a directory service as the default, and change the order of directory services.

**Action** Lets you choose actions from a submenu. Actions include sending mail to the selected contact or group, dialing the contact's phone number, and making an Internet call.

**TIP** You can also access these options by right-clicking a contact or group in the contacts list and choosing Action.

**Synchronize Now**

**AUTHOR'S NOTE** Unfortunately, neither myself (the author) nor the technical editor were able to get the Synchronize Now feature to activate. The feature wouldn't activate for us in beta Release Candidate 2, nor could we activate it once we got the final code (build 2195). We were not able to get a response from Microsoft about this before the book went to print.

## Creating a New Contact

Click New on the toolbar, then choose New Contact to open the Properties dialog box.

**TIP** Alternatively, you can choose File ➢ New Contact, or you can right-click a contact, group, or folder and choose New ➢ New Contact.

The Properties dialog box has seven tabs:

**Name** Enter the first, middle, and last names of the contact, as well as a title and nickname. From the Display drop-down list, select how you want the name to be displayed in the contact list. You can choose from three different formats (first_name last_name; last_name first_name; or last_name, first_name). Alternatively, you can also type a display name into the Display text box.

**TIP** Each contact must have a display name.

On the Name tab, you can also enter one or more e-mail addresses by entering an address in the E-Mail Addresses text box and clicking Add. Select an e-mail address in the list and click Edit to make changes to the e-mail address (click Remove to remove the address). Click Set as Default to select an e-mail address as the default for this contact. If you're not certain the contact can receive e-mails that contain formatting, select the Send E-Mail Using Plain Text Only check box.

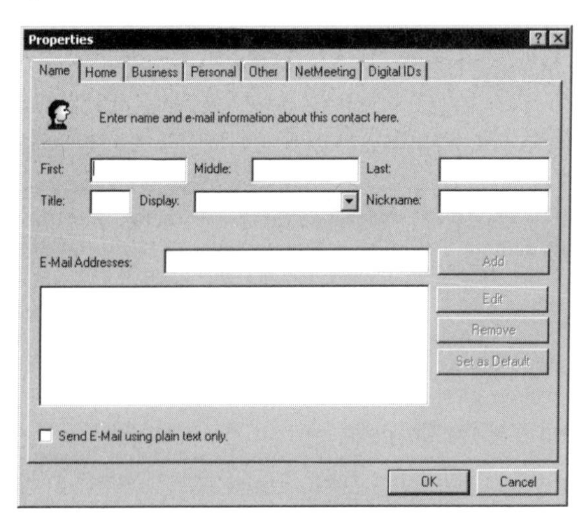


**Home** Lets you enter personal postal address information, such as street address, city, and state/province, as well as phone, fax, and mobile telephone numbers for the contact.

You can designate this address as the default by selecting the Default check box. Then, if an application you use prints addresses from the address book, this address will be printed.

Click View Map to open Internet Explorer and display a map for the address you've entered. Microsoft Expedia provides the map information.

**TIP** Maps can be displayed only if you're connected to the Internet.

If the contact has a personal Web page, you can enter the URL in the Web Page text box and access the Web page by clicking Go.

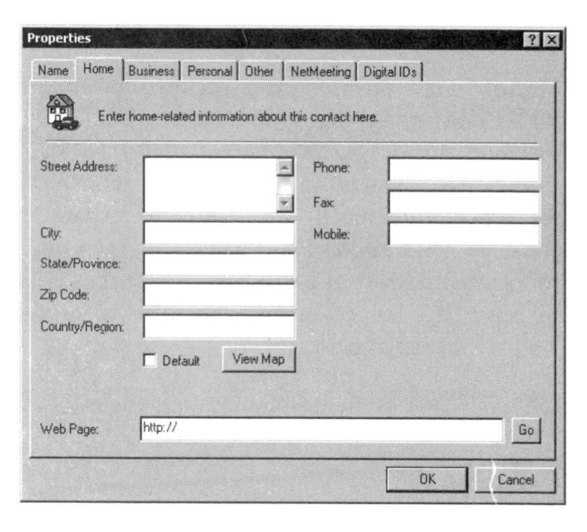


**Business** Lets you add business address information for the contact, such as company name, street address, city, and state/province, as well as other information, such as job title, department, office, and phone, fax, pager, and IP phone numbers. As with the home address, you can select Default to designate this address as the default. You can also click View Map to see a Microsoft Expedia map for the information you entered. If the contact has a business Web page, enter the URL in the Web Page text box and click Go to access the Web page.

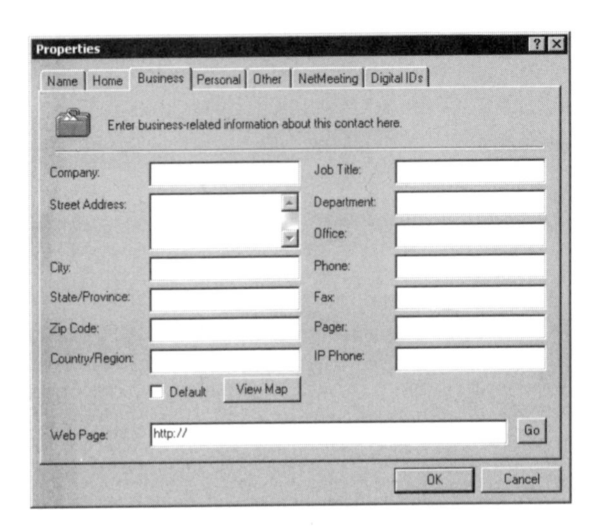


**Personal** Lets you enter other personal information about the contact, such as spouse's and children's names, gender, and birthday and anniversary dates. To change the current date for birthday and anniversary dates, click the arrow next to the respective field and select a date from the calendar. To add a child's name, click Add, then replace the words New Child with the child's name. Select a child's name, then click Edit (to change the name) or click Remove (to remove it from the list).

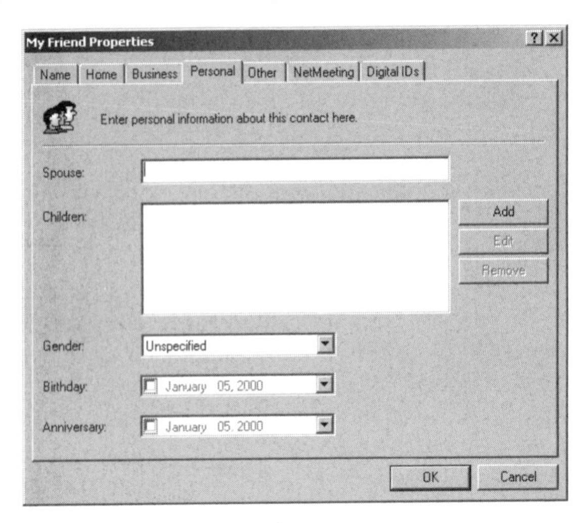

**Other** Lets you enter additional information about the contact in the form of notes. Type the information in the Notes text box. If the contact is a member of one or more Address Book groups, the names of the groups appear in the Group Membership list box.

**TIP** You will not be able to add the contact to a group until you've created the contact.

The Address Book folder in which the contact is stored appears next to Folder Location.

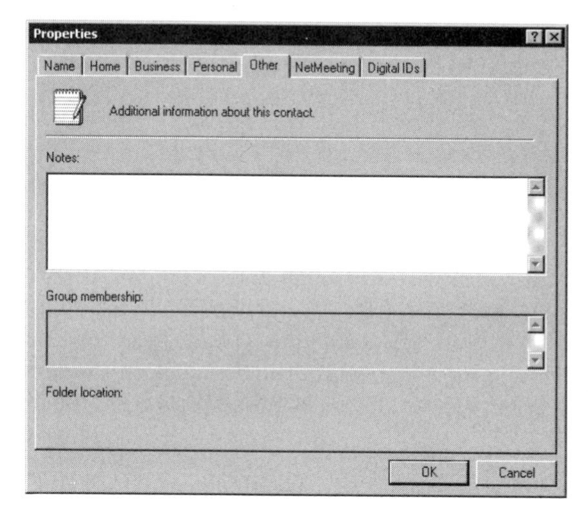


**NetMeeting** Lets you specify NetMeeting-related information, such as the directory server or servers the contact uses for NetMeeting conferences. Enter the name of one or more servers in the Conferencing Server text box. In the Conferencing Address combo box, you can enter the contact's conference e-mail address. Click Add to add the information to the list box. The first directory server you add is automatically set as the default server.

Select an entry in the list and click Edit (to make changes to the entry), Remove (to remove the entry), or Set as Default (to specify the selected server as the default directory server). Click Set as Backup to specify that server as the backup server should the default be busy or not available and a connection can't be established. Click Call Now to open NetMeeting and immediately call the selected directory server.

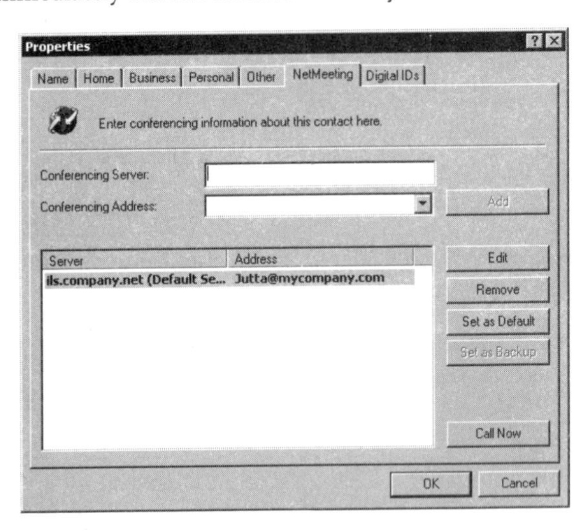


**Digital IDs** Lets you add, remove, and view digital IDs for the contact. To add a digital ID, click Import, browse to the digital ID file, select it, and click Open to add it to the Digital IDs tab. Select a digital ID and click Properties (to view the property sheet for the ID), Remove (to remove the ID), or Set as Default (to use the selected ID as the default).

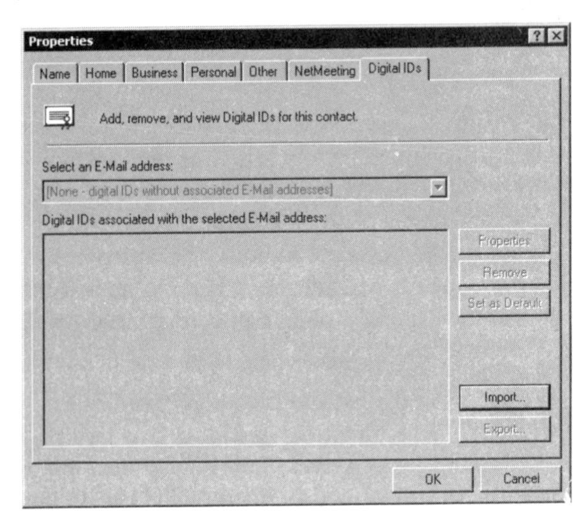

### *Creating a New Contact to Use as a Template*

You can create a new contact that is representative of other contacts you might want to create in the future—such as a contact that contains all of the business information for people in the same organization—and then use this contact as a template to create other contacts. To do this, first create the contact and enter all information that applies to all users you want to create using the template. To create a new contact using the Template contact, select the Template contact in the contacts list and choose Edit ➢ Copy, then Edit ➢ Paste. The property sheet for the Template contact opens, and you can change or add any information that is unique to the new contact you're creating. Finally, click OK to add the new contact to the contact list. Because you don't have to retype the same contact information over and over, this approach saves you a lot of time.

**TIP** You can also create a template group and use it in the same manner.

## Creating a New Group

You can create a new group so you can send e-mail to all members of that group. Click New on the toolbar, then select New Group to open the Properties dialog box. It has two tabs.

**TIP** Alternatively, you can choose File ➢ New Group, or you can right-click a contact, group, or folder and choose New ➢ New Group.

**Group** Lets you enter a name for the group and add contacts to the group (making them members of the group). To assign the group a name, enter a name in the Group Name text box. To add contacts to the group, first click Select Members. Next, choose a member from the Select Group Members dialog box by selecting a contact in the left pane and clicking Select to move the contact to the right (Members) pane. Then click OK. In the Select Group Members dialog box, you can also search for contacts in your address book or on the Internet by typing a name in the text box next to the Find button, or by clicking Find and entering the appropriate information and selecting where you want to search.

Back in the Select Group Members dialog box, you can also specify the folder for which you want to display contacts by selecting that folder from the drop-down list. Click New Contact to create a new contact, and click Properties to view a contact's property sheet.

You can also create a new contact and add the contact to the group at the same time by clicking New Contact on the Group tab. To remove a contact from the group, select the contact in the Group Members list box and click Remove. To view and edit a contact's property sheet, click Properties.

Finally, you can add contacts that are not in your address book by entering a name and e-mail address in the Name and E-Mail text boxes and clicking Add. Contacts added to the group in this manner won't be added to your address book.

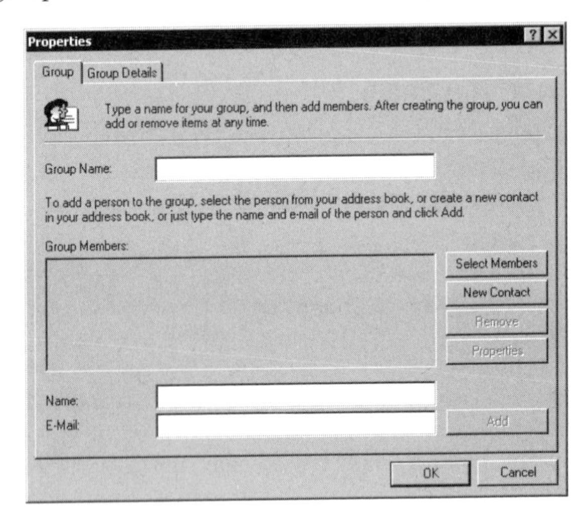


**Group Details** Lets you specify other information for the group, such as postal information (street address, city, state/province, and so forth), phone and fax numbers, and notes about the group. You can view a map for the group address information you enter by clicking View Map, and you can enter a Web page URL for the group in the Web Page text box. Click Go to access the Web page.

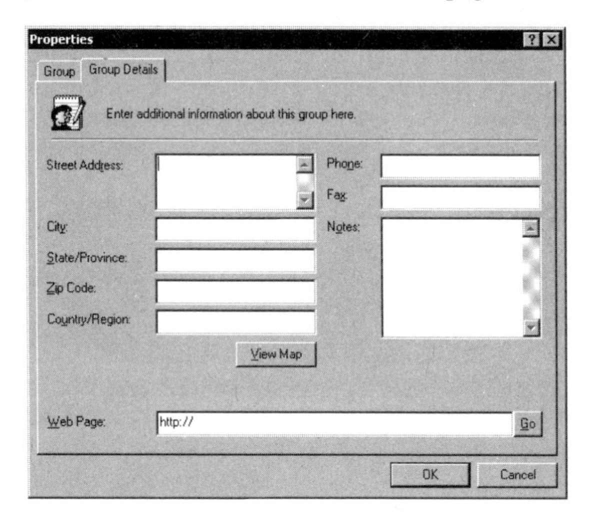


## Folders

Folders let you organize your contacts. Two folders are created by default: the Shared Contacts folder and the Main Identity's Contacts folder. To see folders, choose View ➢ Folders and Groups.

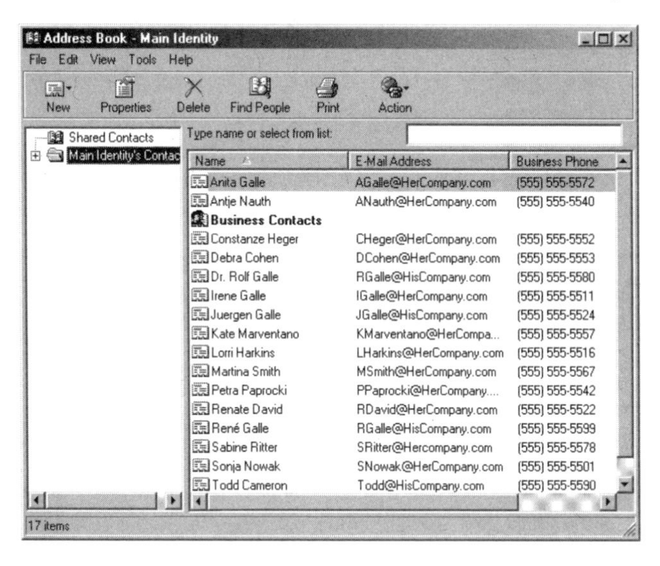

### *Creating a New Folder*

You can create new folders for organizing contacts. New folders are created below the currently selected identity's Contacts folder. Begin by clicking New on the toolbar, then choose New Folder. In the Properties dialog box, enter a name for the folder in the Folder Name text box and click OK to create the folder. The newly created folder then appears in the Folders and Groups view.

**TIP** Alternatively, you can choose File ➢ New Folder, or you can right-click a contact, group, or folder and choose New ➢ New Folder.

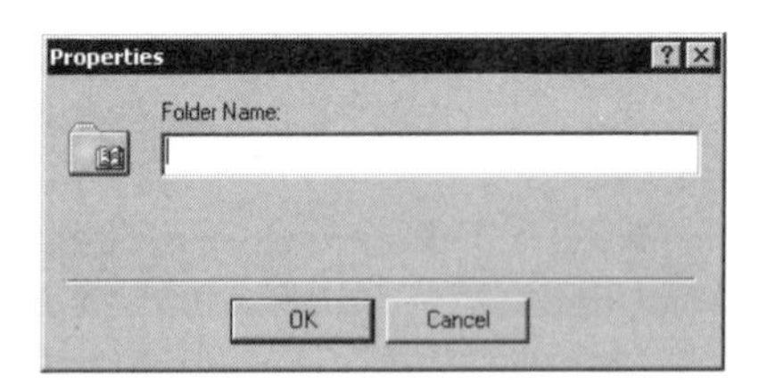


Once you've created other folders, you can select the folder into which you want to place new contacts and groups before you create them. Contacts and groups are always saved in the currently selected folder.

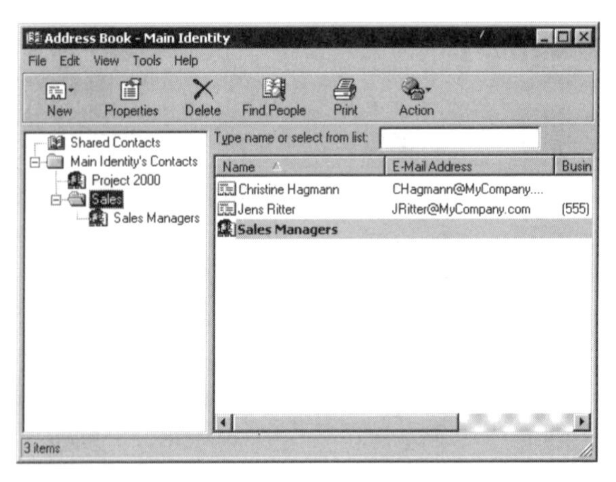

**TIP** If you want to change a folder's name, right-click the folder, then choose Properties. You can change the name by entering a new name in the Folder Name text box and clicking OK.

## Contact and Group Properties

Every contact and group has properties, which you configure on the same tabs you use when you create a contact or group. To access properties, select the contact or group in the list of contacts and click Properties on the toolbar, or choose File ➢ Properties. The property sheet for contacts features an additional tab, called Summary, which contains items from several of the contact's property tabs, such as name, e-mail address, home and business phone, and personal and business Web page addresses.

**TIP** Alternatively, you can right-click a contact or group in the contacts list and choose Properties.

## Creating Additional Identities

By default, one identity, the main identity, is created to use Outlook Express and the address book. You can create additional identities for other users and then share Outlook Express and the address book with those users (all users can read their own mail and see their own contacts and groups). Additionally, you can share contacts and groups among different identities. You can create identities in both Outlook Express and the address book.

To create an additional identity in the address book, follow these steps:

1. Choose File ➢ Switch Identity.
2. In the Switch Identities dialog box, click Manage Identities.
3. In the Manage Identities dialog box, click New.
4. In the New Identity dialog box, enter a name in the Type Your Name text box.
5. If you want to password-protect the identity, select Require a Password, then enter the password in the New Password and Confirm New Password text boxes in the Enter Password dialog box and click OK.
6. Click OK to create the new identity.
7. Click Yes if you want to switch to the new identity right away; click No if you don't want to switch identities at this time. If you click No, you're returned to the Manage

Identities dialog box, where the new identity appears in the list of identities. Click Close, then Cancel to return to the Address Book, or click New to create another identity.

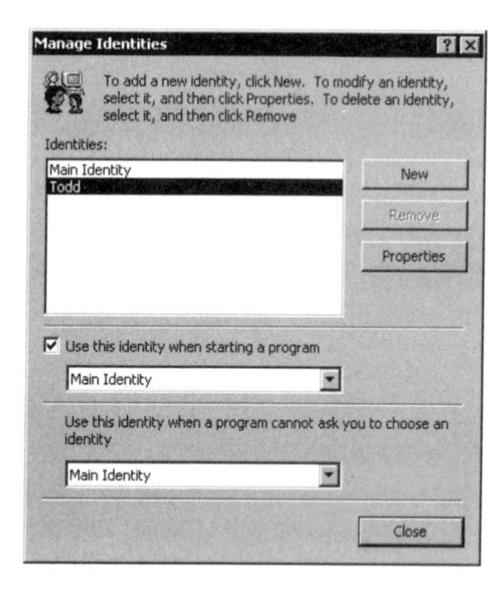


## Switching Identities

To switch identities, choose File ➢ Switch Identity, then select the identity you want to switch to from the list, enter a password if required, and click OK. You will now see the contacts, groups, and folders for the identity you switched to.

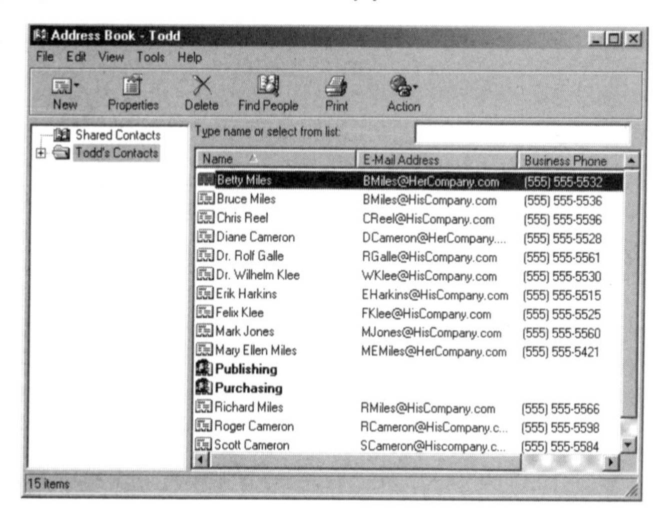

### Sharing Contacts and Contact Folders between Identities

You can share individual contacts with other users (for whom an identity has been created).

With the Folders and Groups view displayed, drag a contact from the list of contacts to the Shared Contacts folder. All other identities can now see the contact by clicking the Shared Contacts folder.

When you share a contact by dragging it to the Shared Contacts folder, you are moving the contact, which means it no longer exists in the original user's list of contacts. You can make a copy, but be aware that any changes to either copy are not replicated and the information about the user can become out of sync. You can't, however, copy a contact into the Shared Contacts folder; if you try, the Paste option will be unavailable (grayed out). Instead, drag the contact to the Shared Contacts folder, then copy it back to the identity's folder from where you moved the contact.

**See Also** Outlook Express, Internet Explorer, Search

# Administrative Tools

Collection of MMC tools you can use to administer every aspect of your Windows 2000 computer configuration. Which tools are available depends on whether the computer is a Windows 2000 Professional or Server computer, whether the computer is a domain controller, and which services are installed on the computer.

To access Administrative Tools, choose Start ➢ Settings ➢ Control Panel, then double-click the Administrative Tools icon.

**TIP** In Windows 2000 Server, you can also choose Start ➢ Programs ➢ Administrative Tools to display a submenu with all currently available Administrative Tools.

Commonly available options in Administrative Tools include Component Services, Computer Management, Data Sources (ODBC), Event Viewer, Local Security Policy, Performance, Services, and Telnet Server Administration. On computers configured as

domain controllers with Active Directory installed, you'll also typically see Active Directory Domains and Trusts, Active Directory Sites and Services, Active Directory Users and Computers, Configure Your Server, DHCP, DNS, Licensing, and many others.

Each of the Administrative Tools available in Windows 2000 Professional and Windows 2000 Server that are available with the Server computer installed as a domain controller with Active Directory installed, and the Professional computer installed in the domain, are covered in separate sections of this book.

**See Also** Component Services, Computer Management, Data Sources (ODBC), Event Viewer, Local Security Policy, Performance, Services, Telnet Server Administration, Active Directory Domains and Trusts, Active Directory Sites and Services, Active Directory Users and Computers, Configure Your Server, DHCP, Distributed File System, DNS, Domain Controller Security Policy, Internet Services Manager, Licensing, Domain Security Policy, Routing and Remote Access, Server Extensions Administrator, Microsoft Management Console (MMC), Active Directory

# Autodial

**See** Network and Dial-up Connections

# Backup

Lets you safeguard the data stored on your computer or on network drives to which you have access by copying the data to a data storage device, such as a tape drive or additional hard drive. Should there be a problem with your live data (such as disk failure, accidental deletion of files, or file corruption), you can restore data from a backup.

**NOTE** Supported file systems include FAT and NTFS.

**NOTE** You must have administrative privileges to perform backup- and restore-related functions.

Choose Start ➢ Programs ➢ Accessories ➢ System Tools ➢ Backup to open Windows 2000 Backup. Backup has four tabs:

**Welcome** Gives you general information about Backup's features and provides you with buttons to access the Backup and Restore Wizards. Another option on this tab guides you through the process of creating an emergency repair disk.

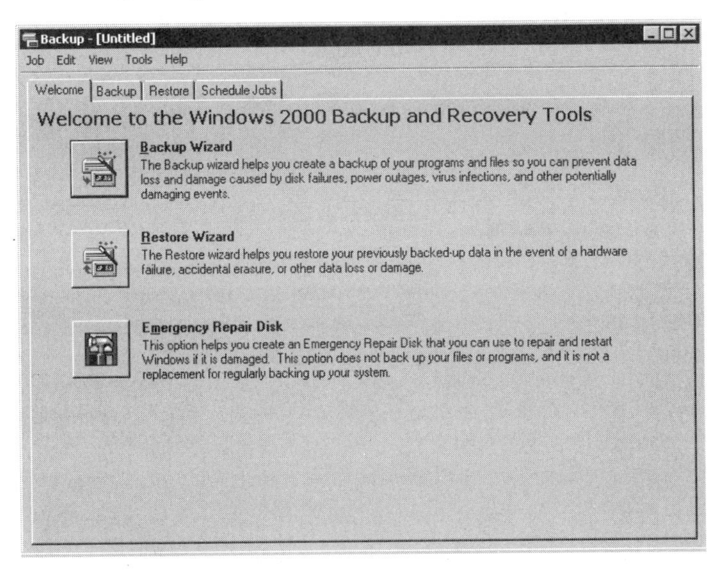

**TIP** You can also access the three options available on the Welcome tab from the Tools menu.

**Backup** Lets you select the files you want to back up, specify a backup destination and backup media or filename, and start the backup by clicking Start Backup.

**TIP** If you back up files to a file, you can then copy the file to a floppy disk, other hard disk, or other storage medium.

The Backup tab has two panes for selecting drives, folders, and files to back up. The left pane lets you select the drives and folders in the entire file system structure (local and network file systems to which you have access). The right pane lets you select the contents of the currently selected drive or folder, including files. You'll also see detailed information about the contents of your left-pane selection, such as name, total size, and free space (for drives), and name, type, size, and modified date and time (for folders and files).

Select drives, folders, and files to back up by clicking the check box to the left of the item.

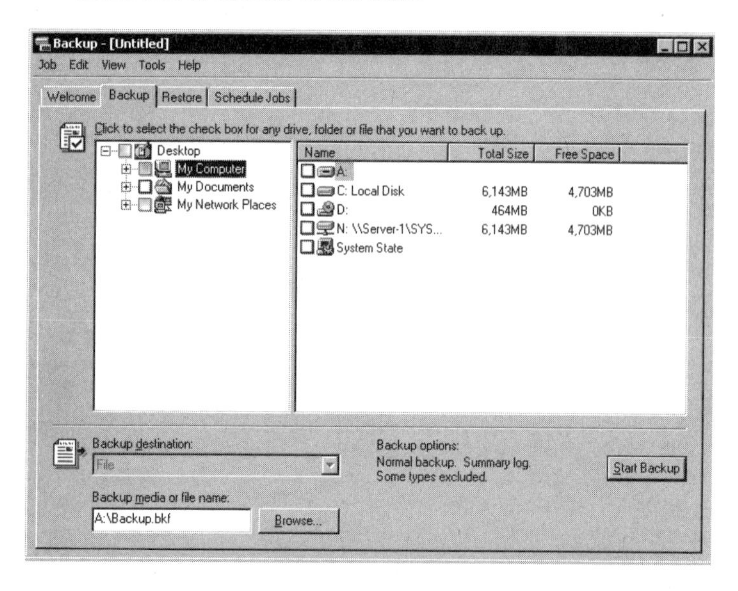


Once you click Start Backup, the Backup Job Information dialog box opens. This dialog box lets you customize the backup job; for example, you can provide a backup description and specify whether you want to append the backup to the media or overwrite existing data on the media. You can also schedule the backup job to run at a later time by clicking Schedule. Click Advanced to specify whether you want to:

- Back up data in Remote Storage (infrequently accessed files that have been moved to a secondary, non-local storage device)
- Verify the backup
- Compress the backup data (if available)

- Back up system protected files (only available if you're backing up system state data)
- Select the backup type

## Catalog Backup Sets

In the Backup Job Information dialog box, you can also specify that only the owner and Administrator have access to the backup data. This option is available only if you've selected the option for overwriting data on the media. After making all selections, click Start Backup in the Backup Job Information dialog box.

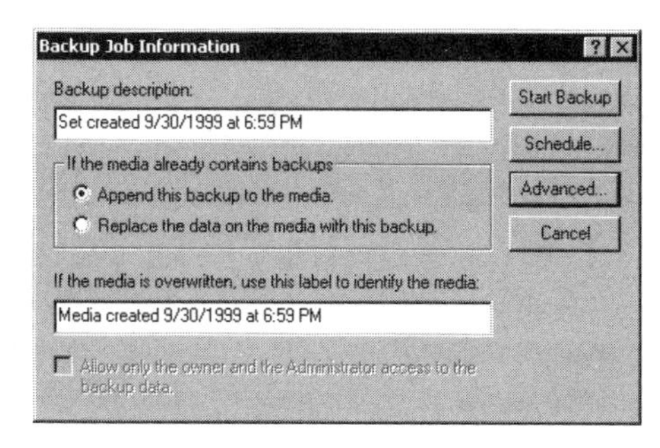


**Restore** Lets you select from any available backup set the files you want to restore from the backup media to disk and lets you start the restore operation.

The Restore tab has two panes for selecting backup sets, folders, and files to restore that are available under each created media under the appropriate media type. The left pane lets you select the backup sets and folders available in backup sets under each created media. The right pane lets you select the contents of the currently selected created media, backup set, or folder, including files. You'll also see detailed information about your selection. For media type, this information includes the name of the created media. For created media, this includes the volume (name), backup set number, the date and time the backup set was created, the method used to create the backup set, and the size and description of the set. For backup sets and folders, this information includes the name, size, and modified date of any folder or file contained in the currently selected backup set or folder.

Choose backup sets, folders, and files to restore by selecting the check box to the left of each item.

For any backup sets that have not yet been cataloged, the backup set icon contains a question mark. To catalog a backup set or media, right-click the backup set or media and choose Catalog to create a catalog on disk. You cannot access files and folders in a backup set until it has been cataloged.

**TIP** Question marks for backup sets that are not cataloged may not appear right away. You may have to close and run Backup again or even restart the computer.

You can also choose a location for the restored files by selecting Original Location, Alternate Location, or Single Folder from the Restore Files To drop-down list. Click Start Restore to start the restore. You'll have a chance to set advanced restore options by clicking Advanced in the Confirm Restore dialog box.

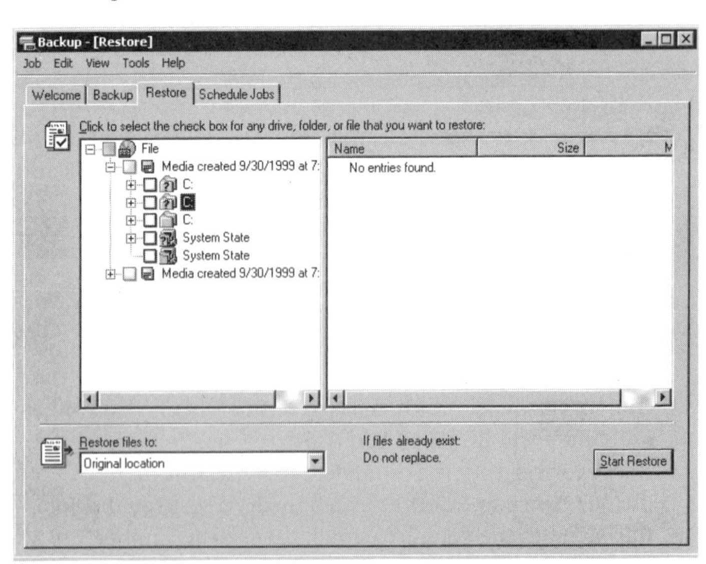


**Schedule Jobs** Lets you choose the start date for a backup job you want to run at a later time and then start the Backup Wizard to create the backup job. Select a date in the calendar, then click Add Job or double-click a date.

Either action will start the Backup Wizard. More information about running the Backup Wizard is provided under the subheading Backup Wizard. In the calendar, navigate to the previous month by clicking the left arrow button, and navigate to the next month by clicking the right arrow button. Click Today to return to the current date.

Backup - [Schedule Jobs]

Job Edit View Tools Help

Welcome | Backup | Restore | Schedule Jobs

Today — September, 1999

| Sun | Mon | Tue | Wed | Thu | Fri | Sat |
|---|---|---|---|---|---|---|
| 29 | 30 | 31 | 1 | 2 | 3 | 4 |
| 5 | 6 | 7 | 8 | 9 | 10 | 11 |
| 12 | 13 | 14 | 15 | 16 | 17 | 18 |
| 19 | 20 | 21 | 22 | 23 | 24 | 25 |
| 26 | 27 | 28 | 29 | | 1 | 2 |
| 3 | 4 | 5 | 6 | 7 | 8 | System Event |

Add Job

## Backup Wizard

The Backup Wizard guides you through the process of configuring the parameters for backup jobs. You can then run these backup jobs to back up files that reside on your computer's storage devices or network storage devices to which you have access to storage media, such as tape or a file.

To create backup jobs using the Backup Wizard, follow these steps:

1. Click the Backup Wizard button on Backup's Welcome tab to start the Backup Wizard. Click Next.
2. Select whether you want to back up everything on the computer; selected files, drives, or network data; or only system state data. Click Next.

**TIP** System state data for Windows 2000 Professional includes the Registry, system boot files, and the COM+ Class Registration database. For Windows 2000 Server, it includes the aforementioned items and the Certificate Services database. If the Windows 2000 Server computer is also a domain controller, system state data includes the Active Directory database and the SYSVOL directory.

**3.** If you chose to back up everything, or to back up system state data only, skip to Step 4. If you chose to back up selected files, drives, or network data, you have to select the files, drives, or network data you want to back up. To do this, navigate the file systems available to you in the What to Back Up area of the Items to Back Up dialog box (use the plus and minus signs to expand and collapse drives and directories), and then select the files, drives, and network data you want to back up by checkmarking the corresponding boxes to the left of the files, folders, or drives. If you select a drive or folder, the utility will back up all folders and files below the drive or folder. When you've finished, click Next.

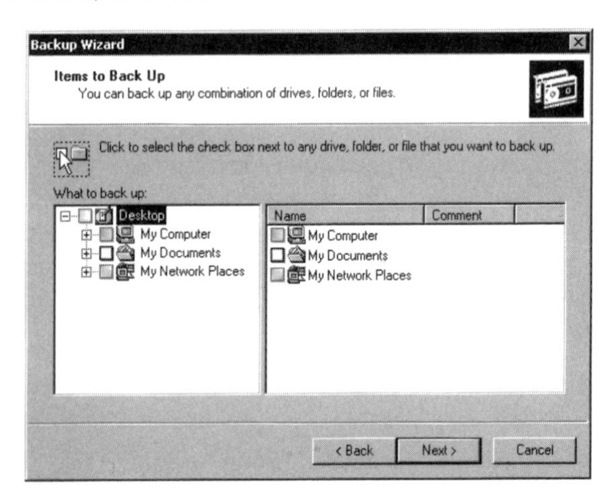

**TIP** You cannot select grayed-out check boxes (such as those for Desktop, My Computer, and My Network Places).

4. Select your media type, such as tape (file is the default if no other media type is installed). Then enter the name of the media—for example, the name of the tape to you which want to back up (or, if you select file as the media type, the name of the file to which you want to back up). Click Next.

5. If you want to specify advanced settings, click Advanced and continue with step 6. Otherwise, skip to step 7.

**TIP** If you don't click Advanced and follow the Advanced dialog boxes, several defaults will be applied to your backup.

6. Follow the dialog boxes to set up advanced options. Items include selecting the type of backup operation you want to perform (Normal, Copy, Incremental, Differential, or Daily) and specifying labels for the backup and the media. In addition, you can specify whether you want to:

   - Back up migrated data
   - Verify your data after it's been backed up
   - Compress files during backup
   - Append the backup to the media or replace the data on the media
   - Allow only the Administrator or owner access to the backup data
   - Run the backup job now or schedule it at a later time

**TIP** For more information on how to schedule a job, see the subheading Scheduling a Backup Job.

**TIP** For more information on backup types, see the information about the Backup Type tab under the subheading Options.

7. Verify that the information on the Summary screen is correct and click Finish. Your backup job either starts immediately or at the scheduled time.

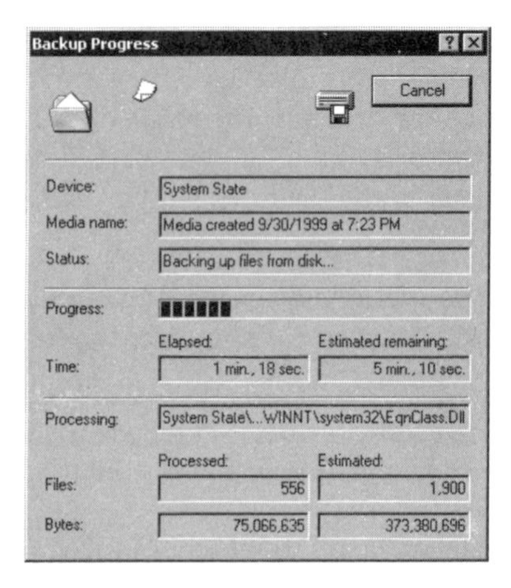


8. When the backup is finished, you'll see a summary in the Backup Progress dialog box telling you that the backup is complete and giving you additional information, such as the media name, status of the backup job, time elapsed during the backup, and the number of files and bytes processed. Click Close to close the Backup Progress dialog box, or click Report to see more detailed information about this backup job.

## Restore Wizard

The Restore Wizard guides you through the process of restoring data you previously backed up in the event that your data was destroyed, deleted, corrupted, or otherwise damaged. To restore files using the Restore Wizard, follow these steps:

1. Click the Restore Wizard button on the Welcome tab to start the Restore Wizard. Click Next on the first screen.

**TIP** Note that the Restore Wizard button and the Backup Wizard button are very similar. The Restore Wizard button has an arrow that points from media to disk; the Backup Wizard button has an arrow that points from disk to media.

2. Navigate the available backup sets by using the plus and minus signs or double-clicking the available media and then folder names. You can select folders to restore in the left pane or files and folders to restore in the right pane of the What to Restore window. The left pane shows you the entire folder structure; the right pane shows only the contents of the currently selected drive or folder.

   When you try to expand a media name or backup set, you may be prompted to catalog the backup set if a catalog does not yet exist. Verify or change the path to the catalog backup file and click OK to create a catalog on disk.

   When you have made your selections, click Next.

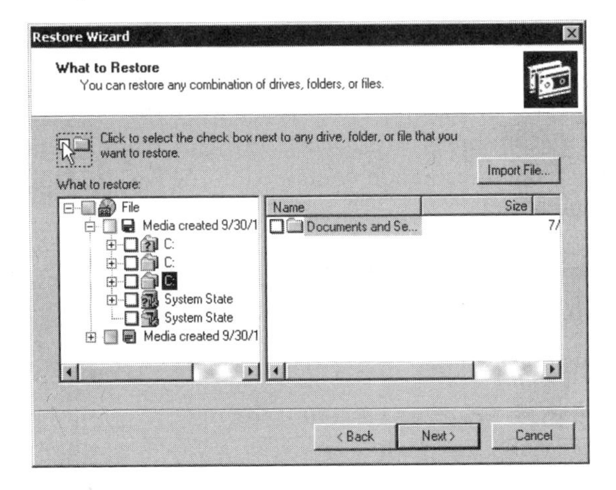


3. Once you've finished making your selections and you don't want to specify advanced restore options, skip to step 7. If you do this, several default restore settings will be used for the restore—for example, files will be restored to their original location and existing files will not be replaced.

   If you want to specify advanced restore settings, click Advanced.

4. Select a location for the restored files from the Restore Files To drop-down list. Your choices include Original

Location, Alternate Location, and Single Folder. Then click Next.

5. Specify what you want to happen if a file that is being restored already exists on disk. You can choose not to replace the file (the default), to replace the file if it is older than the backup file, or to always replace the file. When you've made your selection, click Next.
6. Select advanced restore options if they're available. These may include restoring security, restoring the removable storage database, and restoring junction points. Click Next.
7. Read the summary screen and click Finish to start the restore operation.
8. Follow any additional prompts, which may vary depending on your backup media. When the restore begins, you'll see the Restore Progress dialog box. This dialog box provides the same information contained in the Backup Progress dialog box.

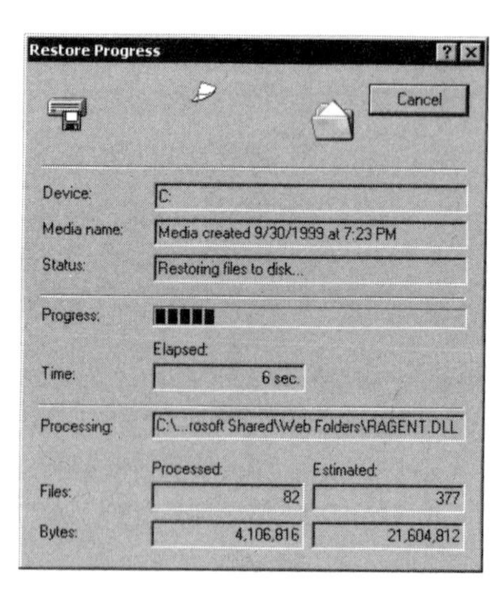


9. When the restore is complete, click Report if you wish to see more detailed information about the process, or click Close to dismiss the Restore Progress dialog box.

## Scheduling a Backup Job

Lets you schedule a backup job to run at a later time. To schedule a backup job, follow these steps:

1. Run the Backup Wizard and follow the steps until you reach the summary screen. Click Advanced.
2. Follow the steps until you reach the When to Back Up dialog box and select Later. If you're prompted, enter the name and password of the user you want to run the backup job and click OK. Next, enter a name for the backup job in the Job Name text box and click Set Schedule.

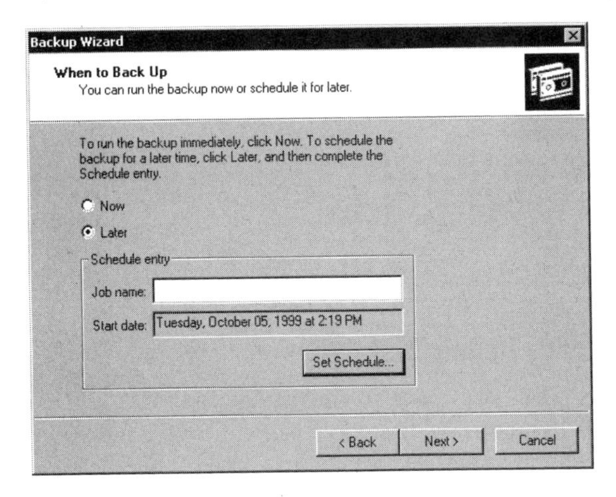


3. When the Schedule Job dialog box opens, you'll notice it has two tabs: Schedule and Settings. Because scheduling a backup job is the same as scheduling any other task to run on the computer, the two tabs available on the Schedule Job dialog box are the same as the Schedule and Settings tabs in the property sheet of any task scheduled with the Scheduled Task Wizard. For more information on these tabs, see the subheading Scheduled Tasks Folder under the heading Scheduled Tasks.

   Make your scheduling choices on these two tabs, then click OK to save them and return to the When to Back Up dialog box in the Backup Wizard. Click Next.

4. Read the summary screen and click Finish to save the scheduled backup job.

To verify that the backup job has been scheduled, select Start ➢ Settings ➢ Control Panel and open Scheduled Tasks. Your backup job should appear in the list of scheduled tasks in the Scheduled Tasks folder.

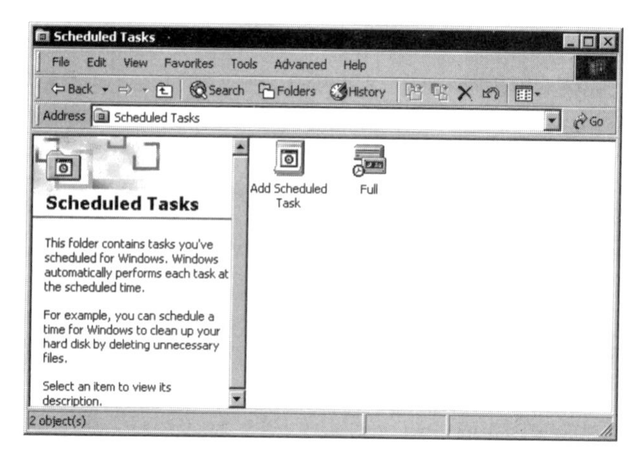


## Emergency Repair Disk

Lets you create an emergency repair disk (ERD), which you can use to try to repair your Windows 2000 system if a system file becomes corrupted, erased, or overwritten and your system does not work properly anymore.

To create an ERD, follow these steps:

1. Click the Emergency Repair Disk button on the Welcome tab of Backup.
2. Place a blank, formatted floppy disk into your floppy drive (typically drive A or drive B). Specify whether you also want to back up the Registry to the repair directory. Click OK.
3. Wait for a moment while the ERD is being created. When the process is finished, a message appears telling you that the repair disk was successfully saved. Click OK, then

remove the floppy disk from the drive, label it ERD for *computer name,* and note the date the disk was created.

4. Store the floppy disk in a safe place.

## Menus

The Backup utility has some familiar and some unique menus and menu options. The options available on each menu change depending on which tab you currently have selected.

### Job Menu

The Job menu contains these options:

**New** Lets you create a new backup job. If any files had been selected on the Backup tab, these selections are removed.

**Start** Lets you start a backup or restore job after you've selected the appropriate files.

**Load Selections** Lets you load a previously saved backup job script.

**Save Selections** Lets you save a backup job as a script so that you can load and use it at a later time. Files are saved as BKS files.

**Save Selections As** Lets you save a backup script under a different name.

**Recent File** Appears if you have not saved any backup jobs as a file using Save Selections or Save Selections As. Once you've saved selections, this option is replaced with the filenames of the most recently saved selections.

**Exit** Closes the backup program.

### Edit Menu

The Edit menu contains these options:

**Select Space** Lets you select a drive, folder, or file (place a check mark in the check box) on the Backup and Restore tabs (in either pane).

**Deselect Space** Lets you deselect a drive, folder, or file (remove a check mark from the check box) on the Backup and Restore tabs (in either pane).

**Move Up** Moves up to the next higher level from the currently selected drive, folder, file, backup set, or created media as applicable on the Backup and Restore tabs.

### *View Menu*

The View menu contains these options:

**Toolbar** Toggles the display of the Backup toolbar, which contains buttons for creating a new backup job, opening an existing backup job, saving a backup job, accessing backup job reports, accessing the Options dialog box, and accessing Help.

**Status Bar** Toggles the display of the status bar at the bottom of the Backup window.

**List** Removes the column headers in the right pane of the Backup and Restore tabs.

**Details** Displays the column headers in the right pane of the Backup and Restore tabs.

### *Tools Menu*

The Tools menu contains these options:

**Backup Wizard** Starts the Backup Wizard.

**Restore Wizard** Starts the Restore Wizard.

**Create an Emergency Repair Disk** Starts the process of creating an ERD.

**Catalog a Backup File** Lets you create a catalog on disk of any backup file you've created.

**Media Tools** If catalogs have been created, contains a suboption, Delete Catalog, which you can use to delete a previously created catalog.

**Report** Lets you access any available backup job report.

**Options** Lets you configure backup and restore options.

## Options

You can access Backup options in two ways: either by choosing Tools ➢ Options, or by clicking the Options button on the toolbar, if it's displayed. The Options dialog box contains five tabs:

**General** Lets you make general choices regarding backups, such as whether you want Backup to:

- Calculate the number of files and bytes to be backed up based on your selections
- Use catalogs available on the media to create catalogs on disk
- Verify the backed-up data after completion of a backup job

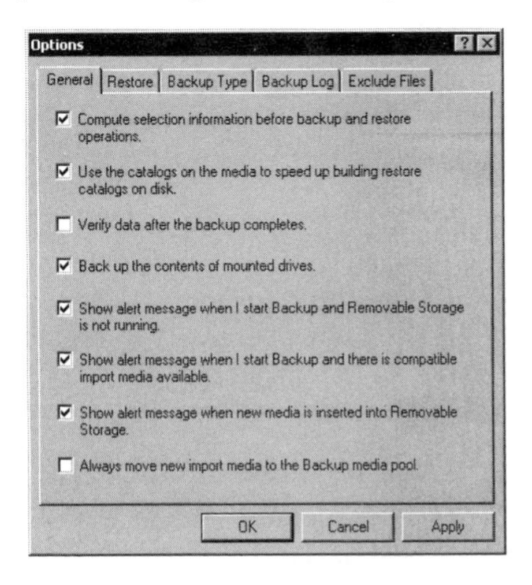


You can also specify that you want Backup to back up the contents of mounted drives as well as display alert messages for several different backup-related scenarios. Finally, you can specify that you want Backup to always move new media (detected by Removable Storage) to backup media pools. Select the appropriate check box to make your choice.

**Restore** Lets you specify the action you want Backup to perform when you're restoring a file and the file already exists on the disk to which you're restoring. Your options include not replacing the file (Microsoft recommends this option and it's the default), replacing the file if the file on disk is older than the file that is being restored, or always replacing the file. Select the appropriate radio button to make your choice.

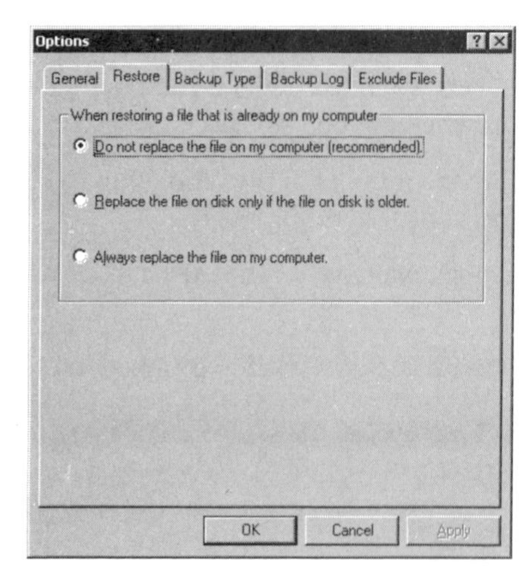


**Backup Type** Lets you select the kind of backup you want to use by default. Your choices are Normal (the default), Copy, Differential, Incremental, and Daily. Select an option from the Default Backup Type drop-down list. When you make a selection, an explanation of the option appears in the Description area below the drop-down list.

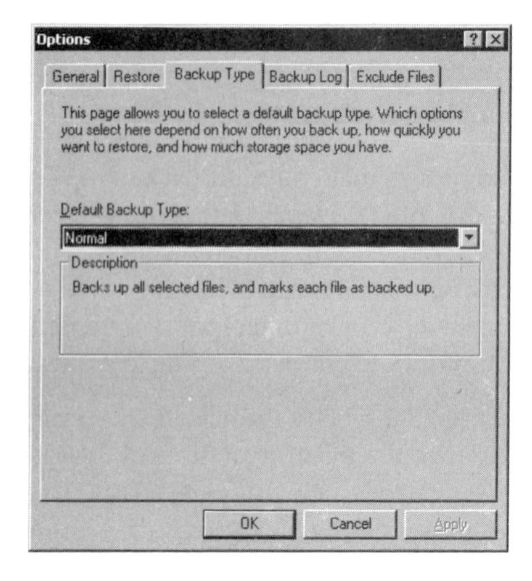

**Backup Log** Lets you specify the type of backup log file you want to create. Different types will provide varying levels of detail. You can choose from Detailed, Summary (the default), and None by checking the appropriate radio button.

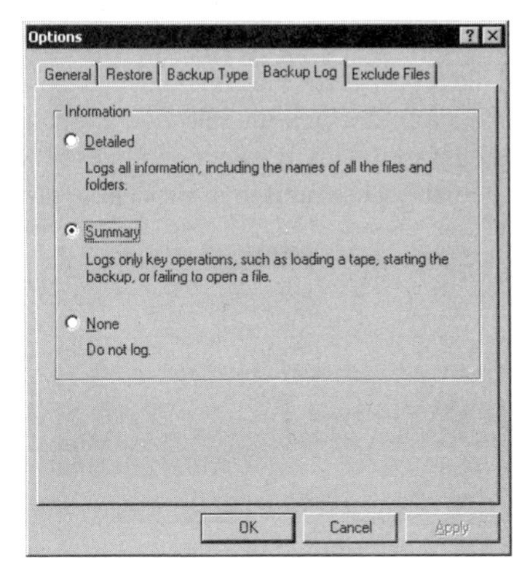


**Exclude Files** Lets you specify certain file types or files you don't want to back up. You can tell Backup to exclude files depending on who owns them. To exclude files that are owned by anyone, you would add the files to the Files Excluded for All Users list box. To exclude only files that are owned by the Administrator, you would add the files to the Files Excluded for User Administrator list box.

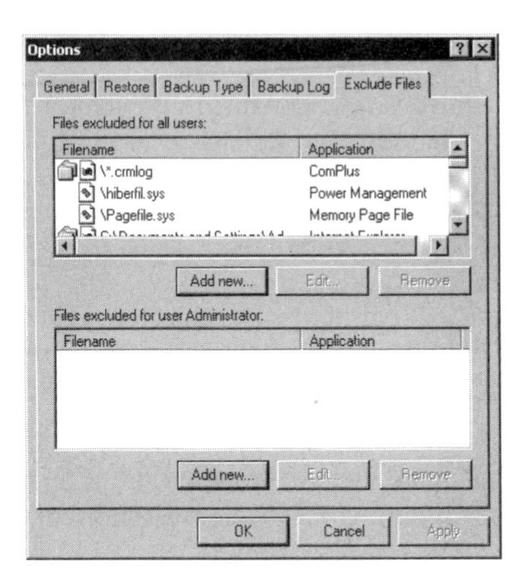

To add a file to either list box, click the corresponding Add New button. You can specify files for exclusion in one of two ways. The first is by type. To do this, select a registered file type in the list. You can use the Shift or Ctrl key to select more than one file type. The second method is by typing a specific filename (or file type if you don't find it in the list of registered file types) in the Custom File Mask text box. Make sure that the path to which the selection applies is correct; otherwise, change it. Finally, select or deselect the Applies to All Subfolders check box, and then click OK to save the change.

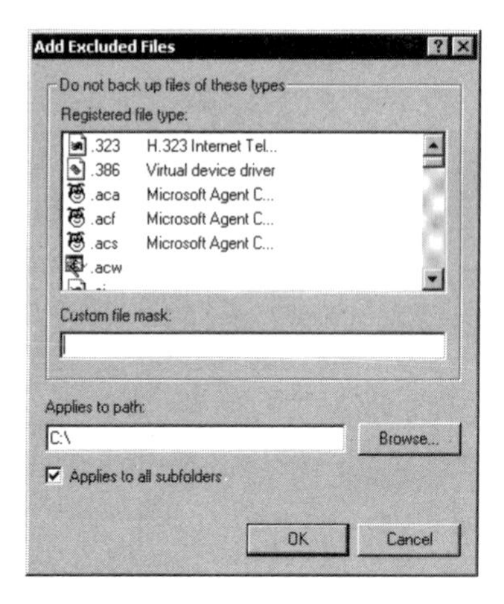


To edit or remove an excluded file or file type, on the Exclude Files tab select it in the list box and click the corresponding Edit or Remove button.

**See Also** Scheduled Tasks (Scheduled Task Folder), System Information

# Browse

Browse...

Used to find files and directories on the computer or in the network. You'll see this button in many dialog boxes where you need to provide the name and path of a file or folder or specify an Internet or intranet address or URL.

When you click Browse, the Browse window opens. On the left side of the window, you can choose a shortcut to different locations on the computer or network where you can look for the files you want. Locations include History, Desktop, My Documents, My Computer, and My Network Places. If you click one of these shortcuts, the location is displayed in the Look In field, and the files and folders found in that location appear in the window to the right. You can also choose a location from the Look In drop-down list. Double-click on folders in the window to move further down the directory structure.

In the Files of Type drop-down list, you can specify which type of files you want to see displayed in the Browse window, or you can specify to see all files of all types.

When you find the file you're looking for, select it in the window, and its name will appear in the Filename field. Then click Open, which will return you to the dialog box from where you were browsing, and enter the name and path of the file in the appropriate field.

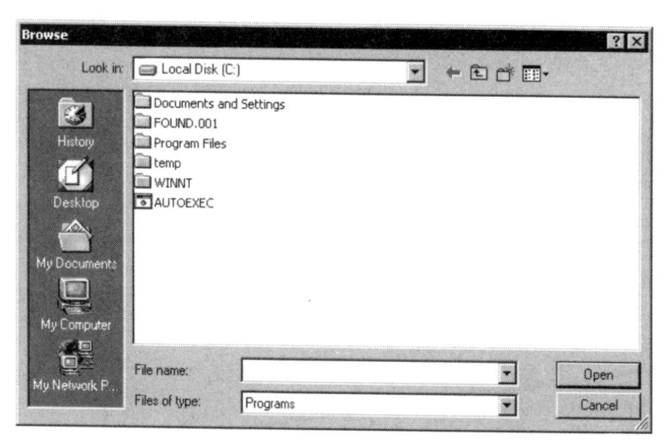


**See Also** My Computer, My Documents, My Network Places

# Calculator

Calculator

Lets you perform mathematical calculations, including standard, scientific, and statistical calculations. To open the Calculator, choose Start ➢ Programs ➢ Accessories ➢ Calculator. You can display the Calculator in either Standard view or Scientific view, depending on which view was used when you last closed the Calculator.

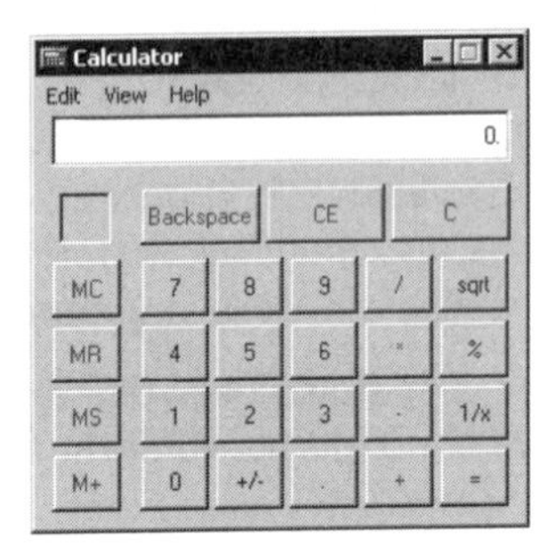


To enter numbers in the calculator, use the mouse and click the number keys in the Calculator, or use the numbers on the keyboard.

Depending on whether you're in Standard or Scientific view, you'll see different Calculator options. However, the following buttons are available in either view:

**Backspace** Deletes a single digit to the left of the cursor.

**CE (Clear Entry)** Erases the last entry. Alternatively, you can press the Delete key to clear the entry.

**C (Clear All)** Erases the entire calculation.

**MC (Memory Clear)** Clears the calculator's memory.

**MR (Memory Recall)** Recalls a number from memory. Also shows the result of adding a displayed number to the number in memory.

**MS (Memory Store)** Stores a number in the calculator's memory. Any previously stored number is erased. When you click MS, an *M* appears in the box to the left of the Backspace button.

**M+ (Add to Memory)** Adds the displayed number to the number in memory.

The operators available in Standard view include: / (division), * (multiplication), – (subtraction), + (addition), sqrt (calculating the square root), % (calculating the percentage of another number), and 1/x (calculating the reciprocal). Use the = sign to obtain the result of your calculation.

You can use the Edit menu to copy and paste. The View menu lets you switch from Standard view to Scientific view as well as activate and deactivate digit grouping.

## Scientific Calculations

Calculator also lets you perform scientific and statistical calculations. To do so, you must change the view to Scientific. This view lets you choose from several different number systems (hexadecimal, decimal, octal, and binary) by selecting the appropriate radio button (Hex, Dec, Oct, or Bin).

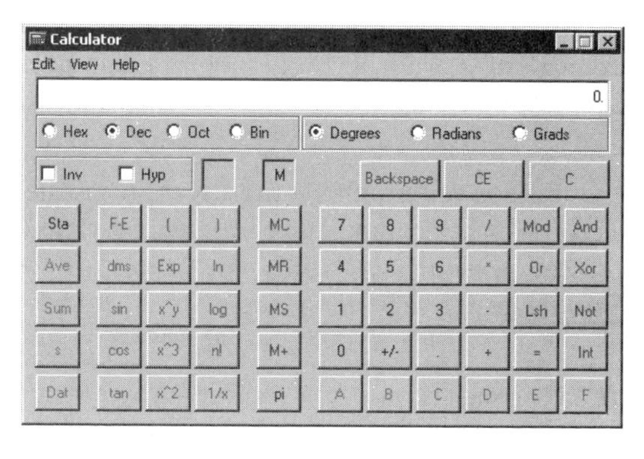


To perform a calculation, select the number system you want to use, enter a number, choose an operator, enter any other numbers and operators necessary for the calculation, and click = to display the result. Use the Calculator's memory functions as necessary.

### *Statistical Calculations*

To perform a statistical calculation, you enter the first number, then click Sta to open the Statistics box. Next, click Dat to enter the number. Enter additional numbers and click Dat after each number. Click Sta to display the statistical data you're entering and Ret to return to the Calculator. In the Statistics box, you can also click Load (to display in the Calculator display area the number selected in the Statistics box), CD (to clear the selected number), or CAD (to clear all numbers).

When you've entered all the data, click the statistical function you want to apply. Choices are Ave (Average), Sum (Sum), and S (Standard Deviation). Calculator will then display the result.

## Callback

**See** Network and Dial-up Connections

## Capturing Images

Windows 2000 lets you capture screen images (full screen or active window), which you can then paste into a document. When you capture a screen image, it's saved to the Windows Clipboard, making it available for pasting at a later point in time. To capture an image and paste it into a document, follow these steps:

1. If you want to capture the entire screen, press the Print Screen key or key combination (often abbreviated as PrtSc and accessed by pressing Shift+Print Screen). If you want to capture an active window, press Alt+Print Screen.

**NOTE** Note that you won't see anything happen on the screen when you capture a screen or window with Print Screen.

2. Place the cursor where you want to insert the image in your document and press Ctrl+V or choose Edit ➢ Paste. Windows will paste the image into your document.

## CD Player

Plays audio CDs from the CD-ROM drive installed in your computer.

**NOTE** You must have a sound card and speakers installed in your computer to use the CD Player.

Choose Start ➢ Programs ➢ Accessories ➢ Entertainment ➢ CD Player to start the CD Player.

## Loading a CD

If you start the CD Player and no audio disk is in the CD-ROM drive, the CD Player displays a message asking you to insert an audio compact disc.

When you insert an audio CD into the CD-ROM player for the first time, you'll see the New Album Found in Drive dialog box. You can choose to download information for the CD from the Internet, such as the artist, title, and track information for only this CD, or to always download the information. If you choose the latter, you won't see this dialog box when you insert a new audio CD into the CD-ROM drive in the future. Click OK, then click Connect to connect to the Internet and download album information. You must already have a connection to the Internet configured. Click Cancel if you don't want to connect and download album information.

**TIP** You can disable downloading album information from the Internet, as explained under the subheading Options.

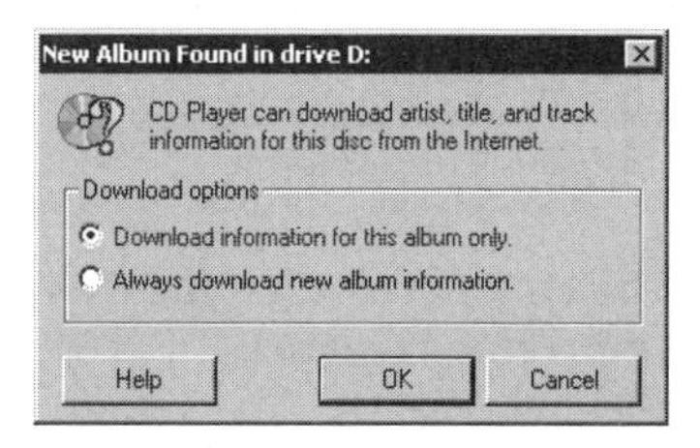


## Using the CD Player

After you load a CD and download album information, the CD starts playing immediately, and the following information is displayed on the CD Player's interface: the CD title, the name of the current track, and the name of the artist. The CD title bar also displays the CD title. During playback, you'll see which track is currently playing and how much of the track's play time has elapsed.

The Windows 2000 CD Player interface looks very similar to a physical CD player. You can control the playback of audio CDs using these buttons and other controls:

**Play** Starts playing the CD. During playback, this button changes to the Pause button, which you can use to pause playing the CD.

**Pause** Pauses playback of the currently playing track. When you click the Pause button, it changes to the Play button, which allows you to resume playback.

**Stop** Stops playing the CD.

**Eject** Ejects the CD-ROM drive's CD tray.

**Scan Back/Scan Forward** Lets you scan through the currently playing track bit by bit, either forward or back.

**Previous Track/Next Track** Lets you skip to the previous or next track.

**Mode** Lets you choose one of five play modes from a drop-down list:

- **Standard** Plays each track in order.
- **Random** Plays tracks in random order.
- **Repeat Track** Repeats the current track until you choose a different play order.
- **Repeat All** Repeats the entire CD after playing the last track.
- **Preview** Plays the first five seconds of each track.

Each mode has an associated symbol. This symbol displays to the left of the CD title in the CD player's interface so that you can quickly identify the current play mode.

**Volume Control** Lets you adjust the playback volume. Move the cursor over the Volume control knob and watch the cursor turn into a hand. You can now click the Volume control knob and drag the hand right or left to turn the volume up or down.

**Mute** Lets you mute the CD.

**Track** Displays a list of all tracks on the CD and their length in minutes and seconds. You can choose the track to play by selecting it from the list. The current track appears in bold.

**Disc** Displays a list of all audio CDs loaded in all CD-ROM drives installed in the computer. Multiple entries will show only if you have multiple CD-ROM drives with multiple audio CDs inserted. If multiple CDs are listed, you can choose a CD from the list to switch to that CD. The current CD appears in bold.

## Options

The Options button lets you configure the CD player.

Click the Options button and select from the following choices:

### *Preferences*

Lets you control playback, time display, preview time, Internet album information, download batching, and playlists. Click Preferences to display the Preferences dialog box, which has three tabs:

**Player Options** Lets you configure playback options, time display options, and the preview time. You can specify whether you want to:

- Automatically begin playback at startup
- Automatically stop playback on exit

- Always make the CD player the top window
- Display the CD control icon on the taskbar

Select or deselect the appropriate check boxes under Playback Options to activate or deactivate these options. By selecting the appropriate radio button under Time Display Options, you can show the elapsed track play time, the remaining track play time, the elapsed CD play time, or the remaining CD play time in the CD Player interface. You can also change how much of the track is played in Preview mode. Under Preview Time, move the slider to the left or right to set a preview time from between 1 and 20 seconds. You can click Use Defaults to return to the default values after you make changes, and you can click Advanced Audio to set advanced volume control options.

**TIP** Clicking the timer in the CD Player switches between Track Time Elapsed, Track Time Remaining, Disc Time Elapsed, and Disc Time Remaining.

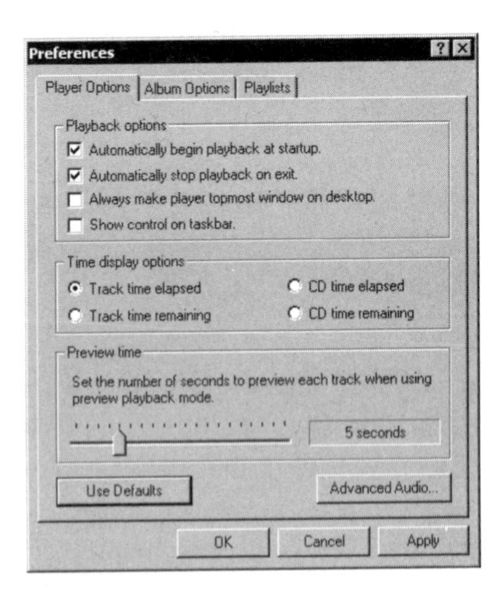


**Album Options** Lets you configure Internet album information and album download batching settings. Under Internet Album Information, you can choose to enable downloading of album information from the Internet, and you can choose to have the player prompt you before downloading information if downloading album information is enabled. You can also select an album information provider from the Primary Provider drop-down list.

In the Album Download Batching section, you can enable or disable album download batching. Use batching to download Internet album information at a later time if album download is disabled or if the album information is not available when you try to download. Click Download Now if you have batched albums (albums for which you were not able to download information either because Internet album information was disabled or information was not available) and want to download the information now. Click Use Defaults to return to the default settings.

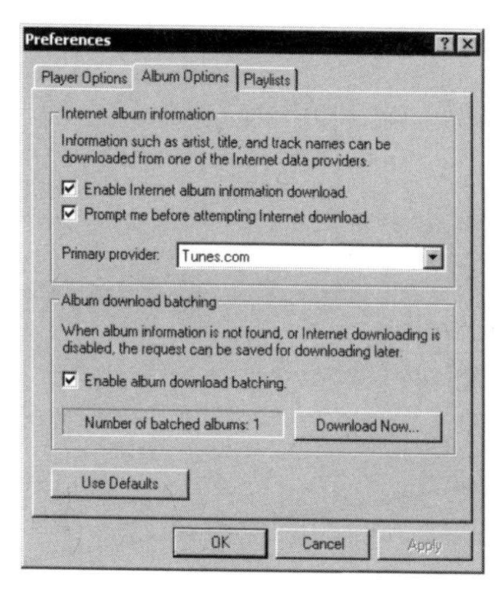


**Playlists** Lets you view and configure album information and playlists. If you've downloaded album information, you can view this information for any audio CDs currently loaded in any CD-ROM drive or contained in the CD Player database in the Album Information list box. Expand a CD title to see that CD's list of available tracks. To remove an album from the list, right-click a CD title and choose Delete Album.

If you haven't downloaded album information yet, right-click the CD-ROM drive's drive letter and select Download Album Information.

You can also view album information by viewing the database. Expand the Albums in Database icon to see albums in the database. By default, they are sorted by album title. Click View Albums by Artist Name to change the sorting of the database list from By Title to By Name.

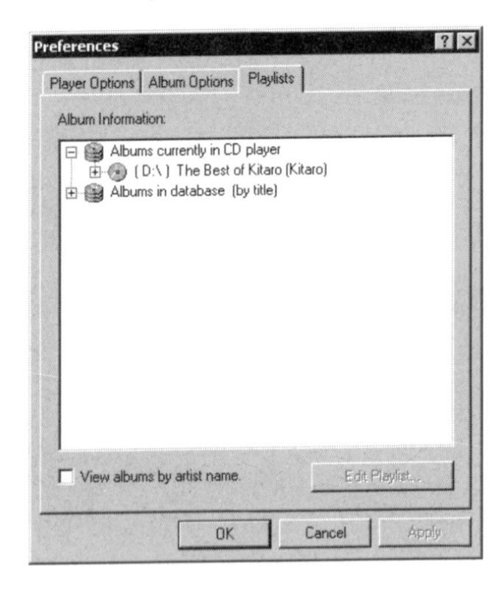


**Playlist Editor** Playlists show the tracks that will be played on each CD for which you have information. You can edit playlists to determine which songs you want to play and in which order. Right-click any CD or song title and choose Edit Playlist, or select a CD or song title and click Edit Playlist. When the Playlist Editor opens, you can change the name of the artist, the title of the CD, and the tracks (songs) you want to play (and in which order).

To remove a single track, select the track in the list and click Remove. To change the order of tracks in the playlist, click Clear All, then select a song from the Available Tracks drop-down list and click Add to Playlist. Continue to select and add tracks until you've created the playlist you want.

**TIP** You can use the Ctrl or Shift key to select multiple tracks in the same manner you would to select multiple files in a Windows 2000 folder.

To return to the default playlist, click Reset. If downloaded information about an album is incorrect, you can make changes and click Internet Upload to send the updated information to the Internet provider that you used to download the information. To save your changes and return to the Playlists tab, click OK.

**TIP** If you don't have information for a CD (either you haven't downloaded it yet or none was available), you can select the drive letter for the CD-ROM and click Create Playlist. You'll be able to enter a name for the artist and the CD title, and you'll be able to select which tracks to play (and in which order). However, the tracks will be titled Track 1, Track 2, and so forth instead of having the actual track names.

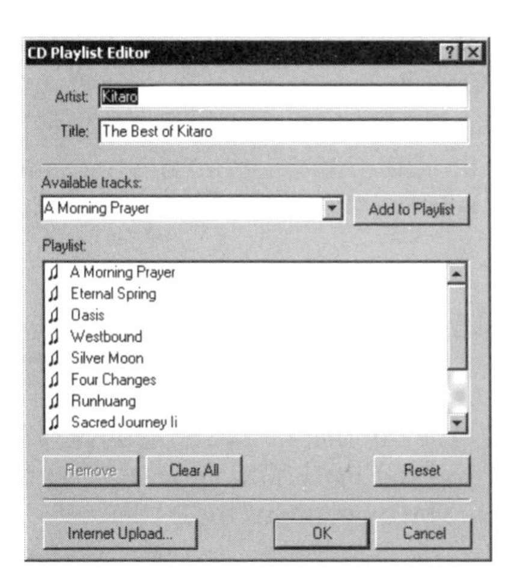


### *Playlist*

Takes you directly to the Playlist tab in the Preferences dialog box, where you can view and edit playlists.

### *Tiny View*

Changes the CD Player interface on the desktop to a smaller view.

**TIP** You can also change to Tiny View by clicking the Change to Tiny View button in the upper-right corner of the CD Player interface. This button looks like the Restore Down button in regular Windows 2000 windows.

Click Options ➢ Normal View to return the CD Player to its normal size.

**TIP** Alternatively, click the Change to Normal View button in the upper-right corner of the CD Player interface.

### *CD Player Help*

Opens the Windows 2000 Help system to the CD Player entries in the Help system's contents.

### *About CD Player*

Shows you information about the CD Player, such as version, copyright, and licensing information, and how much memory is available to Windows 2000.

### *Exit*

Closes the CD Player.

## Internet

The Internet button lets you perform CD-related actions that require accessing Internet sites. The Internet menu contains these options:

**TIP** If you choose an item from the Internet menu and you don't currently have an active connection to the Internet, nothing happens. If you want to automatically be prompted to connect to the Internet when you choose an item from this menu and you're not connected to the Internet, check Always Dial My Default Connection on the Connections tab of Internet Options, which you can access through Control Panel.

**Download Track Names** Downloads the names of the tracks for the CD currently in the CD-ROM drive and adds them to the CD Player database.

**Internet Music Sites** Lets you go to any of the music Web sites available on the submenu by choosing a site from the submenu. Your default Web browser opens to the appropriate page.

Once you've downloaded album information for a CD, the Internet menu may contain additional items that may allow you to search the Internet for additional music information, find more information about the artist and album, and perform other tasks. Options depend on the Internet music data provider you used to download the album information.

**See Also** Network and Dial-up Connections

# Change Password

Lets you change the password for the currently logged–on user or another user. Press Ctrl+Alt+Del, then click Change Password. Either leave the User Name and Log On To information as it is (to change the currently logged–on user's password) or specify a different username and where the user logs onto (to change another user's password). Enter the old password; then enter the new password and reenter it to confirm it. Click OK to change the password.

**See Also** Ctrl+Alt+Del

# Character Map

Character Map

Lets you display and copy the available characters for each font installed on your Windows 2000 computer. This includes private characters you created with the Private Character Editor. Character Map displays Unicode, DOS, and Windows character sets.

To access Character Map, choose Start ➢ Programs ➢ Accessories ➢ System Tools ➢ Character Map. The character set for the first font in alphabetical order is displayed.

**NOTE** By default, the Unicode character set for the selected font is displayed.

You can display character sets for other fonts by selecting a font from the Font drop-down list. Enlarge any character by simply clicking it.

**TIP** If you have created private characters with the Private Character Editor and linked them with either all or selected fonts, (Private Characters) will appear after the appropriate font names in the drop-down list.

When you click a character, the status bar at the bottom of the Character Map dialog box shows you the Unicode value (hexadecimal equivalent) for the character, as well as the name of the character. You may also see a keyboard equivalent displayed for the character if one is available.

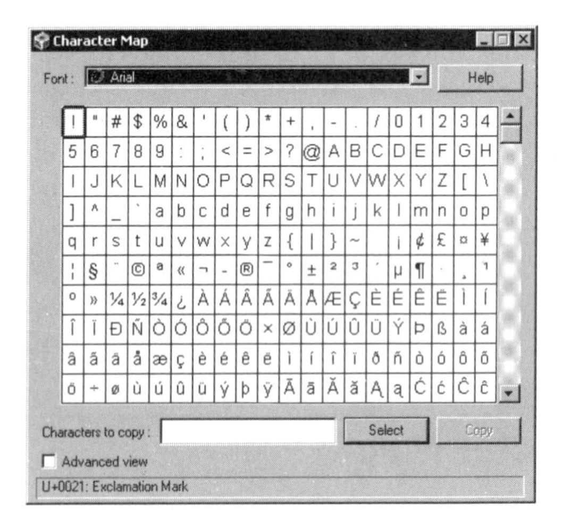


## Copying Characters

Character Map lets you copy characters to the Windows 2000 Clipboard and then paste them into other programs. To do this, first either click a character and then click Select, or double-click a character. Once you do, the character appears in the Characters to Copy text box. You can then click Copy to copy all selected characters to the Windows 2000 Clipboard.

**TIP** If the application into which you want to copy a character supports drag-and-drop, you can also select a character in the character set and then drag and drop it into the application.

## Advanced View

Select Advanced View to display additional Character Map–related options. You can select the character set you want to display, group the Unicode character set by Unicode subrange, search for a specific character, or go directly to a character in the Unicode character set.

**TIP** The entire Character Map window may not fit on your screen, and you can't resize this window. You may have to move the window to see certain portions of it.

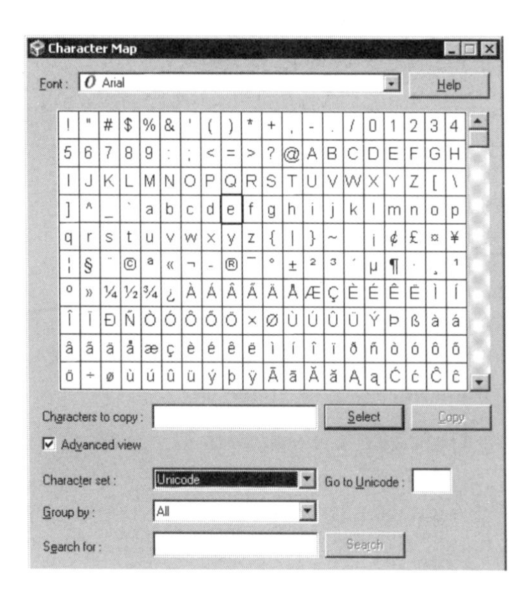

### Selecting a Character Set

To choose the character set you want to display, select a set from the Character Set drop-down list. You can choose from Unicode and from several DOS and Windows character sets.

### Grouping Characters in the Unicode Character Set

With the Unicode character set, instead of displaying all characters, you can group characters by Unicode subrange by selecting Unicode Subrange from the Group By drop-down list. If you do, the Group By dialog box opens, and you can select a subrange, such as Latin, Currency, Arrows, and Symbols & Dingbats. The Character Map dialog box then displays only the characters that are part of the selected subrange. This makes it easier for you to find a specific character.

**TIP** If you're currently displaying a DOS or Windows character set and you select Unicode Subrange from the Group By drop-down list, the character set automatically changes back to Unicode.

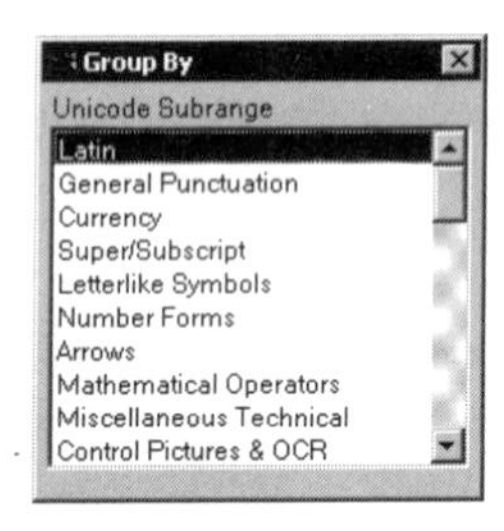


### Searching for Characters

You can search for a character by entering all or part of its name in the Search For text box and clicking Search. Character Map then takes you directly to that character.

### Accessing Unicode Characters Directly

You can access a Unicode character directly by selecting Unicode from the Character Set drop-down list and then entering in the Go to Unicode box the Unicode value for the character to which you want to go. Character Map then takes you automatically to the corresponding character.

**See Also** Private Character Editor, Fonts

## Checking Drives for Errors

You can check a floppy or hard drive for any file system and physical errors on the disk. To do so, perform these steps:

1. Right-click the drive in any Explorer window, then select Properties.
2. Select the Tools tab.
3. In the Error-Checking section, click Check Now.
4. In the Check Disk dialog box, specify whether you want file system errors to be fixed automatically and whether you want to scan for and attempt to recover bad sectors on the disk. Click Start when you've finished.

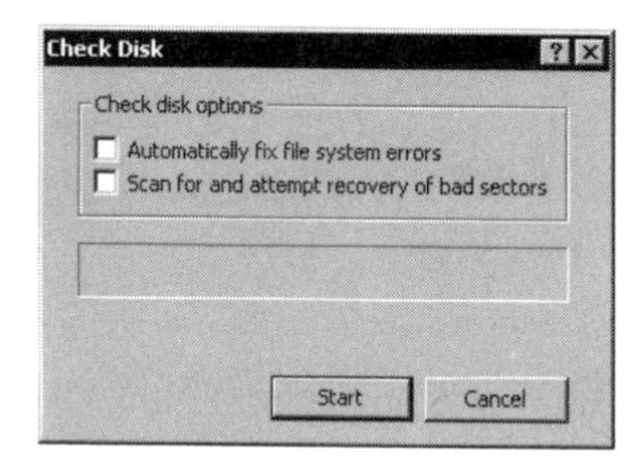


5. Wait for all phases of the check to finish. This may take some time. When the check is done, click OK in the Checking Disk *driveletter* message box.

**See Also** Explorer

## Clipboard

The Windows Clipboard is a temporary holding place for data. When you use the Cut or Copy command in programs running on a Windows 2000 computer, any data you cut or copy is placed onto the Clipboard. You can retrieve the contents of the Clipboard by using the Paste command. To view the contents of the Clipboard, you can paste them into Notepad, for example, or you can use the ClipBook Viewer.

**TIP** ClipBook Viewer is the new name in Windows 2000 for what was called the Clipboard Viewer in Windows NT and Windows 98. The ClipBook Viewer has greatly enhanced features beyond those of the Clipboard Viewer.

**WARNING** You can place only one item onto the Clipboard at any time. If you cut or copy a new item, any contents currently on the Clipboard are erased. You can, however, use ClipBook Viewer to save contents of the Clipboard into your local ClipBook.

**See Also** ClipBook Viewer

# ClipBook Viewer

ClipBook Viewer lets you view and save the contents of the Windows 2000 Clipboard. To open ClipBook Viewer, choose Start ➢ Run, then type **clipbrd** and click OK.

The ClipBook Viewer has two windows: the Local ClipBook and the Clipboard. Maximize or resize the Clipboard to view its contents.

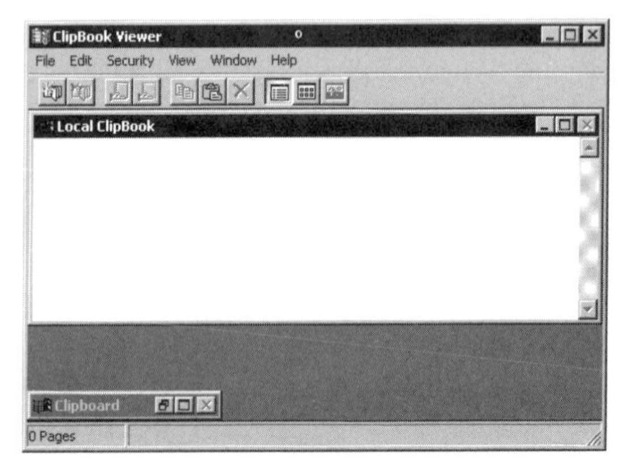


You can save the contents of the Clipboard either to a file or to the local ClipBook. If you do the latter, you can share ClipBook pages with other users. You can also set up permissions as well as auditing for each ClipBook page (for remote user access after you share a page) and take ownership of a page.

## Saving the Clipboard Contents to a File

To save the contents of the Clipboard to a file (with a .CLP extension), perform the following steps. Note that you cannot share files you save in this way.

1. Activate the Clipboard window by clicking somewhere in the window to select it.
2. Choose File ➢ Save As.
3. Browse to the folder where you want to save the file, enter a name for the file, and click Save.

## Saving the Clipboard Contents in the Local ClipBook

To save the contents of the Clipboard to the Local ClipBook in a ClipBook page, perform the following steps. If you save Clipboard contents in this way, you can share them with others.

1. Activate the Local ClipBook window by clicking somewhere in the window to select it.
2. Choose Edit ➢ Paste.
3. In the Paste dialog box, enter a name for the ClipBook page you're creating. Select Share Item Now if you want to share the page.
4. Click OK. The page is added to the ClipBook. If you selected the Share Item Now option, provide the necessary information in the Share ClipBook Page dialog box that opens (see Sharing a ClipBook Page).

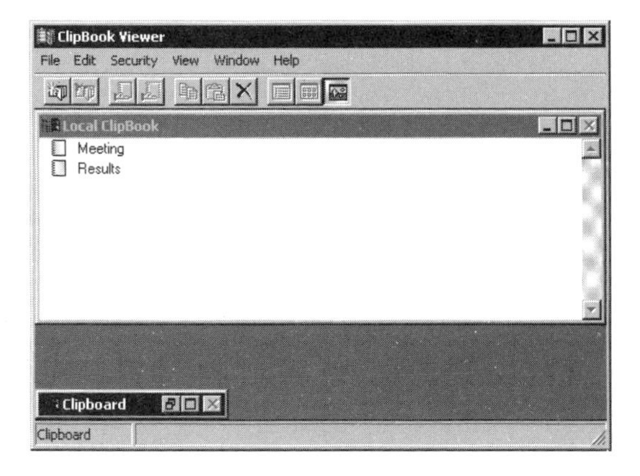

Once you have pages in your Local ClipBook, you can display them using the Table of Contents view (the default), the Thumbnail view, or the Full Page view (which displays the contents of the selected page). You can access the views either from the View menu or by clicking the appropriate button on the toolbar.

## Sharing a ClipBook Page

You can share ClipBook pages with other users. To do this, perform the following steps:

1. In the Local ClipBook, select the page you want to share.
2. Choose File ➢ Share to open the Share ClipBook Page dialog box.

**TIP** You can also click the Share button on the toolbar.

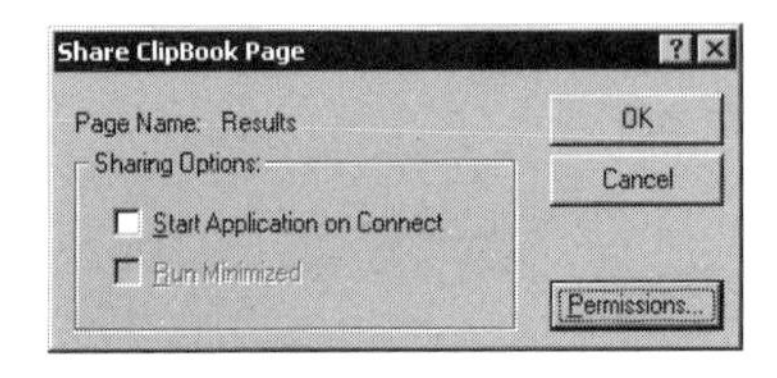


3. Select Start Application on Connect if you want the application used to create the contents of the page to start when another user accesses the page. Select Run Minimized if you want the application to run minimized. Run Minimized is available only if you select Start Application on Connect.
4. Click Permissions to configure the users and groups that you want to have access to the page, and the type of access they should have. Click OK to return to the Share ClipBook Page dialog box.
5. Click OK to share the page. A hand appears at the bottom of the page's icon to indicate that the page is shared.

To stop sharing a page, select the page in the Local ClipBook and choose File Stop Sharing, or click the Stop Sharing button on the toolbar.

## Accessing Pages in Another User's ClipBook

If other users have shared ClipBook pages, you can access these pages through ClipBook Viewer. Follow these steps:

1. Choose File ➢ Connect.

**TIP** You can also click the Connect button on the toolbar.

2. In the Select Computer dialog box, browse to and select the computer to which you want to connect. Click OK.
3. A list of all shared ClipBook pages appears. Double-click the ClipBook page you want to open.

To disconnect from the remote computer, choose File ➢ Disconnect, or click the Disconnect button on the toolbar.

## Security

You can set several security settings for ClipBook pages using the Security menu. It contains these options:

**Permissions** Lets you configure permissions to the selected ClipBook page for users and groups. Access types include Full Control, No Access, Read, Read and Link, Change Full Control, and Special.

**Auditing** Lets you configure the events to be audited for specific users and/or groups for the ClipBook page, such as success and/or failure of the following actions: Read, Delete, Change Permissions, and Change Audit Types.

**Owner** Lets you view the current owner of the ClipBook page or take ownership of the page.

**See Also** ClipBoard

# Close

☒ Closes the currently open window/application. You'll find this button in the top-right corner of any open window, next to either the Restore Down or Maximize button.

**See Also** Maximize and Minimize, Restore Down

# COM+ (Component Services)

Collection of services based on the Component Object Model (COM) and Microsoft Transaction Server (MTS) extensions. COM+ provides application administration and packaging, component load balancing (CLB), improved threading and security, object pooling, transaction management, queued components, and IMDB (In-Memory Database).

**See Also** Component Services

# Command Prompt

Used to execute command-line functions and utilities, such as MS-DOS commands and programs. Many MS-DOS commands and programs are still available in Windows 2000, although some have been removed. Check the Help system for a list of functions that still exist and those that have been removed. Examples of MS-DOS commands are del, dir, path, more, and print. An example of an MS-DOS program is Edit. Microsoft has added some new commands in Windows 2000, such as convert (to convert a FAT file system to NTFS) and start (to run a command or program in a separate window). Other examples of commands you can execute at the command prompt include the IPCONFIG command, used to view TCP/IP configuration information, and Net commands, used to performing Windows 2000 networking tasks, such as Net Use and Net Print. To see a list of many of the available commands, enter help at the command prompt.

To access a command prompt, choose Start ➢ Programs➢ Accessories ➢ Command Prompt. The Command Prompt window opens. You can now enter commands at the command prompt (by default, C:\).

**TIP** You can switch to a full-screen view by pressing Alt+Enter. This may be necessary for some programs that can't run in a Command Prompt window. Switch back by pressing Alt+Enter again.

**See Also** IPCONFIG, NET

# Communications

Communications ▸ Windows 2000 predefined program group from which you access the following communication-related program groups, programs, and functions: Fax, HyperTerminal, Internet Connection Wizard, NetMeeting, Network and Dial-up Connections, and Phone Dialer. These items are described in detail throughout this book. Choose Start ➢ Programs ➢ Accessories ➢ Communications to access the Communications program group.

**See Also** Fax, HyperTerminal, Internet Connection Wizard, NetMeeting, Network and Dial-up Connections, Phone Dialer

# Configure Your Server

Configure Your Server Lets you configure services and options on Windows 2000 Server computers. To access Configure Your Server, choose Start ➢ Programs ➢ Administrative Tools ➢ Configure Your Server.

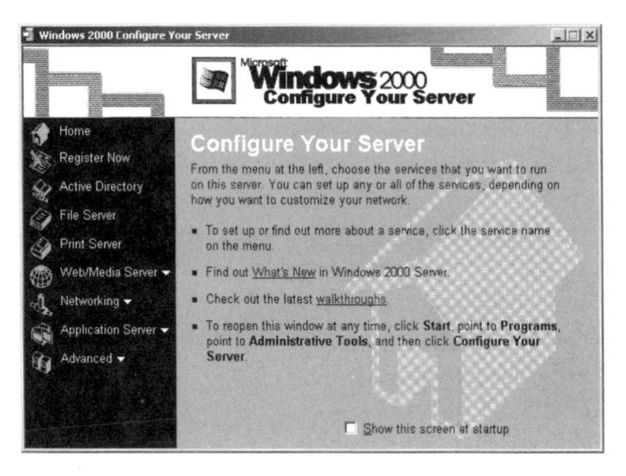

Configure Your Server contains links to the following server configuration options:

**Home** Lets you view and return to the Configure Your Server home page. Also contains a link to new features in Windows 2000 and a link to walkthroughs on the Web. The latter takes you to Microsoft's Web site, where you can find step-by-step instructions for installing and configuring Windows 2000 Server. Back on the Configure Your Server home page, you can also select a check box to specify that you want the Configure Your Server screen to display at startup.

**Register Now** Lets you register your copy of Windows 2000 Server.

**Active Directory** Depending on whether Active Directory is already installed, lets you install Active Directory or access links to Active Directory Users and Computers and Active Directory help.

**File Server** Lets you access links to the Create Shared Folder Wizard (to create shared folders), to Computer Management (where you can manage shared folders), and to shared folders help.

**Print Server** Lets you access links to the Add Printer Wizard, to the Printers folder (for printer management), and to printing help.

**Web/Media Server** Features a submenu that contains two links, Web Server and Streaming Media Server. The Web Server link lets you access the Web Server page, which has links to the Internet Services Manager (where you can perform Web and FTP server configuration) and to Internet Information Services (IIS) help. The Streaming Media Server link lets you access the Streaming Media Server page, which has links to start the Windows Component Wizard (used to set up Windows Media Services) and to Windows Media Services help. The Streaming Media Server page also contains a Next button, which you can click to start using streaming media after using the Component Wizard to set up Windows Media Services.

**Networking** Lets you access links to Network and Dial-up Connections and to the Network Identification tab of System Properties. Also has a submenu that contains four links: DHCP, DNS, Remote Access, and Routing. The DHCP link lets you access links to the DHCP Microsoft Management Console (MMC) snap-in and to DHCP help. The DNS link lets you access links to the DNS MMC console snap-in and to DNS help. The Remote Access and Routing links let you access links to the Routing and Remote Access MMC console snap-in, and to routing and remote access help.

**Application Server** Has a submenu with four links: Component Services, Terminal Services, Database Server, and E-mail Server. The Component Services link lets you access the Component Services MMC console snap-in and application and programming tools help. The Terminal Services link lets you access the Component Services Wizard (also accessible through Add/Remove Programs), which you use to install Terminal Services (an optional Windows 2000 component) and Terminal Services help. The Database Server and E-mail Server let you view screens explaining that Windows 2000 Server computers can be configured and used as database and e-mail servers after you install database or e-mail server applications.

**Advanced** Lets you view information about how you can use Windows 2000 Administration Tools to manage Windows 2000 Server computers from client computers. Also lets you access links to Windows 2000 Administration Tools help and Component and Services checklists. Also has a submenu with three links: Message Queuing, Support Tools, and Optional Components. The Message Queuing link lets you access links to the Message Queuing Installation Wizard and to Message Queuing help. The Support Tools link gives you information about how to install the Windows 2000 Resource Kit Support Tools. The Optional Components link lets you access a link to the Windows Component Wizard, which you use to install other optional Windows 2000 components.

**See Also** Active Directory, Computer Management, Create Shared Folder Wizard, Add Printers Wizard, Printers, Internet

Services Manager, Network and Dial-up Connections, System, DHCP, DNS, Routing and Remote Access, Component Services, Add/Remove Programs, Help, Microsoft Management Console (MMC)

## Component Services

MMC snap-in administrative tool that lets you configure and manage COM and COM+ applications and components. Tasks include, for example, installing COM+ applications and managing component load balancing, application security, distributed transactions, and IMDB (In-Memory Database).

To access Component Services, choose Start ➢ Settings ➢ Control Panel, double-click Administrative Tools, and then double-click Component Services.

**TIP** In Windows 2000 Server, you can also access Component Services by choosing Start ➢ Programs ➢ Administrative Tools ➢ Component Services.

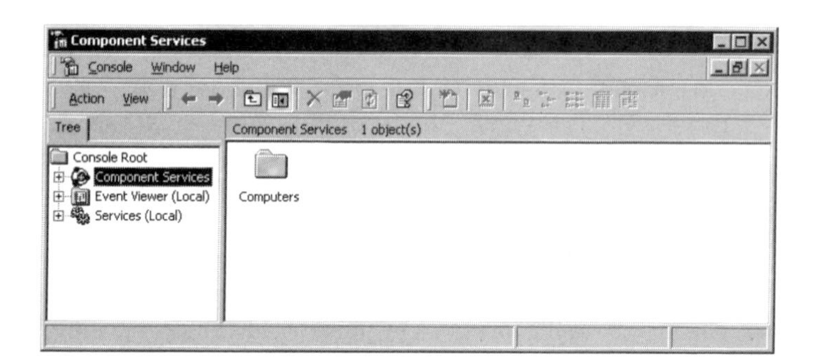


If you expand Component Services in the console tree, you'll see the Computers folder, and below it the My Computer object. Expand the My Computer object to see the currently installed COM+ applications in the COM+ Applications folder. Expand any COM+ application to see the Components and Roles folders, in which you can view and configure components and roles for the application.

Right-click any item in the Computers Folder and below, then choose Properties, if available, to view and configure the item. The tabs and configuration options available on the property sheets will vary depending on the item you've selected.

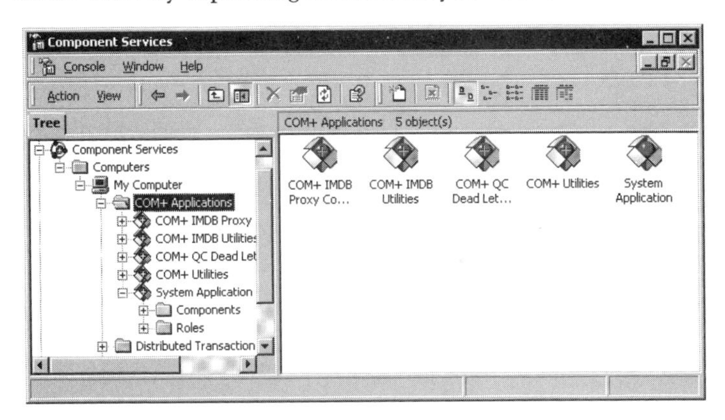


## Enabling Security

To be able to use Component Services, you must first enable security on the System application and assign at least one user to the Administrator role. Microsoft recommends adding users to groups and then assigning the group to the role. Follow these steps:

1. Expand the console tree as follows: Computers, My Computer, COM+ Applications, System Application, Roles, Administrator, Users.
2. Select the Users folder, then choose Action ➢ New ➢ User.
3. Select a user or group from the list and click Add, then click OK.
4. Reboot the computer.

**NOTE** The Administrators group may already be added to the Users folder.

## Adding a Network Computer

By default, only the local computer appears under Component Services in the console tree. To be able to use Component Services on remote computers, you can add those computers to the console tree by following these steps:

1. Select Computers in the console tree.
2. Choose Action ➢ New ➢ Computer, and then enter or browse for the name of another computer in the network. Click OK.

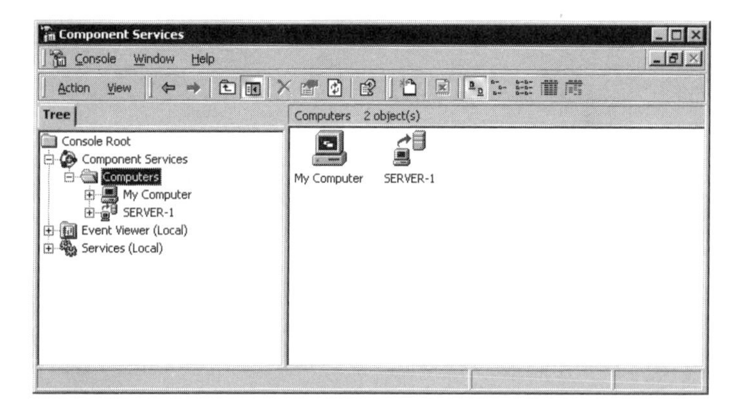


## Installing COM+ Applications

You can install additional COM+ applications on computers that have Component Services installed. Follow these steps:

1. Right-click the COM+ Applications folder of the computer where you want to install the application, and choose New ➢ Application. This starts the COM Application Install Wizard. Click Next.
2. Click Install Pre-Built Application(s).
3. Browse to and select the appropriate MSI file, then click Open.
4. In the Select Application Files screen, click Add to add additional applications, if applicable. Click Next.
5. Select an application identity. This can be either the currently logged–on user (Interactive User) or a user you specify. Click Next.

6. Click Finish. Component Services adds the application to the COM+ Applications folder.

**TIP** Note that applications that are currently running have a moving ball in their application icon box. To start or stop an application, right-click the application icon in the Details pane and choose Start or Shut Down, respectively.

**See Also** COM+, Microsoft Management Console (MMC)

# Compressing Drives, Folders, and Files

You can compress NTFS-formatted drives, as well as individual folders and files on NTFS drives, to save on disk space. If you copy or add a file in a compressed drive or folder, it is automatically compressed.

**TIP** If you move a file into a compressed drive or folder, it is compressed automatically if moved from a different NTFS drive. If it is moved from the same NTFS drive, the file remains in the state it was originally, either compressed or decompressed.

To compress an NTFS drive, follow these steps:

1. Right-click a drive in an Explorer window and select Properties.
2. On the General tab, check Compress Drive to Save Disk Space, and click OK.
3. In the Confirm Attribute Change dialog box, specify whether you want only files and folders at the root of the drive to compress or subfolders and files as well. Click OK.

To compress files or folders, follow these steps:

1. Right-click the folder or file in an Explorer window and select Properties.

2. On the General tab, click Advanced to open the Advanced Attributes dialog box.

**TIP** If the Advanced button is not available, the drive is not formatted with NTFS.

3. In the Compress or Encrypt Attributes section, check Compress Contents to Save Disk Space and click OK.

**WARNING** Before you compress a drive, you should run Scandisk to make sure the drive is free of errors. Also, make sure your data is backed up before you compress files, just in case corruption occurs. Finally, performance may suffer if you compress files that are frequently accessed.

4. Click OK again to close the folder's Properties dialog box. If you're compressing a folder and it contains subfolders, you'll be prompted to confirm the attribute changes. Specify whether you want the changes to apply only to this folder or to any subfolders and files as well. Click OK.

**TIP** You can display compressed files and folders in a different color. To do this, on the View tab in Folder Options, check Display Compressed Files and Folders with Alternate Color.

**See Also** Folder Options, Explorer

# Computer Management

MMC console snap-in that lets you manage various aspects of your computer. To access Computer Management, choose Start ➢ Settings ➢ Control Panel, double-click Administrative Tools, and then double-click Computer Management.

**TIP** In Windows 2000 Server, you can also access Computer Management by choosing Start ➢ Programs ➢ Administrative Tools ➢ Computer Management.

In the console tree of Computer Management under Computer Management (Local), you'll see three categories: System Tools, Storage, and Services and Applications. Each of these items contains other items you use to manage your local computer, which is the computer you can manage by default. You can manage remote computers by selecting Computer Management (Local) in the console tree and choosing Action ➢ Connect to Another Computer, then selecting the computer from the list and clicking OK.

With a default installation, you'll find the following items in the three categories. Other items might be available, and some items might not be available if you did not perform a default installation.

**System Tools** Event Viewer, System Information, Performance Logs and Alerts, Shared Folders, Device Manager, and Local Users and Groups (not on Windows 2000 domain controllers).

**Storage** Disk Management, Disk Defragmenter, Logical Drives, and Removable Storage.

**Services and Applications** WMI Control (Windows Management Instrumentation), Services, and Indexing Service. On Windows 2000 domain controllers, you'll also find DHCP, Telephony, DNS, and Internet Information Services.

Each of these items is covered under a separate heading in this book.

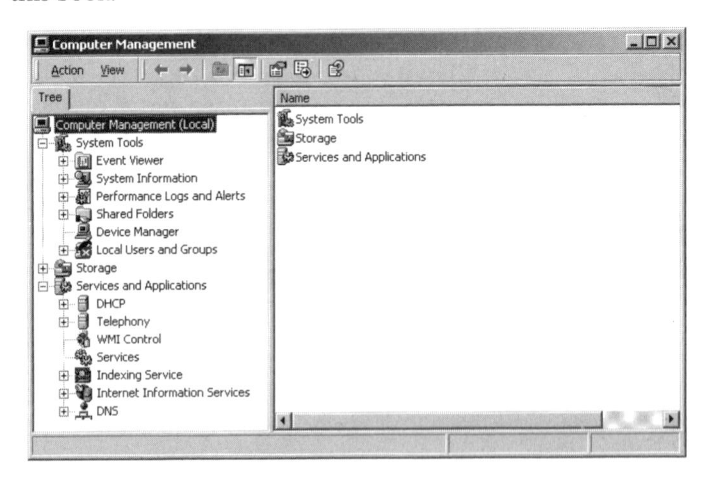


**See Also** Event Viewer, System Information, Performance Logs and Alerts, Shared Folders, Device Manager, Local Users and Groups, Disk Management, Disk Defragmenter, Logical Drives, Removable Storage, WMI Control, Services, Indexing Service, Microsoft Management Console (MMC), DHCP, Telephony, WINS, DNS, Internet Information Services

# Connect to the Internet

Accessible on the Windows 2000 desktop until you've completed the Internet Connection Wizard, which starts if you double-click the Connect to the Internet icon. The Internet Connection Wizard leads you through the process of connecting to the Internet for the first time. After you finish the Internet Connection Wizard, the Connect to the Internet icon is removed from the Windows 2000 desktop. The Internet Connection Wizard is described in detail under Internet Connection Wizard.

**See Also** Internet Connection Wizard

# Control Panel

Control Panel is where you go to configure and personalize settings for many of Windows 2000's functions and features, such as Accessibility Options, Add/Remove Programs, Administrative Tools, Folder Options, Regional Options, and Scheduled Tasks. To access Control Panel, choose Start ➢ Settings ➢ Control Panel. You can also access the Control Panel through My Computer and Windows Explorer.

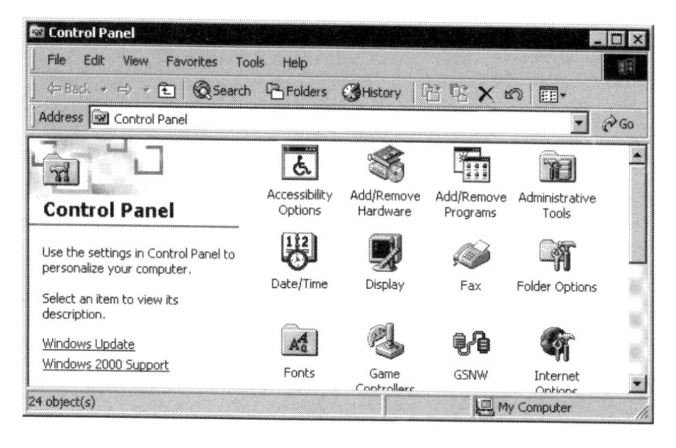


When you select an icon in Control Panel, a short description of the item appears on the left side of the screen. The same description also appears as a ToolTip if you move the mouse pointer over any item.

Control Panel items are listed as individual entries throughout this publication.

**NOTE** Control Panel in Windows 2000 Professional and Windows 2000 Server are not exactly identical. Windows 2000 Professional has an item called Users and Passwords that Windows 2000 Server does not have. Users and Passwords controls the local SAM database. Windows 2000 Server has an item called Licensing that Windows 2000 Professional does not have. Licensing controls how Windows 2000 Server licensing is set up (per server vs. per seat).

**See Also** Accessibility Options, Add/Remove Hardware, Add/Remove Programs, Administrative Tools, Date/Time, Display, Fax, Folder Options, Fonts, Game Controllers, GSNW, Internet Options, Keyboard, Mouse, Network and Dial-up Connections, Phone and Modem Options, Power Options, Printers, Regional Options, Scanners and Cameras, Scheduled Tasks, Sounds and Multimedia, System, Users and Passwords, Licensing

# Copy Disk

Copy Disk...

You can copy a floppy disk to another using the Copy Disk command in Windows Explorer. The two floppy disks must be of the same type; for example, you can copy one 3½-inch high-density disk to another 3½-inch high-density disk.

**WARNING** Make sure that you do not have data you want to keep on the target disk. The Copy Disk command overwrites its contents with the contents from the source disk.

To copy floppy disks, perform the following steps:

1. Open Windows Explorer.
2. Browse to and right-click the source floppy drive.

**TIP** You can copy to and from the same floppy drive.

3. Choose Copy Disk to open the Copy Disk dialog box. If you have only one floppy drive, skip to step 4. If you have more than one floppy drive, select the drive you want to copy from and the drive you want to copy to in the respective list boxes.

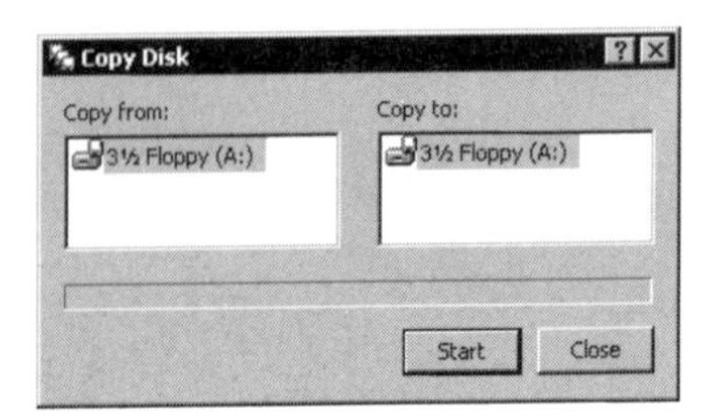

4. Click Start, then click OK (make sure the source disk is inserted; if it isn't, insert it). The progress bar in the dialog box tells you where you are in the process of reading from the source disk and writing to the destination disk. If you have only one floppy drive, you'll be prompted to swap the source and destination disk as necessary.

When the copy operation finishes, Copy Completed Successfully appears in the Copy Disk dialog box. You can now either copy another disk or click Close to close the Copy Disk dialog box.

**See Also** Explorer

# Copy Files and Folders

Copy

You can copy a file or folder to another location, leaving the original intact in the original location. You do this by using the Edit menu, the pop-up menu, or by using drag-and-drop.

## Copy Files or Folders Using the Edit Menu

To copy files or folders using the Edit menu in Windows Explorer, follow these steps:

1. Select the file or folder in the right pane of the Explorer window.

**TIP** To copy multiple files or folders, hold down the Shift key to select contiguous files or folders, or hold down the Ctrl key to select individual files or folders.

2. Choose Edit ➢ Copy.

3. Browse to and select the destination folder in the Folder view of the Explorer Bar.

4. Choose Edit ➢ Paste. The file(s) or folder(s) appear in the destination folder.

### Copy Files or Folders Using the Pop-up Menu

To copy a file or folder using the pop-up menu, right-click the file or folder to open the pop-up menu, then choose Copy. Next, browse to and right-click the destination folder, then choose Paste. Windows copies the file or folder to the destination folder.

### Copy Files or Folders Using Drag-and-Drop

To copy files or folders using drag-and-drop, you must first make sure that both the source and destination folders are visible in the Folders view. Open the source folder, hold down the Ctrl key, then drag the file or folder from the source folder to the destination folder while holding down the left mouse button. When the cursor is over the destination folder (the folder is selected), let go of the mouse button, and then release the Ctrl key. Windows copies the file or folder to the destination folder.

**WARNING** If you don't hold down the Ctrl key, the file or folder is moved, rather than copied.

**TIP** You can also copy a file or folder by selecting the file or folder, pressing Ctrl+C (Copy) on the keyboard, selecting the destination folder, and then pressing Ctrl+V (Paste).

**See Also** Explorer, Move Files and Folders

## Create New Folder

To be able to organize the files on your computer, you'll want to create new folders. You can do this in Windows Explorer by performing the following steps:

1. Select the folder or drive in which you want to create the new folder.
2. Choose File ➢ New ➢ Folder.

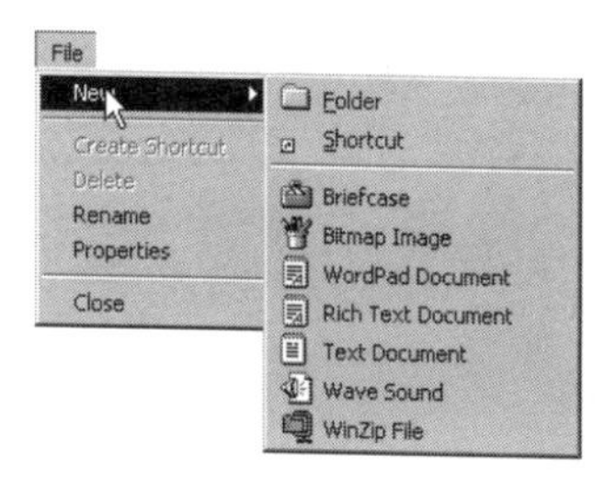

**TIP** You can also right-click anywhere in the right pane of the Explorer window and choose New ➢ Folder from the pop-up menu.

3. A new folder with the name New Folder appears in the folder or drive you chose. Replace the name New Folder with a descriptive name of your choice and press Enter.

**See Also** Explorer

# Create Shared Folder Wizard

Windows 2000 includes the Create Shared Folder Wizard, which walks you through the process of creating shared folders. When you share a folder, it becomes visible and available to other users on the network.

To create a shared folder using the Create Shared Folder Wizard, follow these steps:

1. On a Windows 2000 Server computer, choose Start ➢ Programs ➢ Administrative Tools ➢ Computer Management. On a Windows 2000 Professional computer, choose Start ➢ Settings ➢ Control Panel, then double-click Computer Management.
2. Expand System Tools, expand Shared Folders, and then select Shares.
3. In the Action menu, choose New ➢ File Share to start the Create Shared Folder Wizard. The Create Shared Folder dialog box appears.

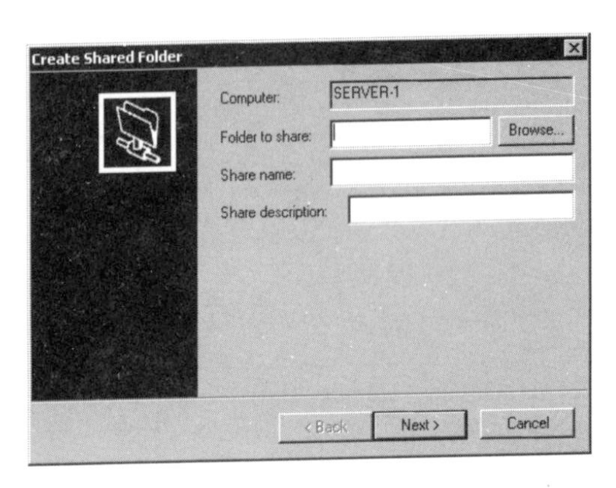


4. In the Folder to Share text box, specify the path to the folder you want to share. The folder does not have to exist already. You can also click Browse to browse to an existing folder.
5. In the Share Name text box, enter a share name. Optionally, in the Share Description text box, enter a description. Click Next.
6. If the folder already exists, skip to step 7. If the folder does not yet exist, you're asked if you want to create it. Click Yes to create the folder, and click No to return to the Create Shared Folder dialog box.
7. Set the permissions you would like to assign for this folder. You can choose from several predefined permissions or select Customize Share and Folder Permissions and click Custom to customize permissions. When you're done, click Finish.
8. You'll see a message that the folder access was successfully set. If you want to share another folder, click Yes. If you do not want to share another folder, click No.

**See Also** Computer Management, Shared Folders

# Create Shortcut

Create Shortcut

Shortcuts let you access programs, files, folders, printers, computers, or Internet addresses without having to go to their permanent locations.

You can create shortcuts by using the File menu, pop-up menus, and drag-and-copy. For information on how to add a shortcut to the Start menu, see the heading Taskbar & Start Menu.

## Using the File Menu in Windows Explorer

In Windows Explorer, select an item in the right pane, then choose File ➢ Create Shortcut. A shortcut to the item is placed into the same folder. You can now drag the shortcut to where you want it (such as another folder, the desktop, or the taskbar).

**TIP** You can also access items through My Computer, My Network Places, and My Documents. They all open Windows Explorer to a different, specific place in the Windows 2000 file system structure.

## Using Pop-up Menus

To create a shortcut using pop-up menus, right-click an item and choose Create Shortcut. If you right-click the desktop and choose New ➢ Shortcut, the Create Shortcut Wizard starts, which will guide you through the process of creating a new shortcut.

## Using Drag-and-Copy

To create a shortcut using drag-and-copy, in Windows Explorer select an item and drag it to where you want the shortcut to reside while pressing Ctrl+Shift. Alternatively, press the right mouse button and drag the item to where you want to place the shortcut, release the mouse button when you have reached the destination, and then choose Create Shortcut(s) Here from the resulting pop-up menu.

## Shortcut Properties

Once you've configured a shortcut, you can see and configure its properties by right-clicking the shortcut and choosing Properties. The Properties dialog box has three tabs on drives formatted with NTFS—General, Shortcut, and Security—and two tabs on drives formatted with FAT—General and Shortcut.

**General** Displays and lets you change the name of the shortcut. Also displays the file type, description, location, size, size on disk, and when it was created, modified, and last accessed. Lets you configure the Read-only and Hidden attributes. On a FAT-formatted drive, you can also configure the Archive attribute on the General tab. On an NTFS drive (recommended for Windows 2000 computers), you can click Advanced to configure the Archive, Index, Compress, and Encrypt attributes.

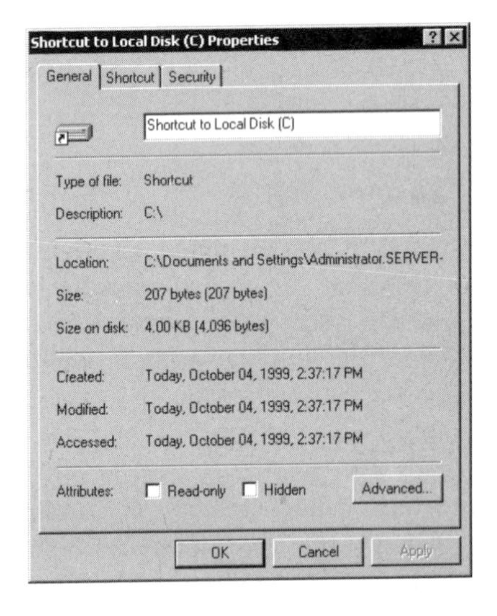


**Shortcut** Lets you configure the shortcut's target name, the location of the original files (Start In), a keyboard shortcut key sequence for the shortcut, and how to run the shortcut (Normal Window, Minimized, or Maximized). You can also add a comment, find the target, and change the shortcut's icon. If available, you can also configure whether to run the shortcut in separate memory space and to run it as a different user.

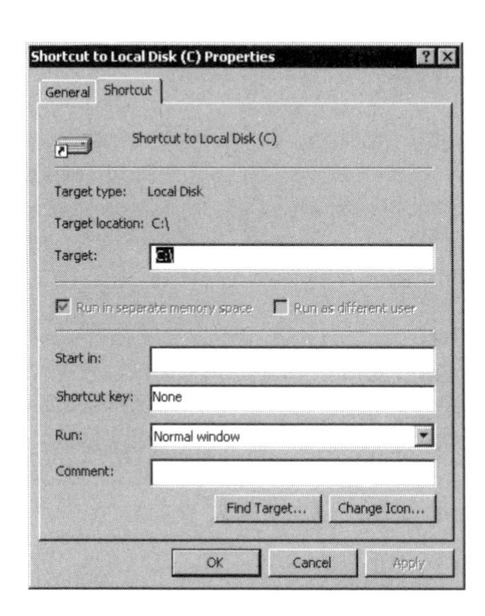


**Security** Available only on NTFS-formatted drives. Lets you configure permissions for the shortcut for users, groups, and computers. Click Advanced to configure advanced permissions and auditing and to assign ownership to a different user or group. You can also configure whether you want inheritable permissions from the parent to propagate to this object.

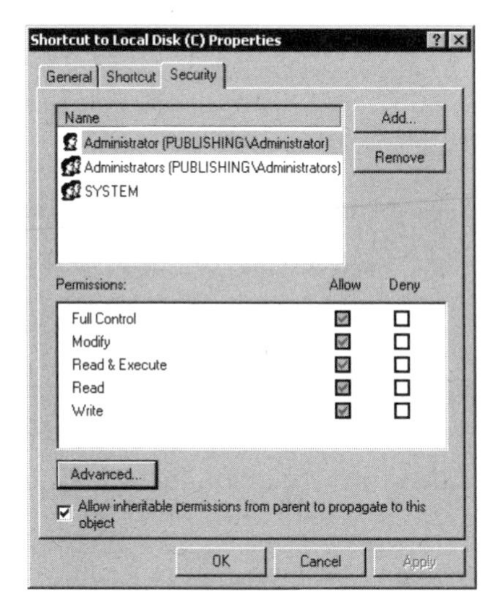


**See Also** My Computer, Taskbar & Start Menu

# Ctrl+Alt+Del

Keystroke combination that lets you access several Windows Security options through the Lock Computer, Log Off, Shut Down, Change Password, and Task Manager buttons. You can press Ctrl+Alt+Del at any time during a Windows 2000 session to access these options. Click Cancel to return to your Windows session without using any of the available options.

**See Also** Lock Computer, Log Off, Shut Down, Change Password, Task Manager

# Data Sources (ODBC)

Data Sources (ODBC)

Lets you add, configure, and remove user, system, and file data sources and drivers so you can access data from multiple database formats, such as FoxPro, dBASE, and Access, using the same interface. To open the ODBC (Open Database Connectivity) Data Source Administrator, choose Start ➢ Settings ➢ Control Panel, double-click Administrative Tools, and then double-click Data Sources (ODBC).

**TIP** In Windows 2000 Server, you can also access Data Sources (ODBC) by choosing Start ➢ Programs ➢ Administrative Tools ➢ Data Sources (ODBC).

ODBC Data Source Administrator has several tabs:

**User DSN** Lets you add and configure data sources that will be available only to the current user on the current computer.

**System DSN** Lets you add and configure data sources that will be available to all users of the computer.

**File DSN** Lets you add and configure data sources that enable users to connect to a data provider.

**Drivers** Displays the name, version, company, filename, and date of all ODBC drivers installed on the computer.

**Tracing** Lets you configure logging of calls to ODBC drivers. Logs can be used for troubleshooting purposes. Also used to start Tracing and Visual Studio Analyzer.

**Connection Pooling** Lets you enable and configure connection pooling. If it's enabled, applications can reuse open connection handles, which increases performance.

**About** Displays information about ODBC core components, including description, version, and the core component's filename and location.

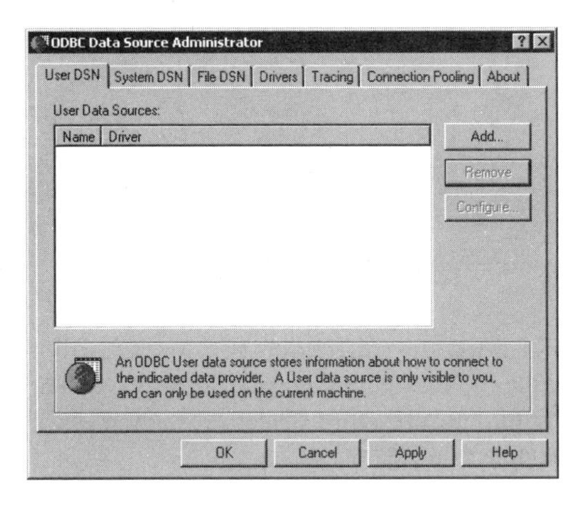


# Date/Time

Used to set the date, time, and time zone for the computer. Choose Start ➢ Settings ➢ Control Panel and double-click the Date/Time icon to open the Date/Time Properties dialog box. Alternatively, you can double-click the system clock on the right side of the taskbar.

It's important that the date and time of the system clock are correct because this time and date information is used to specify when files on your computer are created and modified. The Date/Time Properties dialog box has two tabs: Date & Time and Time Zone.

**Date & Time** Lets you set the date and time. To set the date, select the month from the drop-down list, use the up and down arrows to select the year, and click the desired day of the month. To set the time, select each value (hour, minute, seconds) and enter the correct value, then use the up and down arrows to specify AM or PM. You'll also see the current time zone information at the bottom of the dialog box.

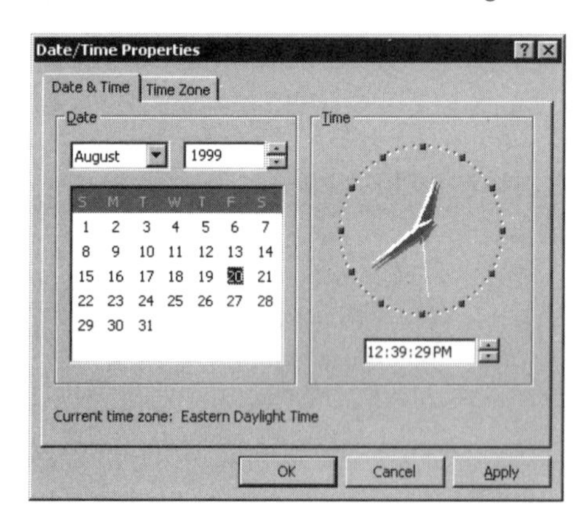


**Time Zone** Lets you set the time zone for the computer. To do so, select the correct time zone from the drop-down list. For many time zones, you can also specify that Windows automatically adjust the clock when daylight saving time changes take place.

Click Apply to apply any changes you make without closing the dialog box, or click OK to save changes and close the dialog box.

**TIP** Use Regional Options in Control Panel to change the format in which the time and date display in the taskbar. Changing the time format also changes how the time appears in the Date/Time Properties dialog box.

**See Also** Taskbar, Regional Options

# Deleting Files and Folders

It will at times be necessary for you to delete files or folders from your computer—for example, to free up space on your hard drive or to keep your files and folders well organized. You can do this in

several ways. The first step is to select the file or folder you want to delete. Next, do one of the following:

- Choose File ➢ Delete.
- Right-click the file or folder and choose Delete from the pop-up menu.
- Press the Delete key on the keyboard.
- Drag the file or folder to the Recycle Bin icon on the desktop (you'll have to make sure that you can see this icon on the desktop).

Using any of the above methods and default settings, you'll have to click OK to confirm that you want to move the file or folder to the Recycle Bin. Windows then moves the file or folder to the Recycle Bin.

**TIP** To undo a file or folder deletion, choose Edit ➢ Undo Delete, or manually restore the file or folder from the Recycle Bin.

**TIP** To delete a file or folder permanently without first sending it to the Recycle Bin, press Shift+Delete. You'll have to confirm this action. Once you do, it can't be undone.

**See Also** Explorer, Recycle Bin

# Desktop

The desktop is what you first see when you run Windows 2000. It is meant to resemble a physical desktop on which you work and organize your papers, telephone numbers, and so forth.

By default, the desktop contains several icons at the left of the screen (including My Documents, My Computer, My Network Places, Recycle Bin, Internet Explorer, and Connect To The Internet) and the Start button and taskbar at the bottom of the screen. As you add new programs and make changes to your environment, new icons are added to the desktop and taskbar, and some may be removed. Any time you work with a program, the program's user interface appears on the desktop so that you can use the program.

You can control the appearance and other settings for your desktop by right-clicking anywhere on the desktop and choosing Properties. This opens the Display Properties, which you use to configure your desktop.

**See Also** Display, Control Panel, Active Desktop

# Device Manager

Device Manager...

Device Manager is a Windows 2000 Microsoft Management Console (MMC) snap-in. It shows you a list of all hardware installed in the computer and provides information about this hardware. Use Device Manager after you install new hardware to verify the installation. Use it also to further configure devices, check a device's status, view and update device drivers, and enable and disable devices.

**TIP** You must have administrative privileges to make certain changes to devices in Device Manager.

To access Device Manager, choose Start ➢ Settings ➢ Control Panel, double-click System, select the Hardware tab, and click the Device Manager button.

**TIP** You can also access Device Manager by choosing Start ➢ Settings ➢ Control Panel, double-clicking Administrative Tools, double-clicking Computer Management, expanding System Tools, and selecting Device Manager. Or you can access Device Manager by right-clicking My Computer on the desktop, choosing Properties, selecting the Hardware tab, and clicking Device Manager.

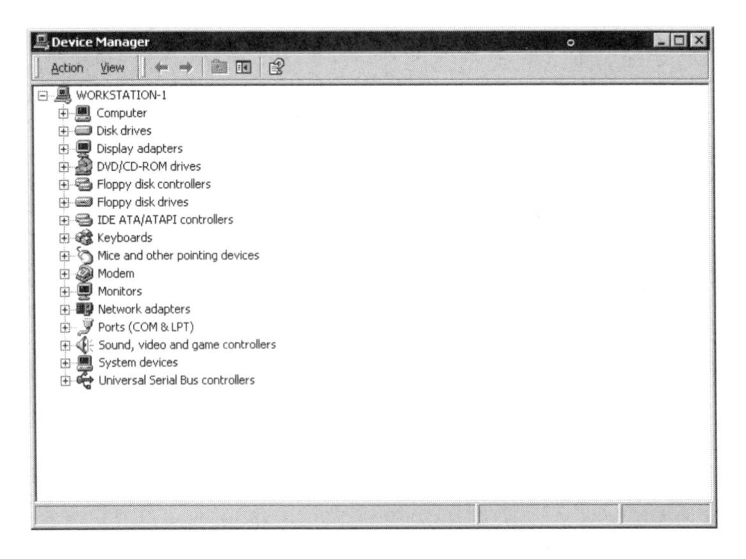


In Device Manager, each hardware class and device is depicted by an icon and then followed by the name of the class or device. To see devices in each class, expand the class by clicking the plus sign to the left of the class icon. Unknown devices are depicted by a yellow question mark item.

As with all MMC consoles and snap-ins, Device Manager has an Action and a View menu that contain options specific to the currently active MMC console snap-in.

## Action Menu

Action

Use the Action menu to access device-related actions. Select a device (expand a device class to list the devices it contains) and click Action to view the choices you have regarding the device in the menu that appears. They can include Disable (toggles to Enable if chosen), Uninstall, Scan for Hardware Changes, and Properties. The menu also contains an item called Help, which opens the Help system to the appropriate Microsoft Management Console Help system entry.

**TIP** An alternative method for accessing the options available under Action is to select a device and right-click. If you select a device class, you'll only have the Scan For Hardware Changes and Properties options available. If you select the workstation itself, a disk driver, or the display adapter, the Disable option won't be available.

### *Disable and Enable*

Disable

Lets you temporarily disable a Plug and Play device. You may want to do this if you're setting up different hardware profiles, such as a hardware profile for your laptop when it is docked and one for when it is not docked. As an example, you might want one profile in which certain devices are disabled (such as a modem for when the laptop is docked) and another in which other devices are disabled (such as a network adapter for when the laptop is not docked). When you disable a device, you don't have to physically remove it from the computer to avoid having Windows 2000 load drivers for the device.

**TIP** The Disable and Enable options appear only if you have administrative privileges.

After you choose Disable, you'll see a prompt asking you to confirm your selection and advising you that disabling the device means it will not function. If you want to enable the device again, select the device, right-click, and choose Enable, or select the device and select Enable from the Action menu.

After you disable a device, the device's icon in the device list has a red *x* through it, indicating that the device is disabled. When you enable the device, the red *x* disappears.

### *Uninstall*

Uninstall... Lets you completely remove a non–Plug or Play or Plug and Play device from the Windows 2000 computer. Once you do this, you'll have to physically remove the device from the computer; otherwise, if it's a Plug and Play device, it will be reinstalled again the next time you start Windows 2000. To reinstall the device, physically install the device in the computer. If it's a Plug and Play device, Windows 2000 installs the device and loads the appropriate drivers automatically the next time it's started. For a non–Plug and Play device, you can use the Add/Remove Hardware Wizard to install the device.

**NOTE** The Uninstall option is available only if you're logged on as a user with administrative privileges.

**TIP** An alternative method for removing a non–Plug and Play device is to use the Add/Remove Hardware Wizard. See Add/Remove Hardware Wizard for more information.

**TIP** Another way to uninstall a Plug and Play device is to shut down the computer (necessary for most devices), physically remove the device, and then start Windows again. The device is then automatically removed from Windows 2000.

When you choose to uninstall a device, you'll be asked to confirm the device removal. Click OK to uninstall the device.

### *Scan for Hardware Changes*

Scan for hardware changes Lets you manually start a scan of Plug and Play devices to see if any changes have occurred, such as removal or addition of a device from/to the computer.

If changes occurred, Windows 2000 takes the appropriate action (such as removing or adding the device from/to the list of devices) and may also display messages regarding the change. One such message is the Unsafe Removal of Device message, which appears if you remove or unplug a device from the computer without first disabling the device.

**WARNING** You should always disable a device before removing it from the computer; otherwise, serious problems may result. Many devices also require that you power off the computer before you remove the device. Consult your hardware documentation for more information.

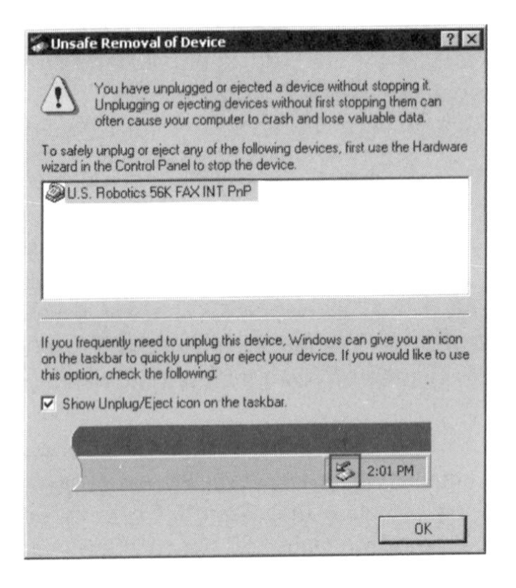


### *Properties*

To display the Properties dialog box, choose Properties either after right-clicking a device or by selecting a device and choosing Properties from the Action menu. The tabs and settings available on the device's Properties dialog box will vary depending on the device. Commonly available tabs are General, Driver, and Resources.

**TIP** You can also display a device's properties by selecting it and clicking the Properties button in the toolbar.

**General** Displays general information about the device, such as device type, manufacturer, location of the device (for example, if you've selected an adapter, you'll see the bus it's installed on), and the device status (whether it's working properly). To troubleshoot a device that's not functioning properly, you can click Troubleshooter to open the appropriate Windows 2000 hardware troubleshooter. On the General tab, you can also choose to enable or disable the device by making a selection from the Device Usage drop-down list.

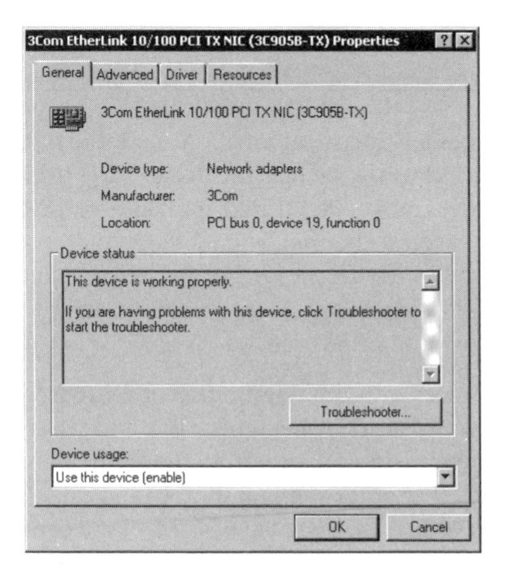


**Driver** Displays information about the currently installed driver for the device. This may include items such as driver provider, date, and version. To see the actual driver files, click Driver Details. On the Driver tab, you can also remove a driver by clicking Uninstall and confirming your selection, and you can update drivers to a newer version of the driver by clicking Update Driver and following the instructions in the Upgrade Device Driver Wizard.

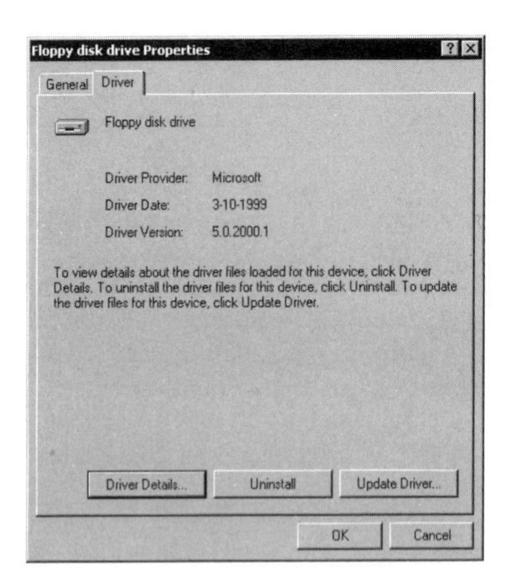


**Resources** Displays information about the system resources the device is using, such as the device's I/O (Input/Output) port address range, IRQ (Interrupt Request), DMA (Direct Memory Access) channel, and memory address range. For Plug and Play devices, resources are assigned automatically. For non–Plug and Play devices, you may have to manually configure resource settings.

In some cases, you can select different settings by deselecting the Use Automatic Settings check box and selecting a different hardware configuration from the Setting Based On drop-down list. If another configuration would cause resource conflicts with other installed devices, or if a conflict currently exists, these conflicts appear in the Conflicting Device list and the icon representing the conflicting resource type would have a red circle with a red slash through it. You can also manually change a resource setting by deselecting Use Automatic Settings, selecting a resource under the Resource Type heading, and clicking Change Setting. Some resource settings cannot be changed.

**WARNING** Change resource settings only if you're very comfortable with device hardware settings. Otherwise, the device or other devices may no longer function properly after you make a change.

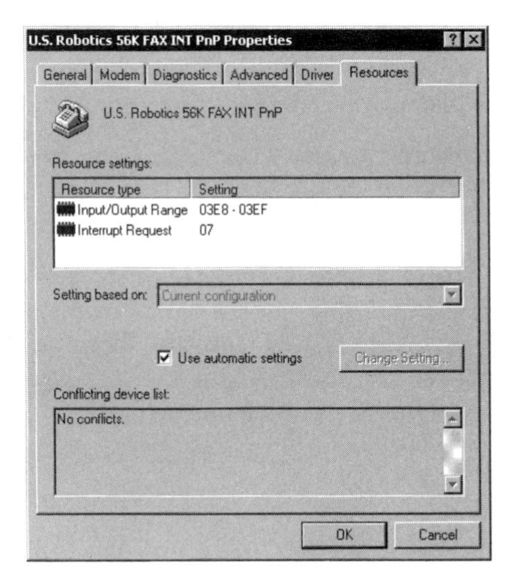


## View Menu

The View menu lets you display devices and resources by using various sorting methods, display hidden devices, print one of three types of reports, and customize the view.

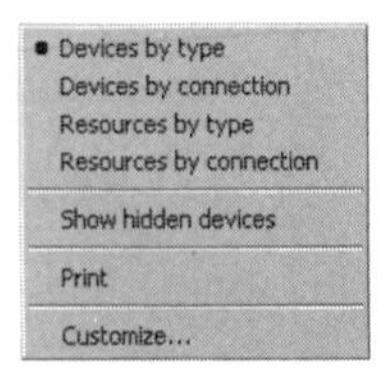


**Devices by Type** Displays hardware devices in alphabetical order by device type (the default setting).

**Devices by Connection** Displays hardware devices in alphabetical order by device connection (permanent—typically internally connected, or removable—typically externally connected).

**Resources by Type** Displays usage of DMA, I/O, IRQ, and memory resources by device type.

**Resources by Connection** Displays usage of DMA, I/O, IRQ, and memory resources by device connection.

**Show Hidden Devices** Displays devices not visible by default. They can include items such as non–Plug and Play drivers, Printers, and Other (unknown) devices.

**Print** Enables you to print one of three reports: a system summary, a report for a selected class or device, or a report for all devices and a system summary. Reports include such items as device class, device name, resources used, driver name, size and version, and manufacturer.

**Customize** Enables you to customize the MMC view by selecting which items to show or hide. Items include the console tree, the standard menus (Action and View), the standard toolbar and description bar, taskpad navigation tabs, and the menu and toolbar snap-ins.

## Additional Toolbar Buttons

In addition to Action and View, the Device Manager MMC console snap-in toolbar contains some of the buttons commonly found on MMC consoles, such as Back, Forward, Up One Level, Show/Hide Console Tree/Favorites, and Help. It can also contain one or more of the following buttons (depending on whether you selected the workstation, a device class, or a device, and whether a device is disabled or enabled):

**Disable** Used to disable a device.

**Enable** Used to enable a device.

**Uninstall** Used to uninstall a device.

**Scan for Hardware Changes** Used to scan for changes made to the hardware in the computer.

**See Also** System (Hardware tab), Administrative Tools, Microsoft Management Console (MMC), Add/Remove Hardware Wizard, Administrative Tools, Computer Management

# DHCP

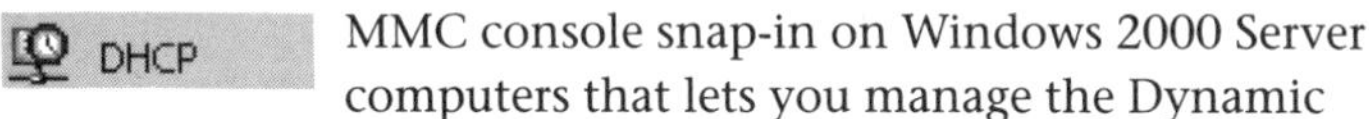


MMC console snap-in on Windows 2000 Server computers that lets you manage the Dynamic Host Configuration Protocol (DHCP) service. DHCP eases the administrative burden of IP address management and overall IP client configuration. Every computer in an IP network must have a unique IP address assigned to be able to communicate with other computers in the network. This IP address assignment can be done either manually or automatically (via DHCP). DHCP also enables automatic configuration of associated configuration options on DHCP-enabled client computers. Any client computer that runs a Microsoft Windows operating system can function as a DHCP client.

To be able to perform the above functions, the DHCP service in Windows 2000 Server enables the Windows 2000 Server computer to function as a DHCP server.

To access the DHCP MMC console snap-in, choose Start ➢ Programs ➢ Administrative Tools ➢ DHCP.

## DHCP Terminology

To be able to configure your DHCP server, you must understand several DHCP-related terms.

### *Scopes*

A scope is a contiguous range of IP addresses and typically comprises a physical subnet to which you will provide DHCP services. You create scopes using the DHCP MMC console snap-in and use them to manage and configure automatic IP address assignment.

**Superscope** A superscope consists of a list of several scopes that are grouped together. This enables support for multiple logical IP subnets that exist within a physical subnet. You configure the scopes contained in the superscope (also called member scopes) by configuring each individual scope.

### Exclusion Range

An exclusion range is a range of addresses within a scope that will not be available for automatic IP address assignment.

### Address Pool

An address pool consists of the IP addresses available in a scope exclusive of the IP addresses specified in the scope's exclusion ranges. Thus:

IP addresses in a scope – IP addresses in exclusion ranges = Address pool

Addresses in an address pool are available for automatic client IP address assignment by the DHCP server.

### Lease

A lease is the length of time that a client computer can use an IP address that the DHCP server dynamically assigned to the client. The DHCP server specifies this value. Once the DHCP server assigns a lease, the lease is considered active. To be able to continue using the assigned IP address, the client must request a renewal of the lease from the DHCP server before the lease expires. If the DHCP server does not renew the lease, or if the lease expires or is deleted, then the IP address is returned to the address pool and the DHCP server can assign it to a different client. Additionally, you can manually release or renew a lease at the client workstation.

### Reservation

A reservation is a permanent lease of an IP address to a client. Because the lease never expires, the client will always have the same IP address.

### Option Types

Option types are additional client configuration parameters that you can configure using the DHCP MMC console snap-in. Some examples are:

- IP addresses of computers such as default gateways, WINS servers, and POP 3 servers
- UCT time offset
- DNS domain name for client address resolution
- Client host name
- Broadcast address

Default option types are defined through the RFC 2132 standard; however, you can also create and add new option types, and you can edit predefined option types.

### Options Classes

Options classes contain option types. You can add new option classes to enable further configuration of client settings. They fall into two categories: user class (user defined) and vendor class (vendor defined).

## DHCP MMC Console Snap-in Window

By default, the Windows 2000 server on which DHCP is installed is configured to function as a DHCP server. Use the DHCP MMC console snap-in to configure the DHCP server. You can also add DHCP servers to the MMC console snap-in.

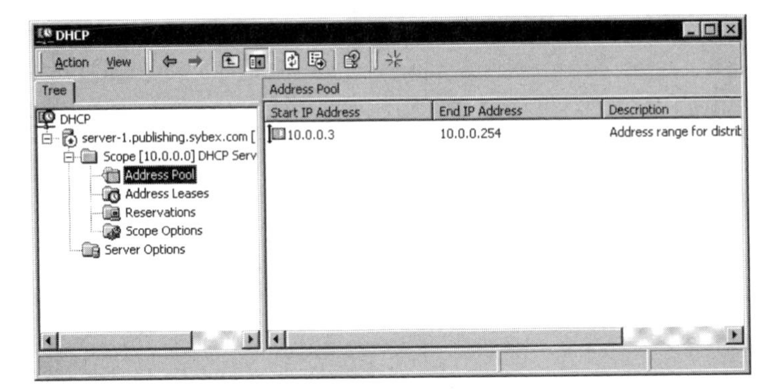

### *Action Menu*

Use the Action or pop-up menus to perform DHCP-related functions, among them:

- Add DHCP servers
- Define vendor and user classes
- Customize predefined options
- Start, stop, pause, resume, and restart the DHCP service
- Display DHCP service and scope statistics
- Create new scopes and superscopes
- Activate scopes
- Configure scope properties (such as scope address range and lease duration)
- Create exclusion ranges
- View currently active leases
- Create reservations
- Configure options

The options available on the Action or pop-up menus will depend on which item you have selected in the console tree or Details pane.

## Enabling DHCP on a Windows 2000 Client

To be able to have an IP address dynamically assigned by a DHCP server to a Windows 2000 client, you must verify that DHCP is enabled at the client. To do so, follow these steps:

1. Choose Start ➢ Settings ➢ Network and Dial-up Connections.
2. Double-click the Local Area Connection icon, then click Properties.
3. Select Internet Protocol (TCP/IP) in the list of components used by this connection and click Properties.
4. Check Obtain an IP Address Automatically. Click OK, then click OK again and click Close.

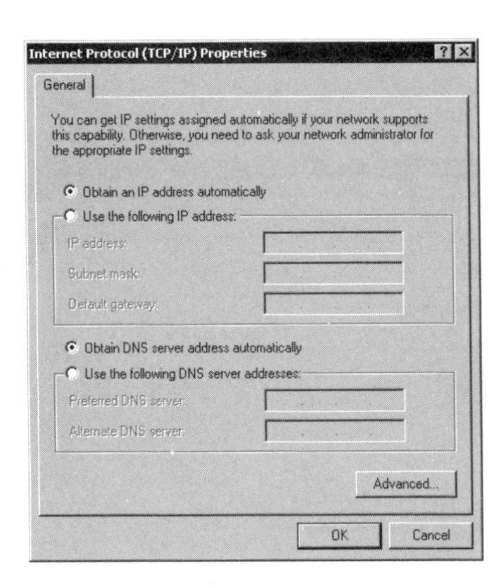


**See Also** Microsoft Management Console (MMC), Network and Dial-up Connections, DNS

# Dial-in

**See** Network and Dial-up connections

# DirectX Diagnostic Tool

DirectX Diagnostic Tool Lets you obtain information about Microsoft DirectX application programming interface drivers and components installed on your computer. You can also use it to check components and to disable some hardware acceleration features. You can provide the information you obtain to support personnel who are helping you troubleshoot a problem.

To access the DirectX Diagnostic Tool, choose Start ➢ Settings ➢ Control Panel, double-click Administrative Tools, double-click

Computer Management, expand System Tools, select System Information, and then choose Tools ➢ Windows ➢ DirectX Diagnostic Tool.

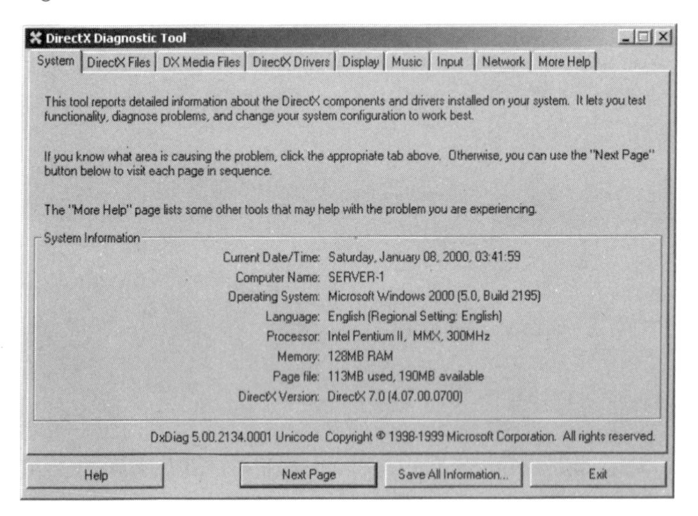


## Problem Types

If you have problems with a DirectX application, they might be caused by one or more of the following, as well as other causes not listed here:

- Incorrect or beta versions of DirectX components
- Uncertified drivers
- No hardware acceleration
- Devices that are not connected

You can find helpful information about these types of situations on the various DirectX Diagnostic Tool pages.

## DirectX Diagnostic Tool Pages

The DirectX Diagnostic Tool consists of 10 pages that provide information about DirectX components, any problems the tool has detected, buttons to test components, and buttons to disable hardware acceleration features.

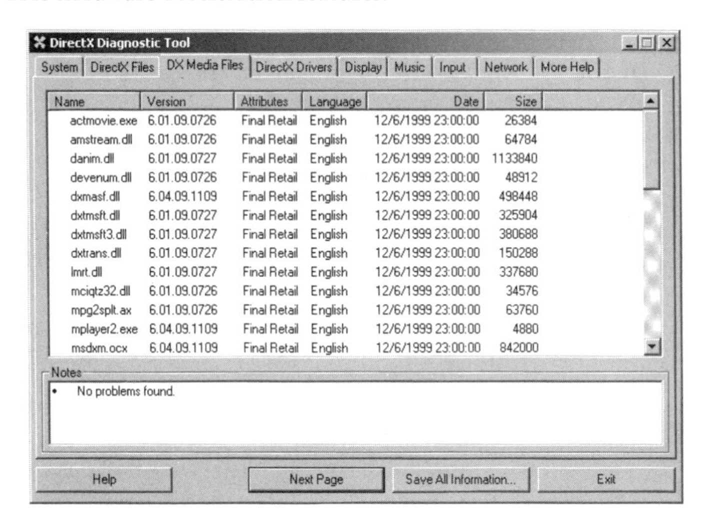


To move from page to page, click Next Page or select a specific page by clicking it. Each page contains information specific to its page topic and a Notes section where you can see any problems the DirectX Diagnostic Tool found as well as help suggestions. If you want, you can save the information contained on all of the pages by clicking Save All Information, specifying a filename, and clicking Save. Windows saves the information in a text file.

**System** Displays information about your system, such as date, time, computer name, operating system, language, processor, amount of memory, page file size, and the DirectX version.

**DirectX Files** Displays DirectX files installed on your computer. Information includes name, version, attributes (such as Final Retail or Beta Retail), language, date, and size.

**DX Media Files** Displays DirectX media files installed on your computer. Information includes name, version, attributes (Final Retail or Beta Retail), language, date, and size.

**DirectX Drivers** Displays DirectX drivers installed on your computer. Information includes name, version, certification status, language, date, and size.

**Display** Displays information about your installed display device (name, manufacturer, chip type, DAC type, total memory, display mode, and monitor), its driver (such as name, version, and certification status) and DirectX features, such as hardware acceleration. Click Disable to disable hardware acceleration or other DirectX features. Click Test DirectDraw or Test Direct3D to test these two DirectX components on the monitor attached to your computer. Follow the prompts to complete the tests. Results appear in the Notes section.

**Music** Displays information about each of your installed music ports (description, type, kernel mode, input/output, whether the port supports DLS, whether the port is an external device, and whether the port is the default port), and DirectX features, such as port acceleration. If DirectX features are available, you can disable them. To test a port, select the port from the drop-down list, then click Test DirectMusic. Follow the prompts; results appear in the Notes section.

**Input** Displays information about each of your installed input devices and drivers. Input device information includes device name, provider, device ID, status, port name, port provider, port ID, and port status. Device driver information includes registry key, whether the driver is active, device ID, matching device ID, driver (16-bit), and driver (32-bit).

**Network** Displays information about your installed DirectPlay service providers (such as Internet TCP/IP Connection for DirectPlay) and registered lobbyable DirectPlay applications. Service provider information includes name, registry, file, and version. DirectPlay application information includes name, registry, file, version, and globally unique identifier (GUID). You can test DirectPlay by clicking the Test DirectPlay button. Enter a username, choose the service provider, and specify that you want to create a new session. Click OK to start the session. Now have another user join this session from a computer on the network by following the above procedure (this time, select the option for joining an existing session). Once both users have joined the session, enter messages and press Send to test the chat session. Both computers should display all messages. Click Close to finish; results appear in the Notes section.

**More Help** Contains additional options. The options available depend on the release of the DirectX Diagnostic Tool you are running. Some options are available only with the developer release of the tool. Options might include Report (to create and send a bug report), Restore (to run the DirectX setup program), and Override (to override the monitor refresh rate). Click MSInfo to start the Microsoft System Information Tool, an MMC console snap-in that provides you with information about your system hardware and software.

**See Also** System Information

# Disk Cleanup

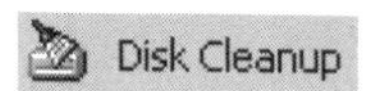


Finds files on your hard disk that can be deleted to free up hard disk space. Includes temporary files, unnecessary program files, no longer used Windows 2000 components, cache files, and files in the Recycle Bin. You then have the option to delete either some or all of the files, components, or programs.

## Using Disk Cleanup

To free up space on your hard disk, follow these steps:

1. Choose Start ➢ Programs ➢ Accessories ➢ System Tools ➢ Disk Cleanup to start Disk Cleanup.

**TIP** Alternatively, you can access Disk Cleanup by right-clicking a disk in an Explorer window, selecting Properties, and clicking Disk Cleanup, or by choosing Start ➢ Settings ➢ Control Panel, double-clicking Administrative Tools, then double-clicking Computer Management, selecting System Information, and choosing Tools ➢ Windows ➢ Disk Cleanup.

2. Select the drive you want to clean from the Drives drop-down list. Click OK. Wait for Disk Cleanup to scan the drive. This may take some time.

3. On the Disk Cleanup tab in the Disk Cleanup for *driveletter* dialog box, place a check mark next to the type of files you want to delete. You can also select a file type from the Files to Delete list box (without placing a check mark) and click View Files to see which files will be affected if you place a check mark next to the file type.

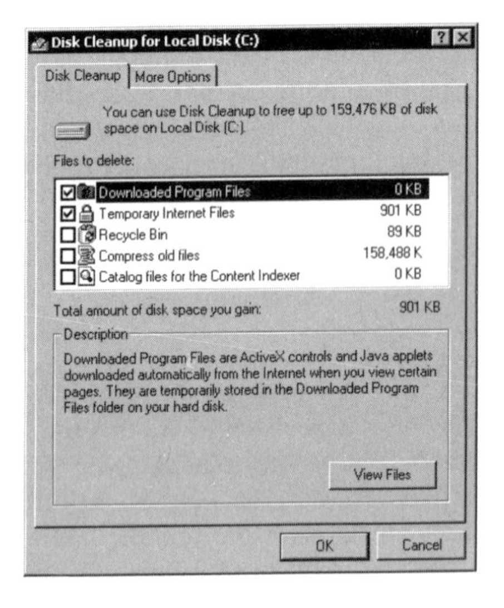


Select the More Options tab to specify that you want to remove optional Windows components and programs you no longer use by clicking the appropriate Clean Up button. This will start the Windows Component Wizard or Add/Remove Programs, respectively. You can then remove any Windows components or other installed programs you no longer use.

4. When you've finished making selections, click OK.

5. Confirm that you want to delete the files by clicking Yes.

6. Wait for the utility to remove the files. This may take a while, depending on the number of files you selected for deletion.

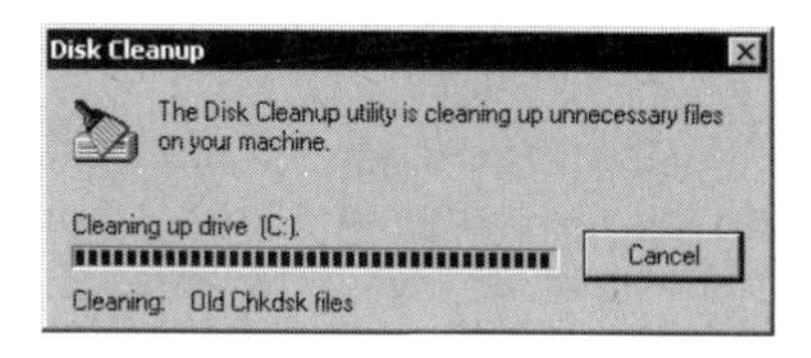


7. Windows returns you to the desktop when Disk Cleanup has finished.

**See Also** Add/Remove Programs, System Information

# Disk Defragmenter

A Microsoft Management Console (MMC) snap-in that lets you change the order of files and unused space on your computer's hard disk so that programs can run more efficiently, which increases overall response time.

Choose Start ➢ Programs ➢ Accessories ➢ System Tools ➢ Disk Defragmenter to start Disk Defragmenter.

**TIP** You can also access Disk Defragmenter by choosing Start ➢ Settings ➢ Control Panel, double-clicking Administrative Tools, and then double-clicking Computer Management. You'll find Disk Defragmenter under Storage.

## Disk Defragmenter MMC Console

In the top pane of the Disk Defragmenter MMC console, you'll see the volumes available for defragmentation. Take note of the other information available regarding the volume, such as Session Status (for example, analyzing or defragmenting), File System, Capacity, Free Space, and % Free Space.

In the lower portion of the console, you'll see a graphical representation of the data on the volume during and after analysis or defragmentation. The console also contains some of the MMC toolbar buttons, such as Action and View, as well as a status bar at the bottom of the window.

During volume analysis or defragmentation, the graphical displays Analysis Display and Defragmentation Display represent the volume's current state (during or after analysis or defragmentation). Fragmented files are indicated in red, contiguous files in blue, system files in green, and free space in white. Also, in the left portion of the status bar, you'll see the current action being performed, and to the right of this, a blue indicator bar shows you the progress of the current action.

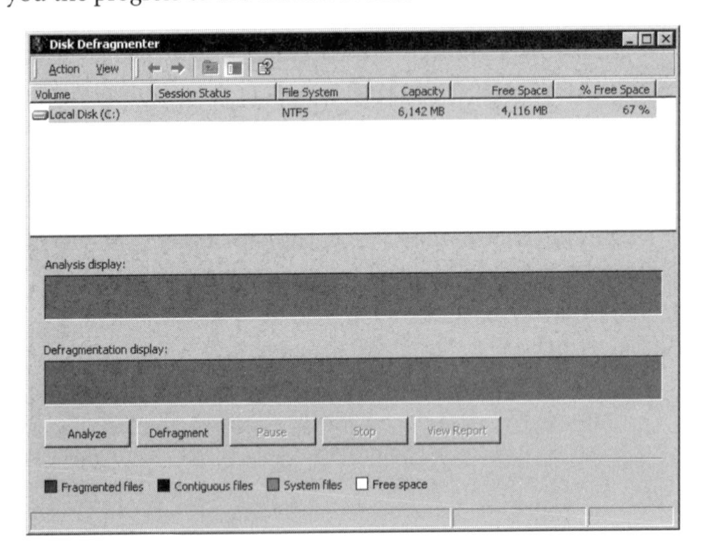


## Analyzing a Volume

To analyze a volume on your computer, perform these steps:

1. Select a volume in the list of available volumes in the upper pane of the Disk Defragmenter MMC console.

2. Click the Analyze button to start analyzing the volume. Click Pause or Stop at any time to pause or stop the drive analysis.

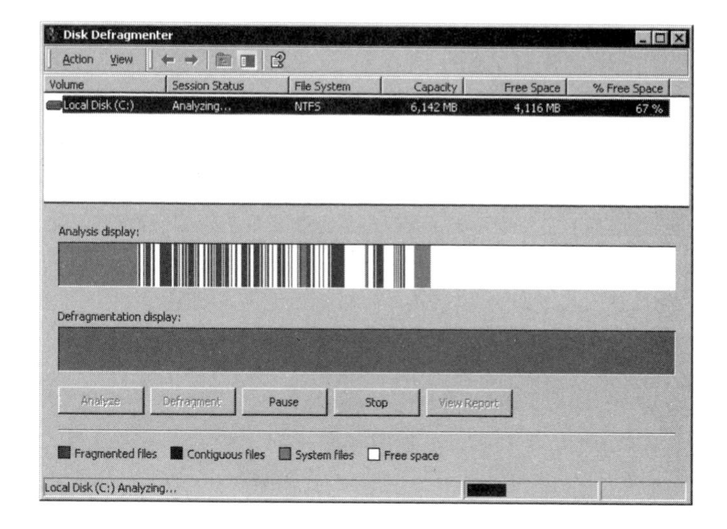

**TIP** Alternatively, you can choose Action ➢ Analyze to start the analysis.

3. When Disk Defragmenter finishes, you'll receive a message indicating that the analysis is complete. The message also advises you whether you should defragment the volume. Click View Report to see a report about the analysis, click Defragment to defragment the volume now, or click Close to close the message and return to Disk Defragmenter.

## Defragmenting a Volume

To defragment a volume on your computer, perform these steps:

1. Select a volume in the list of available volumes in the upper pane of the Disk Defragmenter MMC console.

2. Click the Defragment button to start the defragmentation. First, the volume is analyzed (or reanalyzed if it was previously analyzed), and then the defragmentation begins. This process may take quite some time to finish, depending on the size and state of the volume. Click Pause or Stop at any time to pause or stop the defragmentation process.

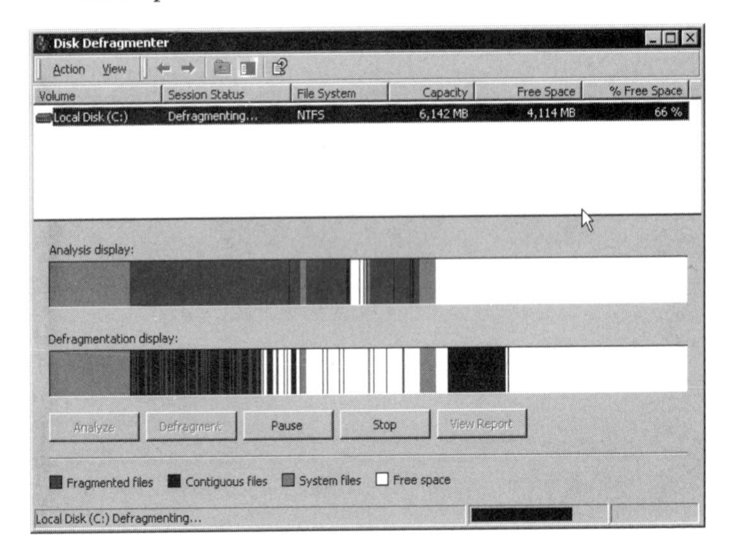


3. When Disk Defragmenter finishes, a message appears telling you that defragmentation is complete. You can click View Report to see a detailed report regarding the defragmentation, or you can click Close to return to Disk Defragmenter.

## Viewing Reports

After you analyze or defragment a volume, a report is created that provides you with detailed information about the action. You can view this report either at the end of the operation by clicking View Report in the message that appears when the operation is finished, or you can choose Action ➢ View Report to view the report most recently created. You can also click the View Report button.

A report contains information about the volume, volume fragmentation, file fragmentation, pagefile fragmentation, directory fragmentation, and Master File Table (MFT) fragmentation. It also includes information about files that did not defragment during the defragrementation process. If you wish, you can print the report or save it to a file.

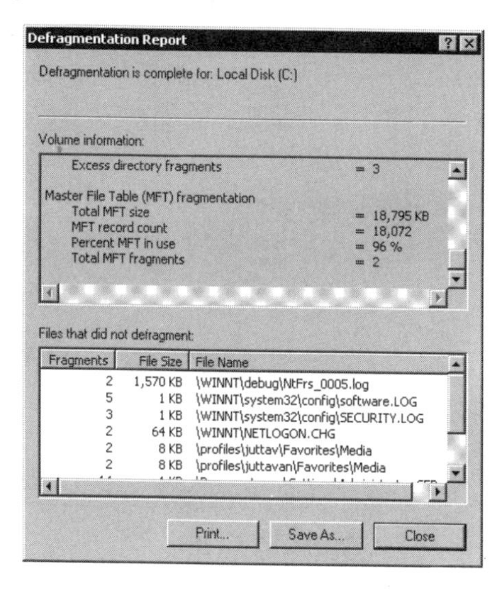

**WARNING** If you want to later refer to a report, make sure you save it after the analyze or defragment operation has finished. If you start another action, the report will be overwritten Using Action ➢ View Report lets you access only the report the most recently performed action.

**See Also** Microsoft Management Console (MMC), Computer Management

# Disk Management

Disk Management MMC console snap-in that lets you manage disks and volumes in a graphical environment. To access Disk Management, choose Start ➢ Settings ➢ Control Panel, double-click Administrative Tools, and then double-click Computer Management. You'll find the Disk Management snap-in under Storage.

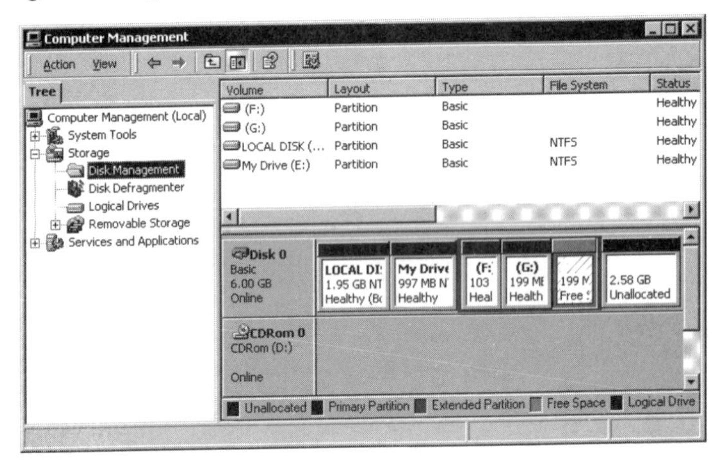

**TIP** You must be a member of the Administrators group to use Disk Management.

Use Disk Management to perform operations such as changing drive letters and paths, formatting your disk, deleting partitions, creating partitions, upgrading basic disks to dynamic disks, and ejecting removable media (such as CDs). You can also create and work with simple volumes, spanned volumes, striped volumes, mirrored volumes, and RAID-5 volumes for both basic and dynamic disks.

**WARNING** If you upgrade a basic disk to a dynamic disk, it can no longer be accessed by any operating system other than Windows 2000.

The Disk Management Details pane by default displays a top and bottom window, with the volume list in the top window and a graphical view of your disks in the bottom window.

## Basic Disks

Basic disks are hard disks that can contain primary and extended partitions, and logical drives, as well as mirrored volumes, striped volumes, spanned volumes, and RAID-5 volumes. Basic disks can be accessed by Windows 2000, as well as Windows NT 4.0, Windows 3.1, 95, and 98, and MS-DOS. Basic disks have these limits: four primary partitions per disk or three primary partitions and one extended partition. You can set up multiple volumes (logical drives) on an extended partition.

### *Action Menu with Basic Disks*

With basic disks, you'll find many unique items on the Action menu or its All Tasks submenu. The options available depend on which item you've selected in the Details pane, and which view you've selected (Disk List or Volume List).

**Refresh** Updates the disk and volume views.

**Rescan Disks** Rescans all available disks.

**Restore Basic Disk Configuration** Restores the disk configuration that was saved from a previous version of Windows NT.

**Change Drive Letter and Path** Lets you change the drive letter and path of a volume.

**Eject** Ejects the removable media from the drive.

**Properties** Opens the drive's properties.

**Upgrade to Dynamic Disk** Lets you upgrade a basic disk to a dynamic disk.

**Open** Opens the drive in Windows Explorer without an Explorer Bar view selected.

**Explore** Opens the drive in Windows Explorer with the Explorer Bar Folders view selected.

**Mark Partition Active** Marks the currently selected partition as active.

**Format** Lets you format the drive. You can choose a volume label, file system (NTFS or FAT32), and allocation unit size.

**Delete Logical Drive** Deletes the selected logical drive.

**Delete Partition** Deletes the selected partition.

### *Creating Partitions*

To create a partition or logical drive using unallocated space, right-click unallocated space in the Graphical view and choose Create Partition, then follow the wizard's instructions.

### *View Menu with Basic Disks*

The View menu contains the following unique options when working with basic disks:

**Top** Contains a submenu that lets you select what to display in the top window of the Details pane. Choices include Disk List, Volume List, and Graphical View.

**Bottom** Contains a submenu that lets you select what to display in the bottom window of the Details pane. Choices include Disk List, Volume List, Graphical View, and Hidden.

**Settings** Lets you configure the color and pattern for each of the disk regions in the Graphical view, such as primary partition, free space, and simple volume. Also lets you configure the proportion for how disks and disk regions display in the Graphical view.

**All Drive Paths** Displays all drive paths.

## Dynamic Disks

Dynamic disks are hard disks that contain dynamic volumes, which you create using Disk Management. A dynamic disk can also contain dynamic mirrored, striped, spanned, and RAID-5 volumes. Dynamic disks can be accessed only by the Windows 2000 operating system. There is no limit as to how many volumes you can create on a dynamic disk. No partitions or logical drives can exist on dynamic disks. Portable computers cannot contain dynamic disks.

## Upgrading a Basic Disk to a Dynamic Disk

You can upgrade basic disks to dynamic disks using Disk Management. However, once you've done that, you cannot revert the disk to a basic disk. To upgrade a basic disk to a dynamic disk, follow these steps:

**WARNING** Perform these steps only if you are absolutely sure that no operating system other than Windows 2000 needs to be able to access files stored on this computer. For example, once you upgrade a disk to a dynamic disk, you can't save a file from that disk, copy it to a floppy, and read it on a Windows 98 computer. You can save the file to a floppy, but Windows 98 won't be able to read it.

1. Choose View ➢ Top ➢ Disk List.
2. Right-click the disk you want to upgrade in the Details pane and choose Upgrade to Dynamic Disk.
3. Verify that the correct disk is selected, then click OK.
4. In the Disks to Upgrade dialog box, verify that the information is correct, then click Upgrade.
5. Read the warning message that you won't be able to boot previous versions of Windows from any volume on the disk. Click Yes to confirm the upgrade.
6. Click Yes to verify force dismount of file systems.
7. Click OK to reboot the computer.

After you upgrade the disk, the changes are reflected in Disk Management, showing the type as dynamic in the Details pane.

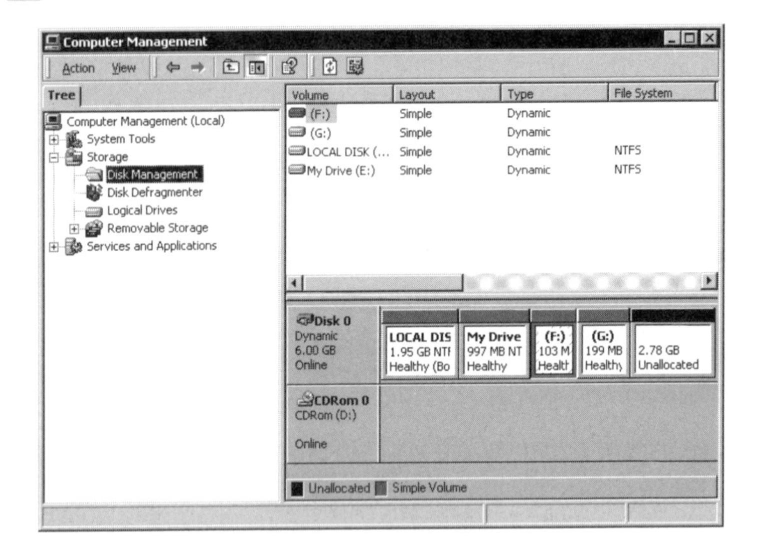


**See Also** Microsoft Management Console (MMC)

# Disk Quotas

Let you control how much disk space each user can use on a local or network NTFS-formatted volume. You can also use disk quotas to track disk space usage without restricting disk space.

Disk quotas are set up on the Quota tab of a volume's Properties page. To access this tab, right-click a volume in an Explorer window, select Properties, and then select the Quota tab.

## Quota Tab

The Quota tab lets you enable and configure disk quotas. To enable disk quotas, select the Enable Quota Management check box. If you want to use disk quotas only to track disk space usage, leave the Deny Disk Space to Users Exceeding Quota Limit check box deselected. Otherwise, select it. If this option is selected, users receive an *Insufficient Disk Space* message when they try to save a file after exceeding their disk space quota.

To specify default disk usage limits, select the radio button next to Limit Disk Space To and enter the amount of disk space in the text box. Choose a unit of measurement (KB, MB, GB, TB, PB, or EB) from the corresponding drop-down list. You can also set a warning level in the same manner next to Set Warning Level To. You can also specify that you want Windows to log an event in the Event log when users exceed their quota limit and/or warning level. To do this, select the appropriate check box. You can view events with Event Viewer (to make disk quota events easier to find, you can filter the Event log for Disk events). Click OK twice to implement your settings (enable disk quotas).

Windows applies the disk space and warning levels you set here to any new user the first time the user accesses the quota-enabled volume. To add quotas to existing users, you have to add a new quota entry.

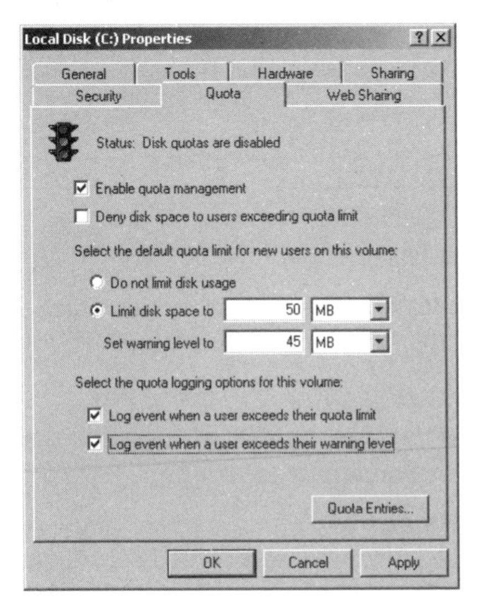


## Quota Entries

Quota entries give you specific disk quota information for each user. This information includes such items as the amount of disk space used, the quota limit, the warning level, and the percentage of allowed disk space used.

## Quota Entries Window

To access the Quota Entries window for a quota-enabled volume, click Quota Entries on the Quota tab of the volume. The Quota Entries window consists of menus, a toolbar, the quota entry list box, and a status bar.

The quota entry list box contains information about each quota entry, including Status, Name, Logon Name, Amount Used, Quota Limit, Warning Level, and Percent Used.

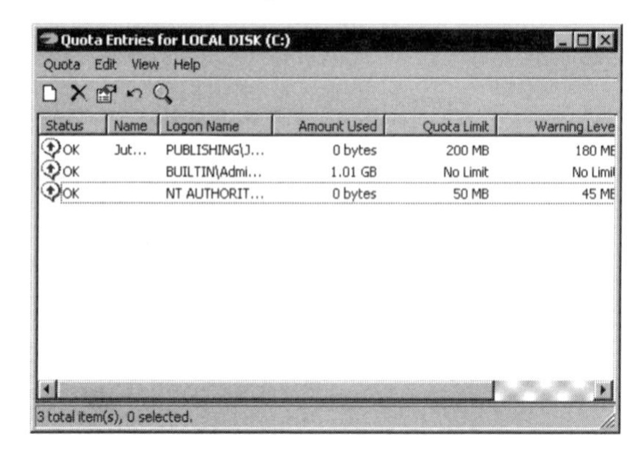


## Quota Entries Menus

The Quota Entries window has four menus: Quota, Edit, View, and Help. The Help menu contains typical Windows Help menu options.

### *Quota Menu*

The Quota menu contains these options:

**New Quota Entry** Lets you create a new quota entry (for example, for a user who existed before you enabled quotas on the volume).

**Import** Lets you import quota settings from another volume.

**Export** Lets you export quota settings for this volume.

**Delete Quota Entry** Removes the selected quota entry.

**Properties** Displays the properties of the selected quota entry. Properties include quota used, quota remaining, and disk space limit and warning levels. You can also specify that you don't want to limit disk usage for this quota entry.

**Close** Closes the Quota Entry window.

### *Edit Menu*

The Edit menu contains familiar Windows Edit menu options, such as Undo, Copy, Select All, and Invert Selection, as well as one additional option—the Find option. Use Find to locate a quota entry by Logon name.

### *View Menu*

The View menu contains familiar Windows View menu options, such as Toolbar, Status Bar, and Refresh. It also contains two unique options:

**Containing Folder** Toggles the display of the In Folder column.

**Arrange Items** Lets you sort quota entries by each of the column headers.

## Quota Entry Toolbar

The Quota Entry toolbar contains shortcut buttons to the most commonly performed quota entry functions. They include New Quota Entry, Delete Quota Entry, Properties, Undo, and Find Quota Entry.

## Creating a New Quota Entry

You'll need to create a new quota entry for any user who existed before you enabled disk quotas for a volume.

To create a new quota entry, perform these steps:

1. Choose Quota ➢ New Quota Entry to open the Select Users dialog box.
2. From the Look In drop-down list, select the domain for which you want to display users, or select Entire Directory to display all users in the Active Directory.

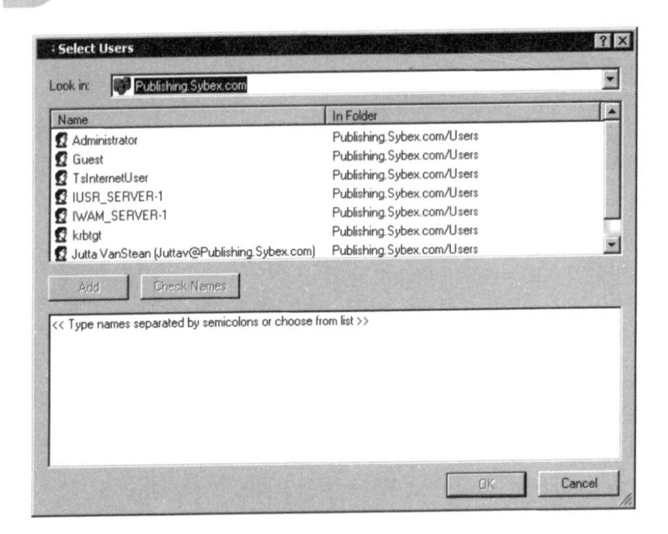


3. Select one or more users in the list, then click Add to add the users to the list of users for which a quota entry will be created. Optionally, click Check Names to verify that the names you selected are valid. Click OK.

4. In the Add New Quota Entry dialog box, you can select Do Not Limit Disk Usage or you can select Limit Disk Space To and enter the appropriate amounts and unit of measurement for disk space limits and warning levels. Click OK.

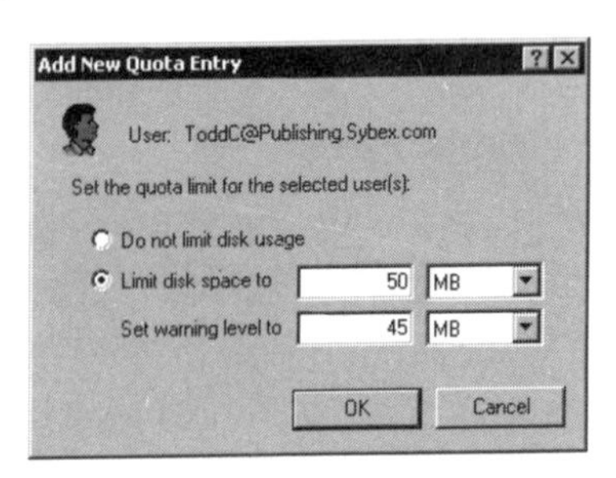


You can change the properties for any quota entry by right-clicking an entry and selecting Properties. The resulting Quota Settings dialog box contains a General tab that tells you the

amount of the quota used (percent) and the quota remaining. In addition, the tab lets you change the quota disk space limit and warning level for the entry, as well as disable disk usage limits.

# Disk Space

You can see how much disk space a file or folder uses. To do so, in any Explorer window, select a folder in the Folders Explorer Bar or a file in the right pane. The amount of space the file or folder uses appears in the status bar at the bottom of the window (the status bar must be turned on).

You can also choose File ➢ Properties, or right-click a file or folder and choose Properties from the pop-up menu. You'll find the size on the General tab. For folders, you'll also see how many files and folders are contained in the folder.

**See Also** Explorer

# Display

Used to configure the look of your desktop, including backgrounds, screen savers, appearance of program windows, Web options, desktop icons, visual effects, number of colors, and resolution.

Choose Start ➢ Settings ➢ Control Panel and double-click the Display icon. The Display Properties dialog box has six tabs, on which you can make configuration changes. These six tabs are Background, Screen Saver, Appearance, Web, Effects, and Settings. Click Apply any time you want changes applied to your desktop without closing the Display Properties dialog box.

**TIP** An alternative method for accessing the Display Properties dialog box is to right-click anywhere on the desktop and choose Properties, or choose Active Desktop ➢ Customize My Desktop.

## Background Tab

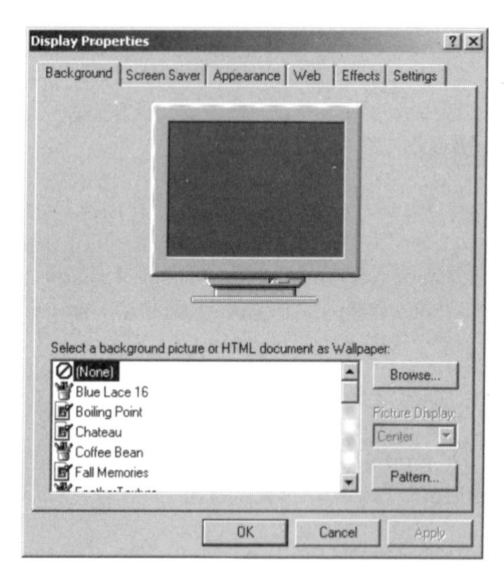


You can choose to use either a picture or an HTML document as the wallpaper for your desktop. In the list box, select the background you want to use. As you make selections, you'll see a preview in the picture of the monitor above the list. If you don't like any of the selections shown, click Browse to browse for a picture. By default, Windows 2000 looks in the `C:\WINNT` directory for additional files. You can browse other drives and folders if you wish.

**TIP** File types you can use as backgrounds include .JPG, .JPEG, .GIF, .BMP, .DIB, .PNG, .HTM, and .HTML.

Once you've selected a background, you can choose to center, tile, or stretch it. Center means the picture or document appears centered in the middle of the screen and may not occupy the entire screen. Tile means that the picture or document is repeated over and over to fill the entire screen. Stretch means the picture or document is stretched to fill the entire screen.

You can also choose a pattern either as a background (to fill the entire screen) or to fill in areas around a background that are blank (as is usually the case with centered backgrounds). Click Pattern and select the pattern you want in the Pattern list. You'll

see a preview of your choice in the Preview box. Click OK when you're satisfied with the pattern.

## Screen Saver Tab

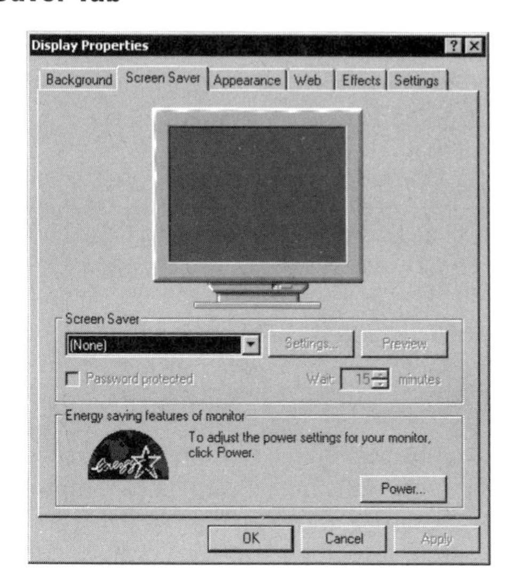


Used to select a screen saver. Screen savers display continuously changing images and are activated after the computer has been idle for a certain amount of time. You can specify how long the computer has to be idle before starting the screen saver. Screen savers have two functions:

- You can use a screen saver together with a screen saver password to secure your desktop when you're away from your desk. Once the screen saver starts, hiding your desktop, you can't return to the desktop without entering the password.
- You can use a screen saver to prevent a static image from being burnt into the display. If you're away from your desktop for long periods of time and the display is on, over time, the displayed static image can burn itself permanently into the display. This is a great concern if the computer and display are frequently left on overnight.

The following options are available on the Screen Saver tab:

**Screen Saver** Drop-down list of available screen savers.

**Settings** Available only when a screen saver has been selected. Opens a dialog box to configure the screen saver. The options in this dialog box are different for each screen saver.

**Preview** Available only when a screen saver has been selected. The screen saver starts to give you a full-screen preview of its moving image and then returns you to the Display Properties dialog box.

**TIP** Should the preview continue to run and not return you to the Display Properties dialog box, press any key to stop it.

**Password Protected** Assigns your logon password to the screen saver. You must enter the password to terminate the screen saver once it has started.

**Wait** Amount of time in minutes that must elapse before the screen saver starts. The default is 15 minutes. The range is 1 minute to 999 minutes.

### *Power Options*

If you have a computer with energy-saving power management options, you can configure them from the Screen Saver tab. Click the Power button to open the Power Options Properties dialog box.

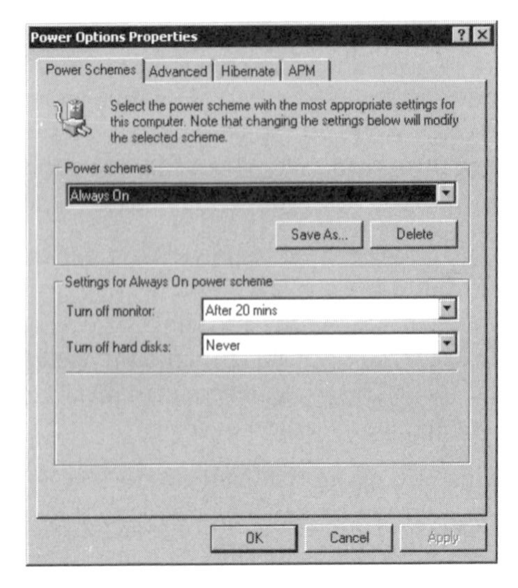

The Power Options Properties dialog box has several tabs that you can use to select specific hardware/usage power schemes and configure their settings, specify advanced settings, configure hibernation settings, and, if available, enable Advanced Power Management (APM), or configure UPS settings.

This dialog box is identical to the Power Options dialog box that opens when you double-click the Power Options icon in Control Panel.

## Appearance Tab

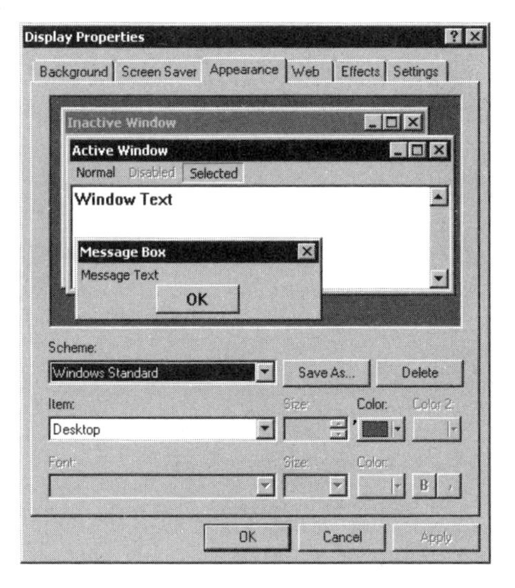


Controls how the desktop and desktop components such as program windows and dialog boxes will look on your desktop. You can configure the color, size, or font for certain items, including title bars, icons, menus, and scroll bars. You can pick from a list of predefined schemes, or you can use a scheme as a basis for configuration, then further configure individual items. If you wish, you can save your custom configuration, thereby creating a new scheme that you can access at any time from the Scheme drop-down list.

### *Setting Up a Preconfigured Scheme*

To set up a preconfigured scheme, first select one from the Scheme drop-down list and verify in the preview that this is the scheme you want. Then click OK (to save the scheme) or Apply (to apply the settings without closing the dialog box).

### *Setting Up a Custom Scheme*

To set up a custom scheme, select a preconfigured scheme and then choose an item from the Item drop-down list. You can now configure the size and color of the item and, if applicable, the font you want to use, as well as its size and color, by using the provided configuration boxes. You can also choose to apply bold or italics to the font. If you want to save your settings as a new scheme, click Save As, give the scheme a name, and click OK. The new scheme will appear in the Schemes drop-down list. Otherwise, just click OK or Apply to apply the settings without setting up a new scheme. You can also delete schemes by selecting a scheme and clicking Delete.

## Web Tab

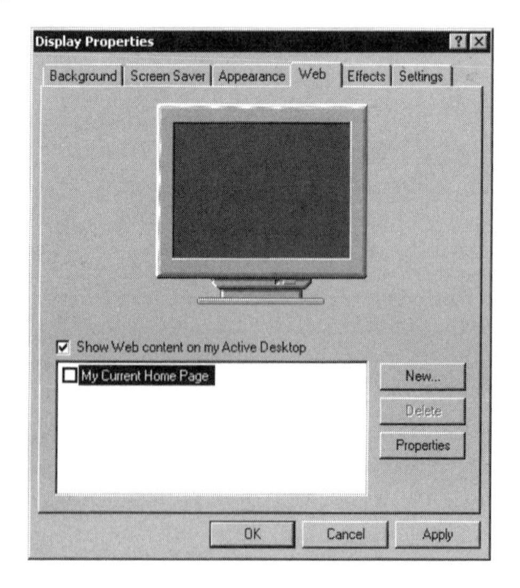


Gives you the ability to add interactive items from the Web to your desktop and configures what items you want to display.

Select Show Web Content on My Active Desktop to activate the Active Desktop. This means you can display Web pages, interactive items such as weather information, stock tickers, news, sports scores, and other Web content on your Active Desktop. By default, your current home page is listed as an item you can add to your Active Desktop. Simply select the check box to add it. To add a new item, click New, then enter the URL in the Location text box on the New Active Desktop Item dialog box or browse for a URL. You can also add items from Microsoft's Active Desktop Gallery by clicking Visit Gallery. Just follow the instructions on the site. Once you add content, it appears in the list of available Web content with a check mark in its check box. Deselect an item if you don't want to display it but you aren't ready to remove it. To remove an item, select it in the list and click Remove.

**TIP** Another way to access the New Active Desktop Item dialog box is to right-click in a blank area on the desktop and choose New Desktop Item.

### *Properties*

Each item has its own set of properties. Select the item and click Properties. The resulting property sheet has three tabs:

**Web Document** Here you can view information about the item, such as the URL, number of visits, last synchronization, download size, and download result. You can also specify whether the page should be available offline when you're not connected to the Internet (the default).

**Schedule** Lets you set up a schedule for synchronization of live content with the offline content.

**Download** Lets you specify which portions of a Web site's content you want to download. You can also set a maximum limit for how much hard disk space the content can take up, and you can specify that you want to receive e-mail notification when the page changes. Finally, if you have to enter a username and password for a site, you can click Login and provide that information. When you actually connect to the site, Windows provides the username and password information automatically.

### *Web Content on the Desktop*

Content that's added to your Active Desktop appears in a floating window with scroll bars on the right and bottom. Move the cursor toward the top of the window to bring up the top bar, where you can click the various resizing buttons to resize the window, or click the Close button to close the window.

If you click the down arrow at the left of the bar, you'll see a menu that you can use to synchronize the offline content with the online content and edit properties of this item. You can also use the menu to open the Display Properties dialog box to the Web tab to customize your Active Desktop and configure how the content should display.

## Effects Tab

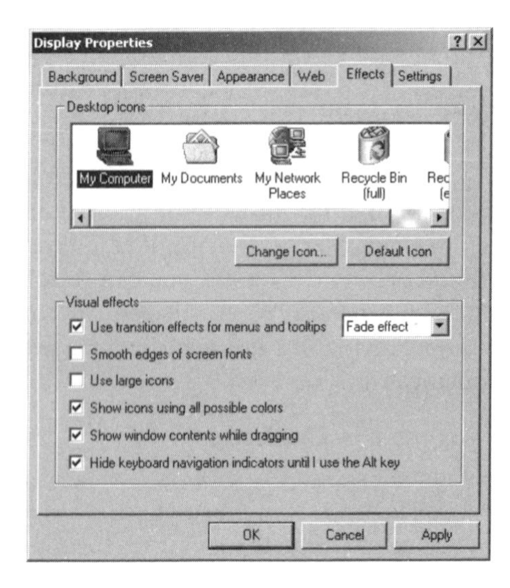

Used to customize desktop icons and desktop visual effects. At the top of the tab, in the Desktop Icons list, you'll see icons for the following items available on your desktop: My Computer, My Documents, My Network Places, Recycle Bin (Full), and Recycle Bin (Empty). Select an icon, then click Change Icon. You'll see a list of icons available in the file `C:\WINNT\SYSTEM32\SHELL32.DLL`. Select an icon from the list and click OK to assign it to the item. If you don't find an icon in the list, you can also browse for other files that contain icons.

Visual effects are used to customize how desktop items appear on the screen. Options are:

**Use Transition Effects for Menus and Tooltips** Changes how menus and windows appear when they are opened or closed. Examples are fading and scrolling of items. Works only with High Color (16-bit) or higher color palette settings.

**Smooth Edges of Screen Fonts** Smoothes the edges of large fonts, making them easier to read. Best results are achieved if 16-bit color is supported; the minimum requirement is 256 colors.

**Use Large Icons** Uses large icons for items on your desktop instead of the default icon size. Makes icons easier to see; however, displaying large icons uses more memory and can negatively affect performance.

**Show Icons Using All Possible Colors** Makes use of the entire range of colors supported by your display adapter, monitor, and color setting.

**Show Window Contents While Dragging** If you select this option, you'll see all of the contents of a window you're dragging to a different position on the desktop. If you leave the option deselected, you'll see only an outline of the window when you're dragging it.

**Hide Keyboard Navigation Indicators Until I Use the Alt Key** If you select this option, you won't see the underlined letters in menus (keyboard navigation indicators) or dotted lines around items that are active (focus indicators) until you press Alt, Tab, or any of the arrow keys.

Pressing these keys indicates that you want to use the keyboard for navigation, and the keyboard indicators then become visible. If you leave this option deselected, keyboard indicators and focus indicators are always displayed.

## Settings Tab

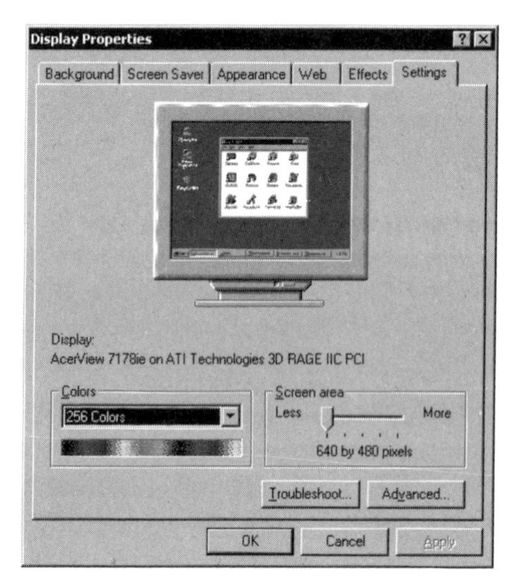


Used to specify the color palette and display resolution you want to use for your display adapter, whose name appears under Display.

## Color Palette

In the Colors section, you can choose your color palette from a drop-down list. Choices will vary depending on your display adapter and may include 256, High Color (16-bit), True Color (24-bit), or True Color (32-bit). The higher your color palette setting, the truer colors appear on the desktop.

## Display Resolution

In Screen Area, you can set the display resolution (indicated in pixels). The higher the resolution, the more information you can display. However, the size of each item on the desktop decreases with an increase in resolution. Move the slider left or right to set the number of pixels you want to display.

### Other Options

If you have problems with your display, click Troubleshoot to open the Windows 2000 Display troubleshooter in Help. For additional options, click Advanced. You'll be able to further configure your display adapter and monitor, perform more troubleshooting, and set color profiles.

**See Also** Power Options, Active Desktop

# Distributed File System

MMC console snap-in available on Windows 2000 servers (member servers or domain controllers) that enables you to make files located on different servers (distributed) appear to users as if they are in one location. Distributed File System (Dfs) thus eliminates the need for users to try to find related files that are located on different servers. With Dfs, there is no need for drive mappings, and users are not affected if you move the physical location of a shared folder. If you use Dfs for Web servers, HTML links will still function even if you move the location of Web server resources.

To access Dfs, choose Start ➢ Programs ➢ Administrative Tools ➢ Distributed File System.

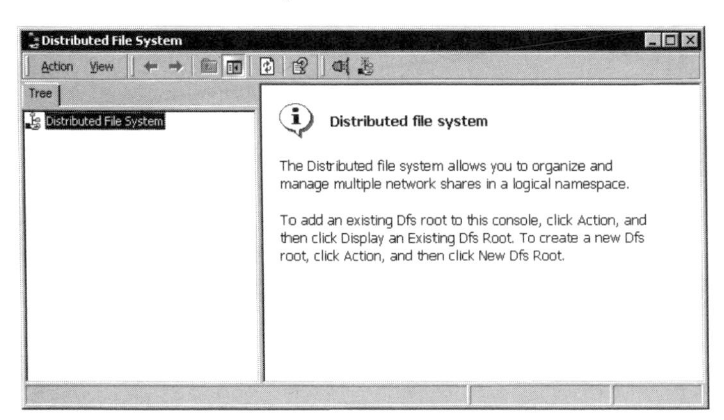

## Dfs Types

You can implement Dfs using one of two types:

**Stand-alone Distributed File System** Not stored in Active Directory. Does not support automatic replication.

**Domain-based Distributed File System** Stored in Active Directory. Supports automatic replication.

## Dfs Architecture

Dfs consists of three components:

**Dfs Root** Contains files and Dfs links. A server can host only one Dfs root; a domain can host multiple Dfs roots.

**Dfs Link** A link between a Dfs root and shared folders, domain volumes, or a different Dfs root.

**Dfs Shared Folder** A shared folder added to a Dfs link. The first shared folder is added when you create the Dfs link. Dfs shared folders can participate in replication, making them replicas in a replica set. When you create new replicas (adding another shared folder to a Dfs link), you can specify manual or automatic replication. Automatic replication, which ensures that changes to a Dfs shared folder remain synchronized among replicas, is configured via replication policy. You'll have to specify one shared folder as the master folder. Additional shared folders must reside on a server different from the one that holds the master folder.

**TIP** Automatic replication is supported only on NTFS-formatted drives.

## Action Menu

You can use the Action or pop-up menu to create and delete Dfs roots, Dfs links, and Dfs replicas (either root or folder replicas). Dfs root objects are depicted by a shared server icon, Dfs link objects are depicted by a linked folder icon, and replica objects are depicted by a shared folder icon.

You can also use the Action or pop-up menu to:

- Display existing Dfs roots
- Check the status of Dfs roots, links, and replicas (offline/online)
- Take folder replicas offline/online
- Configure replication policy
- Open any Dfs link, root, or replica

You can also remove the display (stop displaying) of a Dfs root in the MMC console snap-in (users will continue to be able to see and access the Dfs root) and later redisplay it. The options available will depend on which item you've selected in the console tree or Details pane. Some of the options will also be available as buttons on the toolbar.

## Creating a Domain-based Distributed File System

To create a domain-based Dfs, follow these steps:

1. Right-click Distributed File System in the console tree pane and choose New Dfs Root to start the New Dfs Root Wizard. Click Next.
2. Select Create a Domain Dfs Root and click Next.
3. Select the domain you want to host this Dfs root. Click Next.
4. Type or browse for the server you want to host this Dfs root. Click Next.
5. Select to use an existing share and choose one from the drop-down list, or select to create a new share and enter the necessary share information. Then click Next.
6. Type a name for the Dfs root in the Name text box. Type a comment in the Comment text box if you wish. Click Next.
7. Verify the information. If you need to make changes, use the Back button. Click Finish to create the Dfs root.
8. Reboot the computer. (If you don't, Dfs won't work.)
9. Run Distributed File System again.
10. Right-click the Dfs root in the console tree and choose New Dfs Link.

11. In the Create a New Dfs Link dialog box, type a name for the link in the Link Name text box; then type the path to or browse to the folder you want opened when a user opens the Dfs link.

12. If desired, type a comment in the Comment text box and change how long clients keep the Dfs link referral in cache.

13. Click OK to create the Dfs link.

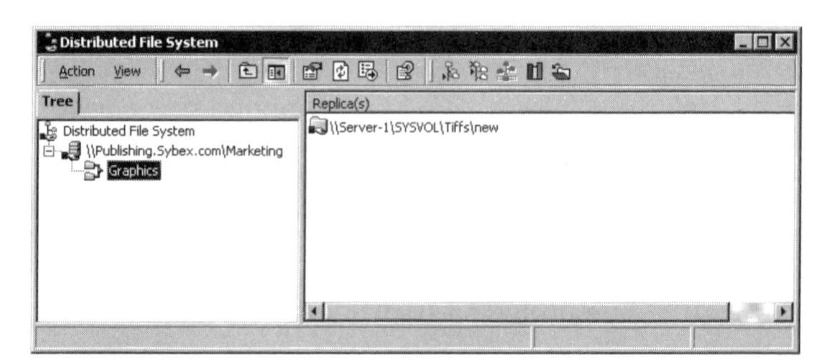


14. To verify the creation and accessibility of the distributed file system you created, open Windows Explorer (you can do this at a client computer if you wish) and navigate My Network Places to the server where you created the distributed file system. The Dfs root appears as a network share below the server. Navigate to the Dfs link you created, which appears as a folder below the Dfs root. Verify that the contents of the folder are the same as those of the folder you specified in the Create a New Dfs Link dialog box to open when the Dfs link is opened.

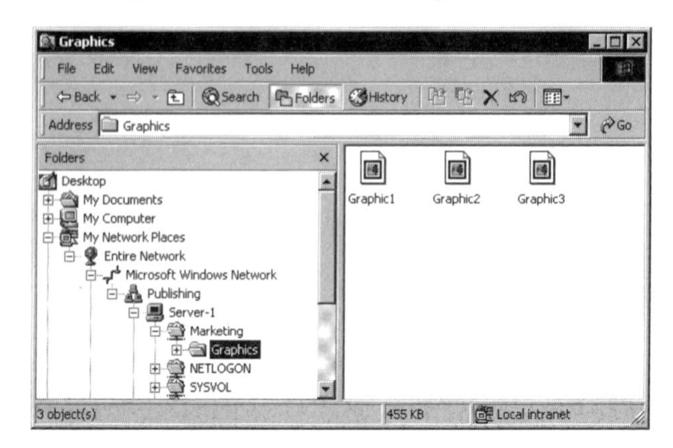

**See Also** Microsoft Management Console (MMC)

# DNS

DNS Domain Name System (DNS) service and also Administrative Tools menu option that takes you to the DNS MMC console snap-in installed by default on Windows 2000 domain controllers with Active Directory installed. The DNS MMC console snap-in lets you manage Windows 2000 Domain Name System (DNS) servers.

**TIP** Use Add/Remove Programs to install DNS if it isn't yet installed on a Windows 2000 Server computer.

DNS is a system for assigning user-friendly names (DNS names) to computers in a TCP/IP network (such as the Internet) using a domain hierarchy. This makes it easier for people to locate computers (hosts) and services in the network; for example, it's easier to remember `microsoft.com` than it is to remember the IP address `207.46.130.149`. However, hosts use each other's IP addresses to communicate. DNS names are registered with their corresponding IP addresses in DNS databases, and then the data in DNS databases is used to resolve DNS names to IP addresses when hosts request services from each other. An entry in a DNS database is called a resource record. Resource records can be one of several types, among them:

- Host—also called an A record; maps a DNS domain name to an IPv4 address
- Alias—maps an alias to an existing DNS domain name
- IPv6 hosts—maps a DNS domain name to an IPv6 address

**TIP** DNS is required for Active Directory to function.

A DNS implementation requires a DNS domain name space, resource records, a DNS server, and DNS clients.

## DNS Domain Name Space

The DNS domain name space is organized to represent a conceptual tree of named domains, consisting of branch and leaf levels.

At the branch level, several names represent groups of resources; at the leaf level, a single name denotes a single resource.

Each level in the domain name space has an associated name that corresponds to its function. Levels are separated by periods.

**Domain Root** This is an unnamed level and is denoted by two empty quotation marks (" "). In a DNS domain name, the domain root is denoted by a trailing period at the end of the DNS name, such as `"publishing.sybex.com."`. When a DNS name is used this way, it indicates an exact location in the tree hierarchy and is called a fully qualified domain name (FQDN). Contains top-level domains.

**Top-Level Domain** Consists of two or three letters and denotes a country, region, or organization type. Organization type examples are `.com` and `.org`; country/region examples are `.ca` (Canada) and `.de` (Germany). Contains second-level domains.

**Second-Level Domain** Name that an individual or organization registers to use on the Internet, such as `sybex.com`. Can contain either subdomains or host names.

**Subdomain** Added to an organization's second-level domain name to further organize an organization's structure, such as `publishing.sybex.com` (a fictitious example used throughout this book). Contains host names.

**Host Name** Identifies a single resource in the domain, such as a computer or other device. An example might be `workstation-5.publishing.sybex.com`.

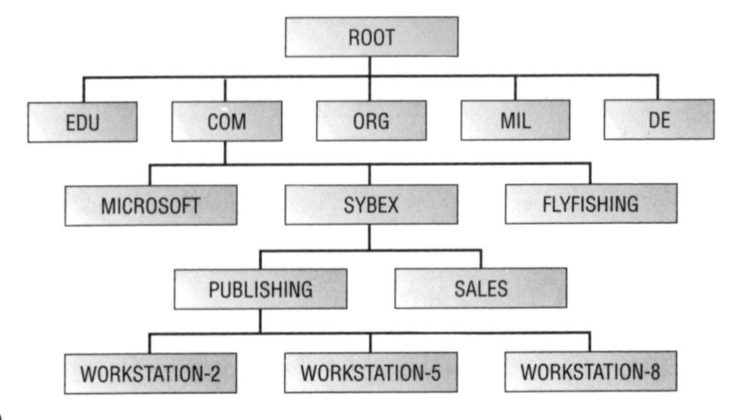

## Zones

Zones are databases of one or more DNS domain names and store name information for the domain names they include. For example, a zone could contain `sybex.com` and `publishing.sybex.com`, or you could have a separate zone for each. At the time the `sybex.com` domain is created at a server, a single zone is created for the `sybex` name space. When you add subdomains, you can either add them to the existing zone or create a new zone for them (called delegation).

Two types of zones exist:

**Forward Lookup Zones** Assumes that IP addresses are required as the response to queries.

**Reverse Lookup Zones** Assumes that DNS domain names are required as the response to queries.

## Zone Transfers

To provide fault tolerance, you must make zones available from more than one DNS server. You accomplish this through zone transfers, which ensure that zone data is replicated and synchronized between multiple DNS servers. When a second server is configured to host a zone that exists on another server, a full zone transfer (transferring all data) is made. After that, in Windows 2000 Server incremental zone transfers occur as changes are made to the zone.

**TIP** Earlier DNS implementations allowed only for complete zone transfers. Incremental zone transfers generate much less network traffic.

## DNS MMC Console Snap-in

Use the DNS MMC console snap-in to view and configure DNS services. In the DNS console snap-in window, you can view and configure the DNS server and zones.

### *Action Menu*

The Action and pop-up menus contain options to perform such functions as starting, stopping, pausing, resuming, and restarting the DNS service; configuring the DNS server; creating new zones;

creating new resource records; adding a new domain to a zone; configuring item properties; and accessing Help. The options available depend on which item you've selected in the console tree or Details pane.

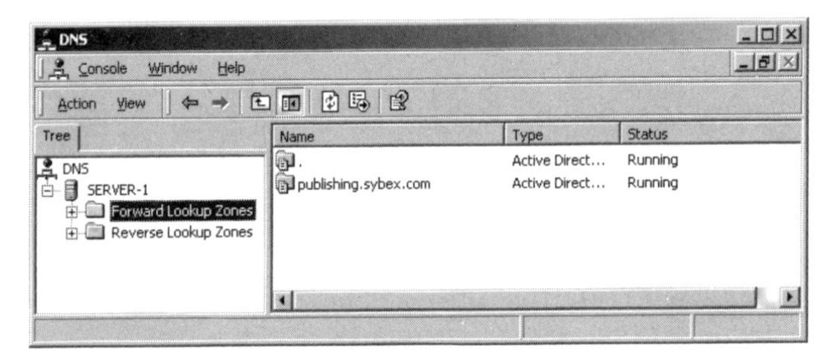


## DNS Client Configuration

In order for Windows clients to be able to use DNS services, they must know the IP address of one or more DNS servers in the network. You can have the client obtain DNS server addresses automatically (via DHCP), or you can specify an IP address for the preferred DNS server, as well as for an alternate DNS server and additional DNS servers. Follow these steps:

1. Choose Start ➢ Settings ➢ Network and Dial-up Connections.
2. Double-click the Local Area Connection icon, then click Properties.
3. Select Internet Protocol (TCP/IP) in the list of components used by this connection and click Properties.
4. To use DHCP to obtain DNS server addresses, select Obtain DNS Server Address Automatically. Otherwise, select Use the Following DNS Server Addresses and enter the IP address of the preferred DNS server. To provide fault tolerance, enter the IP address of an alternate DNS server, if available.

**NOTE** For a client to be able to use DHCP to obtain DNS server IP addresses, option 006 (provided by the DHCP server) must be enabled (use the DHCP MMC console snap-in to verify this configuration).

5. Optional: To specify additional DNS server IP addresses, click Advanced, select the DNS tab, click Add, enter a DNS server's IP address, and click Add. Repeat this step until you've added all DNS server IP addresses, then click OK.

6. Click OK, click OK again, then click Close.

**See Also** Microsoft Management Console (MMC), DHCP

# Documents

Provides access to a list of shortcuts Windows 2000 maintains to the 15 most recently accessed documents so that you can quickly access them again if you need to. Choose Start ➢ Documents to access the list. Click any item in the list to open the document in the appropriate application, saving you time and effort.

**NOTE** The submenu also contains a shortcut to My Documents, the default folder when saving documents in many applications that run on Windows 2000.

The list of documents is maintained even if you shut down and restart Windows 2000.

To clear the list of documents, choose Start ➢ Settings ➢ Taskbar & Start Menu and click Clear on the Advanced tab.

**See Also** Taskbar & Start Menu, Start Menu

# Domain Controller Security Policy

**See** Security Policy

# Domain Security Policy

**See** Security Policy

# Drag-and-Drop

You can use drag-and-drop to copy, move, and delete files and folders in many application programs and on the desktop. To do so, place the mouse pointer over an item, press and hold the left mouse button, and drag the item to its destination by moving the mouse. A destination might be a folder, a drive, the desktop, and so forth. Place the pointer over the destination and release the left mouse button. The result of the drag-and-drop items can differ, as outlined below:

- If you drag a file or folder to a folder on the same disk, Windows moves the item. To copy the item, hold down the Ctrl key while dragging and dropping.
- If you drag a file or folder to a folder on a different disk, Windows copies the item.
- If you drag a file or folder to the Recycle Bin, Windows deletes the item (not permanently until you empty the Recycle Bin).
- If you drag a file to a printer shortcut on the desktop, Windows prints the file.

**See Also** Explorer

# Dr. Watson

Error-debugging program that automatically diagnoses and logs Windows 2000 program errors. Support personnel can then use this information to troubleshoot the problem. Dr. Watson starts automatically when a Windows 2000 program error occurs.

To access and configure Dr. Watson, and to view application errors, choose Start ➢ Settings ➢ Control Panel, double-click Administrative Tools, double-click Computer Management, expand Systems Tools, select System Information, and then choose Tools ➢ Windows ➢ Dr Watson.

**TIP** Alternatively, you can start Dr. Watson by entering **drwtsn32** in the Run dialog box after choosing Start ➢ Run.

## Configuration Options

In the Dr. Watson window, you can configure the following items:

- Log file path
- Crash dump file path (if Create Crash Dump File is selected)
- Wave file path (if Sound Notification is selected)
- Number of instructions
- Number of errors to save

You can also set several options; for example, you can choose to dump the symbol table (which might make your log file very large) and to dump all thread contexts (not just the one causing the error, which is the default). You can also specify that you want to append information to an existing log file, to receive visual and/or sound notification when a Windows 2000 program error occurs, and to create a Crash Dump file.

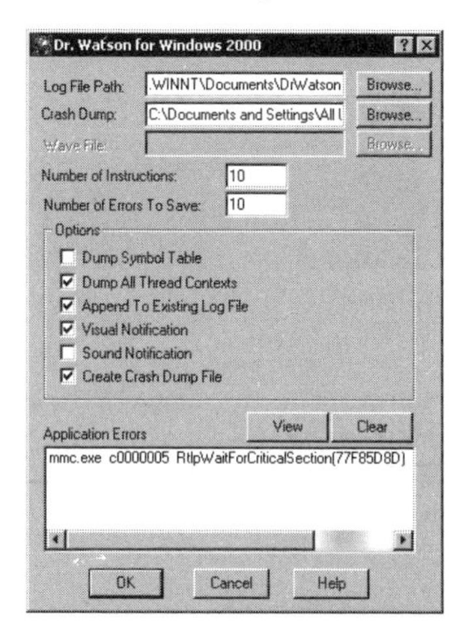


## Viewing Errors

Once application errors have occurred, they appear in the Application Errors list box toward the bottom of the Dr. Watson window. Two buttons are available:

**View** Opens the Log File Viewer after selecting an error so that you can view detailed information about the error in the log file.

**Clear** Clears the selected error from the file.

### Help

To access Dr. Watson help topics, click the Help button at the bottom of the Dr. Watson window.

## Entertainment

Windows 2000 default program group that provides access to the following entertainment programs: CD Player, Sound Recorder, Volume Control, and Windows Media Player. These items are discussed in detail under their respective headings in this book. You access the Entertainment program group by choosing Start ➢ Programs ➢ Accessories ➢ Entertainment.

**See Also** CD Player, Sound Recorder, Volume Control, Windows Media Player

## Event Viewer

Event Viewer

Displays information about events that are logged by Windows 2000 and other installed applications. Used to monitor and troubleshoot Windows 2000 hardware and software. Also lets you manage the logged information.

To access Event Viewer, choose Start ➢ Settings ➢ Control Panel, double-click Administrative Tools, then double-click Event Viewer.

**TIP** You can also access Event Viewer by double-clicking the Computer Management icon in Control Panel. You'll find Event Viewer listed under System Tools in the console tree.

**TIP** In Windows 2000 Server, you can also access Event Viewer by choosing Start ➢ Programs ➢ Administrative Tools ➢ Event Viewer.

## Event Viewer Logs

By default, Event Viewer in Windows 2000 contains three logs—the Application, Security, and System logs. Each log displays different types of events. Additional logs may appear, depending on your configuration and on whether the computer is running Windows 2000 Professional or Windows 2000 Server.

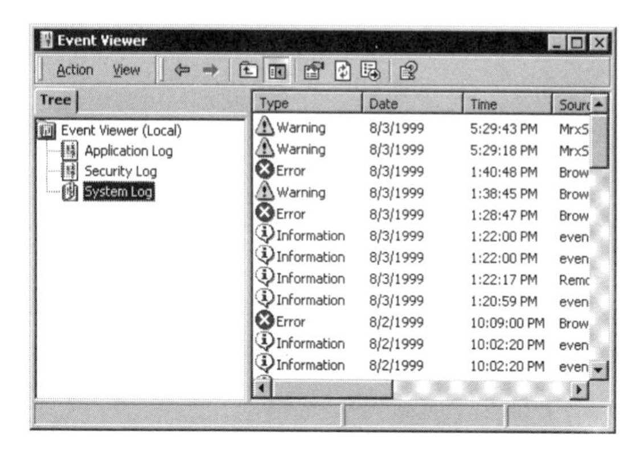


### *Application Log*

The Application log displays events generated by such ap ica-tions as installation programs and database programs. Tl appli-cation developer programs the events to be logged into t application.

### *Security Log*

The Security log displays such events as successful and failed login attempts, as well as events related to working with files and folders, such as creating, opening, and deleting files and folders. Security auditing is not enabled by default, and events are logged only after audit policies are set up. You must use Group Policy on a domain or Local Security Policy on a loc computer to enable it. If your computer is part of a domai Group Policy settings on the domain take precedence over Local Security Policy settings.

### *System Log*

The System log displays events that are logged by Windows 2000 components. Examples are when drivers fail to load, a hard disk is renamed, or user disk quota data is rebuilt.

### Event Types

The Event Viewer Details pane displays the following event types:

**Information** Describes a successful event, such as loading a service successfully.

**Warning** Describes an event that is not problematic right now but that may indicate a problem in the future, such as the browser not being able to obtain a list of servers from the browser master on a domain controller.

**Error** Describes a serious problem, such as a service that fails to load.

**Success Audit** Describes a successful, audited event, such as a successful system logon.

**Failure Audit** Describes an unsuccessful, audited event, such as an unsuccessful system logon.

### Event Log Properties

You can customize event log properties for each log. Select the log in the console tree and choose Action ➢ Properties. The Properties dialog box has two tabs: General and Filter.

**General** Here you can change the log's display name and the maximum log size, configure log wrapping (when the maximum log size is reached), clear the log, and restore default settings. You can also view information about the log file, such as its current size and creation date, and when it was last modified and accessed.

**Filter** Lets you filter the log by certain criteria. You can specify the types of events you want to view, the source and category of events you want to view, and the user, computer, or event ID for which you want to view events. You can also specify a timeframe for viewing events. Click Restore Defaults to return to the default settings.

**TIP** You can also access the Filter tab by choosing View ➢ Filter.

## Event Information

When you select an event log in the console tree, the Details pane displays all events currently in the log. You can see some preliminary information about each event under the column headings. The column headings give you information about the event, such as its type; the date and time the event occurred; the source and category of the event; an event ID, if applicable; and the name of the user and computer on which the event occurred.

### *Viewing Detailed Information*

To view additional, more detailed information about an event, right-click the event and choose Properties, or double-click it. In addition to the information available in the Details pane, you'll see a detailed description of the event and, if available, record data on the Event Detail tab. To see details for the next or previous event, click the up or down arrow button, respectively. You can also click the copy button (depicted by two sheets of paper) to copy the details of the event to the Windows Clipboard.

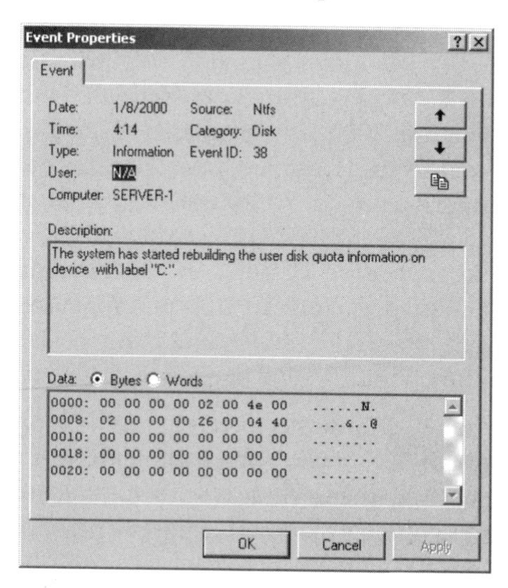


### *Ordering Events*

By default, events in the Details pane display chronologically with the newest event first. You can reverse this order by choosing View ➢ Oldest First.

### *Finding Events*

If you're looking for a specific event, it might be difficult to find the event in the log. You can search for a specific event by choosing View ➢ Find and then specifying information about the event you want to find (such as type, source, category, and user) in the Find In dialog box. Click Find Next to start your search.

## Viewing Logs on a Remote Computer

By default, Event Viewer displays the event log files for the local computer. You can also access log files on remote computers. Select Event Viewer (Local) and choose the option Connect to Another Computer from the Action menu to connect to and view log files on a remote computer.

**See Also** Microsoft Management Console (MMC), Computer Management, Clipboard

# Explorer

Windows Explorer

Program used to work with files and folders on your computer and in the network in Windows 2000. The program's full name is Windows Explorer. It displays and lets you navigate the hierarchical structure of drives, folders, and files on your computer and of any mapped network drives. Using Explorer, you can accomplish such tasks as creating, copying, moving, renaming, and deleting files and folders. You can also run programs, search for files, view the properties of files, and many other file- and folder-related functions.

To open Explorer, choose Start ➢ Programs ➢ Accessories ➢ Windows Explorer. When you open Explorer in this manner, it opens to the My Documents folder (a desktop folder). Alternatively, you can right-click Start and choose Explore. This will open Explorer to the Start Menu folder.

**TIP** To access Windows Explorer quickly, double-click the My Documents folder on the desktop. If you access Windows Explorer this way, it opens without an Explorer Bar open.

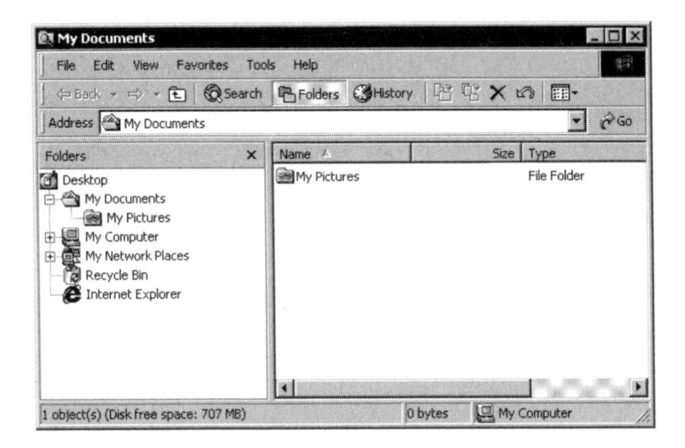


Windows Explorer consists of the menu bar and toolbars at the top of the window, the Explorer Bar in the left pane, and the main Explorer view in the right pane. The status bar is at the bottom of the window.

## Explorer Menus

The Explorer menus let you perform all necessary file- and folder-related functions. The options available—or even visible—on each of the menus depend on what type of object you have selected in the main Explorer view. Some of the items available on the Explorer menus are also available from the toolbars.

**TIP** You'll find many of the same menu options when you open My Computer, My Network Places, and the Recycle Bin.

### *File Menu*

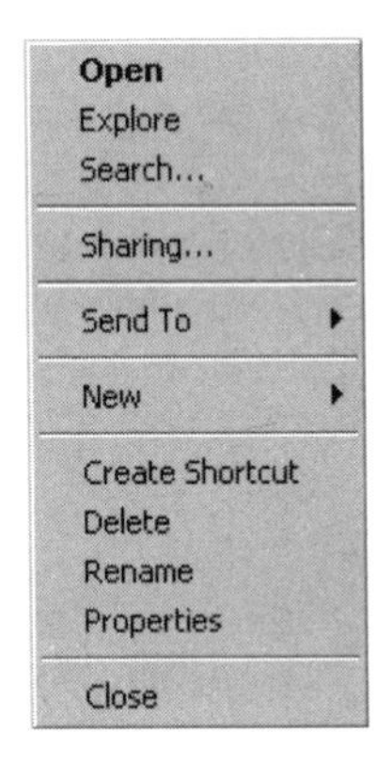


Presents you with file management choices you can use to perform the functions below. Some functions are available on the File menu only when the item is selected in the right pane, not in the Explorer Bar, or when you right-click the item in the Explorer Bar to open a pop-up menu.

- Open a file or folder.
- Explore the contents of a folder, disk, or computer (expand to display the next level in the hierarchy). If you select

Explore from the pop-up menu by right-clicking an item in the Explorer Bar, the item opens in a new window. If you select an item in the right pane and choose Explore from the pop-up or File menu, the item opens in the right pane, replacing the current contents of the pane.

- Open a file with a program you specify. Available only when you've selected a file.
- Open Search to search for files, folders, computers, people, printers, or sites on the Internet.
- Configure sharing of a folder with other users.
- Send the selected file(s) or folder(s) to a floppy disk, to the My Documents folder, or as e-mail to a mail recipient, or create a shortcut to the file on the desktop.
- Create a new folder, shortcut, or document.
- Format the selected drive (available only by right-clicking when selecting a physical floppy disk or hard drive).
- Map a network drive (available only when a network folder is selected).
- Print a file or display a preview of a selected file (a preview appears only when one is available).
- Create a shortcut for the selected files or folders.
- Delete the selected file(s) or folder(s).
- Rename the selected file or folder.
- View the properties of the selected file, folder, or drive.
- Close the selected item.

### *Edit Menu*

Lets you perform editing functions. Some functions are not available if you select an item in the Explorer Bar. You can do the following:

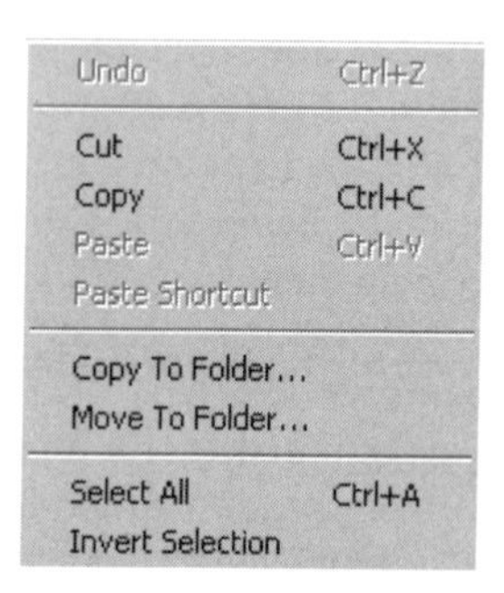


- Undo the last action.
- Cut, copy, or paste a file or folder.
- Paste a cut or copied item as a shortcut.

- Copy or move an item to a specific folder.
- Select all items in the main window (files and folders).
- Select all files that are currently not selected and deselect those that are.

### View Menu

Lets you configure what is displayed in the Explorer window and how it appears. You can exclude and include toolbars, the status bar, and the Explorer Bar. Toolbars include the Standard Buttons, Address Bar, Links, and Radio toolbars. You can also use the View menu to customize toolbars. The Explorer Bar can display the Search, Favorites, History, and Folders view. Additionally, you can display a tip of the day in a separate pane.

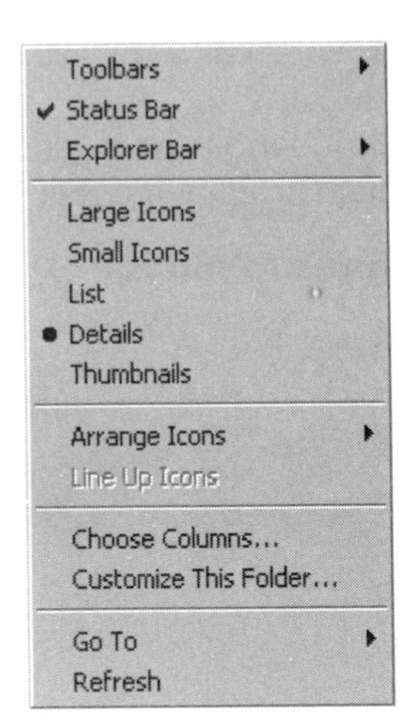


You can choose to display files and folders as:

- Large or small icons
- A list
- A list with details (by default, this includes file size, type, and modification date)
- Thumbnails

In addition, you can do the following:

- Arrange icons by name, type, size, or date or have Explorer auto-arrange icons.
- Arrange icons in a grid (Line Up Icons). Not available with the List and Details views.
- If you selected the Details view, you can choose which columns to display. Many additional columns are available along with the default columns that appear.
- Change the appearance of a folder (Customize This Folder).
- Go directly to a specific place, such as the previous view, the next view, up a level, to your home page, and to folders you've previously opened.
- Redisplay the current view (Refresh).

### Favorites Menu

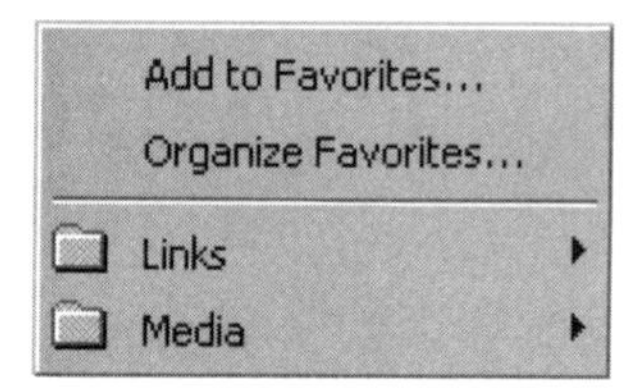


Lets you add and organize your favorite Web sites or local addresses (drives and folders) in the Favorites folder. Any address you've added appears in the appropriate folder in the list at the bottom of the Favorites menu for quick access. For more information about adding and organizing favorites, see the main heading Internet Explorer.

### Tools Menu

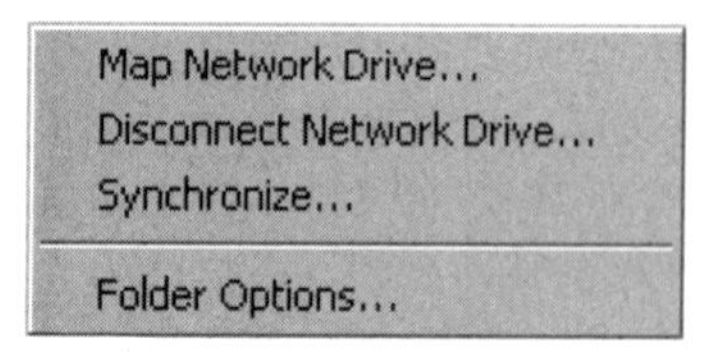


Lets you map and disconnect network drives, configure synchronization of offline files and folders and synchronize them, and configure folder options.

### Help Menu

Lets you access the Windows 2000 Help system and find out information about Windows 2000, such as available memory and version and licensing information.

## Explorer Toolbars

Windows Explorer includes four toolbars: Standard Buttons, Address Bar, Links, and Radio. Windows displays the Standard Buttons and Address Bar toolbars by default in Windows Explorer.

### Standard Buttons Toolbar

The Standard Buttons toolbar contains these buttons by default:

**Back** Lets you go back to the last item you displayed. You can also go directly to items you displayed in this Explorer session by clicking the down arrow to the right of this button and selecting an item from the list.

**Forward** Lets you go to the item you displayed before going to the current item with the

Back button. You can also go directly to items you displayed in this Explorer session by clicking the down arrow to the right of this button and selecting an item from the list.

**Up** Lets you go up one level in the directory structure displayed in the Explorer Bar. The display in the right (main) pane changes accordingly.

Search **Search** Changes the Explorer Bar view to the Search view, where you can find files and folders, computers, people, printers, and sites on the Internet.

Folders **Folders** Changes the Explorer Bar view to the Folders view, where you can see and navigate the desktop folder structure (this means you can see and navigate the directory structure of your computer and any network to which you're attached).

History **History** Changes the Explorer Bar view to the History view, where you can see and access all the pages and files you've viewed today, yesterday, the day before yesterday, and in the weeks starting last week and three weeks ago.

**Move To** Lets you move the selected item directly to a folder you specify. Available only with items selected in the right pane.

**Copy To** Lets you copy the selected item directly to a folder you specify. Available only with items selected in the right pane.

**Delete** Lets you move the selected item(s) to the Recycle Bin.

**Undo** Lets you undo the last action. This button's label changes according to your last action (for example, Undo Move or Undo Delete).

**Views** Lets you select how you want items in the right pane to appear. You can choose from Large Icons, Small Icons, List, Details, and Thumbnails.

**Customizing the Standard Buttons Toolbar** Not all available buttons appear on the Standard Buttons toolbar by default. You can add and remove buttons from the Standard Buttons toolbar to customize the toolbar for your needs. To do so, follow these steps:

1. Choose View ➢ Toolbars ➢ Customize to open the Customize Toolbar dialog box.
2. To add a button to the toolbar, select it in the left list box and click Add. To remove a button from the toolbar, select it in the right list box and click Remove.
3. If you want to change the order of buttons, select a button in the right list box and click Move Up or Move Down to change the position of the button in the toolbar.
4. Select how you want text and icons to display from the Text Options and Icon Options drop-down lists. Items include Show Text Labels, Selective Text on Right, and No Text Labels (Text Options), and Small Icons and Large Icons (Icon Options).
5. Click Close.

**TIP** To reset the toolbar to the default settings, click Reset in the Customize Toolbar dialog box.

### *Address Bar Toolbar*

The Address Bar toolbar contains these buttons:

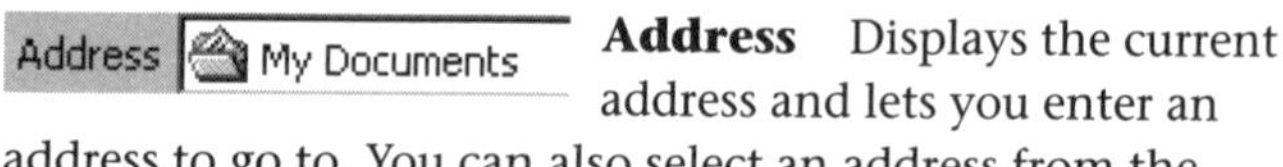


**Address** Displays the current address and lets you enter an address to go to. You can also select an address from the drop-down list by clicking the down arrow at the end of the Address bar.

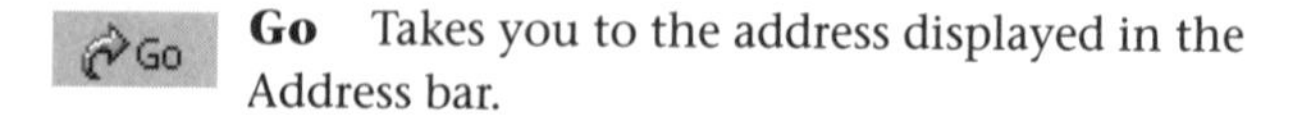


**Go** Takes you to the address displayed in the Address bar.

### *Links and Radio Toolbars*

Two other toolbars are available:

**Links** The Links toolbar contains buttons that you can click to go to certain Web pages on Microsoft's Web site. You can also access these pages through Favorites ➢ Links.

**Radio** Lets you access radio stations that broadcast on the Internet. Using the Play, Stop, and Mute buttons and the Volume Control slider respectively, you can start playback of audio streams, stop playback of audio streams, mute the sound, and adjust the volume.

## Explorer Bars

Explorer bars display in the left pane of the Explorer window and give you different views for navigation. Four views are available: the Search view, Favorites view, History view, and Folders view. Additionally, you can select the Tip of the Day view.

If you don't choose an Explorer Bar view, the contents of the currently selected folder or drive appear in the right pane, and information about the selected folder or drive appear in the left pane. This information can include such items as name, size, modification date, and attributes of the folder or drive. Use the Address field on the toolbar to navigate the hierarchical structure without an Explorer Bar view or with any Explorer Bar view except the Folders view displayed.

### *Search View*

Lets you search for files and folders, people, computers, printers, and sites on the Internet. See the subheading Search for more information on the Search view.

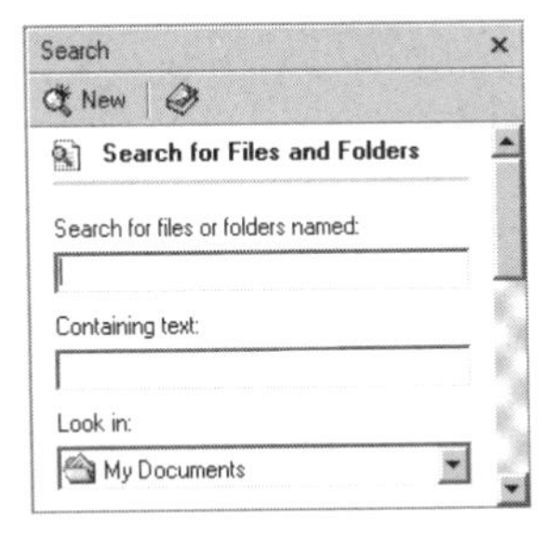


### *Favorites View*

Lets you navigate to the items you've added to your Favorites folder (and subfolders). You can also use this view to add and organize favorites. To navigate, click an item or sub-item. To add a page, click the Add button. To organize pages, click the Organize button.

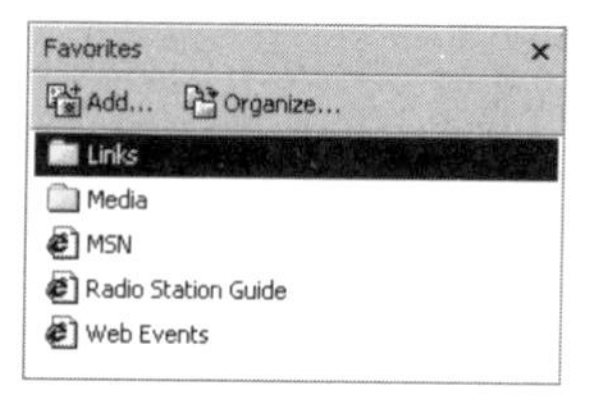

**TIP** Be selective with the items you add to your Favorites folder, as it can quickly become cluttered and unmanageable. Add only items you truly access often and periodically remove items you no longer access frequently, if at all.

### History View

Lets you view and access pages you've opened previously. You can viem items by date, site, most-visited, and by order visited today by choosing the appropriate selection from the History View's View menu. To navigate, click an item or sub-item.

### Folders View

Lets you view and navigate the folders available on your desktop, including My Documents, My Computer, My Network Places, the Recycle Bin, and Internet Explorer.

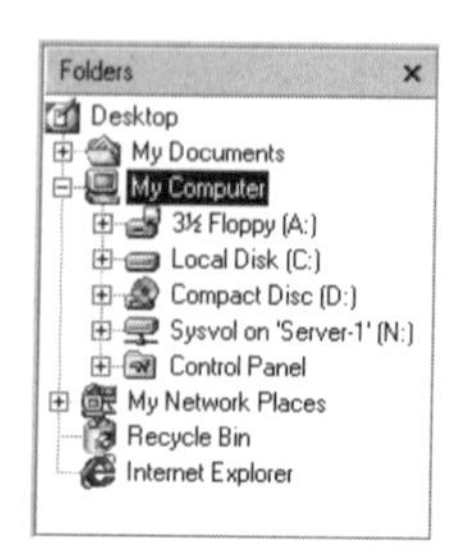

The contents of the Folder view represent all items available on your computer and those that are shared in the network. The name of each item appears to the right of the item icon. Items that have a plus sign (+) next to them contain other items, typically folders, but also other items, such as drives. Click the plus sign to expand an item and display its contents. When an item is expanded, the plus sign changes to a minus sign (–). Click this sign to collapse an item. Use the scroll bars to display items that do not fit into either of the panes.

To display the contents of an item in the right pane, including files, folders, and drives, select an item in the Folders view rather than expanding it. When you select a folder, the folder icon changes to an open folder. You can also expand folders and drives in the right pane by double-clicking them in this pane. When you do this, the selection in the left pane automatically changes accordingly to show you where you are in the hierarchical structure.

## Customize a Folder

You can change the appearance of a folder by customizing it. To do so, select a folder and choose View ➢ Customize This Folder. This opens the Customize This Folder Wizard. The wizard lets you choose from these options:

**Customize** Lets you do the following:

**Choose or Edit an HTML Template for This Folder** Lets you choose or edit the HTML template that is used to display this folder.

**Modify Background Picture and Filename Appearance** Lets you add a background picture and specify the text and background color.

**Add Folder Comment** Lets you add a comment to the folder using HTML.

**Remove Customizations** Lets you remove any folder customization from the folder.

Follow the wizard to finish customizing the folder. Options depend on the choice you made in the first customizing dialog box.

### Status Bar

The status bar appears at the bottom of the Explorer window. It provides such information as how many objects the selected object contains, how much free space is available on the disk, and how much disk space is taken up by files in a folder.

**See Also** My Documents, Folder Options, Synchronize, Search, Map Network Drive, My Computer, My Network Places, Recycle Bin, Internet Explorer, Help

## Fax

Configures Microsoft Fax properties, such as user information, cover pages, and fax monitoring. Choose Start ➢ Settings ➢ Control Panel and double-click the Fax icon to open the Fax Properties dialog box. It contains four tabs: User Information, Cover Pages, Status Monitor, and Advanced Options.

**NOTE** Microsoft Fax is part of Windows 2000 and is used to send faxes via a fax modem, also called a fax device. If one is installed, you can create a document you want to fax and then send it, as if you were printing a document. Choose File ➢ Print in any Windows application program (such as Microsoft Word) and select the fax device to which you want to send the document. Click Print and follow the instructions in the Send Fax Wizard.

**TIP** Fax devices cannot be shared across the network.

## User Information Tab

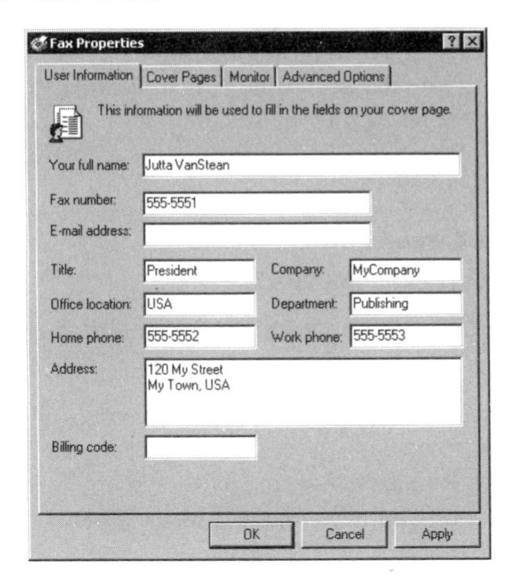


On the User Information tab, you can enter your personal information. Some of this information can be used to fill in fields on a cover page, if you create and use one. Items on this tab include name, fax number, e-mail address, title, company, office location, department, home phone, work phone, address, and billing code.

## Cover Pages Tab

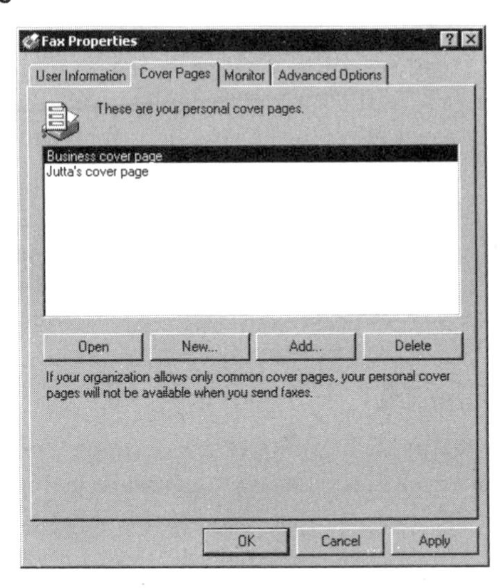

Lets you configure personal fax cover pages that are sent as part of your fax. When you create a cover page, you can create fields for sender and recipient information and other information, such as subject and date and time sent. You can also manipulate how the fields appear on the page. You'll be able to choose one of the cover pages you create when sending a fax using the Send Fax Wizard.

### *Creating a Cover Page*

To create a cover page, follow these steps:

1. On the Cover Pages tab, click New, and then click OK to open the Fax Cover Page Editor.
2. To create fields, choose Insert ➢ Recipient, Sender or Message, and choose a field from the list. Place the field where you want it to appear on the page. Add any fields you want to appear on your cover page and place them on the page.
3. Add other elements using the available text and drawing tools, and use other menu options, such as Format and Layout, to further design how the page will look.
4. When you finish, choose File ➢ Save and give your cover page a name. Windows will save it as a .COV (Fax Cover Page) file, by default in the Personal Coverpages folder. Close the Cover Page Editor.
5. Your cover page appears in the list of personal cover pages.

You can open any existing cover pages to edit them by selecting the cover page in the list and clicking Open, or you can add other existing cover pages by clicking Add. To delete a cover page, select it in the list and click Delete.

**TIP** You may not be able to use the cover pages you create here if only common cover pages have been allowed through Fax Service Management.

## Status Monitor Tab

Controls Fax Status Monitor options. Fax Status Monitor monitors fax-related events, such as sending and receiving faxes. It also tells you the status of Microsoft Fax and enables you to

interrupt incoming faxes. In addition, Fax Status Monitor lets you specify that you don't want to manually answer a second incoming call. This is handy if you share a line for voice and fax calls, and callers phone you first to tell you that they're about to send a fax. You then know that the next call is a fax call that you want the fax device to pick up.

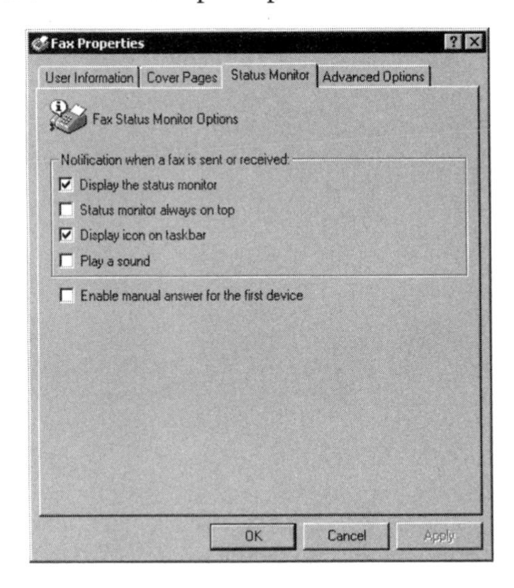


On the Status Monitor tab of Fax Properties, you can specify that you want Windows to:

- Display Status Monitor or an icon on the taskbar when a fax is sent or received.
- Always display Status Monitor on top of other windows.
- Play a sound when you receive faxes.

Simply check any or all of these options.

You can also select the option Enable Manual Answer for the First Device. If you do, you'll be able to share a phone line with a fax device and have a chance to answer the call before the fax device picks up the call. You'll be asked if you want to answer the call. If you hear a fax tone, answer No; if you don't, answer Yes. You don't need to check this box if your phone line is dedicated to the fax device.

## Advanced Options Tab

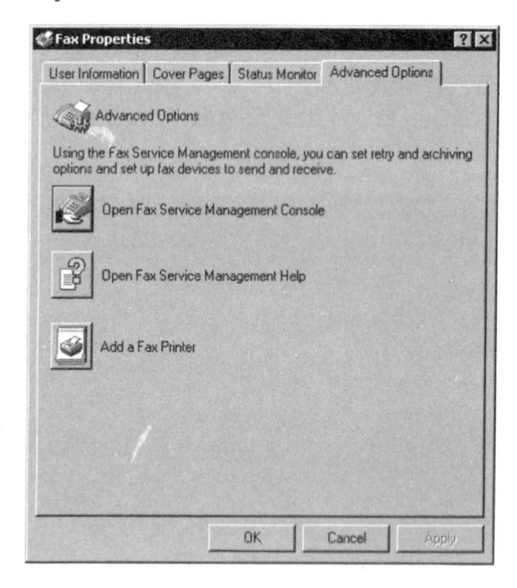


Lets you perform several actions:

- Start Fax Service Management by clicking the Open Fax Service Management Console button. Fax Service Management is a Microsoft Management Console (MMC) snap-in. You can use it to view fax devices installed on your computer, change their properties, and configure how much detail you want the Application log to record for NT Fax events for each logging category.

**TIP** You can access the Application log through Start ➢ Settings ➢ Control Panel ➢ Administrative Tools ➢ Event Viewer ➢ Application Log. Check the right pane for events of Source NT Fax, or click the Source header to sort events alphabetically and then find events of Source NT Fax.

- Access Fax Service Management Help by clicking the Open Fax Service Management Help button.
- Automatically create a fax printer object called Fax (if no object of that name exists), or create a copy of an existing fax printer object called Fax. To do this, click the Add a Fax Printer button.

After you've configured the various Fax (Properties) tabs and clicked OK, Windows automatically adds a Fax printer object to the list of printers in the Printers folder.

**See Also** Fax Service Management, Fax Queue, My Faxes, Send Cover Page Fax, Fax Status Monitor, Send Fax Wizard

# Fax Status Monitor

Fax Status Monitor monitors fax-related events, such as sending and receiving faxes. It also tells you the status of Microsoft Fax as well as the status and other information, such as the elapsed time, of faxes currently being sent or received. It also enables you to interrupt incoming and outgoing faxes, and lets you specify that you don't want to manually answer a second incoming call.

Fax Status Monitor is available only during fax activity (after you send a job to the fax printer or while the job is being sent, for example).

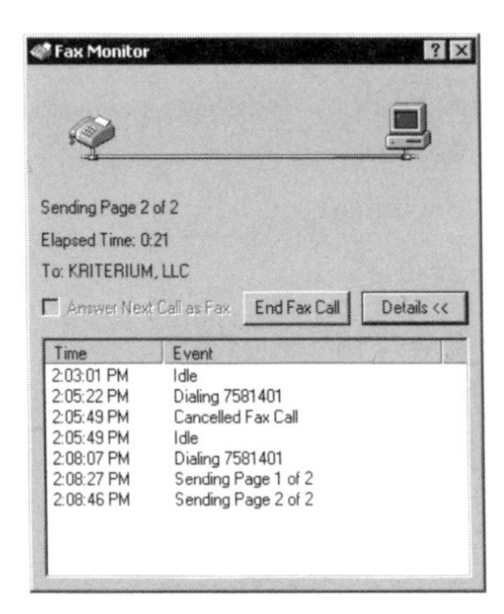


**See Also** Fax

# Fax Queue

Holds faxes after they're sent from an application to the fax printer until they are sent or until the number of retries has been exceeded without successfully sending the fax. Also stores faxes that are scheduled to be sent at a later time. Choose Start ➢ Programs ➢ Accessories ➢ Communications ➢ Fax ➢ Fax Queue to open the fax queue.

**TIP** You can also open the fax queue for any device by double-clicking the desired fax printer in the Printers folder in Control Panel.

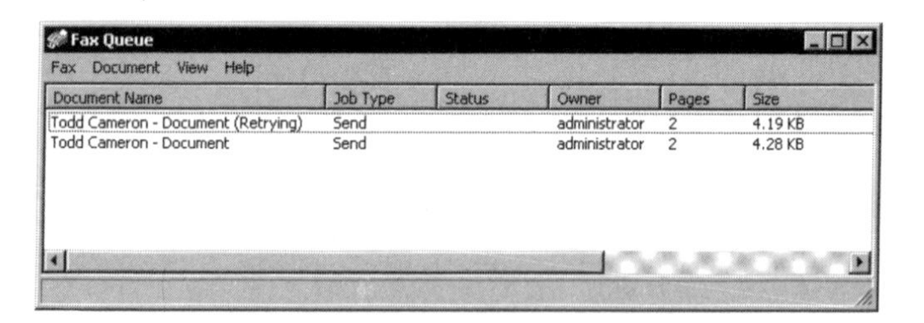


In the fax queue, you can see information about each fax in the queue, such as:

- Name of the document
- Job type (for example, send)
- Status (such as dialing)
- Username of owner
- Number of pages
- Size of the document
- Time the fax is scheduled to be sent
- Port that should be used

The fax queue is very similar to the print queue. In the Fax menu, you can perform such actions as setting the fax printer as the default printer, pausing faxing, canceling all faxes, and accessing the fax printer's properties. The Document menu lets you perform such actions as pausing, resuming, and canceling a fax job, as well as accessing the document properties for the job.

**See Also** Send Fax Wizard, Fax Service Management, Printers

# Fax Service Management

MMC console snap-in used to configure fax services on the local computer, such as fax job default settings, security default settings for Fax Service Management, fax device properties, and logging levels. Choose Start ➢ Programs ➢ Accessories ➢ Communications ➢ Fax ➢ Fax Service Management to open Fax Service Management.

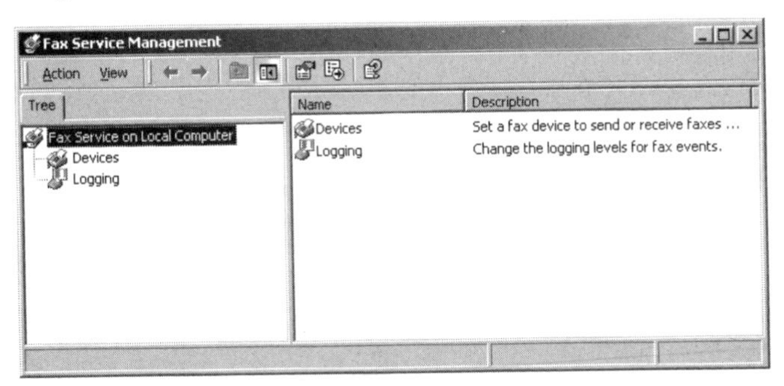


The console tree of Fax Service Management has three items: Fax Service on Local Computer, Devices, and Logging.

**TIP** You must have administrative privileges to use Fax Service Management to configure fax service, devices, and logging.

## Fax Service on Local Computer

Configures Fax Service on the local computer. Right-click Fax Service on Local Computer and choose Properties to open the Properties dialog box. It contains two tabs: General and Security.

**TIP** You can also open the properties of Fax Service on Local Computer by clicking Action on the toolbar and choosing Properties or by clicking the Properties button on the toolbar.

**General** Configures retry options and send settings. Options include:

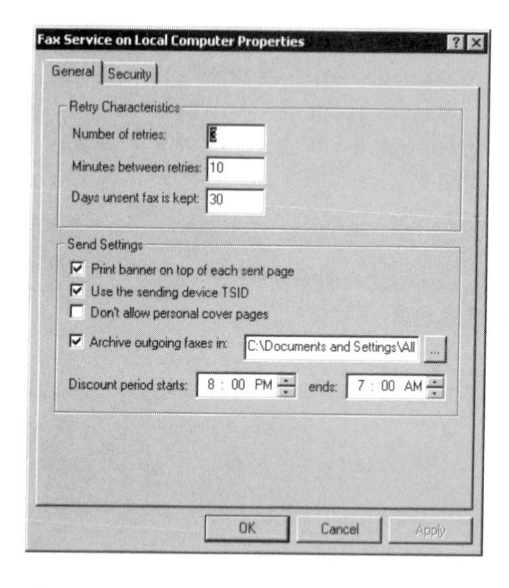


- **Number of Retries** The number of times Fax Service Management should try to send fax jobs that did not send successfully on the first attempt.
- **Minutes between Retries** The number of minutes that should elapse between each attempt to send the fax.
- **Days Unsent Fax Is Kept** The number of days a fax is kept in the fax queue after unsuccessful send attempts.

- **Print Banner on Top of Each Sent Page** Includes user information from the User Information tab on every page of the fax.

---

**TIP** You can access the User Information tab by either opening Fax in Control Panel or by right-clicking a fax device in Printers and selecting Properties.

- **Use the Sending Device TSID** Displays the Transmitting Station Identifier (TSID) on cover pages. The TSID is configured manually for each fax device. If this option is unchecked, the fax number specified in User Information is used instead.

---

**TIP** The TSID is configured on the General tab of each fax device's properties in Fax Service Management.

- **Don't Allow Personal Cover Pages** Disables the ability to pick a personally created cover page when sending a fax with the Send Fax Wizard. Only system-provided cover pages will be available in the list of cover pages from which to choose.
- **Archive Outgoing Faxes In** Tells Windows to save faxes after they've been sent; if you select this option, you also specify the path to the directory in which Windows saves the sent faxes.
- **Discount Period Starts/Ends** Specifies the time during which costs for making calls over a phone line is cheaper. This is the time range used for sending faxes if you choose When Discount Rates Apply in the Send Printer Wizard.

**Security** Sets permissions for fax jobs and fax service. Possible permissions are:

- Submit Fax Jobs
- View Fax Jobs
- View Fax Service
- View Fax Devices

- Manage Fax Jobs
- Manage Fax Service
- Manage Fax Devices

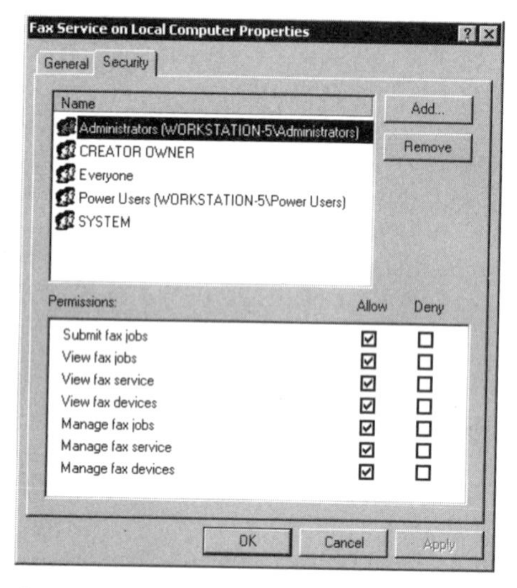


By default, the group Everyone is allowed the Submit Fax Jobs and all View permissions but none of the Manage permissions. The groups Creator Owner, System, and Administrators are allowed all permissions. On a Windows 2000 Professional Computer, the group Power Users is also allowed all permissions. Select the respective Deny check box to deny one or more permissions. You can add users or groups by clicking Add, selecting a group or user, clicking Add, and clicking OK. If neither Allow nor Deny is checked, the user or group is implicitly denied the permission. To delete a user or group from the list, select the object and click Remove.

## Devices

Devices Configures fax device settings. When you click Devices in the console tree of Fax Service Management, all installed devices appear in the Details pane. You can see information about the devices, such as the device name, whether the device can send or receive, the device's Transmitting Station Identifier (TSID) and the Called Subscriber Identifier (CSID), the device status, and the send priority.

To configure settings for any of the installed devices, select the device in the Details pane, right-click, and choose Properties. The device Properties dialog box has two tabs: General and Received Faxes.

**General** Enables and disables sending and receiving of faxes for the device. By default, sending faxes is enabled. Check Enable Send to enable sending faxes; deselect it to disable sending faxes. Check Enable Receive to enable receiving faxes; deselect it to disable receiving faxes. In the TSID and CSID text boxes, enter the name you want to use to identify the sender or recipient of a fax, respectively. If Enable Receive is checked, you can specify how many rings are allowed before the device answers the call. The default is 2.

**TIP** A quick way to enable or disable sending and receiving faxes is to right-click the device and choose Send or Receive from the menu. A check mark next to the choice indicates enable; no check mark indicates disable.

**TIP** If you're sharing the telephone line for voice and fax calls, a higher setting, such as 4 rings, might make sense.

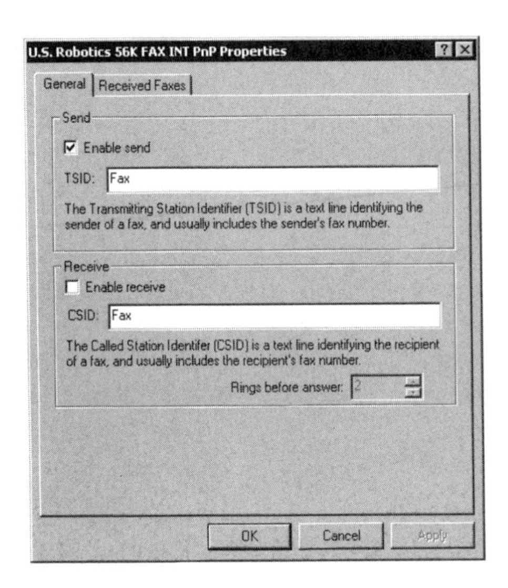

**Received Faxes** Specifies actions that will be performed when the fax device receives a fax. You can choose to have incoming faxes print on a local or network printer. To do this, select Print On and choose a printer from the drop-down list. If you want incoming faxes to be saved to a file, check Save in Folder and enter the path or browse for a directory. By default, incoming faxes are saved to the `C:\Documents and Settings\All Users (WINNT)\Documents\My Faxes\Received Faxes` folder. If Microsoft Exchange is installed and configured in the network, you can also check Send to Local E-mail Inbox and enter a Microsoft Messaging profile name in the Profile Name text box or select one from the drop-down list.

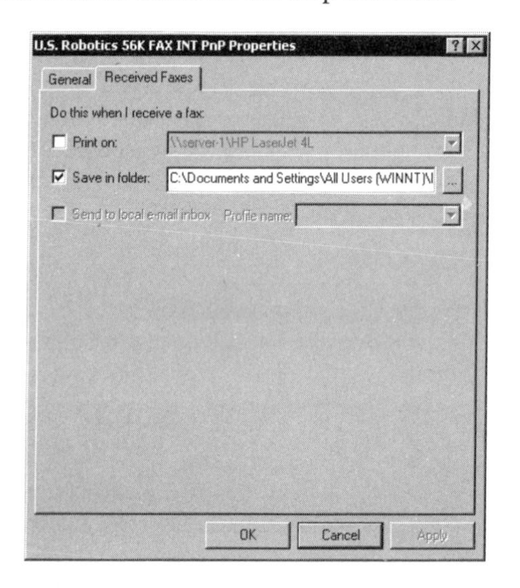


### *Send Priority*

When you select a fax device in the Details pane of Fax Service Management, arrows appear at the right side of the toolbar. Click the up arrow to increase the device's send priority in relation to other devices; click the down arrow to decrease the send priority.

**NOTE** A minimum of two fax devices must be installed to change the send priority.

## Logging

Logging Controls the level of fax event logging in the Application log. In the Fax Service Management console tree, select Logging. In the Details pane, you will see several different logging categories, including Inbound, Initialization/Termination, Outbound, and Unknown.

**Inbound** Logs events that relate to incoming faxes.

**Initialization/Termination** Logs events that relate to starting and stopping of Microsoft Fax Service.

**Outbound** Logs events that relate to outgoing faxes.

**Unknown** Logs any other events that relate to faxing.

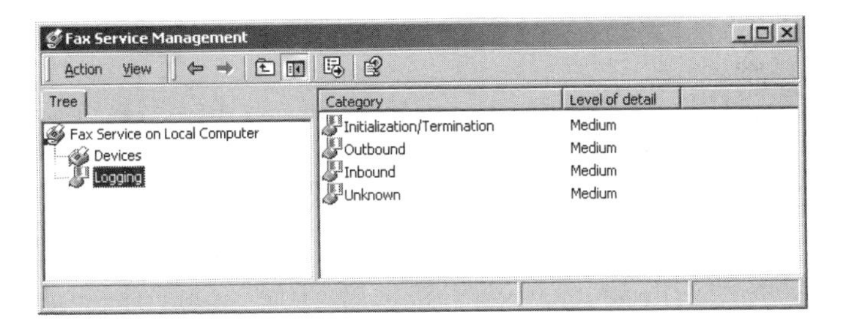


By default, each category is set to record a medium level of logging. To change the logging level, right-click a category, choose Level of Detail, and then choose the level you want from the menu. Available levels are None, Minimum, Medium, and Maximum. Logged information might include such items as the sender's username, the computer name, the date and time of the event, the type (such as Error or Information), the Event ID, the source, the category, and a description of the event.

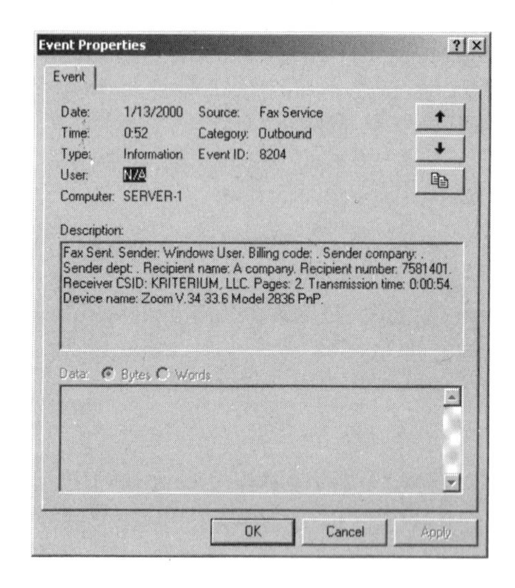


**See Also** Fax (Properties), Fax Queue, Send Fax Wizard, Microsoft Management Console (MMC), Event Viewer

# File Signature Verification Utility

File Signature Verification Utility

To maintain system integrity and detect changes to system files, system files are digitally signed. The File Signature Verification utility lets you check for critical system files that should be digitally signed but aren't.

To start the utility, choose Start ➢ Settings ➢ Control Panel, double-click Administrative Tools, double-click Computer Management, expand System Tools, and select System Information. Then choose Tools ➢ Windows ➢ File Signature Verification Utility.

To perform file signature verification, follow these steps:

1. In the File Signature Verification dialog box, you can click the Advanced button to configure verification options on the two tabs of the Advanced File Signature Verification Settings dialog box. On the Search tab, you can specify that you want to be notified of unsigned files, or you can specify that you want the utility to search for files of other

file types that aren't digitally signed. On the Logging tab, you can specify that you want to save results to a log file, set logging options, and assign a filename for the log file. Click OK when you've finished setting advanced options.

After you've created a log, you can return to the Logging tab in the Advanced File Signature Verification Settings dialog box at any time and click View to view the log file in Notepad.

2. Click Start to begin the file signature verification process. Wait for the process to finish. You'll see a progress bar while the utility is scanning files.
3. If all files have been digitally signed, you'll be prompted by the SigVerif message box advising you that all files have been scanned and digitally signed. Click OK and skip to step 6. If one or more files have not been digitally signed, continue with step 4.
4. The Signature Verification Results dialog box opens and lists all system files (or other files, if you selected the option for searching other files) that are not digitally signed. Information about each file includes name, folder, modified date, file type, and version. The status bar tells you how many files were found, how many were signed, how many were not signed, and how many were not scanned.

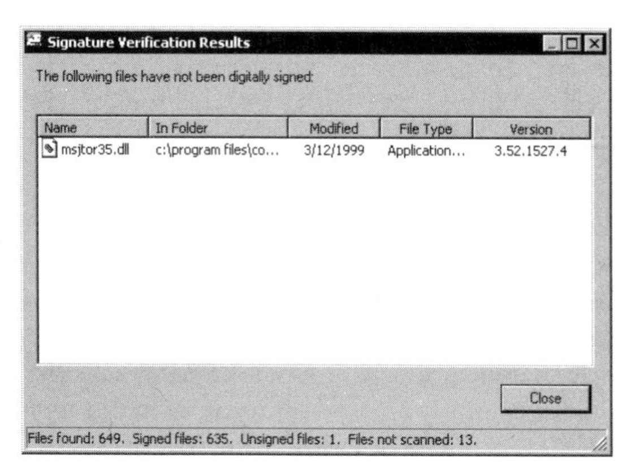


5. Click Close to dismiss the Signature Verification Results dialog box.
6. Click Close again to close the utility.

# Folders

Folders are part of the Windows 2000 file system structure. You use folders to organize files on your computer. In addition to files, folders can contain subfolders.

To view a folder, open a Windows Explorer window and use Explorer's navigation tools to find the folder. To view and access folder contents, double-click the folder.

## Folder Properties

Right-click a folder and select Properties to access the folder's properties. It can have any or all of the following tabs:

**General** Displays general information about the folder, such as its name (which you can change), type, location, size, size on disk, the items it contains, and creation date. You can also choose to apply the Read-only and Hidden attributes (and the Archive attribute if formatted with FAT). If the drive is formatted with NTFS, click Advanced to configure additional attributes, such as archiving, indexing, compression, and encryption attributes.

**Web Sharing** Lets you share a folder on a Web site. Available on Windows 2000 Server computers with IIS started and a Web site created.

**Sharing** Lets you share a folder so that other users in the network can access it. For more information, see the main heading Sharing.

**Security** Available on NTFS-formatted drives. Used to set permissions to the folder for users, groups, and computers. Click Add to add a user, group, or computer, and click Remove to remove a user, group, or computer. Under Permissions, check or uncheck Allow or Deny to set permissions for a user, group, or computer. Specify whether you want permissions from a parent to apply to this folder.

Click Advanced to configure advanced options. This includes adding permission entries, specifying whether the object inherits permissions from parent objects (such as folders), and specifying whether permissions are propagated to child objects (such as subfolders and files). Use the Auditing tab to add and configure auditing entries (users and groups). Use the Owner tab to change the current owner of the folder, and the owner of subcontainers and objects.

**See Also** Explorer, Shared Folders, Sharing, Web Sharing

# Folder Options

Controls the appearance and use of files and folders, activates the Active Desktop, configures file associations, and enables offline use of network files. Any settings you make are reflected in how folders are displayed and used in Windows Explorer (this includes My Documents, My Network Places, My Computer, and Control Panel). Choose Start ➢ Settings ➢ Control Panel and double-click the Folder Options icon to open the Folder Options dialog box, which contains four tabs—General, View, File Types, and Offline Files.

**TIP** You can also access Folder Options from the Tools menu of any Windows Explorer window.

## General Tab

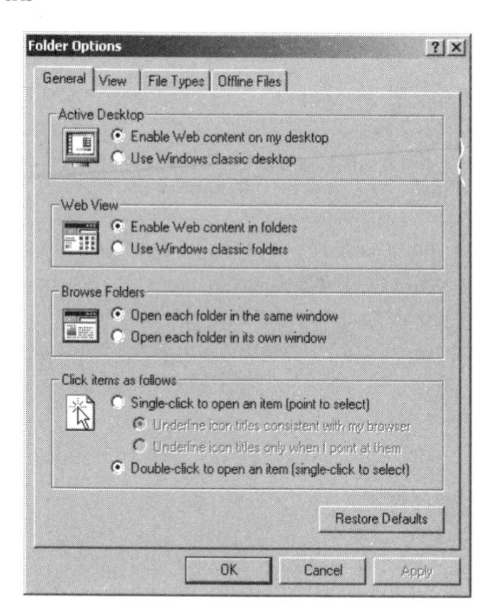

Controls how folders appear and work. The tab is divided into four sections:

**Active Desktop** Choose Enable Web Content on My Desktop to activate the Active Desktop. You can then add Web content to your desktop. The default is Use Windows Classic Desktop.

**TIP** You must have Internet connection settings configured to be able to choose Enable Web Content on My Desktop. You can use the Internet Connection Wizard to configure those settings. Configure Active Desktop settings on the Web tab of Control Panel ➢ Display.

**Web View** Lets you specify that you want Windows to display the contents of folders as Web pages. The default is Enable Web Content in Folders.

**TIP** My Computer and Control Panel always display contents as Web pages and are not influenced by the selection you make in Web View.

**Browse Folders** Lets you specify whether you want to use the same window or open a new window each time you open a new folder. The default is Open Each Folder in the Same Window.

**Click Items as Follows** Lets you specify whether you want to open items with a single click or by double-clicking. The default is Double-click to Open an Item.

**TIP** If single-clicking is specified, move the mouse pointer over an item to select it.

You can return to default values by clicking Restore Defaults.

## View Tab

Controls the View setting and advanced settings for folders. You can configure all of your folders to use the same view as that set up in the View menu in the current folder—simply click Like Current Folder. The Like Current Folder button is available only if you accessed Folder Options from the Tools menu of a Windows Explorer window, not through Control Panel. You can reset the view of all folders to the default setting (Large Icons) by clicking Reset All Folders.

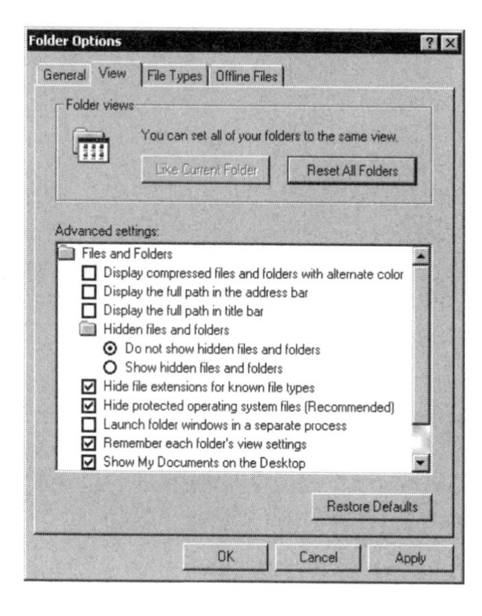


In the Advanced Settings list box, you can configure file and folder settings, such as displaying the full path in the title bar, hiding file extensions for known file types, and showing hidden files and folders.

**TIP** Deselect Show My Documents on the Desktop to remove the My Documents folder from the desktop.

Select the check boxes for settings you want to apply.

## File Types Tab

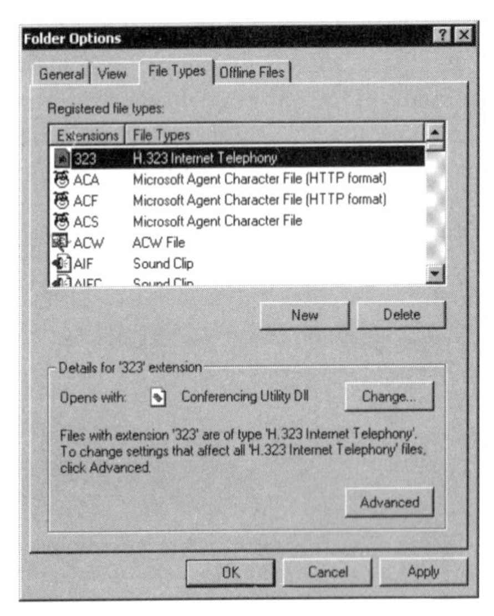


Controls which file types are associated with which file extension (.XXX) and which application Windows uses to open a file. The Registered File Types window shows registered file types and their extensions. When you select a file type in the list, the Details For area tells you which application is used to open files of this type and displays a quick description.

The following buttons are available on the File Types tab:

**New** Lets you create a new file extension. You can associate a new or existing file type with the new extension by clicking Advanced and making the appropriate selection from the drop-down list. You can also enter an existing file extension and then change which file type is associated with the extension.

**Delete** Lets you delete an existing file extension and associated file type.

**Change** Lets you change the application that Windows uses to open files of the selected extension and file type.

**Advanced** Lets you change the selected file type's associated icon and actions. Any configured actions appear in the File menu and shortcut menu for the item. You can configure a new action by clicking New and then specifying the action as well as the application that is supposed to perform that action. You can also edit or remove existing actions, and you can specify whether you want files to open immediately after they have finished downloading. Finally, you can choose to always show file extensions and to enable browsing in the same window.

## Offline Files Tab

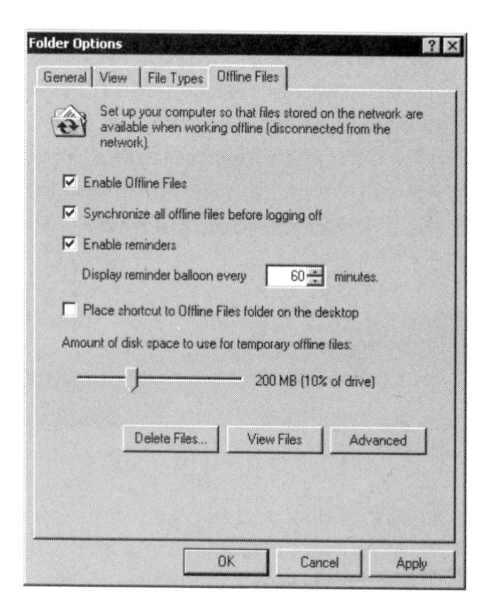


Used to configure whether files on the network can be available when you are not connected to the network. On this tab, you can enable or disable offline files, you can specify whether to synchronize online with offline files before you log off, and you can enable reminders and specify when to show them. Reminders are pop-up messages that tell you that you're working offline. Additionally, you can create a shortcut on the desktop to the Offline Files folder, where you can see, access, and synchronize files marked to be available offline.

You can also specify the amount of disk space that can be used by temporary offline files. The default setting is 10% of total disk space. Move the slider left or right to adjust this value.

The following three buttons are also available on the Offline Files tab:

**Delete Files** Deletes offline files. You'll have to specify if you want to delete only temporary offline files or all offline files.

**View Files** Displays offline files in the Offline Files folder.

**Advanced** Lets you choose what you want to happen when you lose your connection to the network. You can specify that you want to be notified and then work offline, or you can choose to never allow the computer to go offline. You can also specify exceptions for certain computers. Click Add, type the name of a computer or browse for it, and then specify the behavior for that computer when a network connection is lost.

**See Also** Explorer, Internet Explorer, Synchronize, Make Available Offline

# Fonts

Fonts

Folder used to view and manage fonts (type styles) used by Windows 2000 and applications. To open the Fonts folder in an Explorer window, choose Start ➢ Settings ➢ Control Panel and double-click Fonts. You'll see a list of all currently installed fonts.

Font types supported by Windows 2000 include TrueType fonts, Open Type fonts (an extension of TrueType), Type 1 fonts (by Adobe Systems, Inc.), Vector fonts, and Raster fonts. The font type is indicated by the look of the font icon in the Fonts folder. For example, Open Type fonts show an O in the font icon; TrueType fonts show two T's in the icon.

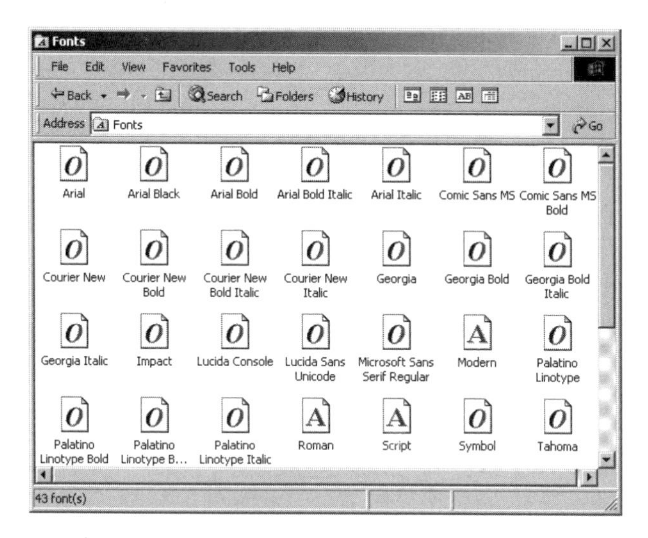


## Viewing Font Examples

You can see what each font looks like by double-clicking a font icon. This opens a window containing examples of the font in different sizes. You'll also see information regarding the font, such as type, typeface name, file size, version, and copyright information. In this window, you can also print the font example by clicking Print.

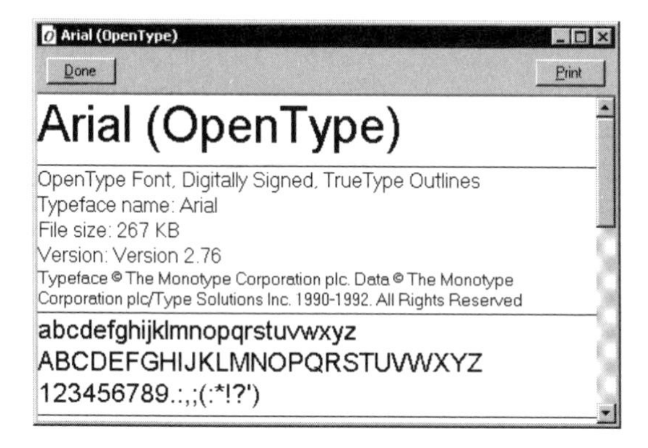


If you have a lot of fonts installed on your system, it can get difficult to keep track of what fonts you have available and what they look like. The View menu of the Fonts folder includes two options that make it easier to keep track of your fonts:

**List Fonts by Similarity** Lets you choose a font you know from the List Fonts by Similarity To drop-down list and then lists all other installed fonts by name with information about how similar to the chosen font each of the fonts is. You can also click the Similarity button on the toolbar to display this view.

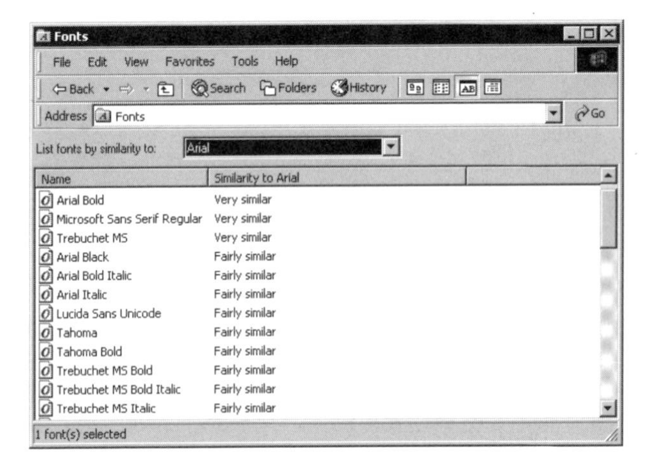


**Hide Variations (Bold, Italic, Etc.)** Lists only main fonts, without showing all of the fonts' variations (such as bold or italic). This reduces the number of fonts for you to look at and makes it easier to find or choose a font you're looking for.

## Adding New Fonts

You can add new fonts to your computer at any time by following these steps:

1. Choose File ➢ Install New Font.
2. Browse for the directory and folder where the new fonts are located.
3. Select one, several, or all fonts in the List of Fonts list box. Click OK. Windows installs the fonts and returns you to the Fonts folder.

**See Also** Explorer

# Format

Format...

Lets you format floppy disks for first-time use, or completely erase the floppy disk's contents. Also lets you format fixed disks, such as your hard drive. Formatting is required in order for Windows to be able to save information to and read information from any disk device, including floppy disks.

To format a floppy disk, perform steps 1 through 12; to format a hard disk, perform steps 2 through 12:

1. Insert a floppy disk into the floppy disk drive.

**WARNING** Make sure this is either a blank disk or a disk whose contents you don't need anymore. Formatting a used disk erases all of the contents of the disk.

2. Open My Computer (or Windows Explorer).
3. Select the floppy or hard disk drive (navigate to the drive, if necessary).
4. Choose File ➢ Format, or right-click the disk drive and choose Format.

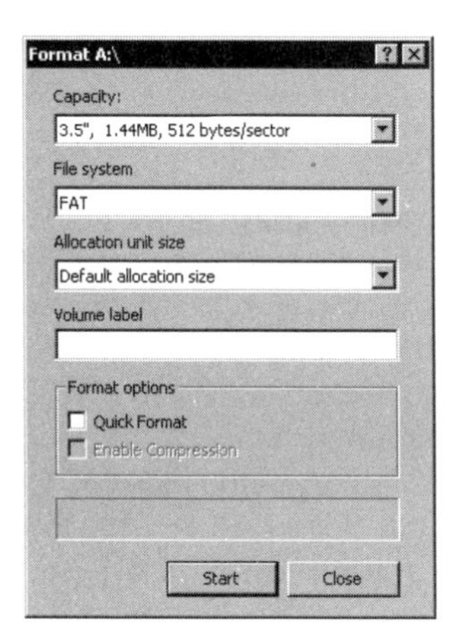


5. If applicable, select the disk capacity (multiple options are available only for floppy disks), file system, and allocation

unit size (multiple options are available only for hard disks) from the respective drop-down lists.

6. Enter a label for the disk in the Volume Label text box.
7. Choose whether you want to perform a quick format. Do this only if you know that the disk does not have any bad sectors. A quick format takes less time because the disk is not scanned for bad sectors.

**TIP** You cannot quick-format a blank disk.

8. If you're formatting a hard disk with NTFS, specify whether you want to enable compression.

**TIP** You cannot format a floppy disk with the NTFS file system.

9. Click Start.
10. Click OK to confirm the action.
11. Click OK when the format is complete.
12. Click Close.

**See Also** My Computer, Windows Explorer, NTFS

# FTP

Acronym for File Transfer Protocol, which is a part of the TCP/IP protocol suite used for Internet and other network communications. It is also a utility that is included with Windows 2000 that lets you transfer one or more files to or from a remote host (a computer on an IP network). It supports many file types, including American Standard Code for Information Interchange (ASCII), binary, and Extended Binary-Coded Decimal Interchange Code (EBCDIC). You can also use FTP to display directory lists and file lists.

In Windows 2000, FTP is a text-based program that you run from a Windows 2000 command prompt. To run it, follow these steps:

1. Choose Start ➢ Run.
2. Enter **ftp** and click OK. A command prompt window opens to an FTP prompt (ftp>).

You can type **?** or **help** at the ftp> prompt to display all available FTP commands. You can also type **help** followed by the name of a command to see an explanation of what the command does.

**TIP** If you just type **he** followed by the command, FTP still recognizes that you're looking for help on the command and displays the information. This is for those people who like to minimize keystrokes.

Many of the commands are used for troubleshooting purposes and to navigate the local or remote directory structure, but the following are what you need to know to use FTP for file transfer purposes:

**open** Opens a connection to the remote computer. You can then enter the IP address of the computer to which you want to connect to establish the connection. You can use **anonymous** as the username and your e-mail address as the password.

**TIP** You don't have to use a valid e-mail address; as long as you're following e-mail address format, you'll be allowed access to the remote computer.

**ascii** Establishes the file transfer type as ASCII.

**binary** Establishes the file transfer type as binary.

**put** Transfers a file you specify from your computer to the remote host.

**get** Transfers a file you specify from the remote host to your computer.

**quit** Closes the connection to the remote host and ends the FTP session. You can also use the bye command for the same purpose. You'll be returned to the Windows 2000 desktop.

# Game Controllers

Installs, removes, and configures game controllers, such as game pads, joysticks, and flight yokes. Choose Start ➢ Settings ➢ Control Panel and double-click the Game Controllers icon to open the Game Controllers dialog box. It has two tabs: General and Advanced.

**General** Lets you add, configure, troubleshoot, test, and remove game controllers. To add a game controller, click Add and select the type of controller you want to add from the list. Click Custom to define a custom game controller, and click Add Other to install a device driver for a device not listed.

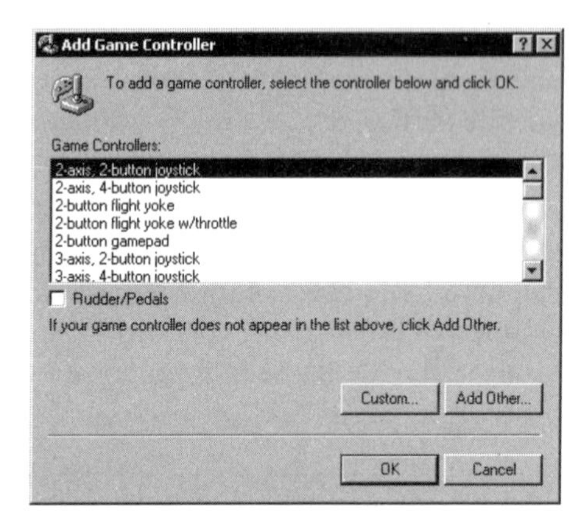


To test a controller, select the controller on the General tab, click Properties, and then click Test. If the test is unsuccessful, select the Settings tab to perform a calibration. To troubleshoot a controller, select the controller and click Troubleshoot to open the appropriate Windows 2000 troubleshooter. To remove a controller, select it and click Remove.

**Advanced** Lists all installed game controllers and their controller IDs. Use this tab to change the game controller's controller ID Assignment.

# Games

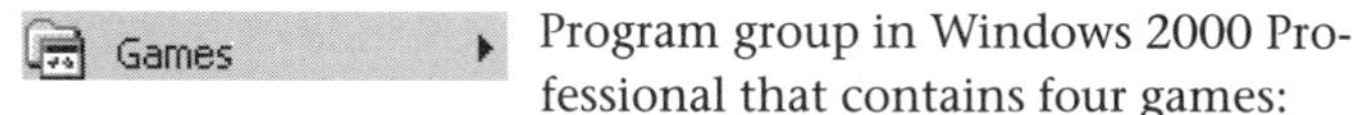

Program group in Windows 2000 Professional that contains four games: Freecell, Minesweeper, Pinball, and, on computers running Windows 2000 Professional, Solitaire. To access the Games program group, choose Start ➢ Programs ➢ Accessories ➢ Games. (Some users claim that Solitaire helps people new to computers to learn how to control the mouse—you'll have to decide for yourself on that one.) Pinball can be played with more than one player. If you want help learning how to play any of these games, choose Help from the menu.

# Getting Started

Getting Started — Lets you access information and services for Windows 2000 Professional. Choose Start ➢ Programs ➢ Accessories ➢ System Tools ➢ Getting Started to open the Getting Started with Windows 2000 dialog box.

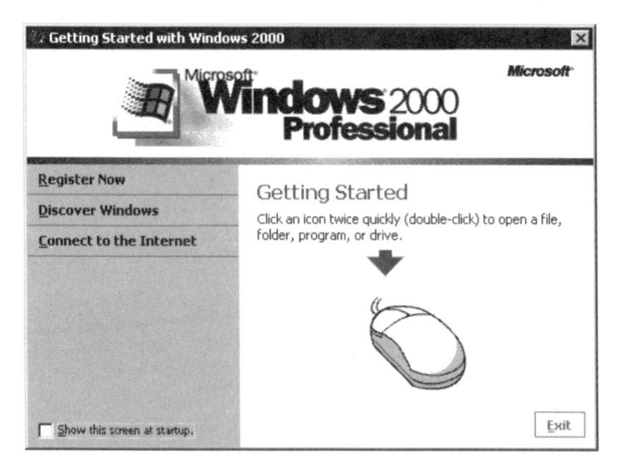

**NOTE** The Getting Started dialog box opens automatically the first time a user logs into Windows 2000 Professional. He or she can then decide not to show this dialog box by unchecking Show This Screen at Startup. Also, when you open Getting Started through Start ➢ Programs ➢ Accessories ➢ System Tools ➢ Getting Started, you can use this check box to specify whether you want Getting Started to appear at startup.

The Getting Started with Windows 2000 dialog box has three options:

**Register Now** Lets you register your Windows 2000 product so that you can receive support, software upgrades, and new product information.

**Discover Windows** Takes you on a tour of new Windows 2000 Professional features.

**Connect to the Internet** Starts the Internet Connection Wizard.

**See Also** Internet Connection Wizard

# Group Policy

Microsoft Management Console (MMC) snap-in and Windows 2000 Server component that lets you control the desktop environment of users in your network, including the programs users can access, the programs that are displayed on users' desktops, the options that appear on users' Start menus, and the script files that run at certain times. Group policies consist of settings that can be applied to all users in a site, domain, or organizational unit (OU). Group policies are useful because they:

- Reduce the amount of administration needed to configure user environments.
- Enable you to control and automate application and file access.
- Reduce the number of problems that result from users making changes to their environments.
- Make the user's environment easier to work in.

Group policies are usually set for an entire site or domain by group policy administrators and are a good way to enforce company policies, such as limiting the use of applications to certain users. A group policy administrator should belong to the default Group Policy Creator Owners security group, which provides the necessary rights to modify group policies in a domain; Administrator is a member of this group by default.

## Group Policy Types

Several types of group policies exist that apply settings for specific purposes:

**Security** Lets you restrict user access to files and folders and specify the number of incorrect password entries before Windows locks out the user account. Also lets you specify user rights—for example, who can log onto a Windows 2000 Server computer.

**Application Deployment** Lets you define application access for users. Applications can then be distributed to users in one of two ways: application assignment or application publication. With application assignment, applications and application upgrades are automatically installed on a user's computer, or a permanent connection to an application is automatically established. With application publication, an application is published to the Active Directory, making it available for installation by users using Add/Remove Programs in Control Panel.

**File Deployment** Lets you specify files that Windows copies automatically to certain folders on a user's computer, such as My Documents.

**Software** Lets you specify settings that will be applied to user profiles. Examples include Start menu and desktop settings.

**Scripts** Lets you specify scripts or batch files that should run automatically on users' computers at certain times—for example, when the user logs in or when the system starts. Using scripts enables task automation, such as automatically mapping network drives.

## Group Policy Inheritance

Group policies are inherited in the following order: site, domain, OU. Group policies defined for a container object closer to the user override those defined for a container object farther away from the user. For example, for a user that belongs to a specific OU, a group policy applied to that OU overrides a group policy applied to the site in which the user exists.

## Group Policy Objects and Templates

Group policy objects (GPOs) contain group policy configuration settings that can be applied to a site, domain, domain controller, or OU. A default GPO called Default Domain Policy is automatically created for each domain, and a default GPO called Default Domain Controllers Policy is automatically created for each domain controller.

GPOs use two different locations to store group policy configuration settings. These locations are group policy containers (GPCs) and group policy templates (GPTs). GPCs are stored in Active Directory and contain GPO properties, such as version and GPO status information. GPCs also contain subcontainers that contain user and computer group policy information. A GPT is a folder structure that is created in the system volume (`sysvol`) folder of a domain controller when a GPO is created. It contains all settings for all policies created in the group policy object.

## Working with GPOs

You can perform many functions related to GPOs by using the Group Policy tab of site domain objects, the Domain Controllers OU, and other OU objects. Functions include creating new GPOs, adding links to existing GPOs, applying options, deleting GPOs or links to GPOs, viewing and editing GPO properties, and editing GPOs. To access the Group Policy tab, follow these steps:

1. Choose Start ➢ Programs ➢ Administrative Tools. If you want to work with GPOs applied to a domain, domain controller, or OU, choose Active Directory Users and Computers. If you want to work with GPOs applied to a site, choose Active Directory Sites and Services.
2. Right-click the appropriate object or folder (domain, the Domain Controllers OU, other OU, or site) and choose Properties.
3. Select the Group Policy tab.

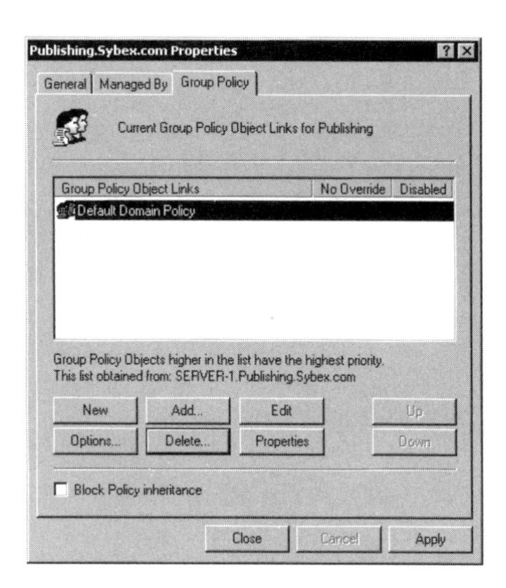


In addition to offering each of the functions related to the available buttons (which will be described in more detail below), the Group Policy tab lets you specify whether you want to block policy inheritance from linked GPOs defined at higher levels than the current object. Simply select the Block Policy Inheritance check box.

### *Creating a New GPO*

You can create new GPOs to allow further customization of your client environment. To create a new GPO, follow these steps:

1. On the Group Policy tab, click New.
2. Type a name to replace the default name New Group Policy Object and press Enter. This creates the new GPO and automatically adds it to the list of GPOs linked to this object (site, domain, domain controller, or OU).

**TIP** You can change the order of priority of linked GPOs by selecting a GPO in the list and clicking the Up or Down button.

### *Adding a Link to Another GPO*

You can apply one or more GPOs to a site, domain, or OU, and more than one site, domain, or OU can use the same GPO. Use the Group Policy tab to add a link to GPOs defined for a different site, domain, domain controller, or OU. Follow these steps:

1. On the Group Policy tab, click Add to open the Add a Group Policy Object Link dialog box.

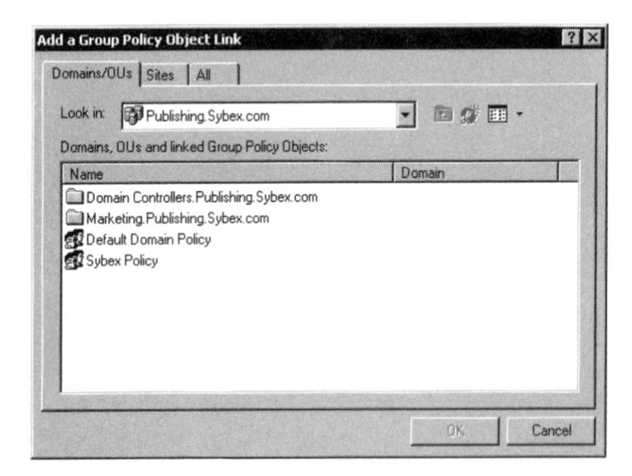


2. Select the Domains/OUs, Sites, or All tab to view the currently existing GPOs. Navigate to a GPO if necessary.

3. Select the GPO to which you want to add the link and click OK. A link to the GPO will appear in the list of GPO links.

### *Deleting a GPO or GPO Link*

You can use the Group Policy tab to delete GPOs or GPO links. Follow these steps:

1. Select a GPO in the list of linked GPOs and click Delete.

2. To delete only the link to the GPO, select Remove the Link from the List. To delete the link to the GPO and the GPO itself, select Remove the Link and Delete the Group Policy Object Permanently.

**WARNING** Exercise great caution when selecting a link and GPO to delete permanently. Be absolutely certain that you want to delete the GPO. All settings associated with the GPO will be deleted, and if you delete a GPO by mistake, you'll have to re-create the GPO and all its settings.

### *GPO Link Options*

You can set two GPO link options: No Override and Disabled. A GPO link that has the No Override option set will not have its settings overridden by settings in other GPO objects. A GPO link that has the Disabled option set is not applied to the container.

To change GPO link options, follow these steps:

1. On the Group Policy tab, click Options to open the Link Options dialog box.
2. Select the check box next to the option(s) you want to set and click OK. A check mark appears in the appropriate column for the affected GPO in the list of linked GPOs.

### *GPO Properties*

You can view GPO properties on the Group Policy tab. Select the appropriate GPO in the list, then click Properties. You'll see three tabs:

**General** Displays general information about the GPO, such as creation date and revision. You can also disable or enable the user or computer settings of the GPO.

**Links** Lets you view all sites, domains, or OUs that are linked to the GPO. To display locations, select a domain from the list and click Find Now.

**Security** Displays the permissions assigned to users and groups for the GPO. You can also add users and groups to the list and modify permissions. Click Advanced to access more detailed permission information and to further configure permissions, auditing, and ownership.

### *Group Policy Editor*

To allow you to customize settings in policies contained in a GPO, Windows 2000 provides you with the Group Policy Editor, an MMC console snap-in. To access the Group Policy Editor, on the Group Policy tab select a group policy, then click Edit.

**TIP** Alternatively, you can add the Group Policy MMC console snap-in for a specific group policy to an MMC (see Microsoft Management Console (MMC) for more information on how to do this), and then add the new MMC to the Administrative Tools program group. This allows you to access it easily and more directly using the Start menu.

The Group Policy Editor has two nodes: Computer Configuration and User Configuration. Policies defined under Computer Configuration apply to computers in the network and take effect when the client operating system is initialized. Policies defined under User Configuration apply to users in the network and take effect when the user logs onto a computer in the network.

Each node has three extensions (folders)—Software Settings, Windows Settings, and Administrative Templates—which in turn can contain additional extensions and policies.

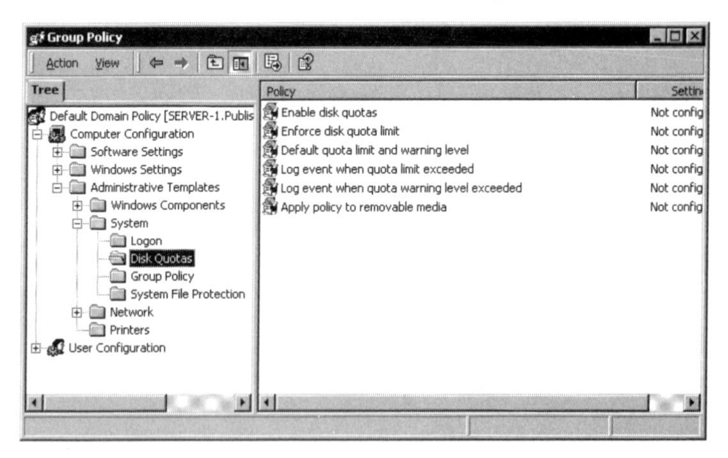


Navigate the extension structure and then use the Action menu to perform actions related to policy setting, such as changing the properties of and configuring a policy. The items available on the Action menu will vary depending on which item you have selected in the console tree or Details pane.

### *The Windows Settings extension*

If you expand the Windows Settings extension for the Default Domain Controllers Policy or the Default Domain Policy, you'll find a node called Security Settings. The Security Settings node is where the default Domain Controller Security Policy and default Domain Security Policy, respectively, are defined and configured. The Security Settings node, in turn, has one or more levels of subnodes that contain individual policies, such as password, user rights, and event log related policies. Here you can also configure settings for Registry security, system service security, file security, and restricted groups.

**NOTE** You can also access the default Domain Controller Security Policy and default Domain Security Policy directly by choosing Start ➢ Settings ➢ Control Panel, then double-clicking Administrative Tools and selecting Domain Controller Security Policy or Domain Security Policy, respectively.

**See Also** Active Directory Users and Computers, Microsoft Management Console (MMC), Add/Remove Programs, Control Panel, Start Menu, Profiles, Local Security Policy

## Hardware

**See** Add/Remove Hardware

## Help

The Windows 2000 Help system. Includes extensive explanations and step-by-step instructions for Windows 2000. You can access the information contained in the system by browsing its contents, querying the index, searching by keyword, or bookmarking and checking favorite areas of Help. The Help system pages are written in HTML, and as a result, if you're connected to the Internet, you can also follow links that point to Web pages on the Internet.

## Additional Help Tools

The following additional tools are available in or through the Help system. Some of these have direct links on the Help system's home page:

- Web Help (in the toolbar), which provides you with a link to Microsoft's support Web site.
- Search Tips, designed to help you with your search.
- Windows 2000 Troubleshooters, which let you interactively troubleshoot various hardware- and software-related problems.
- Information and Support on the Web/Additional Resources, which offers links to additional information related to Windows 2000 on the Web.
- If You've Used Windows Before (Windows 2000 Professional) and New Ways To Do Familiar Tasks (Windows 2000 Server), which show you where items from Windows 98 and Windows NT 4.0 have moved to or what they are now called.
- Best Practices (mainly for Windows 2000 Server), which are topics that explain best practices you should apply when using many of Windows 2000 Server's features. You can find a lot of valuable information here that will enable you to use and manage your Windows 2000 network much more effectively.
- Checklists (mainly for Windows 2000 Server), which are included with the Help system to make sure you're performing all necessary steps for specific procedures (for example, configuring system security, backing up and restoring data, and installing and configuring virtual private networks). Each of these handy checklists provides you with the necessary steps to perform the procedure, the ability to checkmark steps you've performed, and links to other reference materials.
- New Features, which are topics that tell you what's new in Windows 2000.
- Find It Fast, which contains help on how to optimize using the Search tab.

**TIP** Some best practices and checklists are available in the Windows 2000 Professional Help system as well.

## Help System Window

Choose Start ➢ Help to open the Help system. The Help system window that opens is called the Help viewer.

### *Help System Toolbar*

You can use the Help system toolbar to perform a variety of functions:

- Use the Hide button to hide the left pane of the Help system window, making it easier to read the help information in the right pane. When the left pane is hidden, the Hide button turns into a Show button. Click Show to display the left pane again.
- Use the Back and Forward buttons to navigate through Help pages you've opened.
- Use the Options button to display the Options menu, where you can choose to hide the left pane (Hide Tabs), navigate through opened Help pages (Back and Forward), return to the Help system home page (Home), stop a search (Stop), refresh the right pane (Refresh), access Internet options (Internet Options), go to Web Help (2 Web Help), print Help pages (Print), and turn off and on the feature that highlights search terms in the right pane (Search Highlight On/Off) when Help pages are displayed in the right pane after a search.
- Use the Web Help button to display the Online Support and Information page in the Help system. From there, you can choose from several links that will take you to various areas on Microsoft's Web site for specific areas of help available online.

### *Help System Tabs*

The left pane of the Help viewer contains four tabs that provide you with different options to search the Help system. When you first open Help, the right pane shows the Help system home page, which contains links to some or all of the additional Help tools mentioned earlier. When you select entries on one of the left pane's four tabs, the right pane displays detailed help information that may contain links to additional information. Use the Back and Forward buttons in the toolbar to navigate previously opened pages. The four Help system tabs are as follows:

**TIP** To return to the Help system's home page at any time, click Options on the toolbar and then choose Home.

**Contents Tab** Here you can browse the Help system's table of contents. Each topic has a book icon next to it that, when double-clicked, expands to show the topics' entries, as well as other topics (reflected by book icons). Each entry is a link that, when clicked, displays the relevant information in the Help system's right pane.

**TIP** If you want to print the contents of a category or subject, place the pointer over the category or subject and right-click. Then select Print.

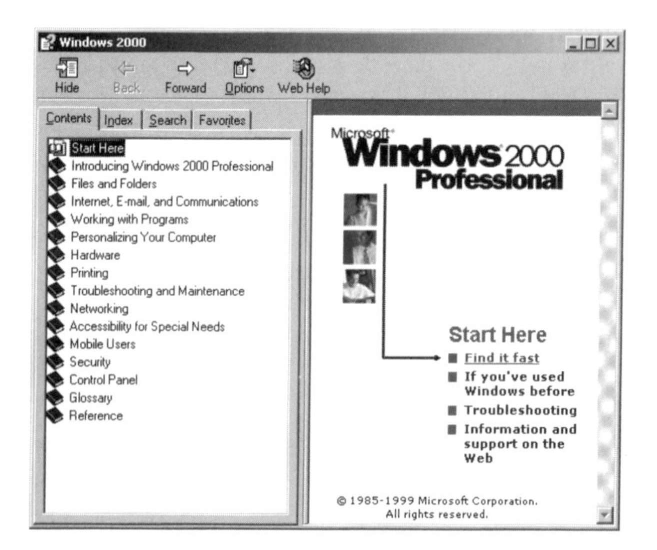

**Index Tab** The first time you click the Index tab, a wizard prepares the Help system's alphabetical index. On this tab, you can enter keywords that are matched against the index. When you start typing a word in the provided text box, the list automatically scrolls to any matching or closely matching words in the index. Alternatively, you can manually use the scroll bars to scroll to the topic you're looking for. When you find the topic, select it, or if the topic has subtopics, select the subtopic you're interested in. Double-click or click Display to display detailed information in the right pane. If this subtopic contains additional subtopics, Windows will present you with a list. Select the topic you're interested in and click Display.

**TIP** On the Index tab, if you double-click a main topic that contains subtopics you'll see a message advising you to select a subtopic.

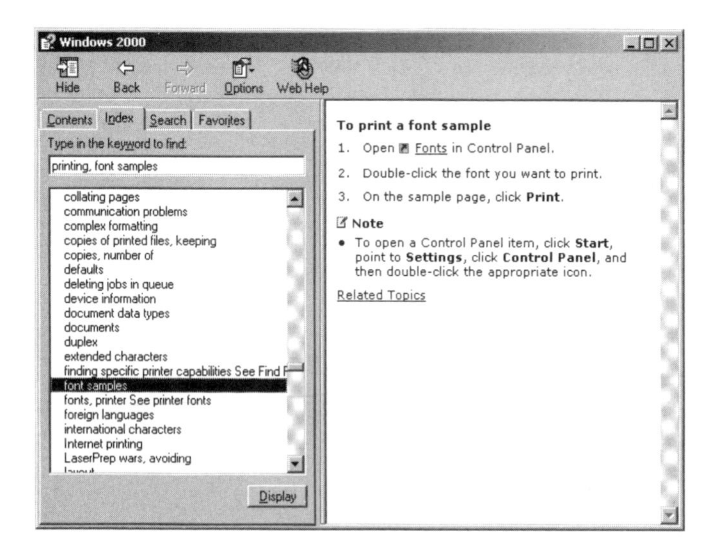


**Search Tab** On this tab you can enter a keyword or phrase in the provided text box and then click List Topics (or press Enter) to search the entire Help system for every occurrence of the word (or words). Relevant topics will appear in the list box. Select and double-click a topic, or select it and click Display to display detailed information in the right pane.

In Windows 2000 Server, you can also click the right arrow next to the text box and select AND, OR, NEAR, or NOT to combine several words or phrases to refine or narrow your search. (You can also use these qualifiers in Windows 2000 Professional, but you have to manually type them in because there is no drop-down list from which to choose. See Search tips for more information.) In addition to the topic title, in the list of topics found you'll see information regarding the location of the topic in the Help system and its rank in terms of relevance to your search criteria. You can sort the list by title (alphabetical), location (alphabetical), or rank by clicking the respective column header. Refine your search by selecting one or more of the check boxes at the bottom of the screen: Search Previous Results, Match Similar Words, and Search Titles Only.

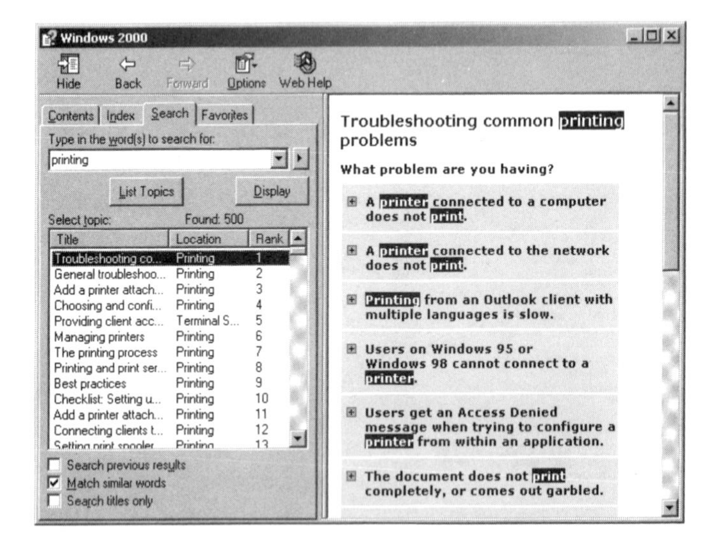


**Favorites Tab** On this tab, you can bookmark a topic you previously selected on one of the other three tabs. Select the topic, then click the Favorites tab. The topic appears in the Current Topic text box. Click Add to add the topic to your list of favorite topics. Later, you can return to the Favorites tab, select a bookmark from the list, and click Display or double-click to display that topic's detailed information. Click Remove to remove the bookmark.

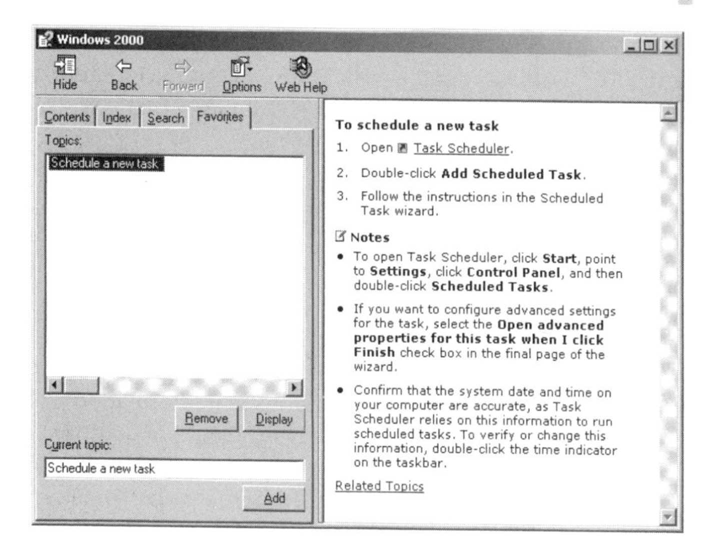

**TIP** Once you've found information you're looking for, you can hide the left pane of the Help system by clicking Hide on the toolbar. Click Show to redisplay the left pane.

## Using the Troubleshooters

The Windows 2000 troubleshooters provide you with an interactive resource to try to isolate and correct problems. Troubleshooters present you with specific questions relating to various subjects (such as networking, printing, and system setup) and common problems, then make recommendations based on your answers.

How you access the troubleshooters varies slightly for Windows 2000 Professional and Windows 2000 Server.

### *Windows 2000 Professional:*

On the Contents tab, double-click Troubleshooting and Maintenance ➢ Windows 2000 Troubleshooters.

### *Windows 2000 Server:*

On the Contents tab, double-click Troubleshooting and Additional Resources ➢ Troubleshooting ➢ Troubleshooter Overview ➢ Troubleshooters.

**TIP** You might also find links to specific troubleshooters embedded in Help pages you're viewing.

Then, in the right pane, find and click the link for the troubleshooter you want to use. Check the radio button that corresponds to the problem you're having and click Next. Windows will present you with troubleshooting suggestions and information. Follow the instructions, and then answer the next set of questions. Click Next to continue. If a suggestion or instruction doesn't apply to your situation, click I Want to Skip This Step and Try Something Else, then click Next. A different set of suggestions and information is displayed. Continue until your problem is resolved. Click start over to start from the beginning of the troubleshooter you selected.

**TIP** The option I Want To Skip This Step And Try Something Else is not always available.

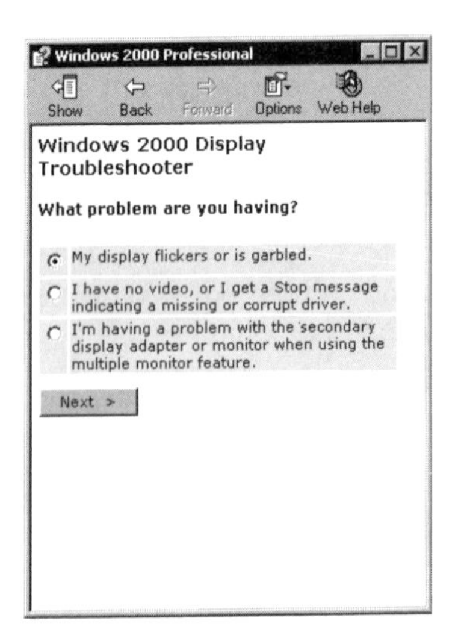

**TIP** Another way to access troubleshooters is by running the Add/Remove Hardware Wizard and choosing the option for troubleshooting a device. After you select the device, the appropriate troubleshooter starts automatically. You can also access certain troubleshooters by double-clicking the System icon in Control Panel, selecting the Hardware tab, clicking Device Manager, displaying the properties for a device, and clicking Troubleshooter.

## Context-Sensitive Help

In addition to using the Help system by choosing Start ➢ Help, you'll find that context-sensitive help is often available in dialog boxes. If it is, you might see a button with a question mark next to the Close button in the upper-right corner of the dialog box. If you click this button, a question mark attaches itself to the mouse pointer. Move the pointer over an item for which you want more information and click once. A ToolTip pops up containing information about the item. Click again to close the ToolTip. An alternative method is to right-click an item and then click the What's This? pop-up message (if it's available). This also brings up the item's ToolTip. And, if there's a Help menu option, you might also find a What's This choice in the drop-down menu. Select it, and the question mark attaches itself to your mouse pointer. Some dialog boxes might feature a Help button that you can click for additional information.

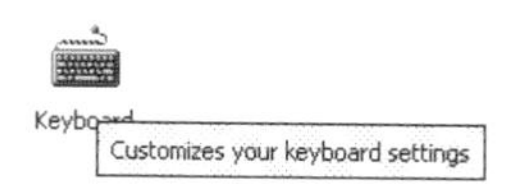


Most applications also have a Help option in their menu that offers you additional information about that particular program.

**See Also** Add/Remove Hardware Wizard, System

# HyperTerminal

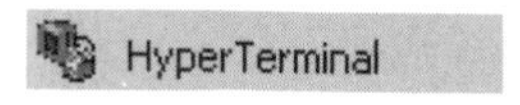


Used to connect to Internet Telnet servers, online services, Bulletin Board

Systems (BBS), TCP/IP hosts, and other computers via a modem or null-modem cable connection. You can use the connection to browse file systems and upload and download files.

## Creating a New HyperTerminal Connection

To create a new HyperTerminal connection, choose Start ➢ Programs ➢ Accessories ➢ Communications ➢ HyperTerminal. Follow these steps:

1. In the Connection Description dialog box, enter a name for the connection in the Name text box, and choose an icon from the list of icons. Click OK.

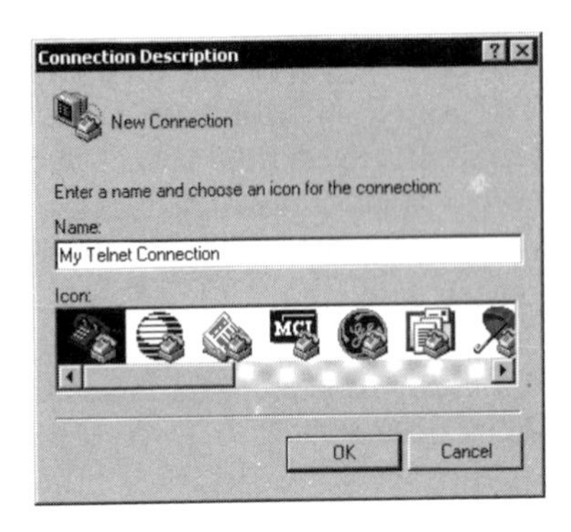


2. In the Connect To dialog box, specify whether you want to use a modem, COM port, or TCP/IP to make the connection. Depending on your choice, you may have to enter phone number information (for modem connections) or the host address and port number (for TCP/IP connections). No additional information is required for COM port connections. Click OK.
3. If you chose a TCP/IP connection, HyperTerminal tries to establish the connection. If you chose a COM port connection, select your port settings and click OK to try to establish a connection. If you chose a modem connection, click Dial to try to establish the connection. Click Cancel to go directly to the HyperTerminal window without trying to establish a connection.
4. To be able to use the connection later, you need to save it as a session file. In the HyperTerminal window, choose File ➢ Save.

Windows saves the session (connection) in the HyperTerminal folder using the name you assigned to the connection.

**TIP** HyperTerminal session files use an .HT extension.

**TIP** You'll also be prompted to save the current session as a file if you close HyperTerminal, or if you try to open an existing connection or create a new connection.

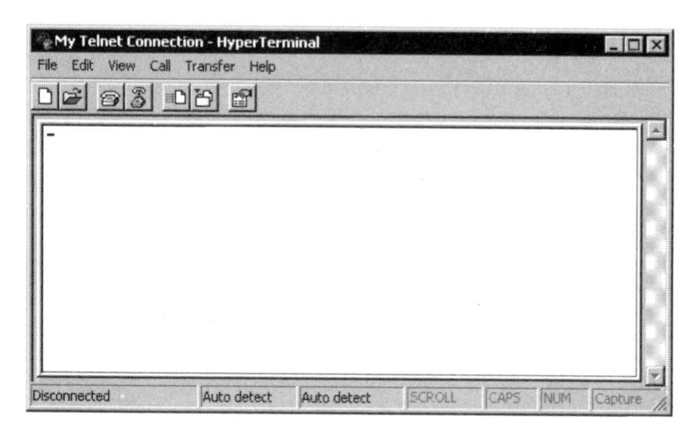

**TIP** Once you create a HyperTerminal connection, Windows adds a new program group called HyperTerminal to the Communications program group. From there you can directly access your connections and captured text files (discussed later) without having to first manually open HyperTerminal and the connection.

## Opening an Existing Connection

To open an existing connection, follow these steps:

**TIP** Opening a connection does not imply that you must establish a connection. You can have a connection open without being connected. You must, however, have a connection open before you can establish the connection.

1. Choose File ➢ Open to open the HyperTerminal folder.
2. Double-click the connection you want to open.

## HyperTerminal Window

The HyperTerminal window has several menu items and toolbar buttons you can use to call other computers, create new connections, transfer files, and configure connections, among other things.

### *Toolbar*

The toolbar has the following buttons:

 **New** Lets you create a new HyperTerminal connection.

 **Open** Lets you open an existing connection from the HyperTerminal folder.

 **Call** Tries to establish the connection you last opened.

 **Disconnect** Ends the currently active connection.

 **Send** Lets you transfer files from this computer to the remote computer or service (upload the file). You'll have to enter or browse for the file you want to transfer, and choose the protocol you want to use (such as Zmodem, Xmodem, or Ymodem).

 **Receive** Lets you transfer files from the remote computer or service to your computer. You'll have to enter or browse for the directory into which you want to place files, and choose the protocol you want to use.

 **Properties** Lets you change the properties of the connection you last opened.

### *Menus*

The HyperTerminal menus have a number of unique items on several menus:

**File Menu**

- New Connection—Used to create a new connection.

**Edit Menu**

- Paste to Host—Used to transfer terminal window contents copied to the Windows Clipboard to the remote host.

### Call Menu

- Call—Used to establish a connection to a remote computer.

**TIP** If you don't currently have a connection open and you click Call, you'll be prompted to create a new connection.

- Wait for a Call—Used to wait for an incoming call from a remote computer.
- Stop Waiting—Used to stop waiting for an incoming call from a remote computer.
- Disconnect—Used to disconnect a currently established connection.

### Transfer Menu

- Send File—Lets you transfer (upload) a file from this computer to the remote computer.
- Receive File—Lets you receive (download) a file from the remote computer to this computer.
- Capture Text—Lets you start saving incoming text in a HyperTerminal session to a text file. You'll have to specify the path to the file and click Start. Text is captured until you choose Transfer ➢ Capture Text ➢ Stop (or Pause). If you pause capturing text, you can continue again by choosing Transfer ➢ Capture Text ➢ Resume.
- Send Text File—Lets you send a text file to a remote computer.
- Capture to Printer—Lets you print text coming from the remote computer to the printer.

# Imaging

Lets you view and change graphical image files. Examples of this are digitized text documents (such as scanned documents or faxes received on a computer), photographs, or line drawings. You may want to send images in e-mails, use them in a newsletter or other document that calls for images, print them, or make annotations. Imaging lets you work on existing files, or you can send images directly into Imaging using a scanner or digital camera. Imaging lets you work with TIFF, BMP, JPG, and GIF files, and PCX/DCX, XIF, and WIFF documents.

Choose Start ➢ Programs ➢ Accessories ➢ Imaging to open Imaging.

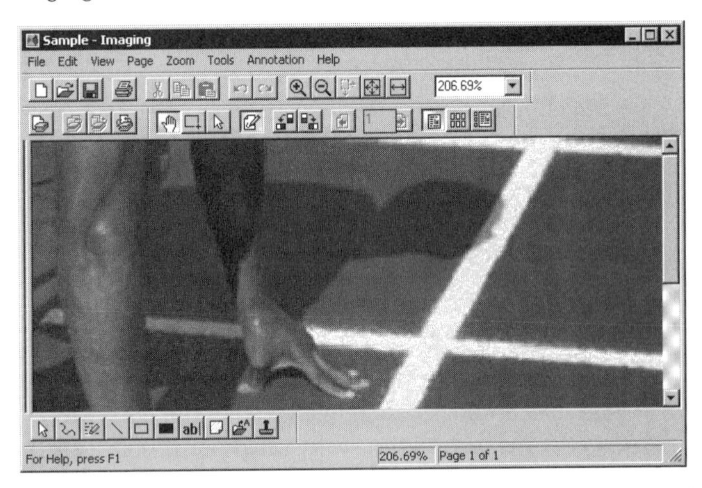

**TIP** You can find the sample image displayed here in the My Pictures folder (located in the My Documents folder). An image has to be open for many of the Imaging functions to be available.

## Toolbars

Imaging contains four toolbars that group related functions together. You can turn individual toolbars on and off by choosing View ➢ Toolbars and making the appropriate selection in the Toolbars dialog box. The Toolbars dialog box also lets you toggle the display of color buttons, large buttons, and ToolTips.

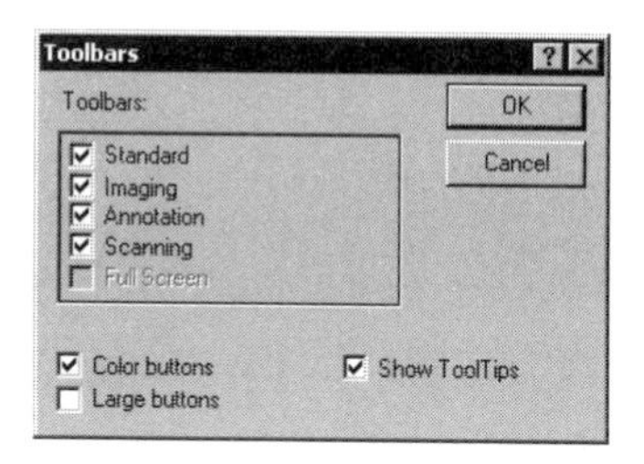

**TIP** You can also right-click anywhere on the Standard, Imaging, and Scanning toolbars and toggle any of the toolbars off or on by selecting the appropriate toolbar name. A selected (active) toolbar has a check mark next to its name.

### *Standard Toolbar*

The Standard toolbar contains buttons for such actions as opening, saving, cutting, and pasting images, and zooming in and out.

**New** Lets you create a new TIFF, BMP, or JPG image. You'll also be able to specify color, compression, resolution, and size settings for the image.

**Open** Lets you open an existing image file or document.

**Save** Lets you save the current image or document.

**Print** Lets you print the current page or the entire document.

**Cut** Lets you place the selected item on the Windows Clipboard.

**Copy** Lets you copy the selected item onto the Windows Clipboard.

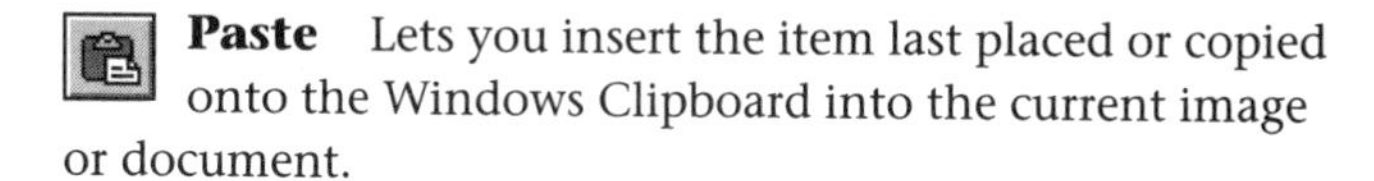

**Paste** Lets you insert the item last placed or copied onto the Windows Clipboard into the current image or document.

**Undo** Lets you reverse the last performed action.

**Redo** Lets you repeat the last Undo action.

**Zoom In** Lets you enlarge the image to twice its current size.

**Zoom Out** Lets you reduce the image to half its current size.

**Zoom to Selection** Lets you zoom to the current selection.

**Best Fit** Lets you change the size of the image to best fit the window (this does not necessarily mean that the entire window will be filled).

**Fit to Width** Lets you change the size of the image to fit the window width.

75%

**Zoom** Lets you specify a zoom factor from the drop-down list, or enter a zoom factor in the combo box.

### *Imaging Toolbar*

The Imaging toolbar contains items that are used to manipulate the current image and other toolbars.

**Drag** Activates the dragging tool.

**Select Image** Activates the image selecting tool.

**Annotation Selection** Activates the Annotation Selection tool and selects the Annotation Selection button on the Annotation toolbar.

**Annotation Toolbar** Toggles the display of the Annotation toolbar.

**Rotate Left** Turns the image 90 degrees to the left.

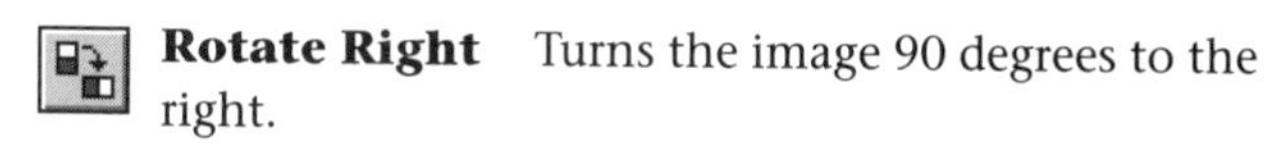

**Rotate Right** Turns the image 90 degrees to the right.

**Previous Page** Displays the document's previous page.

**Page** Lets you enter the page you want to display.

**Next Page** Displays the document's next page.

**One Page View** Displays the document one page at a time.

**Thumbnail View** Displays all document pages as thumbnails. Thumbnails are small previews of the full-page image.

**Page and Thumbnails View** Displays thumbnails and the active page.

### *Annotation Toolbar*

The Annotation toolbar displays at the bottom of the Imaging window and contains items that relate to creating image annotations. Annotations are like overlays to the image, and thus are not part of the image. You can merge annotations into an image. Once you do, you can no longer change the annotations.

You can right-click any tool button in the Annotation toolbar to access and configure properties of the tool. For example, if you right-click the Text button and select Properties, you can choose the font, font style, size, effects, and script you want to use.

**TIP** Whenever you choose a tool from the Annotation toolbar, your mouse pointer changes to an icon that represents the currently selected tool.

**Annotation Selection** Activates the Annotation Selection tool, which you can use to move, resize, change, or delete annotations.

**Freehand Line** Activates the Freehand Line annotation tool, which you can use to draw freehand lines.

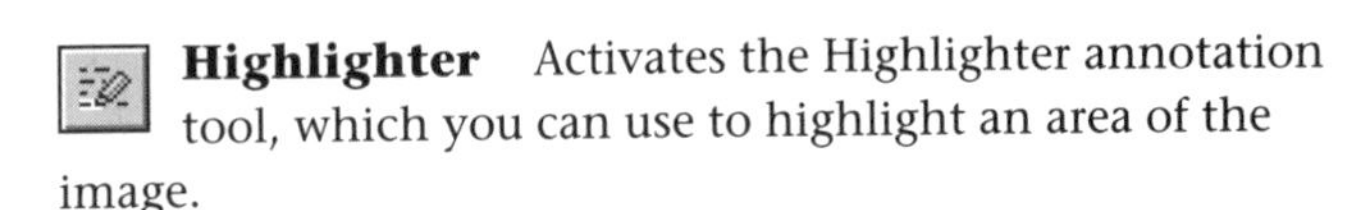

**Highlighter** Activates the Highlighter annotation tool, which you can use to highlight an area of the image.

**Straight Line** Activates the Straight Line annotation tool, which you can use to draw straight lines.

**Hollow Rectangle** Activates the Hollow Rectangle annotation tool, which you can use to draw hollow rectangles.

**Filled Rectangle** Activates the Filled Rectangle annotation tool, which you can use to draw filled rectangles.

**Text** Activates the Text annotation tool, which you can use to place text into the image.

**Attach-a-Note** Activates the Attach-a-Note tool, which you can use to attach a comment to an image.

**Text from File** Activates the Text from File annotation tool, which you can use to add text from a specified file to the image.

**Rubber Stamp** Activates the Rubber Stamp annotation tool. When you click the Rubber Stamp button, a submenu appears from which you can select stamps to add to the image. Stamps include Approved, DRAFT, Received, and Rejected.

**TIP** The Approved, Received, and Rejected stamps automatically add the current date (using the system clock) to the stamp.

### *Scanning Toolbar*

The Scanning toolbar contains items that relate to scanning a document directly into Imaging. A scanning device must be installed on the computer to use these functions.

**Scan New** Scans a new document into Imaging.

**Insert Scanned Page** Inserts a scanned page before the currently active page.

**Append Scanned Page** Appends a scanned page to the end of the current document.

**Rescan Page** Replaces the currently active page with a newly scanned page.

## Imaging Menus

The menus in Imaging let you access menus of the tools and other options available through the toolbars as well as many other familiar options. Several unique items do exist, however.

### *File Menu*

The File menu contains the following unique options:

**Acquire Image** Lets you scan a new document.

**Select Device** Lets you select a TWAIN service, such as a scanner or a camera.

**Color Management** Lets you enable/disable color management. If it's enabled, you can configure how you want colors to display on your printer or monitor, and set proofing options.

**Send** Lets you send the image in an e-mail.

### *Edit Menu*

The Edit menu contains the following unique options:

**Copy Page** Copies the entire page to the Windows Clipboard.

**Delete Page** Deletes the entire page.

### *View Menu*

The View menu contains the following unique options:

**Scale to Gray** Toggles displaying black-and-white images as grayscale images.

**Full Screen** Displays the image using the entire width and length of your monitor. Click the Full Screen icon to return to the Imaging window.

### *Page Menu*

The Page menu contains the following unique options:

**First** Displays the first page of the document.

**Last** Displays the last page of the document.

**Print Page** Prints the currently active page.

**Rotate Page** Lets you rotate the currently active page by 90 degrees left or right, or by 180 degrees.

**Rotate All Pages** Lets you rotate all pages in a document by 90 degrees left or right, or by 180 degrees.

**Properties** Lets you configure colors, compression, resolution, and size for the current page.

### *Zoom Menu*

The Zoom menu contains the following unique options:

**Fit to Height** Changes the image's size to fit the window height.

**Actual Size** Displays the image at its real (actual) size.

### *Tools Menu*

The Tools menu contains the following unique options:

**General Options** Displays the General Options dialog box, where you can specify how documents appear when they are first opened. Items to configure include zoom options and scroll bar display. You can also specify the default file location and whether images are opened in Imaging for Windows or Imaging for Windows Preview.

**NOTE** Imaging for Windows Preview is a scaled-down version of Imaging for Windows used only for viewing. You cannot edit an image in Imaging for Windows Preview.

**Scan Options** Lets you configure how you want to compress scanned images, such as for best quality or smallest file size. You can also specify custom settings. Click Advanced to specify the image transfer mode. You can choose from Native (which gives you faster transfer but requires more memory) and Memory (which results in slower transfer but requires less memory).

**Thumbnail Size** Lets you specify the size you want Imaging to use to display thumbnail images. You can configure the aspect ratio, width, and height. If an image is currently open, you can drag the image out from the bottom-right corner to adjust the size.

### *Annotation Menu*

The Annotation menu contains this unique option:

**Make Annotations Permanent** Merges annotations into the image, where they can no longer be changed.

**See Also** Paint

## Indexing Drives, Folders, and Files

You can enable Indexing Service to index the contents of an NTFS-formatted drive, as well as individual folders and files, so that accessing files when you use Search, for example, is faster. Before you can index any drive, folder, or file, Indexing Service must be running on the computer. See the sub-heading Indexing in the entry Indexing Service to learn how to start Indexing Service. Once it's started, you can include disks, folders, and files for indexing.

To index a disk, perform the following steps:

1. Right-click the drive in any Explorer window, then select Properties.
2. On the General tab, check Allow Indexing Service to Index This Disk for Fast File Searching. Click OK.

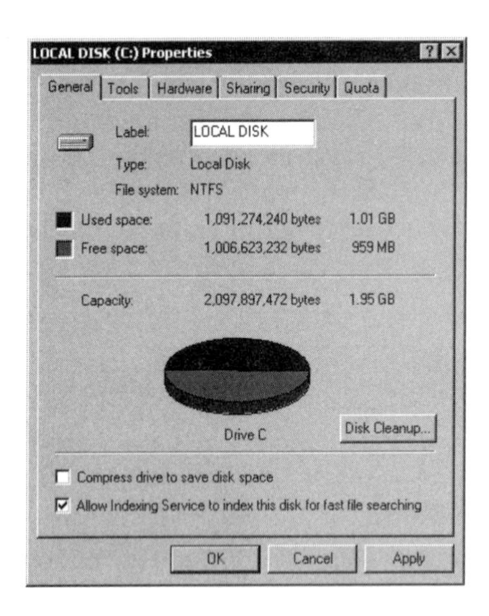


To index a file or folder, follow these steps:

1. Right-click the file or folder in any Explorer window and select Properties.
2. On the General tab, click Advanced to open the Advanced Attributes dialog box.

**TIP** If the Advanced button is not available, the drive is not formatted with NTFS.

3. Check the For Fast Searching, Allow Indexing Service to Index This Folder (File) option. Click OK, then click OK again to close the folder's or file's Properties dialog box.

**See Also** Indexing Service

# Indexing Service

Indexing Service Microsoft Management Console (MMC) snap-in that lets you index (extract information from documents and organize it in a catalog) documents on the computer for faster access. This works only with NTFS-formatted drives. Indexing Service can index different types of documents, such as HTML, Text, Microsoft Office 95 and higher, Internet mail and news, and other documents for which a filter is available. The indexed information is stored in catalogs. Indexing documents makes searches, such as those with Search or a Web browser, faster. You can also perform queries on any catalogs that have been created by using the Indexing Service Query Form.

To access Indexing Service, choose Start ➢ Settings ➢ Control Panel, double-click Administrative Tools, then double-click Computer Management. You'll find Indexing Service under Services and Applications.

**TIP** In Windows 2000 Server, you can also access Indexing Service by choosing Start ➢ Programs ➢ Administrative Tools ➢ Computer Management. You'll find Indexing Service under Services and Applications.

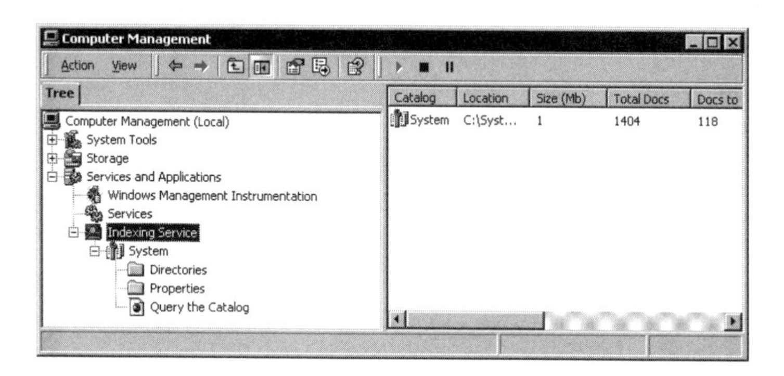


## Action Menu

The Action menu in Indexing Service contains familiar options and some unique options. The options available depend on which Indexing Service console tree or Details pane item you have selected (Indexing Service, a catalog, the Directories folder, directories, the Properties folder, or properties) and whether Indexing Service is running. Some options may be available only via the All Tasks submenu. No unique options are available with the Query the Catalog console tree item. The following are possible unique items on the Action menu in Indexing Service:

**Empty Catalog** Removes indexing information from the selected catalog. Available only if Indexing Service is stopped.

**Start** Starts the indexing service.

**Stop** Stops the indexing service.

**Pause** Pauses the indexing service.

**Merge** Merges indexes in the selected catalog. Available only if Indexing Service is stopped.

**New** Lets you add a new catalog or directory, depending on your selection in the console tree.

**Rescan (Full)** Manually starts a complete rescan of the selected directory. Available only if Indexing Service is running and with a directory selected in the Details pane.

**Rescan (Incremental)** Manually starts a scan of all documents in the selected directory that were modified while Indexing Service was inactive, or since the last scan. Available only if Indexing Service is running and with a directory selected in the Details pane.

**Tune Performance** Enhances the Indexing Service indexing performance.

**Refresh List** Updates the Properties list.

## Catalogs

A default catalog, called System, is created when Indexing Service is installed. This catalog contains an index of the information contained on all disks attached to the computer. On a Windows 2000 Server computer that has Internet Information Services (IIS) installed, another catalog, called Web, is created by default. This catalog contains an index of IIS. To see the available catalogs in the Details pane, select Indexing Service in the console tree.

### *Indexing*

Columns containing information for each catalog in the list include Catalog (name), Location, Size (Mb), Total Docs, Docs to Index, Deferred for Indexing, Word Lists, Saved Indexes, and Status. Information in all but the Catalog and Location columns appears only if Indexing Service is running. To start it, right-click Indexing Service and choose Start. If automatic indexing is not enabled, you'll see the Enable Indexing message box, which asks whether you want Indexing Service to start automatically when you start the computer. Click Yes or No. Indexing continues to occur from this point on until you stop the service. To do so, choose Stop from the pop-up or Action menu. You can also choose Pause to pause indexing. To resume, select Start again. When you restart Indexing Service, an incremental scan is performed automatically.

You can also start and stop indexing of a particular catalog by right-clicking the catalog and choosing All Tasks ➢ Start or All Tasks ➢ Stop, respectively.

### *Configuring a Catalog*

Right-click a catalog and choose Properties from the pop-up menu to view and configure properties on the General, Tracking, and Generation tabs. By default, some of the available settings are inherited from the Indexing Service Properties.

**General** Lets you view the catalog name, location, and size of the index and property cache in megabytes.

**Tracking** Lets you specify whether you want network share aliases automatically added. Also lets you specify whether you want to inherit this setting from the Indexing Service properties. On a computer with IIS installed, you can also specify whether you want to associate a virtual WWW server with the catalog.

**Generation** Lets you specify whether you want to index files with unknown extensions, and whether you want abstracts generated for files found in a search. If you choose to have abstracts generated, you can specify the maximum number of characters that can be used for the abstract. Abstracts are returned with the results of a query. You can also specify whether you want to inherit the settings from the Indexing Service properties. Uncheck to inherit the settings to be able to make changes.

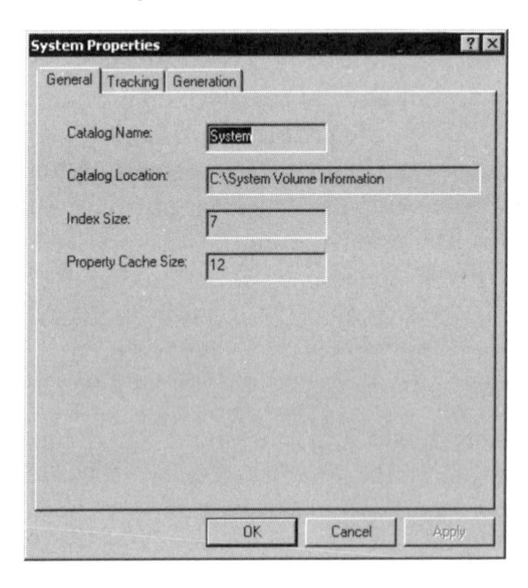


### *Directories Folder*

You can see the Directories folder in the console tree if you expand a catalog. This folder contains all of the directories that are included or excluded in the index. You can see information about each directory in the Details pane, such as the directory name, the alias name (if applicable), and whether the directory will be included in the catalog.

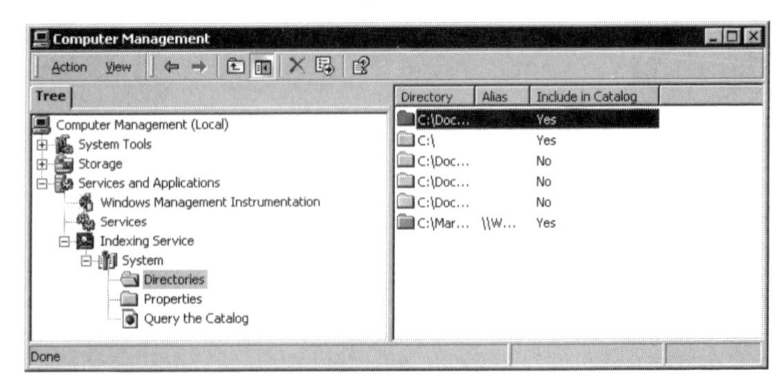

**Adding a Directory** To include or exclude specific directories, you use the Add Directory dialog box. Follow these steps:

1. With either a catalog or the Directories folder selected, choose Action ➢ New ➢ Directory.

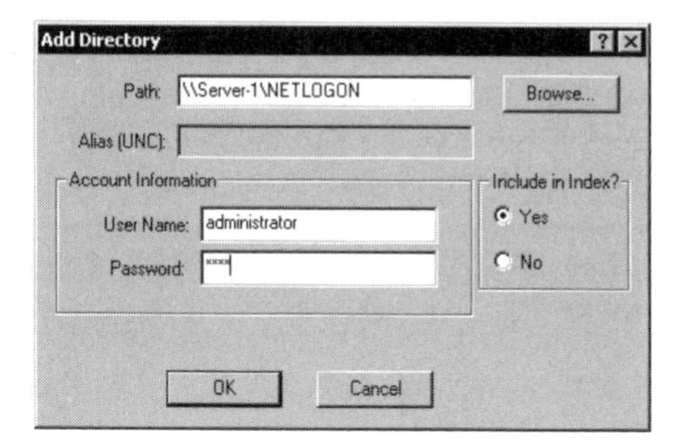


2. Enter the path to the directory and the network share alias (if applicable). If the directory is on a remote computer, enter a username and password for a user who can access the computer.

3. Specify whether you want to include the directory in the index by selecting either Yes or No. Click OK to add the directory to the list.

**WARNING** If you exclude a directory, all subdirectories are automatically excluded, even if you add such a subdirectory as a separate directory entry and specify to include it in the index.

**Changing Directory Information** You can change a directory's path or network share alias, and whether the directory should be included in the index, by double-clicking the directory in the Details pane and modifying information as necessary. This dialog box is identical to the one you use to add a new directory.

## *Properties Folder*

The Properties folder contains the properties and values that can be stored in the property cache. Properties that are stored in the property cache will appear in the results page of a query. Some properties are added to the property cache by default. You can identify them by scrolling to see properties that display a value in the Cached Size column. They include such properties as Document Title, Size, and Path. To add a property to the property cache, select it in the Details pane, right-click, choose Properties, and select the Cached check box.

**WARNING** Adding properties to the property cache can negatively affect Indexing Service performance.

Details about each property include Property Set, Property, Friendly Name, Data Type, Cached Size, and Storage Level. The Friendly Name column should give you an idea of what each property represents. You can also find detailed information in the Windows 2000 Help system about the properties that are cached by default.

## Querying a Catalog

You can query Indexing Service catalogs using the Query form. To access the query form, select Query the Catalog in the console tree. The Indexing Service query form is displayed in the Details pane. You might want to hide the console tree to be able to see the form better.

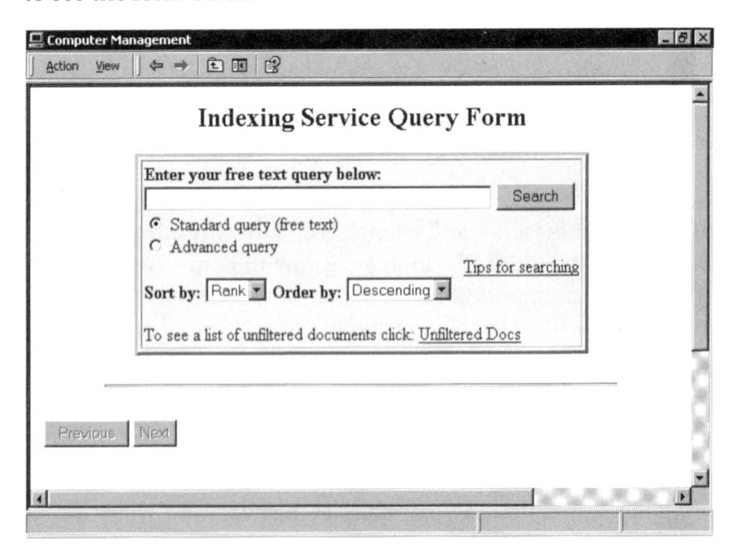

To perform a query, choose whether you want to perform a standard or advanced query, enter your query text in the text box, and then make your choices from the Sort By and Order By drop-down lists. Click Search to start the search. For detailed information on standard and advanced queries and syntax, see the Queries, Overview entry in the Windows 2000 Help system.

The results of your query will appear at the bottom of the query form. Scroll down and click the link to any document you would like to open. If your results contain several pages, click Next or Previous to navigate the results pages.

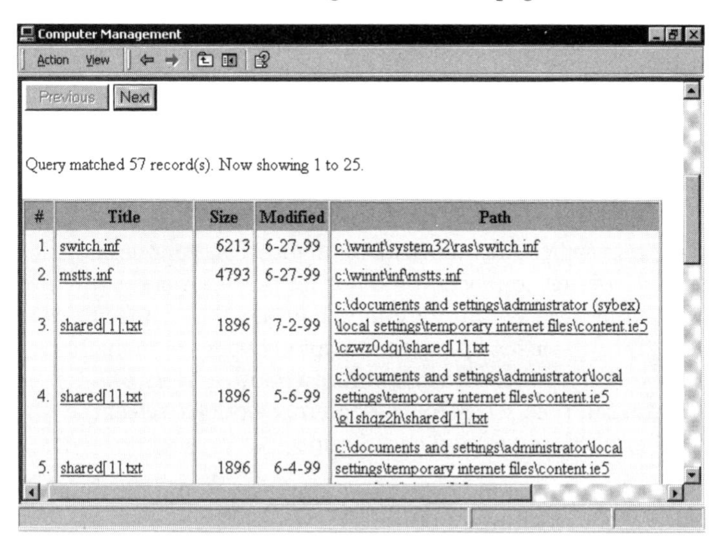


**See Also** Microsoft Management Console (MMC), Computer Management, Indexing

# Internet Connection Wizard

Internet Connection Wizard

Guides you through the process of setting up either a dial-up or LAN connection to the Internet and setting up Internet e-mail. Once you have created a connection, you can use it to connect to the Internet, where you can browse Web sites, download files, and send and receive e-mail (if you've configured e-mail account information). You can access the Internet Connection Wizard in several ways:

- Choose Start ➢ Programs ➢ Accessories ➢ Communications and select Internet Connection Wizard from the menu.
- Double-click the Connect to the Internet icon on the desktop.

**TIP** The Connect to the Internet icon is on your desktop if you're not yet connected to the Internet. Once you set up a connection, Windows will remove it from the desktop.

- Choose Start ➢ Settings ➢ Control Panel, double-click Internet Options, select the Connections tab, and click Setup.
- Double-click the Internet Explorer icon on your desktop. If an Internet connection has not yet been set up, the Internet Connection Wizard starts automatically. If a connection has already been set up, Internet Explorer opens (you might be asked to connect or work offline; choose to work offline). You can then select Tools ➢ Internet Options, select the Connections tab, and click Setup.

When the Internet Connection Wizard starts, the Welcome screen gives you three options:

- You can sign up for a new Internet account, meaning that you don't have an Internet Service Provider (ISP) yet. If you choose this option, you can select from a list of ISPs or you can supply the necessary information for the ISP you want to use.
- You can transfer an existing Internet account.
- You can manually set up your Internet connection, or you can connect through a LAN.

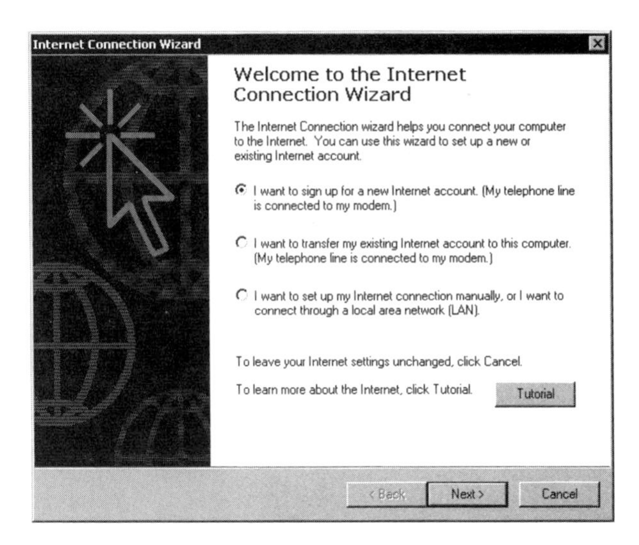


A common scenario is to set up your Internet connection manually (you already have an account set up with an ISP, you have a modem installed, and you're connected to a phone line). This is called a dial-up connection. Many companies also have their users access the Internet through the company LAN. In order for you to be able to connect to the Internet through a LAN, a proxy server has to be set up on the network and you may need the name of the proxy server to establish the connection (if the Internet Connection Wizard was unable to automatically discover the proxy server and you have to manually configure the connection to the proxy server or servers). If you want to set up sending and receiving e-mail, you'll need to know your e-mail address, the type of mail server your company uses, and the names of the servers that process your company's incoming and outgoing e-mail.

**TIP** If you already have an account set up with an ISP and you use different computers frequently, it might be a good idea to keep your account and connection information saved to a file on disk. Then, you can use the Internet Connection Wizard and the information on disk to quickly set up an Internet connection on a new computer.

## Setting Up a Dial-up Internet Connection and E-mail

To set up a connection to the Internet for the first time using a modem installed in your computer (an account with an ISP is already established) and to set up Internet e-mail, follow these steps:

1. Access the Internet Connection Wizard using one of the methods described above.
2. On the Welcome screen, choose I Want to Set Up My Internet Connection Manually or I Want to Connect through a Local Area Network (LAN). Then, click Next.
3. Choose I Connect through a Phone Line and a Modem. Click Next.
4. If no locations have been previously set up on your computer, the Location Information dialog box appears. (Otherwise, skip to step 6.) Choose your country or region from the drop-down list, enter the area code for your city, and, if applicable, enter any numbers that you need to dial to access an outside line. Also choose whether to use Tone or Pulse dialing. Click OK.
5. On the Dialing Rules tab of the Phone & Modem Options dialog box, select your location. Multiple locations can be set up on the same computer. You can also create a new location by selecting a location and clicking New or edit an existing location by selecting it and clicking Edit. Click OK.

**TIP** Multiple locations can be helpful—for example, if you're using a laptop and travel internationally, or if you travel within your country and must access the Internet from cities with different area codes.

6. Enter your ISP's phone number in the Telephone Number field. If you're calling long-distance, verify that your country/region information is correct; otherwise, select a different country/region from the list. If the call to your ISP is a local call, deselect the option Use Area Code and Dialing Rules. The fields Area Code and Country/Region Name and

Code are grayed out if you deselect this box because that information is not applicable to a local call. Click Next.

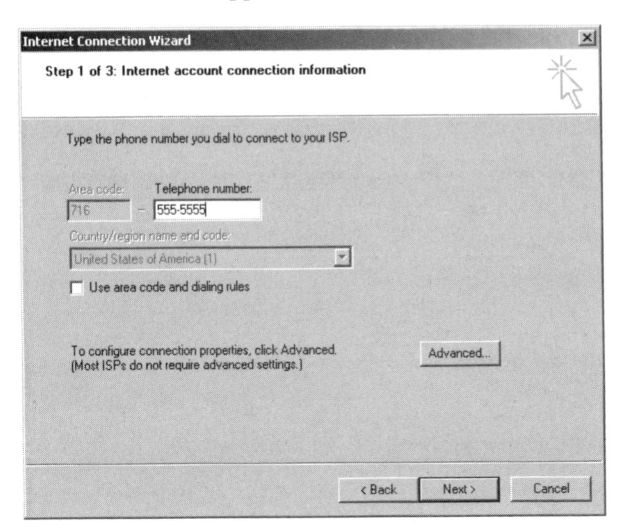

**TIP** If your ISP requires it, you can specify the connection protocol, such as PPP or SLIP; any specific logon procedures; and specific IP and DNS server addresses. To do this, click Advanced to access the Advanced Connection Properties dialog box and configure the necessary settings on the Connection and Addresses tabs.

7. Enter the name and password of the account you have set up with the ISP. Click Next.
8. Enter a name for the connection. This is the name that will appear in your Network and Dial-up Connections folder. Click Next.
9. Specify whether you want to set up Internet e-mail. Windows 2000 includes Outlook Express, which you can configure as your e-mail client if you choose Yes. Click Next.
10. If you chose No in step 9, skip to step 14. If you chose Yes, enter the name you want to show in the From field of any e-mail messages you send to other people. A common choice is first and last names. Click Next.

11. Enter your e-mail address. Your ISP should have provided you with this information. Click Next.

12. Specify the type of the e-mail server for incoming mail. Choices are POP3, IMAP, and HTTP. Also enter the name of the incoming and outgoing mail servers. Your ISP should provide you with this information. Click Next.

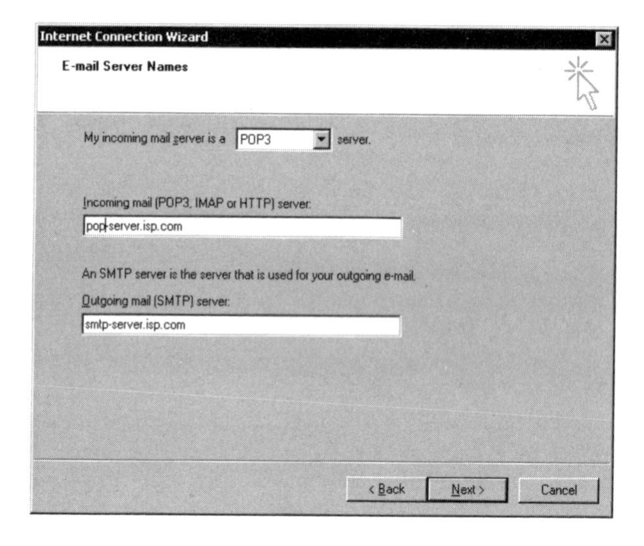


13. Enter the e-mail account name and password you received from your ISP. If you want your password to be remembered so that you don't have to enter it when you connect, check Remember Password. Your ISP may require you to use Secure Password Authentication to log on to your mail account. If so, select the appropriate check box and click Next.

14. The Completing the Internet Connection Wizard screen appears, indicating that you have completed the setup process. You can choose to connect to the Internet immediately. If you deselect that option, you can connect to the Internet later through the dial-up connection you just created—you can access it in your Network & Dial-Up Connections folder. Click Finish.

**TIP** To access Network & Dial-Up Connections, choose Start ➢ Settings ➢ Control Panel ➢ Network & Dial-Up Connections. To connect to the Internet, double-click the dial-up connection you created with the Internet Connection Wizard and click Dial.

**15.** If you chose to connect immediately, you're presented with the Dial-Up Connection dialog box.

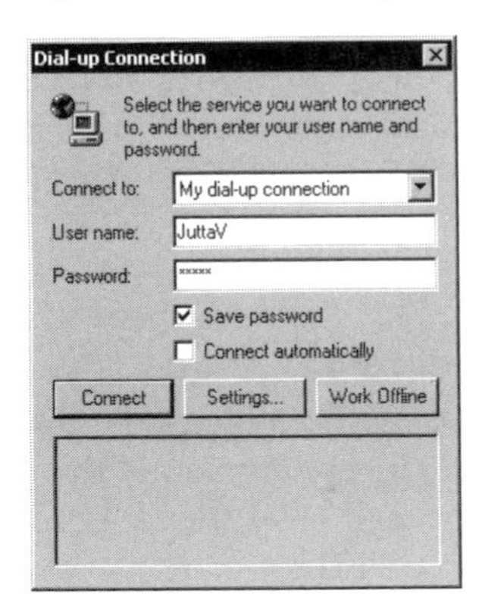


If you have more than one dial-up connection set up, choose the appropriate connection from the Connect To drop-down list. Verify that the username and password are correct; if they aren't, enter the correct information now. You can choose to save the password so that you don't have to enter it in the future. You can also choose to connect automatically. If you do, from then on when you open Internet Explorer, you'll connect automatically using this connection.

The Dial-up Connection dialog box also has the following buttons:

**Connect** Connects you to the Internet.

**Settings** Lets you configure Internet properties.

**Work Offline** Lets you open a browser window but doesn't connect you to the Internet.

**16.** Click Connect to the Internet. The modem starts dialing your ISP. In the box at the bottom of the dialog box, you'll see messages that you're connected to the remote computer and that the username and password are being verified. Internet Explorer then opens to your home page. You can now browse the Internet and download files. You can also send and receive e-mail using Outlook Express.

**TIP** Once you're connected, an icon with two overlapping (connected) computers appears in the status area (the right side of the taskbar) to tell you that a connection is established. You can double-click this icon to obtain information about the connection, such as how long you've been connected, the speed of the connection, how many bytes have been sent and received, the server type used, and the client and server's IP addresses.

### *Closing a Connection*

One method for closing the connection is to close Internet Explorer and choose Disconnect Now in the Auto Disconnect window. You can also right-click the connection icon in the status area and choose Disconnect, or you can double-click the connection icon and click Disconnect.

### *Connecting through a LAN*

To set up a connection to the Internet using your company's LAN, start the Internet Connection Wizard and select the option I Want to Set Up My Internet Connection Manually or the option I Want to Connect through a Local Area Network (LAN). Next, choose to connect through a LAN. You must then choose to manually specify proxy servers or specify that you want Windows to automatically discover proxy servers. If you choose to manually specify proxy servers, enter the names and ports for the proxy server or servers. Specify any Internet addresses you don't want users to access via proxy servers. This can include intranet addresses. If you want to set up Internet e-mail, follow steps 9 through 12 earlier in this section. Click Finish when the wizard prompts you. With a connection through a LAN, all you have to do to browse the Internet and download files is open Internet Explorer and point your browser to the sites you're interested in. No other action (such as dialing a phone number) is required because your connection is made through the proxy server on the LAN, not a modem, and the proxy server is permanently connected to the Internet.

**See Also** Network and Dial-up Connections, Internet Options, Internet Explorer, Outlook Express

# Internet Explorer

Lets you view and download information and Web pages on the Internet or a corporate intranet. To access information on the Internet, you must have a connection established to the Internet—for example, via a modem connection and an Internet account at an ISP, or via your corporate LAN. See the main heading Internet Connection Wizard for more information on how to connect to the Internet.

To access Internet Explorer, use one of the following methods:

- Double-click the Internet Explorer icon on the desktop.
- Choose Start ➢ Programs ➢ Internet Explorer.
- Open any Web file from within Windows Explorer.
- Enter a Web URL in the Run dialog box.
- Enter a Web URL in the Address bar in any Windows Explorer window and click Go.
- Open an Internet network place from within My Network Places.
- Select Internet Explorer in the Folders view (the Explorer Bar of any Windows Explorer window).
- Click a link to an Internet address in an Outlook Express e-mail.
- Choose View ➢ Go To ➢ Home Page in any Explorer window.

## Internet Explorer Window

When you open Internet Explorer, you see the Internet Explorer window. It's very similar to a standard Windows Explorer window. It contains menus, toolbars, the main viewing area, and a status bar. Many of these items are the same as in a Windows Explorer window; however, some of the toolbar buttons that appear by default, as well as several menu items, are different.

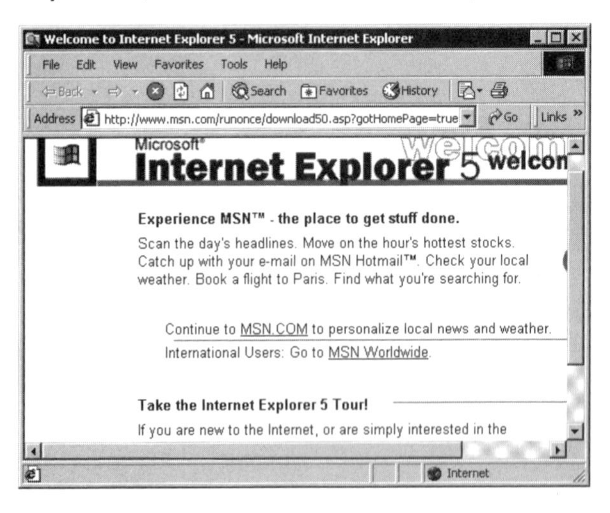


## Viewing Documents

To view Internet or intranet documents in Internet Explorer, you enter the page's address in the Address bar on the Address toolbar, such as `http://www.sybex.com`, and press Enter or click Go on the toolbar. The page then loads and appears in the viewing area.

## Internet Explorer Toolbars

The Internet Explorer toolbars are very similar to the Windows Explorer toolbars. By default, the Standard Buttons toolbar displays several buttons not found on the Windows Explorer toolbar, although all buttons are available in both the Internet Explorer and the Windows Explorer Standard Buttons toolbars. The Internet Explorer Address Bar, Links, and Radio toolbars have the same buttons as the Windows Explorer toolbars, and the Links toolbar appears by default in Internet Explorer.

### *Standard Buttons Toolbar*

The Internet Explorer Standard Buttons toolbar by default contains the following buttons, which don't appear by default on the Windows Explorer Standard Buttons toolbar. Use View ➢ Toolbars ➢ Customize to customize the Internet Explorer Standard Buttons toolbar. For more information on the remaining buttons, see the main heading Explorer.

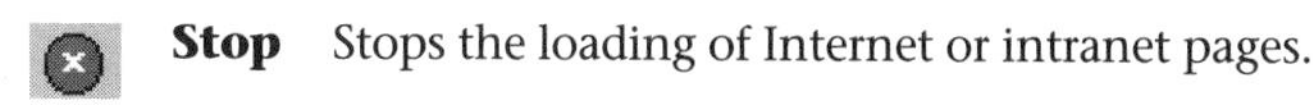

**Stop** Stops the loading of Internet or intranet pages.

**Refresh** Updates the currently displayed page.

**Home** Displays your Internet Explorer home page.

**Mail** Lets you select options from a drop-down menu that allow you to read mail, create a new message, send the current page's address as a link in an e-mail message, send the contents of the current page in an e-mail message, and open your Internet newsreader application.

**Print** Prints the current document to your default printer.

## Internet Explorer Menus

The Internet Explorer menus contain some familiar Windows options, as well as many unique options.

### *File Menu*

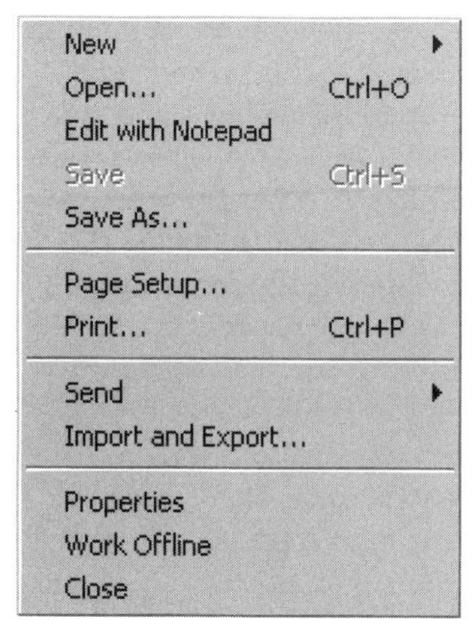


The File menu lets you perform basic tasks, such as opening a new Internet Explorer window; creating a new message, post, or contact; or making a new Internet call using NetMeeting. You can perform these tasks using options that appear on the submenu that appears when you select New on the File menu. Using the File menu, you can also open new Web documents or folders, edit the contents of the current page in Notepad, and save entire Web pages to your local drive. You can configure your printing settings, and, using options that appear when you select Send on the File menu, send the page to someone as a link or its entire contents via e-mail, as well as send the page as a shortcut to the desktop. Additionally, the File menu lets you import and export favorites and bookmarks, view the property sheet of the current Web document, work offline, and close Internet Explorer.

### Edit Menu

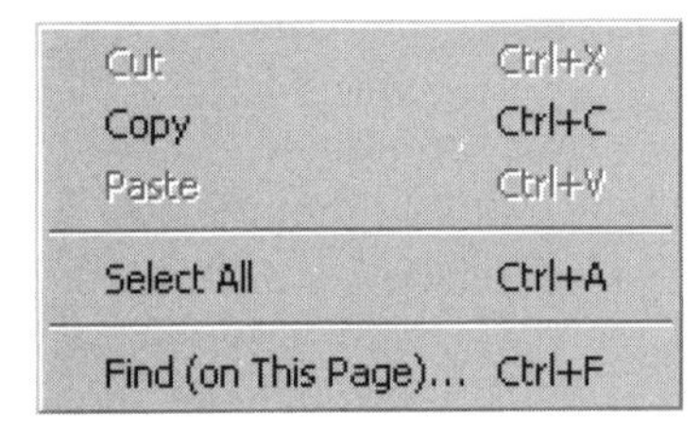


The Edit menu lets you perform editing functions, such as cut, copy, and paste. You can also choose the Select All option, which selects the entire document, and find words on the current page.

### View Menu

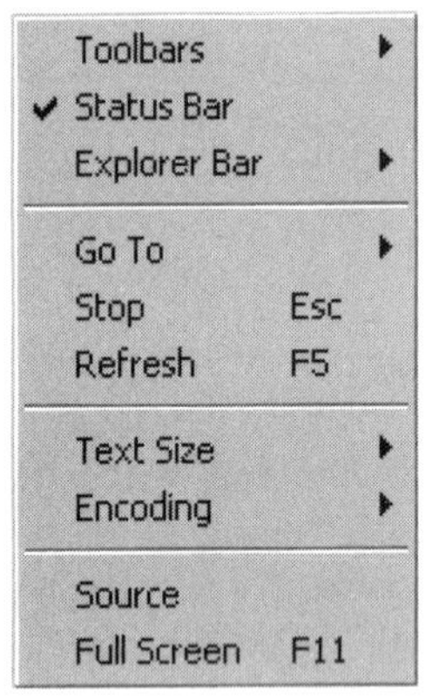


Using the View menu, you can choose which toolbars and Explorer Bar view you want to display, and whether you want to display the status bar. For more information on the toolbars, Explorer Bar, and status bar, see the main heading Explorer and the subheading Internet Explorer Toolbars in this section. You can also return to the previous page, forward to the next page, go directly to your home page, or go to other pages you've accessed. You can stop loading the current page and update the current page. Additionally, you can specify the size in which you want text to display, choose from several character sets for displaying the current page, view the HTML source code of the current page, and view the current page full screen. You'll also be able to access the Microsoft Script Debugger via the View menu.

### *Favorites Menu*

Use the Favorites menu to add Web pages to your Favorites list and to organize your list. Your Favorites list is added to the bottom of the Favorites menu so that you can quickly access your favorites using this menu. Alternatively, you can click Favorites on the Standard Buttons toolbar to access your favorites.

**TIP** By default, the Favorites menu uses Personalized menus for your favorites (displaying only the most recently accessed links). To turn Personalized Favorites Menu off, choose Tools ➢ Internet Options, select the Advanced tab, and uncheck Enable Personalized Favorites Menu. Click OK to save the change.

### *Tools Menu*

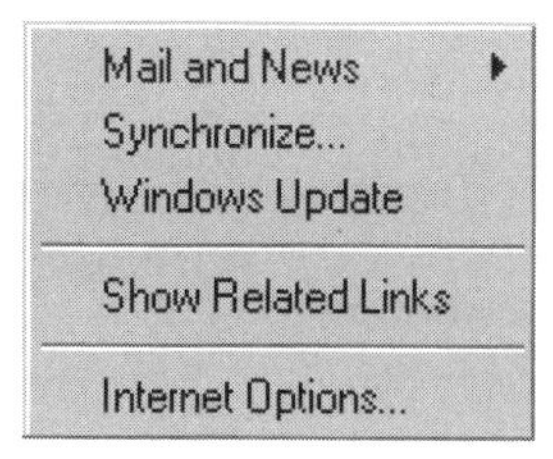


The Tools menu lets you perform mail- and news-related actions, including reading your mail, creating a new message, sending the current page as a link or its contents via e-mail, and accessing your newsreader. It also lets you synchronize offline Web pages, access the Microsoft Windows Update page, view links related to the current page, and configure Internet options. For more information about configuring Internet options, see the heading Internet Options.

### *Help Menu*

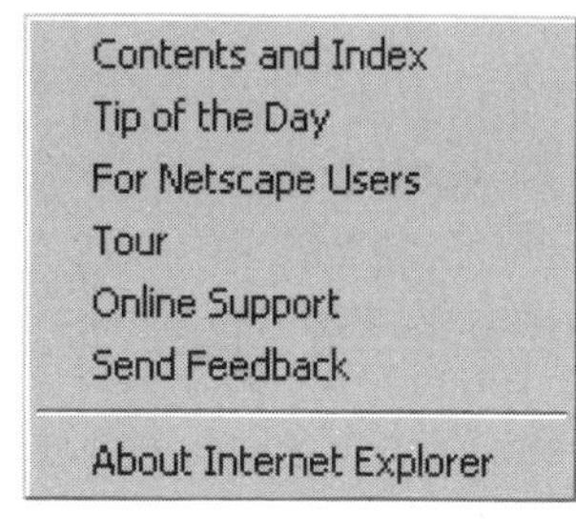


Use the Help menu to access Internet Explorer-related Help topics and to view information about Internet Explorer, such as version and licensing information. Using this menu, you can also access daily tips, see help for switching from Netscape, go to the Web tutorial page on the Internet, access the Microsoft Product Support page, and send feedback to Microsoft about Internet Explorer.

## Editing the Current Page

Internet Explorer lets you open the source code of the current page in Notepad, where you can edit it. To do so, follow these steps:

1. With the document you want to edit open in your active Internet Explorer window, choose File ➢ Edit with Notepad. The source code opens in a Notepad window.
2. Make changes as necessary.
3. Save the document.

## Changing the Web Page Text Size

You can change the size used for the text that displays on Web pages. For example, you might want to use a bigger size to make text easier to read. To do so, choose View ➢ Text Size, then select a size from the submenu.

## Adding Favorites

You can add your favorite (most often visited) places on the Internet or your corporate intranet to the Favorites folder. Then, you can access these favorites easily through the Favorites menu or the Favorites Explorer Bar.

To add a page to your Favorites list, perform these steps:

1. Choose Favorites ➢ Add to Favorites, or click Add in the Explorer Bar Favorites view to display the Add Favorite dialog box.
2. If you want to be able to work on the page while you're not connected to the Internet or network, check Make Available Offline. If you select this option, you can click Customize and use the Offline Favorite Wizard to specify what content you want available offline (just the current document, other pages to which there are links on this page, etc.) and set up synchronization options.
3. If you want to add the page directly to the Favorites folder, click OK. If you want to add it to a subfolder in the Favorites folder, click Create In, then select the folder to which you want to add the page from the list or click New Folder to create a new folder. Click OK when you've selected the appropriate subfolder.

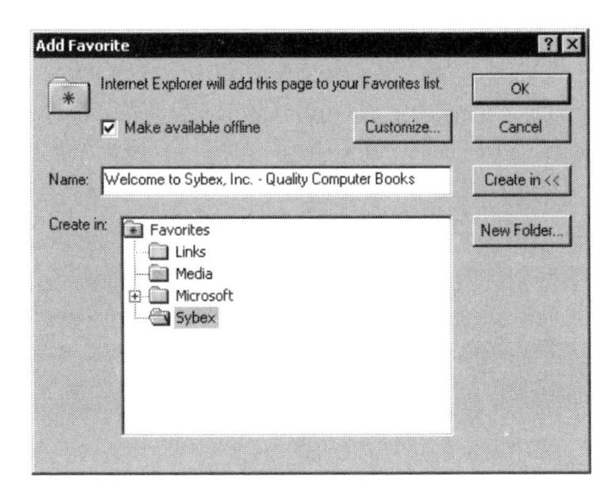


Once you've added pages to your Favorites list, instead of having to enter the page's address in the Address bar or navigating to it via other pages, just select the page from the Favorites menu or in the Explorer Bar Favorites view and it starts loading automatically.

**TIP** You can also access your favorites from within any Windows Explorer window.

## Organizing Favorites

Once you've added pages to your Favorites list, you can organize them—for example, you can delete pages from the list that you no longer want to access, move pages to a different folder, change whether they're available offline, create new folders, and rename items.

To organize your favorites, either choose Favorites ➢ Organize Favorites or click Organize in the Explorer Bar Favorites view to open the Organize Favorites dialog box.

In this dialog box, you can use the following buttons:

**Create Folder** Lets you create a new folder in the Favorites folder. To create a new folder in a subfolder, double-click the subfolder to open it, then click Create Folder.

**Rename** Lets you assign a different name to a folder or page. To do so, select the folder, click Rename, and enter a new name.

**Move to Folder** If you want to move a folder or page to another folder, select them, click Move to Folder, then select the destination folder and click OK.

**Delete** Select a page or folder and click Delete to remove it from your Favorites list.

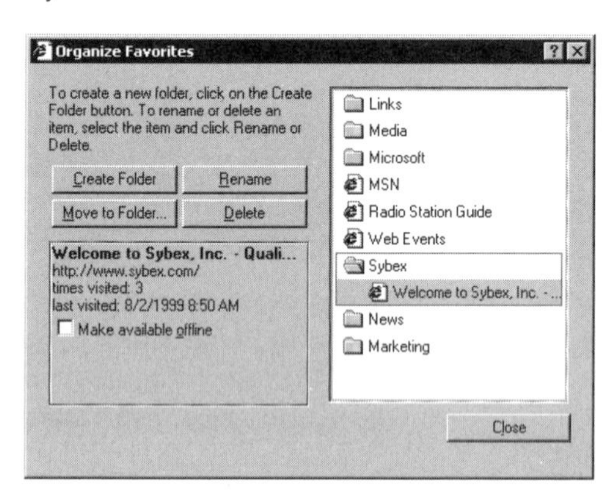


In the Organize Favorites dialog box, you can see additional information about each page you have saved, such as its URL, how many times you've visited the page, and when you last visited the page. You can also choose to make any page available offline or to no longer have it available offline.

**See Also** Explorer, Internet Options, Internet Connection Wizard, Network Connection Wizard, Network and Dial-up Connections

# Internet Options

Lets you configure Internet settings and display options for your Windows 2000 computer. Among other things, Internet Options lets you:

- Configure your home page.
- Manage temporary files.
- Configure Web content colors, fonts, and languages.
- Set up security.
- Specify which applications to use for e-mail and Internet newsgroups.

Choose Start ➢ Settings ➢ Control Panel, then double-click Internet Options to open the Internet Properties dialog box. This dialog box has six tabs: General, Security, Content, Connections, Programs, and Advanced.

**TIP** You can also access Internet Options by choosing Tools ➢ Internet Options in Internet Explorer.

## General Tab

The General tab lets you configure your Internet home page and specify how you want to handle temporary Internet files and files in the History folder. The tab contains three sections: Home Page, Temporary Internet Files, and History.

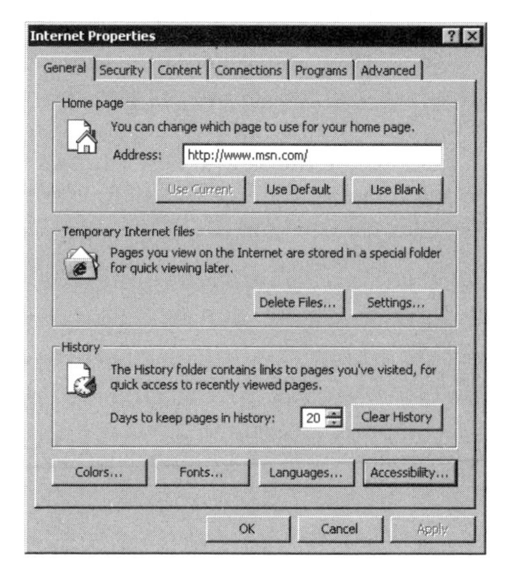


**Home Page** Lets you specify a URL you want to use as your home page, the first page that Internet Explorer displays every time you open it or whenever you click Home in Internet Explorer. If you currently have a Web page open, click Use Current to use that site's address as your home page. To use the default address (`http://www.msn.com`), click Use Default. To show a blank page as your home page, click Use Blank. To specify any other Web page, enter the Web site address in the Address text box.

**Temporary Internet Files** When you access a page on the Internet, the file is stored in a folder on your computer. When you access the same page again, Windows 2000 displays the copy stored in this folder so that access is quicker. If you want to configure when Windows 2000 updates the page with the latest version available on the Internet, click Settings to open the Settings dialog box. This dialog box also lets you configure how much space the files should take up (by using the slider), move the location of the Temporary Internet Files folder (by clicking Move Folder), view the files in the folder (by clicking View Files), and view any ActiveX and Java controls that may have been downloaded to your computer (by clicking View Objects). Back on the General tab, you can click Delete Files to remove the files from the computer if you're running out of disk space.

**History** The History folder holds links to any pages you've accessed, and you can specify how long to keep those links by entering a value in the Days to Keep Pages in History field. You can also use the up and down arrows next to this field to specify the value. To remove all links from the History folder, click Clear History.

Four additional buttons are available on the General tab to configure how Internet Explorer displays Web page content:

Colors...

**Colors** Lets you configure the colors for Web page text, backgrounds, and links. The default selection is Use Windows Colors.

**TIP** To change the Windows colors, right-click the desktop and choose Properties, then select the Appearance tab and make your changes.

Fonts...

**Fonts** Lets you configure the language script and fonts for Web content that does not specify that a certain font be used.

Languages...

**Languages** Lets you configure which languages and the order of languages Internet Explorer should use for Web pages that have multiple language content. To be able to view multiple language content, you must add the appropriate language character set to your Windows 2000 computer using Regional Options.

Accessibility...

**Accessibility** Lets you choose to continue to use your personalized Accessibility settings when viewing Web pages. You can decide to ignore colors, font styles, and font sizes that are specified in Web documents. You can also choose to use a style sheet you create and apply the style sheet settings to Web content. Style sheets are used to define default settings for font color, style, and size, as well as heading and text background.

## Security Tab

Lets you control the security level for different Web site zones. You can add Web sites to some of the zones to determine which security level to apply to a specific Web site. Several security levels are available to control how Internet Explorer handles dynamic content—for example, Java applets and ActiveX controls. Here are the levels of security you can apply:

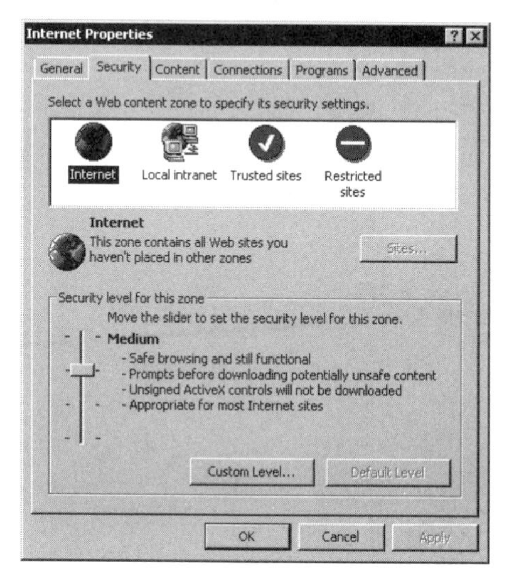


**High** The most secure setting. Some features may be disabled; cookies are disabled. This setting will reduce functionality.

**Medium** Before downloading ActiveX controls or Java applets, you will be prompted by a warning message. Unsigned ActiveX controls won't download.

**Medium-low** You won't be prompted before downloading ActiveX controls or Java applets. Unsigned ActiveX controls won't download.

**Low** Provides little security. Most dynamic content is downloaded without prompting. A few warning prompts may display. Do not use unless you know the Web site can be trusted.

**Custom Level** Lets you create your own security level. Click Custom Level to open the Security Settings dialog box, where you can specify your own settings by choosing Disable, Enable, Prompt, or specific safety levels for different types of dynamic content. Options include ActiveX Controls and Plug-ins, Cookies, Downloads, Microsoft Virtual Machine Content, Miscellaneous, Scripting, and User Authentication settings. To reset custom settings to a specific security level, select a level from the drop-down list and click Reset.

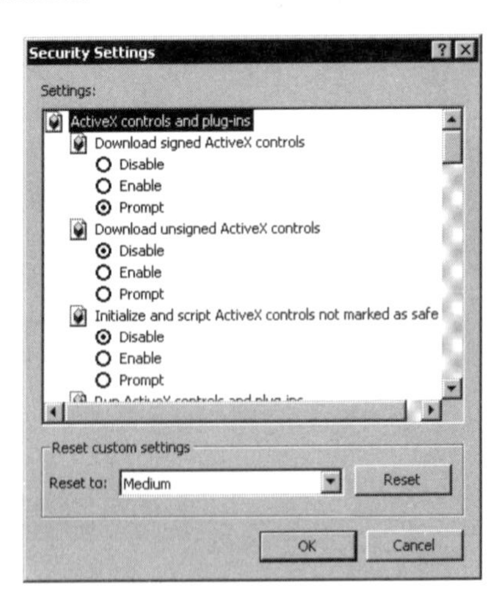

Back on the Security tab, to apply a security setting to a zone that is different from the default, select the appropriate zone, then move the slider to the security level you want to use. If you change the security level to a level below the default for that zone, you will be prompted to confirm your selection.

Following are the four available zones and their default settings:

**Internet** All Web sites that are not contained in one of the other zones. The default security level is Medium. You cannot add specific sites to this zone.

**Local Intranet** Web sites that you access in your company's intranet. The default security level is Medium.

**Trusted Sites** Web sites that you are certain will not try to download harmful content to your computer. The default security level is Low.

**Restricted Sites** Web sites that you access but do not trust; you suspect that the sites may send potentially harmful content to your computer. The default security level is High.

To add a site to the Trusted Sites or Restricted Sites zone, select it and click Sites. Enter the address of the Web site in the Add This Web Site to the Zone text box and click Add. To remove a site, select the site in the Web Sites list box and click Remove.

For the Local Intranet zone, after you click Sites, you'll be prompted to define which Web sites are included, such as all local sites not listed in other zones, all sites that bypass the proxy server, and all UNCs. Make the appropriate choice. To specify a certain URL, click Advanced and add the URL. Click OK either once or twice (depending on whether you clicked Advanced) to save your settings.

## Content Tab

The Content tab lets you restrict access to certain sites, manage certificates, and manage and configure personal information. Three different areas are available on the Content tab: Content Advisor, Certificates, and Personal Information.

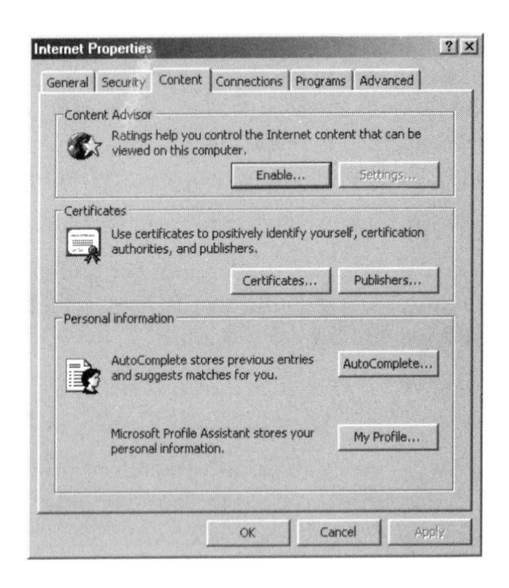


**Content Advisor** Lets you restrict access to certain sites on the Internet. Must be enabled before settings are effective. Click Enable to open the Content Advisor dialog box. Use the four tabs—Ratings, Approved Sites, General, and Advanced—to configure access restrictions.

**TIP** Content Advisor is very useful for restricting Internet access for children.

**Ratings** Enables you to use a rating system for the type of content users are allowed to see for the categories' language, nudity, sex, and violence. The rating system installed by default has been developed by the Recreational Software Advisory Council on the Internet (RSACi). By default, the level for all categories is set to the lowest level (greatest restriction). To adjust the level, move the slider to the desired position. A description of each level appears in the Description area of the tab as you change levels. Clicking More Info takes you to RSAC's Web site, where you can find more information about the organization, the rating system, and how the system is implemented.

**Approved Sites** Lets you specify Web site addresses that users can either never or always view, regardless of the settings you made on the Ratings tab. Enter a Web site address in the Allow This Web Site text box; then click Always to allow it or Never to never allow it. To remove a Web site from the list, select the site and click Remove.

**General** Lets you specify whether users can see sites that haven't been rated by the rating organization. You can also choose to use a Supervisor password that, when entered, allows the user to view restricted documents. You assign the Supervisor password when you first click OK after opening (and possibly making changes to) Content Advisor. To change the Supervisor password, click Change Password. You must know the old password to change it. You can also add and remove ratings systems by clicking Rating Systems and then clicking Add to add a system or selecting a system in the list and clicking Remove. In addition, you can learn more about other rating systems for Internet Explorer at Microsoft's Web site by clicking Find Rating Systems.

**Advanced** Lets you view ratings bureaus from which some rating systems can receive ratings, and allows you to view, import, or remove PICSRules files that can be used to determine whether a specific site should be viewed by the user.

When you're done configuring access restrictions using the Content Advisor dialog box, click OK. You'll be prompted to create the Supervisor password. This prevents children from turning off Content Advisor or changing settings. Enter and confirm the password in the appropriate text boxes, then click OK. You'll see a message that Content Advisor has been enabled. Click OK. Click Settings on the Content tab to change Content Advisor settings. You'll have to provide the Supervisor password.

After you enable Content Advisor, you can disable it by clicking Disable on the Content tab. Again, you'll have to provide the Supervisor password.

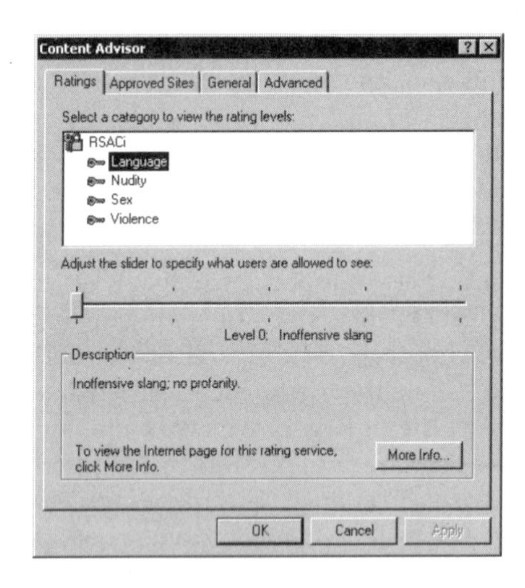


### *Accessing a Restricted Page*

With Content Advisor enabled, if you try to access a page that has not yet been rated or for which access is restricted, Content Advisor displays a dialog box informing you that you're not allowed to see the site. If you know the Supervisor password, you can choose to:

- Always allow the site to be viewed
- Always allow the specific Web page to be viewed
- Allow viewing only this time

Check the appropriate radio button and enter the Supervisor password to effect the change.

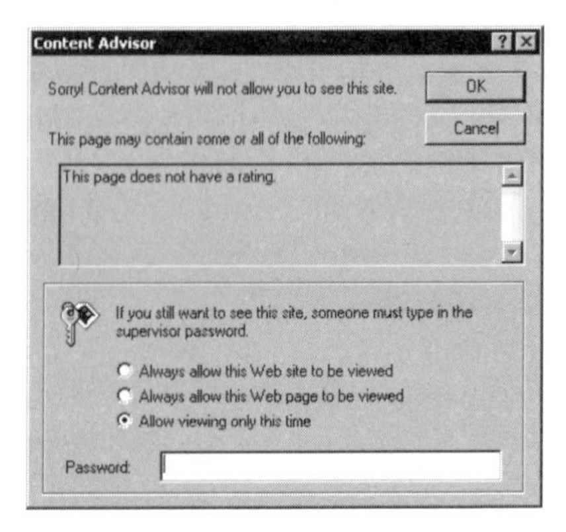

**Certificates** Lets you manage digital certificates used by applications and certain security services. Certificates enable secure communication, authentication, and data integrity over the Internet or other insecure networks. Click Certificates to open the Certificate Manager, where you can manage (import, export, remove, and configure) your own (personal) certificates, certificates for other people, certificates for Immediate Certification Authorities, and certificates for Trusted Root Certification Authorities. Click Publishers to view software publishers and credential issuers you've specified as trusted. You can also remove software publishers and credential issuers from the list.

Select a certificate and click the Advanced button to configure certificate purposes and export format. The selected certificate purposes will display in the Certificate Intended Purposes area of the Certificate Manager. You can display certificates by purpose by selecting the appropriate option from the Intended Purpose drop-down list. By default, all certificates display (no certificate purpose filter is applied).

**TIP** You must have administrative privileges to manage certificates.

**Personal Information** Use to configure AutoComplete and your personal profile.

**AutoComplete** Click AutoComplete to open the AutoComplete Settings dialog box, where you can specify in what situations Windows 2000 should try to match items you've previously typed so that you don't have to type the same information over and over. You can configure Windows 2000 to use AutoComplete for Web addresses, forms, and usernames and passwords on forms. If you specify AutoComplete for usernames and passwords, you can also choose to be prompted to save passwords. If you do, you'll have the option to save passwords you enter on a Web page. The next time you access the Web page and enter the corresponding username, you won't be prompted for the password again. You can also choose to remove AutoComplete entries used for forms by clicking Clear Forms, and you can remove saved passwords by clicking Clear Passwords. To remove Web address AutoComplete entries, you'll have to clear the History folder on the General tab of Internet Options.

**WARNING** Saving passwords poses a potential security risk if you leave your computer unattended without logging out of Windows 2000. Anyone could walk up to your computer and access password-protected sites for which you saved the password.

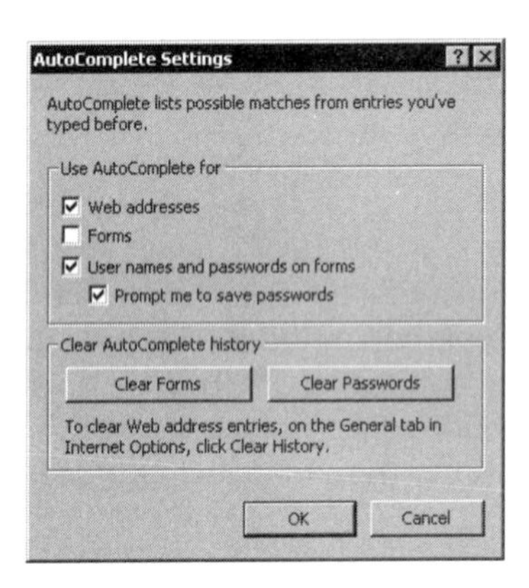


**My Profile** Lets you set up a profile for yourself that you can send to Web sites that request personal information. Click My Profile to open the Address Book—Choose Profile dialog box. Here you can either choose an existing profile from your Address Book or create a new entry in the Address Book to use as your profile.

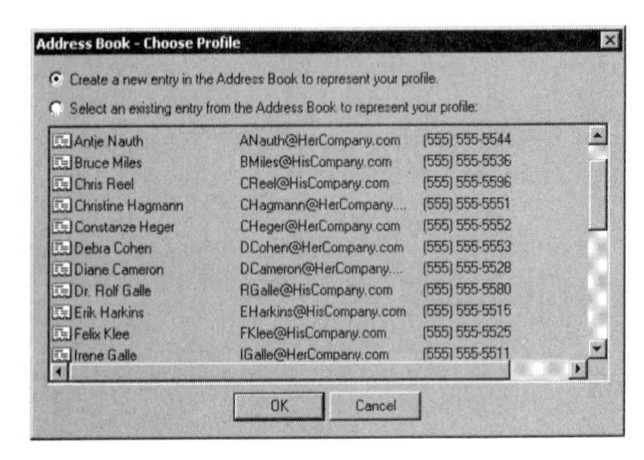

## Connections Tab

Use to configure Internet dial-up and LAN connections. You can create new dial-up connections, edit and remove existing dial-up connections, and configure LAN connection settings.

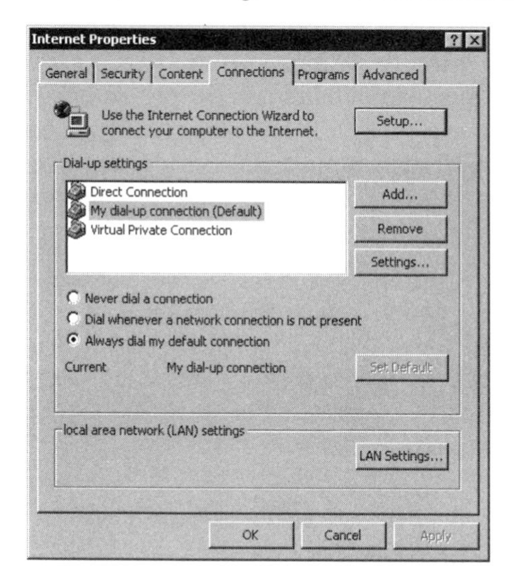


### *Connecting to the Internet*

You can start the Internet Connection Wizard to configure a connection by clicking Setup. The Internet Connection Wizard is explained in detail under the heading Internet Connection Wizard.

### *Configuring Dial-up Connections*

You can configure your existing dial-up connections by selecting a connection in the Dial-up Settings list and clicking Settings. You can also add a new connection by clicking Add and following the prompts in the Network Connection Wizard (see Network Connection Wizard), or you can remove a connection by selecting a connection in the list and clicking Remove.

You can also specify what action Internet Explorer should take if you're trying to access Internet resources and a connection to the Internet is not yet established. The default selection is to never dial a connection. Alternatively, you can choose to dial your default dial-up connection when a network connection is not available, or to always dial your default connection. If you choose to dial a connection, you can change your default connection setting by selecting a different connection in the Dial-up Settings list and clicking Set Default.

### Configuring LAN Connection Settings

If you're connecting to the Internet over a LAN, you can click LAN Settings and choose to automatically detect your proxy server settings, specify an address for an automatic configuration script, or specify a physical address and port for your company's proxy server. If you do this, you can also specify to bypass the proxy server if you're accessing local addresses. Click Advanced to specify addresses for individual proxy servers (such as HTTP, FTP, and Gopher).

## Programs Tab

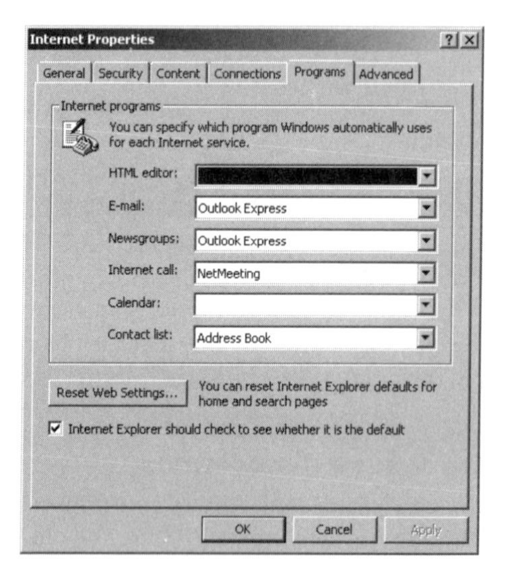


Use this tab to identify which programs you want to use for various Internet services. The types of programs from which you can choose depend on the service. Examples are Outlook Express for E-mail and Microsoft NetMeeting for Internet Calls. You can specify an application for each of the following services:

- HTML editor
- E-mail

- Newsgroups
- Internet call
- Calendar
- Contact list

If you've installed another browser and your default settings for home and search pages have been changed, you can click Reset Web Settings to make Internet Explorer settings the default settings again. If you want to have multiple browsers installed on your computer but want to retain Internet Explorer as your default browser, select the Internet Explorer Should Check to See Whether It Is the Default check box. If Internet Explorer determines that another browser has been set as the default browser, a prompt will ask if you want to make Internet Explorer the default browser again.

**TIP** If that option is enabled, Internet Explorer checks to see if it's the default browser each time it starts up.

## Advanced Tab

Use to configure Advanced Internet settings, such as settings relating to Accessibility, Browsing, HTTP 1.1, Microsoft Virtual Machine (VM), Multimedia, Printing, Searching, and Security.

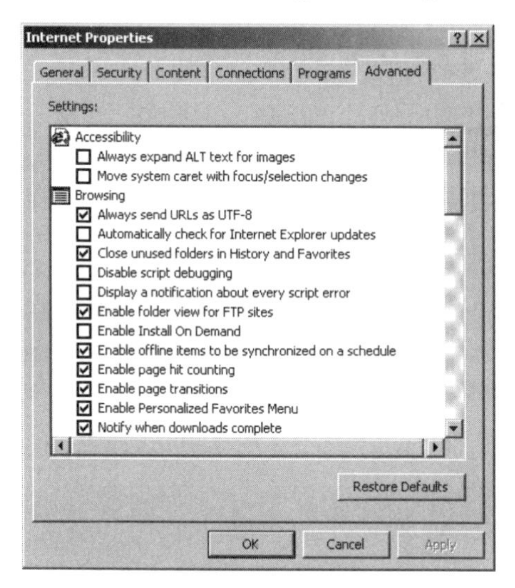

If you make changes on the Advanced tab and want to return to the Windows 2000 defaults, simply click Restore Defaults.

**See Also** Internet Explorer, Regional Options, Accessibility, Internet Connection Wizard, Network Connection Wizard

# Internet Services Manager

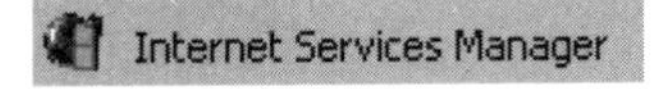


MMC console snap-in installed by default on Windows 2000 Server that lets you manage Internet Information Services (IIS) version 5.0. Internet Information Services lets you create and manage Internet and intranet Web and FTP sites. Web and FTP sites enable you to share information and files with users connected to the Internet or intranet by publishing information to the site and then having users access pages and files using a browser (or, in the case of FTP, a browser or FTP utilities). Publishing information to a Web site involves creating Web pages and copying them to a directory that is part of the Web site. Publishing files to an FTP site involves copying the files you want to share to a directory that is part of the FTP site.

IIS version 5.0 provides support for the following, among others:

- Web Distributed Authoring and Versioning
- FrontPage Server Extensions
- Internet Standards (such as HTTP 1.1)
- Multiple Web sites using one IP address
- News and mail using SMTP and NNTP
- Platform for Internet Content Selection (PICS) Ratings
- HTTP Compression
- FTP and FTP Restart
- Active Server Pages (ASP)
- Performance-enhanced objects
- XML integration

- Windows Script Components
- Browser Capabilities Component
- ASP Self-Tuning
- Encoded ASP scripts
- Application Protection
- Active Directory Service Interfaces (ADSI) 2.0
- Multihosting
- Multiple user domains
- User management delegation
- Process Throttling
- Per Web site bandwidth throttling
- Setup and Upgrade integrated with Windows 2000 Server
- Command-line administration scripts
- Process accounting
- Custom error messages for clients
- Granular configuration
- Remote Administration
- Terminal Services
- Centralized administration
- Kerberos security, Digest Authentication, Server-Gated Cryptography (SGC), Fortezza
- Secure Sockets Layer (SSL) 3.0 and Transport Layer Security (TLS)
- IP and Internet Domain restrictions
- Certificate storage

## Internet Information Services MMC Console Snap-in Window

To access Internet Services Manager, choose Start ➢ Programs ➢ Administrative Tools ➢ Internet Services Manager. By default, during the Windows 2000 Server installation, a default Web site is installed and appears in the Internet Information Services

MMC console snap-in window. Additionally, an Administration Web site and default SMTP Virtual Server are installed.

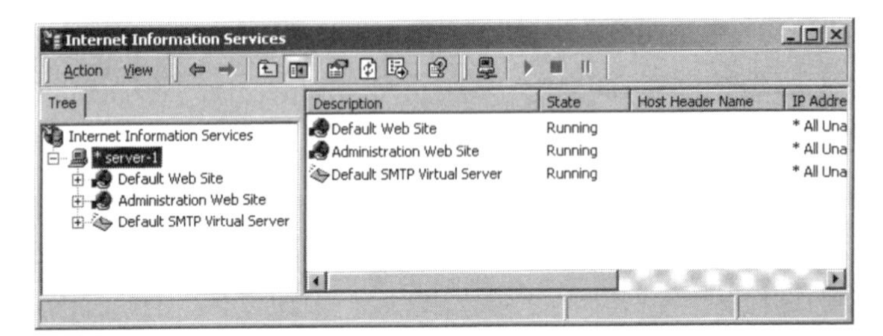

**NOTE** If you upgrade to Windows 2000 Server from a previous version, IIS is installed only if it was previously installed.

## Action Menu

Use the Action menu (or pop-up menus) to create, configure, and manage Web and FTP sites, as well as SMTP Virtual Services. Web and FTP site configuration is very complex, and the options available on the Action or pop-up menus will vary greatly depending on which item you've selected in the console tree or Details pane. Some options are also available via buttons on the toolbar.

**See Also** Microsoft Management Console (MMC), FTP

# IPCONFIG

Command that lets you view TCP/IP configuration information for each network card in your computer. Accessible from the command prompt, without the use of switches it displays basic configuration information, such as IP address, subnet mask, and default gateway IP address.

To access IPCONFIG, choose Start ➢ Programs ➢ Accessories ➢ Command Prompt, then type **IPCONFIG** at the command prompt.

```
Command Prompt
Microsoft Windows 2000 [Version 5.00.2072]
(C) Copyright 1985-1999 Microsoft Corp.

C:\>ipconfig

Windows 2000 IP Configuration

Ethernet adapter Local Area Connection:

        Connection-specific DNS Suffix  . :
        IP Address. . . . . . . . . . . . : 190.190.15.2
        Subnet Mask . . . . . . . . . . . : 255.255.0.0
        Default Gateway . . . . . . . . . :

C:\>_
```

You can use switches with IPCONFIG. Examples include:

**/all** Displays additional, detailed IP configuration information, such as host name; whether IP Routing, WINS Proxy, and DHCP are enabled; physical address; and IP addresses of DNS servers.

**/release adapter name** Releases the currently assigned IP address.

**/renew adapter name** Renews the DHCP lease for the currently assigned IP address.

**/?** Displays IPCONFIG help (syntax and switches).

Additional switches are available. Enter **IPCONFIG /?** at the console prompt to see all switches and their explanations.

**See Also** DHCP, Command Prompt

# Keyboard

Lets you configure your keyboard's settings, such as character repeat settings, cursor blink rate, input locales, and hardware-related settings.

Choose Start ➢ Settings ➢ Control Panel and double-click Keyboard to open the Keyboard Properties dialog box, which contains three tabs: Speed, Input Locales, and Hardware.

## Speed Tab

Use this tab to configure character repeat and cursor blink rate options. You can adjust the following settings:

**Repeat Delay** Lets you adjust the amount of time that elapses before a character starts to repeat after you hold down the corresponding key. Move the slider left or right to adjust the delay time to a setting between long and short.

**Repeat Rate** Lets you adjust the speed with which a character is repeated when you hold down the corresponding key. Move the slider left or right to adjust the repeat rate to a setting between slow and fast.

You can test your settings for Repeat Delay and Repeat Rate by placing the cursor in the provided text box and then pressing and holding down a key.

**Cursor Blink Rate** Lets you adjust the speed at which the cursor blinks. Move the slider left or right to adjust the cursor blink rate to a setting between slow and fast. To the left of the slider you'll see an example of a cursor and how fast it blinks at the currently selected setting.

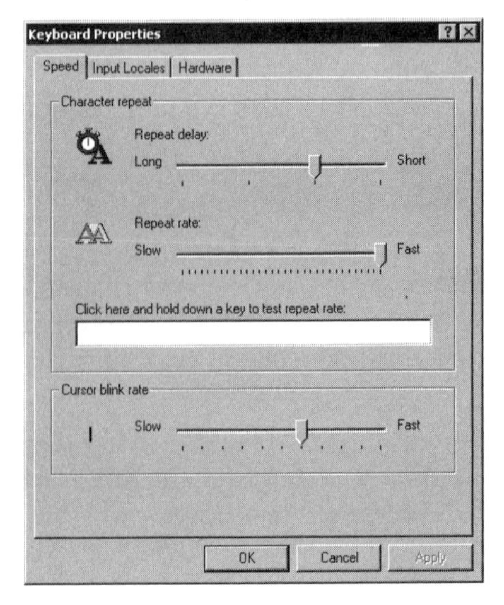


If you make changes to any of the above settings, they take effect immediately for testing purposes. This means that when you make a change to the Character Repeat options and then test them in the text box, the changes are effective, even though you haven't clicked Apply or OK yet. The same holds true for changing the cursor blink rate. The sample cursor's speed adjusts as you make changes. However, to apply the changes to your keyboard outside the Keyboard Properties dialog box, you must click Apply or OK.

## Input Locales Tab

Use this tab to control Windows 2000 input locales. Input locales specify the languages and keyboard layouts you want to be able to use to create new documents using programs that have been written for Windows 2000 and that can use this feature.

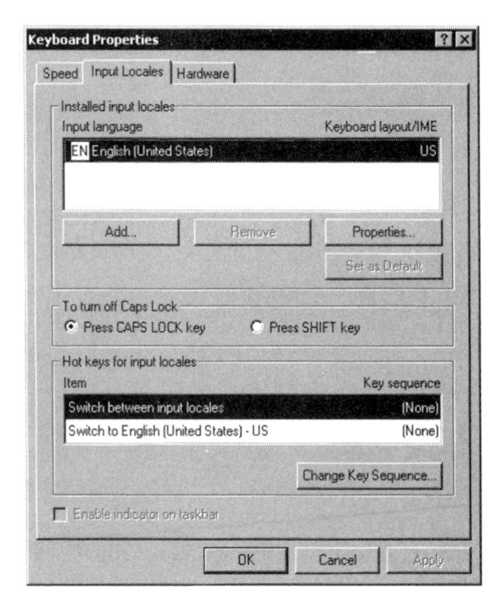


On this tab, you can:

- View installed input locales.
- Add and remove input locales.
- Change the properties of an installed input locale.
- Set an input locale as the default input locale.
- Specify how to turn off Caps Lock.
- Configure hotkey sequences to switch between input locales.

- Enable or disable the display of the input locale indicator on the taskbar if more than one input locale is installed.

The section Regional Options covers the Input Locales tab in greater detail.

**TIP** You can also access the Input Locales tab by choosing Start ➢ Settings ➢ Control Panel, double-clicking Regional Options, then selecting the Input Locales tab.

## Hardware Tab

Use this tab to view, configure, and troubleshoot your keyboard's hardware settings.

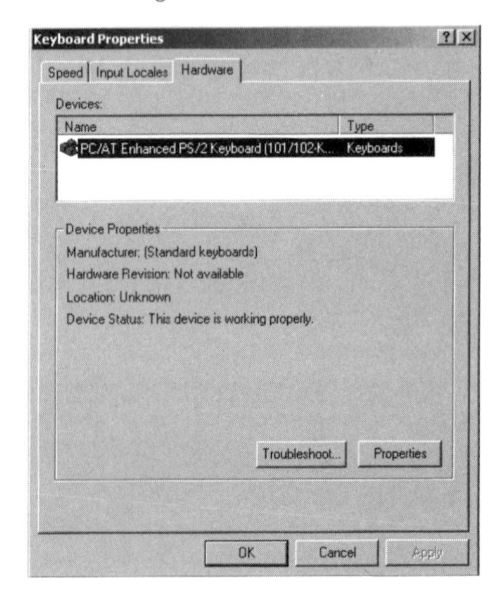


In the Devices list, you'll see the name and type of your installed keyboard. The Device Properties area displays information regarding your keyboard. This includes such information as the manufacturer, hardware revision, location (such as SCSI ID or bus number), and device status. The Device Status line either indicates that the device is working properly, or it displays a description of the problem, a problem code, and a suggested solution, if available.

Two additional buttons are available:

Troubleshoot...

**Troubleshoot** Click Troubleshoot to start the Windows 2000 Hardware Troubleshooter for keyboard problems. Follow the prompts in the troubleshooter to resolve keyboard-related hardware problems.

Properties

**Properties** Click Properties to display the keyboard device's Properties dialog box. It has three tabs: General, Driver, and Resources.

**TIP** One or more of these tabs exist for all installed hardware devices. They display information specific to the device and enable you to configure device properties.

- **General** Displays some of the same information about the device that you saw in the Device Properties area of the Hardware tab in the Keyboard Properties dialog box. From here, you can also click Troubleshooter to start the Windows 2000 Hardware Troubleshooter. In addition, you can enable or disable the device by choosing the corresponding selection in the Device Usage drop-down list.

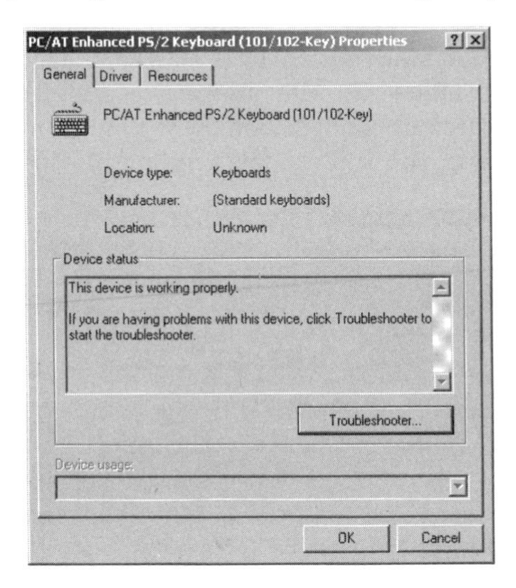


- **Driver** Displays information regarding the device's driver, such as the driver provider, date, and version. You can also see driver details (by clicking Driver Details) or remove the driver (by clicking Uninstall). In addition, you can update the driver by clicking Update Driver, which starts the Upgrade Device Driver Wizard. Simply follow the wizard's instructions to update the driver.

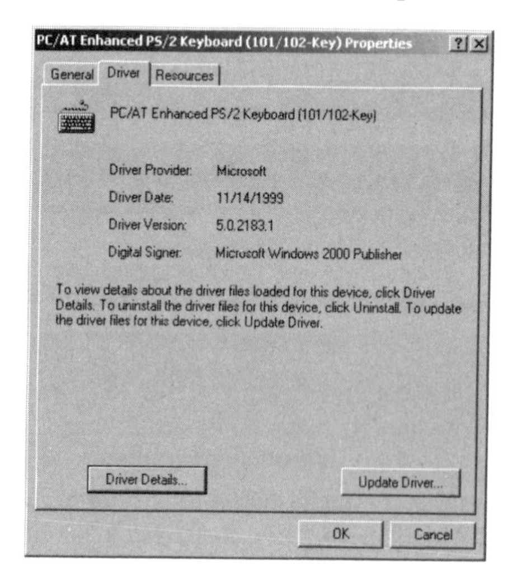


- **Resources** Displays resource information such as I/O range and the IRQ used by the device. You'll also see if any conflicts exist with other devices. This tab displays the hardware configuration the settings are based on; however, you won't be able to change the configuration.

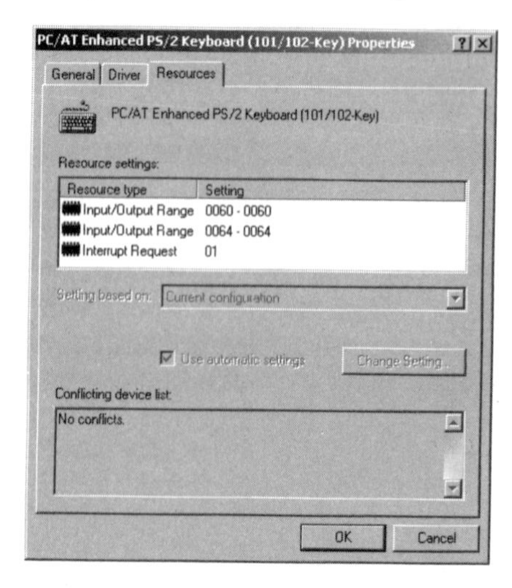

**TIP** You can also access these tabs by choosing Start ➢ Settings ➢ Control Panel, double-clicking Systems, selecting the Hardware tab, clicking Device Manager, expanding Keyboards, right-clicking the keyboard, and choosing Properties.

**See Also** Regional Options, Upgrade Device Driver Wizard, System, Device Manager

# Licensing

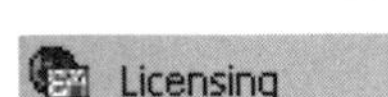


Lets you manage client access licenses to one or more Windows 2000 Server computers. Two licensing items exist in Windows 2000 Server—one accessible through Administrative Tools and one accessible through Control Panel. Licensing accessible through Administrative Tools lets you manage licenses for an enterprise; licensing accessible through Control Panel lets you manage licenses for a single Windows 2000 Server computer. To manage licensing for the enterprise, choose Start ➢ Programs ➢ Administrative Tools ➢ Licensing. To manage licensing for a single Windows 2000 Server computer, choose Start ➢ Settings ➢ Control Panel, then double-click Licensing.

## Licensing Modes

Two licensing modes exist: Per Seat and Per Server.

**Per Seat** Requires a unique Client Access License (CAL) for each computer that needs to access a Windows 2000 Server computer. The CAL can be used to access any Windows 2000 Server in the network.

**Per Server** CALs are assigned to the server, rather than the client, allowing one client connection per CAL. The number of maximum concurrent connections to the server equals the number of available CALs.

## Licensing Window (For Enterprise Management)

The Licensing window consists of menus, a toolbar, four tabs, and a status bar. The tabs in the Licensing window give you different views of licensing information. They include the following:

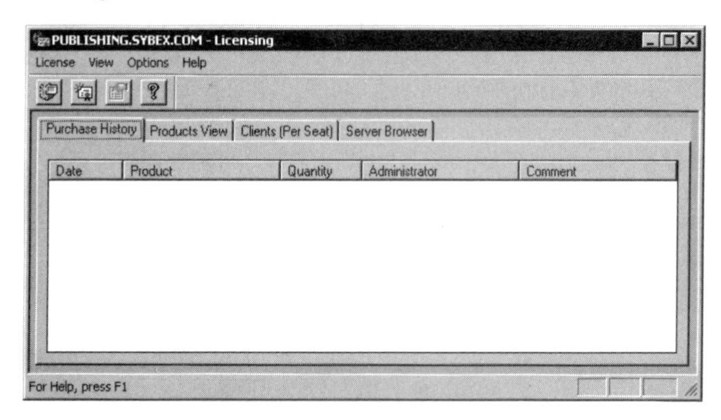


**Purchase History** Displays your license purchase and deletion history for licensed products. Information includes the date and quantity added or deleted, the name of the administrator who added or deleted licenses, and comments.

**Products View** Lets you view license information for server products (such as Windows Server and Microsoft BackOffice). Depending on the licensing mode, you can view how many licenses have been purchased and allocated per seat, or how many licenses have been purchased or used (reached) per server. In the Products view, three different icons are used to provide you with information about the product license. A package icon means that the product complies with licensing requirements. A yellow triangle with an exclamation mark means that the product does not comply with licensing requirements. An up arrow hitting a line means that the licensing limit has been reached for the product.

**Clients (Per Seat)** Lets you view Per Seat license information, such as which user has used per seat licenses and information about licensed and unlicensed usage of a product. Two icons give you information about a user's licensing status. A person icon means that the user is in compliance with licensing requirements; a yellow triangle with an exclamation mark means that the user is not in compliance with licensing requirements.

**Server Browser** Lists sites, domains, and servers. On this tab, you can browse to and administer licenses on any site, domain, or server to which you have the appropriate rights.

## Menus

The Licensing window contains four menus you can use to view and manage licenses:

**License** The License menu contains options for adding new licenses, deleting existing licenses, editing license properties, and selecting the domain for which you want to view and manage licenses.

**View** Lets you toggle the display of the toolbar and status bar, choose which tab you want to display, and refresh license information.

**Options** Lets you change the font, format (icon size, list, details), and sort options. Also lets you create and edit license groups and toggle whether changes should be saved when exiting the Licensing utility.

**Help** Lets you access licensing help.

## Changing Licensing Mode

You can switch licensing mode from Per Server to Per Seat—but only once. Once you have switched, you cannot switch back. If your licensing mode is Per Seat to begin with, you can't switch to Per Server mode.

**WARNING** Switch licensing mode only if you're absolutely certain that this is how you want to handle licensing.

To access the Choose Licensing Mode dialog box for enterprise licensing management, follow these steps:

1. Select the Server Browser tab in Licensing and browse to the appropriate license.
2. Choose License ➢ Properties.

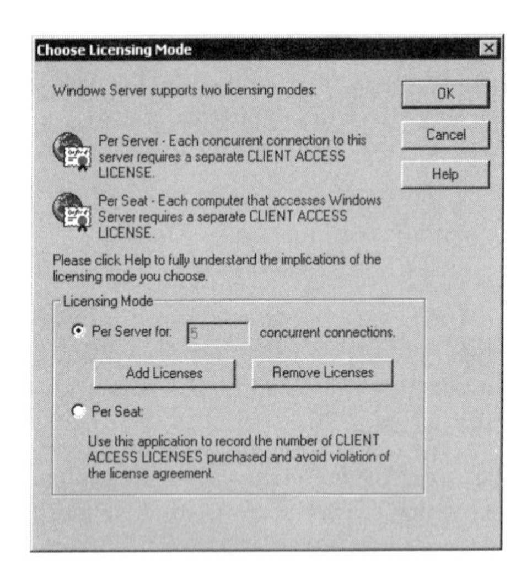


To access the Choose Licensing Mode dialog box for a single Windows 2000 Server computer, choose Start ➢ Settings ➢ Control Panel, then double-click Licensing.

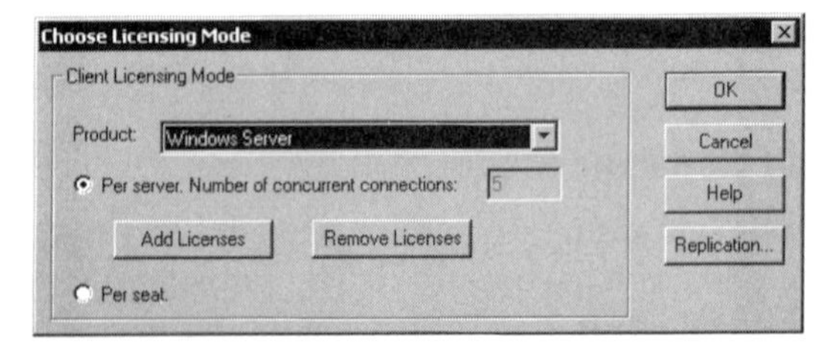


## Replication

In Windows 2000, licensing information is automatically replicated to a central database on a server called the site license server. Typically, this is the first domain controller installed in the network. You can configure replication either on the local server through Licensing in Control Panel, or on a remote server through Licensing in Administrative Tools.

**TIP** You can find out which server is the site license server through Active Directory Sites and Services (and change it if desired). Open Active Directory Sites and Services, browse to and select the appropriate site, then, in the Details pane, right-click Licensing Site Settings and choose Properties. In the Licensing Site Settings Properties dialog box, you'll see which computer (in which domain) is currently the licensing computer (site license server). Click Change to assign this role to a different server.

To access replication configuration options on the local server, follow these steps:

1. Choose Start ➢ Settings ➢ Control Panel, then double-click Licensing.
2. Click Replication to open the Replication Configuration dialog box.

To access replication configuration options on a remote server, follow these steps:

1. Choose Start ➢ Programs ➢ Administrative Tools ➢ Licensing, then select the Server Browser tab.
2. Browse to the server you want to manage, right-click it, and choose Properties.
3. Select the Replication tab.

**TIP** Alternatively, you can select the Products View tab, right-click the server product, choose Properties, select the Server Browser tab, select the server you want to manage, click Edit, then select the Replication tab.

### *Replication Options*

You can configure licensing replication either to start at a specific time each day (using the Start At option) or to start at a specific interval (using the Start Every option).

**TIP** You may see unavailable options regarding a master server. These options are available only on Windows NT 4.0 servers and enable you to specify the server to which to replicate.

## License Groups

If you're using Per Seat licensing, a license is assigned to a user when he or she logs onto the network the first time, which fulfills the licensing requirement of one license per computer. This works well if the number of users equals the number of computers and each user logs on only from one computer. However, if there are more users than computers, more than one user logs on from the same computer, or a user uses multiple computers, licensing information may become incorrect. To get around this problem, you can create license groups. When you create a license group, you assign multiple users to the group and allocate one license for each computer used to access the server. When a user who belongs to a license group logs on, the group license is used and licensing information remains correct.

To configure license groups using Licensing accessible through Administrative Tools, follow these steps:

1. In the Licensing window, choose Options ➢ Advanced ➢ New License Group.
2. Enter a name and description for the license group, and specify how many licenses to allocate (the number of computers used to access the server by members of the group). Next, click Add to add users.
3. In the Add Users dialog box, select one or more users in the Users list and click Add to add the user(s) to the Add Users list. Repeat this process until all users you want to add to the group appear in the Add Users list. To display users from a different domain, change the selection in the List Users From drop-down list. Click OK when you've finished.
4. Click OK.

**See Also** Control Panel, Active Directory Sites and Services

# Local Security Policy

Local Security Policy

Lets you view and configure account, local, public key, and IP security policies for the local computer.

To access Local Security Policy, choose Start ➢ Settings ➢ Control Panel, double-click Administrative Tools, then double-click Local Security Policy.

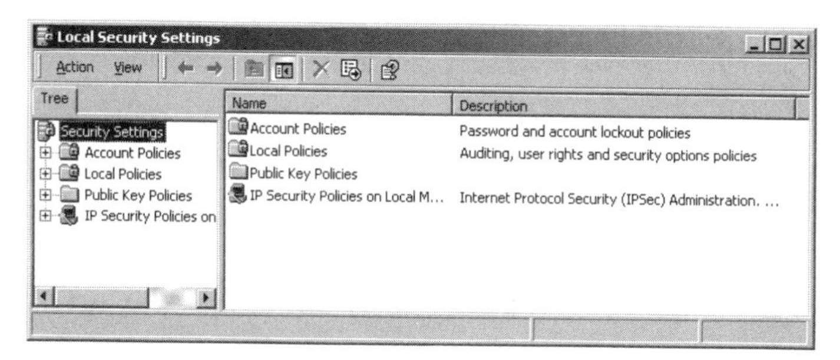


## Configuring Security Policies

To configure a specific security policy, navigate the console tree until individual policies appear in the Details pane. The Details pane displays each policy's name, local setting, and effective setting. To configure the policy's local setting, right-click a policy and select Security, or double-click a policy. If the computer is part of a domain and domain-level policy settings are configured, local policy settings are overridden by domain-level policy settings.

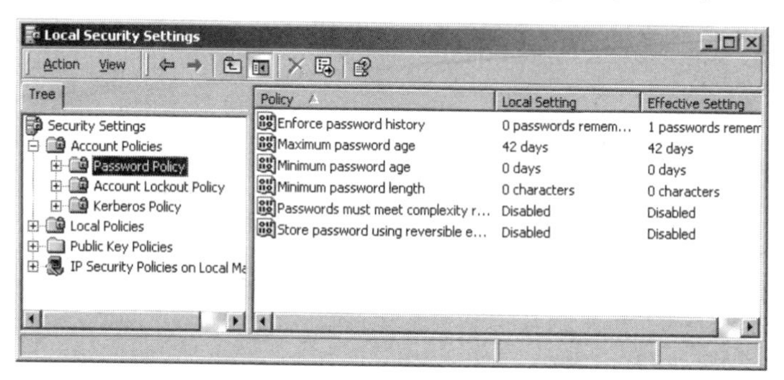

### Account Policies Node

Lets you configure settings for password, account lockout, and Kerberos policies. Kerberos is an Internet standard security protocol that is used for user or system identity authentication. Policy examples for password policies include Maximum Password Age, Minimum Password Age, and Minimum Password Length. Policy examples for account lockout policies include Reset Account Lockout Counter After and Account Lockout Duration. Policy examples for Kerberos policies include Enforce User Logon Restrictions and Maximum Tolerance for Computer Clock Synchronization.

### Local Policies Node

Lets you configure settings for audit policies, user rights assignments, and security options. Policy examples for audit policies include Audit Account Logon Events and Audit Directory Service Access. Policy examples for user rights assignments include Add Workstations to Domain, and Manage Auditing and Security Log. Policy examples for security options include Allow System to Be Shut Down Without Having to Log On, and Digitally Sign Client Communication (Always).

### Public Key Policies Node

Enables you to:

- Have computers submit certificate request to a CA (Certification Authority) automatically, and then automatically install the certificate.
- Add encrypted data recovery agents and change policy settings for encrypted data recovery.
- Establish trust in a common, external root certification authority.
- Create and distribute a signed list of root certification authority certificates, also called a certificate trust list.

### IP Security Policies on Local Machine

Lets you configure Windows Internet Protocol security (IPSec) to thwart network attacks (internal, private network, and Internet or extranet) by encrypting data that traverses between computers in the network. Several policies are predefined for use on computers that are part of a domain. They include Server (Request Security), Secure Server (Require Security), and Client (Respond Only).

Each policy has certain rules that apply to any computer to which the policy is assigned. You can change these rules by double-clicking a policy and making changes, or by right-clicking the policy and selecting Properties from the pop-up menu.

**Assigning an IP Security Policy** To assign an IP security policy to a computer, right-click the policy and select Assign. To remove the assignment, right-click the policy and select Un-Assign.

**TIP** Alternatively, you can assign a policy as follows: Choose Start ➢ Settings ➢ Network and Dial-up Connections, right-click your Local Area Connection, choose Properties, select Internet Protocol (TCP/IP), click Properties, click Advanced, select the Options tab, select IP Security, click Properties, select Use This IP Security Policy, and select a policy from the drop-down list.

**Creating a New IP Security Policy** You can create new IP security policies. To do so, right-click IP Security Policies on Local Machine and select Create IP Security Policy. Follow the steps in the IP Security Policy Wizard.

**TIP** You can also click the Create an IP Security Policy button on the toolbar to create a new IP security policy.

**Managing IP Filter Lists and Actions** You can create new IP filter lists and actions. To do so, right-click IP Security Policies on Local Machine and select Manage IP Filter Lists and Filter Actions. In the dialog box that opens, select the Manage IP Filter Lists tab, click Add, click Add again, then follow the wizard's instructions to create a new IP filter list. Or, select the Manage Filter Actions tab and click Add, then follow the wizard to create a new filter action. If you don't want to use the wizards, deselect the check box Use Add Wizard in the appropriate dialog box.

**TIP** You can also click the Direct Management of the Available IP Filter Lists and Filter Actions button on the toolbar to perform these actions.

**See Also** Network and Dial-up Connections, Microsoft Management Console (MMC), Group Policy

# Local Users and Groups

Local Users and Groups MMC console snap-in that lets you create and configure user and group accounts on the local computer. Local user and group accounts let you control access to resources on the local computer by assigning rights and permissions as necessary. Any user who has a local user account set up can log onto the computer using his or her username and password. Groups allow you to assign access to resources to multiple people at the same time rather than to each individual user. To do this, you create a group and add users and groups to the group. You then assign rights and permissions to a resource to the group. All users and groups added to the group then have the same rights and permissions the group has.

**TIP** Local Users and Groups is only available on Windows 2000 Professional computers and Windows 2000 member servers.

To access Local Users and Groups, choose Start ➢ Settings ➢ Control Panel, double-click Administrative Tools, then double-click Computer Management. You'll find Local Users and Groups under System Tools. Local Users and Groups contains two subfolders: Users and Groups.

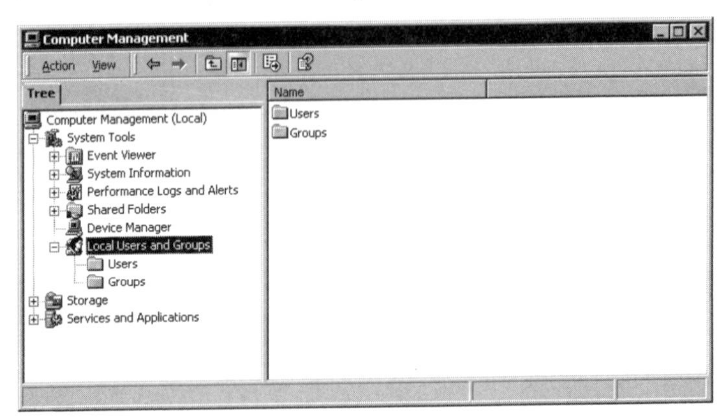

**TIP** Use Active Directory Users and Computers to manage domain users and groups.

## Action Menu in Local Users and Groups

While the Action menu for Local Users and Groups and its subcategories has many familiar options, it also has some unique options. Available options change depending on whether you select an item in the console tree or in the Details pane.

**New User** Lets you create a new user account. Available with Users selected in the console tree.

**Set Password** Lets you change the password for the selected user account. Available with a user account selected in the Details pane.

**Delete** Deletes the user or group account selected in the Details pane.

**Rename** Lets you rename the user or group account selected in the Details pane.

**Properties** Opens the property sheet for the user or group selected in the Details pane.

**New Group** Lets you create a new group. Available when you select Groups in the console tree.

**Add to Group** Lets you add users or groups to the group selected in the Details pane.

## Users Node

Lets you view and configure existing user accounts and create new accounts. Details about each user account in the Details pane include Name, Full Name, and Description. An account icon for a disabled user account has a red circle with an x in it.

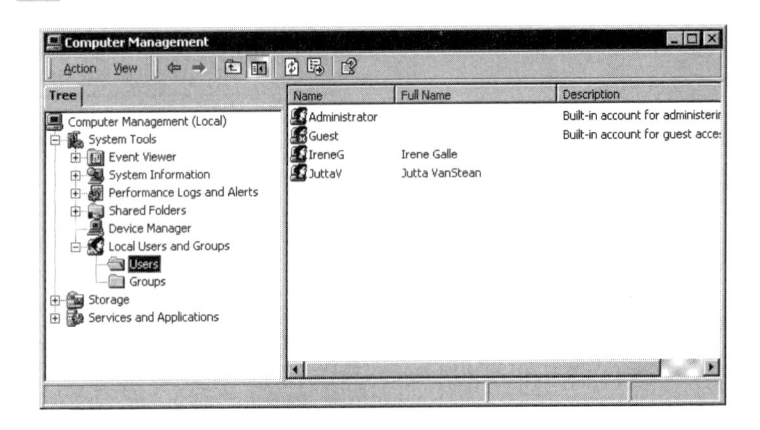


### *Built-in User Accounts*

Built-in user accounts are accounts that are created by the system during installation. Windows 2000 has two built-in user accounts: Administrator and Guest. Windows 2000 Server may have additional built-in user accounts. The server's configuration determines which built-in accounts exist.

**TIP** To view built-in user accounts on a Windows 2000 Server domain controller, you must use Active Directory Users and Computers. A Windows 2000 Server domain controller installed with default options has two additional built-in user accounts: IUSR_servername (for anonymous access to Internet Information Services) and IWAM_servername (for starting Internet Information Services out of process applications).

**Administrator** User account that gives you access and all-encompassing rights and permissions to all areas of Windows 2000 computers. Administrator is a member of the Administrators group. You cannot delete or disable this account, or remove it from the Administrators local group.

**Guest** User account that can be used to enable users to log onto a Windows 2000 computer without having an account set up on the computer. By default, Guest does not have a password assigned, although you can assign one later. As a security feature, the Guest account is disabled by default. By default, Guest is a member of the Guests group.

### Creating a New User Account

To create a new user account, follow these steps:

1. Select Users in the console tree, then choose Action ➢ New User.
2. In the New User dialog box, enter a username, full name, and description. Then enter a password and confirm the password.
3. Make any applicable choices relating to the user's password, such as User Must Change Password at Next Logon, User Cannot Change Password, Password Never Expires, and Account Is Disabled.
4. Click Create to create the account. If you want to create another user account, repeat steps 1 through 4. Otherwise, go to step 5.
5. Click Close.

### Configuring a User Account

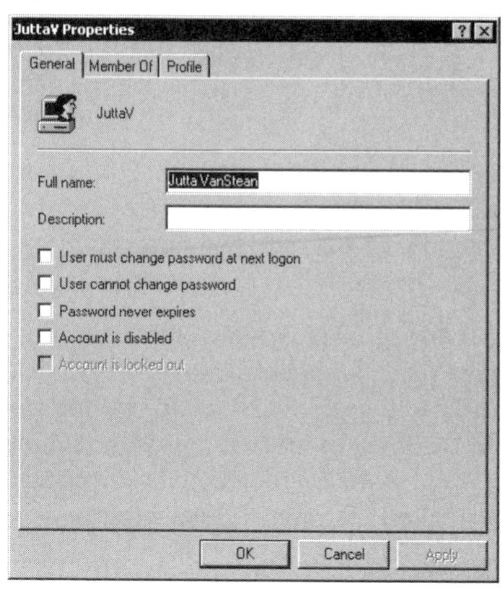

To configure a user account, you use the account's Properties dialog box, which you can access from the Action menu or the pop-up menu. The Properties dialog box has three tabs: General, Member Of, and Profile.

**General** Lets you specify the full name and description for the user account. Also lets you set password options. If a user has exceeded the number of unsuccessful logon attempts specified in the Password policy, Account Is Locked Out will be checked on this tab. Deselect it to unlock the account.

**Member Of** Lets you add a user to a group or groups. Click Add, select one or more groups, click Add, then click OK to add the user to one or more groups. To remove a user from a group, select that user and click Remove.

**Profile** Lets you specify the path to the user's roaming profile (this enables roaming profiles to be used), to a logon script, and to a home folder located either on the local computer or on the network.

## Groups Node

Lets you view and configure currently existing groups, create new groups, and add users and groups to groups. Details about each group account in the Details pane include name and description. Two types of groups exist: local and global.

**Local Groups** For Windows 2000 Professional and Windows 2000 member servers, groups that are assigned rights and permissions to the local computer. You can add global and local groups, as well as local users, to local groups.

**Global Groups** For Windows 2000 Server, groups that are assigned rights and permissions. They can also be added to local groups in their own domain, workstations that participate in the domain, trusted domains, and member servers. Windows 2000 Professional computers can also become members of domain global groups.

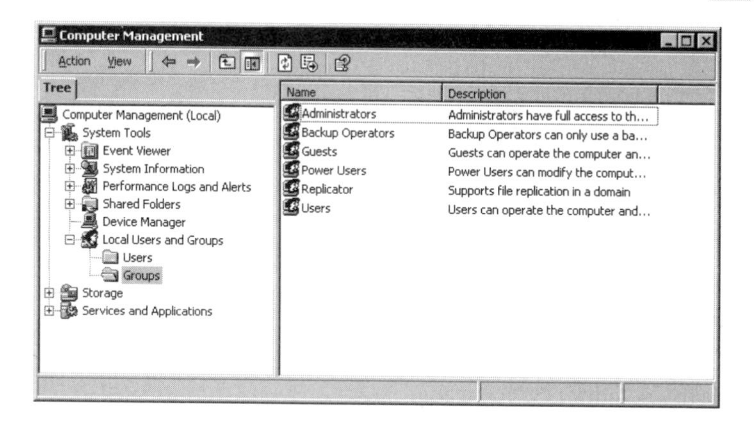


### *Built-in Groups*

Several built-in groups exist. Some examples are Administrators, Backup Operators, Guests, Power Users, and Users. Built-in groups are created during the Windows 2000 installation. These groups have rights and permissions assigned by default to enable members of the groups to perform certain functions, such as perform administrative tasks, back up files or folders, and install programs.

**TIP** Additional built-in groups are available on a Windows 2000 Server computer installed as a domain controller, such as Domain Administrator, Domain Users, and Domain Controllers. You would view and administer these groups with Active Directory Users and Computers.

### *Creating a New Group*

To create a new group, follow these steps:

1. Select Groups in the console tree, then choose Action ➢ New Group.
2. Enter a name and description for the group.
3. Click Add and select one or more global groups or users from the list. Click Add. To see users and groups on other computers or in the Active Directory, make the appropriate

choice from the Look In drop-down list. Click OK when you've finished adding users and groups.

4. Click Create. You can now create another group or click Close to return to Local Users and Groups.

### *Configuring Group Properties*

To configure group properties, right-click a group in the Details pane and choose Properties. It contains the General tab, which displays the name of the group, a description of the group's rights, and the members of the group. To add a new member, click Add, then select a user or global group from the list, click Add, and click OK. To remove a user or group from the list, select the user or group, then click Remove.

**See Also** Microsoft Management Console (MMC), Active Directory Users and Computers

# Lock Computer

Lets you secure the computer by locking it. Press Ctrl+Alt+Del, then click Lock Computer to lock the computer. To unlock the computer, press Ctrl+Alt+Del, then enter the name and password of the user you're logged on as or the administrator name and password to unlock the account. No other user will be able to unlock the computer.

# Logical Drives

Logical Drives A Windows Management Instrumentation (WMI) utility that lets you manage drives (both mapped and local) either on a local or remote computer.

To access Logical Drives, choose Start ➢ Settings ➢ Control Panel, double-click Administrative Tools, then double-click Computer Management. You'll find Logical Drives under Storage.

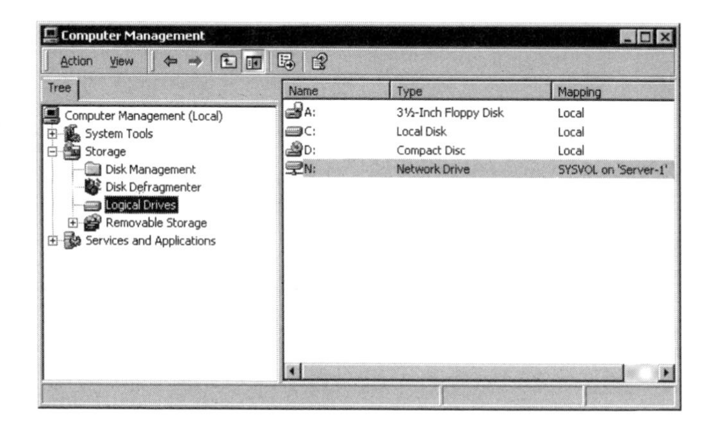


To work with logical drives, right-click a drive in the list and choose Properties from the pop-up menu. You can then perform actions such as changing the drive label and assigning security (on NTFS-formatted drives). You can also view the drive type, the file system with which the drive is formatted, the amount of space used, the amount of free space, and the total capacity of the drive.

**See Also** Microsoft Management Console (MMC), Computer Management, WMI Control

# Log Off

Lets you log the current user off a Windows 2000 computer. Each user in Windows 2000 has his or her own user profile that contains such items as desktop preferences, password, synchronization options, and accessibility options. When a user logs on, this profile is used to ensure that the environment is restored to the way the user previously configured it. Logging off enables you to log off as the current user and then log back on as another user without having to shut down the computer.

You can log off in one of two ways:

- Choose Start ➢ Shutdown, then select Log Off *username* from the drop-down list and click OK.
- Press Ctrl+Alt+Del, then click Log Off. Click Yes to confirm that you want to log off.

**See Also** Log On, Shutdown, System

# Log On

Lets you log onto a Windows 2000 computer. Each user in Windows 2000 has his or her own user profile (either a local profile, or, if you're connected to a network and roaming profiles are configured, a roaming profile) that contains such items as desktop preferences, password, synchronization options, and accessibility options. When a user logs onto Windows 2000, this profile is used to ensure that the environment is restored to the way the user previously configured it. This means that several users can use the same computer at different times while retaining individual desktop and other settings.

When you start Windows 2000 or after logging off as the current user, press Ctrl+Alt+Del and you're prompted to log on as a specific user, either to the local computer, or, if you're connected to a network, to the applicable workgroup or domain. Enter your username, password, and the computer, workgroup, or domain you want to log onto in the respective fields in the Log On to Windows dialog box. If you're connecting from a remote computer via a modem connection, check Log On Using Dial-up Connection. Click OK to log on.

**TIP** You may have to click Options to see all fields available in the Log On to Windows dialog box.

**See Also** Shutdown, System

# Magnifier

Used to enlarge certain areas of the screen so that they are easier to view for users with vision problems. Choose Start ➢ Programs ➢ Accessories ➢ Accessibility ➢Magnifier. Read the message about the limitations of Magnifier. If you don't want this message to appear the next time you start Magnifier, select the Do Not Show This Message Again option. Click OK to open the Magnifier window and the Magnifier dialog box. The Magnifier window appears at the top of the screen by default.

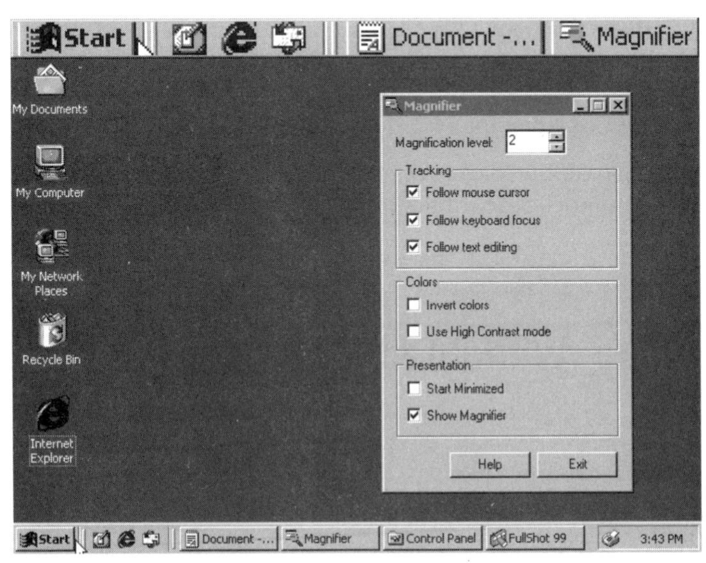


To use the Magnifier, move the mouse pointer anywhere in the desktop, and the Magnifier window displays that area, enlarged. You can change the size of the Magnifier window by dragging its bottom edge downward. Click and drag the Magnifier window to turn it into a floating window. You can also change how the Magnifier is set up in the Magnifier dialog box. When you make changes in this dialog box, you can immediately see how the changes affect the Magnifier window. The following options are available:

**Magnification Level** Lets you adjust the amount of magnification. Range is from 1 (no magnification) to 9.

**Tracking** Follow the Mouse Cursor means that wherever you move the mouse pointer, that area of the screen is enlarged. Follow Keyboard Focus means that areas are magnified as you use keyboard keys to navigate, such as the Tab or arrow keys. Follow Text Editing means that the magnified area follows the insertion point while you are typing information.

**Colors** Invert Colors means that the colors in the magnification window will invert. Use High Contrast Mode means that the color scheme used for Windows will use high-contrast colors, making text easier to read.

**Presentation** Start Minimized means that the Magnifier dialog box will be minimized when the Magnifier starts. Show Magnifier controls whether the Magnifier window appears when the Magnifier dialog box is open.

To turn off the Magnifier, click Exit in the Magnifier dialog box or right-click Magnifier in the taskbar and select Close.

**See Also** Accessibility, Accessibility Options, Display

# Make Available Offline

✔ Make Available Offline

Makes network or shared files or folders available for use when you're not connected to the network.

**WARNING** This menu option is available only if Enable Offline Files is checked on the Offline Files tab of Folder Options (accessible through Control Panel). It's also strongly recommended that you select the Place Shortcut to Offline Files Folder on the Desktop check box for easy access to the Offline Files folder.

To make a file or folder available offline, right-click the item in Windows Explorer and choose Make Available Offline. The first time you do this, you have to follow the Offline Files Wizard as outlined here:

1. Right-click the file or folder in Windows Explorer and choose Make Available Offline. This starts the Offline Files Wizard.

2. In the Welcome dialog box, click Next.
3. If you don't want files to synchronize automatically when you log on and off the computer, uncheck the option Automatically Synchronize The Offline Files When I Log On An Log Off My Computer. Click Next.
4. If you don't want a message to display that reminds you that you're working offline when you're working offline, uncheck Enable Reminders, otherwise leave the option checked. If you want to have a shortcut to the Offline Files folder on your desktop, check the option Create A Shortcut To The Offline Files Folder On My Desktop. Click Finish. The file or folder is synchronized to the Offline Files Folder and you're returned to Windows Explorer.

When you subsequently choose to make files or folders available offline by right-clicking the item and choosing Make Available Offline, the item is automatically synchronized to the Offline Files folder.

**TIP** To undo making a file available offline, access the Make Available Offline menu option and select it. This will remove the check mark on the menu item, and the file won't be available offline any longer.

Files that are made available offline are marked with a smaller icon in the bottom-left portion of the icon so that you can easily identify files that have been made available offline. This smaller icon contains two opposite-facing arrows.

Once you go offline, you'll be able to access the files or folders that you've made available offline as if you were still connected to the network. When offline, you'll see a computer icon in the status area of the taskbar. Click this icon to see your current offline files status. If you have reminders set up, a pop-up message periodically tells you that you're working offline. Use the Folder Options in the Control Panel to further configure Reminders.

To work on a file offline, use Windows Explorer or My Network Places to browse to the file. Open it and make any changes you need. Alternately, access files in the Offline Files folder.

**TIP** When you're browsing offline folders, a message tells you on the left side of Windows Explorer that the folder is offline.

The next time you connect to the network, synchronization occurs automatically (unless you've changed default settings in Synchronization or in the Offline Files Wizard). If you need to synchronize manually, go to the Offline Files folder using the shortcut on the desktop (created through Folder Options or the Offline Files Wizard). If necessary, change the view to Details. For files that have been modified, the Synchronization column displays Local Copy Data Has Been Modified. To synchronize all files, choose Tools ➢ Synchronize, then click Synchronize. To synchronize an individual file, select the file and choose File ➢ Synchronize, or right-click the file and choose Synchronize.

**TIP** You cannot have files you want to synchronize open during the synchronization process. Make sure you close all files before choosing File ➢ Synchronize.

**TIP** If you uncheck Synchronize All Offline Files Before Logging Off on the Offline Files tab of Folder Options (to specify that you don't want to synchronize files when logging off) and also check When I Log Off My Computer on the Logon/Logoff tab in the Synchronization Settings dialog box of Synchronize (to specify that you want to automatically synchronize items when logging off; you can display this dialog box by choosing Start ➢ Programs ➢ Accessories ➢ Synchronize, and then clicking Setup in the Items to Synchronize dialog box), the setting in Items to Synchronize takes precedence and your offline files are synchronized when logging off.

## Offline Files Folder

Offline files are also accessible through the Offline Files folder. You can create a shortcut to this folder by selecting Place Shortcut to Offline Files Folder on the Desktop on the Offline Files tab in Control Panel's Folder Options or by making the appropriate selection in the Offline Files Wizard. Double-click the shortcut and the Offline Files folder opens, displaying all files marked to be available offline. You'll also see information regarding the synchronization status, availability, and the access rights you have to each file. You can also delete items in this folder. If you do, only the offline version of the file is deleted, not the network version.

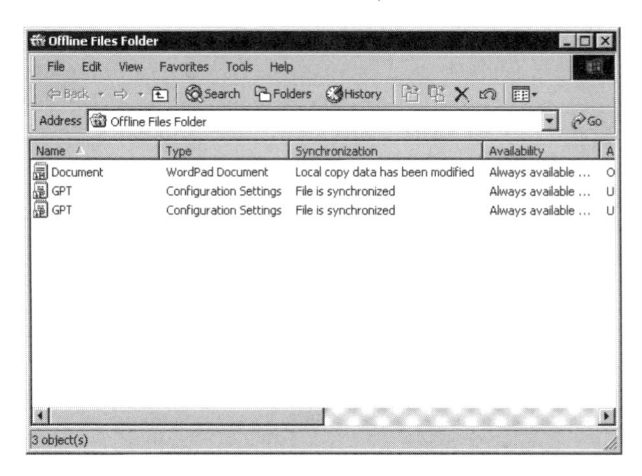

**TIP** If you make changes to a file in the Offline Files folder while you are connected to the network, the file is synchronized automatically with the file on the network.

**See Also** Folder Options, Synchronize

# Make New Connection

**See** Network and Dial-up Connections

# Map Network Drive

Map Network Drive...

If you're connected to a network, you can assign a drive letter to a share on the network (either on another workstation or a server). This is called mapping a drive. Assigning a drive letter lets you easily access specific shares from within Explorer windows or applications—for example, those shares that you need to access frequently.

## Mapping a Network Drive

To map a network drive, perform these steps:

1. Open an Explorer window (by opening Windows Explorer, My Computer, My Network Places, or My Computer).

2. Choose Tools ➢ Map Network Drive to open the Map Network Drive dialog box. Select the drive letter you want to assign from the Drive drop-down list, and enter the UNC path to the folder in the Folder text box. You can also browse to the folder by clicking Browse.

**TIP** Alternatively, you can right-click My Computer or My Network Places and select Map Network Drive.

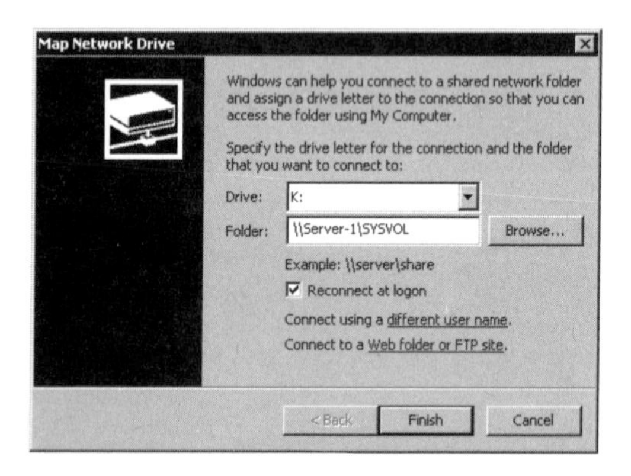


3. If you want this drive mapping to be permanent, select Reconnect at Logon. Otherwise, the drive mapping will be in effect for this Windows 2000 session only. You can also connect as a different user by clicking the link Connect Using a Different User Name and entering the username and password, or you can connect to a Web folder or FTP site by clicking that link and following the prompts in the Add Network Place Wizard.

4. Click Finish to map the drive. The mapped drive is added to My Computer, and you can see it in any Explorer window or in the Open, Save, and Save As windows when working with applications.

## Disconnecting a Mapped Network Drive

After you map a drive, you can disconnect it to free up the drive letter, for example, or if you no longer need the mapping. Follow these steps:

1. In any Explorer window, choose Tools ➢ Disconnect Network Drive to open the Disconnect Network Drive dialog box.

**TIP** Alternatively, you can right-click My Computer or My Network Places and select Disconnect Network Drive.

2. Select the mapped network drive you want to disconnect and click OK.

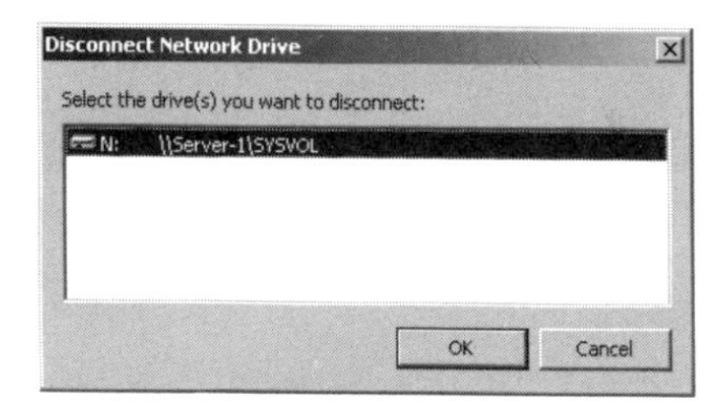


# Maximize and Minimize

Lets you change the size of any Windows 2000 application program window.

When you click the Maximize button, the application window changes to full screen size. The Maximize button then changes to the Restore Down button (represented by two overlapping windows). Click this button to restore the window to its original size.

When you click the Minimize button, Windows minimizes the application window and places it on the taskbar. To bring the application window back to its original size, click the application's icon on the taskbar.

**TIP** An alternative method for resizing an application window is to place the mouse pointer over any edge of the window until the pointer turns into a double-pointing arrow. Then drag to the left or right, or up or down, to change the window size.

**See Also** Taskbar

# Microsoft Management Console (MMC)

Used to create, save, and open administrative tools, which are called MMC consoles. MMC consoles can contain tools, containers, folders, Web pages, and other administrative items, such as snap-ins, snap-in extensions, tasks, wizards, and documentation. You use MMC consoles to administer all aspects of your computer, domain, and Active Directory.

Many MMC consoles and console snap-ins already exist in Windows 2000, including Component Services, Computer Management, Event Viewer, Performance, Active Directory Users and Computers, and Services, to name just a few. You can also create new consoles using MMC.

To start MMC, choose Start ➢ Run, then enter **mmc** to open MMC. Here you can create new and open existing consoles.

## MMC Window

The MMC window consists of a menu, a toolbar, and a main area, called the workspace, in which you can display existing MMC consoles or create new ones.

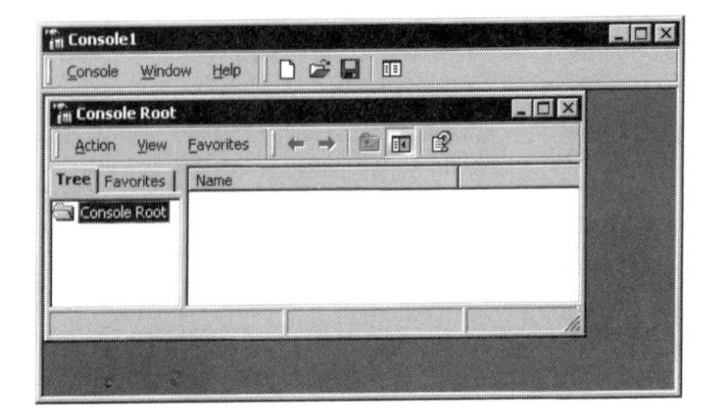

### *MMC Menus*

MMC has three menus—Console, Window, and Help—that you can use to work with MMC consoles.

**Console Menu** The Console menu lets you work with MMC consoles and contains the following options:

**New** Lets you create a new MMC console.

**Open** Lets you open an existing MMC console.

**Save** Lets you save an MMC console you've created or changed.

**Save As** Lets you save an MMC console using a different name than the current name.

**Add/Remove Snap-in** Lets you add snap-ins to (or remove them from) the currently open console.

**Options** Lets you change the name of the current console, change the console's icon, choose a console mode (consoles modes determine the type of access for the console), and configure additional console settings.

**Exit** Closes MMC.

The Console menu also contains a list of the most recently accessed consoles for quick access.

**Window Menu** The Window menu lets you control MMC console windows. It contains these options:

**New Window** Opens another console in a new window.

**Cascade** Cascades open console windows.

**Tile Horizontally** Displays console windows horizontally next to each other.

**Arrange Icons** Arranges icons.

**AUTHOR'S NOTE** Unfortunately, neither myself (the author) nor the technical editor were able to get the Arrange Icons feature to have any visible effect. The feature wouldn't activate for us in beta Release Candidate 2, nor could we activate it once we got the final code (build 2195). We were not able to get a response from Microsoft about this before the book went to print.

At the bottom of the Window menu, a list of all currently open console windows appears. The currently active console window has a check mark next to it. Select a console window from the list to make it the active window and bring it to the front.

**Help Menu** The Help menu contains the following options:

**Help Topics** Opens MMC-related help topics in the Windows 2000 Help system.

**Microsoft on the Web** Contains a submenu that contains links to several Microsoft Web sites where you can obtain snap-ins, product news, and answers to frequently asked questions, as well as send feedback to Microsoft. Also contains a link to Microsoft's home page.

**About Microsoft Management Console** Displays information about MMC, such as version number and licensing information.

### *MMC Toolbar*

The standard MMC toolbar contains buttons to the most commonly used items also available from the MMC menus. They include Create a New Console, Open an Existing Console, Save the Current Console, and New Window.

## MMC Consoles

MMC consoles are used to administer some aspect of your computer or network. They do not perform functions themselves, but rather host the tools that do.

MMC consoles have two panes. The left pane is called the console tree, where snap-ins, extension snap-ins, and other console items appear. The right pane, called the Details pane, contains functions for and information about any item you select in the console tree.

Although all MMC consoles have some menus and toolbar buttons in common, individual menu options and additional buttons may be available depending on the item you've selected in the console tree.

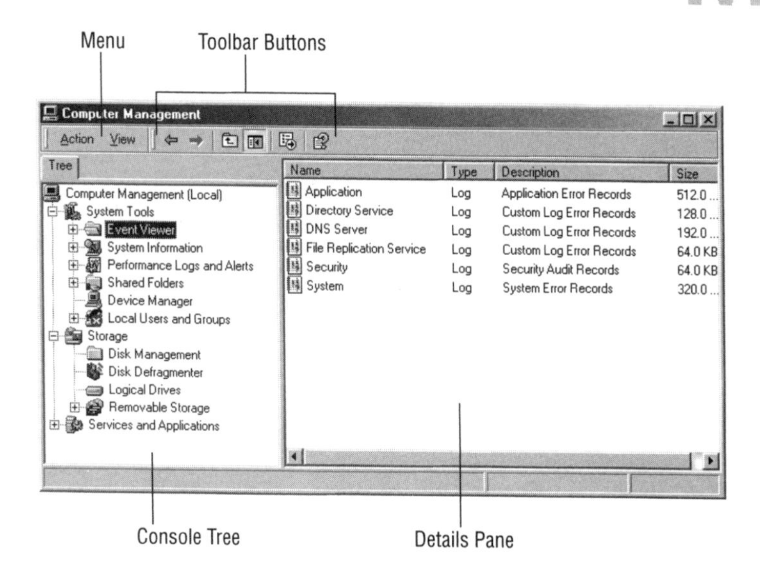


The Details pane in an MMC console can also display taskpad views. You can create taskpad views and add commonly used actions (tasks) to them to make using the console easier, especially for users who are not very familiar with MMC console functions and how to find actions. A taskpad view contains the items normally displayed in the Details pane along with icons for the tasks you added to the taskpad view.

### MMC Console Modes

MMC consoles can be saved and then used in one of four modes:

**Author Mode** Users of the console can perform all MMC functionality, including adding and removing snap-ins and extension snap-ins, and creating new windows, taskpad views, and tasks. Users can also see the entire console tree.

**User Mode—Full Access** Users of the console can create new windows and see the entire console tree. They cannot add or remove snap-ins, taskpad views, and tasks or otherwise change the properties of the console.

**User Mode—Limited Access, Multiple Window** Users of the console can see only the portion of the console tree that was visible when the author of the console saved it. They can open new windows but cannot close existing windows.

**User Mode—Limited Access, Single Window** Users of the console can see only the portion of the console tree that was visible when the author of the console saved it. They cannot create new windows.

To open a console in Author mode that was saved in one of the user modes, use one of the following methods (you must be a member of the Administrators group):

- Choose Start ➢ Run, then enter **mmc** ***pathname*** **/a**, where *pathname* represents the complete path to the console file.
- Right-click the console file in a Browse dialog box and choose Author from the pop-up menu.

### *MMC Console Menus*

MMC console menus include the Action, View, and Favorites menus. The Action and View menus are available in all MMC consoles; the Favorites menu is available only in some consoles.

**Action Menu** The Action menu contains options related to actions you can perform for items that appear in the right pane.

**TIP** If you right-click either an item in the right pane or in a blank area of the right pane, you'll see the same options on the pop-up menu as those that are available on the Action menu with or without an item selected.

The options available in the Action menu will vary greatly depending on the console snap-in or extension snap-in you have selected. Some options, however, are often available on a console's Action menu. They include:

**New Window from Here** Not available if the console is opened with User Mode—Limited Access, Single Window. Opens another window of the same console.

**New Taskpad View** Only available for consoles that are opened in Author mode. Lets you create a new taskpad view.

**Edit Taskpad View** Only available for consoles that are opened in Author mode and after taskpad views have been created. Lets you edit the selected taskpad view.

**Delete Taskpad View** Only available for consoles that are opened in Author mode and after taskpad views have been created. Lets you remove the selected taskpad view.

**All Tasks** Brings up a submenu that contains tasks that can be performed on the selected object.

**Export List** Lets you export the current list of items in the view pane to a text file.

**Refresh** Refreshes the contents of the object currently selected in the console tree.

**Properties** Displays properties of the object currently selected in either pane, including version, location, operating system, folder properties (in case of a folder), and any other applicable properties.

**Help** Opens the Help system to the topic related to the selected item.

**Connect to Another Computer** Lets you access the same type of information currently displayed for the local computer for a remote computer. For example, if you're currently viewing event logs in Event Viewer (Local), you can connect to another computer and display that computer's event logs. To connect to another computer, follow these steps:

1. Select Item (Local) in the console tree.
2. Choose Action ➢ Connect to Another Computer.
3. Select Another Computer and enter the name of the computer in the field or browse for it. Click OK.

**View Menu** The View menu contains options pertaining to how items are displayed in MMC consoles. The options available depend on the item you have selected in the console tree pane; however, you'll often see these choices:

**Choose Columns** Lets you specify which columns to display in the Details pane.

**Customize** Lets you specify which MMC options and snap-in options to display, such as MMC and/or Snap-in menus and toolbars.

Additionally, you'll often see the menu options Large Icons, Small Icons, List, and Detail, which you would use to configure how the Details pane displays items.

**Favorites Menu** The Favorites menu, which is not available in all consoles views, lets you add items from the console tree to your MMC favorites. This allows you to quickly access them via the Favorites menu or the Favorites tab in the console tree pane. Adding and organizing favorites in MMC functions the same way as it does in Internet or Windows Explorer. The options on the Favorites menu also are the same: Add to Favorites and Organize Favorites.

### MMC Console Standard Toolbar

The buttons available on the MMC console standard toolbar depend on the item you have selected in the console tree. All or some of the following buttons are commonly available on the standard MMC console toolbar:

**Back** Goes back to the previously selected item in the console tree.

**Forward** Returns to the item in the console tree that was selected before you clicked the Back button.

**Up One Level** Moves up one level in the console tree.

**Show/Hide Console Tree** Toggles the display of the console tree on and off.

**Export List** Exports the contents of the display pane to a text file.

**Help** Opens the Windows 2000 Help system to the related topic.

**Refresh** Updates the currently selected item.

**Properties** Displays properties for the currently selected item.

## Creating a New MMC Console

You can use MMC to create new MMC consoles. Follow these steps:

1. Choose Console ➢ New or click Create a New Console on the toolbar to open a new MMC console window in MMC.
2. Choose Console ➢ Add/Remove Snap-in to open the Add/Remove Snap-in dialog box.
3. On the Standalone tab, click Add, then select a snap-in in the list and click Add. If a wizard starts, follow the prompts.
4. Select any additional snap-ins you want and click Add. When you've finished, click Close. To add a snap-in below another snap-in, select the snap-in from the Snap-ins Added To drop-down list in the Add/Remove Snap-in dialog box, then click Add. If you want to remove a snap-in you've added, select it in the list and click Remove.

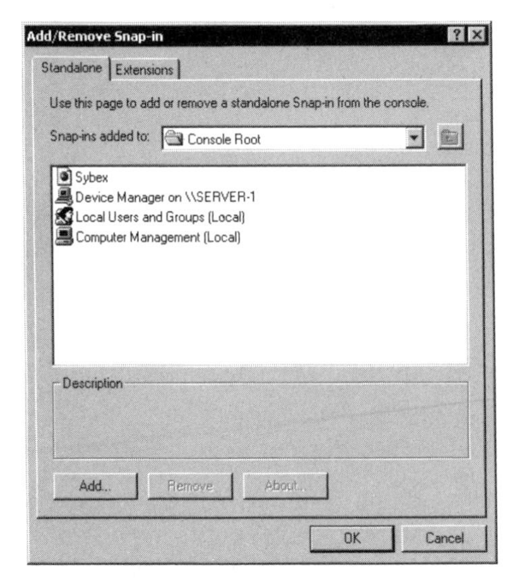


5. To configure which extension snap-ins to enable (if any are available), select a snap-in in the list, then select the Extensions tab.

6. If extension snap-ins are available, uncheck Add All Extensions, then select and deselect extension snap-ins to specify which extensions you want to enable. Click OK to return to the Add/Remove Snap-in dialog box.

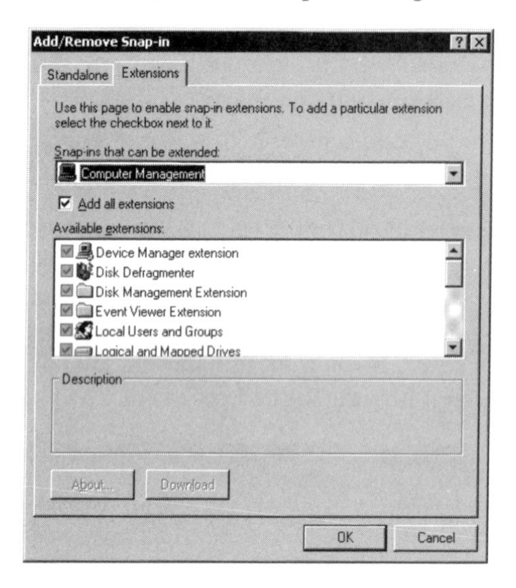


7. Click OK to return to the console window.

8. Choose Console ➢ Options to open the Options dialog box.

9. On the Console tab, enter a name for the console. If you want to change the console's icon, click Change Icon.

10. In the Console Mode drop-down list, select the console mode you want to use for this console.

11. If you selected one of the three user modes, specify whether you want to enable context (pop-up) menus on taskpads, save changes that are made to the console, or allow the user to customize views. Click OK to save your changes.

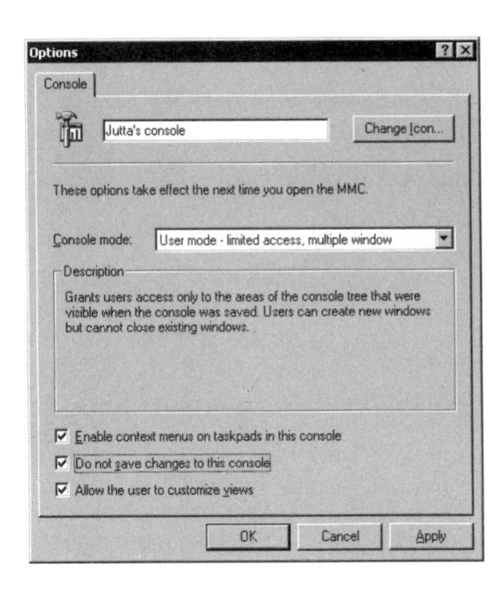


12. Choose Console ➢ Save As, enter a name for the console, browse to the folder where you want to save the console, and click Save. Console files are saved as files with an .MSC extension and by default are saved in the logged-on user's Administrative Tools folder. If you use this default, you'll be able to access newly created MMC consoles by choosing Start ➢ Settings ➢ Control Panel, then double-clicking Administrative Tools and double-clicking the new console.

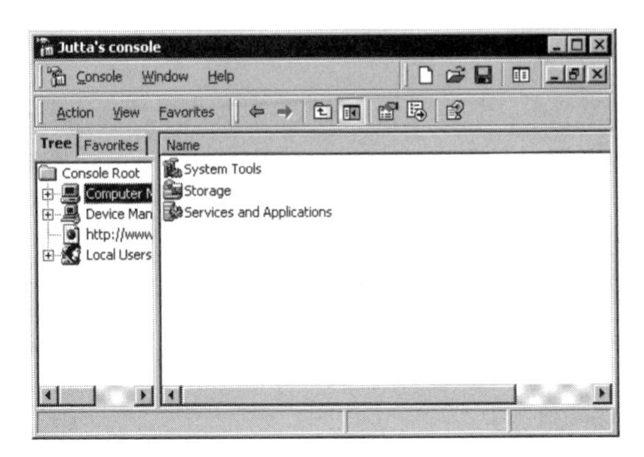

## Creating Taskpad Views and Tasks

To make working with an MMC console easier for users, you can create taskpad views and add commonly used tasks to the view.

To create a taskpad, perform these steps:

1. Open an MMC console in Author mode.

**TIP** See the subheading MMC Console Modes in this entry to see how to open a console in author mode.

2. Select a snap-in or extension snap-in in the console tree.
3. Choose Action ➢ New Taskpad View to open the New Taskpad View Wizard and click Next.
4. Choose how you want the Details pane and task descriptions to appear (vertical list, horizontal list, or no list, and text or infotip). If you choose a list display, also specify the list size (large, medium, or small). Click Next.
5. Specify whether you want the taskpad view to apply only to the currently selected console tree item or to all console tree items of this type. Click Next.
6. Enter a name and description for the taskpad view. Click Next.
7. If you want to add a new task to the taskpad view, leave Start New Task Wizard checked. Otherwise, deselect it. Click Finish.
8. If you didn't check the Start New Task Wizard option, Windows returns you to the console where the new taskpad view appears. Otherwise, the New Task Wizard starts, and you can continue with step 9.
9. Click Next.
10. Select the type of command you want to add to the taskpad view, such as Menu Command, Shell Command, or Navigation. Click Next.

11. The next item depends on the choice you made in step 10. Follow the screen and enter information as necessary. Click Next.

12. Enter a name and description for the task and click Next.

13. Select an icon that will represent the task from the list of icons. Click Next.

14. If you want to add another task, select Run This Wizard Again, then click Finish. Otherwise, just click Finish.

The new taskpad view and new task(s) appear in the Details pane.

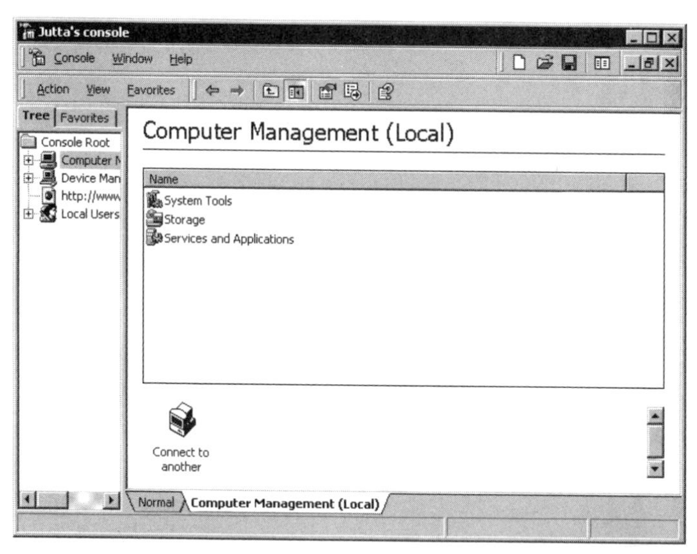


**See Also** Explorer, Internet Explorer

# Microsoft Script Debugger

Microsoft Script Debugger Installed by default on Windows 2000 Server computers. Lets you debug (troubleshoot) and test both client and server scripts written with ActiveX-enabled scripting languages—for example, Jscript and VBScript. Additionally, you can use Microsoft Script

Debugger to debug ActiveX components, Java applets, and JavaBeans. Client scripts, which are found in HTML pages, are executed when an HTML page loads or when the user clicks a button that executes a script. Server scripts are embedded in Active Server Page (ASP) files; Internet Information Service (IIS) executes server scripts when an ASP page is requested, prior to sending page content to the browser.

Use Microsoft Script Debugger to view source code, view and configure the values of properties and variables as well as script flow, and specify the pace at which a script executes.

To access the Microsoft Script Debugger, choose Start ➢ Programs ➢ Accessories ➢ Microsoft Script Debugger ➢ Microsoft Script Debugger.

## Microsoft Script Debugger Window

The Microsoft Script Debugger window consists of menus, a toolbar, a main viewing area, and a taskbar.

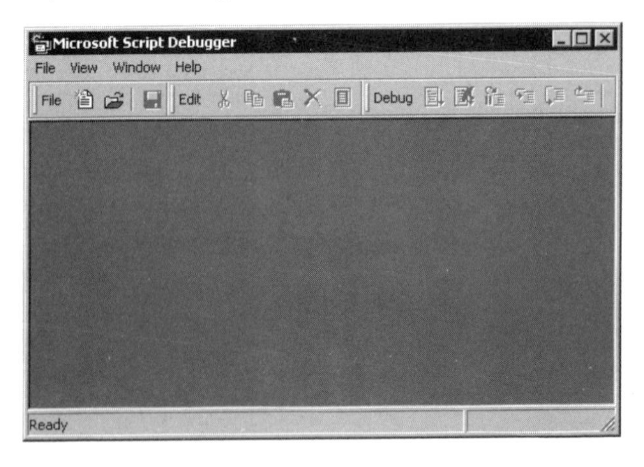


### *Menus*

The menus available in Microsoft Script Debugger are as follows:

**File** Contains options for creating a new script, opening an existing script, and closing or saving scripts.

**Edit** Contains standard document editing options, such as copy and paste. Available only when a script is open.

**View** Contains options for toggling the display of the toolbar and status bar, displaying a list of running documents that can be debugged, displaying the current calling stack, opening the command input/output window, and accessing program options (to enable/disable Java debugging).

**Debug** Contains options for running (executing) the current script (document), breaking execution at the next statement, stopping debugging, stepping into or over the next statement, stepping out of the function that is currently executing, inserting or removing a breakpoint at the current line, and clearing all breakpoints. Available only when a script is open.

**Window** Contains options for manipulating open windows, such as closing one or all windows, moving to the next or previous undocked window, and physically arranging windows (cascade, tile, etc.).

**Help** Contains options for accessing Microsoft Script Debugger help topics in the Windows 2000 Help system, accessing various Microsoft Web pages on the Internet, and accessing version and copyright information.

### Toolbar

The Toolbar is broken into three sections—File, Edit, and Debug—and contains buttons that let you quickly access commonly used items also available through the menus. Buttons visible by default in the File section include New, Open, and Save; buttons visible by default in the Edit section include Cut, Copy, Paste, Clear, and Select All; and buttons visible by default in the Debug section include Run, Stop Debugging, Break at Next Statement, Step Into, Step Over, and Step Out. You can resize each toolbar to display additional available buttons, such as Save All in the File section, Find in the Edit section, and Toggle Breakpoint, Clear All Breakpoints, Running Documents, Call Stack, and Command Window. To resize a toolbar, grab the line to the left of the section name and drag left or right. You can also drag down to place the section below the current toolbar area

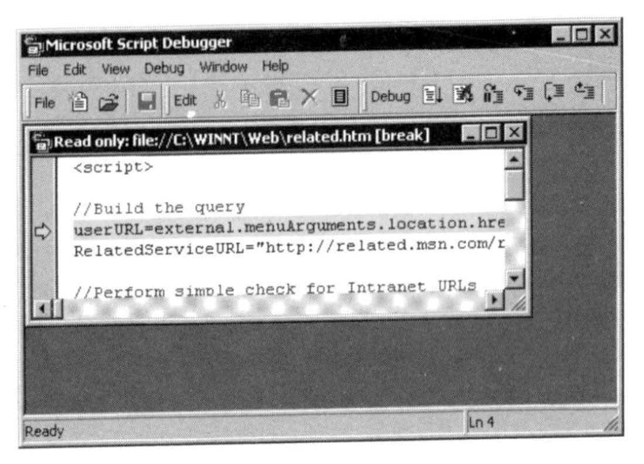


# Mouse

Lets you control the settings of your mouse, such as mouse button and pointer usage, pointer speed, and hardware configuration settings.

Choose Start ➢ Settings ➢ Control Panel, then double-click Mouse to open the Mouse Properties dialog box, which contains four tabs: Buttons, Pointers, Motion, and Hardware.

## Buttons

Use this tab to control how your mouse buttons function. Three configuration areas are available:

**Button Configuration** You can configure the mouse for left-handed or right-handed use. Click the appropriate radio button to make your choice. If you select Right-handed, the left button lets you select and perform normal drags, and the right button lets you open up context menus and perform special drags.

**Files and Folders** You can configure to open items (for example, documents or Control Panel icons) by either single-clicking or double-clicking them. If you choose Single-click to Open an Item, you can select an item by placing the pointer over it. If you choose Double-click to Open an Item, you can select an item by single-clicking it.

**Double-click Speed** You can set the speed at which a double-click is recognized. Move the slider left or right to adjust the speed between slow and fast. You can test your setting in the Test area. Double-click the pink box; if you click fast enough, the box opens and a jack-in-the-box pops out. If the box doesn't open, you may want to adjust the double-click speed to a lower setting.

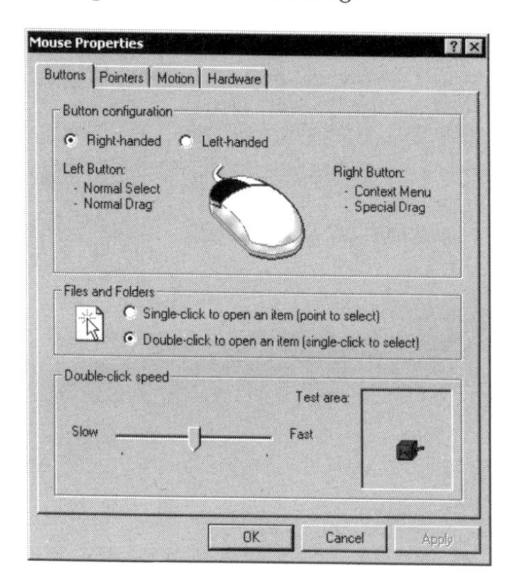


## Pointers

Use this tab to set up a scheme for the pointer's appearance during various actions, such as when you select a help, text, or normal item; when the pointer is unavailable; and when you want to resize an item.

Windows 2000 comes with several predefined pointer schemes. You can select a scheme from the drop-down list in the Scheme area of the Pointers tab. When you select a scheme, you'll see the default pointer icons for that scheme in the Customize list. You can use the scheme as is by clicking OK or Apply, or you can create a custom scheme by selecting an item in the list, clicking Browse, and selecting a different pointer icon from the list in the Cursors directory. Or you can point to any directory that contains a pointer icon you want to use. When you return to the Pointers tab, click Save As to save your custom scheme.

To delete a scheme, select it in the list and click Delete.

**TIP** Cursor files use the extensions .ANI and .CUR.

Also, when you select an item in the list, you'll see an example of how the pointer looks or will behave (for animated pointers) in the upper-right corner of the tab.

To return to the Windows 2000 default pointer settings, click the Use Default button (only available if a scheme has been selected).

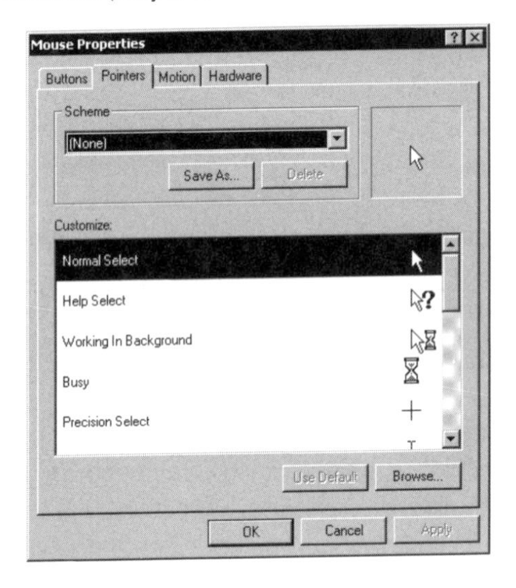


## Motion

Use this tab to control how your pointer moves, including its speed, acceleration, and placement in dialog boxes. The tab consists of three areas: Speed, Acceleration, and Snap to Default.

**Speed** Lets you specify your pointer's speed when you're moving the pointer. Move the slider left or right to adjust the pointer to a setting from between slow and fast.

**Acceleration** Lets you specify your pointer's acceleration when you increase the speed with which you're moving the pointer. The higher you set the Acceleration setting, the faster you can move across your screen with the smallest amount of mouse movement.

**TIP** As you make changes to these settings, they become immediately effective. Try different combinations of pointer speed and acceleration to find a pointer movement that works for you.

**Snap to Default** Every dialog box has what is considered a default button, over which the pointer will move automatically when a dialog box opens if you select Move Pointer to the Default Button in Dialog Boxes.

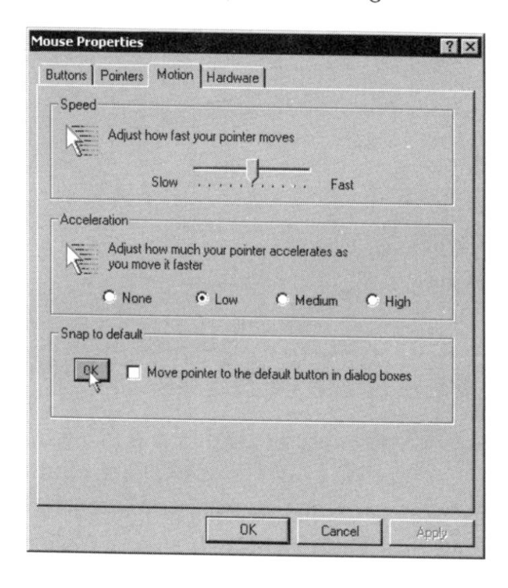


## Hardware

Use this tab to view and change the hardware configuration and properties of your mouse. You'll find the name and type of your mouse in the Devices list, and device properties below the list.

You can click Troubleshoot to start the Windows 2000 Hardware Troubleshooter for mouse problems, and you can click Properties to configure the hardware properties of your mouse. These settings will vary depending on your hardware. You will, however, find the three tabs that are present for most hardware devices installed on the system (General, Driver, Resources), where you can enable or disable the device, view information about the device, make changes to the driver, and view and configure hardware resources the device is using.

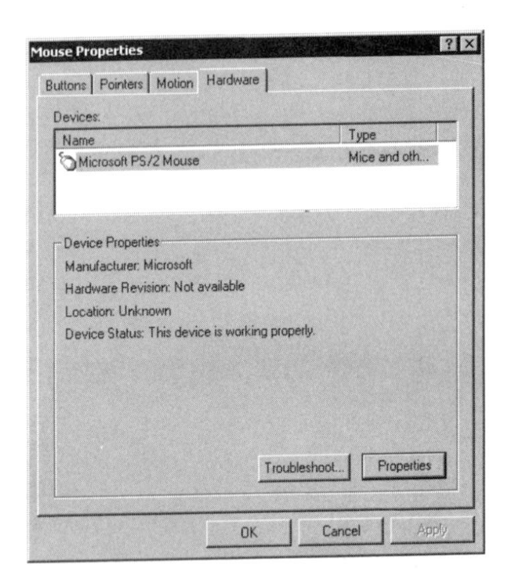


**See Also** System

# Move Files and Folders

Windows 2000 lets you move files and folders in a variety of ways. You can use the Edit menu in Windows Explorer windows, drag and drop, or use the pop-up menu that appears when you right-click a file or folder. When you move a file or folder, Windows removes it from the original location and places it in the new location.

## Using the Edit Menu

To move files or folders using the Edit menu, perform these steps:

1. In any Explorer window, select a file or folder you want to move.
2. Choose Edit ➢ Cut.
3. Select the destination folder.
4. Choose Edit ➢ Paste.

## Using the Pop-up Menu

You can right-click files and folders to bring up the pop-up menu, which lets you perform various functions, including cutting and pasting. To move files or folders using the pop-up menu, perform these steps:

1. In any Explorer window, right-click a file or folder you want to move and select Cut.
2. Right-click the destination folder and select Paste.

### Using Drag-and-Drop

To move files or folders using drag-and-drop, you must first make sure that both the source and destination folders are visible in the Folders view. Open the source folder, and then drag the file or folder from the source folder to the destination folder while holding down the left mouse button. When the cursor is over the destination folder (the folder is selected), release the mouse button. Windows will move the file or folder to the destination folder. If you want to use this procedure to move a file or folder, the source and destination folders must reside on the same drive. If the destination folder is on a different drive, Windows will copy the file or folder, not move it.

To move a file or folder to a different drive using drag-and-drop, you must use the right mouse button to drag the item. When you release the right mouse button, a pop-up menu appears, and you can choose to move or copy the item, or create a shortcut.

**TIP** You can also move a file or folder by selecting the file or folder, pressing Ctrl+X (cut), selecting the destination folder, and then pressing Ctrl+V (paste).

**See Also** Explorer, Copy Files and Folders

## My Computer

Lets you view and navigate the contents of your computer, such as drives, folders, and files. By default, Windows places a shortcut to the My Computer folder on the desktop. To open My Computer, double-click the My Computer shortcut or right-click it and select Open.

**TIP** You can also access My Computer by selecting it from the Address drop-down list of any Explorer window.

The My Computer folder is part of the Windows hierarchical structure and as such opens in an Explorer window. By default, an Explorer Bar view is not selected, so you'll see the name My Computer in the left portion of the window and the top-level contents of your computer in the right portion of the window (using large icons). These contents include physical drives, mapped network drives (logical drives), and the Control Panel folder. You can change views in this window the same way you can in any Explorer window.

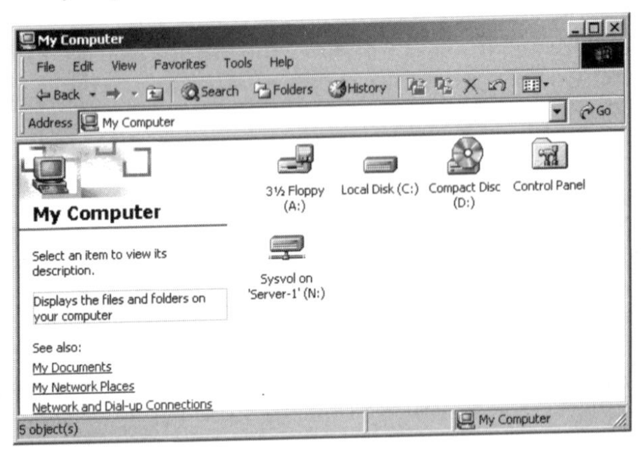


To see the contents of a drive, network share, or folder in My Computer, double-click the item. The right pane changes to display the contents of the item you double-clicked, and the left pane displays information about the item. Alternatively, you can choose an item from the Address drop-down list.

You can use the My Computer desktop shortcut to quickly access System properties. To do so, right-click the My Computer icon on the desktop and select Properties. This opens the System Properties dialog box. To quickly open Computer Management, right-click My Computer and choose Manage.

**See Also** Explorer, System, Computer Management

# My Documents

Folder that, by default, Windows 2000 uses to store documents that you save in such applications as WordPad and Paint. Lets you organize and quickly access your documents. A shortcut to My Documents appears on the desktop by default. Each user of the computer has a unique My Documents folder. To change the location of the My Documents folder, right-click the My Documents shortcut on the desktop and choose Properties. Then, on the Target tab, enter a new path in the Target text box and then click OK. Alternatively, you can click Move and then browse to the new target folder.

To open My Documents, double-click the My Documents shortcut on the desktop, or navigate to it using the Address bar in any Explorer window. By default the My Documents folder contains the folder My Pictures, which stores documents created with Paint. Additional folders might be created automatically in the My Documents folder as you work with Windows 2000. One example is the Fax folder, which is created when you create and then save personal fax cover pages using default save options.

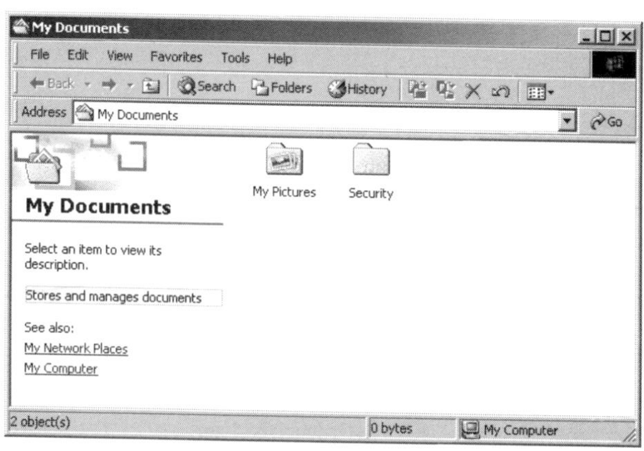


The My Documents folder is part of the Windows hierarchical structure and as such opens in an Explorer window. By default, an Explorer Bar view is not selected. You'll see the name My Documents in the left portion of the window, as well as links to My

Network Places and My Computer. The top-level contents of the My Documents folder appear in the right portion of the window (using large icons).

**See Also** Explorer, My Pictures, Fax

# My Faxes

My Faxes

Folder that stores sent and received faxes as well as cover pages included with Microsoft Fax. Choose Start ➢ Programs ➢ Accessories ➢ Communications ➢ Fax ➢ My Faxes to open the My Faxes folder. The My Faxes folder contains three folders: Common Coverpages, Received Faxes, and Sent Faxes.

**TIP** The default path to the My Faxes folder is `C:\Documents and Settings\All Users (WINNT)\Docments\My Faxes`. You can change this path on the General tab in the Fax Service on Local Computer property sheet, which you access through Fax Service Management.

**TIP** Cover pages you create yourself are by default stored in `C:\Documents and Settings\your_user_name\My Documents\Fax\Personal coverpages`.

In the right pane of the Received Faxes or Sent Faxes folder, with the Details view selected, you'll see information about each fax, such as the name, size, and type of the document and the modified date. You can customize columns to include other items, such as the type of the transmitting device, the name of the receiving device, Caller ID information (if available), routing information (if available), the name of the sender, the name of the recipient, the fax number, the transmission time, and soon. To do so, choose View ➢ Choose Columns, then check the columns you want to display. Use the Move Up and Move Down buttons to change the order of columns. Click OK to save your changes.

If you right-click any column header, you can choose to display or hide any of these information categories, with the exception of Name. Double-click any fax document to view it with Imaging for Windows Preview.

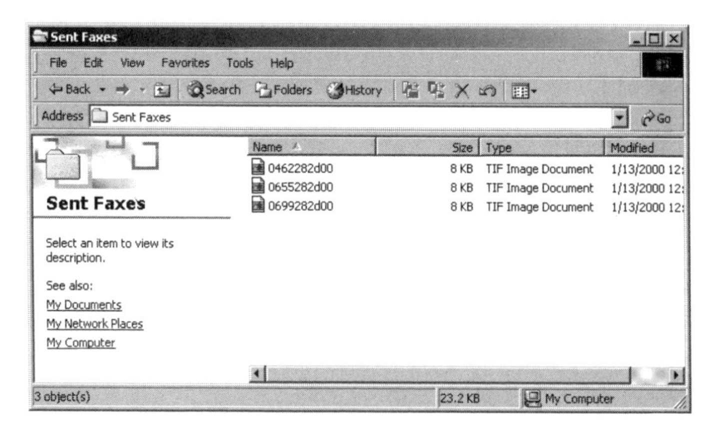

**TIP** Fax documents are saved as TIF (Tagged Image File Format) files.

To view a system-created cover page, in the Common Coverpages folder, double-click a cover page, and it will open in the Fax Cover Page Editor.

**See Also** Fax, Fax Queue, Fax Service Management

# My Network Places

Lets you view and navigate network resources, such as network shares and other computers. By default, a shortcut to the My Network Places folder appears on the desktop. To open My Network Places, double-click the shortcut, or right-click it and select Open.

**TIP** You can also access My Network Places by selecting it from the Address drop-down list of any Explorer window.

The My Network Places folder is part of the Windows 2000 hierarchical structure and as such opens in an Explorer window (without an Explorer Bar view selected). You'll see the My Network Places name in the left pane (and several related links) and the top-level contents in the right pane. Top-level contents include the Entire Network icon. Double-click this icon to navigate the network hierarchy, including domains, and computers belonging to the domains, all the way down to the file level.

In the My Network Places folder, you'll also see the Add Network Place icon, which you can double-click to add shortcuts to network, Web, and FTP servers using the Add Network Place Wizard.

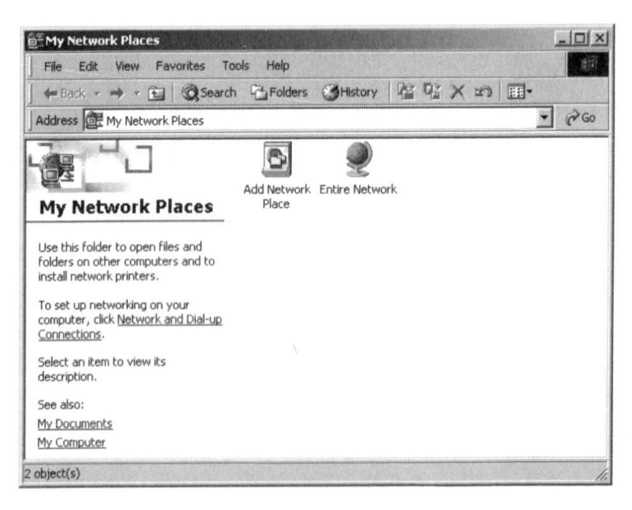

**TIP** You can use the My Network Places shortcut to quickly access Network and Dial-up Connections. To do this, right-click the My Network Places icon on the desktop, then select Properties. This opens the Network and Dial-up Connections folder.

## Navigating My Network Places

My Network Places lets you navigate network resources using the Entire Network icon.

If you double-click Entire Network, you'll see links that let you search for printers, computers, people, and files and folders, and a link that lets you view the contents of the entire network. This can include Microsoft Windows networks, Novell NetWare networks, and the Active Directory (if it has been installed). Double-click the item you want to navigate to access down-level information, such as domains, computers and shares, and Active Directory components, including group, user, and computer accounts and domain controllers.

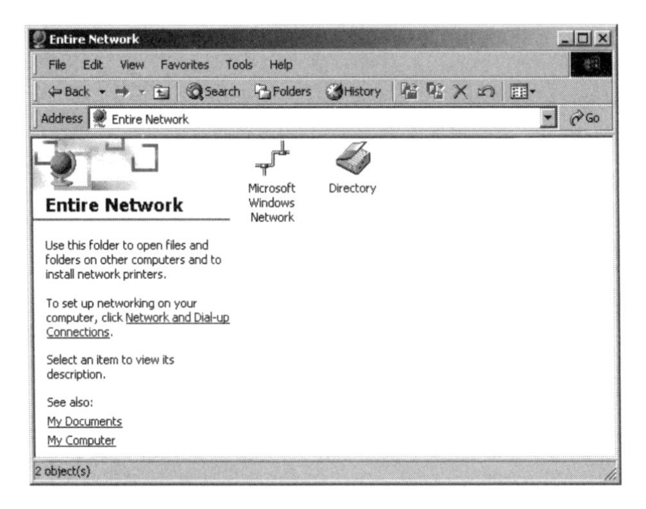


## Add Network Place

Lets you add shortcuts to network shares and servers, Web folders, and FTP sites using the Add Network Place Wizard. To open the Wizard, double-click Add Network Place. Then perform these steps:

1. In the text box, type the location of the network place you want to add (use UNC paths for network servers). You can use the Browse button if you wish. Click Next.

2. Enter the necessary information and click OK until you reach the Completing the Add Network Place Wizard screen. The type of information you'll have to provide depends on the type of network place you specified (network server, Web page, or FTP server).
3. Enter a name for the network place and click Finish. The new network place is added to the My Network Places folder.

**See Also** Explorer, Network and Dial-up Connections

# My Pictures

My Pictures

Folder under the My Documents folder that is used as the default folder for storing image files. For example, if you're creating an image with a program such as Paint, the default location for storing the file is My Pictures. Using the My Pictures folder to store image files means that you can easily find your image files later in this centralized location.

## Previews in Explorer

If you don't have an Explorer Bar view selected, you can perform some basic functions in the left pane of the Explorer window relating to an image you select in the right pane. The left pane gives you information about the file, such as name, modify date, size, and soon, and also shows you a preview of the image contained in a file. In the Preview area, you can perform such functions as zooming in and out or changing the size of the picture to actual size or to best fit the preview area. You can also view a full-screen preview of the image or print the image by clicking the appropriate button. If you switch to Full Screen view, you can switch back to Explorer by pressing Alt+Tab.

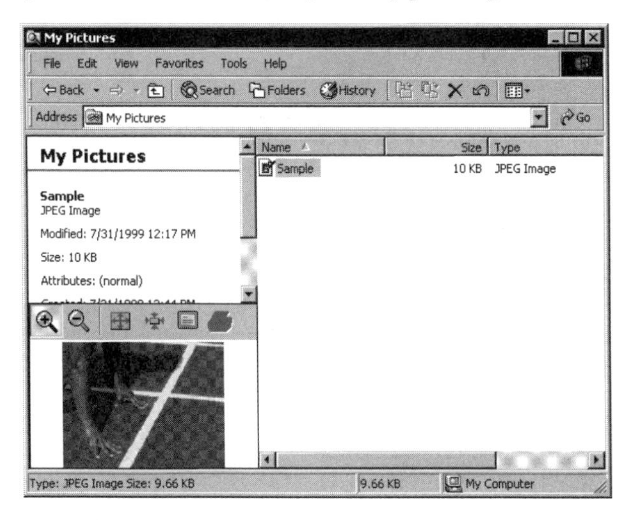


**See Also** My Documents, Explorer

# Naming a Disk

You can add a label (name) to a floppy or hard drive. To name a disk, perform the following steps:

1. Right-click the disk in an Explorer window and select Properties.
2. In the Label text box, enter a name for the disk.
3. Click OK to save your changes.

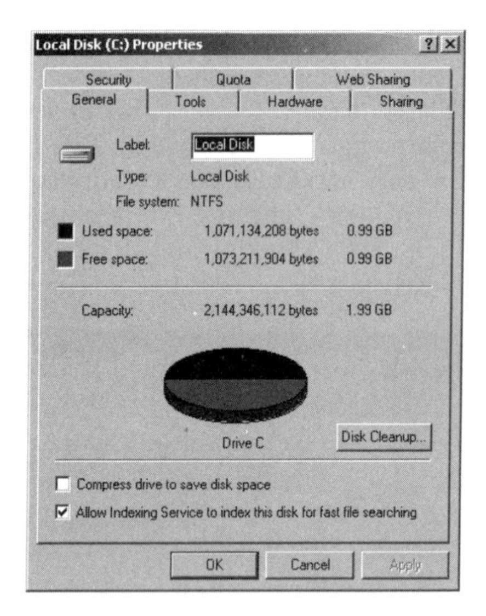


## Narrator

Aids users with vision impairments by "narrating" (reading aloud) on-screen text, menus, buttons, and dialog boxes. A sound card and speakers, or some other output device must be installed. Choose Start ➢ Programs ➢ Accessories ➢ Accessibility ➢ Narrator to open Narrator. You'll have to click OK to acknowledge a message dialog box explaining that Narrator has limited functionality. You can specify that you don't want Windows to display this dialog box the next time you start Narrator.

Four choices are available in the Narrator dialog box:

- Announce Events on Screen
- Read Typed Characters
- Move Mouse Pointer to the Active Item
- Start Narrator Minimized

Place a check mark in the check box next to the option you want to activate.

Three buttons are available:

**Help** Opens the Windows Help system to the Narrator entry.

**Voice** Lets you change voice settings, including speed, volume, and pitch, for each installed voice.

**Exit** Closes Narrator.

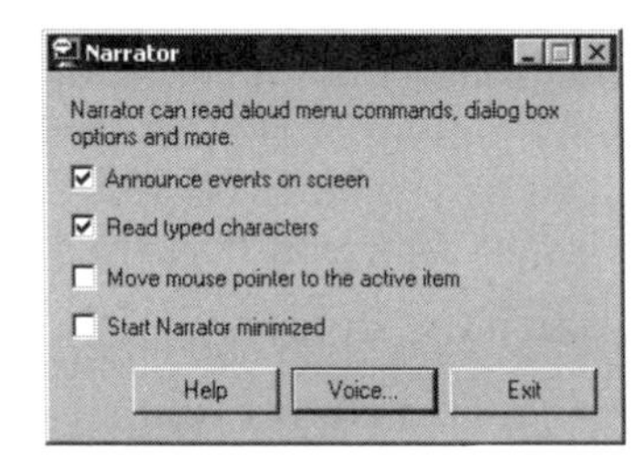


**See Also** Accessibility, Accessibility Options

# Net

Net commands enable you to perform networking-related functions from the command prompt. Examples of this command include net print (to display print jobs and shared queues) or net group (to display all groups in the security database). To see a complete list of net commands available, at the command prompt enter **net help** or **net /?**. To see information about the net help syntax, enter **net help syntax**. To see what services you can start using the net command, enter **net help services**. To view more detailed help information about a specific net command, enter **net help *command name***—for example, **net help group**.

If the command you're executing will prompt you to enter either yes or no at certain times, you can use the /yes and /no switches at the end of the command to automatically answer yes or no to those prompts.

**See Also** Command Prompt

# NetMeeting

NetMeeting Lets you communicate with other people over the Internet using voice and video. This feature enables you to see images of and talk to people during meetings you conduct over the Internet. NetMeeting also enables you to engage in real-time chats, work together in shared applications, send files, and create drawings together on a shared Whiteboard.

The first time you run NetMeeting, a wizard will guide you through the process of configuring NetMeeting and tuning your audio settings. Subsequently, you will be brought directly to Microsoft NetMeeting. To be able to configure NetMeeting correctly, you'll have to have your speakers or headphones, your microphone, and a video camera installed in the computer.

To configure NetMeeting for first-time use, follow these steps:

1. Choose Start ➢ Programs ➢ Accessories ➢ Communications ➢ NetMeeting to start the Microsoft NetMeeting Wizard. Read the introduction and click Next.

2. Enter personal information about yourself that you want to use with NetMeeting. The first name, last name, and e-mail address fields are required. When you've finished, click Next.

3. To be able to meet with people using NetMeeting, you have to log onto a directory server. Once you're logged on, your name will appear in the directory and other people can then call you. Leave the Log On to a Directory Server when NetMeeting Starts check box selected, and choose a directory server from the list of available directory servers. Alternatively, enter the name of the directory server you want to use. Other users with whom you want to communicate will have to log onto the same directory server.

   If you don't want to have your name displayed, select Do Not List My Name in the Directory. When you've finished, click Next.

**TIP** The directory servers you log onto are called Internet Locator Servers, or ILS servers. Use your browser and favorite search engine to find available ILS servers.

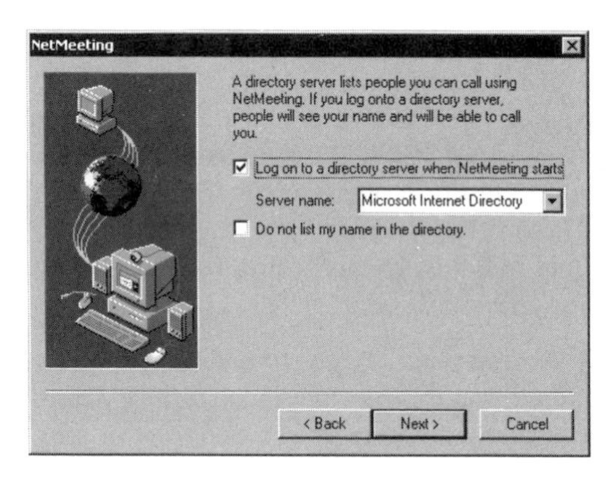


4. Specify the speed/type of connection you use to connect to the Internet. Click Next.
5. Specify whether you want to place a shortcut to NetMeeting on the desktop and/or on the Quick Launch bar. Click Next.
6. The Audio Tuning Wizard starts, which you use to configure your audio settings for NetMeeting. If you have any programs open that play sound, close them and then click Next.
7. Click the Test button to test the volume of your speakers or headphone. A sound plays, and you can use the slider to adjust the volume. When you've finished, click Stop, then click Next.

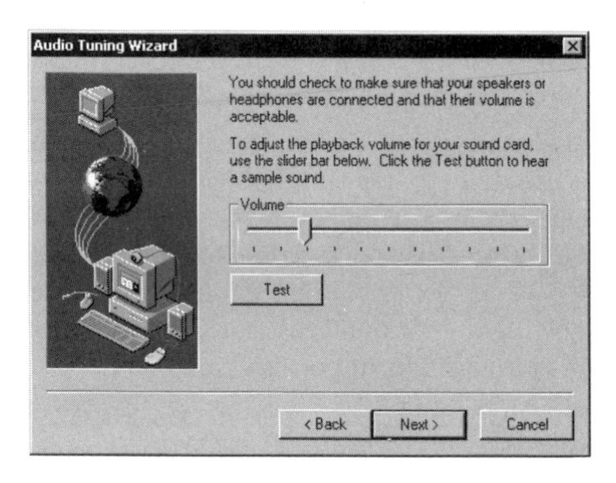

8. Speak into your microphone. You can use the text provided in the dialog box, or you can choose other text. While you are speaking, a colored line indicates the recording volume. If the line is not visible, turn up the volume. If the line is green, the recording volume is about right. If the line changes to yellow or red, lower the recording volume. Use the slider to adjust the recording volume. When you've finished, click Next.

9. Read the message advising you that your audio settings have been tuned. You can run the Audio Tuning Wizard again at a later time should other people using NetMeeting have difficulty hearing or if you're having trouble hearing others. Click Finish to start Microsoft NetMeeting. NetMeeting automatically tries to log onto the directory server you specified in step 2, and will be successful only if you currently have a connection to the Internet established.

**WARNING** If you're not connected to the Internet, a warning message appears telling you that the directory server can't be found. Connect to the Internet, then choose Call ➢ Log On to *directory server name* to log onto the directory server.

**TIP** To run the Audio Tuning Wizard again, choose Tools ➢ Audio Tuning Wizard in NetMeeting.

## NetMeeting Window

After you configure NetMeeting and click Finish, or when you choose NetMeeting from the Communications program group menu any time after configuring NetMeeting, Microsoft NetMeeting opens and by default automatically logs you onto either the default directory server or the directory server you specified under Tools ➢ Options. Once you are logged on, by default all other NetMeeting users around the world can see the personal information you specified and place a call to you.

**TIP** You must be connected to the Internet to be able to log onto a directory server.

The Microsoft NetMeeting window consists of several different areas, including the NetMeeting menus; several NetMeeting buttons; the video area, which displays video images of other users or of yourself; the data area, which displays the names of participants in a call or meeting; and the status bar.

## NetMeeting Menus

Four NetMeeting menus are available to work with and configure NetMeeting: Call, View, Tools, and Help.

### *Call Menu*

The Call menu has the following options:

**New Call** Opens the Place a Call dialog box. You can enter the address of the user you want to call (directory username, e-mail address, computer name, telephone number, or IP address), select how you want the user to be located (using the network, a directory, or automatic), and click Call to place the call. You can also choose to require data security for the call.

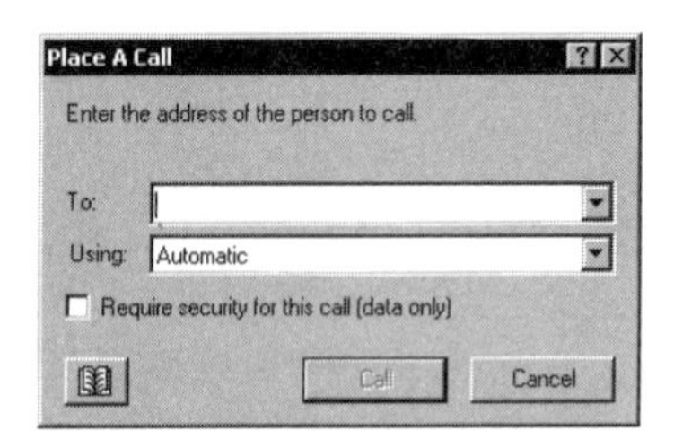

**TIP** Alternatively, you can enter the user's address in the Address bar in the NetMeeting window (to the left of the New Call button) and then click the New Call button.

If you don't know the user's address and want to search the directory you're currently logged onto or other available directories, the Speed Dial list, the history list, or the Windows Address book, click the directory button in the bottom-left corner of the Place a Call dialog box. In the Find Someone dialog box, select a directory from the drop-down list, then select a name from the list and click Call.

When you call another user, he or she receives a notification message that you are calling. The user can either accept or ignore the incoming call. To establish the call, the user must click Accept.

After a call is established, you'll see the names of the participants in the data area of the NetMeeting window.

**Host Meeting** When you host a meeting, others can join. Tell the other participants when the meeting will take place, then at the specified time, choose this menu option to start hosting the meeting. You can also configure meeting options, such as establishing a meeting password, specifying who can place incoming and outgoing calls during the meeting, and specifying who can start meeting tools, such as sharing or chat.

Others can then call you and automatically join the meeting. Once a meeting is started, it is active until you hang up.

**Meeting Properties** Displays meeting properties, such as the name of the meeting, whether you can place incoming and outgoing calls, and whether you can start Sharing, Whiteboard, Chat, and File Transfer.

**Log On to *directory server name*** Logs you onto the directory server name you specified on the General tab of the Options dialog box (which you access by selecting Tools ➢ Options). You must have an Internet connection established in order to log onto a directory server. Once you're logged on, this option changes to Log Off from *directory server name*. You can then use this option to log off from the server.

**Directory** Opens the Find Someone dialog box. Here you can select the directory where you want to search for a user, type a name in the Type Name text box, or select a user from the list of users.

**Do Not Disturb** When you activate this option, NetMeeting can't notify you of calls by other users. You have to disable Do Not Disturb to start receiving calls again. When it's activated, a check mark appears next to this menu option. To disable Do Not Disturb, select it again from the Calls menu.

**TIP** A person who tries to call you when you have Do Not Disturb active will have the option to send you e-mail instead.

**Automatically Accept Calls** If you enable this option, all incoming calls are automatically accepted. To turn off this feature, select Automatically Accept Calls again to remove the check mark.

**Create SpeedDial** Opens the Create SpeedDial dialog box, where you can manually create a Speed Dial entry. You can enter the address of the user and how you want to place the call, then you can choose to add the Speed Dial entry to your Speed Dial list or save it on the desktop.

**Hang Up** Ends the current call or meeting.

**Exit** Closes Microsoft NetMeeting.

### View Menu

The View menu contains these options:

**Status Bar** Toggles the display of the status bar.

**Dial Pad** Displays the dial pad instead of the video view in the NetMeeting window. Use the dial pad to place calls to an automated telephone system.

**Picture-in-Picture** Lets you display the video image you're sending to other computers in a small window within the video window.

**My Video (New Window)** Displays your own video image in a new window.

**Compact** Toggles the NetMeeting window to display only the video area, not the data area of the window.

**Data Only** Toggles the NetMeeting window to display only the data area, not the video area of the window.

**Always on Top** Specifies that Windows should always display the NetMeeting window on top of other open windows.

### Tools Menu

The Tools menu contains these unique options:

**Video** Contains a submenu that lets you choose to send or receive video. Also lets you specify the size of the video window (100, 200, 300, or 400 percent).

**Audio Tuning Wizard** Starts the Audio Tuning Wizard, which you use to configure your audio settings, such as playback and recording volume.

**TIP** The Audio Tuning Wizard option is available only when you are not in a call.

**Sharing** Lets you share an application with other people in the meeting. Sharing is explained in more detail later in this topic.

**Chat** Opens a chat window you can use to send messages to one or more people in a call or meeting. Enter text in the

Message text box, select a recipient from the Send To drop-down list, then click the Send button. Sent and received messages appear in the upper portion of the Chat window.

**Whiteboard** Opens the Whiteboard on all computers of all users in the call or meeting. You can use the Whiteboard to work together as if working on a physical whiteboard; for example, you can jot down meeting notes or agendas. When you're done, you can save the Whiteboard contents as a Whiteboard (.WHT) file.

**TIP** The Whiteboard works similar to Paint. See the heading Paint in this book for more information about Paint.

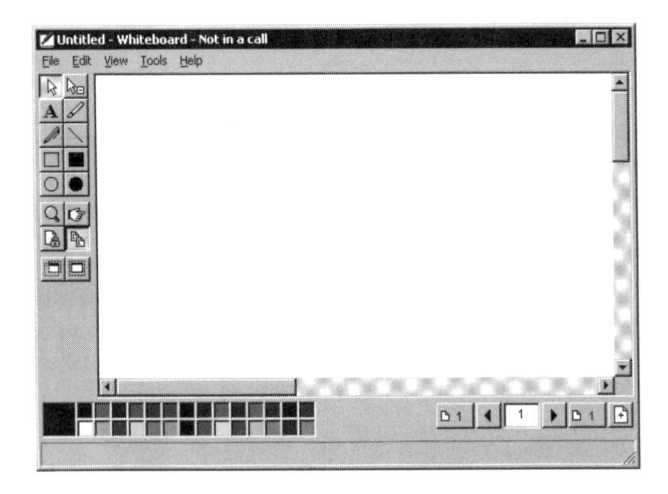

**File Transfer** Opens the File Transfer window, where you can send files to (and receive files from) other NetMeeting users' computers while in a call or meeting. Also lets you open the Received Files folder, which holds files you received from other users, and open other file folders.

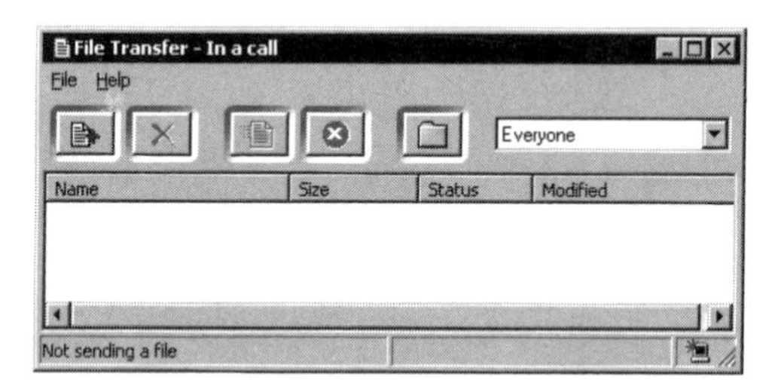


**Whiteboard (1.0–2.x)** Opens the NetMeeting 2.1 Whiteboard.

**Remote Desktop Sharing** When you select this option for the first time, it starts the Remote Desktop Sharing Wizard, which lets you set up your computer so you can control it from a remote computer when NetMeeting is not running. Any time after that, you use this option to enable or disable Remote Desktop Sharing, but you can also run the Wizard again by clicking the Wizard button that will appear. When you control a desktop remotely, you can access files, run programs, and transfer files to the remote computer. Once this option is enabled, you can activate Remote Desktop Sharing by right-clicking the Remote Desktop Sharing icon in the system tray on the taskbar and choosing Activate Remote Desktop Sharing. You can then call this computer from another computer using NetMeeting and use the desktop remotely.

To do so, choose Call ➢ New Call, then enter the DNS name or IP address of the computer you're accessing, select the Require Security for This Call (Data Only) option, and click Call. When prompted, enter the username, password, and domain (if applicable) of an administrator account and click OK. The remote computer's desktop appears in a separate window. To stop using the desktop remotely, end the call by choosing Call ➢ Hang Up or by clicking the End Call button in NetMeeting.

Turn off Remote Desktop Sharing by right-clicking the Remote Desktop Sharing icon in the system tray and choosing Turn Off Remote Desktop Sharing.

**TIP** You must have administrator privileges to access a computer using Remote Desktop Sharing.

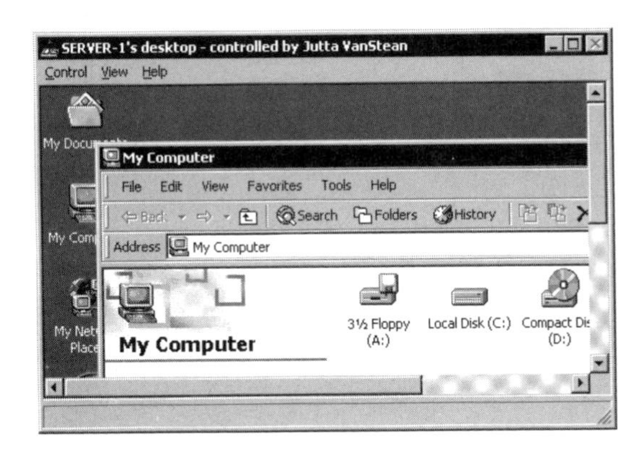


**Options** Lets you configure NetMeeting options relating to directory and general information as well as security and video settings.

### *Help Menu*

The Help menu contains these options:

**Help Topics** Opens NetMeeting Help in the Windows Help system.

**Readme** Opens the NetMeeting readme file.

**Microsoft on the Web** Contains a submenu from which you can access NetMeeting-related pages on Microsoft's Web site, as well as Microsoft's home page.

**Online Support** Opens Microsoft's NetMeeting online support site.

**Get a Camera** Starts a search on Microsoft.com for companies that sell cameras for your computer and displays the search results.

**About Windows NetMeeting** Displays version and licensing information for NetMeeting. Also displays the computer's IP address.

## NetMeeting Options

You can configure NetMeeting to best serve your Internet conferencing needs using the NetMeeting Options dialog box.

Choose Tools ➢ Options to open the Options dialog box. It has four tabs: General, Security, Audio, and Video.

### *General Tab*

Lets you specify general, network bandwidth, and advanced calling settings. It contains these areas:

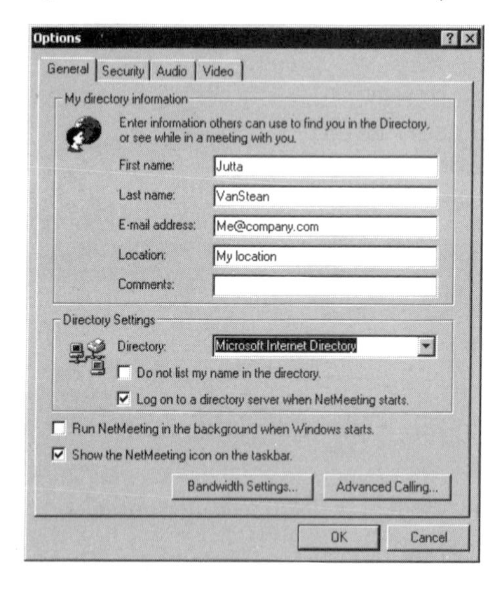


**My Directory Information** Here you can enter your personal information, such as first name, last name, e-mail address, location, and any comments you would like to add. This is the information other NetMeeting users see about you when you're logged onto an ILS server.

**Directory Settings** Here you can choose whether you want to automatically log onto a directory server when NetMeeting starts and select or enter the name of the default directory server in the Directory combo box. You can also specify whether you want to list your information in the directory.

On the General tab, you can also specify whether you want NetMeeting to run in the background when Windows starts, and whether you want Windows to display the NetMeeting icon on the taskbar. The General tab also contains the following two buttons:

**Bandwidth Settings** Opens the Network Bandwidth dialog box, where you can select the speed of your network connection. Choices include 14400 bps modem, 28800 bps modem, Cable, xDSL or ISDN, or Local Area Network.

**Advanced Calling** Opens the Advanced Calling Options dialog box, where you can choose to use a gatekeeper to place calls and to use a gateway to call telephones and videoconferencing systems.

### *Security Tab*

On this tab you can configure whether you want incoming and/or outgoing calls to be secure and configure certificate use.

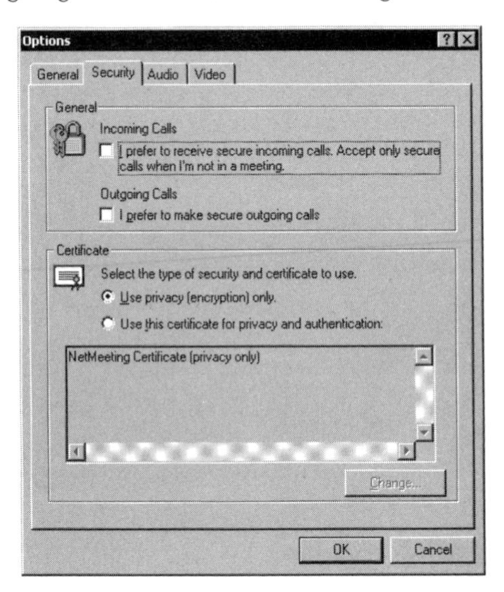

### Audio Tab

This tab lets you configure audio settings. It has two areas:

**General** Here you can configure such settings as enabling full duplex audio and auto-gain control, automatically adjusting your microphone's volume while in a call, and enabling DirectSound for better audio performance. You can also start the Audio Tuning Wizard by clicking the Tuning Wizard button, and you can configure audio compression settings by clicking Advanced.

**Silence Detection** Here you can configure whether you want the silence detection sensitivity adjusted automatically or manually. Use the slider to adjust it manually. This feature is helpful if the background noise in the room you are in varies.

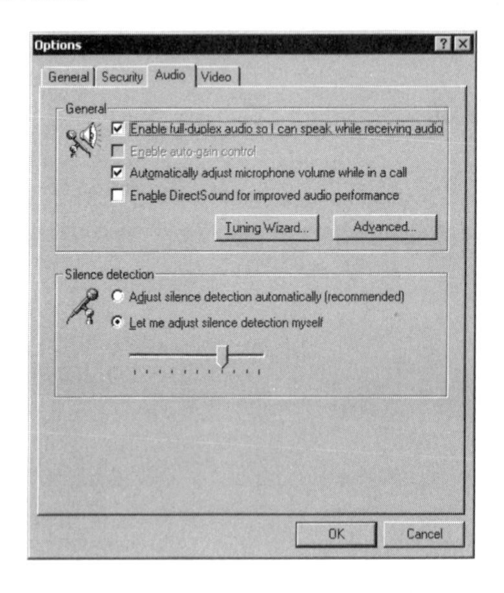


### Video Tab

Use this tab to configure your video settings. Three areas are available:

**Sending and Receiving Video** Here you can specify whether you want to automatically send and/or receive video when you start a call.

**Send Image Size** Choose from a small, medium, or large image size.

**Video Quality** Lets you adjust the video quality from faster video (lesser quality) to better quality (slower video).

**Video Camera Properties** Here you can select which video capture device you want to use and click Source to configure video card settings (provided by the manufacturer). If the Source button is grayed out or missing, the Format button may be available, which serves the same function as the Source button.

**TIP** The Source button may be available only if you're viewing an image in the Video window.

On the Video tab, you can also check the Show Mirror Image in Preview Video Window option to display the preview image as a reversed image (as if you're looking in a mirror).

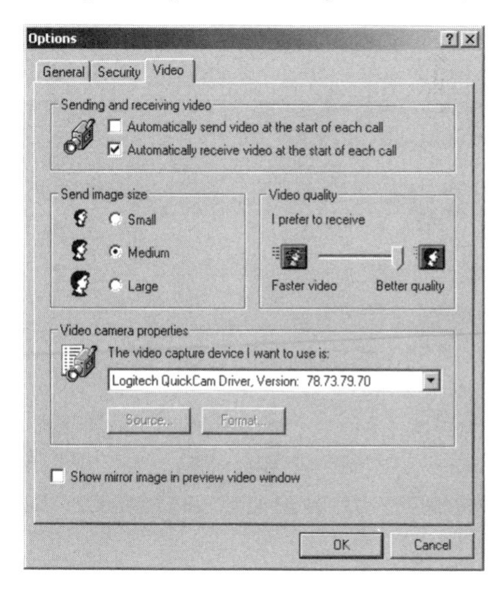


## Status Bar

The left side of the status bar tells you whether you are currently in a call. The right side of the status bar tells you graphically whether you're in a call and whether you're logged onto an ILS server. If you're logged onto an ILS server, place the mouse pointer over the server icon to see which server you're logged onto.

## NetMeeting Buttons

Most of the NetMeeting buttons perform functions you can also access via the NetMeeting menus. These include (with the equivalent menu option name in parentheses, if different from the button name): New Call, End Call (Hang Up), Find Someone in a Directory (Directory), Start Video/Stop Video, Picture-in-Picture, Share Program (Sharing), Chat, Whiteboard, and Transfer Files (File Transfer).

You'll see one unique button—the Adjust Audio Volume/View Participant List button. This button toggles the data area to display either the participants in the current call or meeting, or sliders to adjust the microphone and speaker volume.

## Finding a User

If you want to place a call but don't know the user's directory address, you can search for users in any directory. Choose Call ➢ Directory, or click the Find Someone in a Directory button to open the Find Someone dialog box.

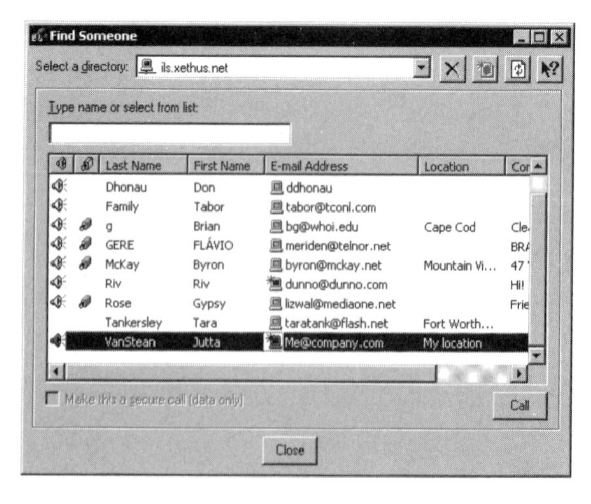

### *Choosing a Directory*

In the Select a Directory combo box, select a directory, the Speed Dial or History view, or the Windows Address Book from the list, or enter the name of a directory in the combo box. All available entries then appear in the list box below. Choosing a different directory from the list does not change which directory you are logged onto, but only the display of users logged onto the directory you're selecting.

Once you've made a selection in the combo box, you can then either type a user's name in the Type Name or Select from List text box (you're taken to the closest match automatically), or select a user in the list.

### *User Information*

Information about logged-on users includes whether a user has audio or video (if yes, an audio and/or video icon is visible), last name, first name, e-mail address, location, and comments. To the left of each person's e-mail address is an icon representing a computer that shows whether the person is currently in a call. If the user is in a call, the monitor in the icon is blue and a red star appears in the top-left corner of the icon. If the user is not in a call, the icon is grayed out.

You can sort the list of users in any view by any of the column headers in ascending or descending order by clicking a column header either once or twice. You can also rearrange the order of the columns by dragging a column header to a different position in relation to other column headers.

### *Available Actions*

You can right-click any user listed in the directory and choose from several actions, such as:

- Make a call to the user
- Access the user's properties
- Add the user to your Speed Dial list
- Add the user to the Address Book
- Refresh the directory list (or stop NetMeeting from refreshing the directory)

## Sharing an Application

To share an application with other people in the call or meeting, choose Tools ➢ Sharing to open the Sharing—Programs dialog box. Select the application you want to share in the list of applications and click Share. Any currently open application appears in the list. When you share an application, meeting participants can see the information you enter in the application, but they cannot make any changes themselves. To stop sharing an application, select it in the list and click Unshare. Click Unshare All to stop all sharing. Placing a check mark in the Share in True Color check box means that you can share the application using true colors. If you choose this option, more than 16 million colors can be displayed.

**WARNING** Microsoft recommends that you don't check the Share in True Color option, as it makes application sharing very slow, especially over dial-up connections.

**TIP** The shared application must be the active window and on top of all other windows on the computer of the person who is sharing the application for it to be properly viewed by other people.

To make shared applications easier to view on the desktop, remote users can choose Full Screen in the shared application's View menu.

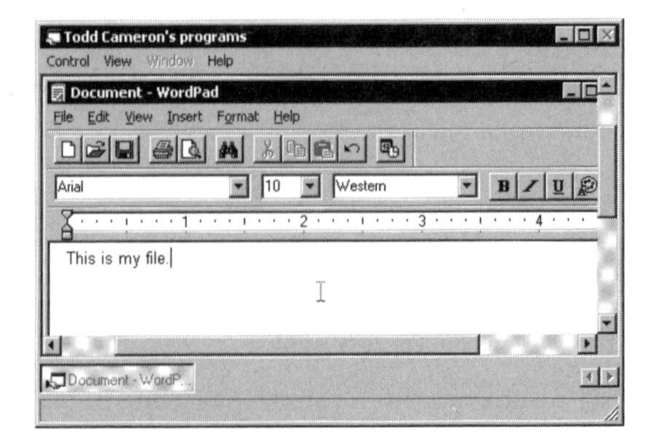

### *Enabling Control by Other Users*

In the Sharing—Programs dialog box, you can also allow other users to make changes in your shared application. To do so, click the Allow Control button. It is toggled to say Prevent Control (which prevents others from making changes to your application). You can now also specify that you want to automatically accept requests for control or to temporarily not allow requests for control (Do not Disturb Me with Requests for Control Right Now).

**Requesting Control** Once Allow Control is enabled, other users sharing the application can choose Request Control from the Control menu of the shared application window to ask you to take control of the application. If you specified that you want to automatically accept all requests for control, control is switched without further action. If you didn't select that option, you'll receive a message stating that the remote user would like to take control of the shared programs. You can click Accept to honor (or Reject to deny) the request. To stop controlling, a user needs to choose Control ➢ Release Control. This turns control back over to the person sharing the application.

You can also grant control directly to a user (without him or her requesting it first) by right-clicking the user's name in the data area of the main NetMeeting window and choosing Grant Control (this option is available only if you've shared at least one application).

### *Removing a User from a Meeting*

You can remove a user from a meeting you are hosting by right-clicking the user's name in the data list of the main NetMeeting window and choosing Remove from Meeting. The user is automatically removed from the meeting.

**See Also** Address Book, Paint

# Network and Dial-up Connections

Network and Dial-up Connections Opens the Network and Dial-up Connections folder, where you can view and configure existing and create new network and dial-up connections on the computer. You use network and dial-up connections to establish communications (connections) between computers, such as between two computers, between a computer and a local area or wide area network, or between a computer and host on the Internet. Once a connection is established, you can access and use resources on the computer, network, or Internet. Examples of this are using files located on the computer or network to which you are connected, and printing to printers connected to the computer or network to which you are connected. If the connection is to the Internet, you may choose to view Web sites and download files. Connections can be either local or remote. Dial-up connections you create with the Network Connection Wizard or Internet Connection Wizard appear in this folder.

You can configure security for network and dial-up connections by using such features as callback, data encryption, authentication, and Windows 2000 login and domain security.

## Network and Dial-up Connections Folder

To open the Network and Dial-up Connections folder, where you can view, configure, and create network and dial-up connections, choose Start ➢ Settings ➢ Network and Dial-up Connections.

**TIP** If, when you place the cursor over Network and Dial-up Connections, a submenu appears showing your established connections and the menu option Make New Connection, you can still open the Network and Dial-up Connections folder by right-clicking Network and Dial-up Connections and choosing Open.

**TIP** You can also choose Start ➢ Settings ➢ Control Panel and double-click Network and Dial-up Connections to open the Network and Dial-up Connections folder, or choose Start ➢ Programs ➢ Accessories ➢ Communications ➢ Network and Dial-up Connections. Finally, you can right-click the My Network Places shortcut on the desktop and choose Properties to open the Network and Dial-up Connections folder.

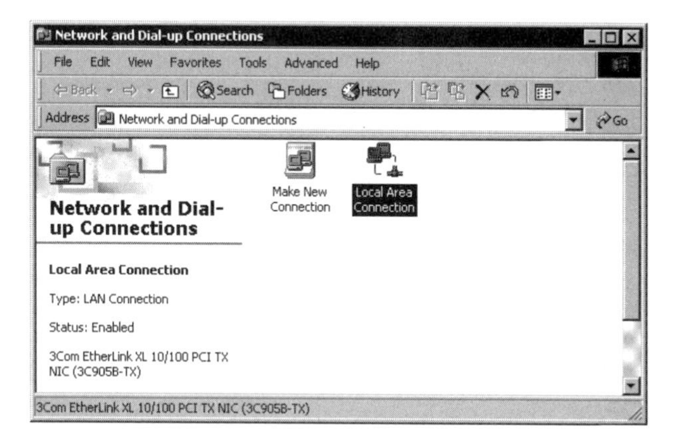


When you open the Network and Dial-up Connections folder, you'll see an icon for each connection currently configured on the computer, as well as the Make New Connection icon used to create a new connection. If you select a connection in the folder, on the left side of the window you'll see some information about the connection. This information can include the name of the connection, the connection type, the current status of the connection, and the name of the device used for the connection.

You can tell by the look of each icon whether a connection is currently active. With active connections, the screen areas of the two connected computers in the icon are blue. With inactive connections, the two connected computers are grayed out.

### *Network and Dial-up Connection Types*

Windows 2000 supports five types of network and dial-up connections: Dial-up, Local Area, Virtual Private Network (VPN), Direct, and Incoming. Each connection type has a different icon and default name associated with it that appears when you create a connection in the Network and Dial-up Connections folder.

**Dial-up Connection** A connection to the remote computer is established via standard telephone lines using a modem, via ISDN lines using ISDN cards, or via an X.25 network. Typically used for connections to the Internet or to connect remote users to the corporate network.

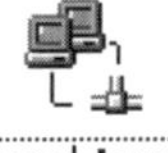

Local Area Connection

**Local Area Connection** A connection to another computer in a network, typically over Ethernet, Token Ring, cable modem, Fiber Distributed Data Interface (FDDI), Digital Subscriber Line (DSL), T1, Frame Relay, and others. Typically used to connect computers in a corporate local area network (LAN).

Virtual Private Connection

**Virtual Private Connection** A dedicated, secure connection between two LANs over Point-to-Point Tunneling Protocol (PPTP) or Layer-2 Tunneling Protocol (L2TP). Lets you establish a secure connection between a remote computer and a computer on a corporate network over the Internet.

**TIP** VPN connections over PPTP use MPPE (Microsoft Point to Point) encryption and connections over L2TP use IPSec (IP Security Protocol) DES (Data Encryption Standard) encryption.

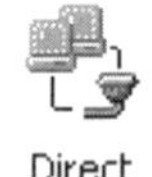

Direct Connection

**Direct Connection** A direct serial, parallel, or infrared connection between two computing devices. Typically lets you connect desktop computers with handheld computing devices.

**TIP** Use an RS-232C null modem cable to make a serial connection between two computers. The computers cannot be located more than 50 feet from each other.

**TIP** In the Help system, go to the index entry Null Modem Cabling to find information on the exact pinout for 9-pin and 25-pin null modem cables used to create direct serial connections.

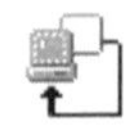

Incoming Connections

**Incoming Connections** A connection that allows other computers to connect to this computer via dial-up, VPN, or direct connection. The computer then acts as a dial-in server. You can configure both Windows 2000 Professional and Windows 2000 Server for incoming connections;

however, you must use the Routing and Remote Access management console (accessible through Administrative Tools) to configure incoming connections for a Windows 2000 Server that belongs to or controls a domain. Windows 2000 Professional supports up to three incoming sessions, but only one of each type (dial-up, VPN, or direct). Windows 2000 Server supports up to 256 incoming dial-up connections.

## *Local Area Connection*

If you have a network card installed in a computer and you install Windows 2000 on the computer, a local area connection is created automatically. The icon for this connection appears in the Network and Dial-up Connections folder. When you connect the computer to the network, this connection automatically activates without further action required by the user. If you install additional adapters, a local area connection is created for each adapter and an icon for each connection appears in the Network and Dial-up Connections folder.

If the connection to the network is broken (for example, if you disconnect the patch cable from the hub or network card, or if a cable connecting the computer to the network is faulty), the icon grays out, indicating that this connection is no longer connected. When the connection to the network is reestablished (for example, you plug the patch cable back in), the local area connection automatically reconnects.

As with all other connections, you can manually disconnect a local area connection by right-clicking the appropriate icon and choosing Disconnect. If you do this, the local area connection no longer connects automatically. This can be useful if you're using a laptop and don't want the adapter to try to establish a connection when you're traveling (and not connecting to the network via a local area connection). When you're back in the office and want to use the connection again, just right-click the connection's icon and choose Connect, or double-click the connection icon.

**Local Area Connection Properties** To configure local area connection properties, such as installed network clients and protocols, right-click the Local Area Connection icon and choose Properties. The Properties dialog box has one tab: the General tab.

**General** At the top of the tab, you'll see the network adapter used for the connection. Click Configure to access the network adapter's properties. The General tab also displays the clients, services, and protocols that are used by the connection. To configure a component, select it in the list and click Properties.

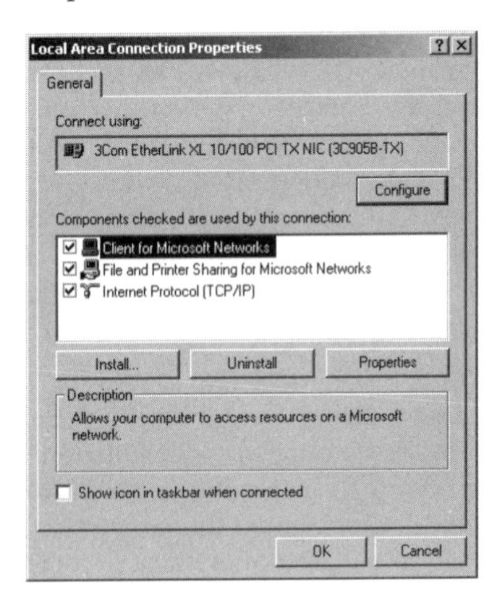


For example, to configure your IP address, select Internet Protocol (TCP/IP) and click Properties. You can then enter your IP address, subnet mask, default gateway address, and DNS server addresses. Or you can choose to obtain your IP and DNS server addresses automatically from a DHCP server. For advanced IP, DNS, and WINS settings, click Advanced.

On the General tab, you can also click Install to install new clients, services, and protocols, or select a client, service, or protocol and click Uninstall to remove it from the system.

Select the Show Icon in Taskbar when Connected option if you want to have a visual reminder in the taskbar after you establish a connection to the local area network.

## *Make New Connection*

Make New Connection

Starts the process of creating a new network or dial-up connection. Double-click the Make New Connection icon to start the Network Connection Wizard, which will guide you through the process of creating a new network or dial-up connection. First, you'll be presented with the Welcome screen. Click Next to display the Network Connection Type dialog box, where you can choose the type of connection you want to create.

**TIP** You can also choose File ➢ New Connection to start the Network Connection Wizard.

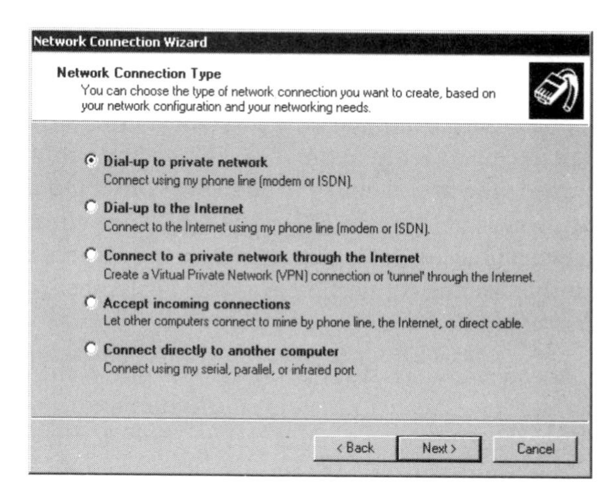


The following choices are available:

**Dial-up to Private Network** Lets you create a dial-up connection to a computer on a corporate network that is set up as a dial-in server. Once the connection is established, you can access resources on the network as if you were locally attached to the network. The creation process of this type of connection is very similar to that of a dial-up connection to the Internet. During the creation of the connection, you'll have to provide the telephone number you want Windows to use to establish the connection with the dial-in server. You also have to provide an account and password on the dial-in computer or in the domain to be able to log into the computer or domain.

**Dial-up to the Internet** Lets you create a dial-up connection to an Internet Service Provider (ISP). You must have administrative privileges to create this type of connection. If you choose this option, the Internet Connection Wizard starts and guides you through the process of setting up the connection. You'll need to know the phone number to dial your ISP, and the account name and password you established with the ISP. Or, you can create a connection to the Internet through your network's proxy server. In that case, you may need to know the name and port of your company's proxy server.

**Connect to a Private Network through the Internet** Lets you create a secure, dedicated connection between your computer and a computer on a corporate network over the Internet. During setup of the VPN connection, you'll have to provide the host name or IP address of the computer to which you want to connect. If you're logged on with administrative privileges, you'll also be able to specify that you want to make the connection available to all users (instead of just yourself).

Before you can successfully connect via a VPN connection, you must have created a dial-up connection to the Internet on the computer and you must be connected to the Internet. You can choose to have the dial-up connection dialed automatically when you double-click the VPN connection, or you can choose not to have this done (in that case, you'll have to separately establish a connection to the Internet before you can connect via the VPN connection).

**Accept Incoming Connections** Lets you configure a Windows 2000 computer to act as a dial-in server. The computer must be running Windows 2000 Professional, or if it's a standalone computer, it can be running Windows 2000 Server. If you don't have administrative privileges, this option is grayed out. If you choose this option after you've already configured the computer for incoming connections, you're effectively changing the properties of the current configuration.

**NOTE** To configure a Windows 2000 Server for incoming connections that acts as a domain controller or is part of a domain, you must use the Routing and Remote Access management console (accessible through Administrative Tools).

**Connect Directly to Another Computer** Lets you create a connection between two computers using a serial or parallel cable, or an infrared connection. You'll have to specify whether the computer is the host (the computer that will be accessed) or the guest (the computer that will access the host computer), and choose the device you want to use for the connection (serial, parallel, or infrared port). Depending on whether the computer is the host or the guest, you'll have to specify the users that are allowed to access the computer (host) or specify if you're creating the connection for yourself or all users of the computer (guest).

**TIP** If you're logged in without administrative privileges, the connection is automatically set up for the computer to act as guest and it is created only for you. The only item you can specify is the device you want to use for the connection.

**TIP** When you set up a direct connection with the machine acting as a host, you're effectively setting up the machine to accept incoming connections. If the computer has already been configured to accept incoming connections and you use the Network Connection Wizard to try to create a direct connection with the machine acting as host, you will effectively only change the parameters of the already existing incoming connection.

**Accepting Incoming Connections** To configure an eligible Windows 2000 computer to accept incoming connections and thus become a dial-in server, do the following:

1. Double-click Make New Connection in the Network and Dial-up Connections folder to start the Network Connection Wizard. Click Next.
2. Select Accept Incoming Connections. Click Next.

3. Select the device or devices you want to use to accept incoming connections (such as a modem or serial or parallel cable). If necessary, you can change the properties of any device by selecting it and clicking Properties. Properties depend on the device. They can include such items as port speed and flow control, whether the call should be operator assisted, whether the call should be disconnected after a certain amount of idle time, and hardware settings for the device. Click OK when you've finished changing a device's properties. Then click Next to continue.

4. Select whether you want to allow VPN connections. Click Next.

**NOTE** You must have a valid Internet host name or IP address to allow VPN connections.

5. In the Allowed Users dialog box, specify the users that are allowed to connect to the computer. All users that currently have an account on the computer are displayed in the Users Allowed to Connect list. Place a check mark next to any user you want to allow to use this incoming connection.

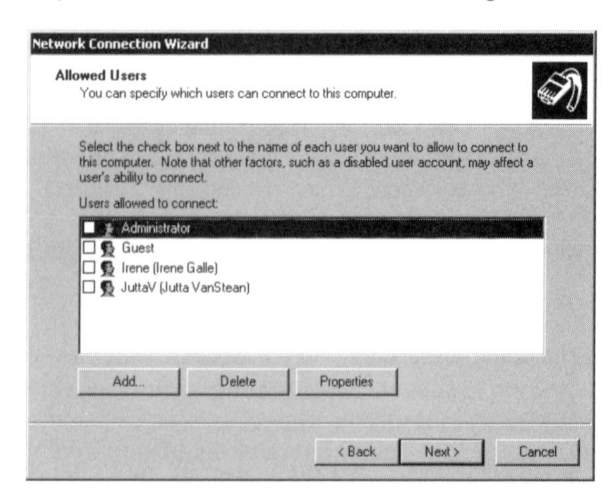


You can also add new users in this dialog box. Click Add and specify a logon name, full name, and password for the user. Then click OK. The user is automatically added to the local SAM database and appears in the Users Allowed to Connect list with a check mark in the user's check box. To change the full name, password, or callback properties of any user in the list, select a user and click Properties. On the General tab, you can change the full name and password.

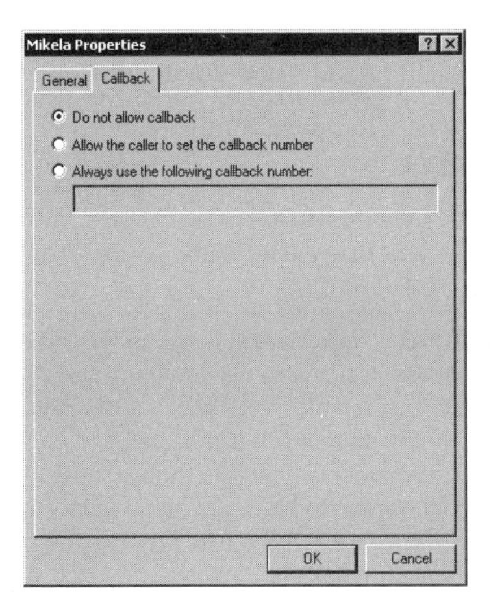


On the Callback tab, you can configure the following callback options for incoming connections:

**NOTE** Callback means that after a connection to the dial-in server is established, the dial-in server verifies the user's logon name and password, then disconnects and calls the user back at a specified phone number. This has two advantages. First, the cost to the user is reduced because the dial-in server calls the user back; thus any phone charges apply to the phone line used by the server, not the user. Second, callback adds a level of security by preventing incoming connections made from unknown or unauthorized telephone numbers. Callback is not supported for VPN connections.

**Do Not Allow Callback** Callback cannot be used for this user.

**Allow the Caller to Set the Callback Number** The user can specify the number at which he or she wants the server to call him or her back. This option can reduce the cost to the user.

**Always Use the Following Callback Number** Allows the administrator to specify a telephone number that should always be used when the server makes a callback call to the user. This option can reduce the cost to the user and provides additional network security.

Click OK when you have configured a user's general and callback properties.

You can also delete users from the Users Allowed to Connect list by selecting a user and clicking Delete.

**WARNING** If you delete a user in this dialog box, keep in mind that the user is also deleted from the SAM database. Do not delete a user here unless you're absolutely certain that this is what you want to do. If you don't want a user to be able to make an incoming connection to this computer, simply leave the check box next to his or her name empty.

When you've finished, click Next.

6. In the Networking Components dialog box, select and configure the networking components, such as protocols, file and printer sharing services, and client services you want to have enabled for incoming connections. All currently installed services appear in the Networking Components list. If a check box for a service is grayed out, it means that the service cannot be disabled. Protocols (such as TCP/IP, IPX/SPS, NetBEUI, and AppleTalk) can be further configured for incoming connections. Select the protocol and click Properties.

   For example, you can configure the following settings for incoming TCP/IP connections:

   - Allow incoming callers to access the LAN to which the computer is attached.
   - Assign IP addresses automatically using a DHCP server.

- Specify a range of TCP/IP addresses that should be used for incoming connections.
- Allow the incoming caller to specify his or her own IP address.

Click OK when you're done making changes.

**WARNING** Allowing incoming callers to specify their own IP address can leave your network security compromised. The caller could use the IP address of a client that connected to the computer prior to this caller, and obtain access to those resources on the network the previously connected client had accessed.

You can click Install to install additional networking components, and you can select a component and click Uninstall to remove that component from the computer. Do the latter only if you're absolutely sure this is what you want to do. Click Next to continue.

7. You cannot change the default name for incoming connections. Click Finish to create the incoming connection. Windows returns you to the Network and Dial-up Connections folder and displays the Incoming Connections icon in the folder.

**Changing Your Incoming Connections Configuration** If you need to make changes to your Incoming Connections configuration, right-click the Incoming Connections icon and choose Properties. Use the General, Users, and Networking tabs to make configuration changes. These settings are almost identical to the settings you were able to configure when you created the connection, with some exceptions.

For instance, on the General tab you have one additional option. You can specify whether you want Windows to display an icon on the taskbar when users are connected to the computer. On the Users tab, you have two additional options. You can choose to require users to secure their passwords and data, and you can choose to allow directly connected devices (for example, palmtop computers) to connect without a password. If you require users to secure their passwords and data, they must select Require Secured Password and Require Data Encryption on the Security tab of the connection they are using to connect to this computer.

## *Connection Properties*

Every connection has properties you can use to further configure the connection. To access the properties of any connection, right-click the connection and choose Properties. The Properties dialog box has five tabs: General, Options, Security, Networking, and Sharing. (This applies to all connections but the Incoming Connections connection, which we described earlier, and the Local Area Connection, which has only one tab.)

**General** This is the only tab that differs significantly for each of the connection types.

**Dial-up Connections** On the General tab for dial-up connections, you'll see which device will be used to make the connection. You can click Configure to configure device settings, such as connection speed and hardware features. The configuration options available will depend on the device you're using. On the General tab, you can also change the phone number the device is dialing. If you click Alternates, you can add numbers for Windows to use if the first number doesn't work, and choose to move to the top of the list the number to which the device successfully connects. Back on the General tab, you can specify to use a country/region code as well as dialing rules. Finally, you can specify whether an icon should appear in the taskbar when a connection is established.

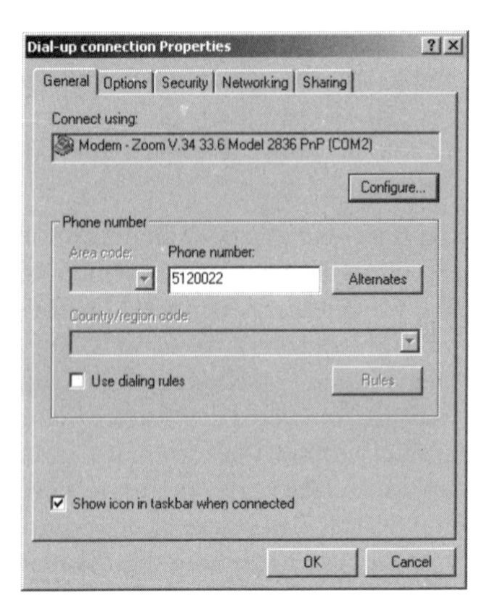

**Local Area Connections** The General tab for local area connections is very similar to the Networking tab for the other connection types. You can view and configure the device you are using to make the connection (the network adapter installed in the computer), and view and configure the networking components the connection uses (such as clients, services, and protocols). You can also install and uninstall networking components, and choose whether you want the taskbar to display an icon when the connection is active.

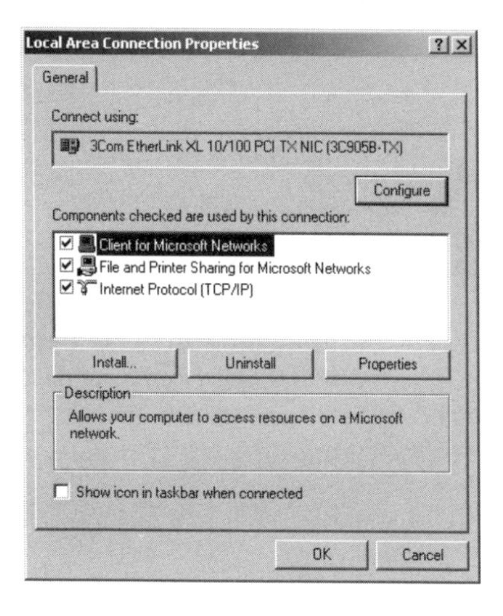

**TIP** If you click Configure to configure the network adapter, you'll see the same Properties dialog box you would see when configuring the network adapter through Device Manager.

**Virtual Private Connections (VPN)** The General tab for the Virtual Private Connection Properties dialog box lets you specify the host name or IP address of the destination server to which you want to connect. You can specify that you want Windows to automatically dial your dial-up connection to the Internet before trying to establish the VPN connection. The dial-up connection must be established before you can establish the VPN connection. Finally, you can choose whether to display an icon in the taskbar when this connection is active.

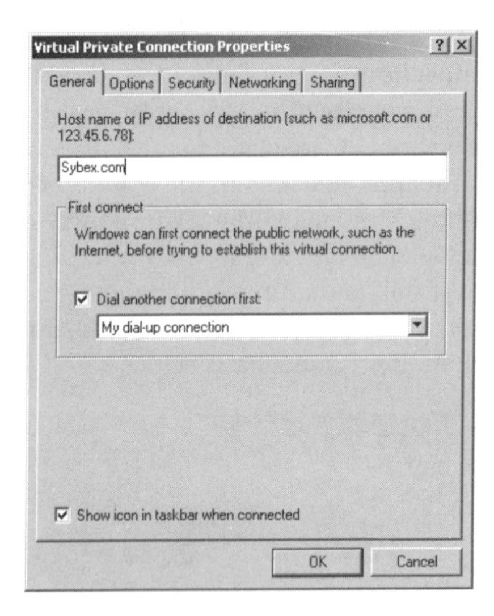


**Direct Connections** On the General tab for direct connections, you can specify and configure the device (such as parallel or null modem) used to make the connection. The configuration options available depend on the selected device. You can also choose whether to show an icon in the taskbar when the connection is active.

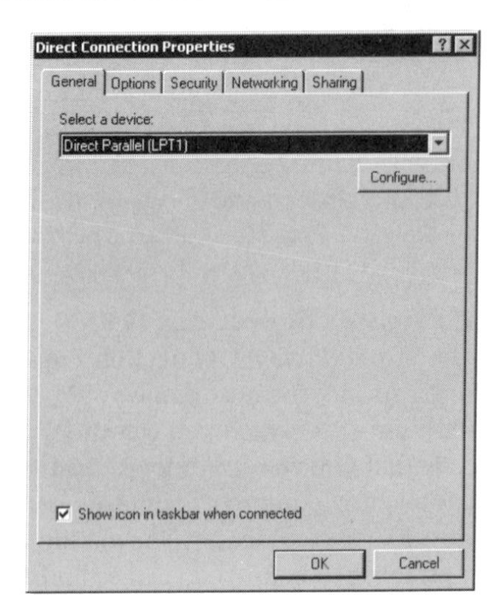

**Options** Lets you configure dialing and redialing options. You can specify whether you want Windows to:

- Show information on the connection's progress while the connection is being established.
- Prompt for authentication information such as name and password, certificate, and so on before establishing the connection.
- Include the Windows logon domain information.
- Prompt for the phone number to be used for the connection (available for dial-up connections).

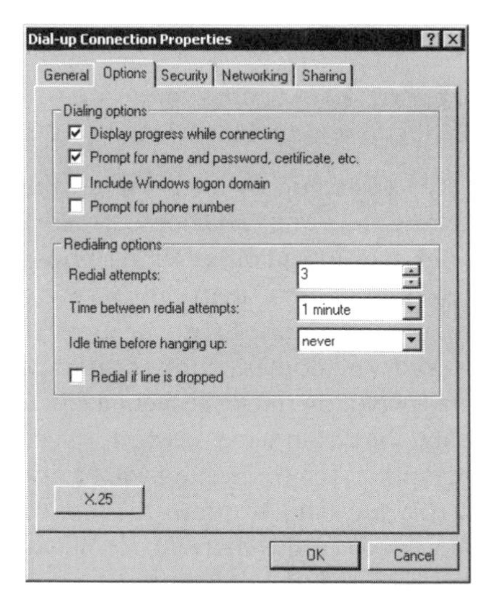

**TIP** If you use smart cards, a certificate may be required for authentication. Smart cards are similar to credit cards and store authentication information such as certificates, passwords, and public and private keys. In order to use smart cards to authenticate, you must have a smart card reader attached to your computer and Use Extensible Authentication Protocol (EAP) must be enabled in the Advanced Security Settings of the connection's Security tab.

You can also specify how many times you want the device to redial if a connection cannot be established (the default is three times), how much time should elapse between each redial attempt (the default is one minute), and how long the connection can be idle before it disconnects (the default is never). Finally, you can specify that you want Windows to redial the connection if the line is dropped. This will work only if you have started the Remote Access Auto Connection Manager under Services in Component Services or Computer Management.

**TIP** To access Services, choose Start ➢ Control Panel, double-click Component Services, and select Services. Or right-click My Computer, choose Manage, expand System Tools, and select Services.

From the Options tab of dial-up connections, you can also specify X.25 logon settings by clicking the X.25 button.

**Security** Lets you set up the level of security used when making a connection. You can choose to allow unsecured passwords (for dial-up and direct connections), require secured passwords, or use a smart card. If secured passwords are required, you can choose to use the user's Windows logon name, password, and domain during authentication and whether data encryption should be required. If data encryption is required, and the dial-in server to which you connect doesn't use data encryption, the connection will be disconnected. If you specify that you want Windows to use a smart card for authentication, you can also choose to require data encryption.

**TIP** If Require Data Encryption is not checked, it simply means that it is not required but will nonetheless be attempted. If the dial-in server doesn't use encryption, the connection will stay connected and not use data encryption.

Alternatively, you can select Advanced (Custom Settings) and click Settings to configure advanced security settings, including making encryption optional, not allowing encryption, or requiring encryption, as well as specifying the security protocols that can be used for the connection.

**TIP** When you select Advanced and then click Settings, the settings shown on the Advanced Security Settings dialog box reflect the default settings for whichever choice you had made when Typical was checked under Security Options on the Security tab.

Finally, on the Security tab of dial-up connections, you can also choose to display a terminal window after connecting. The remote terminal server prompts you for logon information in the terminal window, and you'll be authenticated after providing the necessary information (such as logon name and password). To automate this process, you can create a script with the necessary information, and then specify to use the script for the connection.

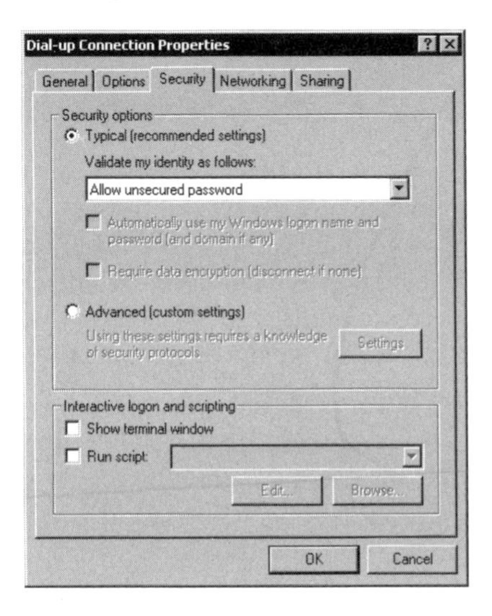


**Networking** Lets you specify the type of dial-up server you're connecting to. For dial-up and direct connections, your choices are PPP: Windows 95/98/NT4/2000, Internet, or SLIP: UNIX Connection. PPP is by far the most common connection type for dial-up connections. For VPN connections, your choices are Automatic (which means Windows will attempt to connect via PPTP first, then via L2TP),

Point-to-Point Tunneling Protocol (PPTP), or Layer-2 Tunneling Protocol (L2TP).

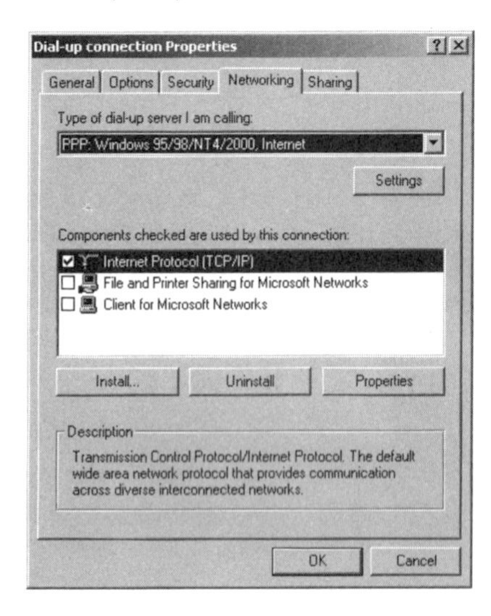


You can also specify the installed networking components the connection will use (by placing a check mark in the box next to the appropriate component). Additionally, on the Networking tab of dial-up connections, you can install new networking components, uninstall existing networking components, and change the properties of some of the existing networking components.

**Sharing** Lets you enable or disable the ability of other computers on the network to use this connection to access external resources. If you enable this option, you can also enable or disable on-demand dialing, which means that when another computer tries to access external resources, this connection is dialed automatically.

Click Settings to configure the network applications you want to enable for any computer that shares this connection, and to specify and configure the services that will be provided to the remote network.

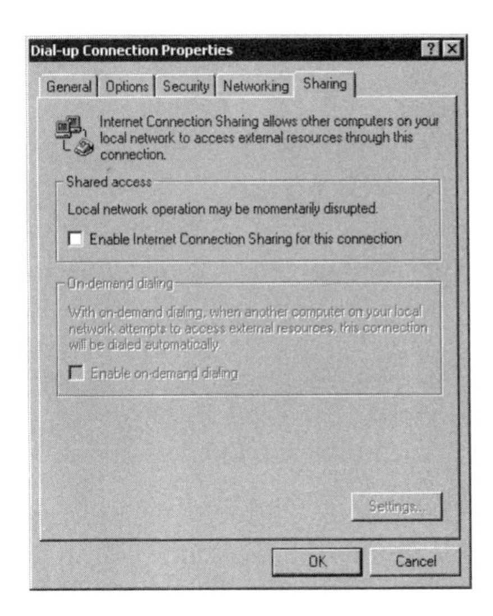


### *Connection Status*

In order to see connection information about any active connection, right-click the connection and choose Status from the menu. This opens the Status dialog box, which always has a General tab and can also have a Details tab.

**TIP** If you specified to have an icon appear in the taskbar when the connection is active, you can also either right-click this icon and choose Status or single- or double-click the icon. Both actions also open the Status dialog box. If you place the cursor over the icon, you'll see information about the connection, such as the name of the connection, the connection's speed, and the number of bytes sent and received.

**General** Provides information about the connection, such as the status (for example, Connected) and the duration and speed of the connection. It also gives you activity information, such as the number of bytes sent and received, the compression ratio, and any errors that occurred during the connection.

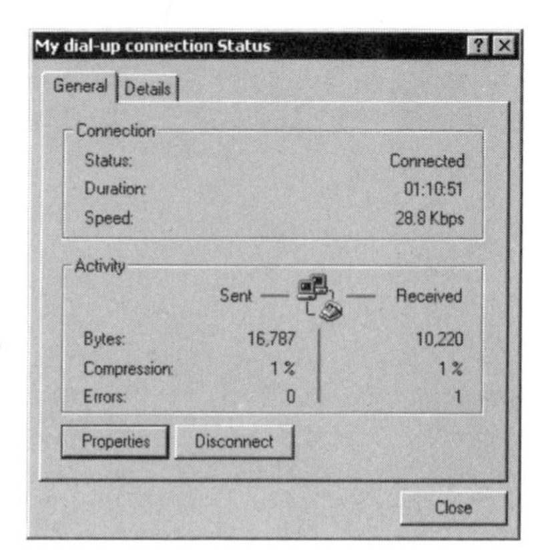


You can also access the connection's properties (by clicking the Properties button) and disconnect the connection (by clicking Disconnect, or, if avilable, disable it by clicking Disable).

**Details** Provides additional information and depends on the type of connection. It is not available for all connection types. It can include items such as the server type, compression level, and server and client IP addresses.

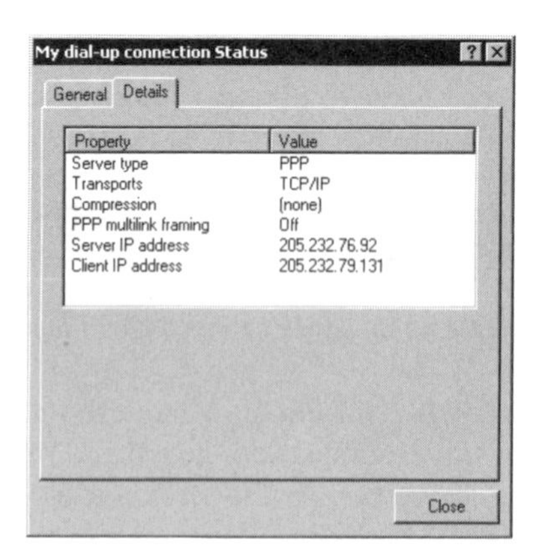


### Connecting and Disconnecting a Connection

To establish a connection, select the connection and double-click the connection's icon, or right-click the connection's icon and choose Connect.

To disconnect a connection, either right-click the connection's icon and choose Disconnect or open the connection's Status dialog box and click Disconnect on the General tab.

Finally, if you chose to display an icon in the taskbar when the connection is active, you can also right-click the taskbar icon and choose Disconnect.

## Advanced Menu

Advanced

The Network and Dial-up Connections folder menu bar contains an additional menu, Advanced, that lets you enable or configure advanced connection options. The menu contains five options: Operator-Assisted Dialing, Dial-up Preferences, Network Identification, Advanced Settings, and Optional Networking Components.

### *Operator-Assisted Dialing*

Operator-Assisted Dialing

If you desire, you can configure dial-up connections to allow you to either dial the number of the connection yourself through a telephone handset or have an operator dial the number for you. To enable Operator-Assisted Dialing, in the Network and Dial-up Connections folder choose Advanced ➢ Operator-Assisted Dialing (this places a check mark next to the option, indicating that it is activated). Now, after you double-click the connection, you can either dial the number yourself through a telephone handset or have an operator dial the number for you. When you finish dialing, click Dial in the connection's Connect dialog box. Don't hang up the handset until the modem takes control of the telephone line (you may hear a click in the line, and the line becomes silent). To turn off Operator-Assisted Dialing, choose Advanced ➢ Operator-Assisted Dialing again to remove the check mark from the menu option.

### *Dial-up Preferences*

Dial-up Preferences...

Choose Advanced ➢ Dial-up Preferences to open the Dial-up Preferences dialog box, where you can set preferred settings that will apply to all of your dial-up connections. The Dial-up Preferences dialog box has two tabs: Autodial, and Callback.

**Autodial** Lets you configure Autodial options. Autodial learns which connections you used to access remote resources, and when you try to access resources on a remote network a second time without being connected, Autodial automatically dials the connection. Options you can configure on this tab include the location(s) for which you want to enable Autodial, whether you want to be prompted before Autodial automatically dials the connection, and whether you want to disable Autodial for the current session.

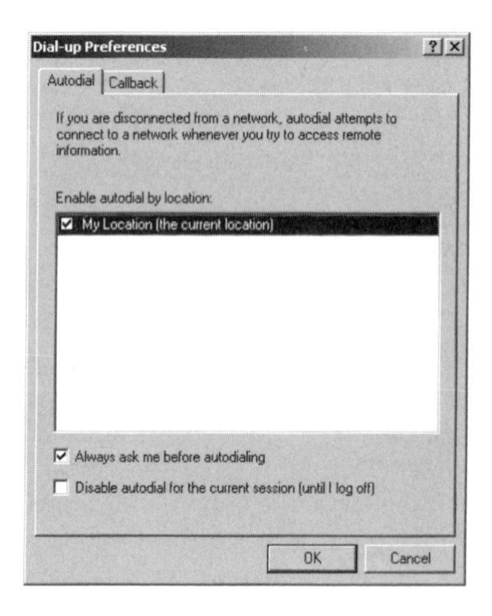


**Callback** Lets you configure callback options for outgoing connections if you're dialing into a server that will request callback. You can specify to not use callback, to decide whether to use callback when you're dialing the connection, and to always have the server call you back at the phone number(s) you specify for your device(s) in the provided list box. Callback is not supported for VPN connections.

**TIP** Callback settings that are specified for individual users through the dial-in server's Incoming Connections connection (on the Callback tab of individual users who have been granted the right to establish an incoming connection) take precedence over settings made by users on the Callback tab of Dial-up Preferences for outgoing connections.

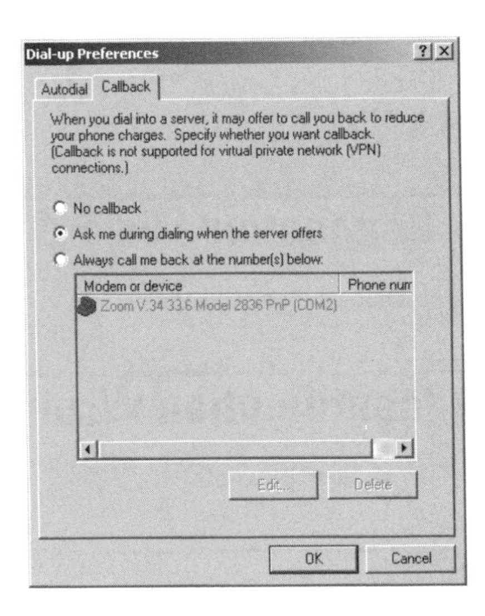


### *Network Identification, Advanced Settings, and Optional Networking Components*

The Network Identification menu option takes you to the Network Identification tab of System Properties. Here you can change the computer's name, as well as the domain or workgroup the computer belongs to. From here you can also run the Network Identification Wizard to connect the computer to a network.

The Advanced Settings menu option lets you configure advanced network adapter options, such as connections and their bindings (if applicable), NetBIOS network route LANA numbers (applicable only if NetBIOS is used), and the order in which the computer accesses network resources and information (through what are called Providers).

The Optional Networking Components menu option lets you install additional Windows networking components that are not yet installed on the computer (when you select this menu option, the Windows Optional Networking Components Wizard starts and guides you through the process of adding components).

**See Also** Internet Connection Wizard, Routing and Remote Access, Administrative Tools, System, Device Manager, System Information, DNS, DHCP, WINS

# Network Connection Wizard

**See** Network and Dial-up Connections

# Network Identification Wizard

**See** System (Network Identification tab)

# Notepad

Program used to view, create, and edit small text files, such as configuration text files, readme files, or the contents of the Windows Clipboard.

## Notepad Window

Choose Start ➢ Programs ➢ Accessories ➢ Notepad to open Notepad. The Notepad window consists of a menu bar and a text area.

The Notepad menus contain standard options, as well as some unique options.

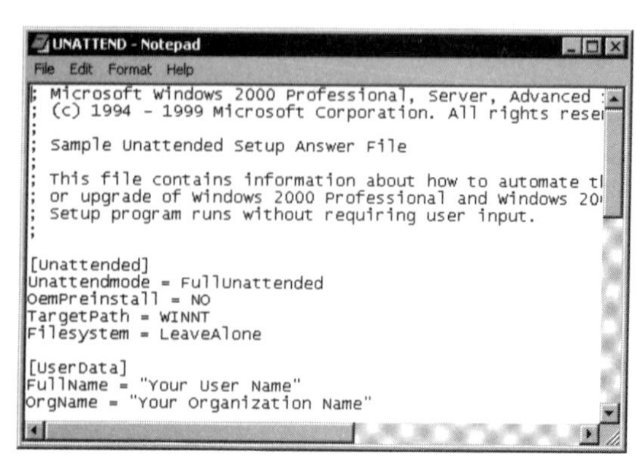

### File Menu

The File menu does not contain unique options; however, when a file is opened in Notepad, any existing formatting is stripped from the file, turning it into ASCII format.

### Edit Menu

The Edit menu contains the following unique options:

**Find** Lets you search for words in the document.

**Find Next** Finds the next occurrence of your search term.

**Replace** Lets you find a word and replace it with another.

**Go To** Lets you go directly to a specific page number.

**Select All** Selects all text in the document.

**Time/Date** Adds the current time and date to the document at the insertion point.

### Format Menu

The Format menu contains the following unique options:

**Word Wrap** Toggles Word Wrap on and off. If this option is enabled, words automatically wrap around to the next line.

**Font** Lets you choose a font for your text.

## Working with Text

You can work with text in Notepad in one of the following ways:

- Create a new text file by typing in the text area and saving the file.
- Open an existing text file by choosing File ➢ Open.
- Place the contents of the Windows Clipboard into Notepad by choosing Edit ➢ Paste.

**See Also** WordPad

# NTFS

File system for Windows 2000 computers. NTFS has many advantages over older file systems, such as FAT and FAT32. Windows 2000 Server computers that act as domain controllers require NTFS. You can format a disk partition with the NTFS file system during the Windows 2000 operating system installation, or you can convert an older file system (FAT or FAT32) to NTFS either during the Windows 2000 operating system installation or later on using `convert.exe`.

**TIP** For more information on how to convert a file system using `convert.exe`, choose Start ➢ Programs ➢ Accessories ➢ Command Prompt, then type **help convert** at the C:\> command prompt.

Features that are available only if you're using NTFS include, among others:

- Active Directory
- File encryption
- Permissions set on files
- Remote Storage
- Disk Quotas

**See Also** Active Directory, Disk Quotas, Command Prompt, Permissions

# On-Screen Keyboard

Displays a keyboard on the screen that you control with the mouse or switch input device. This feature is designed to aid users who have difficulty using a keyboard. Choose Start ➢ Programs ➢ Accessories ➢ Accessibility ➢ On-Screen Keyboard to bring up the on-screen keyboard. Alternatively, you can use the Windows Logo key+U shortcut. You'll have to click OK to acknowledge a message dialog box explaining that the on-screen keyboard has limited functionality. You can specify that you don't want Windows to display this dialog box the next time you start the on-screen keyboard.

By default On-Screen Keyboard is added to Utility Manager so that On-Screen Keyboard can be one of the accessibility options that Utility Manager can start automatically when starting Windows or Utility Manager. You can choose File ➢ Remove from Utility Manager to remove it. If you remove it and then want to add it again, choose File ➢ Add To Utility Manager.

**NOTE** You must have administrative privileges to add On-Screen Keyboard to Utility Manager.

## Keyboard Options

Use the Keyboard menu to choose the type of keyboard you want to display. Your choices are Enhanced Keyboard (with a numeric keypad) or Standard Keyboard, Regular or Block Layout, and 101 (U.S. Standard), 102 (Universal), or 106 (additional Japanese characters) keys.

Use the Settings menu to configure the on-screen keyboard's behavior. You can configure it to always run on top of other windows and to make a clicking sound when a character is entered in the program you're using (imitating the sound of a keyboard).

You can set up different typing modes; for example, you can specify that either clicking a key or hovering over a key selects that key. Alternatively, you can choose Joystick or Key to Select and then set up a scan interval to activate scanning of the keyboard. During the scan, each key on the on-screen keyboard is highlighted and you can select keys by using a dedicated key on the physical keyboard or an external switching device. To specify a dedicated physical key or external switching device, click Advanced and select Serial, Parallel, or Game Port, or select Keyboard Key and choose the key you want to use from the drop-down list.

Back on the Settings menu, you can also change the font used for the keys on the keyboard, perhaps making it larger to make it easier to read.

**NOTE** The program in which you want to enter text must be active when you're using the on-screen keyboard.

**See Also** Utility Manager

# Outlook Express

Program you can use to send and receive Internet e-mail, and to post messages to newsgroups. Choose Start ➢ Programs ➢ Outlook Express to start Outlook Express. Alternatively, you can start Outlook Express by clicking the Launch Outlook Express button on the Quick Launch toolbar.

**TIP** You can also open Outlook Express from within Internet Explorer by choosing any option from Tools ➢ Mail and News.

**TIP** You must have an e-mail account set up with an ISP to use Outlook Express, and you must have created a mail account in Windows 2000 using the Internet Connection Wizard. A quick way to do this in Outlook Express is to choose Tools ➢ Accounts, click Add, and choose Mail, then follow the steps for creating an e-mail account using the Internet Connection Wizard. If you don't have an Internet account set up yet on the computer, the Internet Connection Wizard will start automatically when you try to open Outlook Express. For more information, see Internet Connection Wizard.

## Outlook Express Window

The Outlook Express window in Windows 2000 consists of the menu bar and toolbar at the top of the window, the Folders and Contacts panes to the left of the window, and the main Outlook Express pane to the right of the Folders and Contacts panes. The main pane displays changes depending on the folder you select in the Folders pane.

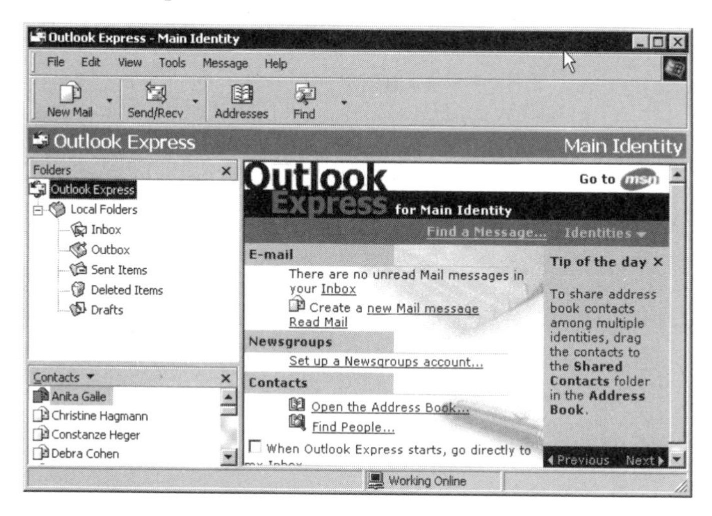


## Outlook Express Toolbar

When you first open Outlook Express, the toolbar contains the following options:

**New Mail** Opens the New Message dialog box, where you can create a new e-mail message. Click the arrow on the New Mail button to open a list of stationery options for the message. Choose Stationery to see the complete list and preview all available stationeries. Choose No Stationery if you don't want to use stationery, and click Web Page to create an e-mail using a saved HTML file.

**Send/Recv** Sends all messages currently held in the Outbox and receives all messages waiting on the mail server. Click the down arrow and choose to send and receive all messages, to only receive all messages, or to send all messages. You can also select the mail server you want to query. Any mail server you define is added to the bottom of this menu.

**Addresses** Opens the Address Book.

**Find** Opens the Find Message dialog box, which you can use to find a message in any of Outlook Express's folders. Click the arrow on the Find button and choose to look for messages in a specific folder, or to find the next message containing the search criteria. You can also choose to find people, or text contained in a specific message.

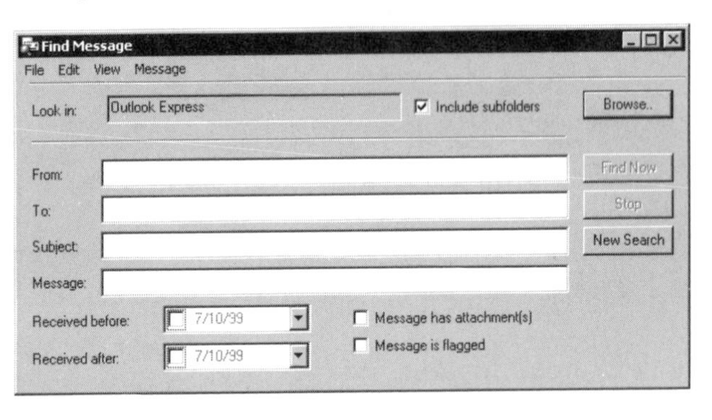


When you select a folder other than the Outlook Express or Local Folders folder (such as Inbox, Outbox, or Sent Items), the following e-mail message–related options are also available on the toolbar.

**Reply** Opens the selected message and places the cursor above it so that you can write a reply to the author of the message. The original message is included in the new message; attachments to the original message are not.

**Reply All** Opens the selected message and places the cursor above it so that you can write a reply to all recipients of the original message as well as the sender. The original message is included in the new message; attachments to the original message are not.

**Forward** Opens the selected message so you can forward it to a different recipient. You can add a new message above the original message. Attachments to the original message are also forwarded.

**Print** Prints the currently selected message(s).

**Delete** Deletes the currently selected message(s).

### *Customizing the Toolbar*

You can customize the Outlook Express toolbar by right-clicking anywhere on the toolbar and choosing Customize. This opens the Customize Toolbar dialog box, where you can add and remove toolbar buttons, choose whether and how you want text labels to display, select an icon size, and change the order of buttons on the toolbar. Click Reset to return to toolbar defaults.

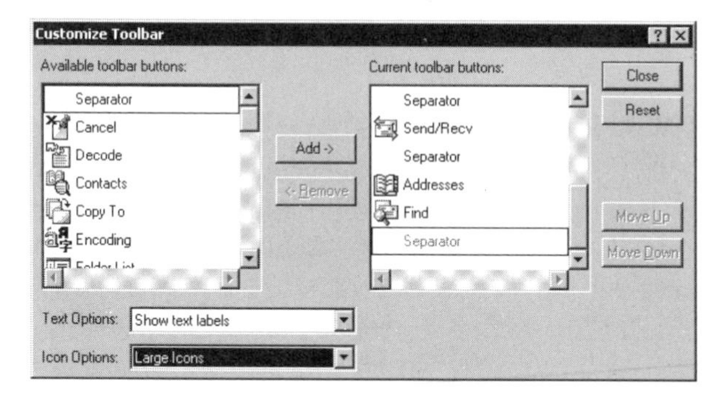


## Folders Pane

Use the Folders pane to navigate the Outlook Express folder structure. Several default folders exist to help you organize your messages. They include Inbox (which holds messages when they are first received), Outbox (which holds messages that haven't yet been sent), Sent Items (which holds messages you've sent), Deleted Items (which holds messages you've deleted), and Drafts (which holds messages you're still working on). Outlook Express automatically places messages in these folders, as appropriate. If you have unread messages in a folder, the number of unread messages appears in parentheses next to the folder.

You can also create new folders to further organize your messages.

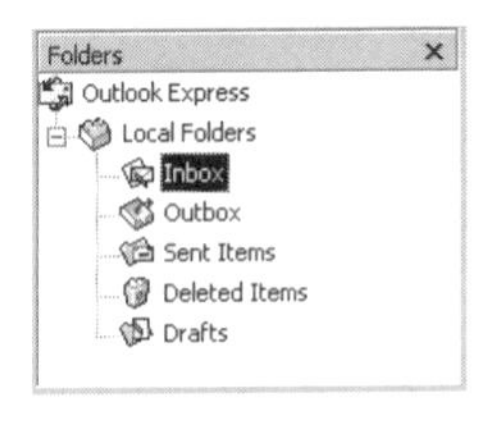


## Contacts Pane

Displays contacts from the address book for the currently selected identity. Right-click a contact and choose Send E-Mail to open a new mail message that is automatically addressed to the selected contact. Use the Shift and Ctrl keys to select more than one contact. Right-click a contact and choose Properties to display the contact's entry in the Address book.

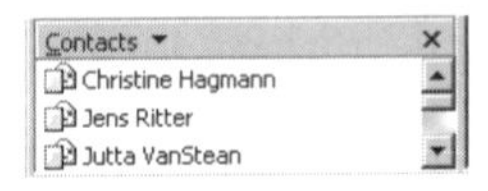


## Outlook Express Menus

The Outlook Express menus contain many of the familiar Windows 2000 menu options, all of the options that are accessible via the toolbar buttons, and many additional options for configuring Outlook Express. Whether an option is available on a menu depends on where you are in Outlook Express and what selections you have made. Some of the actions you can perform using menu options are importing and exporting address books, messages, and account settings; marking messages as read; moving messages; changing views; synchronizing Outlook Express; creating rules for messages; and setting up and configuring accounts.

## Creating and Sending a Message

To create and send a new message, follow these steps:

1. Click New Mail on the toolbar, or choose File ➢ New ➢ Mail Message.
2. Type the recipient's e-mail address in the To text box. Separate multiple addresses with semicolons or commas. If

you have entered contacts in your address book, you can click the To icon and select addresses from the list.

3. If you want to send copies to other recipients, type their addresses in the CC text box.

4. Type a subject for the message in the Subject text box.

5. Type the message in the New Message body area in the lower part of the New Message window. You can format the message by selecting a font, font size, and other attributes for the text.

**TIP** You can add other items to the message—such as attachments, text files, images, and business cards—by using the Insert menu. You can further format your message by choosing options from the Format menu, and you can perform other functions—such as spell-checking or encrypting your message, or requesting a read receipt—by using the Tools menu. You can also assign a priority to the message by choosing Message ➢ Set Priority and then selecting a priority.

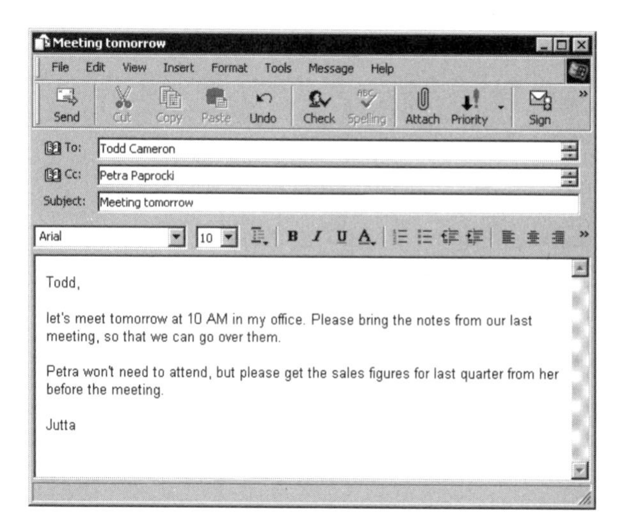


Once you've created the message, you're ready to send it. When you send a message, it goes to the Outbox and is then sent to the mail server from there. You can send a message in one of several ways:

- Click Send on the toolbar.
- Choose File ➢ Send Message.
- Choose File ➢ Send Later.

If you're not connected to the Internet, the message stays in the Outbox until the next time you connect. If you chose File ➢ Send Later, then the message won't be sent until you perform a manual send of all messages in the Outlook Express window (click Send/Recv or choose Tools ➢ Send and Receive ➢ Send and Receive All or Send All), even if you are currently connected to the Internet.

### *Attaching a File to a Mail Message*

You will at times want to send files you have created in other programs to other people using e-mail. To attach a file to a mail message, follow these steps:

1. Create a new mail message.
2. Choose Insert ➢ File Attachment, or click the Attach button on the toolbar (the button may not be visible by default; you may have to resize the New Message dialog box to see it).
3. Browse for and select the file, then click Attach.
4. You'll see the attached file in the Attach field, including the file's size (this field is only visible after you've attached a file).

## Reading Mail

To read new mail, select the Inbox folder in the Folders pane, and then select the message header for the message you want to read in the upper portion of the Preview pane to the right of the Folders pane. The actual message displays in the lower portion of the Preview pane. You can read messages in any other folder in the same fashion.

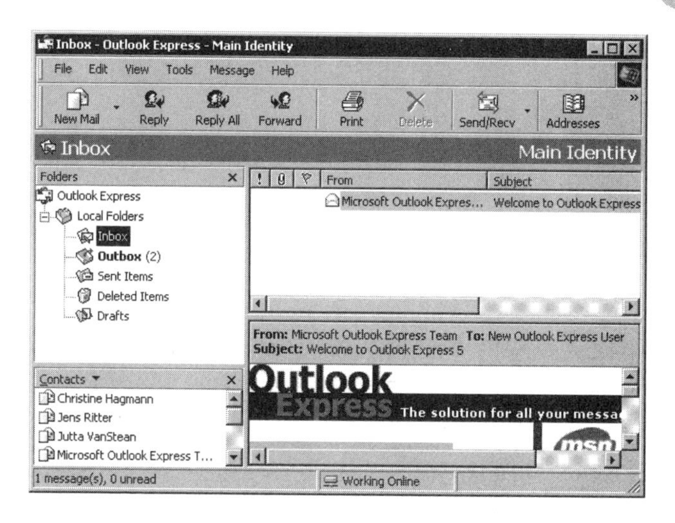


You can right-click any message header and select from several options. You can choose to open the message, print it, reply to the sender or all recipients, or forward the message either as a mail message or as an attachment. You can also mark the message as read or unread, move or copy it to a different folder, or delete it. Finally, you can add the sender to your address book and access message properties.

## Reading News

You can use Outlook Express as a newsreader for Internet-based newsgroups. Before you can do so, you must set up a news account by choosing Tools ➢ Accounts, clicking Add, and choosing News. Follow the Internet Connection Wizard's instructions to complete the account setup. Once you have created an account, you can download a list of newsgroups to which your ISP has access. You can then search the groups and select those that interest you. You can read articles others have posted and post your own articles to newsgroups using Outlook Express's e-mail functions.

## Working with Identities

You can share Outlook Express with others by setting up and using multiple identities. Each identity sees its own mail messages, uses its own contacts, and so forth. You can see which identity is currently in use by checking the far-right corner of the bar right below the toolbar, where the current identity's name displays.

When you first open Outlook Express, the default identity, Main Identity, is used.

**TIP** You can also use identities when in the Address Book.

### *Creating a New Identity*

To create a new identity in Outlook Express, follow these steps:

1. Choose File ➢ Identities ➢ Add New Identity.
2. In the New Identity dialog box, type your name in the text box.
3. Check Require a Password if you want to password-protect your identity.
4. If you selected Require a Password, enter your password in the Enter Password dialog box that appears and click OK. Otherwise, skip to step 5.
5. Click OK.
6. Click Yes to switch to the new identity now or click No to continue using the current identity.

### *Switching to Another Identity*

To switch to another identity, follow these steps:

1. Choose File ➢ Switch Identity.
2. In the list box, select the identity to which you want to switch.
3. Enter the password if necessary.
4. Click OK.
5. If you're connected to the Internet, you're prompted to choose whether you want to keep the current connection

for the next identity. Choose Yes to stay connected or No to break the connection.

### *Logging Off Identities*

To log off the current identity, follow these steps:

1. Choose File ➢ Switch Identity.
2. Click Log Off Identity.
3. Click Yes to confirm.
4. If you're connected to the Internet, you'll have to choose whether you want to keep the current connection for the next identity. Click Yes or No accordingly. Outlook Express then closes. If you're connected to the Internet and Auto Disconnect is enabled, you'll have to specify whether you want to stay connected or disconnect from the Internet.

After logging off an identity, the next time you start Outlook Express, the Identity Login dialog box appears and you'll have to log in using one of the available identities.

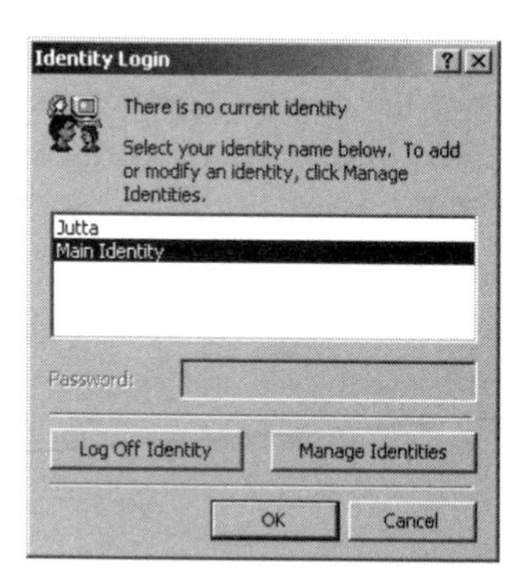


## Configuring Outlook Express Options

You can further configure Outlook Express through several tabs in the Options dialog box. To access Outlook Express options, choose Tools ➢ Options. The tabs are as follows:

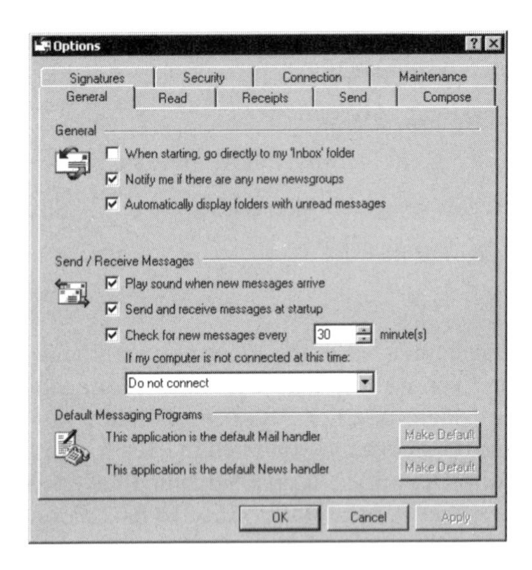


**General** Contains options for configuring Outlook Express startup and sending and receiving messages. Also lets you set Outlook Express as the default mail and news program.

**Read** Lets you configure how you want Outlook Express to display mail and news messages and select fonts to use for reading messages.

**Receipts** Lets you request receipts that tell you when a recipient has read a message, and configure whether you want read receipts sent when you read a message. You can also separately configure secure receipts for digitally signed messages.

**Send** Contains options for configuring how messages are sent, as well as the mail and news sending format (HTML or Plain Text).

**Compose** Lets you specify which fonts Outlook Express should use for creating messages, which stationery it should use with HTML messages, and whether it should include your business card with new messages.

**Signatures** Lets you specify whether you want to sign each outgoing message and lets you define your signature.

**Security** Lets you select the security zone you want to use for Internet Explorer, obtain and manage Digital IDs, and specify whether you want to encrypt and digitally sign outgoing messages.

**Connection** Contains options for configuring dial-up and Internet connection settings.

**Maintenance** Lets you configure how you want Outlook Express to handle the cleaning up of your messages and whether you want to create error log files for troubleshooting purposes. The Cleaning Up Messages section includes such options as Empty Messages from the "Deleted Items" Folder on Exit, and Compact Messages in the Background.

## Creating Mail Message Rules

You can create rules for your incoming messages that will help you keep your messages organized. For example, you might create a rule specifying that you want Outlook Express to:

- Move certain messages to certain folders
- Highlight messages from specific senders
- Automatically forward messages from certain senders to other people

To create a rule that will be applied automatically to all incoming messages, follow these steps:

1. Choose Tools ➢ Message Rules ➢ Mail.
2. In the New Mail Rule dialog box, in list box number 1, select one or more conditions for the rule you want to create. For example, you can choose Where the From Line Contains People and Where the Message Is Marked as Priority. A description for the rule appears automatically in list box number 3.

**TIP** Once you've created a rule and you want to create another new rule starting with step 1, the Message Rules dialog box appears instead of the New Mail Rule dialog box after you select Mail. To access the New Mail Rule dialog box, click New.

3. In list box number 2, select the action(s) you want performed if the rule is met. Examples are moving the message to a specific folder, deleting the message, and forwarding the message.

4. In list box number 3, click each of the hyperlinks to specify the details of the conditions and to specify the details of the selected actions. This might include specifying the name(s) of sender(s) for whom you want the rule to apply, or specifying folders to which you want a message to be moved.

**TIP** If you have multiple conditions, click the AND link to open the And/Or dialog box, where you can specify whether a message must match all of the criteria (AND) or any one of the criteria (OR).

**WARNING** You must specify details for each condition and action; otherwise, you won't be able to save the rule.

5. In text box number 4, type a name for the rule.

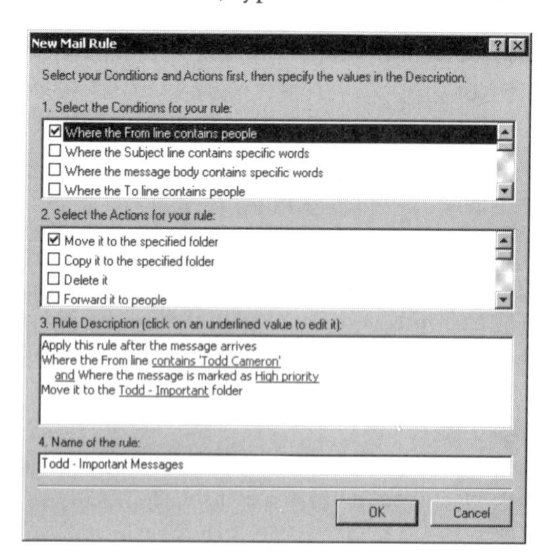

6. Click OK. The Message Rules dialog box displays the name and rule description for the rule you just created. Here you can create another rule; modify, copy, or remove existing rules; and change the order of rules.

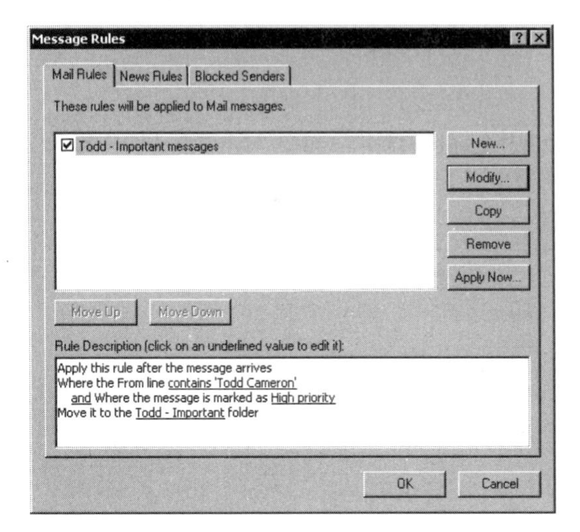


7. If you want the rule to apply to existing messages, click Apply Now (otherwise, skip to step 8). In the Apply Mail Rules dialog box, select the rule(s) you want to apply, browse to the folder to which you want to apply the rule(s), and click Apply Now. Click OK, then click Close.

8. Click OK.

## Blocking Senders

Outlook Express lets you specify e-mail addresses from which you don't want to receive mail and/or news messages (blocking the sender). If a mail message arrives from a blocked sender, the message is automatically moved to the Deleted Items folder. This can help you keep your Inbox uncluttered. An example of e-mail addresses you might want to block are known spamming e-mail addresses.

To block a sender, perform these steps:

1. Choose Tools ➢ Message Rules ➢ Blocked Senders List.
2. On the Blocked Senders tab in the Message Rules dialog box, click Add.
3. Type the e-mail address or domain name you want to block in the Address text box.
4. Check the appropriate radio button to block mail, news, or mail and news messages.
5. Click OK.

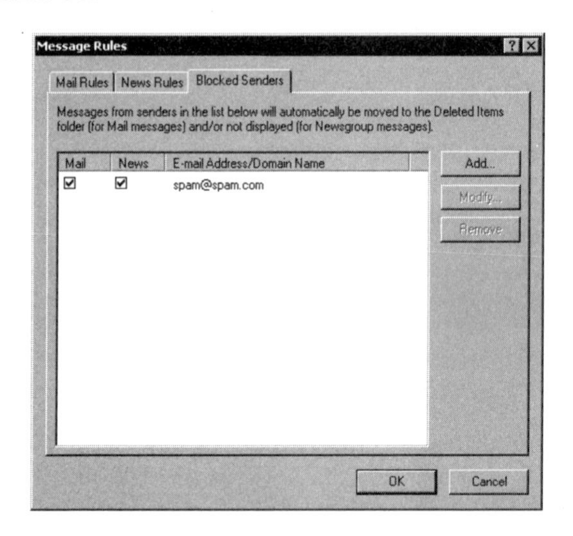


6. On the Blocked Senders tab, you'll see the e-mail address you just added to the list of blocked senders. Verify that the information is correct, make any changes if necessary, and click OK.

**TIP** An alternative method for blocking senders is to select a message in any folder and choose Message ➢ Block Sender. The message sender's e-mail address is then automatically added to the Blocked Senders list.

## Watching and Grouping Conversations

Outlook Express lets you keep track of conversations (the original message and replies) by either watching or grouping conversations.

### *Watching a Conversation*

Watching a conversation means that you tell Outlook Express which conversation you want to watch and then all new messages pertaining to that conversation are marked with the watch icon (depicting glasses).

To watch a conversation, perform these steps:

1. Choose View ➢ Columns.
2. Select Watch /Ignore to turn on the Watch/Ignore column and click OK.

**TIP** You have to turn this column on separately for each folder in which you want to watch conversations.

3. Select a message.
4. Choose Message ➢ Watch Conversation. The watch icon will appear next to all messages pertaining to that message. Also, messages in a conversation will be highlighted in the color you specified on the Read tab in Tools ➢ Options.

### *Grouping Messages*

You can group all messages in a conversation together so that it's easier for you to track conversations. To do so, select a message, then choose View ➢ Current View ➢ Group Messages by Conversations. Outlook Express then groups all messages by conversation (the original message and all replies). After you activate Group Message by Conversations, the original message of any conversation displays a plus sign to the left of the message header. You can expand the grouped conversation (by clicking the plus sign) and collapse the conversation (by clicking the minus sign).

**See Also** Address Book, Internet Connection Wizard, Internet Explorer, Network and Dial-up Connections

# Paint

Paint Lets you create black-and-white or color drawings, which you can save as bitmap (.BMP) files. Drawings created in Paint can be pasted into other documents, printed, or used as Windows 2000 backgrounds.

Choose Start ➢ Programs ➢ Accessories ➢ Paint to open Paint.

The Paint window consists of a menu bar at the top of the window, a toolbox at the left side of the window, and a drawing area to the right of the toolbar. It also contains a color box at the bottom of the toolbox and drawing area, and a status bar at the bottom of the window.

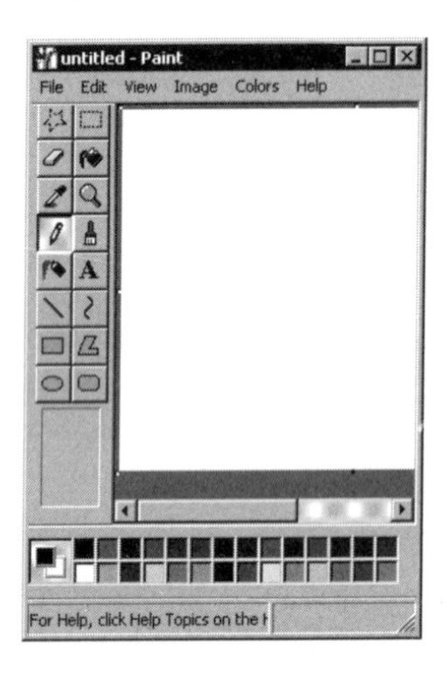


## Paint Toolbox

The Paint toolbox consists of many buttons that activate drawing tools, such as a pencil, brush, and magnifier. When you activate a drawing tool by clicking its button, additional selections might appear in the field beneath the toolbox. An example of this is the Brush drawing tool. When you activate it, you can also choose from a variety of available brushstrokes, which Paint displays below the toolbox.

To use a drawing tool in Paint, click its button to activate it, select a tool shape if available, and then draw in the drawing

area by dragging the mouse to create the lines and shapes you want.

The Paint toolbox contains the following buttons:

**Free-Form Select** Lets you select an irregularly shaped portion of the drawing and move, edit, or copy it. You can choose from an opaque or transparent background.

**Select** Lets you select a rectangular portion of the drawing and move, edit, or copy it. You can choose from an opaque or transparent background.

**Eraser/Color Eraser** Lets you erase a portion of the drawing by moving the eraser over a portion of the drawing. You can choose from several eraser shapes.

**Fill with Color** Lets you fill portions of the drawing. You can select any color from the color palette to use as fill color.

**Pick Color** Lets you pick a color in the drawing and then use it for subsequent line or shape drawing. Useful for matching colors within drawings.

**Magnifier** Lets you change the magnification of the drawing. You can choose from several magnification strengths.

**Pencil** Lets you draw a free-form line using a width of one pixel.

**Brush** Lets you draw a brush stroke. You can choose from several brush shapes and sizes.

**Airbrush** Lets you draw using an airbrush. You can choose from several airbrush sizes.

**Text** Lets you add text to the drawing. You can choose from an opaque or transparent background.

To create a text box, click in the drawing and drag the mouse pointer to the right. When you release the mouse button, the Text toolbar appears, and you can choose the font, font size, and font style for your text box.

**Line** Lets you draw a straight line. You can choose from several line widths.

**Curve** Lets you draw a curved line. You can choose from several line widths. To draw a curved line, first draw a straight line using the Curve tool, then click anywhere on the line and drag the mouse to create the curve. You can then select another point and drag again to change the curve or create another curve. You can drag only twice to create the curve.

**Rectangle** Lets you draw a rectangle. You can choose from several fill styles.

**Polygon** Lets you draw a polygon, or figure consisting of multiple lines that connect at any angle. You can choose from several fill styles. To create a polygon, draw a straight line to begin, then click where you want the next line to end. Paint creates a line that automatically connects to the end of the first line. Continue until your polygon is completed, then double-click to finish.

**Ellipse** Lets you draw an ellipse. You can choose from several fill styles.

**Rounded Rectangle** Lets you draw a rectangle with rounded edges. You can choose from several fill styles.

**TIP** If you draw by dragging the mouse pointer while holding down the left mouse button, the foreground color is used. You can use the background color by holding down the right mouse button.

## Color Box

By default, lines and shapes you draw are black on white. To choose a color for lines and shapes, click the appropriate color in the color palette before or after selecting a drawing tool and start drawing.

## Status Bar

When you select a drawing tool in the toolbar, you'll see a helpful description in the left portion of the status bar. Next to the description area of the status bar you can see where in the image the mouse pointer is currently positioned.

## Paint Menus

The Paint menus contain many standard Windows options as well as some unique options. The Edit and Help menus do not contain any unique options.

### *File Menu*

The File menu contains the following unique items:

**Select Source** Lets you select a scanning device.

**Scan New** Lets you scan a new image into Paint.

**Set as Wallpaper (Tiled)** Lets you designate the current drawing as the desktop wallpaper. The wallpaper will be tiled.

**Set as Wallpaper (Centered)** Lets you designate the current drawing as the desktop wallpaper. The wallpaper will be centered.

### *View Menu*

The View menu contains the following unique options:

**Tool Box** Toggles the display of the toolbox.

**Color Box** Toggles the display of the color box.

**Status Bar** Toggles the display of the status bar.

**Text Toolbar** Toggles the display of the Text toolbar. The Text Toolbar option is available only after you create a text box in the drawing and while the Text tool is still selected.

**Zoom** Lets you choose various zoom options from a submenu. Options include Normal Size, Large Size, and Custom. The Zoom submenu also contains two other options: Grid and Show Thumbnail. Grid lets you display a grid over a selected portion of the drawing, and Show Thumbnail displays a selected portion of the drawing as a thumbnail.

**NOTE** The Grid and Show Thumbnail options are active only if the drawing is zoomed to a size other than normal.

**View Bitmap** Lets you see a full-screen preview of the current bitmap image. Press any key or click anywhere in the bitmap to return to the Paint window.

### *Image Menu*

The Image menu contains the following unique items:

**Flip/Rotate** Opens the Flip and Rotate dialog box, where you can choose to turn the drawing horizontally or vertically or by a 90-, 180-, or 270-degree angle.

**Stretch/Skew** Opens the Stretch and Skew dialog box, where you can choose to stretch or skew the image horizontally or vertically by a percentage you specify.

**Invert Colors** Reverses colors of the drawing or a selection or changes them to their complementary color.

**Attributes** Opens the Attributes dialog box, where you can adjust the width and height of the drawing; specify its measurements in inches, centimeters, or pixels; and specify whether to use black and white or colors. You can also choose to use a transparent color and specify which color to use. Simply click Default to return to the default settings.

**Clear Image** Erases the image from the screen. You can restore it by choosing Edit ➢ Undo.

**Draw Opaque** Toggles opaque or transparent drawing. Opaque means the drawing covers the existing image; transparent means the underlying image shows through.

### *Colors Menu*

The Colors menu contains the following unique item:

**Edit Colors** Opens the Edit Colors dialog box, where you can create custom colors.

**See Also** Imaging

# Performance

Performance

Microsoft Management Console (MMC) console that displays system performance data as graphs and lets you configure alerts and data logs.

To open Performance, choose Start ➢ Settings ➢ Control Panel, double-click Administrative Tools, and then double-click Performance.

Performance contains two MMC console snap-ins: System Monitor and Performance Logs and Alerts.

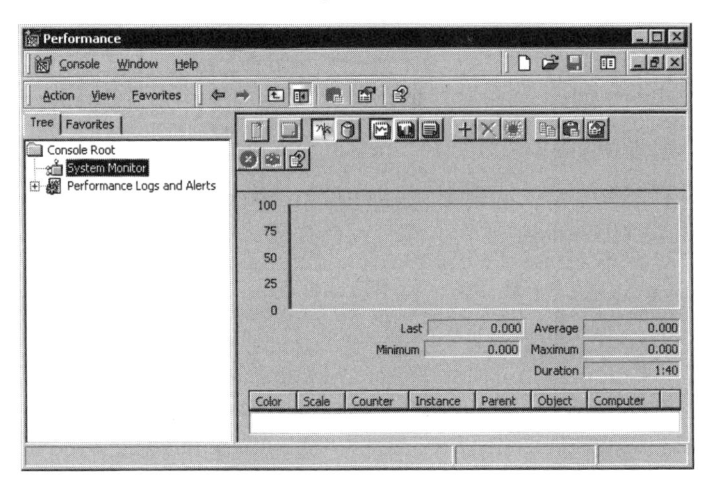

**TIP** You can also access Performance Logs and Alerts through Computer Management in Administrative Tools. You'll find it under System Tools in the console tree.

## System Monitor

The System Monitor snap-in displays system performance in one of three views: chart, histogram, or report. You can view many different performance counters for several different performance objects. Performance objects include such items as Browser, Cache, Indexing Service, Memory, Network Interface, and Processor, to name but a few. Available performance counters depend on the performance object you have selected.

### Viewing Performance Information

To be able to view performance information, select System Monitor in the console tree, then add one or more counters for a performance object to the list of monitored objects. Follow these steps:

1. Right-click anywhere in the Details pane and choose Add Counters, or click the Add button (+) on the toolbar.
2. Check Select Counters from Computer, and select the computer from the drop-down list.
3. Select a performance object from the drop-down list.
4. Check All Counters to display all counters available for the performance object, or check Select Counters from List and choose the counter or counters you want to display.
5. Click Add. If you selected All Counters, System Monitor adds all counters to the Details pane. If you checked Select Counters from List, System Monitor adds the counter or counters you selected to the Details pane. To add other counters, select one or more additional counters in the list and click Add. Continue in this fashion until you've added all the counters you wish to view. If you're not sure which counter to add, select a counter and click Explain for a description of the counter.
6. Check All Instances, or check Select Instances from List and make your selection in the list.
7. Click Close.

Each counter has an assigned color so that you can distinguish it in the graph. You'll see color assignments in the legend (the list of counters) below the graph. There, you'll also see the counter scale, counter name, instance, parent, object, and computer.

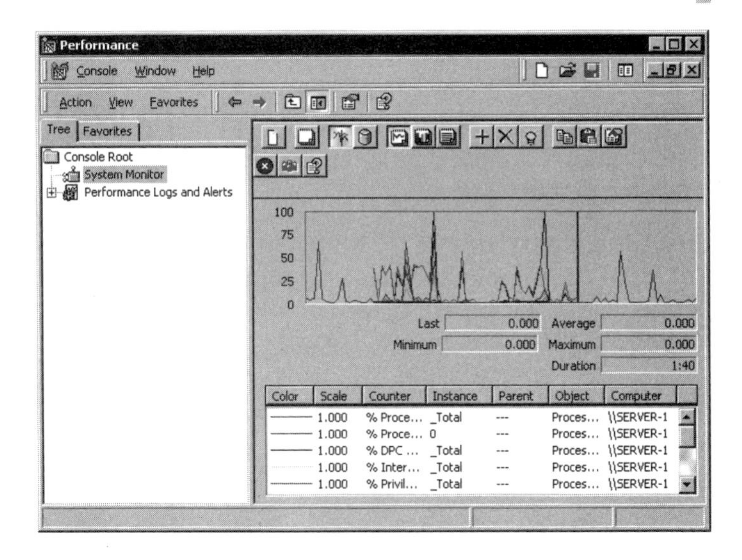


To see counter values for a specific counter, select a counter in the legend, then view the values for that counter (last, average, minimum, maximum, and duration) in the value bar directly below the graph.

### Highlighting Counters

If you have many counters selected, it might be difficult to see each counter in the graph. You can click the Highlight button on the toolbar and then click a counter in the list to bring that counter to the front in the graph and change the counter's color to white.

### Deleting Counters

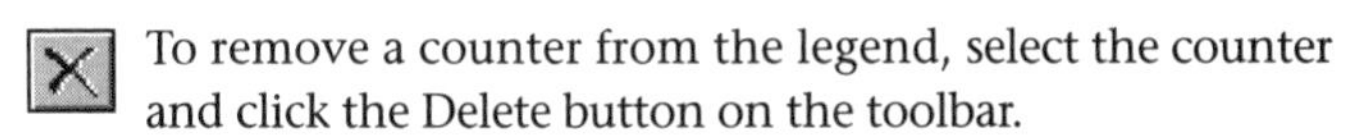

To remove a counter from the legend, select the counter and click the Delete button on the toolbar.

To remove all counters and start over, click the New Counter Set button on the toolbar.

### Changing Views

To change the view from chart to histogram, click the View Histogram button.

To change the view to report, click the View Report button on the toolbar.

### Clearing the Display

To clear the display for the current counters, click the Clear Display button on the toolbar.

### Stopping the Display

To stop the counters temporarily, click the Freeze Display button on the toolbar. To continue the counters, click the Freeze Display button again.

After you have stopped counters, you can update the data to the most current data (snapshot) by clicking the Update Data button. This button becomes unavailable when you click the Freeze Display button again to continue displaying counter data continuously.

### Displaying Data from a Log File

To display data from a log file instead of the current activity, click the View Log File Data button on the toolbar and open the log file you want to view.

### Changing System Monitor Properties

Right-click anywhere in System Monitor in the Details pane and choose Properties to customize System Monitor. Use the General, Source, Data, Graph, Colors, and Fonts tabs to choose items such as which elements to display and which counters to view (and the colors for each counter). Among other items, you can also change the view, update interval, source (current activity or log file), graph properties, and System Monitor colors and fonts.

## Performance Logs and Alerts

MMC console snap-in that lets you configure performance-related logs and alerts. Two log types exist: counter logs and trace logs. Started logs (and alerts) have a green icon; stopped logs have a red icon. Right-click a log and choose Start or Stop from the shortcut menu to start or stop logging, or select the log or alert and choose Action ➢ Start or Action ➢ Stop. To delete a log or alert, select it in the Details pane, then click Delete on the toolbar.

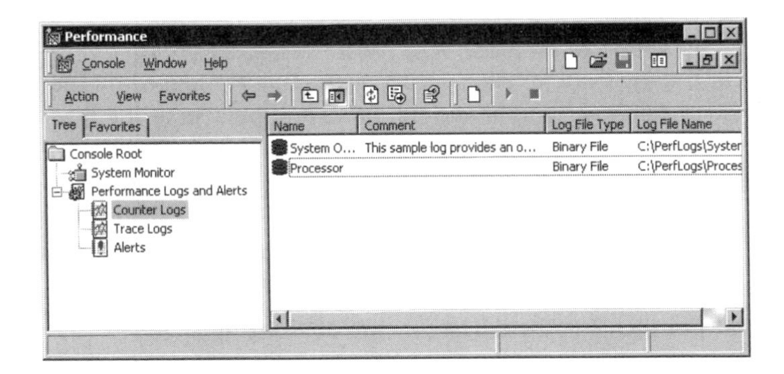


### Counter Logs

Counter logs record information obtained from System Monitor counters you specify. To create a counter log, perform these steps:

1. Select Counter Logs in the console tree.
2. Right-click anywhere in the Details pane and choose New Log Settings.
3. Enter a name for the log and click OK.
4. On the General tab, click Add to add counters to the log. The process is the same as adding counters in System Monitor.
5. On the Log Files tab, configure options for the log file, such as location, name, type, and size.
6. On the Schedule tab, specify when you want the log to be started and stopped.
7. Click OK.

To view the data in the log, use System Monitor.

### Trace Logs

Trace logs record data when an activity occurs, such as a process creation/deletion, disk I/O operation, or page fault. These logs are different from counter logs, which record all activity data during a specified interval.

To create a new trace log, follow these steps:

1. Select Trace Logs in the console tree.
2. Right-click anywhere in the Details pane and choose New Log Settings.

3. Enter a name for the log and click OK.
4. On the General tab, specify events that are logged by the system provider, or add non-system providers to the list. Providers might include the Windows 2000 Kernel Trace Provider (system provider), Active Directory: Kerberos, Active Directory: NetLogon, Active Directory: SAM, Local Security Authority (LSA), and others. Click Provider Status to see a list of providers.
5. On the Log Files tab, set up log files settings, such as location, name, type, and size. On the Schedules tab, create a schedule for starting and stopping the log. The Advanced tab lets you configure buffer settings.
6. Click OK to create the log.

**TIP** Each system or non-system provider can be used by only one trace log at a time.

To view the data in the log file, use System Monitor.

### *Alerts*

You can use alerts to send messages, run programs, or start a log when a counter value equals, exceeds, or is less than the value specified in the alert setting.

To create a new alert, follow these steps:

1. Select Trace Logs in the console tree.
2. Right-click anywhere in the Details pane and choose New Alert Settings.
3. Enter a name for the alert and click OK.
4. On the General tab, add a comment for the alert, then click Add to add a counter using the same method you do when adding counters to the legend in System Monitor. Next, specify when you want System Monitor to trigger the alert and how frequently it should sample data.
5. On the Action tab, select the action you want to take place when an alert is triggered, such as logging an entry in the application event log, sending a message to a user you specify, starting a performance log, or running a program.

6. On the Schedule tab, choose when you want to start and stop alert scans. You can also specify whether to start a new scan when one scan is done.

### *Creating New Logs and Alerts from Saved Files*

You can save logs and alerts as HTML files and then use them to create other logs and alerts. Right-click the log or alert, choose Save Settings As, then enter a name and click Save. To use the saved file to create a new log or alert, right-click anywhere in a blank area of the Details pane and choose New Log Settings From or New Alert Settings From. Then select the applicable HTML file and click Open.

**See Also** Microsoft Management Console (MMC), Computer Management

# Permissions

Permissions specify what kind of access is granted to users or groups for objects or object properties. The permissions you can assign depend on the object type. Some permissions are common to all object types. They include the following:

- Read
- Modify
- Change Owner
- Delete

Additional examples of permissions are Full Control, Read & Execute, Write, and so forth.

**NOTE** For detailed information on available permissions, see the entry Permissions in the Windows 2000 Help system. This entry will also provide you with more detailed information on other permission-related information.

## Explicit and Inherited Permissions

Permissions can be assigned either directly to an object (this is called an explicit permission) or inherited from a parent object (this is called an inherited permission). Explicit permissions are those permissions Windows assigns when an object is first created and those that are manually assigned, by an administrator, for example. By default, any permissions assigned to a container object are automatically inherited by objects that are created in that container. For example, if you create a folder called Data and then create subfolders and files in that folder, the subfolders and files inherit the permissions assigned to the Data folder. This means that the Data folder's permissions are explicit and permissions of subfolders and files in the Data folder are inherited.

**See also** Help

# Personalized Menus

Feature that displays only the most frequently and most recently accessed menu items on Start menu menus. Enables faster access of favorite programs and menu items. You can turn off this feature by deselecting the option Use Personalized Menus on the General tab of the Taskbar & Start Menu property sheet. To access this tab, choose Start ➢ Settings ➢ Taskbar & Start Menu.

**See Also** Taskbar & Start Menu

# Phone and Modem Options

Phone and Modem ...

Lets you configure modem properties and telephone dialing rules. Modem properties determine the modem's configuration, and dialing rules are used to specify how you want Windows to dial phone numbers from each defined location. Choose Start ➢ Settings ➢ Control Panel, then double-click the Phone and Modem Options icon to open the Phone & Modem Options dialog box. This dialog box has three tabs: Dialing Rules, Modems, and Advanced.

**Dialing Rules** Use this tab to specify dialing rules for each location listed in the Locations list box. You can also add new locations by clicking New or delete locations by selecting a location and clicking Delete. To edit the dialing rules for a location, select the location in the Locations list box and click Edit to display the Edit Location dialog box. This dialog box has three tabs: General, Area Code Rules, and Calling Card.

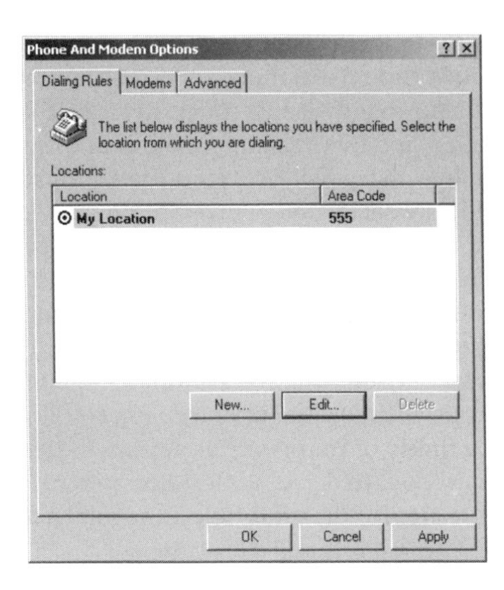


**General** Use this tab to specify the location's name, the country/region from which you're calling, and the area code for the location. In the Dialing Rules area of the General tab, you can specify a number for Windows to dial in order to reach an outside line for either local or long-distance calls. You can also choose to disable call waiting (and provide the number Windows must dial to disable call waiting) and specify whether to use tone or pulse dialing.

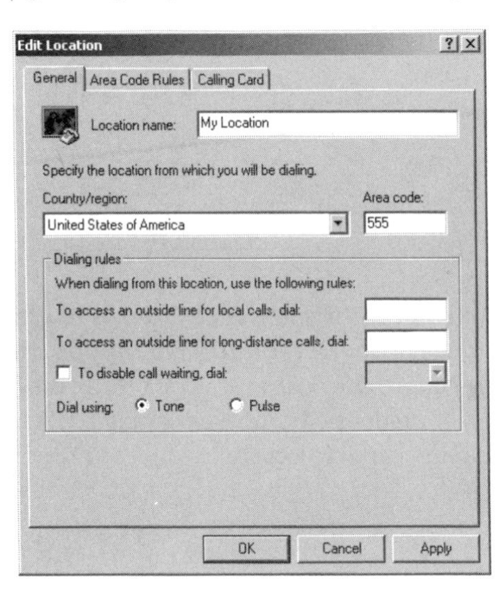

**Area Code Rules** This tab lets you configure how Windows should dial numbers to specific area codes (including your own area code). To create a new rule, click New and fill in the information in the New Area Code Rule dialog box. You must specify an area code for the rule. By default, all prefixes in this area code are affected by the rule. Alternatively, you can specify prefixes to which you want the rule to apply. Finally, specify the rules. Rules include the number(s) Windows should dial before dialing phone numbers (such as 1 for a long-distance call) and whether Windows should include the area code when dialing phone numbers. Click OK when you've finished. Your new rule appears in the Area Code Rules list box. To delete a rule, select it in the list and click Delete. To edit a rule, select the rule in the Area Code Rules list box and click Edit.

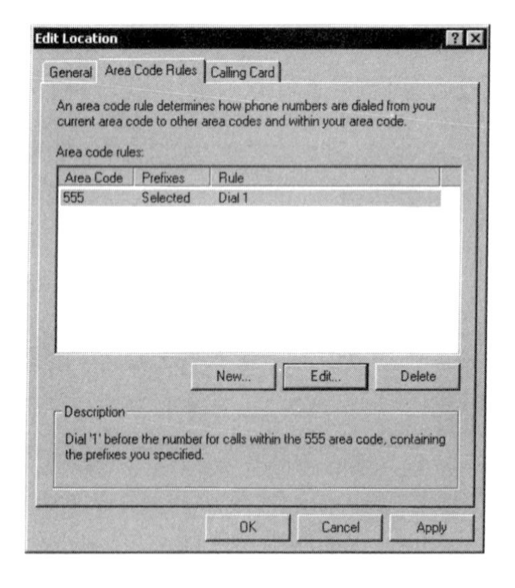


**Calling Card** If you want Windows to use a calling card to make phone calls, this tab lets you specify which calling card to use. Either select a calling card type from the list of predefined card types or click New to create a new calling card type entry if your card isn't in the list. If you're using a predefined card type, all you have to do is specify your account number and PIN number. If you're creating a new card type, you'll have to assign a name to the card type, specify your account number and PIN number, and create rules for the card type on the Long Distance, International, and Local Calls tabs in the New Calling Card dialog box that appears after you click New. On these tabs, you can specify the access phone number(s) to dial for long-distance, international, and local calls, and specify the dialing steps required to make a call using the card. To add a dialing step, click the appropriate button below the Calling Card Dialing Steps list box (Access Number, PIN, Wait for Prompt, Account Number, Destination Number, and Specify Digits). Use the Move Up and Move Down buttons to change the order of rules. After you configure the Long Distance, International, and Local Calls tabs, the General tab will show you when the calling card will be used (rules).

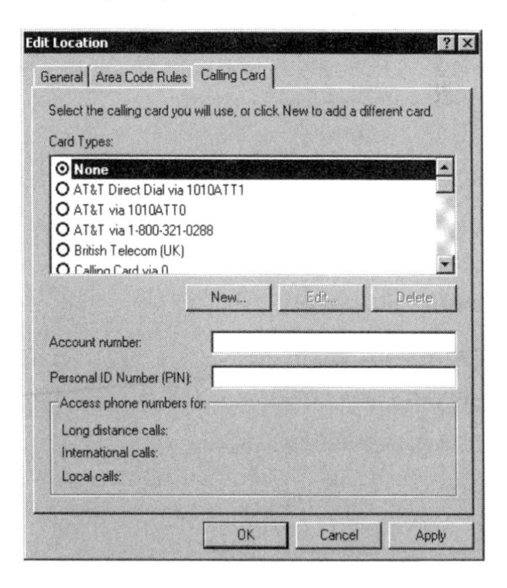


**Modems** Use this tab to view modems installed in the computer, view and change the properties of any installed modem, and add and remove modems. If you select a modem and click Properties, you'll see the modem's property sheet, which has three tabs: General, Diagnostics, and Advanced.

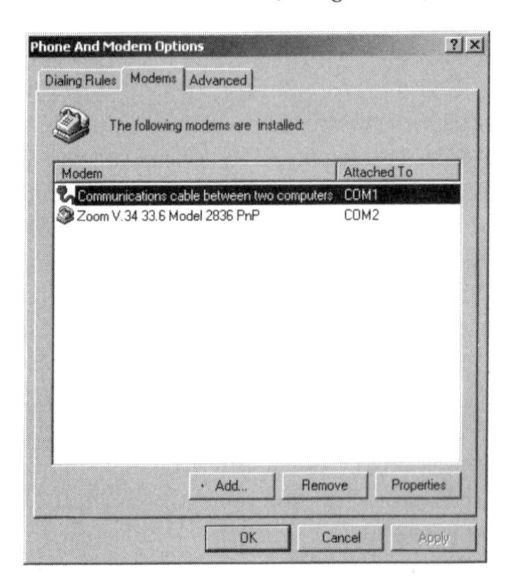


**General** On this tab, you can configure such items as the speaker volume and maximum port speed. You can also specify whether you want Windows to wait for a dial tone before dialing.

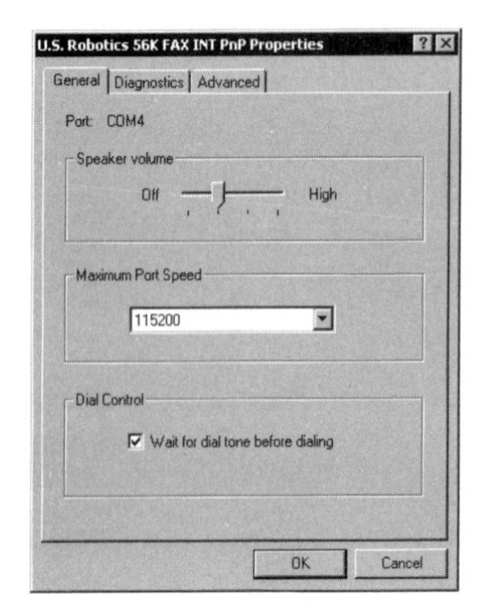

**Diagnostics** On this tab, you can run diagnostics on the modem to see if it is functioning properly by clicking Query Modem. Standard AT commands are sent to the modem, and the commands and the modem's responses are displayed in the list box. In Windows 2000 Professional, click Append to Log if you want Windows to append this log file to an existing log file rather than overwrite it. In Windows 2000 Server, click Record a Log to turn on the logging feature.

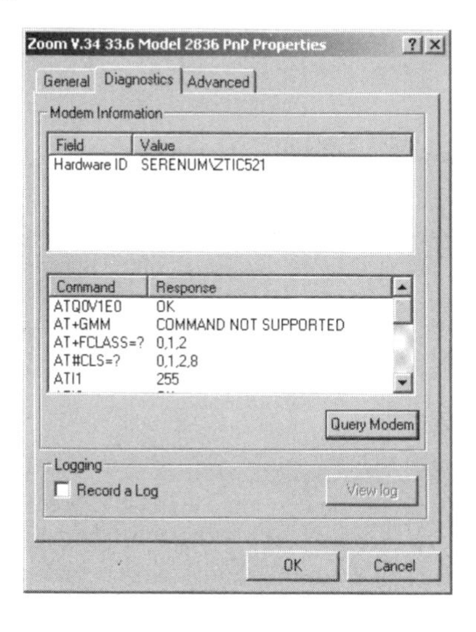

**TIP** In Windows 2000 Professional, logging is automatically turned on and the log file is overwritten unless you check Append to Log. In Windows 2000 Server, logging is not turned on by default. You turn it on by selecting the Record a Log check box.

**Advanced** On this tab, you can configure advanced options, such as specifying additional modem initialization commands. These commands override all other settings previously made because they are sent after other commands are sent to the modem.

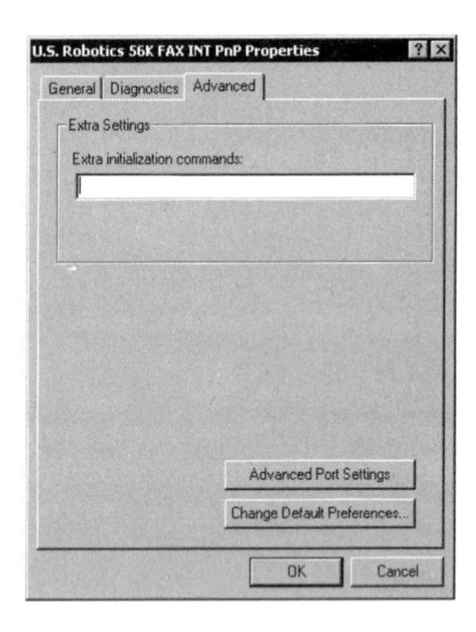


The Change Default Preferences button is also available on the Advanced tab. You click the Change Default Preferences button to change default preferences for your modem.

Change Default Preferences...

In the resulting dialog box, you can specify whether and when to disconnect calls if the computer is idle and when to stop the call if a connection cannot be established. Additional options depend on your hardware but typically include data connection preferences (such as port speed, data protocol, compression, and flow control) and hardware settings (such as data bits, parity, stop bits, and modulation).

Advanced Port Settings

For some modems, you might also see the Advanced Port Settings button on the Advanced tab. Click this button to configure advanced port settings. The available settings will depend on your hardware.

**TIP** You can also access the three tabs found on the modem property sheet by choosing Start ➢ Control Panel ➢ System, selecting the Hardware tab, clicking Device Manager, expanding Modem, and then right-clicking the modem in question and choosing Properties. Note that additional tabs are available in Device Manager, giving you general information about the modem, driver information, and resource usage information.

**Advanced** Use this tab to view telephony drivers installed on the computer, configure any installed telephony driver, and add and remove telephony drivers.

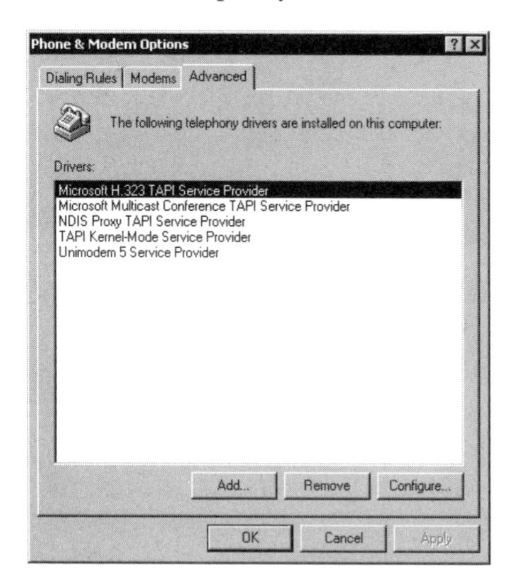


**See Also** System

# Phone Dialer

Phone Dialer Lets you make voice or video calls, or participate in video conference calls from your computer. You can connect by using a telephone connected to your computer, using a modem, over a network, through a telephone switch that's connected to your LAN, or via an Internet address. You'll also have to have a microphone and speakers connected to your computer, and you'll need to know the telephone number, DNS address, or IP address of the person you're calling. If you want others to see a video image of yourself, you'll need a camera attached to the computer. If you don't have a camera, you can still see video images of other people who do have a camera attached to their computer.

To open Phone Dialer, choose Start ➢ Programs ➢ Accessories ➢ Communications ➢ Phone Dialer.

## Phone Dialer Window

The Phone Dialer window consists of menus and toolbars at the top of the window, a left and right pane that take up the majority of the window, and a status bar at the bottom.

The left pane lets you view and select Directories and Directory entries, as well as access the Phone Dialer conference room for video conferences. The right pane displays the contents of any item selected in the left pane, such as people, conferences, and speed dial entries.

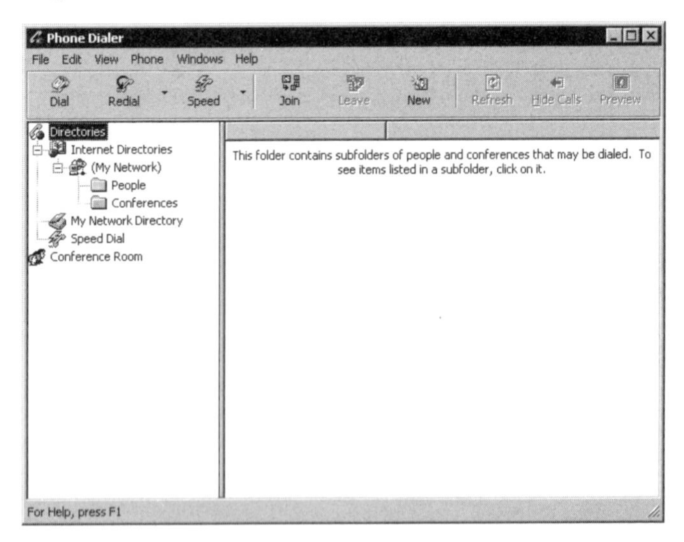


## Phone Dialer Menus and Toolbars

The Phone Dialer has several menus that enable you to use and configure Phone Dialer. Some choices on menus are available only when you have selected certain items in the left pane of the Phone Dialer window.

The Phone Dialer toolbars contain buttons for the most commonly used Phone Dialer functions, such as Dial, Redial, Speed Dial, Join Conference, Leave Conference, and Refresh. These functions are also available from the menus, with one exception: The Preview button on the toolbar is not accessible from any menu. It is available only when you're placing a call and toggles the display of the Preview window.

Additionally, you can access many of the functions available in the menus and on the toolbars by right-clicking an item in the left pane and making a selection from the pop-up menu.

### *File Menu*

The File menu lets you perform the following actions:

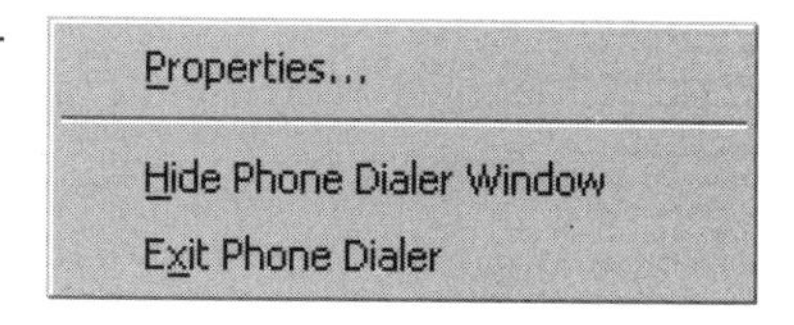


- View and configure properties of the selected item.
- Run the Phone Dialer in the background by hiding it.
- Exit the Phone Dialer.

### *Edit Menu*

The Edit menu lets you perform the following actions:

- Add an entry to the speed dial list. Information includes the name and phone number or network address.
- Edit the speed dial list.
- Add users and directory servers.
- Delete the selected item.
- Configure Phone Dialer options, such as which lines to use and audio and video settings.

### View Menu

The View menu lets you perform the following actions:

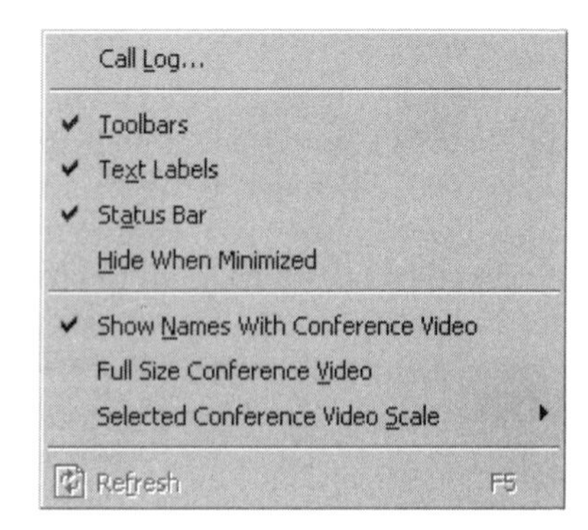


- View the Phone Dialer call log in Notepad.
- Toggle the display of toolbars, text under toolbar buttons, and the status bar.
- Run Phone Dialer in the background when it's minimized.
- Toggle the display of names when using Conference Video.
- Toggle the use of larger or smaller video screens for the video conference participants.
- Adjust the Conference Video scale. Values are 100, 200, and 400 percent.
- Refresh the current view.

### Phone Menu

The Phone menu lets you perform the following actions:

- Place a new Internet, phone, or conference call.
- Redial a previously made call.
- Choose an entry from the speed dial list and edit the speed dial list.
- Start a new conference.
- Start participating in a conference that is already in progress.
- Stop participating in a conference.

### *Windows Menu*

The Windows menu lets you perform the following actions:

- Run current calls in the background.
- Toggle the display of call windows on top (through the Call Windows submenu).
- Automatically close the call window when a call is ended (through the Call Windows submenu).
- Slide call windows left or right as new call windows are added (through the Call Windows submenu).
- Select a call window to make it the active window.

## Placing a Call

To place a call using Phone Dialer, perform these steps:

1. Click Dial on the toolbar to open the Dial dialog box.

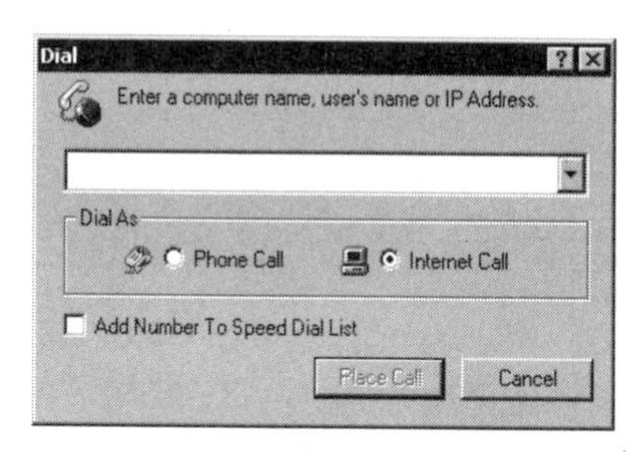


2. Enter the phone number, a user's name, or an IP address for the computer you're calling. You can alternatively make a choice from the drop-down list.
3. Select whether you want to dial as a phone call or as an Internet call. Optionally, you can choose to add the number to your speed dial list.
4. Click Place Call. A dialog box opens, which tells you that Phone Dialer is waiting for an answer. If the call is answered by the recipient, the message changes from Waiting for Answer to Connected. If the call is rejected, a message advises you of this fact. If the call is not answered, a message

tells you that you are connected. Click Disconnect to end the call.

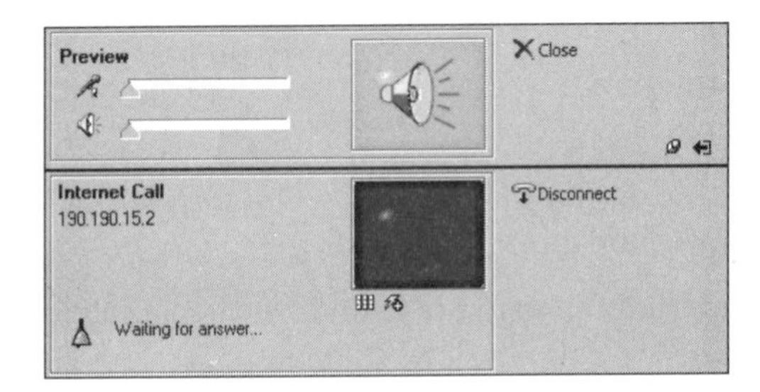


# Ping

Lets you send packets to a host's IP address on a network (LAN, WAN, Internet, intranet) to see if the host responds. Ping is often used to troubleshoot IP connectivity problems.

To use ping, choose Start ➢ Programs ➢ Accessories ➢ Command Prompt. At the command prompt, enter **ping *host IP address***.

```
Command Prompt
Microsoft Windows 2000 [Version 5.00.2072]
(C) Copyright 1985-1999 Microsoft Corp.

C:\>ping 190.190.15.2

Pinging 190.190.15.2 with 32 bytes of data:

Reply from 190.190.15.2: bytes=32 time<10ms TTL=128
Reply from 190.190.15.2: bytes=32 time<10ms TTL=128
Reply from 190.190.15.2: bytes=32 time<10ms TTL=128
Reply from 190.190.15.2: bytes=32 time<10ms TTL=128

Ping statistics for 190.190.15.2:
    Packets: Sent = 4, Received = 4, Lost = 0 (0% loss),
Approximate round trip times in milli-seconds:
    Minimum = 0ms, Maximum =  0ms, Average =  0ms

C:\>_
```

# Power Options

Controls the settings designed to reduce the amount of power your computer consumes. Conserving energy is becoming ever more important, both from an environmental and a cost-savings perspective. Power options can help you conserve valuable resources, such as electricity coming from standard wall outlets used to power desktop machines, as well as power from laptop batteries. The latter option extends the time you can effectively use your laptop while running on battery power. The power options you'll be able to control depend on your hardware and your hardware's configuration.

Choose Start ➢ Settings ➢ Control Panel and double-click Power Options to open the Power Options Properties dialog box. The tabs available depend on your hardware's support for power management. Common tabs include Power Schemes, Advanced, Hibernate, and UPS. If your computer supports Advanced Power Management, you'll also see a tab called APM, where you can enable or disable Advanced Power Management. Advanced Power Management helps you reduce your computer's overall power consumption and provides battery status information if the computer is running on battery power.

## Power Schemes Tab

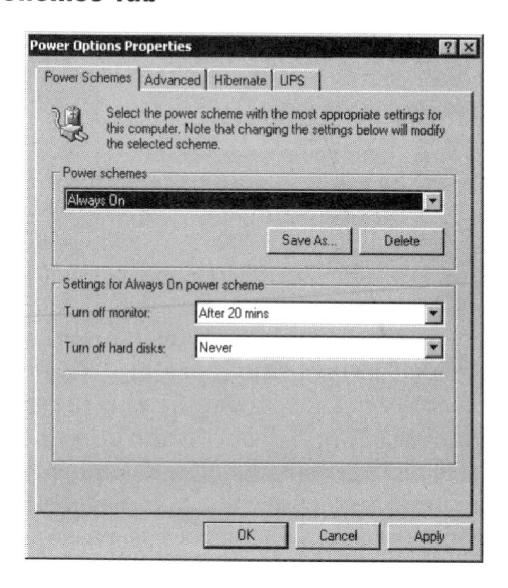


Power schemes are preset collections of power usage settings. Several power schemes are included with Windows 2000; however, you can also create your own power schemes. The options available on this tab depend on your hardware and your hardware's configuration. Possible power scheme power settings include:

- Placing the system on standby (where it will use less power)
- Placing the system into hibernation
- Turning off the monitor or hard disks (controlled separately)

You can specify the period of inactivity that must elapse before these settings take effect. Time frames extend from Never to After 5 Hours.

You may also be able to place your computer on standby manually by configuring Windows to place the computer on standby when you press the power button on a desktop or close the lid on a laptop computer.

If you have a laptop, you can control settings for both AC and battery power.

**WARNING** When a computer enters standby mode, any open files are not saved to disk. Should you lose power to the system while in standby mode, you may lose any unsaved data. Be sure to save your data before leaving the computer idle for extended periods of time.

**TIP** If standby is supported by your hardware, you can also choose Start ➢ Shutdown and then select Standby to manually place the computer on standby.

To activate a power scheme, select one from the list of available power schemes and click Apply or OK. To create your own power scheme, select a power scheme, modify the settings for the scheme, and click Save As. You can also delete power schemes by selecting a power scheme and clicking Delete.

## Advanced Tab

This tab contains advanced power options that depend on your hardware and its configuration. Examples of options are:

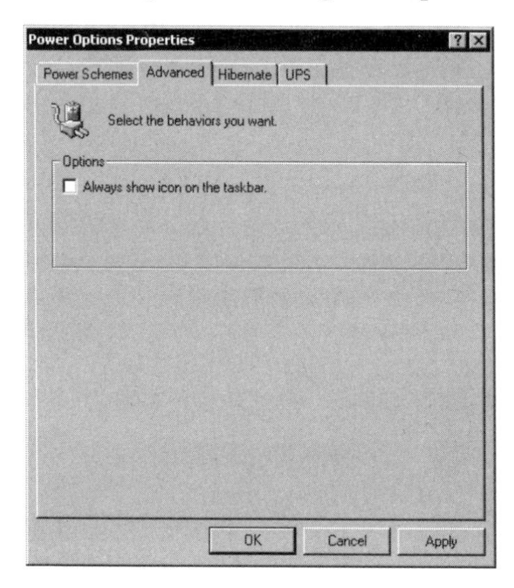


- Displaying a power icon on the taskbar
- Displaying a power meter on the taskbar (on a laptop for battery usage)
- Prompting for a password when the computer comes out of standby mode

## Hibernate Tab

This tab lets you configure hibernation and may or may not be available on your system, depending on whether your hardware supports hibernation. Hibernation means that all data in memory is saved to the computer's hard disk, and then the computer is shut down. When you bring the computer out of hibernation, the data that was in memory before hibernation is retrieved again from the computer's hard disk (Windows opens the necessary programs automatically), and your environment is restored to its state before hibernation.

Again, your options will vary, depending on whether your hardware supports hibernation. You may be able to configure manual or automatic hibernation. To manually place the computer into hibernation, select the Enable Hibernate Support check box and click OK or Apply. Then choose Start ➢ Shutdown. A new item, Hibernate, appears on the list of items in the Shut Down Windows dialog box. Choose Hibernate to place the computer into hibernation. If hibernation is supported, you may also be able to specify the period of inactivity that must elapse before the computer enters hibernation automatically.

Finally, the Hibernate tab also shows you how much disk space is necessary to enter hibernation and how disk space is available on your hard disk.

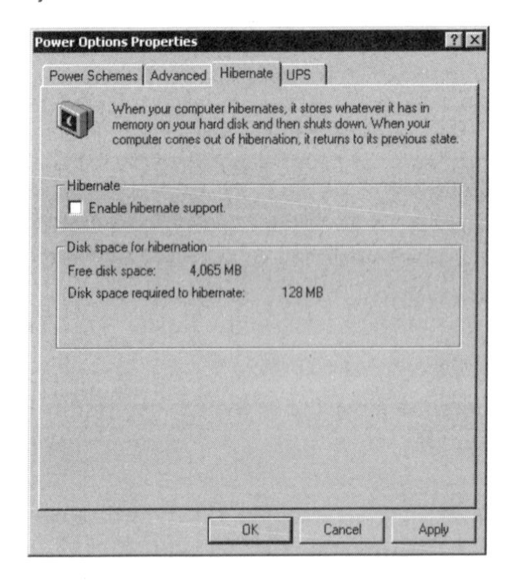


## UPS Tab

This tab lets you configure settings for an uninterruptible power supply (UPS). The Status area contains such information as power source, estimated run-time and capacity, and battery condition. In the Details pane, you can see information about the manufacturer and model of the UPS. To define your UPS, click Select and select the manufacturer and model of your UPS, as well as the port to which the UPS is connected. Click Finish to add the information to the UPS tab. Click Configure to configure UPS settings, such as notifications and alarms. You can also specify the actions you want Windows to take in case of power failure, and choose whether to turn off the UPS after the computer actions have been carried out (such as shutdown).

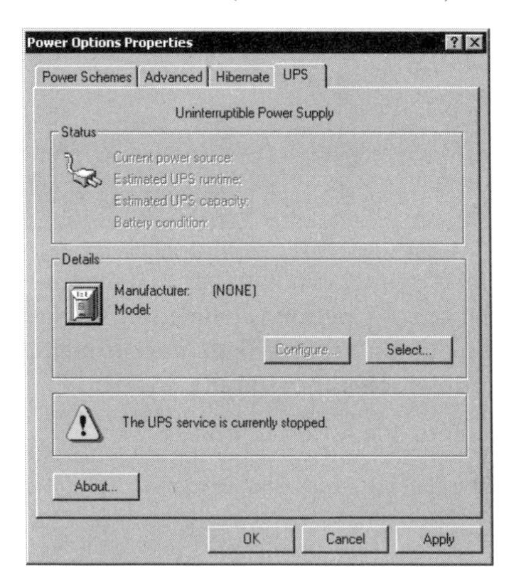


# Printers

Printers Used to manage all aspects of printing. From here you can perform such tasks as adding, removing, and sharing printers; assigning permissions; setting the default printer; changing printer properties; setting printer defaults; viewing and managing job queues; pausing printing; canceling printing; and setting up print server properties.

Printing in Windows 2000 is handled through the Printers folder. You can access the folder by choosing Start ➢ Settings ➢ Printers. Alternatively, you can access the Printers folder through My Computer, Windows Explorer, or Control Panel.

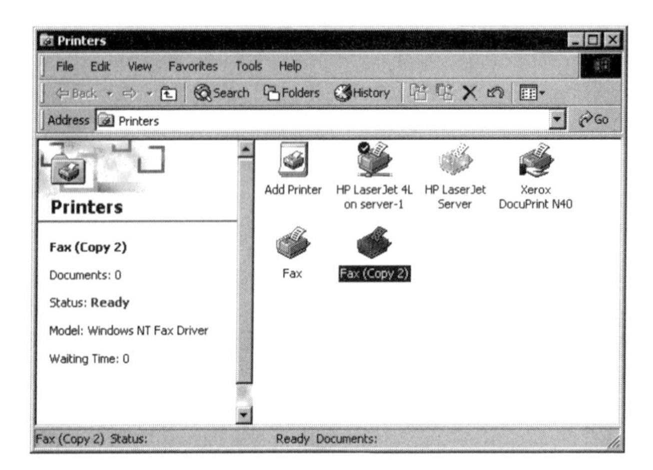


The majority of printer configuration is done through printer properties. You can also perform some printing-related actions or access configuration pages through the File menu or by right-clicking any printer icon. For example, you can:

- Set a printer to be the default printer
- Access the printing preferences pages
- Pause printing
- Cancel printing of all documents
- Share a printer
- Use a printer offline
- Create a shortcut to the printer
- Delete and rename the printer
- Access the printer property sheet
- Access the print server property sheet (available only on the File menu)

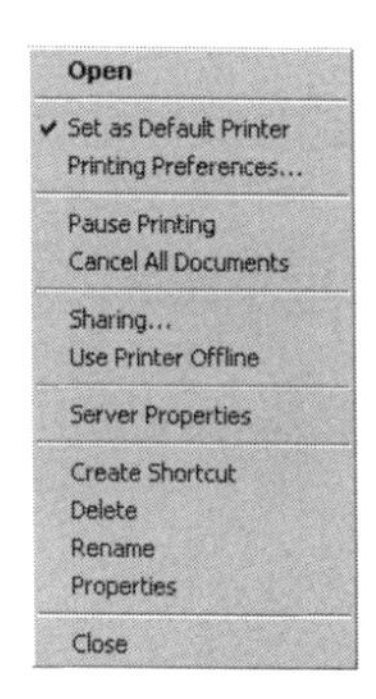


## Add Printer Wizard

Walks you through the process of adding either a new local or a new network printer.

### *Adding a New Local Printer*

To add a new local printer, follow these steps:

1. Double-click the Add Printer icon to start the Add Printer Wizard.
2. Click Next.
3. Specify that the printer is a local printer and specify whether you want Windows to automatically detect the printer. Click Next.
4. If you selected Automatically Detect and Install My Plug and Play Printer, Windows tries to find the printer. If it cannot find the printer, Windows displays a message prompting you to click Next to install the printer manually. Click Next to continue. If Windows detects the printer, it will add the printer automatically and return you to the Printers folder. You can now customize printer settings. If you did not select Automatically Detect and Install My Plug and Play Printer, on the next screen choose the port the printer uses, or create a new port and click Next.
5. Select your printer manufacturer and model, then click Next.

6. Enter a name for the printer. Also specify whether the printer should be the default printer for Windows applications. Click Next.

**NOTE** It's recommended that printer names consist of no more than 31 characters. This is because some clients can't handle longer names and some applications can't print to printers with longer names. If you're planning to share the printer, this recommendation also applies to the name of the print server.

7. Specify whether you want to share the printer. If you do, enter a shared printer name. This name can be different from the printer name. Do not use more than eight characters and a three-character extension separated by a period if you have Windows 3.*x* or MS-DOS–based clients that need to access the printer. Otherwise, select Do Not Share This Printer. Click Next.

**TIP** By default, a shared printer will be listed in Active Directory. If you don't want to list the printer in Active Directory, after the printer is created, right-click the printer, choose Properties, select the sharing tab, and uncheck List In The Directory.

If you chose not to share the printer, skip to step 9.

8. If you chose to share the printer, enter a location for the printer. This can be the name of a building or office, for example. You can also add a comment to further identify the printer. Click Next.
9. Specify whether you want to print a test page. Click Next.
10. Review your choices and settings and click Finish. This closes the Add Printer Wizard, and Windows adds the printer to the Printers folder.

**TIP** In the Printers folder, a check mark appears at the top of the default printer's icon.

### *Adding a New Network Printer*

To add a new network printer, follow these steps:

1. Double-click the Add Printer icon to start the Add Printer Wizard. Click Next.
2. Specify that the printer is a network printer. Click Next.
3. You can find the printer in one of three ways: Search for the printer in the Active Directory, enter the name of the printer (the qualified name, such as `\\server-1\hp laserjet`), or browse for it. If the printer is located on the Internet or on an intranet, you can specify its URL. Make your choice, enter any necessary information, and click Next.
4. If you chose to find the printer in the directory, the Find Printers dialog box appears and you can search for the printer. You can search for all printers by clicking Find New. Refine your search by entering information on the Printers, Features, and Advanced tabs, and then click Find Now. Once you find the printer, select it and click OK. If you chose the browse option, you can browse for and select the printer in the Shared Printers list. Click Next. If you specified the printer's name or URL, skip to step 5.
5. Specify whether you want this printer to be the default printer for Windows programs. Click Next.
6. Review your choices, then click Finish to close the Add Printer Wizard.

**NOTE** When you're using the Add Printer Wizard, some steps might be different if settings for certain group policies have been changed from their defaults.

## Printer Properties

Right-click the appropriate printer icon and choose Properties. The Properties dialog box has six tabs for configuring different aspects of the printer: General, Sharing, Ports, Advanced, Security, and Device Settings. Because each printer has different features and functionality, the options available and features shown on some of these tabs differ from printer to printer.

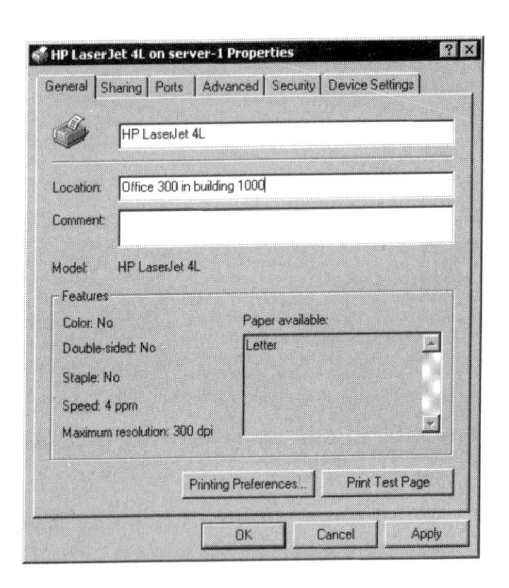


**General** Used to specify the printer name and location. You can also add comments, such as who typically uses the printer and who to contact if there's a problem. The General tab also tells you about the features of the printer. This information will be different for each printer type and model.

Click the Printing Preferences button to configure settings regarding page layout and paper source and quality as well as other advanced printing features (click Advanced to access advanced features). Click the Print Test Page button to verify that the printer is connected and functioning properly. If the test page doesn't print, you can click the Troubleshoot button, which automatically opens the Windows 2000 Print Troubleshooter in the Help system.

**Sharing** Lets you specify that you want the printer to be used only as a local printer or shared with other users in the network. Shared printers can be published in the Active Directory (select the List in the Directory option). On this tab, you can also specify additional drivers for the printer to allow people using a different hardware and/or operating system platform to easily access the printer (the correct drivers download automatically when a computer connects to the printer).

**WARNING** You can share a printer only if you're logged on as a member of the Administrators group or if you've been assigned the Manage Printers permission.

**Ports** Used to specify, delete, and configure the port to which the printer is attached. You can also enable bidirectional support and printer pooling.

**Advanced** Used to configure advanced options, such as printer availability, logical printer priority, printer drivers, spooling options, printing defaults, print processor options, and separator pages.

**Security** Used to assign printing permissions to users, groups, and computers. Permissions that can be granted include Print, Manage Printers, and Manage Documents.

**Device Settings** The options available on this tab depend on your printer's capabilities and functions. Use this tab to view and manage printer-specific settings. Some examples include:

- Assigning forms to specific paper trays
- Substituting unavailable fonts with available fonts
- Setting printer-specific installation options, such as the amount of installed memory

Refer to your printer documentation for specific settings and their values.

**NOTE** You must be the creator of the printer, be logged on as a member of the Administrators or Power Users group, or have been assigned the Manage Printers permission to change printer properties.

## Sharing a Printer

In order for a printer to be accessible to other users in the network, it must be shared. Choose Start ➢ Settings ➢ Printers, right-click the printer, choose Properties, and select the Sharing tab.

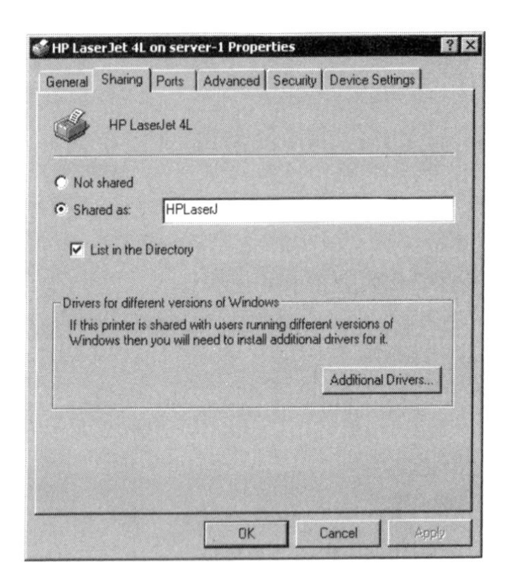


To share the printer, check the Shared As radio button and enter a shared printer name (this can be different from the printer name). This is the name other users will see when browsing the network for shared printers with My Network Places and Windows Explorer.

**TIP** If you have Windows 3.*x* or MS-DOS clients that need to access this printer, you'll have to ensure the shared name consists of no more than eight characters plus a three-character extension separated by a period, as these OSs do not support long filenames.

**NOTE** Printers added on a Windows 2000 Server computer are shared by default; through Plug and Play on a Windows 2000 Professional computer, they are not.

If you want other users on the network to be able to search for the printer, you must publish the printer in the Active Directory. To do this, select the List in the Directory option. Users can then search for the printer by name, location, model, and other printer properties.

If other users who need to have access to this printer use older versions of Windows, such as Windows NT 3.5 or 4.0, Windows 95 or 98, and/or different hardware platforms, click the Additional Drivers button and select the appropriate hardware and OS version. Click OK to install the drivers. When users try to connect to the printer, the correct drivers are automatically downloaded to their workstation.

**TIP** On Windows 95 and 98 workstations, the driver is downloaded only when the workstation connects to the printer the first time. If the driver is later updated, you'll have to manually install the newer driver. Windows 3.*x*, NT 4.0, and 2000 clients automatically download driver updates.

## Printing Documents

You can print documents in Windows 2000 in a variety of ways. To send a print job to the printer without changing default settings, use one of the following methods:

- Open the document in any Windows application and click the Print icon.
- In Windows Explorer, My Documents, My Computer, or My Network Places, select a file, right-click it, and choose Print, or choose Print from the File menu.
- Select a file and drag and drop it onto a printer in the Printers folder or onto a shortcut to a printer on the desktop.

To change default settings before sending a print job, open the document in any Windows application. Then choose File ➢ Print. The Print dialog box opens and you can alter default settings. When you've finished, click the Print button to print.

The tabs in the Print dialog box may vary depending on your printer's capabilities (specified through the printer driver). Below are examples of tabs and settings you'll commonly see in the Print dialog box. Other, printer-specific tabs and settings may be available for your printer. Click Apply to save any changes you make on these tabs without closing the dialog box.

**General** Choose the printer you want to print to and whether you want to print to a file (the default is printing to a printer). You can search for printers, view the status of the currently selected printer, and choose whether you want to print the entire document, only text that is selected in the document, the current page, or a specific range of pages.

You can also specify the number of copies you want to print and whether the copies should be collated.

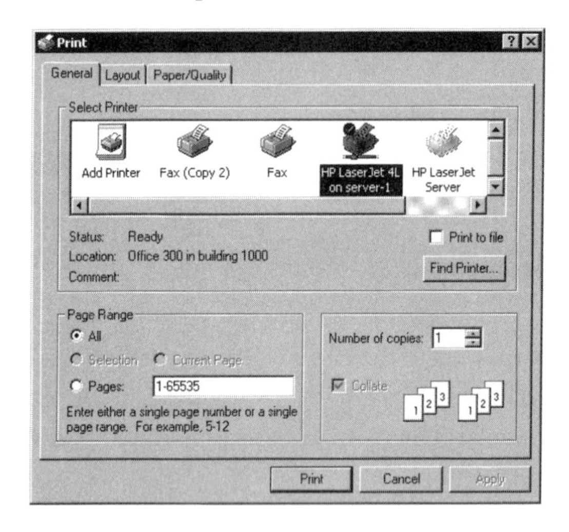


On the next two tabs, you can configure your printer-specific printing preferences:

**Layout** Lets you make document layout choices. Examples are orientation, print order, and pages per sheet.

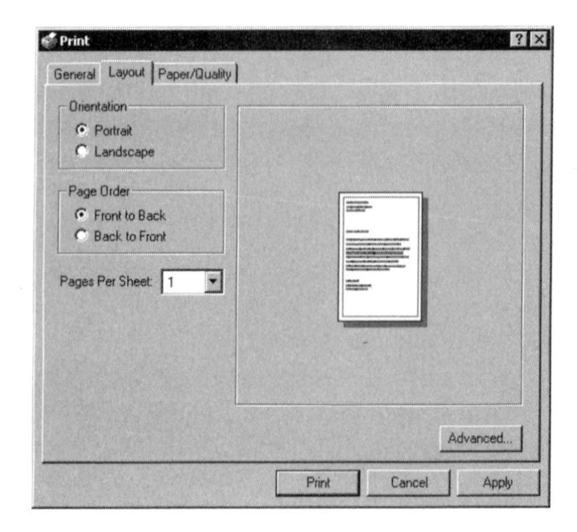

Clicking the Advanced button displays the Advanced Options dialog box, where you can further customize settings. These are printer specific and will vary depending on the printer make and model. Common setting categories are Paper/Output, Graphics, Document Options, and Printer Features. Some examples of settings are Paper Size, Print Quality, Advanced Printing Features (enable/disable), Print Optimizations (enable/disable), and other printer-specific settings. Refer to your printer documentation for specific settings and their values.

**Paper/Quality** Lets you make changes related to paper and paper quality, such as the paper source and media type. Options will vary depending on your printer's capabilities. Refer to your printer's documentation for more information about specific settings. Clicking the Advanced button takes you to the Advanced Options dialog box described under the Layout tab.

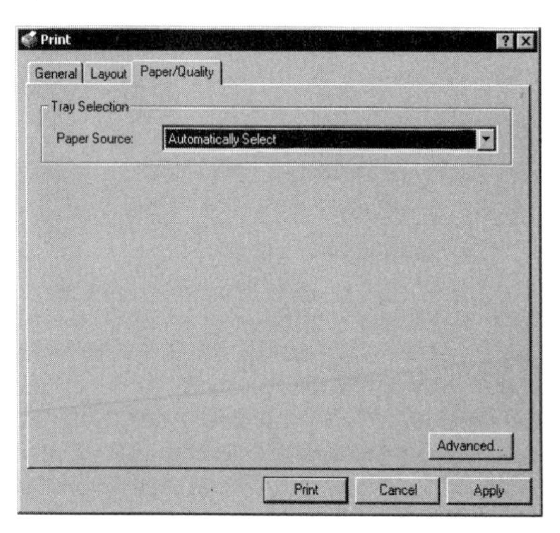

**TIP** You can also access the printing preference tabs by right-clicking any printer icon and choosing Printing Preferences, by choosing File ➢ Menu and selecting Printing Preferences, by clicking the Printing Preferences button on the General tab of the Printer Properties dialog box, or by choosing File ➢ Page Setup ➢ Printer ➢ Properties ➢ in any Windows application.

Unless you have Windows set up to print directly to a printer, once you send the print job, it is sent to the print queue either on the local machine or on the print server, where it waits until it is printed.

## Printing Permissions

Printing permissions are necessary for users to perform printing-related functions. To view and change printing permissions for a printer, right-click the appropriate printer icon in the Printers folder, select Properties, and click the Security tab.

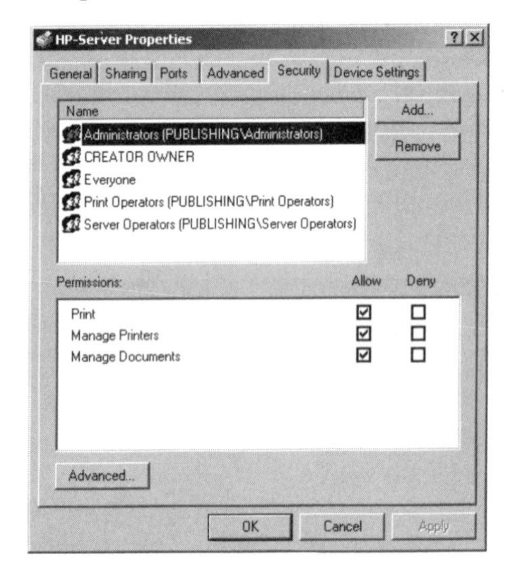


In the Name list box, you'll see the names and locations of all groups and users that are currently assigned printing permissions. To add other users and groups, you have to add them to the Name list on the Security tab. Click Add, select one or more users or groups, and click Add, then click OK. To remove one or more users or groups, select them in the Name list and click Remove.

To view the printer permissions that have been assigned to a user or group, select the object in the Name list box and see which options are enabled in the Permissions list box. Three levels of printing permissions are available:

**Print** User can connect to the printer and print to the printer.

**Manage Printers** User can connect to the printer, print to the printer, and manage the printer. Management tasks include changing printer properties, changing printer permissions, sharing the printer, pausing and restarting the printer, and changing spooler settings.

**Manage Documents** User can control all print jobs (his or her own and all other users' print jobs). This includes pausing, resuming, restarting, and canceling print jobs.

**TIP** The Manage Documents permission does not include the ability to print to the printer.

### *Default Permission Assignments*

In order to facilitate printing and printer management, various default permissions are assigned to various groups as outlined below:

| Group | Permission |
|---|---|
| Everyone | Print |
| Creator Owner | Manage Documents |
| Administrators | Print, Manage Documents, Manage Printers |
| Power Users | Print, Manage Documents, Manage Printers |
| Server Operators | Print, Manage Documents, Manage Printers |
| Print Operators | Print, Manage Documents, Manage Printers |

**NOTE** The Power Users group exists only on Windows 2000 Professional computers, and the Server Operators and Print Operators groups exist only on Windows 2000 Server computers.

**NOTE** Creator Owner refers to the creator of a document, not a printer.

### *Allowing and Denying Permissions*

To assign a permission, place a check mark in the appropriate Allow check box in the Permissions list box. Select the appropriate

Deny option to explicitly deny a specific permission. Denying a permission may disallow more than one assigned permission. (For example, if you deny the Print permission to a group or user that has both the Print and Manage Printers permissions, the Print and Manage Printers permission check boxes are both cleared. This is because the Manage Printers permission implies the Print permission.) If neither an Allow option nor its corresponding Deny option is selected, the permission is implicitly denied.

**TIP** If you see a shaded check box, this means the permission was inherited from a parent object.

## Print Queue

Stores print jobs after they're sent to the printer and until they have printed. Use the print queue to view the status of and manage print jobs. Each printer has a print queue that you can access by double-clicking a printer icon in the Printers folder.

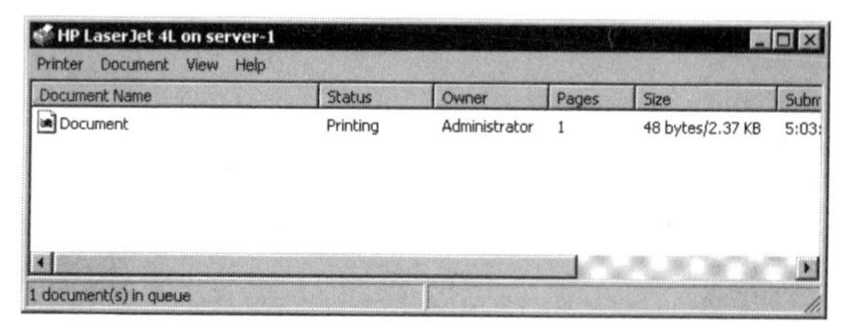


The print queue dialog box displays the following information for every print job in the queue:

**Document Name** Name of the document printing or waiting to be printed.

**Status** Status of the document, such as printing, spooling, paused, or error.

**Owner** Username of the person who sent the print job.

**Pages** If the print job is still waiting in the queue, displays the total number of pages. Once the print job starts printing, displays the number of pages printed and the total number of pages.

**Size** Total and printed document size in kilobytes.

**Submitted** The time and date when the document was sent to the printer.

**Port** The port the printer uses.

The status bar at the bottom of the print queue dialog box displays how many print jobs are in the queue.

Use the Printer menu to connect to the printer, set the printer as the default printer, set up printing preferences, pause printing, cancel all documents, configure printer sharing options, use the printer offline, access printer properties, and perform other functions. Most of these functions are also available on the File menu of the Printers folder when a printer is selected.

**TIP** If you choose to use a printer offline, the printer icon will be grayed out in the Printers folder.

Use the Document menu to perform such functions as pausing, resuming, restarting, and canceling the print job and to access document properties.

**TIP** You can pause, resume, restart, cancel, and access properties for more than one print job at a time by selecting multiple print jobs and then making your choice from the Document menu.

**NOTE** By default, only the creator of a job can manage his or her own print jobs. To be able to manage other people's print jobs, the user has to be assigned the Manage Documents permission or have administrative privileges—for example, through membership in the Administrators group.

## Document Properties

Contains settings related to the document to be printed. Select a print job in the queue and choose Document ➢ Properties.

On the General tab, you can view the document's name, size, number of pages, data type, processor, owner, and the date and time the job was submitted. By default, Windows notifies the owner of the document when the job finishes printing, but you can specify that Windows notify a different user by typing the name in the Notify text box. You can change the priority of the print job in relation to other print jobs in the queue by moving the slider either left or right, which will cause higher priority jobs to print before lower priority jobs. Finally, you can specify when Windows should print the job by selecting a time range.

You can also access other printing preference tabs, such as the Layout and Paper/Quality tabs, from the Document Properties dialog box.

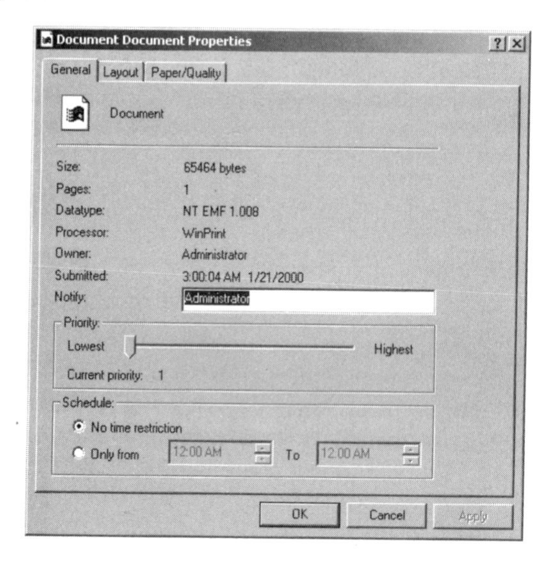


## Print Server

Computer that manages printers in a network. It can be either a Windows 2000 Server or Windows 2000 Professional computer. Windows 2000 Professional, however, does not support Macintosh and NetWare services and allows only 10 connections.

Here's how it works. Designate a computer to be the print server. Add printers on this computer and share them. Have users connect to these shared printers as necessary. Print jobs sent to a shared printer on a print server go into the printer's queue on the print server. This is the queue users will see when they double-click the printer in the Printers folder. They'll be able to see where their job is in relation to other users' print jobs, and can then determine when it's likely to print. When errors occur, error messages appear on all computers that have a connection to the printer, so problems can be resolved quickly (somebody is likely to see the message and either resolve the problem or call a network administrator). Finally, some of the processing involved with the printing of jobs is offloaded to the print server because print jobs are spooled to a folder on the print server rather than the local computer.

Print servers do not have to be dedicated to the function of print server. They are usually Windows 2000 Server computers that perform other server functions as well.

### *Print Server Properties*

In the Printers folder, choose File ➢ Server Properties to access the Print Server Properties dialog box.

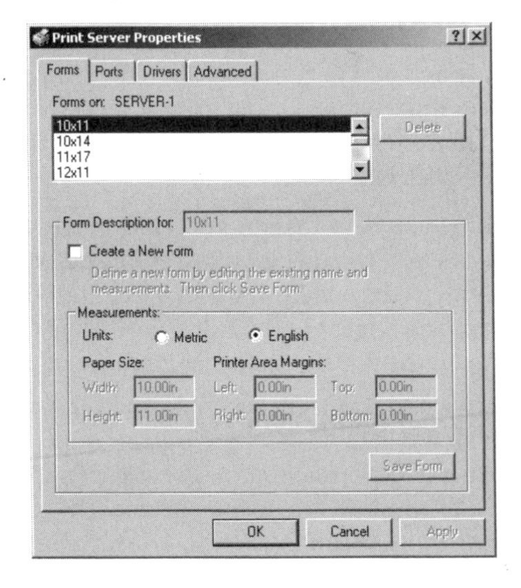


The Print Server Properties dialog box has four tabs you can use to configure the print server: Forms, Ports, Drivers, and Advanced.

**Forms** Lists the printer forms available on the print server and tells you the measurements of each form in either metric or English format. Also allows you to create new forms.

**Ports** Enables you to view, add, delete, and configure print server ports.

**Drivers** Enables you to view, add, remove, and update printer drivers and view and configure printer driver properties.

**Advanced** Enables you to specify the location of the print server's spool folder, as well as log spooler events, such as error, warning, and information events. Lets you specify whether you want Windows to sound an audible alarm when a remote document encounters an error. Also lets you specify whether you want Windows to send out a notification when a remote document is printed, and whether you want that notification sent to the user or to the computer.

# Private Character Editor

Lets you create and add new characters to the Unicode character set. You can link characters to a specific font or all fonts. To start Private Character Editor, choose Start ➢ Run, then type **eudcedit** and click OK.

The first thing you have to do is select a Unicode code for the new character. Select the square in the Select Code dialog box that corresponds to the code you want to assign to the character. Your choice will appear in the Code area below the grid. Click OK to open the Private Character Editor window.

## Private Character Editor Window

The Private Character Editor window consists of a toolbar, a guidebar, an Edit window, and menu options. The toolbar has several drawing tools, including Pencil, Brush, Straight Line, Hollow Rectangle, Filled Rectangle, Hollow Ellipse, Filled Ellipse, Rectangular Selection, Freeform Selection, and Eraser. Click a button to use the corresponding tool to create a new (private) character in the Edit window.

The guidebar displays such items as the character set, code, linked font, and file. The menus contain additional options you can use to create new characters.

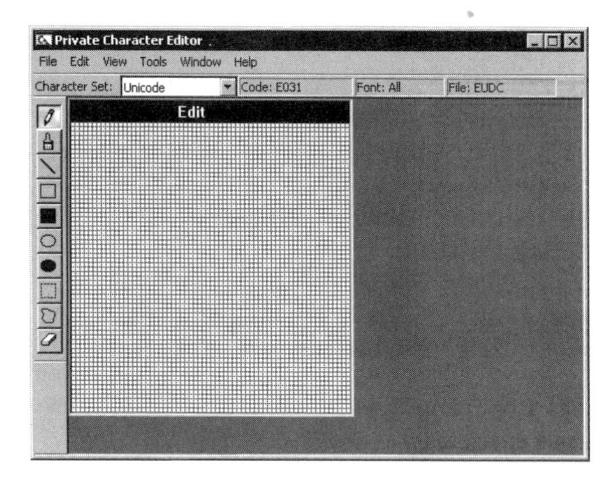


## Menus

The menus in Private Character Editor offer several options specific to Private Character Editor.

### *File Menu*

The File menu contains one unique option:

**Font Links** Lets you link the newly created character with either all available fonts or with fonts you select.

### *Edit Menu*

The Edit menu contains these unique options:

**Copy Character** Lets you copy characters from any available font into the Edit window of Private Character Editor. You can then modify the character in the Edit window.

**Select Code** Lets you select a Unicode code for the character you want to create.

**Save Character** Lets you save the current character using the currently selected Unicode code.

**Save Character As** Lets you save the current character using a different Unicode code.

### *View Menu*

The View menu contains these unique options:

**Guidebar** Toggles the display of the guidebar.

**Grid** Toggles the display of the grid in the Edit window.

**Next Code** Displays the next code in the Edit window.

**Prev Code** Displays the previous code in the Edit window.

**Show Outline** Displays an outline around the line components of the new character in the Edit window.

### *Tools Menu*

The Tools menu contains these unique options:

**Item** Displays a submenu that contains all of the items available in the toolbar, such as Pencil, Brush, and Eraser.

**Flip/Rotate** Lets you flip the character horizontally or vertically, and lets you rotate the character by 90, 180, or 270 degrees.

### *Window Menu*

The Window menu contains these unique options:

**Reference** Lets you select another character from any available font and display the character in a separate window, called the Reference window, next to the Edit window. You can use this to compare your newly created character to an already existing character for reference, which can help you make decisions about the size of the character, the thickness of lines, and so forth.

**Close Reference** Closes the Reference window.

**See Also** Character Map

# Profiles

**See** System (User Profiles subheading)

# Recycle Bin

A folder that holds files and folders you deleted from your hard disk until they are permanently removed from the computer's hard disk. Use the Recycle Bin to restore files that have been deleted but not yet removed from the Recycle Bin.

**NOTE** Files that you delete from a floppy disk or network drive are permanently deleted and not placed into the Recycle Bin.

**WARNING** Never think of the Recycle Bin as a substitute for a tape backup system. The Recycle Bin is limited in size and holds only the most recently deleted files. Consider it a quick way to restore files in a pinch, but that's all.

If deleted files are in the Recycle Bin, the icon will show paper sticking out of the top of the wastebasket. If it is empty (meaning that files have been deleted permanently), no paper shows.

You can put files into the Recycle Bin by deleting them through a pop-up menu, using the Delete key, or dragging and dropping them onto the Recycle Bin.

## Recycle Bin Folder

To access the Recycle Bin folder, double-click the wastebasket icon on the desktop. Alternatively, you can use My Computer or Windows Explorer to browse to and open the Recycle Bin folder.

This folder shows you all of the files contained in the Recycle Bin and information regarding each file's original location, the date it was deleted, its type, and its size.

**TIP** You may have to scroll as well as adjust the size of each column to see some of the detailed file information.

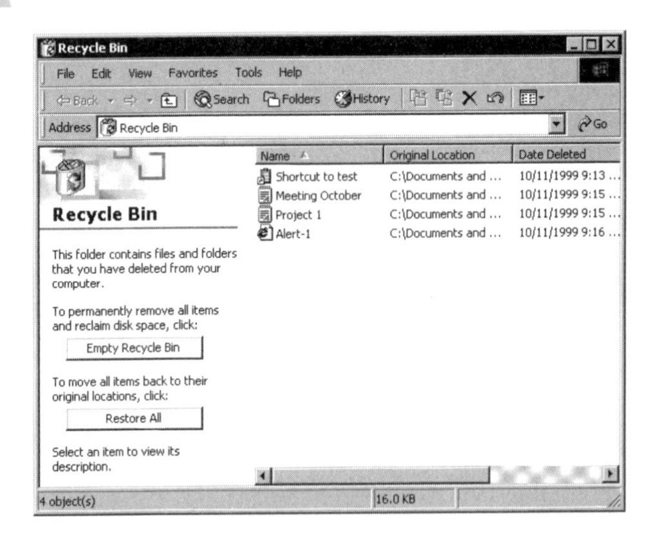


In addition to typical Windows options, this folder has the Restore and Empty Recycle Bin options added to the File menu (the Restore option is visible only when you have selected files to restore).

## Restoring a File

When you restore a file, it is moved back to its original location. To restore a file, follow these steps:

1. Select a file or multiple files in the list of files. The left pane changes to show you a detailed view of the original location of the file, when it was deleted, and its size.

2. Click Restore in the left pane.

**TIP** You can also restore files by right-clicking one or more files and selecting Restore from the shortcut menu, or by selecting one or more files and choosing Restore from the File menu. To restore all files, make sure you have no individual file selected and click Restore All in the left pane.

After you restore a file, it's no longer visible in the Recycle Bin.

## Emptying the Recycle Bin

Files that are in the Recycle Bin still take up space on your hard disk. To reclaim that space, you have to delete some files from the Recycle Bin or completely empty the Recycle Bin. Various methods are available:

To permanently delete selected files:

- Select the file or files you want to delete and choose File ➢ Delete, or right-click and choose Delete.

To permanently delete all files from the Recycle Bin:

- Make sure no files are selected in the Recycle Bin and click the Empty Recycle Bin button in the left pane of the Recycle Bin folder.
- Choose File ➢ Empty Recycle Bin in the Recycle Bin folder.
- Right-click the Recycle Bin icon on the desktop and choose Empty Recycle Bin.
- Choose Edit ➢ Select All to select all files in the Recycle Bin, then choose File ➢ Delete.

As a general rule, you should empty the Recycle Bin once a week.

## Changing the Size of the Recycle Bin

The Recycle Bin is allocated a certain amount of space on the hard drive. If you have multiple hard drives or partitions, each hard drive and partition has its own Recycle Bin. By default, each Recycle Bin is allocated 10 percent of the hard drive or partition space. You can change this setting by following these steps:

**TIP** You must be logged in with administrative privileges to perform these steps.

1. Right-click the Recycle Bin icon and choose Properties.
2. On the Global tab, adjust the amount of space allocated to the Recycle Bin by dragging the slider left to decrease it or right to increase it.

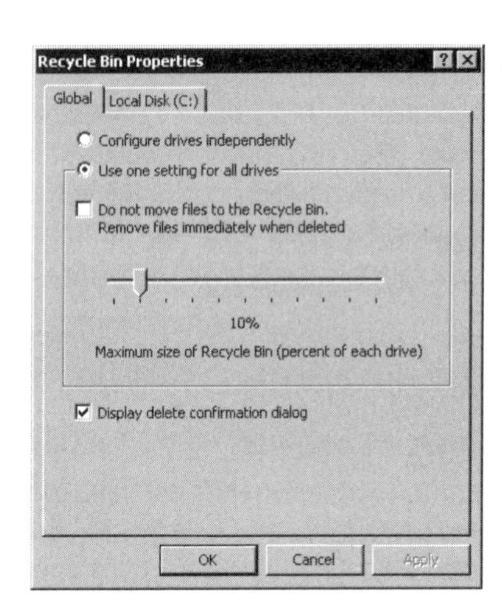


If you have multiple drives or partitions and want to use a different size for each, select Configure Drives Independently. This deactivates the Global tab and activates the tabs for each individual disk and partition. Select each tab and adjust the size of each Recycle Bin. Configuring the size of the Recycle Bin independently for each drive or partition is a good choice if the size of each partition or drive is different, because it gives you control over how much space you want to allocate to the Recycle Bin for each partition or drive. This may also improve your computer's performance.

**WARNING** If you delete a file that is larger than the Recycle Bin's storage capacity, the file will be permanently deleted.

The Global tab also lets you choose not to use the Recycle Bin at all and instead remove files permanently when you delete them; simply select the Do Not Move Files to the Recycle Bin option. Finally, by default, a dialog box pops up when you're deleting a file, asking you to confirm that you want to send the file to the Recycle Bin. To disable this confirmation dialog box, remove the check mark from the Display Delete Confirmation Dialog check box.

# Regional Options

Depending on where you are located geographically, you will use a specific way to display numbers with decimal fractions, large numbers, currencies, dates, and times. You will also use one of two systems of measurement, and your language and language characters will be different. Regional Options enables you to specify your geographic region; how you want Windows programs to display dates, times, numbers, and so forth; and whether Windows programs should use the metric or U.S. system of measurement. Regional Options also enables you to install and use multiple languages and keyboard layouts on the same system. Some programs can take advantage of this and may offer additional functions, such as spell-checkers and fonts for different languages. This enables you to read or type documents using characters used in other language groups (such as Cyrillic or Greek).

Choose Start ➢ Settings ➢ Control Panel, then double-click the Regional Options icon to display the Regional Options dialog box. It contains six tabs: General, Numbers, Currency, Time, Date, and Input Locales.

## General Tab

This tab enables you to choose a locale for the current user, and lets you install language groups.

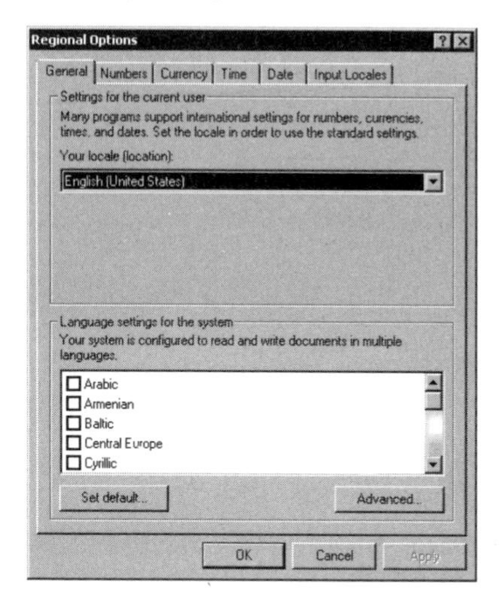

### *User Locale*

A user's locale specifies his or her default settings for number, currency, time, and date conventions, as well as the available languages and keyboard layouts to be used with programs that support creating and reading documents in multiple languages.

To set a user's locale, select a locale from the Your Locale (Location) list. When you do this and then click Apply or OK, the defaults for settings on the Numbers, Currency, Time, and Date tabs change automatically to conform to the regional conventions of the selected locale. Changing a locale also makes it possible for an application's menus and dialog boxes to display in the language associated with the locale. Additionally, when you change a user's locale, the corresponding input locale is installed automatically (an input locale is a combination of a language and its keyboard layout; input locales are discussed in more detail under the Input Locales heading).

**NOTE** Windows 2000 menus and dialog boxes will still be displayed in English.

### *Multiple Language Support*

Windows 2000 supports the use of multiple languages on the same computer. This enables you to read and type documents using any language that is part of any installed language group. By default, the Western Europe and United States language group is installed on a Windows 2000 computer. You can install additional language groups in the Language Settings for the System area of the General tab.

**TIP** The user locales available in the Your Locale (Location) list depend on the language groups you have installed.

**Installing Additional Language Groups** To install additional language groups, follow these steps:

1. Place a check mark in the check boxes next to the language groups you want to install, then click OK or Apply.

2. If necessary, insert the Windows 2000 CD into the CD-ROM drive so that additional files can be installed.

3. When prompted, reboot the computer in order for the settings to take effect.

When you install another language group, the corresponding input locales are added to the list of available input locales (you can see them in the Your Locale (Location) list).

**Adding an Input Locale** To be able to use the keyboard layout and language of a different input locale, you must add the appropriate input locale. To do this, select a locale in the Your Locale (Location) list and click Apply Now. Windows automatically adds the corresponding input locale information.

After you select an additional input locale in this manner, you can see which input locale is currently in use by checking the input locale icon that appears in the status area of the taskbar (for example, this icon displays EN for English or LE for Greek). You will have to switch to the appropriate input locale before you can create or read a document using another language. To do this, press Left Alt+Shift until Windows displays the input locale you want to use.

**TIP** You can also add input locales on the Input Locales tab. You'll find more information on how to do this later in this topic.

**Creating a document using multiple languages** To create a document using another language, perform the following steps (we'll use WordPad in this example):

1. Open WordPad.

2. To switch to the appropriate input locale, press Left Alt+Shift until the correct locale appears in the status area of the taskbar.

3. Now start typing in WordPad. Windows has switched the keyboard layout to that of the language's associated country, and you can type text in the selected language. Note that the font-script list box selection also has changed to coincide with your input locale/language selection.

4. If you want to type in English (or another language), just switch to the appropriate input locale and start typing.

**NOTE** If you send a document that uses multiple languages to another user to read, that user must have the same language groups installed.

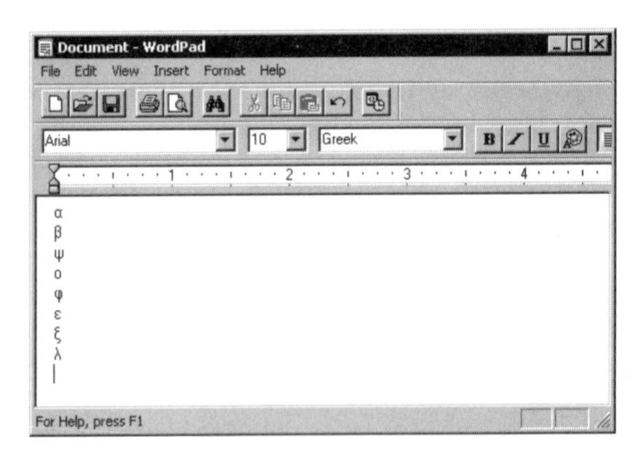


**Removing Language Groups** To remove one or more language groups, deselect the check box next to the appropriate group(s), then click OK. Windows removes the files for the language group(s), and you'll have to reboot the computer to effect the settings.

### *System Locale*

Set default...

Not only can you set a locale for the current user, you can also set a default locale for the system that will be used as the default for all users of the system. Simply click the Set Default button and choose a locale from the list.

### *Code Page Conversion*

You can also use the General tab to install additional code page conversion tables. Click the Advanced button, then select any code page conversion tables you want to install and click OK. To remove a code page conversion table, deselect its check box and click OK.

## Numbers Tab

Use the Numbers tab to specify how you want numbers displayed in Windows 2000. Decimal Symbol, No. of Digits After Decimal, Negative Sign Symbol, Display Leading Zeros, and Measurement System are just some of the options on this tab.

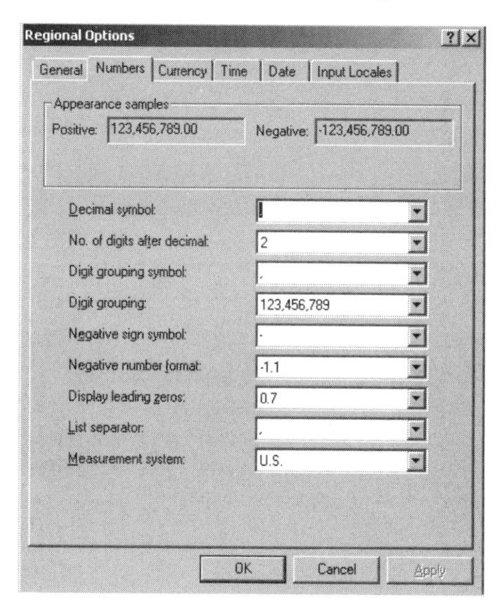


At the top of the tab, you'll see an example of how a large positive or negative number is affected by your changes. Just make a change and click Apply to preview the effect. The default settings of each option will vary depending on the locale you select on the General tab.

## Currency Tab

Use this tab to configure how you want Windows 2000 to display currency values. You can change such items as the currency symbol, the positive and negative currency format, and the decimal symbol.

At the top of the Currency tab, you can see examples of how changes you make affect a large positive or negative currency value. Make any changes, then click Apply to see how the sample numbers change accordingly.

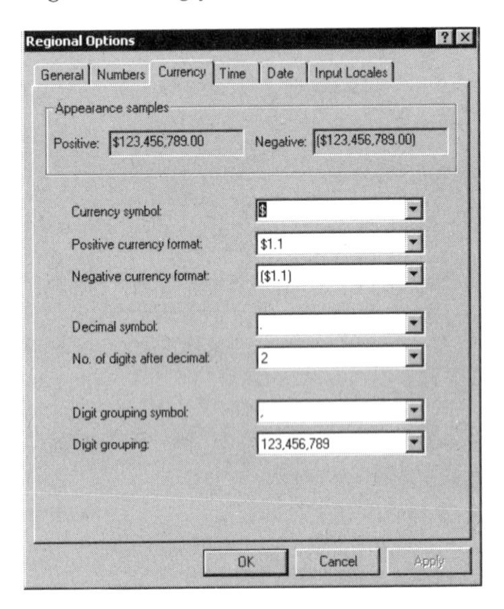


## Time Tab

Use this tab to change how you want Windows 2000 to display the time and date. You can configure such items as the time format (the order in which hours, minutes, and seconds are displayed and whether a 12- or 24-hour clock is used) and the time separator (for example, a colon). You can also specify that Windows 2000 use the AM and PM symbols; if you select a 24-hour time format, the AM and PM symbols automatically are not used.

At the top of the Time tab, you'll see an example of how Windows 2000 will display the time based on the current selections. Make any change, then click Apply, and you'll see how the example changes in accordance with your selections.

At the bottom of the tab, you'll also find a complete explanation of the time format notation.

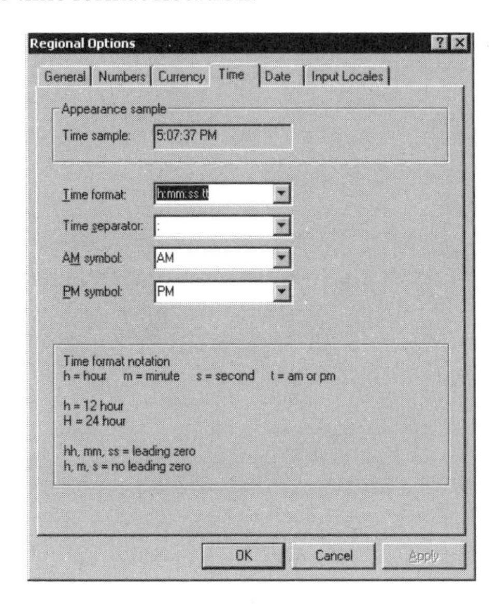


## Date Tab

Use this tab to specify how you want Windows 2000 to display dates.

At the top of the tab in the Calendar area, you can specify how a year is interpreted if you enter only two digits for the year (such as 99 for 1999). This is important for Y2K issues. The default beginning year is specified as 1930, and the default ending year is 2029. This means that any two-digit year entered as a number between 30 and 99 is interpreted as a year starting with 19, so if you enter 79, it would be interpreted as 1979. Any year entered as a number between 00 and 29 is interpreted as a year starting with 20, so if you enter 18, it would be interpreted as 2018. You can change the ending year to a higher value, which automatically adjusts the beginning year value, so that there is always a 99-year difference between the two dates.

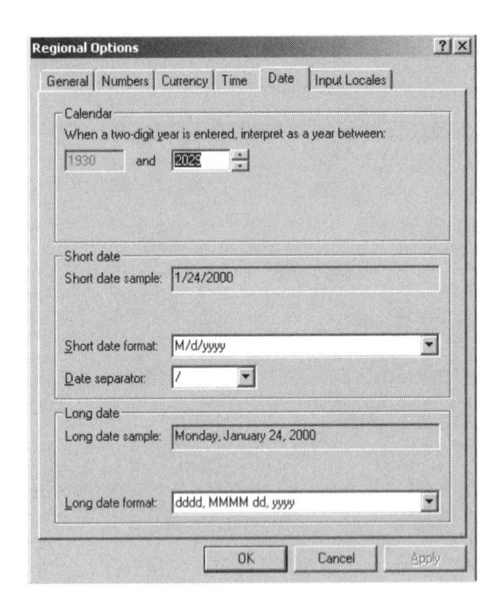


On this tab, you can also specify the format for both short and long dates. Short-date format primarily uses numbers to display a date and never indicates the day of the week. Long-date format uses words for the day of the week and month, and numbers for the day of the month and year.

To see how changes you make will affect how dates are displayed, you can make changes to any of the formats and then click Apply. The examples in the short- or long-date sample area will change according to your selections.

## Input Locales Tab

Use this tab to control Windows 2000 input locales. Input locales specify the languages and keyboard layouts you want available for creating new documents using programs that have been written for Windows 2000 and that can use this feature.

**TIP** You can also access the Input Locales tab by choosing Start ➢ Settings ➢ Control Panel, then double-clicking Keyboard and selecting the Input Locales tab.

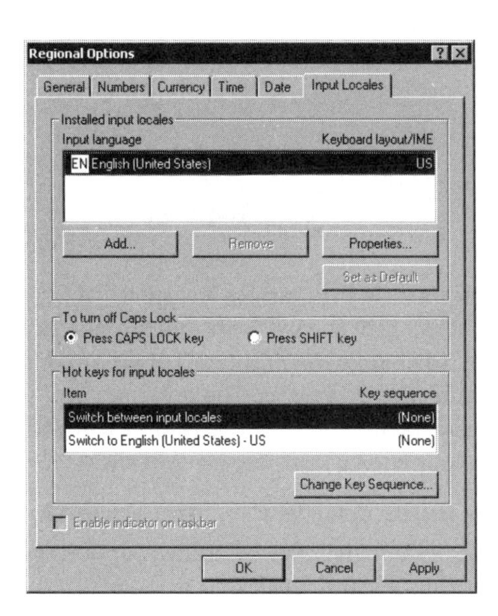


### *Installed Input Locales*

In the Installed Input Locales area of the Input Locales tab, you can see which input locales (language and keyboard layouts) are currently installed on the computer. By default, only English (United States) with a U.S. keyboard layout is installed. When you change the current user's locale, the corresponding input locales are automatically installed and you'll see them in the list on the Input Locales tab.

If you have more than one input locale installed, you can specify which input locale Windows should use as the default. Select an input locale in the list and then click Set as Default. A round icon with a check mark in it appears next to the default input locale.

**Adding an Input Locale** To add an input locale, click Add and select an input locale from the list. You can then either use the input locale's default keyboard layout or select another from the list of keyboard layouts. Click OK when you've finished.

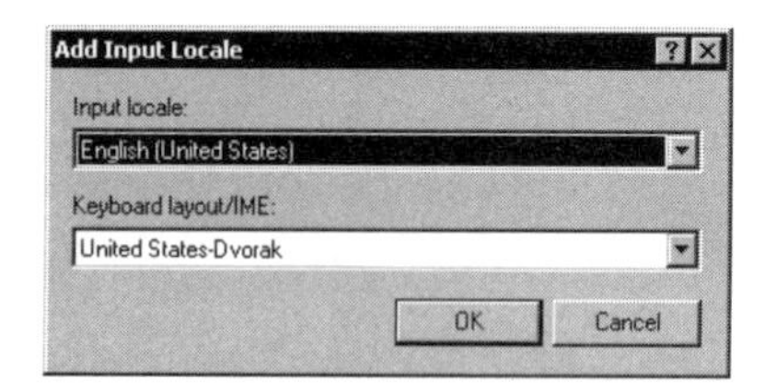


**Removing an Input Locale and Changing Properties** To remove an input locale, select it in the list of installed input locales and click Remove. To change the properties of an input locale, select it in the list and click Properties. The only property you can change is the keyboard layout you want to use for the input locale. Make your choice from the list and click OK.

### *Additional Input Locale Configuration Options*

The Input Locales tab gives you additional options you can use to further customize input locales.

**Turning Off Caps Lock** You can specify whether users turn off the Caps Lock key by pressing the Caps Lock key again or by pressing the Shift key. Whichever you choose, that behavior will apply to all installed input locales.

Change Key Sequence...

**Changing Hotkey Sequences** Once you have more than one input locale installed, you can switch between them by using hotkey sequences. The default hotkey sequence for switching between all installed input locales is Left Alt+Shift. You can also assign a hotkey sequence for switching to a specific input locale. To do this, follow these steps:

1. Select an input locale that does not currently have a hotkey sequence assigned in the Hot Keys for Input Locales list.

2. Click Change Key Sequence.

3. Select Enable Key Sequence.

4. Choose either the Ctrl or Left Alt key by clicking the appropriate radio button and then choose another key in the Key drop-down list. Click OK.

5. The assigned hotkey sequence appears next to the selected item in the Hot Keys for Input Locales list.

To change an assigned hotkey sequence, follow the same procedure but skip step 3.

**Enabling and Disabling the Input Locale Taskbar Indicator** You can enable or disable the taskbar indicator that appears in the status area of the taskbar when you have more than one input locale installed. To do this, select or deselect the Enable Indicator on Taskbar option. This option is enabled by default. If the indicator icon appears in the taskbar, you can also use it to switch between input locales. Click the icon and select the input locale to which you want to switch in the resulting menu.

**TIP** If you right-click the taskbar indicator and choose Properties, Regional Options opens to the Input Locales tab, where you can make changes to your Windows 2000 input locales.

**See Also** Keyboard

# Registry

Database that holds all information about your system, such as defaults and properties for folders, files, users, preferences, applications, protocols, devices, and any other resources.

When you install new applications or hardware, or when you make any changes to your system using Control Panel, information about the installation or changes is saved in the Registry. You can make changes manually to the Registry using the Registry Editor. To run the Registry Editor, choose Start ➢ Run, then type **regedit** and click OK.

**WARNING** Make manual changes to the Registry only if you're very familiar with how the Registry database works; otherwise, you can cause serious problems with your Windows 2000 installation to the point of the system not functioning properly—or at all.

# Removable Storage

Microsoft Management Console (MMC) snap-in that lets you manage hardware libraries. Hardware libraries consist of hardware devices (such as jukeboxes and changers) that can read removable media (for example, tapes and optical discs), and the removable media itself. Use Removable Storage Management to track, label, and catalog your removable media, and to control hardware libraries' physical aspects, such as door, slots, and drives. You can also use Removable Storage Management to clean hardware library drives. Removable Storage Management complements your backup software, which you would use to manage the physical data contained on your removable media. To access Removable Storage, choose Start ➢ Settings ➢ Control Panel, double-click Administrative Tools, then double-click Computer Management. You'll find Removable Storage under Storage. It has four subnodes: Media Pools, Physical Locations, Work Queue, and Operator Requests.

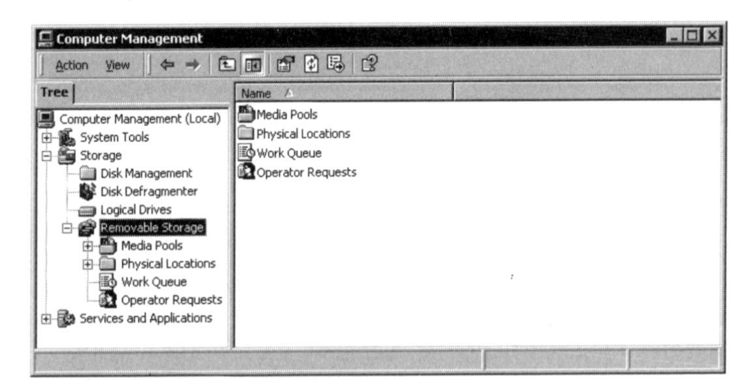


## Media Pools

The removable media in your hardware libraries is organized into logical collections, called media pools. The four types of media pools are Free, Import, Unrecognized, and Application-Specific. Applications then use these pools to control access to specific library tapes or discs.

**Free** Contain currently unused media. Media in this type of media pool can be either automatically or manually moved to Application-Specific media pools.

**Import** Contain media that hasn't been used by Removable Storage but that is recognized in its database. Media in this type of media pool can be moved to Free or Application-Specific media pools.

**Unrecognized** Contain media that is either blank or not recognized. It is recommended that you move this type of media to Free or Application-Specific media pools so that it can be used. If unrecognized media is removed from the library, it is also removed from the Removable Storage database.

**Application-Specific** Contain media that is controlled by data-management applications or by the system administrator. These pools determine which applications can use which media.

### *Creating a New Media Pool*

To create a new Application-Specific media pool, follow these steps:

1. Select Media Pools in the console tree, then choose Action ➢ Create Media Pool.
2. On the General tab, enter a name and description, and specify whether the pool contains other media pools or the type of media it contains. If you select a type of media, you can choose to draw media from a Free media pool or return media to a Free media pool, and to limit reallocations to either the default (100) or a value you specify. Limiting reallocations means specifying how many times media from a Free media pool can be reused (reallocated) in this media pool.
3. On the Security tab, make any changes you need to the permissions assigned to users and groups that will apply to this media pool.
4. Click OK to create the media pool.

## Physical Locations

Lets you view and manage your hardware libraries and offline media. For your libraries, you can perform such actions as injecting and ejecting media, taking an inventory of the media in the library, and viewing and configuring properties from the Action or pop-up menu when you select a library in the Details pane. Alternatively, you can use the Inject Media or Eject Media buttons on the toolbar. If you select physical media, you can perform such actions as ejecting, preparing, mounting and dismounting, and deallocating the media. Actions available when selecting a physical device might include mounting and dismounting the device, as well as marking the device as clean. For offline media, you can perform such actions as ejecting, preparing, mounting, and dismounting the media (if offline media is installed). The options available with any of the media and physical devices in your library will depend on the type of media and device you have installed.

### *Library Properties*

To access the properties of a library, select Physical Locations in the console tree, then right-click the library in the Details pane and choose Properties from the pop-up menu. The Library Properties dialog box has five tabs: General, Media, Components, Device Info, and Security.

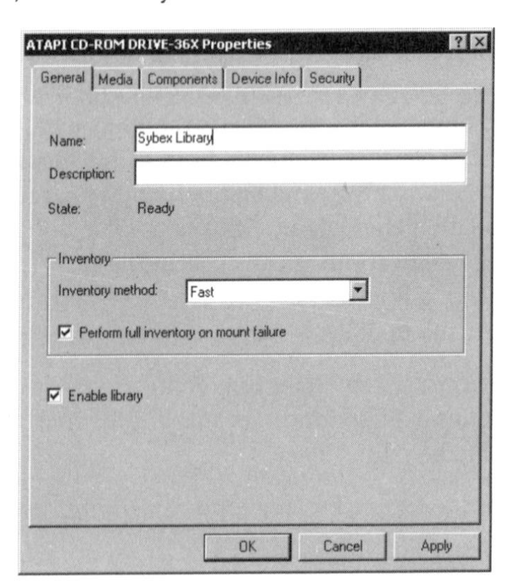

**General** Lets you specify the library name and a description. Also lets you choose the inventory method (None, Fast, or Full) and whether you want to perform a full inventory if media fails to mount. Additionally, you can enable or disable the library by selecting or deselecting the Enable Library option.

**Media** Lets you specify the media type. To change the media type, click the Change button. You can also view the number of slots in the library, as well as the number of the slot that contains the cleaning cartridge. This information does not appear for stand-alone libraries because they do not have these functions.

**Components** If available, lets you specify timeout settings for closing the library door and retracting library ports. If the library door is not closed in the amount of time specified, a warning message is displayed and subsequent actions fail. If you do not insert media into, or remove media from, the port within the amount of time specified, the port retracts. The Components tab also displays the number of drives in the library and indicates whether a library has a barcode reader.

**Device Info** Displays information about the library, such as type, manufacturer, model, serial number, revision, device name, and device addresses.

**Security** Lets you assign permissions for the library to users and groups.

## Work Queue

Select Work Queue in the console tree to display requests submitted to libraries in the Details pane. These requests may have been originated by Removable Storage or by a data-management application, such as Backup. Examples of requests are mounting a tape in a library, ejecting a tape, or marking a drive as clean. Requests are also called work items. After a request is made, the corresponding work item appears in the Work Queue Details pane. Work items can have several states, including Queued, In Process, Waiting, Completed, and Failed.

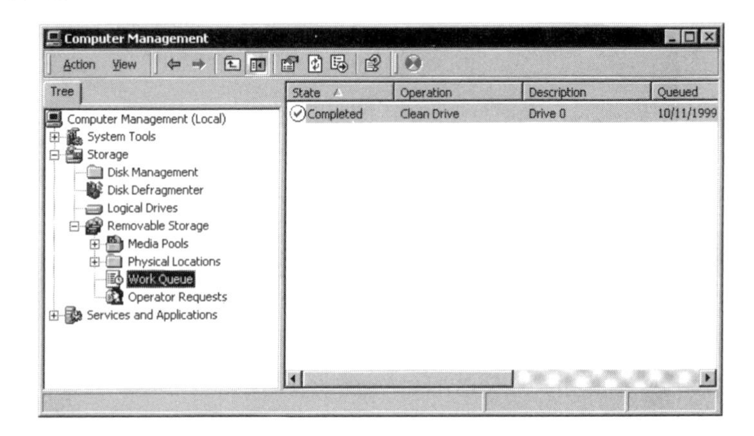


## Operator Requests

If Removable Storage or a data-management application, such as Backup, makes a work request that requires user input or action, an operator request is generated. Select Operator Requests in the console tree to view requests in the Details pane. Examples are:

- Mounting requests for offline tapes
- Requests for service for a malfunctioning or failed library
- Notification that drive cleaning is necessary and that no cleaning cartridge is available
- Notification that media is not available in the appropriate media pool when a request for media is made

**See Also** Microsoft Management Console (MMC), Computer Management

# Restore Down

Button at the top-right corner of windows that lets you return a window to its original size after you have maximized it using the Maximize button.

**See Also** Maximize and Minimize

# Routing and Remote Access

Routing and Remote Access MMC console snap-in that lets you configure and manage Routing and Remote Access services on a Windows 2000 Server computer. Installed by default on Windows 2000 Server computers, but not enabled or configured.

Supported routing services include Virtual Private Network (VPN), Network Address Translation (NAT), and multiprotocol LAN-to-WAN and LAN-to-LAN routing. Routing services enable Windows 2000 Server computers to act as software routers, allowing the computer to forward packets to other computers in the network.

Supported remote access services include VPN and dial-up services, enabling remote users to access the network as if they were locally attached to the network.

To access the Routing and Remote Access MMC console snap-in where you can enable and configure Routing and Remote Access services, choose Start ➢ Programs ➢ Administrative Tools ➢ Routing and Remote Access.

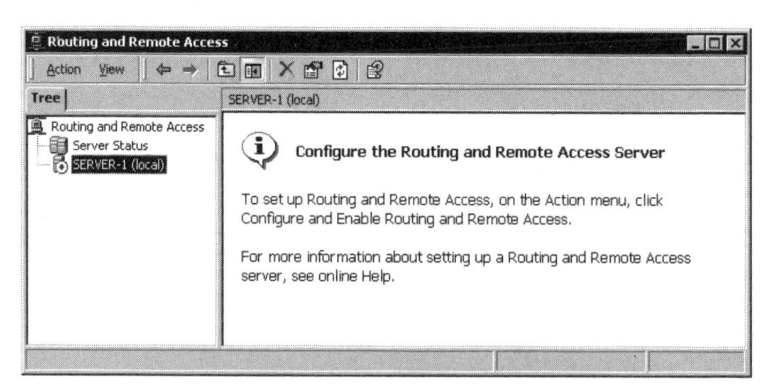


## Routing and Remote Access MMC Console Snap-in Window

Although installed by default on Windows 2000 Server computers, Routing and Remote Access is not enabled or configured by default. In the console tree, you'll see the Server Status node, which provides information about the current routing and remote access status, such as stopped, started, and paused. The Server (local) node (the node's name is your server's name) by default gives you information about how to start the process of setting up and configuring Routing and Remote Access.

### Enabling Routing and Remote Access

To enable Routing and Remote Access, follow these steps:

1. Select the server object in the console tree, then choose Action ➢ Configure and Enable Routing and Remote Access to start the Routing and Remote Access Configuration Wizard.
2. Select one of the Common Configurations. Choices include Internet Connection Server, Remote Access Server, Virtual Private Network (VPN) Server, Network Router, and Manually Configured Server. Click Next.
3. Follow the Wizard's prompts. Selections and options will vary greatly depending on the configuration choice you make in Step 2.
4. When prompted, click Finish to complete the Wizard.
5. Click Yes to start Routing and Remote Access immediately. Click No to leave it stopped for now (you can start the service using the Routing and Remote Access MMC console snap-in).

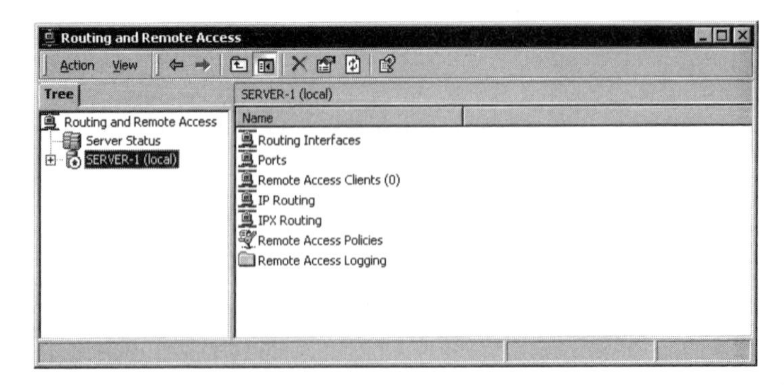


### Action Menu

Use the Action menu to further configure Routing and Remote Access services and access Routing and Remote Access help.

Routing and Remote Access involves complex configuration; accordingly, the available options on the Action (and pop-up) menus will vary greatly depending on the item you have selected in the console tree or Details pane.

**See Also** Microsoft Management Console (MMC)

# Run

Used to open programs, folders, documents, and Internet resources. Most frequently used to run installation programs. Follow these steps:

1. Choose Start ➢ Run to open the Run dialog box.
2. In the Open text box, enter the name of the resource you want to open. Include the full path. If you've used Run before, the path to the most recently opened resource will appear in the Open text box. You can also choose a resource by clicking the drop-down arrow and selecting a resource from the list. If you don't know the exact path to the resource, click Browse and browse for and select it. Click Open to return to the Run menu.
3. Click OK to open the resource.

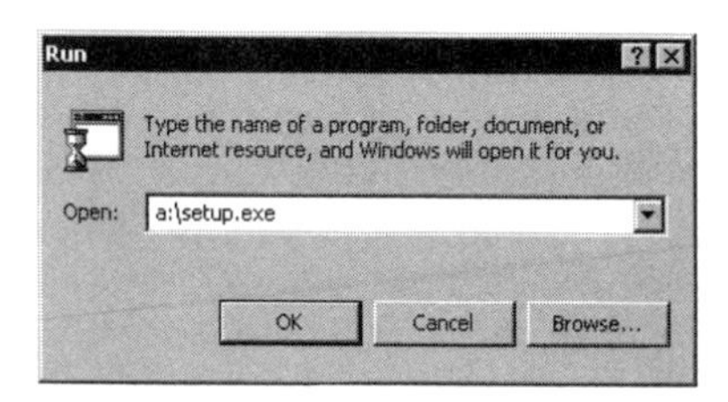


# Run As

Used to run a program or MMC tool as a user other than the one currently logged on (for example, as an administrative user). Follow these steps to access the Run as Other User dialog box:

1. In Windows Explorer, select a program you want to run as another user.

2. Hold down the Shift key and right-click.
3. From the shortcut menu, select Run As.
4. In the Run as Other User dialog box, make sure that the Run the Program as the Following User option is selected and enter the name, password, and domain for the user that you want to run the program.
5. Click OK.

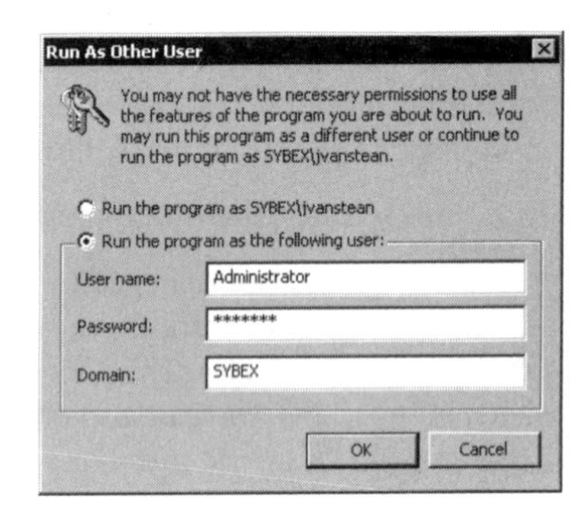


A related dialog box is Install Program as Other User. If you run an installation program such as INSTALL.EXE or SETUP.EXE as a user who does not have administrative privileges, the Install Program as Other User dialog box appears, and you're asked if you want to install the program as an administrative user because some programs won't install correctly if you don't. Enter information the same way you did in the Run as Other User dialog box. You can also specify to always run installation programs as the current user by selecting the corresponding check box.

# Safe Mode

Windows 2000 lets you start up the computer in Safe mode to troubleshoot Windows system problems—for example, if Windows won't start after an application installation. To access the Safe mode startup options on the Windows 2000 Advanced options menu, follow these steps:

1. Choose Start ➢ Shutdown, then select Restart from the drop-down list and click OK.

2. When the Please Select Operating System To Start screen appears, press F8.

3. Choose one of the nine options. Use the up and down arrow keys to highlight your choice and press Enter to select it. NumLock must be off in order for the arrow keys to work.

Each of the menu options serves a specific function, as outlined below:

**Safe Mode** Starts Windows 2000 but bypasses the startup files (such as the Registry) and loads only basic device drivers (standard VGA, keyboard, mouse, and other basic drivers required to start Windows).

**TIP** If you can't start Windows 2000 in Safe mode, you might need to repair your Windows 2000 system using Automated System Recovery. See the heading Backup for more information.

**Safe Mode with Networking** Starts Windows 2000 but bypasses the startup files. Loads network (NIC card) drivers in addition to basic device drivers.

**Safe Mode with Command Prompt** Bypasses the startup files and, after logging on, starts the computer in MS-DOS mode, displaying the command prompt.

**Enable Boot Logging** Starts Windows 2000 and creates a log file of all of the services and drivers that load during startup. The file, called `ntbtlog.txt`, is saved in the `%windir%` directory.

**Enable VGA Mode** Starts Windows 2000 with the standard VGA driver. You can use this mode to troubleshoot problems you might be having after installing a different video driver.

**Last Known Good Configuration** Starts Windows 2000 using the Registry information that was saved the last time you successfully shut down Windows 2000.

**Directory Services Restore Mode (Windows 2000 Domain Controllers Only)** Windows 2000 Server only. Used to restore the Active Directory and the SYSVOL directory on a Windows 2000 domain controller.

**Debugging Mode** Starts Windows 2000 and sends debugging data to another computer via a serial connection.

**Boot Normally** Lets you proceed with a normal boot.

**Return to OS Choices Menu** Lets you return to the Please Select Operating System To Start screen and start Windows normally.

**See Also** Backup

# Scanners and Cameras

Scanners and Cameras

Lets you configure scanners and cameras that are installed on the Windows 2000 computer.

Choose Start ➢ Settings ➢ Control Panel and double-click Scanners and Cameras to open the Scanners and Cameras Properties dialog box, which has one tab: Devices.

## Devices Tab

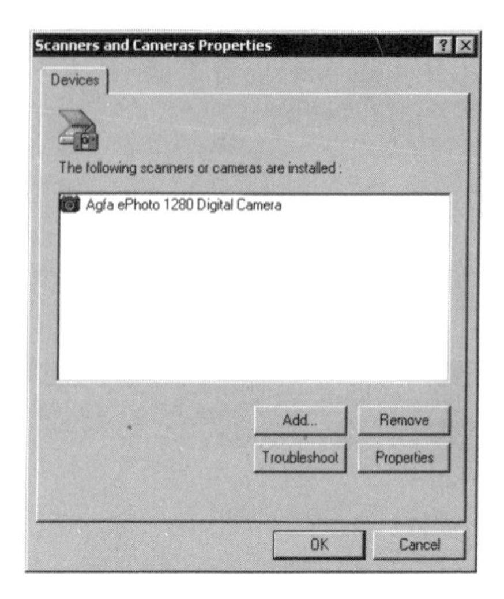

Use this tab to view, add, remove, troubleshoot, and configure the properties of scanners and cameras. Any installed scanners or cameras appear in the list of installed scanners or cameras. You can add new scanners or cameras by clicking Add and following the wizard's instructions. You'll have to provide the manufacturer and model of your hardware, and specify the communications port you want to use for the device.

To remove a scanner or camera, select it in the list and click Remove. If you're experiencing problems with a scanner or camera, select it in the list and click Troubleshoot to start the Windows 2000 Troubleshooter for cameras and scanners.

If you want to view or modify the properties of a scanner or camera, select it in the list and click Properties. The available properties will vary depending on your hardware, but may include such items as port settings used for the device and color management.

# Scheduled Tasks

Scheduled Tasks

Windows 2000 lets you schedule tasks to run at a certain time, date, and interval. Tasks include items such as programs, scripts, and documents. Scheduled Tasks, located in Control Panel, lets you open the Scheduled Tasks folder, where you can create new scheduled tasks as well as view and configure already scheduled tasks.

Choose Start ➢ Settings ➢ Control Panel and double-click the Scheduled Tasks icon to open the Scheduled Tasks folder. By default, no tasks are scheduled and the folder contains only the Add Scheduled Task icon.

**TIP** Make sure your system time settings are accurate if you want to set up scheduled tasks.

**TIP** You can also access Scheduled Tasks by choosing Start ➢ Programs ➢ Accessories ➢ System Tools ➢ Scheduled Tasks.

## Add Scheduled Task

Starts the Scheduled Task Wizard, which guides you through the process of creating scheduled tasks. To create a scheduled task, follow these steps:

1. In the Scheduled Tasks folder, double-click Add Scheduled Task. The Scheduled Task Wizard starts. Click Next.
2. In the list of programs, select a program you want Windows 2000 to run, or click Browse to browse to a program located elsewhere on the computer or network. Click Next.

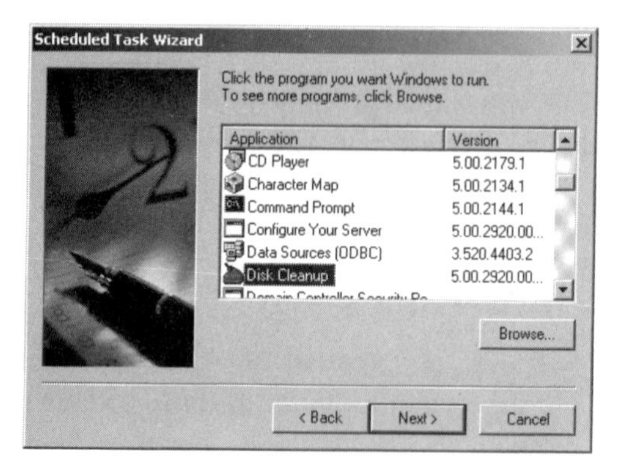


3. Enter a name for the scheduled task. It can be, but does not have to be, the same name as the program.

**TIP** Although a scheduled task icon has a visual indicator to denote that it is a scheduled task, you may find it easier to distinguish scheduled tasks from actual programs if you call the scheduled tasks something different than the name of the program. You may want to indicate in the name of the task that this is a scheduled task, not a program—for example, by calling a scheduled disk cleanup something like My Scheduled Disk Cleanup.

4. Decide how often you want to run this task. You can choose to perform the task, daily, weekly, monthly, only once, every time the computer starts, or every time you

log onto the computer. Select the appropriate radio button and click Next.

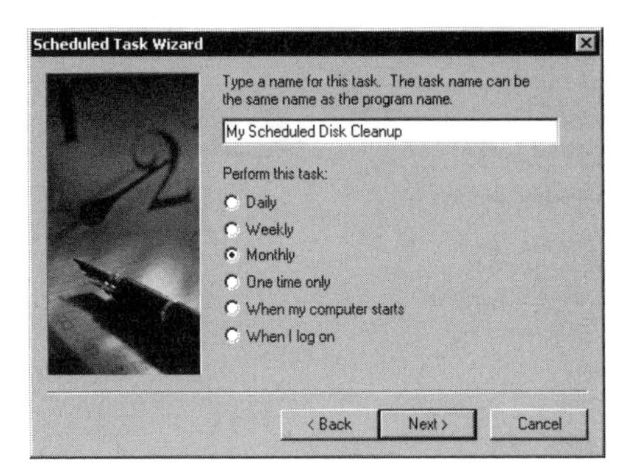


5. The options available in next dialog box will depend on your choice in step 4. If you chose to run the task when you start the computer or when you log onto the computer, skip to step 6. If you chose any of the other options, you will be able to specify such items as the time to start the scheduled task and on which days, weeks, or months you want the task to run. When you finish, click Next.
6. Enter your username and password. Click Next.
7. Select the check box if you want to open the property sheet for the scheduled task after the Wizard creates the task. Click Finish to complete the Wizard.

## Scheduled Tasks Folder

The Scheduled Tasks folder contains all of your scheduled tasks and the Add Scheduled Task icon to run the Scheduled Task Wizard.

You can identify a scheduled task by the small clock icon located in the bottom-left corner of its icon. If you select a scheduled task icon, you'll see information about the task in the left portion of the Scheduled Tasks folder. Information includes the name of the task, the schedule for the task, its next run time, its last run time, the results of the last run, and the task's creator.

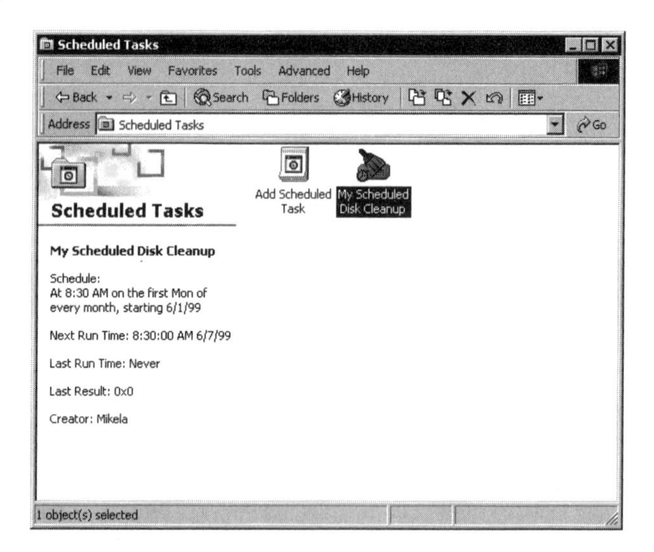


### Run and End Task

When you right-click any task, two options specific to scheduled tasks are available: Run and End Task. Choose Run to run the scheduled task immediately. Choose End Task to stop a scheduled task that is currently running. When a scheduled task is running, you will see status information in the left portion of the Scheduled Tasks folder.

**TIP** End Task is handy when you want to use the computer and a scheduled task is currently running. End the task and then restart it later, using Run Task. It may take several minutes for the task to actually stop.

### Properties

Right-click any task and choose Properties to bring up the properties for the selected scheduled task. The dialog box has four tabs: Task, Schedule, Settings, and Security.

**Task** Use this tab to specify information about the task. In the Run field, you'll see the location of the file currently associated with the task. You can change the path to the file by entering a new path. In the field Start In, you can specify the directory in which the file associated with the task and any other necessary files are located. Additional files necessary for the execution of the task may be located in the same directory as the file that is associated with the task, or they may be found in a different location. In the Comments field, you can enter any comment about the task—for example, a description of what the task does.

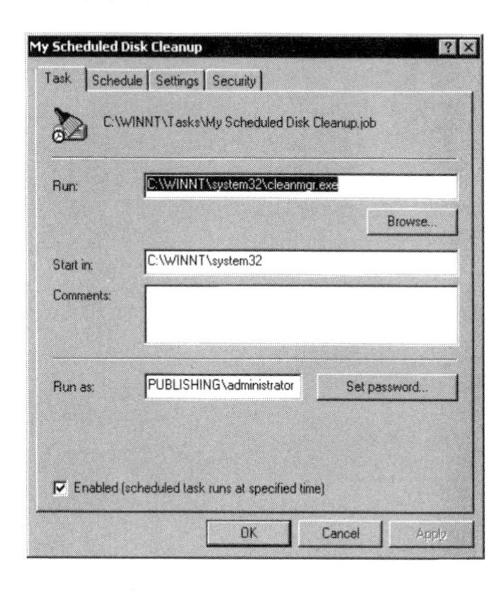

**TIP** If you need to specify command-line parameters for a program, you can enter them in the Run field following the path to the task's associated file.

**TIP** If there are any spaces in the path to the task's associated file, place the path inside double quotation marks.

You do not have to run scheduled tasks as the user you're logged in as or as the user who created the task. If you wish to run the task as a different user, in the field Run As specify the user you would like to run the task. The syntax is `computer_name_or_domain_name\user_name`. By default, the task is run as the creator of the task.

If you change the user to run the task or the task that will be run, click the Set Password button to specify the user's password.

Finally, use this tab to enable or disable the scheduled task by selecting or deselecting the Enabled option.

**Schedule** Use this tab to change the task's schedule—for example, if you want to run the task daily instead of weekly, or you want to change the times the task runs. When you choose an option from the Schedule Task drop-down list, the area below automatically adjusts to reflect the possible scheduling options for the type of schedule you've selected (for example, days of the week for a task that should run weekly). As you make choices on this tab, the scheduling information that appears at the top of the tab is updated to reflect your current choices.

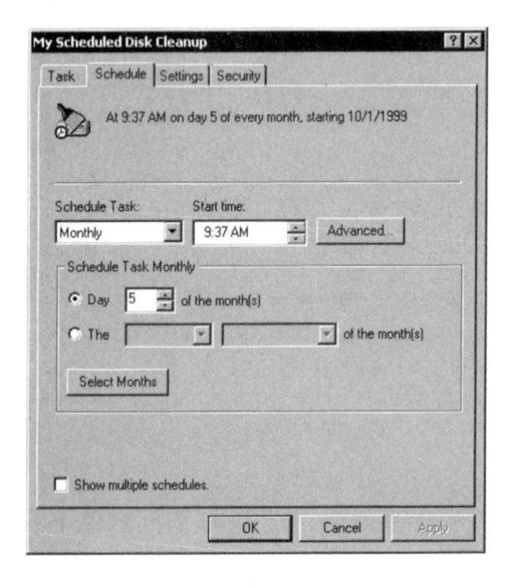

**TIP** If you choose At System Startup or At Logon, you won't be able to further customize when to run the backup job, as it will run every time the system is started or every time you log on, respectively.

You can configure advanced scheduling options, such as start and end dates, by clicking Advanced. In the Advanced Schedule Options dialog box, you can specify a start and end date for the job by selecting the appropriate check box (if applicable) and choosing a date from the drop-down calendar. You can also specify whether you want to repeat the task and, if so, further customize repeat settings. Click OK to save your advanced settings.

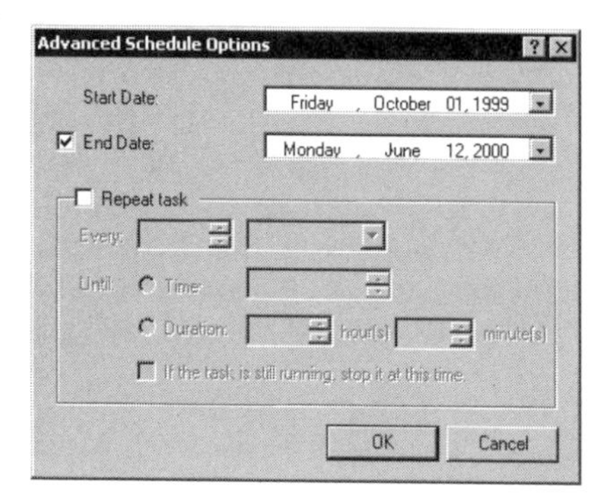


You can also configure more than one schedule for the same task, by selecting Show Multiple Schedules. The top area of the tab changes to display a drop-down list of all configured schedules for the task. Click New to create another schedule for the task. Once you have created multiple schedules, they always appear; you cannot disable the display of multiple schedules unless there is only one schedule.

**Settings** Use this tab to configure what you want to do with the task under certain circumstances, such as when the task is completed, when the computer is idle, or under certain power conditions. Some options are Delete the Task if It Is Not Scheduled to Run Again, Only Start the Task if the Computer Has Been Idle for at Least (you must specify the number of minutes), and Stop the Task if the Computer Ceases To Be Idle.

**TIP** Idle-time configuration can come in handy if you want tasks to run but you still want to be able to use your computer if necessary, without the task tying up your computer's resources.

You can also specify whether you want to run the task if the computer is running on batteries or choose to stop the task if the computer switches to battery power.

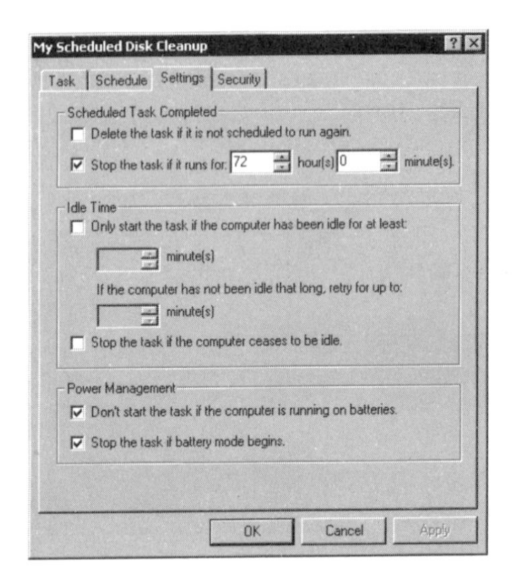


**Security** Available on computers formatted with NTFS. Lets you assign task permissions to groups, users, or computers. Click Advanced to assign advanced permissions and to configure auditing and ownership.

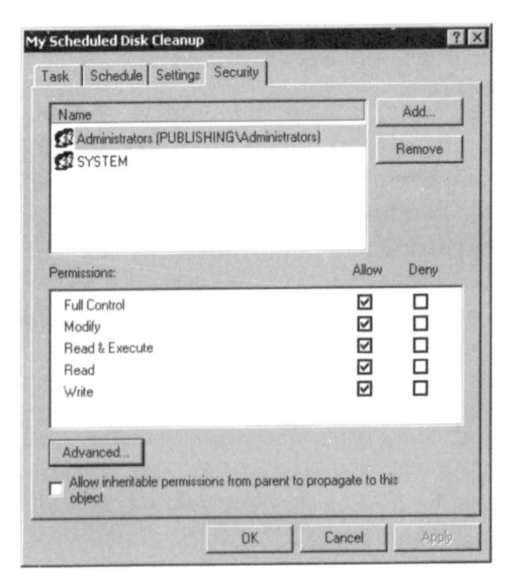

### Advanced Menu

The Scheduled Tasks folder includes a unique menu: Advanced. This menu contains the following five options (the first four are only available for users with administrative privileges):

Stop Using Task Scheduler
Pause Task Scheduler
Notify Me of Missed Tasks
AT Service Account
View Log

**Stop Using Task Scheduler** Stops the task scheduler service. When you stop the service, any tasks that are scheduled to run won't run until the next time they are scheduled to run, providing the task scheduler has been restarted. Choose this option to toggle between Stop Using Task Scheduler and Start Using Task Scheduler. Choose Start Using Task Scheduler to start the task scheduler again after it's been stopped. Stopping the task scheduler also disables two menu options on the Advanced menu: Pause Task Scheduler and AT Service Account.

**Pause Task Scheduler** Available only if the task scheduler is running. Temporarily pauses the task scheduler service. When you pause the service, any tasks that are scheduled to run won't run until the next time they are scheduled to run, providing the task scheduler has been continued. Choose this option to toggle between Pause Task Scheduler and Continue Task Scheduler. Choose Continue Task Scheduler to resume the operation of the task scheduler after it's been paused.

**Notify Me of Missed Tasks** Choose this option to have Windows 2000 notify you if a scheduled task didn't run. Clicking this option places a check mark next to the option, indicating that it's active. Click the option again to turn off notification.

**AT Service Account** Lets you specify which account can run or list scheduled tasks using the command-line AT command.

**TIP** For more detailed information about the AT command, search the Help system's index for the words *AT COMMAND*.

**View Log** View a log of messages relating to scheduled events and the status of the task scheduler. The log file includes success as well as error messages, and messages regarding starting, stopping, pausing, and continuing the task scheduler service.

**See Also** Help

# Screen Saver

**See** Display (Screen Saver Tab)

# Search

Use this Windows 2000 feature to search for files, folders, Internet resources, printers, and people. Choose Start ➢ Search and select one of the options from the submenu. Alternatively, click the Search button in Windows Explorer or Internet Explorer. You'll be able to choose any of the search options in the Search pane at the left of the window. If you ever close the Search pane, you can reopen it by clicking the Search button.

**TIP** You can also right-click the Start button and choose Search to open Search for files and folders. This window contains links to all other search options.

**TIP** Alternative ways of searching the local and network file system for files and folders include browsing My Computer or My Network Places through Windows Explorer or by opening their desktop shortcuts.

## For Files and Folders

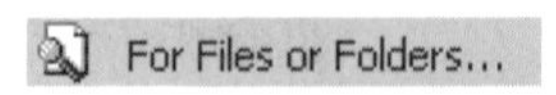


Use this option to search for files and folders on both the local machine and

the network (including the Internet). This is helpful if you don't know the exact name or path of a file or folder.

Choose Start ➢ Search ➢ For Files or Folders to access the Search Results window.

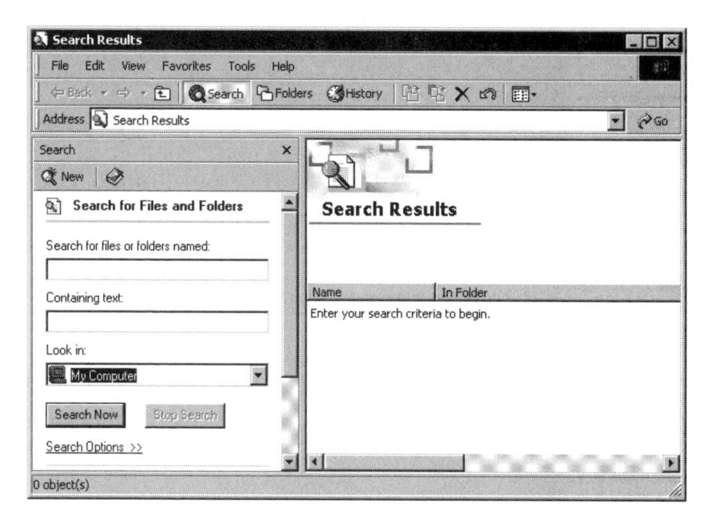


At the left of the Search Results window is the Explorer Bar Search pane. Follow these steps to search for a file or folder:

1. In the Search for Files or Folders Named text box, enter a name for the file or folder you want to find. You can enter the exact name or part of the name. You can also use the * and ? wildcard characters to broaden your search.
2. In the Containing Text text box, you can enter any text that is part of a file you're looking for.
3. In the Look In drop-down list, select the drive or folder you want to search. Click the down arrow and make your selection or click Browse (in the drop-down list) to browse all available folders on the local machine and in the network (including the World Wide Web). When you choose a folder while browsing, its name appears in the Folder text box. Click OK to return to the Search pane.
4. Click Search Now to perform the search. Click the Stop Search button if you want to interrupt the search at any time.

### *Additional Search Criteria*

Specify additional search criteria by clicking the Search Options link beneath the Search Now button and selecting an option you want to configure. You'll also see a status message at the bottom of the Search Options area indicating whether the Indexing Service is currently disabled or building an index. Indexing Service can create an index of files on your computer, which allows for faster seraches. Click the link and use the Indexing Service Settings dialog box.

**Date** Lets you restrict your search to files modified, files created, and files last accessed in a specified number of months and days in a specific date range.

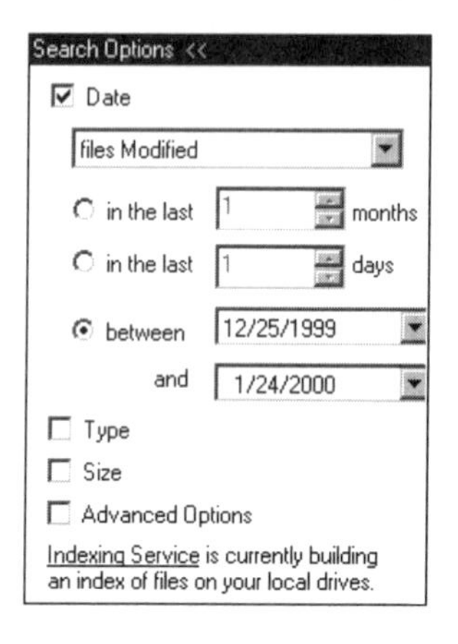


**Type** Lets you specify either all files and folders or files of a specific type. Select the type from the list of available file types.

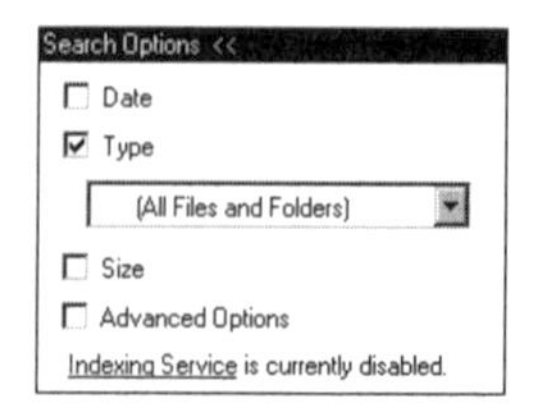


**Size** Lets you specify a minimum or maximum file size.

**Advanced Options** Lets you specify whether you want the search to include subfolders or slow files. You can also specify that you want the search to be case sensitive.

### *Search Results and Saving a Search*

Once you perform a search, your search results appear in the Search Results pane. You will see the name, folder, relevance, size, type, and modification date of each file that matches your search.

To clear all fields and start a new search, click the New button.

Click the Close button in the Search pane to close the Search pane and display only the Search Results window.

You can save your search by choosing File ➢Save Search. Specify where to save the search in the Save In list box and enter a name in the File Name text box, then click Save.

## For Computers

Searching for a computer in the network is done from the Search for Files and Folders Search pane. Scroll down and click the Computers link. Enter the name of the computer you want to find in the Computer Name text box. Click Search Now to perform the search.

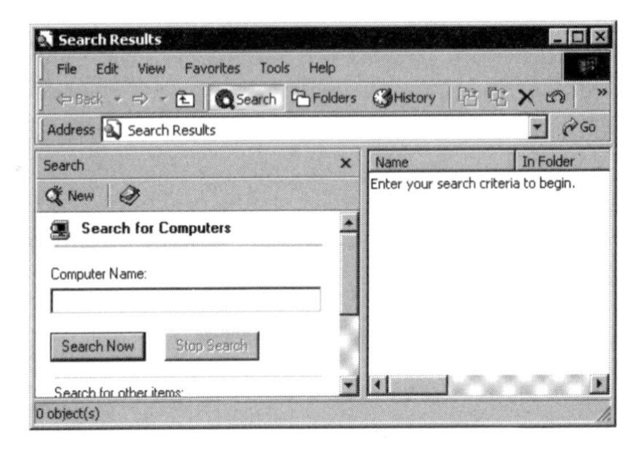


## On the Internet

On the Internet... Used to search the Internet for Web pages, people's addresses, businesses, maps, encyclopedia entries, and newsgroups. Your last ten searches are saved so that you can perform the same search again later without reentering the information. You must be connected to the Internet to successfully perform this type of search.

Choose Start ➢ Search and select On the Internet. This opens Internet Explorer with the Search pane open in the left portion of the screen. In this window, select one of the following categories for your search.

**TIP** You can also perform a search on the Internet by clicking Search on the Windows Explorer toolbar. This opens up the Search pane to the default of For Files and Folders. Scroll down and click Internet. The Search pane displays the same as it does in Internet Explorer.

**Find a Web Page** Lets you search using keywords for Web pages you're looking for. For example, enter **Chrysler** or **Daimler** if you want to find Web sites related to Daimler Chrysler automobiles. You can enter multiple words to refine your search.

**Find a Person's Address** Lets you search for a person's mailing or e-mail address. You can specify the person's first name, last name, city, and state or province.

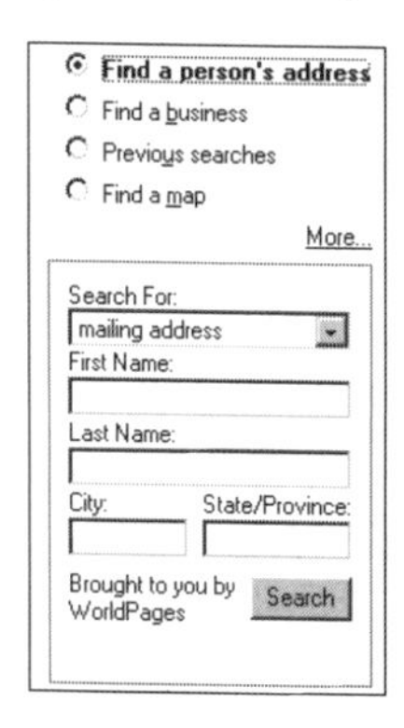


**Find a Business** Lets you search for businesses on the Internet. You can search by business name or category, and enter a name or category, city and state, or province for the business you're looking for.

**TIP** The business search engine WorldPages requires that you fill in the State field.

**Previous Searches** Lets you repeat one of the last ten searches. Select a search from the list and it will be performed automatically.

**Find a map** Lets you search for maps of places you're interested in. You can search for addresses or places and landmarks. You can enter a street address, city, state or province, and zip or postal code, or you can enter the place or landmark you're looking for.

Click the More link to display these additional options:

**Look Up a Word** Lets you perform online encyclopedia, dictionary, or thesaurus searches for any word or subject you enter.

**Find a Picture** Lets you use the Corbis search engine to find a picture relating to a subject you enter.

**Find in Newsgroups** Lets you search Deja.com for newsgroups that are related to a topic you enter.

When you have finished entering your information, click Search to perform the search. The search results appear in the left pane. If the search results are addresses, scroll to find the address you were looking for. If the search results are links, click a link you want to follow to open the corresponding Web page in the right pane. To start a new search, click New. If you want to close the Search pane (but not the entire window), click the Close button in the Search pane.

### *Customizing Your Search*

Each of the categories uses a default search service that is searched first when you perform a search. Other search services are available, and you can specify additional search services you want to use, if any. Click Customize to open the Customize Search Settings dialog box. Each category has an entry in this dialog box. Choose the search service(s) you want to use for each search category. You can also deselect an entire category so that it's not available for searching in the Search pane. Finally, you can choose to use only one search service for all of your searches. Use the Reset button to return to default settings. To change the order of search services, select a service and click the up or down arrow button to change the service's position on the list.

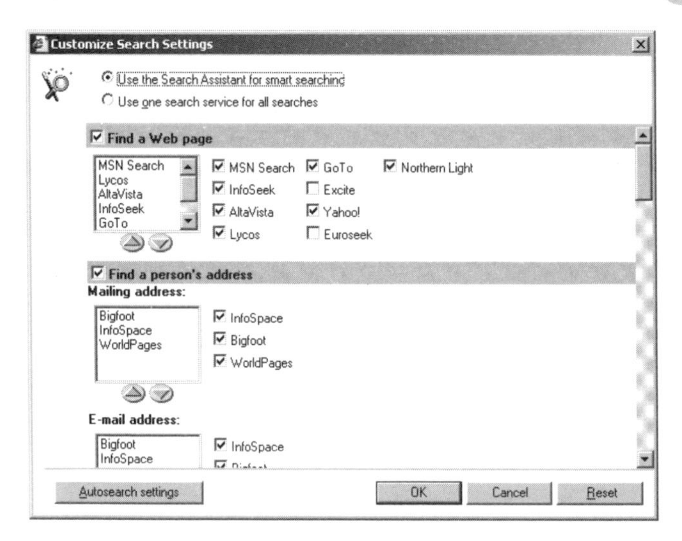


When you've performed a search and you want to use another search service in the list, click Next in the Search pane. If you want to specify which search service to use next, click the drop-down arrow and select the service from the list.

**NOTE** The service that is searched first may change when you make changes to custom settings, even if you don't deselect the service that was previously searched first.

**TIP** You can also perform quick searches by entering **?**, **find**, or **go** followed by any text you'd like to search for in the Address field of Internet Explorer or Windows Explorer.

## Searching for Printers in the Active Directory

For Printers...

To search for printers in the Active Directory (you must be logged into a Windows 2000 domain with Active Directory installed), choose Start ➢ Search ➢ For Printers, or click Search in Windows Explorer, then select the link Printers. Use the In drop-down list to specify that you want to search either the entire directory or a specific domain. Click the Browse button to find domains not listed. The Find Printers dialog box has three tabs: Printers, Features, and Advanced.

**TIP** You can also search for printers when adding a new network printer with the Add Printer Wizard.

**Printers** Lets you enter the name, location, and model of the printer.

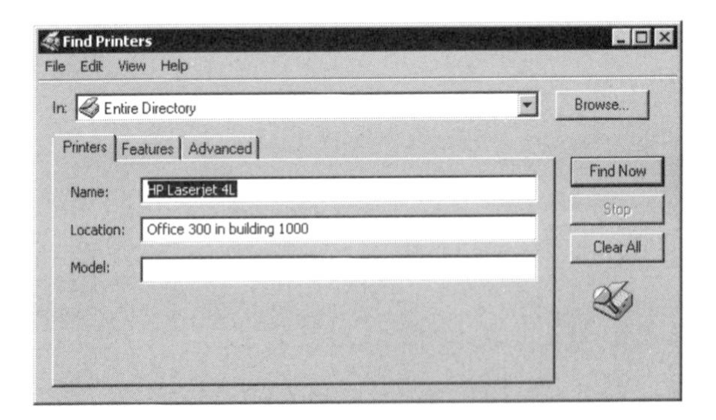


**Features** Lets you refine your search by specifying particular printer features, such as minimum resolution, minimum speed, and print color.

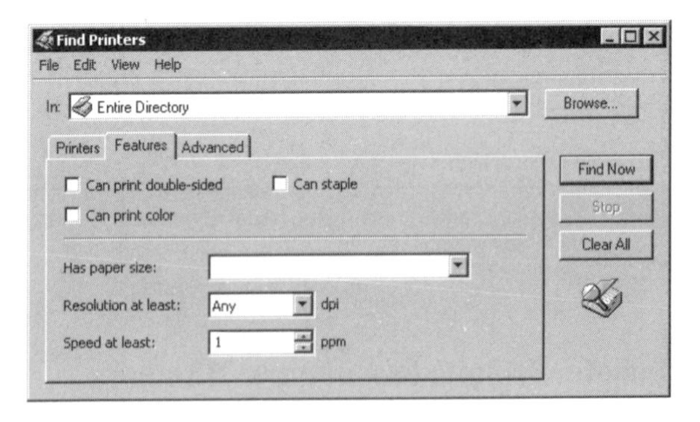


**Advanced** Lets you further refine your search by specifying a value and condition of the value for any of the printer's available fields, such as Asset Number, Contact, Owner Name, and Printer Language.

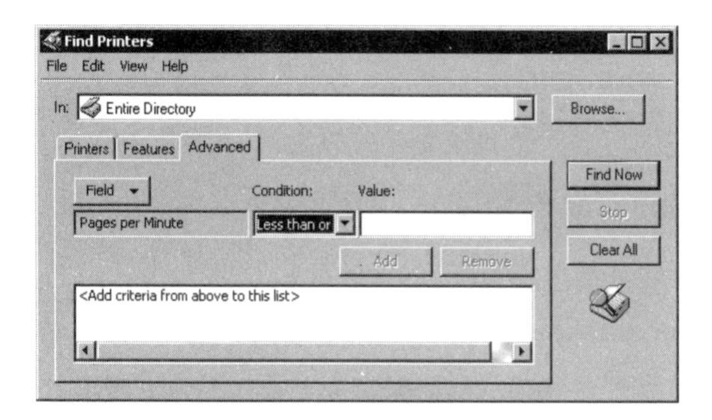


When you have specified all search criteria, click Find Now. Your search results appear in the window below the tabs. You can sort the list by Name, Location, Model, Server Name, or Comment by clicking the corresponding column header.

**TIP** You can connect to any printer in the list by right-clicking it and choosing Connect.

**TIP** To find all printers in the Active Directory, do not specify any search criteria and click Find Now.

Click Clear All to clear all fields and start entering criteria for a new search.

To save your search, select File ➢ Save Search, choose a location, enter a name for the search, then click Save.

### *Filtering Search Results*

If your search produced too many results, you can apply filters to the search results by choosing View ➢ Filter. Enter a value under each search result column against which to filter the results. Click the filter icon next to the value field and select a condition to apply to the value. Conditions include Contains (the default), Does Not Contain, Starts With, Ends With, Is (Exactly), and Is Not. Every time you enter a value or apply a condition, Search sorts the results list with the filter applied.

**NOTE** To be able to apply filters, you must select Details from the View menu.

**WARNING** Do not click Find Now when you want to filter results. Clicking Find Now restarts the search and clears all filters.

## Searching for People

For People...

To search for people, choose Start ➢ Search ➢ For People to open the Find People dialog box. You can also use this dialog box to find groups.

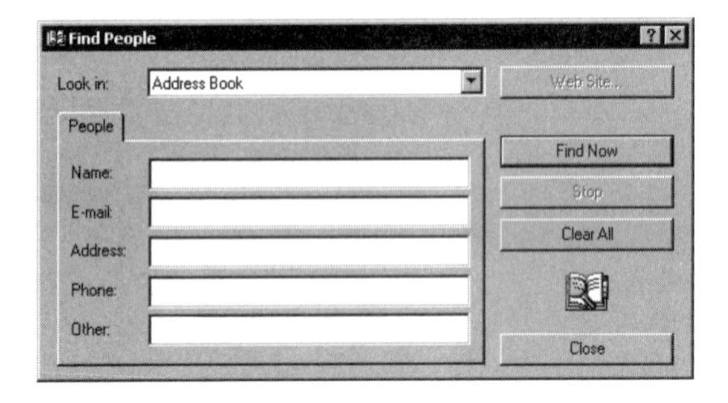


In the Look In drop-down list, you can select where to search for people. Choices include your Address Book, Directory Services such as the Active Directory, or Internet Web sites that provide people-search capabilities.

With the Address Book selected as the place to search for people, the Find People dialog box contains one tab: People. On this tab, you can fill in the following:

**Name** Enter the name, nickname, company name, or organization name of the person or group you're looking for.

**E-mail** Enter the e-mail address for the person or group.

**Address** Enter the address for the person or group. You can search the following fields: address, street, city, state, zip code, and country.

**Phone** Enter a phone number for the person or group. You can search the following fields: phone, fax, pager, and cellular.

**Other** Enter information that might be contained in a person's or group's Address Book or Directory Service entry.

With a directory service selected as the place to search, the People tab only has the Name and E-mail fields. Additionally, the Advanced tab is available, where you can define criteria for your search, much like you apply filters when you perform a search for a printer. Here's an example of defined criteria: Name (you'd select this from a drop-down list), Contains (you'd select this from a drop-down list as well), Jutta (you would type this manually). When you have defined your criteria, click Add to apply the criteria when you start your search. To remove the defined criteria, select the criteria in the list and click Remove.

The following buttons are also available in the Find People dialog box:

**Web Site** Goes directly to the Web site of an Internet search service you selected from the Look In drop-down list.

**Find Now** Starts the search.

**Stop** Stops the search.

**Clear All** Clears information on the People tab so you can start a new search.

**Close** Closes the Find People dialog box.

# Send Cover Page Fax

Send Cover Page Fax

Lets you send a fax that consists only of a cover page. Use this as a quick way to send a short fax without having to open an application and creating a document first.

To send a cover page fax, follow these steps:

1. Choose Start ➢ Programs ➢ Accessories ➢ Communications ➢ Fax ➢ Send Cover Page Fax. If multiple fax printers are installed, choose the one you want to use and click OK. The Send Fax Wizard opens, telling you that you can

only send a cover page now because you started the Wizard outside an application. Click Next.

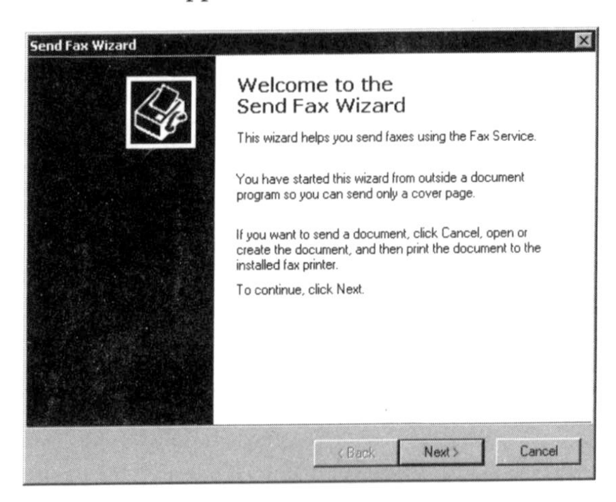


2. Enter the name and fax number information for the recipient, select the country/region code and dialing rules if applicable, or find the recipient in the Address Book. Click Add. Repeat for any additional recipients. When you've finished, click Next.
3. Choose the cover page template you want to use from the drop-down list, enter a subject in the Subject Line field, and enter your message in the Note field. Click Next.
4. Specify when you want to send the fax (now, when discount rates apply, or at a specific time in the next 24 hours). If applicable, enter a billing code. Click Next.
5. Click Finish to add the fax to the fax queue. Your cover page fax is sent at the time you specified.

**See Also** Fax (Properties), Fax Queue, Send Fax Wizard

# Send Fax Wizard

Walks you through the steps of sending a fax via a fax printer installed on the computer. In any Windows application, create a document, then choose File ➢ Print. Select the fax printer you want to use and click Print. This starts the Send Fax Wizard. Follow these steps to finish sending your fax:

1. On the Welcome to the Send Fax Wizard page, click Next.
2. If this is not the first time you've run the Send Fax Wizard, skip to step 4. If this is the first time you've run the Wizard, either you can select Edit the User Information Now, click OK, and continue with step 3, or you can select Keep the Current User Information, click OK, and continue with step 4.
3. In the Fax Properties dialog box, on the User Information tab verify that the user information is correct, or if none appears, fill in that information. On the Cover Pages tab, make sure you have an existing cover page if you want to use a personalized cover page. If not, create one now. When you finish, click OK.
4. Enter the recipient's name in the To field or select it from the Address Book by clicking Address Book. Next, enter the fax number.
5. If the call is long distance, or if you need to make changes to the location from which you're dialing, select Use Dialing Rules. Click Dialing Rules to edit the current location or add a new location. Click OK when you've finished and select the appropriate dialing rule from the drop-down list. If necessary, enter the appropriate area code and/or select a country/region code from the drop-down list.

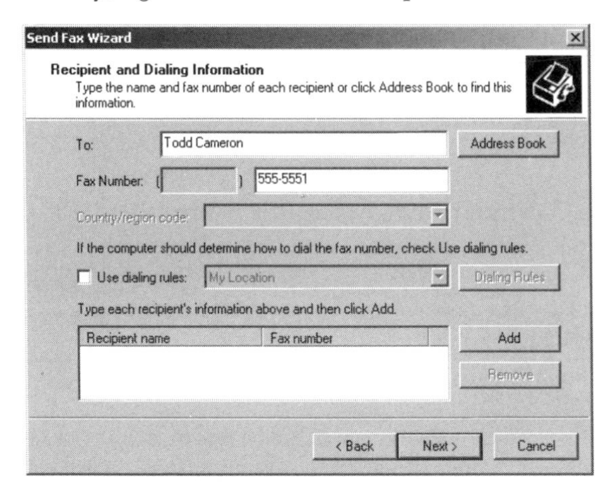

6. Click Add to add the recipient to the list of recipients. If you have more than one recipient, repeat steps 4 and 5. Click Next when you've added all recipients.

7. If you want to use a cover page, select Include a Cover Page, then choose a template from the Cover Page Template drop-down list. Four predesigned templates are available: Confdnet (for a confidential cover sheet), FYI (for a For Your Information cover sheet), Generic (for a generic cover sheet), and Urgent (for an urgent cover sheet).

8. Add a subject line and note by typing text in the respective fields. This text will appear in the Subject and Note fields on your cover page. Click Next.

9. Specify when you want to send the fax. You can send it now, when discount rates apply, or at a certain time within the next 24 hours. Enter a billing code if applicable. Click Next.

**TIP** Times during which discount rates apply are set up through Fax Service Management in the properties of Fax Service on Local Computer.

10. The Completing the Send Fax Wizard page summarizes the information you entered. Make sure it is correct. If it's not, use the Back button to return to any screen on which you want to make changes.

11. Click Finish to add the fax to the fax queue. If you selected to print the fax now, the fax printer will dial the number and send the fax. If you specified to send the fax later, it is held in the fax printer's fax queue until that time.

**See Also** Fax (Properties), Fax Service Management, Fax Queue, Phone and Modem Options, Send Cover Page Fax

# Send To

Send To ▸

Lets you send a file or folder directly to a destination, such as a floppy drive, the desktop (as a shortcut), a mail recipient, and the My Documents folder.

To send an item to a destination using Send To, perform these steps:

1. In any Explorer window, right-click a file or folder to open the pop-up menu.
2. Select Send To, then select the destination.

**See Also** Explorer

# Server Extensions Administrator

Server Extensions Administrator Microsoft Management Console (MMC) snap-in installed on Windows 2000 Server computers that lets you administer FrontPage server extensions for non-IIS and IIS 3.0 virtual servers. For IIS 4.0 or later (Windows 2000 includes IIS 5.0), FrontPage server extensions are already integrated, and you would use the Internet Information Service MMC snap-in (accessible through the Internet Services Manager menu option in the Administrative Tools program group) to administer them.

To access the Server Extensions Administrator, choose Start ➢ Programs ➢ Administrative Tools ➢ Server Extensions Administrator.

**TIP** Alternatively, you can access the Server Extensions Administrator through the Administrative Tools folder in Control Panel.

**See Also** Internet Services Manager, FrontPage Server Extensions

# Services

Services MMC console snap-in that lets you start and stop services that are installed or running on your Windows 2000 computer. Some examples of services are Fax Service, Indexing Service, Event Log, Plug and Play, and Utility Manager.

To access Services, choose Start ➢ Settings ➢ Control Panel, double-click Administrative Tools, then double-click Services.

**TIP** In Windows 2000 Server, you can also access Services by choosing Start ➢ Programs ➢ Administrative Tools ➢ Services.

**TIP** Alternatively, you can access Services by opening Control Panel, double-clicking Computer Management, and then selecting Services under Services and Applications in the console tree.

In the Details pane of the Services MMC console snap-in, you can see information about all services installed on your computer, including name, description, status, startup type, and the account the service uses to log on.

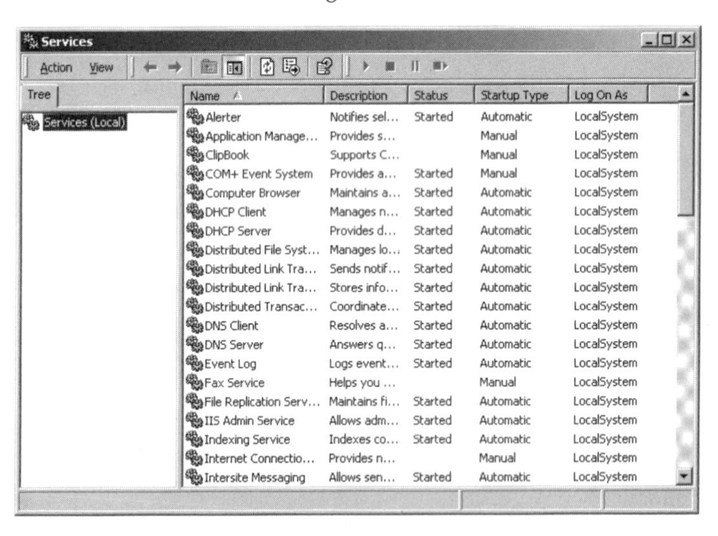


## Working with Services

Services lets you start, stop, pause, resume, and restart services installed on your Windows 2000 computer. To do so, right-click a service and choose the appropriate action from the pop-up menu, or select a service, click Action, and select the action you want to perform. Alternatively, use the Start Service, Stop Service, Pause Service, and Resume Service buttons on the toolbar.

### *Service Properties*

You can view and configure properties for any service installed on your computer. Right-click a service and choose Properties

from the pop-up menu. The Service Properties dialog box has four tabs: General, Log On, Recovery, and Dependencies.

**General** Lets you view and configure general items, such as the display name, description, startup type, status of the service (started, stopped, or paused), and start parameters. You can also click the appropriate button to start, stop, pause, or resume the service. Also lets you enter parameters to apply when the service is started.

**Log On** Lets you specify an account the service should use to log on. This can be either the Local System account or a user account you specify. You can also choose to provide a user interface that anyone logged onto the computer can use to interact with the service. Finally, you can enable or disable the service for specific hardware profiles you have set up on your computer by selecting a profile in the list and clicking Enable or Disable, respectively.

**Recovery** Lets you specify an action Windows 2000 should take if the service fails. You can specify different actions for the first, second, and subsequent failures. The default action varies from service to service. Available options include Take No Action, Run a File, and Reboot the Computer. If you select Run a File, you must specify in the Run File area of the dialog box the file you want Windows to run. If you select Restart the Service, specify the number of minutes that should elapse before the service restarts. If you select Reboot the Computer, click Restart Computer Options to specify the number of minutes that should elapse before the computer reboots and whether you want a custom message sent to network users before the computer reboots. On the Recovery tab, you can also specify the number of days that should pass before Windows resets the fail count.

**Dependencies** Lets you view any services that depend on the currently selected service and any services on which the currently selected service depends. This information can help with troubleshooting service-related problems.

**See Also** Microsoft Management Console (MMC), Computer Management

# Settings

The Settings option on the Start menu gives you access to many Windows 2000 configuration tools, such as Control Panel, Network and Dial-up Connections, Printers, and Taskbar & Start Menu. Choose Start ➢ Settings and make your choice from the submenu.

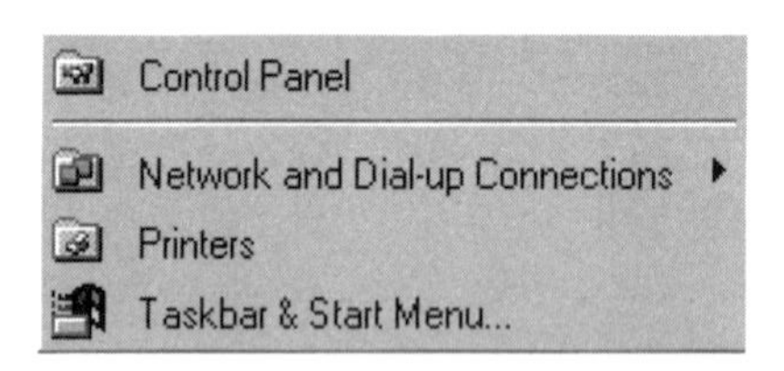


**See Also** Control Panel, Network and Dial-up Connections, Printers, Taskbar & Start Menu

# Shared Folders

Shared Folders MMC console snap-in that lets you view and manage shares on the computer you're using, remote connections to that computer, and files in use by remote users.

**TIP** You must be a member of the Administrators, Power Users, or Server Operators group to use Shared Folders.

To access Shared Folders, choose Start ➢ Settings ➢ Control Panel, double-click Administrative Tools, double-click Computer Management, and select Shared Folders under System Tools in the console tree.

## Shared Folders Nodes

Shared Folders contains three nodes: Shares, Sessions, and Open Files.

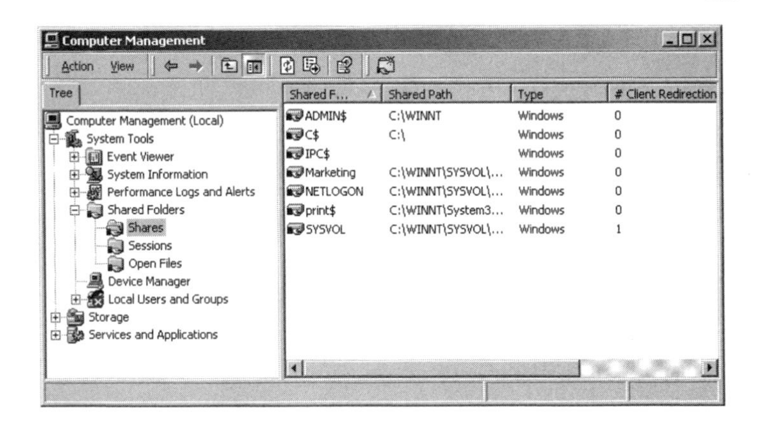


**Shares** Lets you view, stop sharing, and configure properties, such as permissions and security, for existing shares. You can also create new shares. Some default shares for both Windows 2000 Professional and Server are ADMIN$, C$, and IPC$. Windows 2000 Server also has the SYSVOL and NETLOGON default shares. Detail columns for each share include Shared Folder (the name of the share, such as the shared folder's or printer's name), Shared Path (the path to the resource), Type, # Client Redirections (the number of users connected to the share), and Comment.

**Sessions** Lets you see which users are currently connected to the computer, disconnect a single session, or disconnect all sessions. Detail columns for each session include User, Computer, Type, Open Files, Connected Time (the time elapsed since the user connected), Idle Time (the time elapsed since the user performed an action), and Guest (whether the user is connected as Guest).

**Open Files** Lets you see which files are currently open by remote users on shared folders. Here you can also close a single file or all files. Detail columns for each open file include Open File, Accessed By, Type, # Locks, and Open Mode (the permission granted when the file was opened).

## Action Menu

The Action menu in Shared Folders contains many familiar items and some unique ones. The items available depend on whether you're selecting a node in the console tree or an item in the Details pane, and also on the node or item you've selected.

**New File Share** Lets you create a new file share on the computer. Available with Shares selected in the console tree.

**Stop Sharing** Stops sharing the selected share. Available with a share selected in the Details pane.

**Send Console Message** Opens the Send Console Message dialog box, where you can create and send a message to one or more individuals. Available with Shares selected in the console tree.

**Disconnect All Sessions** Lets you disconnect all currently open sessions by remote users. Available with Sessions selected in the console tree.

**Close Session** Closes the selected session. Available with an open session selected in the Details pane.

**Disconnect All Open Files** Closes all files open in shared folders. Available with Open Files selected in the console tree.

**Close Open File** Closes the selected open file. Available with an open file selected in the Details pane.

**See Also** Microsoft Management Console (MMC), Sharing

# Sharing

Sharing...

Lets you share resources on your computer (such as folders, disks, and printers) with users of a network. When you share a folder or disk, you can specify the users who should have access to the resource as well as the permissions they will have to the folder or disk. Sharing settings are configured on the Sharing tab of the resource's property sheet. Users can see and access resources you've shared in any Explorer window by navigating to your computer using My Network Places.

## Sharing a Folder or Disk

To share a folder or disk with users of the network, perform the following steps:

1. In any Explorer window, right-click the folder or disk you want to share and select Sharing.

**TIP** Alternatively, you can right-click the folder or disk, select Properties, and then select the Sharing tab.

**WARNING** On a Windows 2000 Server computer, you can create, view, and navigate folders below the SYSVOL folder. The physical structure for the SYSVOL folder is located under C:\WINNT\SYSVOL on the Windows 2000 Server computer, and you must share folders there. If you right-click a folder under the SYSVOL folder after accessing it—for example, through My Network Places or through a drive mapping—you won't see the Sharing option.

2. On the Sharing tab of the folder's or disk's property sheet, select Share This Folder and enter a name for the share. If you want, you can also enter a comment in the Comment text box.

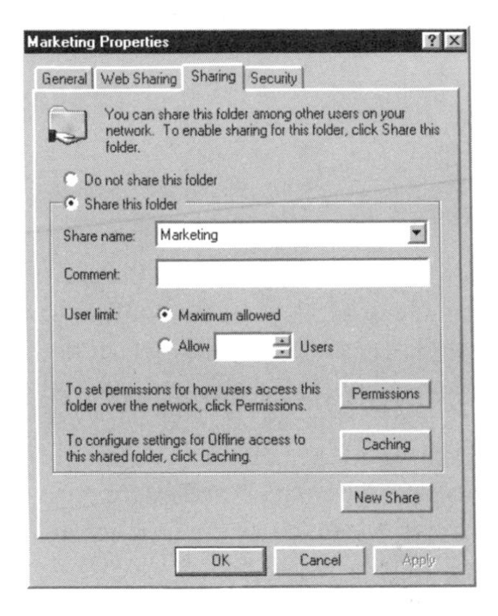

3. Specify whether you want the maximum number of users to be able to connect to the shared folder or disk, or specify a certain number of users who can connect to the folder or disk simultaneously.

4. To change the default permissions (Everyone, Full Control, Change, and Read permissions), click Permissions. In the resulting dialog box, click Add to add users or groups to the list of users with whom you want to share the folder or disk. To remove users or groups, select a group or user in the list and click Remove. To change the permissions, select a group or user in the list, then select the appropriate Allow or Deny option in the Permissions list box. When you've finished, click OK.

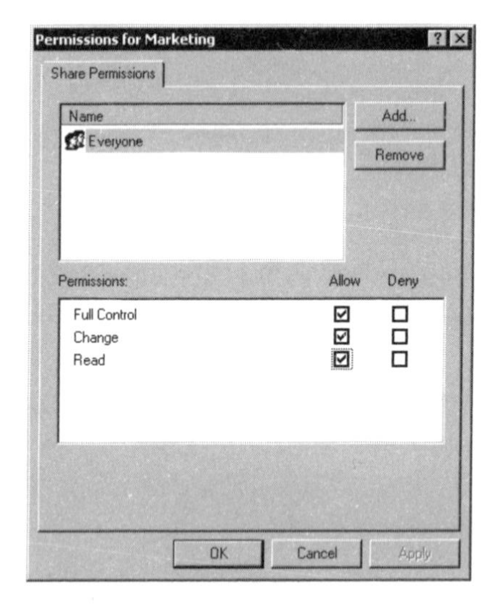


5. To configure offline access, click Caching on the Sharing tab. You can enable or disable caching of files in the folder by selecting or deselecting the Allow Caching of Files in This Shared Folder option. If you select it, you can then choose a setting for caching from the drop-down list. Choices include Manual Caching for Documents, Automatic Caching for Documents, and Automatic Caching for Programs. Detailed explanations are given below the drop-down list as you

make a selection from the list. Click OK when you've made your choices.

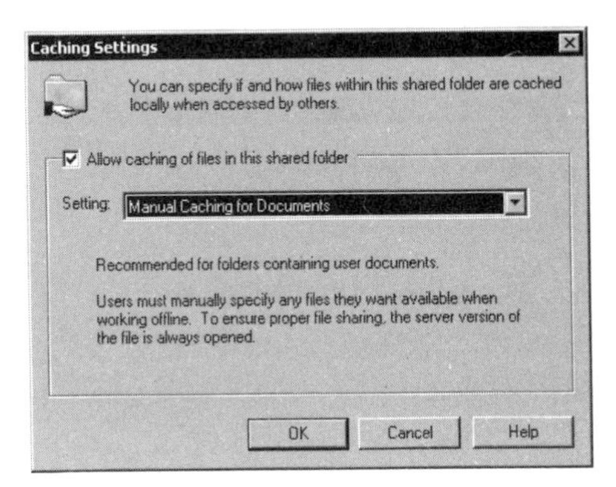


6. If applicable, you can also click New Share to open the New Share dialog box, where you can create a new shared folder. Click OK to finish creating the new share. The New Share button is available only when you are sharing a network folder, not when you're sharing a local folder.

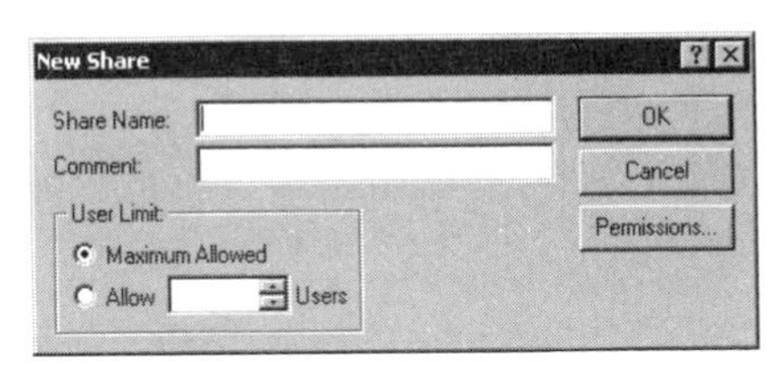


7. Back on the Sharing tab, click OK to save the sharing settings for the folder or disk.
8. In the Explorer window, a hand icon appears at the bottom of the folder or disk, indicating that the resource is shared.

**See Also** Printers, Explorer

# Shut Down

Shuts down the system. Choose Start ➢ Shutdown.

**TIP** Alternatively, you can access Shutdown by pressing Ctrl+Alt+Del and then clicking the Shutdown button.

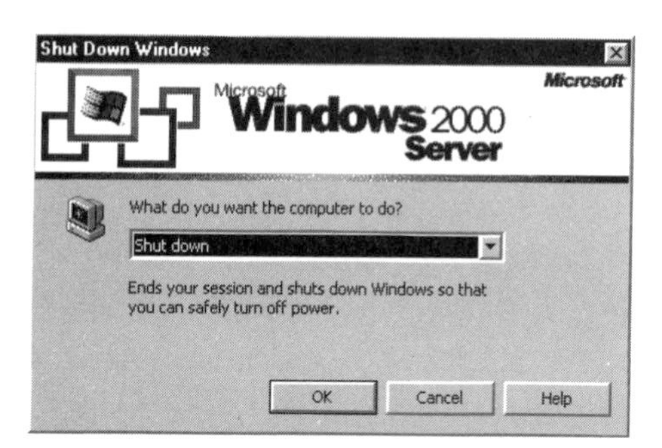


The drop-down list box in the Shut Down Windows dialog box contains three options by default:

**Log Off *current user* (where *current user* is the user you're currently logged on as)** Ends the session by logging off the current user. You'll be presented with the Welcome to Windows window so that you can log on as another user.

**Shut Down** Ends the current session and shuts down Windows. You can then turn off the computer.

**Restart** Ends the current session, shuts down Windows, performs a warm boot, and starts Windows again. You'll be presented with the Welcome to Windows window so that you can log on again.

**See Also** Start, Start Menu, Taskbar & Start Menu

# Sound Recorder

Sound Recorder

Lets you record, edit, play, and mix sounds from audio input devices installed in your computer. Examples of audio input devices are a microphone (using a sound card) and a CD-ROM player.

Choose Start ➢ Programs ➢ Accessories ➢ Entertainment ➢ Sound Recorder to open the Sound Recorder dialog box.

## Sound Recorder Display

The Sound Recorder display provides information about the sound track you're recording or playing back, and you can use several buttons to control recording and playback.

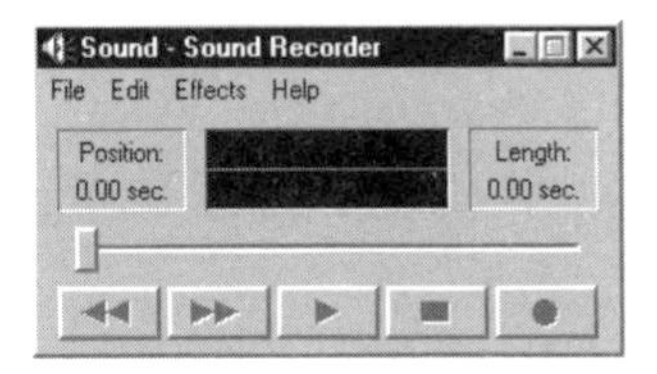


You can view the following information during recording or playback:

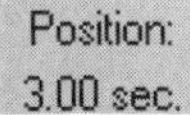


**Position** Displays the current location on the sound track during play and recording.

**Sound Quality Indicator** Visually represents the quality of the sound.

**TIP** If the green line is not visible, the sound file is compressed and can't be modified.

Length:
17.01 sec.

**Length** Displays the total length of the currently open sound track.

In addition to viewing information in the Sound Recorder dialog box, you can use the following controls and buttons:

**Slider** Indicates the relative position in the sound track during recording or playback. You can move the slider to change the position.

**NOTE** As sound plays or records, the slider moves to the right, indicating the position on the track relative to the entire length of the track (the length of the slider represents the entire length of the track). When you record a new track, the entire length of the new track is set to a default of 60 seconds.

**Seek to Start** Places the sound track (and slider) at the beginning of the track.

**Seek to End** Places the sound track (and slider) at the end of the track.

**Play** Plays the currently open sound track from the track's current position.

**Stop** Stops playing or recording of a sound track.

**Record** Starts recording of a sound track.

## Menus

Three menus in Sound Recorder enable you to create and work with sound tracks: File, Edit, and Effects.

### *File*

The File menu has the following options:

**New** Lets you create/record a new sound track (file). If you currently have a sound file open, you'll be asked if you want to save the file.

**Open** Lets you open an existing sound file. The default folder in which Sound Recorder looks for sound files is My Documents.

**Save** Lets you save a sound file. The default folder in which Sound Recorder saves sound files is My Documents.

**NOTE** Sound you record with Sound Recorder is saved as a .WAV file.

**Save As** Gives you the opportunity to save a previously saved file using a new name.

**Revert** Lets you undo the changes you made to a sound file since it was last saved.

**Properties** Displays the property sheet of the currently open sound file. Information includes such items as copyright, length, data size, and audio format. You can also convert the file to a different format to change the sound quality or reduce the size of the file. To convert the format of a file, choose the current file format, click Convert Now, then make your conversion selections.

**TIP** You can also convert a sound file's format by choosing File ➢ Save As, clicking Change, and making your changes.

### *Edit*

The Edit menu has the following options:

**Copy** Lets you copy a currently active sound file.

**Paste Insert** Lets you paste the copied sound file. The sound is appended to the end of the existing sound.

**Paste Mix** Lets you mix the copied sound with the current sound. Mixing starts at the current position. The sound is overlayed.

**Insert File** Lets you insert another .WAV file into the current sound track, beginning at the current position.

**Mix with File** Lets you mix another .WAV file with the current sound track, beginning at the insertion point. The sound is overlayed.

**Delete Before Current Position** Deletes sound from the sound track from the beginning of the track to the current position.

**Delete After Current Position** Deletes sound from the sound track from the current position to the end of the track.

**Audio Properties** Opens the Audio Properties dialog box. This dialog box contains the Audio Devices tab, where you specify the audio devices Sound Recorder should use for playback and recording. This tab also lets you specify volume and advanced settings. More information about the Audio Devices tab is available under Sounds and Multimedia.

### *Effects*

This menu lets you make other changes to the current file. Options include Increase Volume (by 25 %), Decrease Volume, Increase Speed (by 100 %), Decrease Speed, Add Echo, and Reverse. Reverse means that the sound track is reversed and would then play backwards, from the end to the beginning. When you increase or decrease volume or speed or add an echo, the change is applied to the entire sound track.

**See Also** Sounds and Multimedia, Volume Control

# Sounds and Multimedia

Lets you assign specific sounds to Windows 2000 system events, such as receiving e-mail or exiting Windows, and for sound and multimedia device configuration.

Choose Start ➢ Settings ➢ Control Panel, then double-click Sounds and Multimedia to open the Sounds and Multimedia Properties dialog box. This dialog box contains three tabs: Sounds, Audio, and Hardware.

**Sounds** Use this tab to individually assign sounds to specific events, such as starting Windows and receiving an incoming fax, or to assign a sound scheme. With a sound scheme, certain sounds are associated with certain events. You can customize sound schemes, if you wish to do so.

**NOTE** Note that sounds schemes don't assign a sound to every possible event. Thus, even after a picking a scheme, you may still need to assign specific sounds to events that may not currently have a sound assigned.

On the Sounds tab, you can also control the sound volume and specify whether you want the volume control icon displayed on the taskbar. You can use that icon to control the sound volume instead of having to open the Sounds and Multimedia Properties dialog box.

**TIP** If no sound card is installed in the computer, the volume control options are disabled (grayed out).

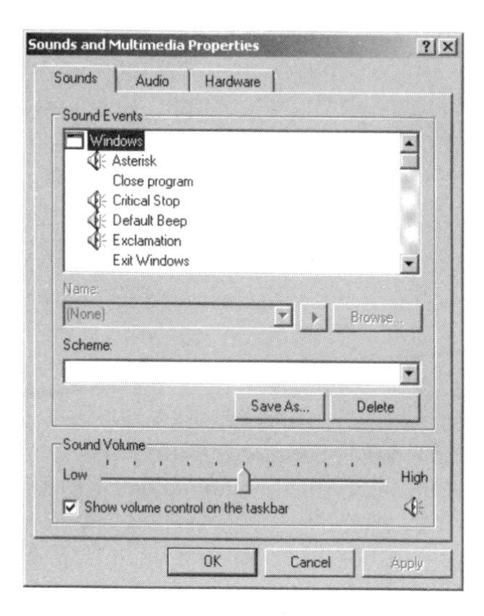


**Audio** Use the Audio tab to specify and control the devices you want to use for playing system sounds, for recording sounds, and for MIDI playback.

Click Volume to open the Volume Control dialog box, where you can control the volume and balance between speakers using the sliders. You can also control the bass and treble settings, if available. Choose Advanced Controls from the Options menu, then click the Advanced button that appears on the Volume Control dialog box. Move the Bass and Treble sliders to the left or right to adjust bass and treble settings from between low and high. More information is available under the entry Volume Control.

If you click the Advanced buttons on the Audio tab for sound playback and recording playback, you can specify the type of speakers you're using and adjust settings such as hardware acceleration and audio sample rate conversion quality.

**TIP** When you move the sliders for hardware acceleration and sample rate conversion quality, the description underneath changes to provide information about the current setting and under which circumstances you should use it.

**Hardware** Use this tab to configure hardware settings for your sound and multimedia devices (including CD-ROM drives).

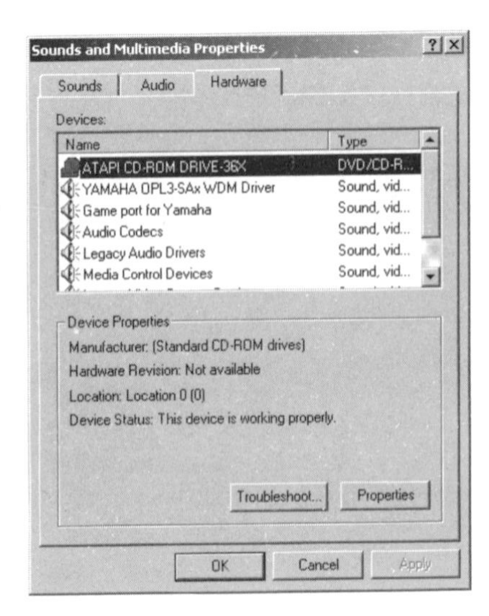

Select a sound device and click Troubleshoot if you're having problems with a sound device. This will start the Windows 2000 Hardware Troubleshooter for sound devices. Click Properties to configure the properties of a sound or multimedia device. Several tabs will be available that will differ depending on the device. Information found on these tabs typically includes such items as device type and manufacturer, device status, the ability to enable or disable the device, driver information, and system resource usage information.

**TIP** You can also access the properties of sound and multimedia devices by choosing Start ➢ Settings ➢ Control Panel, double-clicking Systems, selecting the Hardware tab, clicking Device Manager, expanding the appropriate device heading, right-clicking the device, and choosing Properties.

**See Also** Accessibility, Accessibility Options, System, Volume Control, Sound Recorder

# Start

Used to gain access to system Shut Down options, Windows 2000 Help, files and other resources, configuration options, recently opened documents, programs, and Windows Updates.

By default the Start button is located in the bottom-left corner of the taskbar. Clicking this button activates the Start menu. Right-clicking this button brings up a menu from which you can open the current user's Start Menu folder (click Open), open Windows Explorer (click Explore), and search for files, folders, computers, printers, and people (click Search). If you're logged in as a user with administrative privileges (such as Administrator), you'll have two more options: Open All Users and Explore All Users. These two options open the `C:\Documents and Settings\All Users\Start Menu` folder in Windows Explorer with the Folders Explorer Bar pane either not displayed or displayed.

**See Also** Start Menu, Taskbar, Taskbar & Start Menu

# Start Menu

The Start menu is used to gain access to system Shut Down options, files and folders, Windows 2000 Help, configuration options, recently opened documents, programs, and Windows Updates. To access the Start Menu, click the Start button. The following options are part of the default Start menu:

**Shut Down** Brings up the Shut Down Windows dialog box, from which you can choose to shut down the computer, restart the computer, or log off the current user.

**Run** Brings up the Run dialog box. From here, you can run programs and open folders, documents, or Internet resources.

**Help** Brings up the Windows 2000 Help system. Here you can find answers to all of your Windows 2000–related questions by browsing the contents, querying the index, searching by keyword, or adding and then checking back on your favorite topics.

**NOTE** Windows 2000 Help includes New Ways To Do Familiar Tasks (Windows 2000 Server) and If You've Used Windows Before (Windows 2000 Professional). These sections identify items from Windows 98 or Windows NT 4.0 that have a new name or that are in a new location in Windows 2000.

**Search** Brings up a submenu with options for searching for files or folders on the local computer and on the network, for resources on the Internet (by opening Internet Explorer and activating the IE Search feature), for printers, and for people (in your company or on the Internet).

**TIP** A separate option for searching for a computer is not available on the Search menu. Instead, choose to search for files and folders, then in the Search pane, scroll down and under Search for Other Items, click the link called Computers.

**Settings** Brings up a submenu with options for opening Control Panel to customize and configure your desktop and computer, accessing existing and creating new network and dial-up connections, accessing existing and creating new local and network printers, and customizing the Start menu and taskbar.

**NOTE** If you place the mouse pointer over submenu items (and also items in Windows Explorer), in many cases, a brief explanation of the item or additional information regarding the item is shown as a ToolTip.

**Documents** Brings up a submenu with an option for opening the My Documents folder. Also displays a list of shortcuts to the 15 most recently accessed files. Click a file to open it.

**Programs** Brings up a submenu that gives you access to program groups and programs located on your computer.

**Windows Update** Connects you to `www.windowsupdate.microsoft.com` so that your computer can automatically be updated with new features, device drivers, and so forth.

You can add programs to the Start menu by dragging and dropping a program's icon on the Start button.

**See Also** Taskbar, Start, Taskbar & Start Menu

# System

Controls system properties, including network identification configuration, hardware device configuration (including hardware profile configuration), user profile configuration, and advanced properties, including performance, environment variable, and system startup and recovery configuration.

Choose Start ➢ Settings ➢ Control Panel, then double-click System to open the System Properties dialog box, which contains five tabs: General, Network Identification, Hardware, User Profiles, and Advanced.

**TIP** Alternatively, you can right-click on My Computer and choose Properties to access the System Properties dialog box.

## General

The General tab provides information about your system, such as the version of the operating system you are running, to whom the operating system is registered, and information about the physical computer.

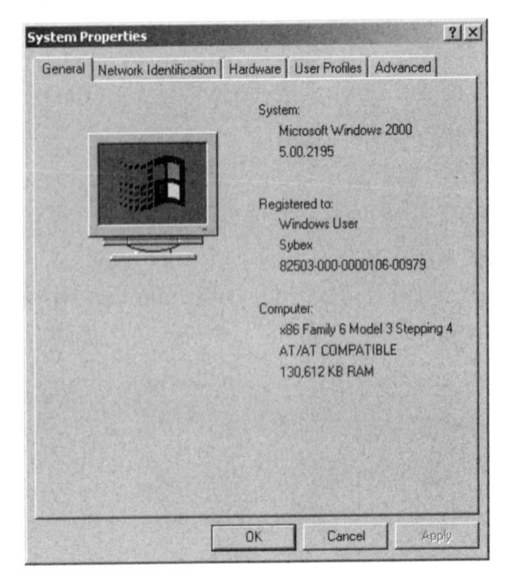

## Network Identification

Use this tab to view and configure the full name of your computer and the workgroup or domain to which it belongs. Each computer in a network must have a unique name by which you and other users can identify it. If the computer is a member of a domain and you've specified a DNS domain name for the computer, then the DNS domain name becomes part of the full name.

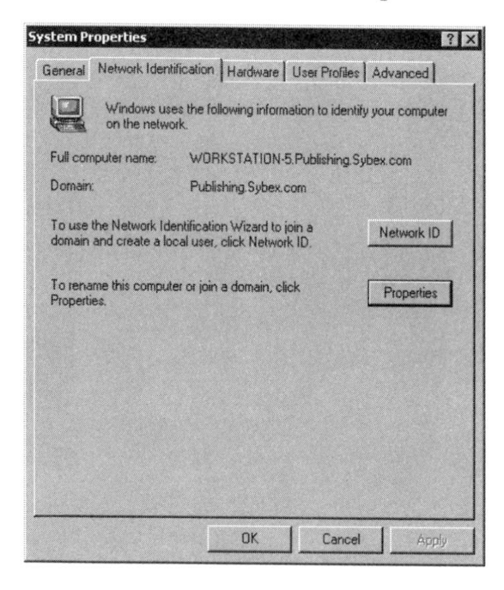


The Network Identification tab has two buttons used for configuration of network identification: Network ID and Properties.

**NOTE** If the computer is a Windows 2000 domain controller, the network identification information cannot be changed. The Properties button is grayed out, and the Network ID button does not exist.

**Network ID** Starts the Network Identification Wizard. Use the Wizard to connect your computer to a different network than the one to which you're currently connected (such as connecting to a workgroup or domain to which you're not currently connected).

**NOTE** You must be logged on as Administrator on the local machine to run the Network Identification Wizard.

**Properties** Opens the Identification Changes dialog box. Here you can change the name of the computer, as well as change the domain or workgroup to which the computer belongs. Click OK after you make your changes. If you're joining a domain, you'll be prompted to supply the username and password for a user who has the proper permissions to enable the computer to join the domain. By default, this is any member of the group Domain Admins. You can also specify the DNS domain name for the computer by clicking More and entering the DNS domain name for the computer. Select the Change DNS Domain Name when Domain Membership Changes option if you want to automatically adjust the DNS domain name when changing domain membership. Click OK to save your changes.

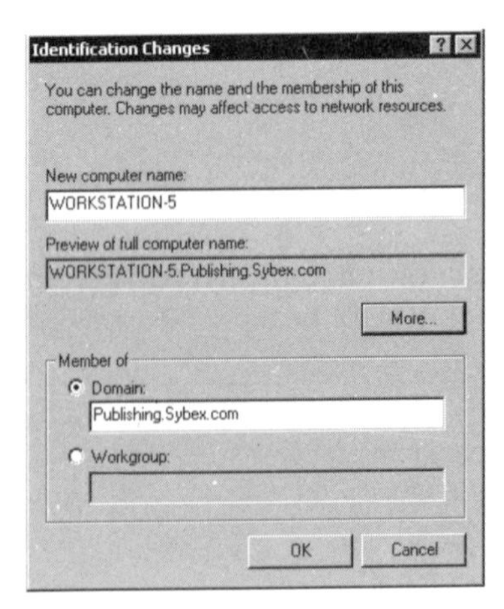


### *Network Identification Wizard*

To change your current workgroup or domain membership, follow these steps:

1. On the System Properties dialog box's Network Identification tab, click Network ID to start the Network Identification Wizard.

2. On the Welcome screen, click Next.
3. Choose This Computer Is Part of a Business Network, and I Use It to Connect to Other Computers at Work. Click Next.
4. Specify whether your company uses a network with a domain or without a domain and click Next.
5. If you specified that your company uses a network without a domain, specify the name of the workgroup to which your computer should belong, click Next, and skip to step 11. If you specified that your company uses a network with a domain, read the Network Information screen and make sure that you have all the necessary information before you proceed. This information includes your username, password, the domain for your user account, and possibly your computer name and the domain for your computer (this may not necessarily be the same domain as the domain in which your user account resides). Click Next.
6. Enter your Windows 2000 username and password, and the domain in which the user account exists. Click Next.

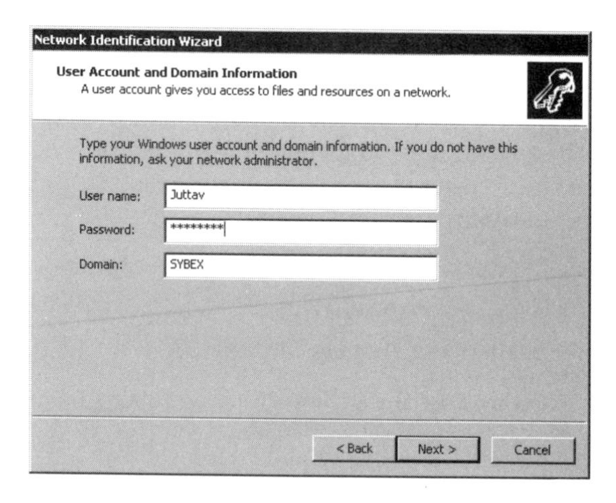


7. If a computer account already exists, the Wizard will ask whether you would like to use the account. Click Yes (if you'd like to use the account) or No (if you don't want to use it). If a computer account does not already exist, or if

you clicked No, enter your computer name and the domain for the computer. Click Next.

8. Enter the name, password, and domain of an administrative user who has the necessary rights to allow the computer to join the domain. Click OK.

**NOTE** By default, this is any user who is a member of the group Domain Admins. However, if you created the computer account in the domain before running the Network Identification Wizard, you had the option to specify users who can allow the computer to join the domain when you created the computer account in the domain.

9. You can add a user who has an account in a domain on the network (either yourself or another user) to the local computer to give that user access to the resources on the computer as well as to shared resources on the network. Enter the name and domain information for the user. Alternatively, you can choose not to add a user at this time. Click Next.
10. If you chose not to add a user, skip to step 11. If you chose to add a user, select the level of access the user should have. Standard means that the user will be added to the Power Users group, and Restricted means that the user will be added to the Users group. Select Other if you want to specify a group. Click Next.
11. Click Finish to complete the Network Identification Wizard.
12. Click OK to acknowledge that you must restart the computer so that your changes can take effect.
13. Click OK to close the System Properties dialog box.
14. Click Yes to restart the computer.

## Hardware

Use this tab to configure your computer's hardware. This tab gives you access to the Add/Remove Hardware Wizard, Device Manager, and Hardware Profiles.

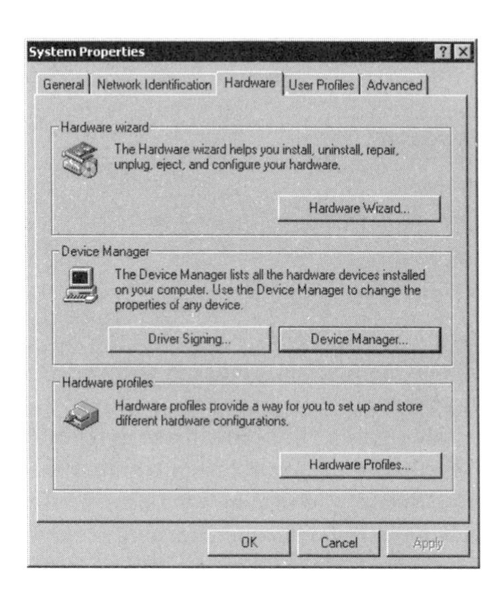


### *Hardware Wizard*

Hardware Wizard...

Click the Hardware Wizard button to start the Add/Remove Hardware Wizard. This Wizard guides you through the steps for:

- Adding new hardware to a Windows 2000 computer after you've physically installed it
- Preparing Windows 2000 to physically remove or unplug hardware from the computer
- Troubleshooting a device that is experiencing problems

The Hardware Wizard automatically makes the necessary changes, such as modifying the Registry and configuration files, and installing, loading, removing, and unloading drivers.

The Add/Remove Hardware Wizard is explained in detail under Add/Remove Hardware.

### *Device Manager*

Device Manager...

Lists all hardware installed in the computer. Also enables you to configure the properties of hardware devices, check the status of installed devices, view and update device drivers, and disable and uninstall devices. Device Manager is explained in detail under the heading Device Manager.

Driver Signing...

The Device Manager area of the Hardware tab contains an additional button, Driver Signing. To maintain file integrity, files can be digitally signed. The integrity of digitally signed files can be verified before they are installed on a computer. For example, all Windows 2000 files are digitally signed and verified during installation.

Click the Driver Signing button to open the Driver Signing Options dialog box, where you can specify how you want to handle digital file signing. You can choose to ignore digital signatures and install all files, regardless of whether they're digitally signed (the default); to display a warning message if an unsigned file is about to be installed; or to not allow the installation of files that are not digitally signed. You can also make your choice the system default by clicking the Apply Settings as System Default check box. Click OK to save any changes you've made and return to the Hardware tab.

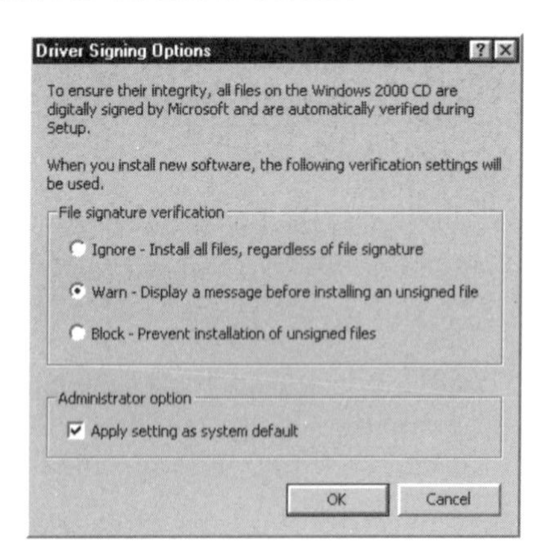


### *Hardware Profiles*

Hardware Profiles...

Hardware profiles specify which drivers you want Windows to load at system startup. You may need different drivers loaded if your hardware changes, such as might be the case if you have a laptop that you place into a docking station when you're back at the office. When the laptop is undocked, you use a modem for dial-up access to the network and a physically attached printer. When it's docked, you use a network adapter to connect to the network, but you don't need the modem or the physically attached printer. To handle these different hardware configuration needs, Windows 2000 allows you to set up multiple hardware profiles. At system startup, you can then choose which profile to use.

To configure hardware profiles, click the Hardware Profiles button, which brings up the Hardware Profiles dialog box. By default, one profile, called Profile 1, is created when you install Windows 2000. It contains the settings for your current hardware. You'll see it in the Available Hardware Profiles list.

Four options are available in the Hardware Properties dialog box: Properties, Copy, Rename, and Delete.

**NOTE** If the computer is a laptop, the default profile will be called either Docked Profile or Undocked Profile.

**NOTE** By default, when you add new hardware, the settings are saved in the Profile 1 hardware profile.

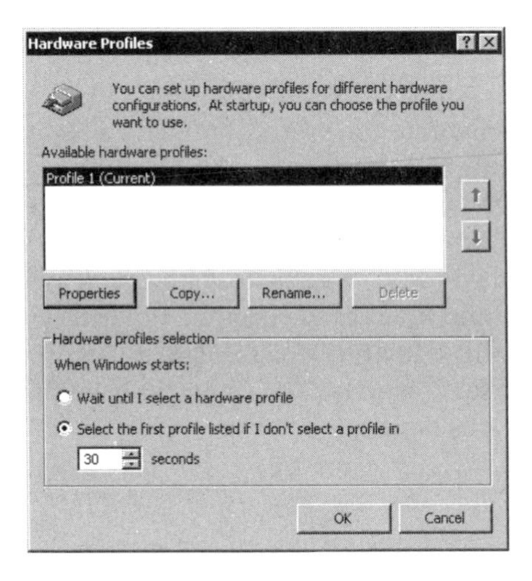

You can copy profiles to create new profiles by selecting a profile, clicking Copy, entering a name for the copy of the profile, and clicking OK. Once you have more than one profile, use the up and down arrows to rearrange each profile's position in the list. The profile at the top of the list is the default profile.

**NOTE** To be able to copy hardware profiles, you must be logged onto the local computer as Administrator.

You can rename a profile by selecting it, clicking Rename, entering a new name for the profile, and clicking OK.

You can delete a profile by selecting it, clicking Delete, and confirming your choice.

**Enabling and Disabling Devices** To enable or disable a device for the current profile, use Device Manager. Right-click a device and choose Disable or Enable, depending on the current state of the device. Device Manager is described in detail under the heading Device Manager.

**Profile Properties** To view and configure the properties of a profile, select the profile in the list and click Properties. In the property sheet, you can see items such as a docking station's Dock ID (provided by the hardware manufacturer) and the serial number.

You can specify that the profile is used for a portable computer by clicking the This Is a Portable Computer check box. If Windows 2000 can determine whether the portable computer is currently docked, the appropriate selection will be made automatically, and you won't be able to change it. If Windows 2000 cannot determine whether the computer is docked or undocked, the selection will read The Docking State Is Unknown, and you can manually select whether the computer is docked or undocked for this profile.

To make the profile available at system startup, select the Always Include This Profile as an Option when Windows Starts check box.

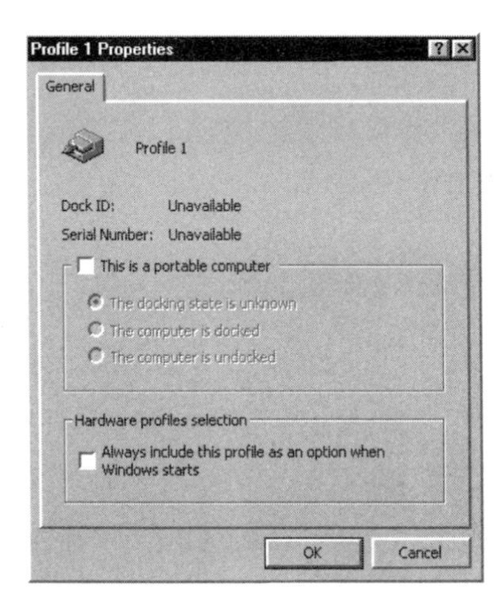


**Hardware Profiles Selection** In the Hardware Profiles Selection area of the Hardware Profiles dialog box, you can choose whether you want Windows to wait at startup until you've made a hardware profile selection, or you can specify that Windows use the first profile in the list after a certain amount of time has elapsed without a choice being made. The range is 0 to 500 seconds.

## User Profiles

User profiles specify the settings for a user's desktop environment when the user logs onto the Windows 2000 computer. Settings include such items as display settings (for example, wallpapers and color schemes), printer connections, mouse settings, Start menu items, and network connections. Three types of user profiles exist: local, roaming, and mandatory (a type of roaming user profile).

The User Profiles tab lets you view, copy, and change the type of user profiles. User profiles are described in more detail under the heading User Profiles.

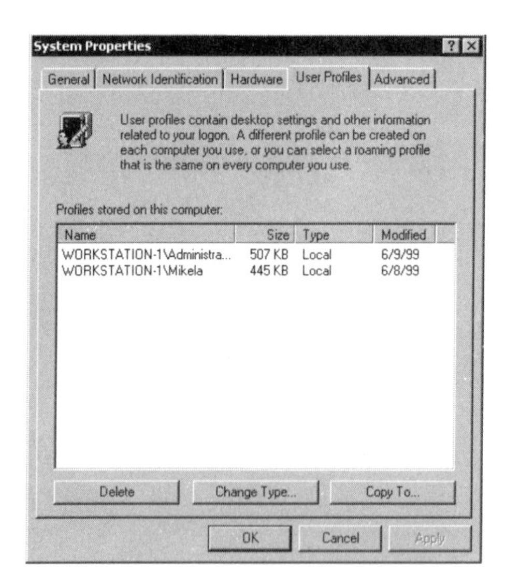


## Advanced

Use this tab to configure advanced system settings related to the computer's performance, environment variables, and startup and recovery.

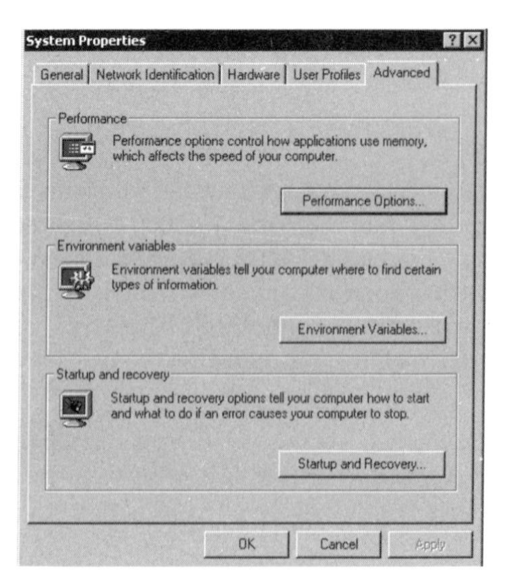

### *Performance*

Performance Options...

Performance Options enables you to configure the computer's virtual memory paging file size, specify the maximum size of the computer's Registry, and optimize performance for applications running either in the foreground or background.

Click the Performance Options button to open the Performance Options dialog box.

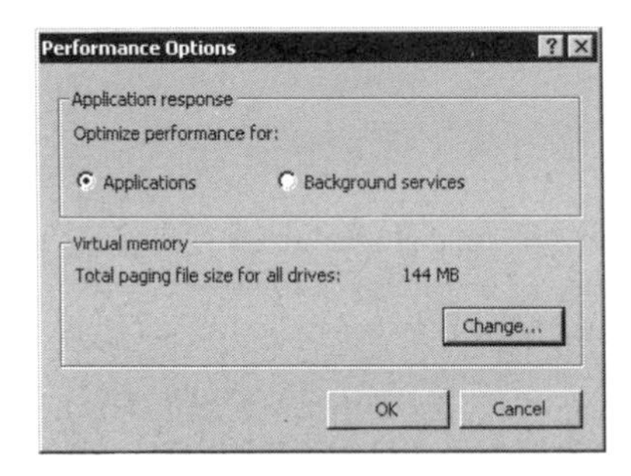


**Application Response** Under Application Response, click the appropriate radio button to optimize performance for either Applications (running in the foreground), or Background Services (running in the background). If you choose the former, foreground applications receive more processor resources than background applications. If you choose the latter, all applications receive equal amounts of processor resources. The default is Applications on a Windows 2000 Professional computer and Background Services on a Windows 2000 Server computer.

**Virtual Memory** A paging file (swap file) lets you hold data on disk that does not fit into physical memory. The combination of the paging file and physical memory is called virtual memory. As data is needed, it is moved out of the swap file into memory (data is moved from memory to disk to accommodate the data that needs to be moved to memory). Each physical disk can hold a separate swap file.

You can view the current size of the paging file in the Virtual Memory area of the Performance Options dialog box. To change the size of a swap file, click Change, select the appropriate drive in the Drive list, and change the values for initial size and maximum size. Click Set to make the change. You can also view information regarding the total paging file size for all drives, such as minimum size, recommended size, and current size.

If you set the initial and maximum size values to zero, you're effectively deleting the paging file.

Finally, on the Virtual Memory tab, you can see the current Windows 2000 Registry size and specify its maximum size in MB.

**TIP** If you specify a smaller value for the initial or maximum size of the paging file, you'll have to restart the computer to make the change effective. If you specify a larger value, rebooting is not necessary.

**TIP** The recommended size for the paging file is calculated as follows: Recommended size = 1.5 x installed RAM.

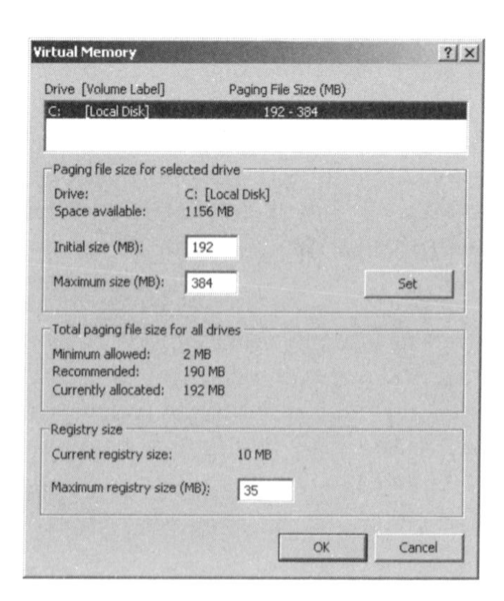

### *Environment Variables*

Environment Variables...

An environment variable is a symbolic name associated with a value (string) that Windows 2000 and programs written to run under Windows 2000 can use to be able to behave in a certain way under certain conditions. Variable values are strings that hold environment information. This information might include items such as paths for saving certain file types (such as Temp files), paths to certain files (such as application files needed by an application to run), the number of processors, and the processor architecture.

Click the Environment Variables button to open the Environment Variables dialog box. Here you can view variables and their values that are already defined for both the current user and the system (these include user- or administrator-created variables as well as application-created variables).

The current user can also create, edit, and delete user-specific variables. Only members of the Administrators group can create new system variables and edit or delete existing system variables.

**TIP** You can also use the SET command at the command prompt to create environment variables.

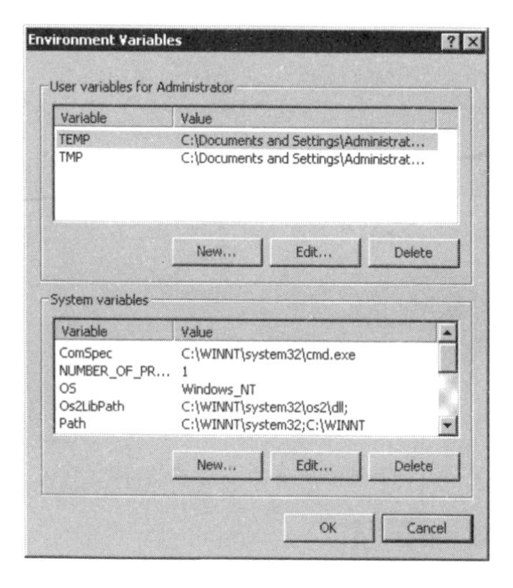

### *Startup and Recovery*

Startup and Recovery...

Lets you specify the operating system the computer should use when it starts, and specify what to do if the computer suddenly stops running.

Click the Startup and Recovery button to open the Setup and Recovery dialog box.

Under System Startup, you can choose the default operating system if you have more than one operating system installed on the computer. You can also specify how long to display the list of operating systems before starting the default operating system if no selection is made.

Under Recovery, specify actions to perform if the computer suddenly stops. Items include writing an event to the system log, sending an administrative alert, and automatically rebooting the computer.

You can also specify whether to write debugging information to a file (this process is called a dump) and how much information you want to record. Under Write Debugging Information, you can select from None (Do Not Write Debugging Information), Small Memory Dump (64 KB), or Kernel Memory Dump. You can specify a path for the dump file and choose whether to overwrite the file if it already exists.

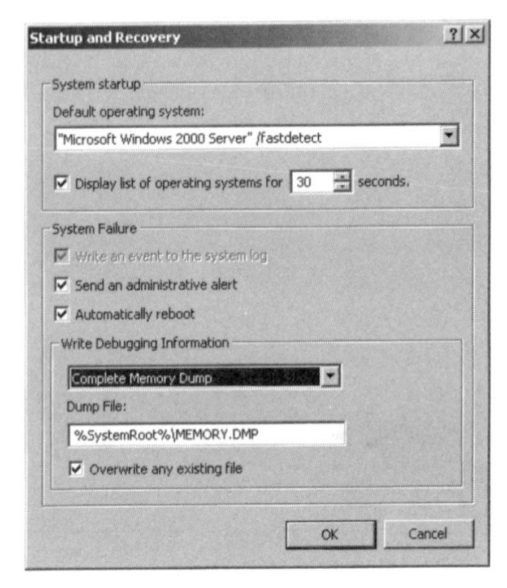

**TIP** You must be logged onto the Windows 2000 computer as a member of the group Administrators to be able to specify startup and recovery options.

**See Also** Add/Remove Hardware, Device Manager, User Profiles

# Synchronize

Synchronize Brings up the Items to Synchronize dialog box, which you use to synchronize offline files with online files and configure synchronization settings. Choose Start ➢ Programs ➢ Accessories ➢ Synchronize to open the Items to Synchronize dialog box.

Items that appear in the Items to Synchronize dialog box are any files or Web pages you've made available offline. If you don't want to synchronize a particular item, deselect its check box.

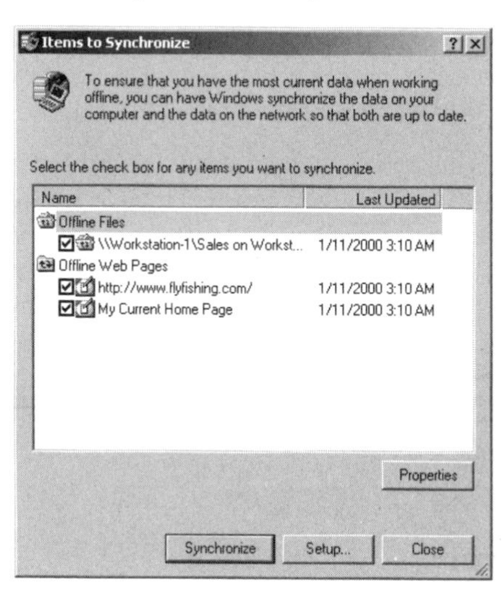


The Items to Synchronize dialog box contains four buttons:

**Properties** Displays properties for the selected item. For offline files, it opens the Offline Files folder, where you can work with and access the properties of any files it contains. For offline Web pages, it opens the Properties dialog box for the selected page.

**Synchronize** Synchronizes the selected items.

**Setup** Opens the Synchronization Settings dialog box. The Logon/Logoff tab lets you specify the items you want to synchronize automatically when you log on or off the computer. The On Idle tab lets you specify the items you want to synchronize when the computer is idle. The Scheduled tab lets you set up a schedule for synchronizing items (using the Scheduled Synchronization Wizard).

**Close** Closes the Items to Synchronize dialog box.

**See Also** Make Available Offline

# System Information

System Information MMC console snap-in that collects and displays information about your Windows 2000 computer. To access System Information, choose Start ➢ Settings ➢ Control Panel, double-click Administrative Tools, double-click Computer Management, then expand and select System Information under System Tools in the console tree.

System Information includes a system summary, along with many different items that are grouped into four categories: Hardware Resources, Components, Software Environment, and Internet Explorer 5. You can see details about your configuration or provide the information collected by System Information to service technicians who are troubleshooting your computer.

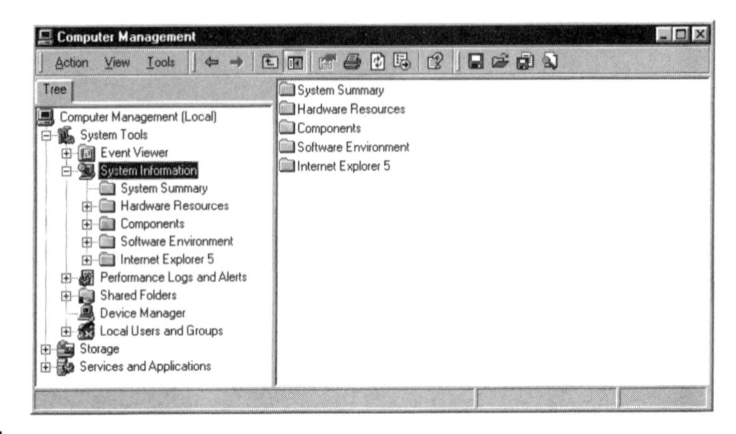

## System Summary

Displays a summary of essential system information, such as operating system name and version, processor type, Windows directory, regional settings, and memory information, just to name a few.

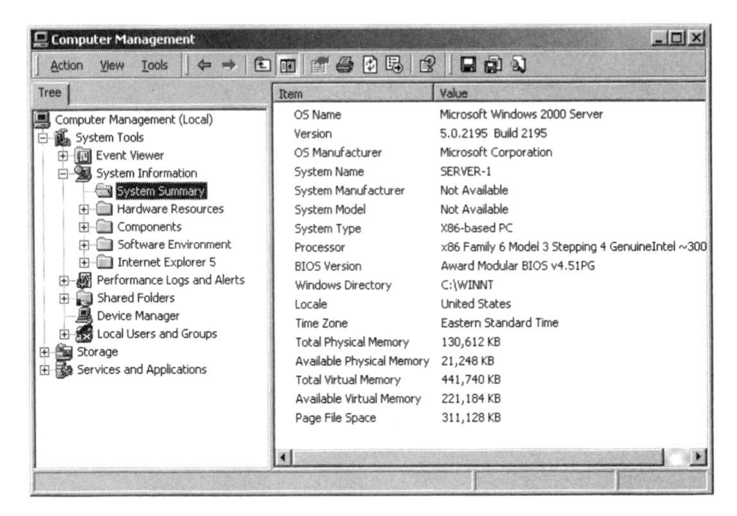


## Hardware Resources

Displays information about your hardware resources in several subfolders, such as DMA, I/O, IRQs, and Memory. Select each subfolder to display detailed information in the Details pane. The type of information you'll see depends on the type of resource you selected. To see if any hardware resources share resources or if resource conflicts exist, select the Conflicts/Sharing folder.

## Components

Displays detailed information about the components of your Windows 2000 computer in several subfolders that may also contain other subfolders. Examples include Multimedia, Display, Input, Modem, Network, Printing, and USB. Select a subfolder to display detailed information about a component. Information displayed in the Details pane includes the item (such as Resolution and Bits/Pixel for display) and the item's value (such as 640 × 480 × 60 hertz and 32).

## Software Environment

Displays detailed information about software currently loaded in memory in several subfolders that may also contain other subfolders. Examples include Drivers, Network Connections, Services, and Program Groups. Select a subfolder to display detailed information in the Details pane. The type of information that appears in the Details pane depends on your selection in the console tree.

## Internet Explorer 5

Displays detailed information about Internet Explorer 5 in several subfolders that can contain other subfolders. Examples include Summary, File Versions, Cache, and Security. The type of information that appears in the Details pane depends on your selection in the console tree.

## Action Menu

The Action menu in System Information contains some of the familiar MMC console Action menu items, as well as some unique items:

**Save as Text File** Saves the information in the selected category and its subcategories to a text file.

**Save as System Information File** Saves the information in the selected category and its subcategories to a System Information file.

**Find** Lets you search System Information categories for specific words.

**Print** Lets you print the system information contained in the selected category and its subcategories.

## View Menu

The View menu contains two unique options:

**Advanced** In addition to the basic system information that is displayed by default, may display other, advanced information for each item.

**Basic** Displays basic system information.

### Tools Menu

System Information has a unique menu called Tools. It has one option, Windows, which contains shortcuts to several system management tools, such as Disk Cleanup, Hardware Wizard (Add/Remove Hardware Wizard), Backup, and Network Connections (Network and Dial-up Connections), to name a few. All tools listed in this menu are covered under separate headings in this book. The names of the items that appear in this menu are not necessarily identical to the name of the corresponding tool.

**See Also** Microsoft Management Console (MMC), Disk Cleanup, Dr. Watson, DirectX Diagnostic Tool, Add/Remove Hardware, Network and Dial-up Connections, Backup, File Signature Verification Utility, Update Wizard Uninstall, Windows Report Tool

## System Tools

Predefined Windows 2000 program group that contains several utilities you can use to perform system maintenance and configure your system. Utilities include Backup, Character Map, Disk Cleanup, Disk Defragmenter, Getting Started (Windows 2000 Professional only), Scheduled Tasks, and System Information.

**See Also** Backup, Character Map, Disk Cleanup, Disk Defragmenter, Getting Started, Scheduled Tasks, System Information

## Taskbar

Primarily used to switch between applications and launch applications. Appears at the bottom of the screen by default. On the left end of the taskbar is the Start button, which brings up the Start menu. Next to it is the Quick Launch toolbar.

Buttons next to the Quick Launch toolbar represent open programs. On the right end of the taskbar is the system clock. This

area of the taskbar is referred to as the status area and can contain other items as well. For example, if you're using a laptop, you'll see an icon that indicates your battery levels. In addition, the status area displays icons that indicate you're printing a document, that you've received e-mail, and that antivirus software is running, among other useful information.

**TIP** Move the cursor over the system clock to display the current date.

**TIP** You can click in an empty area of the taskbar and drag the taskbar to the top, left, or right side of the screen.

## Toolbars

You can display several toolbars on the taskbar by right-clicking an empty area of the taskbar, choosing Toolbars, and selecting a toolbar from the menu. If items on a toolbar don't fit on the taskbar, you can click the double arrows at the end of the toolbar and choose toolbar items from the resulting menu. Resize or move toolbars by moving the pointer over the vertical bar at the left of the toolbar and dragging the toolbar left or right. If you drag a toolbar to the desktop, it turns into a floating toolbar.

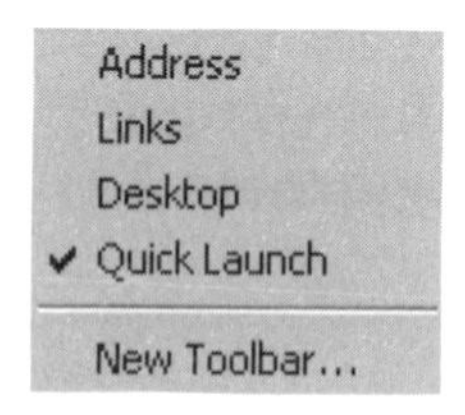


Available toolbars include:

**Address** Lets you enter a URL and click Go for quick access to Web pages (there's no need to open your browser first).

**Links** Provides you with quick, predefined links to Web pages. You can also add custom links.

**Desktop** Places shortcuts found on your desktop, such as My Computer and Connect to the Internet, in the taskbar.

**Quick Launch** Lets you quickly launch applications, such as Internet Explorer and Outlook Express, by clicking the corresponding button. Also contains the Show Desktop button, which you can use to bring the desktop to the front.

**TIP** To add an application to the Quick Launch toolbar, resize the toolbar to make room for another shortcut. Next, drag an application from either My Computer or Windows Explorer to the Quick Launch toolbar. You can remove it at any time by right-clicking the shortcut and choosing Delete.

You can also create new toolbars by clicking the New Toolbar menu option, then choosing a folder or entering a URL and clicking OK.

**TIP** If you create a new toolbar and don't want to display it any longer, right-click the toolbar and click Close.

## Switching Between Applications

With Windows 2000, you can have more than one application open at one time. There are two ways you can switch between those open applications:

- Using the taskbar
- Using the Alt+Tab key combination

### *Switching Using the Taskbar*

When you open an application, a button with the application's icon and name appears on the taskbar. If you have several applications open at the same time, you can click the appropriate button on the taskbar to switch to the application. A taskbar button may at first show the entire name of the application and any open documents or folders. As you open more applications, the buttons become smaller, and the names of the applications will be truncated so that all the buttons can fit on the taskbar. With each application you open, less and less of an application's name and icon is visible on each button, which may make it difficult to figure out which application a button represents.

**TIP** Drag the top of the taskbar upward and you'll have two bars available on which to place buttons. Keep in mind, however, that this reduces the size available to the desktop.

### *Switching Using the Alt+Tab Key Combination*

If you're having trouble identifying which application is which, you can use an alternate method of switching between applications using the Alt+Tab key combination. Hold down the Alt key and press and release the Tab key. This brings up a dialog box that contains an icon for each program that is running. You'll see a border around the icon to the right of the application you last used. This border means that if you release the Alt key, this application will go to the foreground. Press and release the Tab key again to move the border to the next icon on the right. Continue in this manner to move through all open applications. When you've reached the rightmost icon and press and release the Tab key again, the border moves to the leftmost icon. As you're moving through icons in this manner, the name of the application and any open file or folder names appear in the text field below the icons.

**See Also** Start, Taskbar & Start Menu

## Taskbar & Start Menu

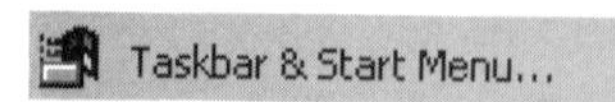


Used to customize the taskbar and Start menu. Choose Start ➢ Settings ➢ Taskbar & Start Menu to display the Taskbar and Start Menu Properties dialog box. It has two tabs: General and Advanced.

## General Tab

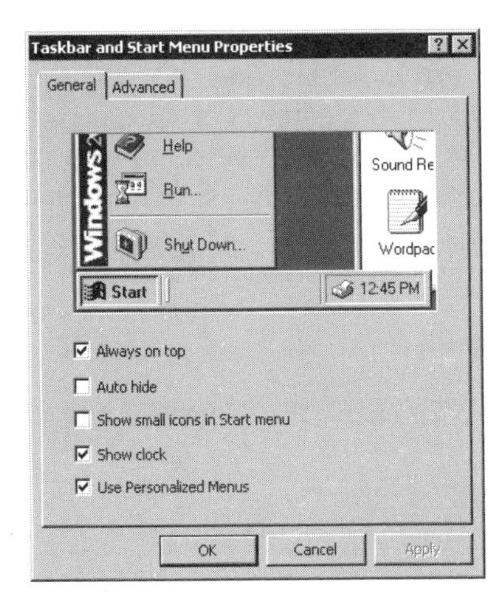


Use this tab to customize the look and placement of the taskbar. You can select or deselect the following options:

**Always on Top** Means that the taskbar will be displayed on top of other windows so that you can always see it. Enabled by default.

**Auto Hide** If you select this option, the taskbar is displayed as a thin line. Move the pointer over this line to display the taskbar.

**TIP** If you want the taskbar to still display as a thin line even if a full-screen window is displayed, select both Always on Top and Auto Hide.

**TIP** A different way to hide the taskbar is to drag its top edge down (or to the side if you've moved the taskbar to the side). Drag the line up (left or right) to display it again.

**Show Small Icons in Start Menu** If you select this option, a smaller Start menu with smaller icons and without the Windows 2000 side bar displays. The Windows side bar is the blue bar on the left of the Start menu that displays the Windows operating system name, such as Windows 2000 Professional.

**Show Clock** If selected, this option displays the clock on the right side of the taskbar. Enabled by default.

**Show Personalized Menus** If you select this option, menus off the Start menu will become personalized, meaning that only recently accessed menu items appear in the menus. You can view and access all other menu items by moving the mouse pointer over the double downward pointing arrows at the bottom of a menu.

## Advanced Tab

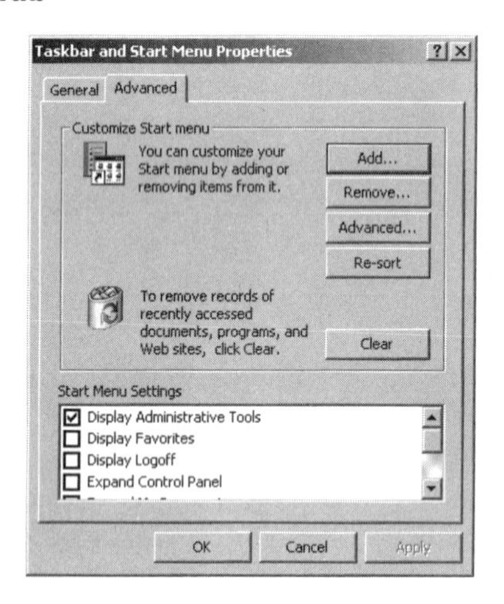


Use this tab to customize the Start menu. Under Customize Start Menu, the following buttons are available:

**Add** When you click this button, the Create Shortcut Wizard helps you through the process of adding a shortcut to the Start menu. Follow these steps:

1. Click Add to start the Create Shortcut Wizard.
2. Type the path for or browse to the location of the item for which you want to create a shortcut. You can specify programs, files, folders, computers, and Internet addresses. Click Next.
3. Choose the Start Menu folder in which you want to place the shortcut or create a new folder. Click Next.

4. Enter a name for the shortcut.

5. Click Finish.

**Remove** Lets you remove shortcuts from the Start menu. Click Remove, select the shortcut, and click Remove. Click Close when you've finished.

**Advanced** Lets you add submenus to the Start menu or the Programs menu. To get started, click Advanced. This opens the Start Menu folder in a Windows Explorer window. Next, choose File ➢ New ➢ Folder and name the folder. To add a submenu to the Programs submenu, double-click the Programs folder, then choose File ➢ New ➢ Folder and name the folder. To add shortcuts to the new submenu, you can use the Add button on the Advanced tab, or you can add items to the submenu folder you created in Windows Explorer.

**TIP** Additionally, you can add items to the Start menu or any Programs submenu by dragging an item from My Computer or Windows Explorer to the Start menu or any Programs submenu. Note that when you start dragging, the Start menu won't be displayed. To display it, drag the item over the Start Menu button. Then continue to drag the item to the desired location within the Start menu or any Programs submenu.

**Re-sort** Sorts the items on the Programs menu so that they appear in their default order.

**Clear** Removes the list of recently accessed resources (files, programs, Web sites) in the Documents Start menu option.

Under Start Menu Settings on the Advanced tab, you can further customize which Start menu options are displayed and how they are displayed. Select the check box that corresponds to a setting you want to activate.

To activate Start Menu Settings changes without closing the Taskbar and Start Menu Properties dialog box, click Apply.

When you've finished customizing the taskbar and Start menu, click OK.

**See Also** Taskbar, Start, Start Menu

# Task Manager

Lets you view the status of and control programs and processes that are running on the Windows 2000 computer. You can also view performance indicators for processes. Using Task Manager, you can see which programs (tasks) are running, end them if they're no longer responding, see which processes are running, and view system resource information about these processes as well as overall system usage information.

To access Task Manager, press Ctrl+Alt+Del and click Task Manager.

## Task Manager Window

The Task Manager window consists of menus at the top of the window, three tabs (Applications, Processes, and Performance) that take up the main Task Manager window, and a status bar at the bottom.

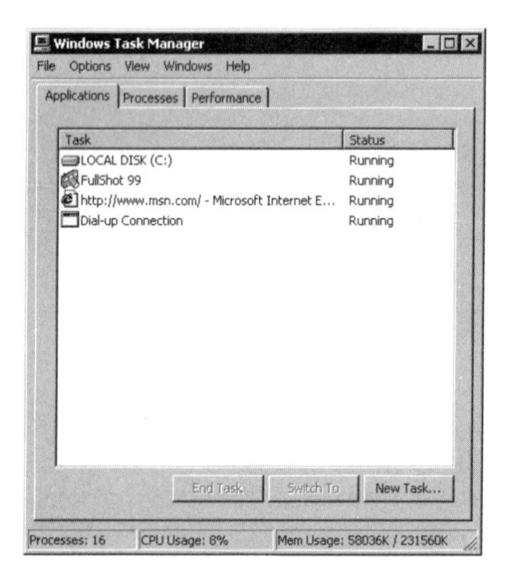

## Task Manager Menus

Task Manager has several menus: File, Options, View, Windows, and Help. The options available on the View menu change depending on the Task Manager tab you have selected.

### File Menu

The File menu contains these options:

**New Task (Run...)** Opens the Create New Task dialog box. Here you can enter the path to a new task and run it (click OK).

**Exit Task Manager** Ends Task Manager.

### Options Menu

The Options menu contains these options:

**Always on Top** If this option is selected, Task Manager always runs on top of other programs.

**Minimize on Use** If this option is selected, Task Manager is minimized when you switch to another running program.

**Hide when Minimized** If this option is selected, Task Manager is hidden when you minimize it and won't appear in the taskbar.

**Show 16-bit Tabs** Displays 16-bit Windows tasks. Look for these tasks under the associated `ntvdm.exe` file. Available only with the Processes tab selected.

### View Menu

The View menu contains these options:

**Refresh Now** Refreshes the Task Manager screen immediately.

**Update Speed** Contains a submenu where you can specify how often the Task Manager screen is refreshed automatically. Choices are High (twice per second), Normal (every two seconds), Low (every four seconds), and Paused (no automatic refresh).

**Large Icons** Displays tasks as large icons. Available only with the Applications tab selected.

**Small Icons** Displays tasks as small icons. Available only with the Applications tab selected.

**Details** Displays tasks with details, such as the task's status. This is the default setting. Available only with the Applications tab selected.

**Select Columns** Lets you select columns you want to display on the Processes tab. Available only with the Processes tab selected.

**CPU History** Lets you specify whether each CPU has its own graph. Available only with the Performance tab selected.

**Show Kernel Times** Displays kernel time in the CPU Usage and CPU Usage History graphs. Available only with the Performance tab selected.

### *Windows Menu*

The Windows menu lets you specify how to display the windows of running tasks on the desktop. It is available only with the Applications tab selected. You can choose from Tile Horizontally or Vertically, Minimize, Maximize, Cascade, or Bring to Front. Bring to Front brings the window to the front but does not switch to it.

### *Help Menu*

The Help menu lets you access Task Manager–specific help topics and information about Task Manager, such as the version number and licensing information.

## Task Manager Tabs

Task Manager contains the Application, Processes, and Performance tabs, which you can use to view and control tasks and processes as well as view performance information.

**Applications** Displays all applications (tasks) that are currently running. You can terminate a task (by selecting it and clicking End Task), you can switch to a task (by selecting it and clicking Switch To), and you can create a new task (by clicking New Task).

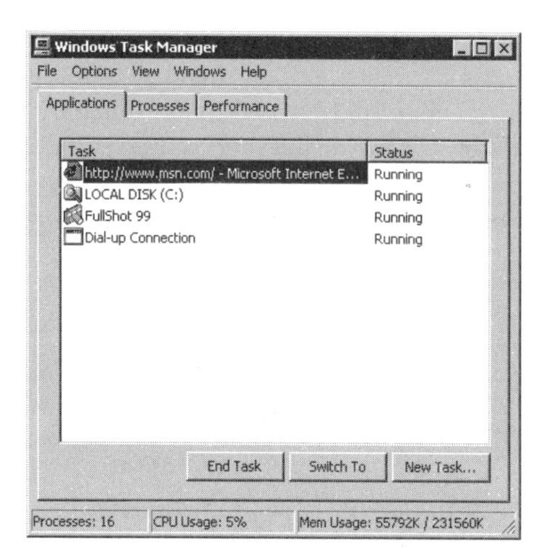


**Processes** Displays the processes currently running on the Windows 2000 computer. Information includes the process name, process identifier (PID), CPU usage, CPU time, memory usage, and many other items. Specify columns you want to display by choosing View ➢ Columns. To terminate a process, select it in the list and click End Process.

You can also assign priorities to processes. Right-click a process, select Set Priority, and select a priority from the list. Choices include Realtime, High, AboveNormal, Normal, BelowNormal, and Low.

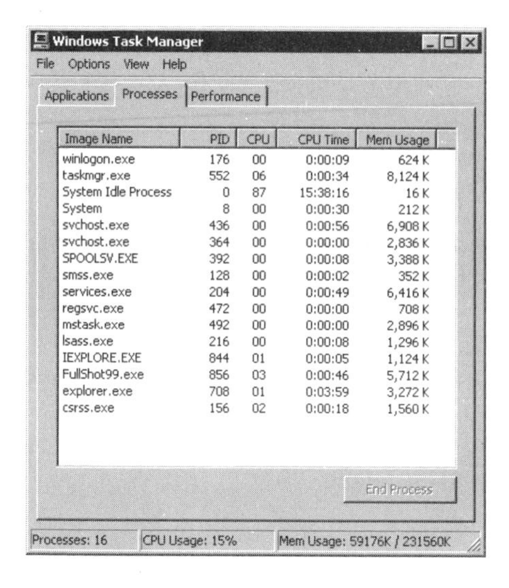

**Performance** Displays system performance information. CPU usage, CPU usage history, memory usage, and memory usage history are displayed as graphs. Total handles, threads, and processes; total, available, and system cache memory; and other system information about commit charge and kernel memory are displayed as text.

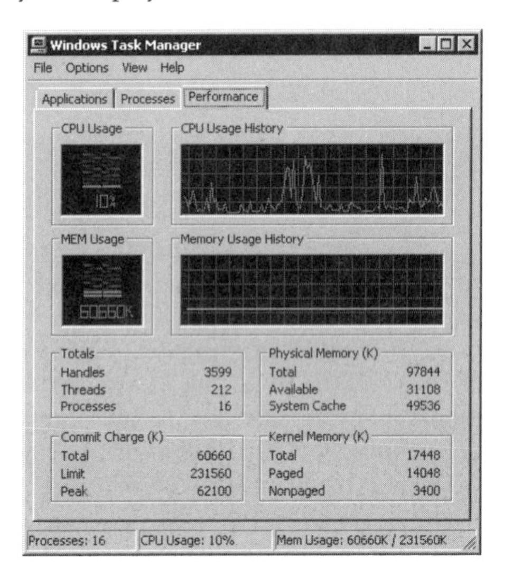


## Status Bar

The status bar at the bottom of the Task Manager window displays information abut the number of processes that are currently running, the current CPU usage, and the current memory usage.

# Telephony

Microsoft Management Console (MMC) snap-in installed on Windows 2000 Server computers that lets you work with telephony service providers on your computer. Telephony services enable the integration of computer application programs and telephony devices. This enables you to use Windows programs to perform such functions as connecting to telephones, sending faxes, and joining a conference. Telephony services are installed but not enabled by default.

During the performance of these functions, three software components are involved: application programs, the Telephony Application Programming Interface (TAPI), and TAPI service providers. Application programs use TAPI functionality to allow you to make phone calls, and send and receive faxes, for example. Examples of application programs include Phone Dialer, NetMeeting, and HyperTerminal. TAPI enables application programs to perform telephony functions. An example of a telephony function is dialing. TAPI service providers translate commands for telephony protocols or devices. This means that if a program wants to perform a function, such as dialing a phone number, TAPI identifies the appropriate TAPI service provider that provides support for the device, and the service provider in turn sends the correct commands to the device.

Several TAPI service providers are installed on Windows 2000. Examples include the TAPI Kernel-Mode Service Provider and the Unimodem 5 Service Provider.

## Making Resources Available

To make network telephony resources available to users, you use the Telephony MMC console snap-in. Network users use what in telephony are called lines to make calls, and they use what are called phones to manage and control calls. Using the Telephony MMC console snap-in, you can make lines and phones available to users. All TAPI service providers provide support for lines, but not all provide support for phones.

### *Lines*

Lines in telephony are media streams (voice, video, or data) that are supported by a TAPI service provider. A line might represent a physical telephone line or other media streams, such as Internet gateways. Users make calls using lines provided by a TAPI service provider.

### *Phones*

Phones in telephony are terminal equipment that is supported by a TAPI service provider. A phone may represent hardware, but it may also be emulated through software. In telephony, a phone encompasses the concepts of a hookswitch, handset, speaker, microphone, display, lamps, and programmable buttons.

## Telephony MMC Console Snap-in Window

To access the Telephony MMC console snap-in, choose Start ➢ Programs ➢ Administrative Tools ➢ Computer Management. You'll find the Telephony node under Services and Applications.

Below the Telephony node you'll see the TAPI service providers installed by default. They include the Unimodem 5 Service Provider, the TAPI Kernel-Mode Service Provider, the NDIS Proxy TAPI Service Provider, the Microsoft Multicast Conference TAPI Service Provider, and the Microsoft H.323 TAPI Service Provider.

If you select a service provider in the console tree, you'll see a list of available lines in the Details pane. Information about the line includes the line name, users, and status. To see available phones, choose View ➢ Phones. Information about each phone includes the phone's name, users, and status.

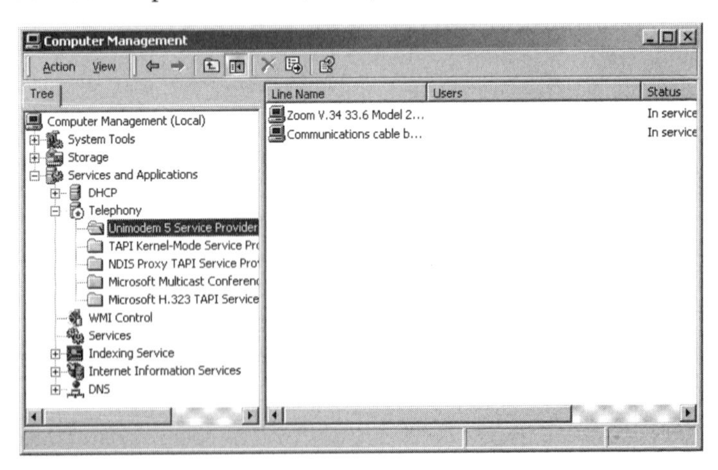


## Action Menu

The Action menu contains several unique items, depending on the item you have selected in the console tree:

**Manage Providers** Lets you add, remove, and configure TAPI service providers. Configuration options vary depending on the type of service provider. Available with the Telephony node selected in the console tree.

**Properties** Displays the Telephony property sheet, where you can enable the telephony service on the server so that it's available to computers connected to the network. Here you can also specify the username and password of the account that will run the telephony service and specify users as Telephony administrators. Additionally, you can enable automatic device status updates and specify an interval for auto updates. Available with the Telephony node selected in the console tree.

**Edit Users** Lets you assign users to a line or phone. This enables the assigned user to use the resource. To assign users, in the Edit Users dialog box click Add, select one or more users from the list, click Add, then click OK, then click OK again. Any assigned users appear in the Details pane under the column Users. Available with a line or phone selected in the Details pane.

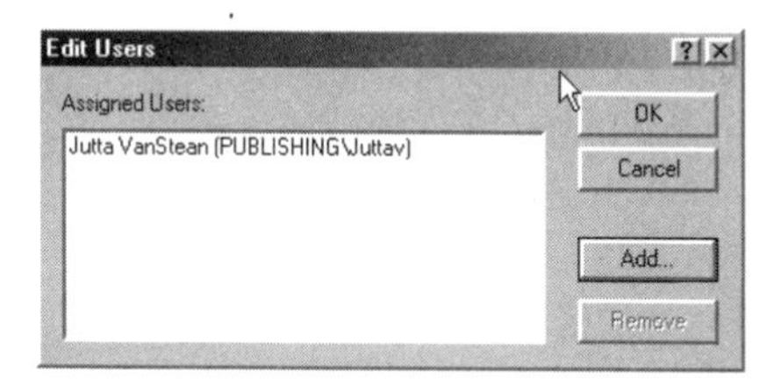


**Configure Provider** Lets you configure the selected provider. Available only with the following providers: Unimodem 5 Service Provider, NDIS Proxi TAPI Service Provider, and Microsoft H.323 TAPI Service Provider.

# Telnet Client

Command-line utility that enables you to connect to a remote Telnet server using the Telnet protocol (part of TCP/IP). Once connected, you can perform character-based functions at the remote computer as if you were directly at the computer.

To start the Telnet Client, perform these steps:

1. Choose Start ➢ Programs ➢ Accessories ➢ Command Prompt.

2. At the command prompt, enter telnet *hostname*. (The host name can be either the remote computer's TCP/IP address or host name). The client connects, and you'll see a message saying Welcome To Microsoft Telnet Server.

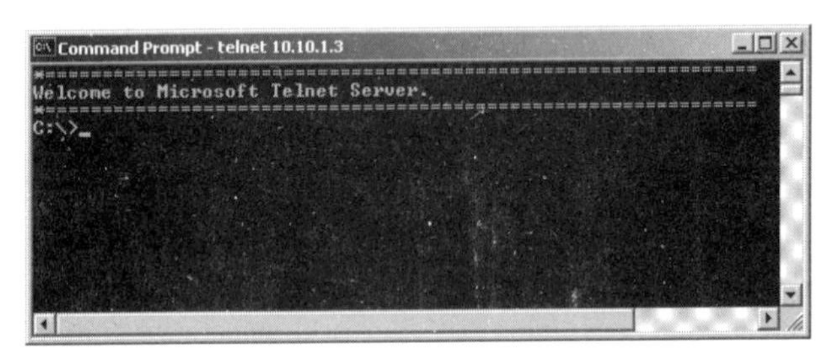


To see a list of many of the commands you can execute at the remote command prompt, type help at the command prompt.

To quit the Telnet Client, perform these steps:

1. At the command prompt, enter **telnet**.
2. At the Microsoft Telnet> prompt, enter **quit**.

**See Also** Telnet Server Administration, Command Prompt, HyperTerminal

# Telnet Server Administration

Lets you administer the Telnet Server service. For example, you use Telnet Server Administration to start and stop the Telnet Server service. The Telnet Server service enables remote computers to connect to the Telnet server via the Telnet protocol (part of TCP/IP). The version of Telnet Server included with Windows 2000 supports two simultaneous connections.

**TIP** If you require more than two simultaneous connections, you can use the version of Telnet Server found in the Microsoft Windows Services For UNIX add-on pack.

To access Telnet Server Administration, choose Start ➢ Settings ➢ Control Panel, double-click Administrative Tools, then double-click Telnet Server Administration. This opens the Telnet Server Administration command-prompt dialog box.

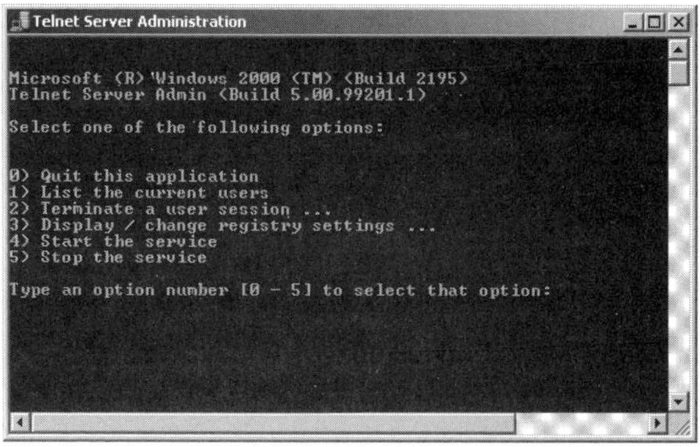

```
Telnet Server Administration

Microsoft (R) Windows 2000 (TM) (Build 2195)
Telnet Server Admin (Build 5.00.99201.1)

Select one of the following options:

0) Quit this application
1) List the current users
2) Terminate a user session ...
3) Display / change registry settings ...
4) Start the service
5) Stop the service

Type an option number [0 - 5] to select that option:
```

At the prompt, type the number that corresponds to the function you want to perform, such as 4 to start the Telnet Server service, or 1 to list current users. Available functions include:

0) Quit This Application

1) List The Current Users

2) Terminate A User Session

3) Display/Change Registry Settings

4) Start The Service

5) Stop The Service

You must use function 4 to start the Telnet Server service before Telnet clients can connect to the Telnet Server. Function 3 enables you display/change registry settings that relate to Telnet Server.

**See Also** Telnet Client, HyperTerminal, Command Prompt

# Update Wizard Uninstall

Update Wizard Uninstall

Lets you uninstall patches, drivers, and system files that were installed using Windows Update, and restore the patch, drive, or system file to the previously installed version. You can also perform this function online on the Windows Update Web site; however, this utility is useful if you don't have a connection to the Internet when you need to restore older versions of installed files.

To access the Update Wizard Uninstall tool, choose Start ➢ Settings ➢ Control Panel, double-click Administrative Tools, double-click Computer Management, expand System Tools, and select System Information. Then choose Tools ➢ Windows ➢ Update Wizard Uninstall.

If no updates are installed, you'll receive a message informing you that no packages are available for uninstall and the process terminates. If updates are installed, follow the wizard's prompts to uninstall options.

# User Profiles

User profiles are a combination of folders and data that specify the settings for a user's desktop environment when the user logs onto the Windows 2000 computer. This way, the user's Windows 2000 environment always looks the same when he or she logs onto the computer. Settings include items such as display settings (for example, wallpapers and color schemes), printer connections, mouse settings, Start menu items, network connections, and desktop shortcuts. Three types of user profiles exist: local, roaming, and mandatory (a type of roaming user profile).

## Local User Profiles

A local user profile, created the first time a user logs onto a Windows 2000 computer, is stored on the local computer. The local user profile is available only on the computer on which it resides. Thus, any changes you make to the user profile are available only on that computer. If you go to another computer and want to have your desktop environment look the same as on your original computer, you'll have to specify all of the settings for your local user profile on that computer.

By default, the local user profile directory (user_name) and its subdirectories are created off the `C:\Documents and Settings` directory. The full path is thus `C:\Documents and Settings\user_name`.

## Roaming User Profiles

A roaming user profile is stored on a server. The first time you log onto the domain after the ability to use a roaming user profile has been set up for you, the local user profile is uploaded to the server. After that, the roaming user profile is downloaded from the server to any Windows 2000 computer in the domain onto which you log on. Thus, you don't have to specify your settings again and again as you move from computer to computer. If you make changes to the desktop environment, when you log off, those changes are copied to the roaming user profile stored on the server. The complete roaming profile is copied to a computer only once; after that, only changes made to the profile are downloaded.

**NOTE** Before you can use a roaming user profile, a roaming user profile directory on a domain server must be created and the path to this directory must be specified in your domain user account's properties. Only users with administrative privileges can perform these two tasks.

### *Creating Roaming User Profiles*

**TIP** You must have administrative privileges on the server to complete this procedure.

To create a roaming user profile for a user, perform the following steps:

1. On a Windows 2000 server, create a shared folder with the shared folder permission Full Control assigned to the Everyone group (the default). This folder will hold roaming user profiles. The path's format should be `\\server_name\shared_folder_name`.

**TIP** To end up with this format, create the folder at the root of C:\.

2. Choose Start ➢ Programs ➢ Administrative Tools ➢ Active Directory Users and Computers, expand the domain, select Users, double-click the user, and select the Profile tab.

3. In the Profile path text box, enter the path to the roaming user profile using the `\\server-name\shared_folder_name\user_name` format. Click OK.

4. Log onto the domain as the user for whom you're creating the roaming profile to create the user's roaming user profile directory on the server and copy the local user profile to the server.

**TIP** This step creates the `user_name` folder under `\\server_name\shared_folder_name\` on the Windows 2000 server, which contains the Cookies, Desktop, Favorites, My Documents, and Start Menu folders.

## Mandatory User Profiles

A mandatory user profile is a roaming user profile whose settings cannot be changed by the user. Only network administrators have the ability to change mandatory user profiles. This way, network administrators can control the settings and options available for individuals, a group of users, or all users, creating a standardized desktop environment, which helps ease administration.

### *Changing a Roaming User Profile to a Mandatory User Profile*

To change a roaming user profile to a mandatory user profile, you must rename the hidden file `NTUSER.DAT` to `NTUSER.MAN`. You'll find this file in the `\\..\user_name` directory for either local or roaming user profiles.

## User Profiles Tab

To view, copy, or change the type of user profiles stored on the local computer, choose Start ➢ Settings ➢ Control Panel, double-click System, and select the User Profiles tab.

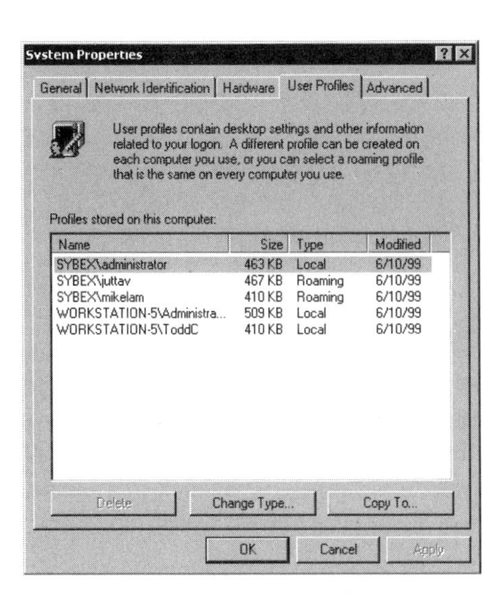


You can see all currently configured user profiles stored on the local computer in the list under Profiles stored on this computer. Three options are available:

**Delete** To delete a user profile, select the profile and click Delete.

**TIP** You cannot delete a domain administrator's user profile.

**TIP** You must have administrative privileges to see and use the Delete button.

**Change Type** To change the user profile type from local to roaming and vice versa, select a profile and click Change Type. This opens the Change Type dialog box. A roaming user profile must exist for the user in order for you to change the profile type (otherwise, the Roaming Profile option is grayed out). Select Roaming Profile to change the user profile from local to roaming.

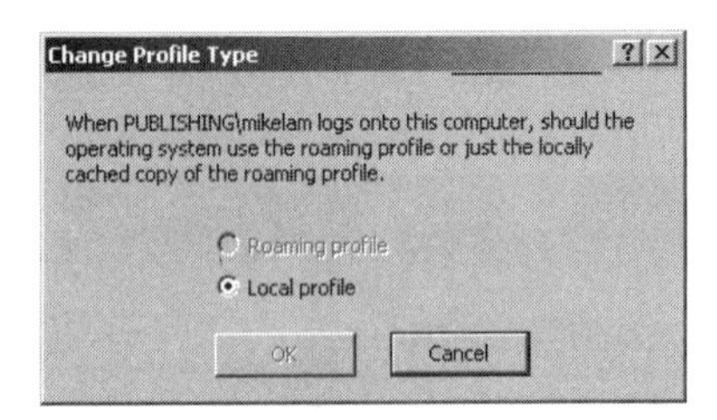

**Copy To** Assume you want to copy user A's profile to user B. Select user A's profile in the list of profiles stored on this computer and click Copy To. Enter the path to user B's roaming profile directory in the Copy Profile To text box (`\\server_name\shared_profile_directory_name\user_name`). Next, click Change under Permitted to Use, click Show Users, select user B, and then click OK.

**TIP** You must have administrative privileges to see and use the Copy To button.

**See Also** System

# Users and Passwords

Users and Passwords

Lets you manage local user accounts and passwords on Windows 2000 Professional computers. If the computer is part of a domain, Users and Passwords also lets you add domain users to a group on this computer to enable them to access this computer using their domain user account password. In addition, Users and Passwords lets you configure boot-up security and certificates, and access Local Users and Groups for more advanced user account management functions.

**TIP** If the computer is part of a domain, you can't use Users and Passwords to create users. You'll have to use Local Users and Groups, which you can access through Computer Management (Local).

**TIP** You also can't use Users and Passwords to perform such actions as creating groups or adding users to multiple groups. For these sorts of actions, you must use Local Users and Groups.

To access Users and Passwords, choose Start ➢ Settings ➢ Control Panel, then double-click Users and Passwords.

Users and Passwords contains two tabs: Users and Advanced.

## Users Tab

The Users tab lists user accounts that have access to this computer. These accounts can be local or network user accounts. The Users tab has the following buttons:

**Add** If the computer is not part of a domain, lets you create a new user. If the computer is part of a domain, lets you add a domain user account to the list of users that can use the local computer.

**Remove** Removes the selected user from the computer's user list. If you remove a local user in this fashion, the local user account is deleted. If you remove a domain user, the user is only removed from the list of users who can use the local computer; the user's domain user account is not affected.

**Properties** For local users, displays the selected user's properties on two tabs: General and Group Membership. You can use these tabs to both view and change the name, full name, description, and group membership properties. For domain users, displays and lets you change only group membership information.

**Set Password** Lets you change the password for the selected local user. You cannot change passwords for domain users.

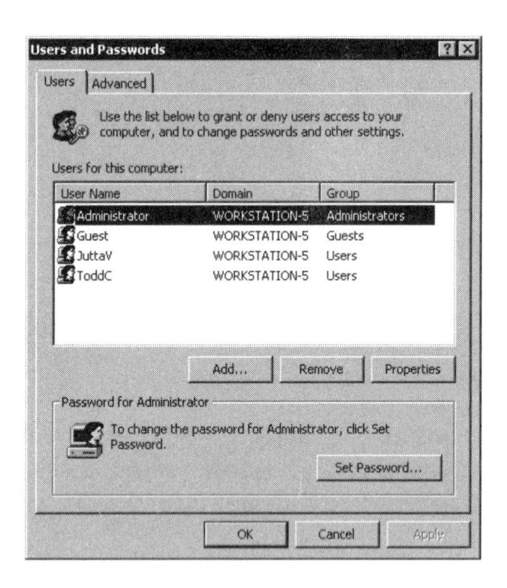


## Advanced Tab

The Advanced tab lets you perform or access additional user management functions.

The Certificate Management area of the tab has two buttons:

**New Certificate** Lets you obtain a new certificate using the Certificate Manager Import Wizard.

**TIP** A Windows 2000 Enterprise certification authority must exist in the domain to which the computer belongs for this button to function.

**Certificates** Lets you view, import, export, and remove certificates. For more information about certificates, see the Content Tab subheading under the main heading Internet Options.

The Advanced User Management area of the Advanced tab contains one button:

**Advanced** Opens Local Users and Groups (Microsoft Management Console), where you can create users and groups, change users' group membership, and perform other advanced user account management functions.

In the Secure Boot Settings area of the Advanced tab, you can specify whether users must press Ctrl+Alt+Del to be able to access the Windows 2000 logon screen. Microsoft recommends requiring users to press Ctrl+Alt+Del to preserve password security and prevent damage that might occur from Trojan horse programs.

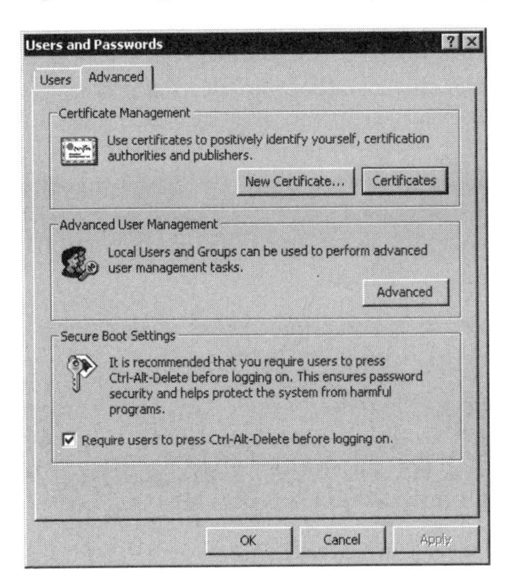


## Adding a User

If your computer is not part of a domain, you can use Users and Passwords to create a new user on the local machine.

To do so, follow these steps:

1. On the Users tab of Users and Passwords, click the Add button.
2. In the Add New User dialog box, enter the user's name in the User Name text box. This name should be unique. Common naming conventions include [First_Letter_of_First_Name][Lastname] and [First_Name][First_Letter_of_Last_Name].
3. You can optionally enter the user's full name in the Full Name text box, and a description in the Description text box; however, the latter two are not required.

4. Click Next and enter a password in the Password text box, then enter the password again in the Confirm Password text box. Click Next to continue.
5. Select one of the three user type options:

   **Standard User** This is the default selection. This type of user is automatically added to the Power Users group. The user can install applications and change computer settings, but cannot read other users' files.

   **Restricted User** This type of user is automatically added to the Users group. The user can use the computer and save files, but cannot install applications or change the computer's settings.

   **Other** Lets you choose from several different groups to which to add the user. Groups include Administrators, Backup Operators, Guests, Power Users, Replicator, and Users. Each group has specific permissions and rights assigned. For more information on these groups, consult the Windows 2000 Help system.

6. Make your selection and click Finish. The user is now added to the list of users for the computer.

If your computer is part of a domain, you can give domain users the ability to access the local computer by adding them to the list of users for this computer and adding them to a local group. They will use their domain user account password to access the computer.

To add a domain user to the local computer's user list, follow these steps:

1. On the Users tab of Users and Passwords, click Add to open the Add New User Wizard.
2. Enter the username of a user in the domain and enter the domain, or use the Browse button to browse to a user in the domain or entire directory. Click Next when you've entered the information.

3. Select the level of access you want to give the user. Standard User adds the user to the Power Users group, Restricted User adds the user to the Users group, and Other lets you specify the group to which you want to add the user, such as Administrators. Click Finish.

After you add a domain user, the user is added to the list of users for this computer. The icon is a head with a globe, indicating that the user is a domain user, rather than a local user. You'll also see that the Set Password button is not available because you can't change passwords for domain users through Users and Passwords.

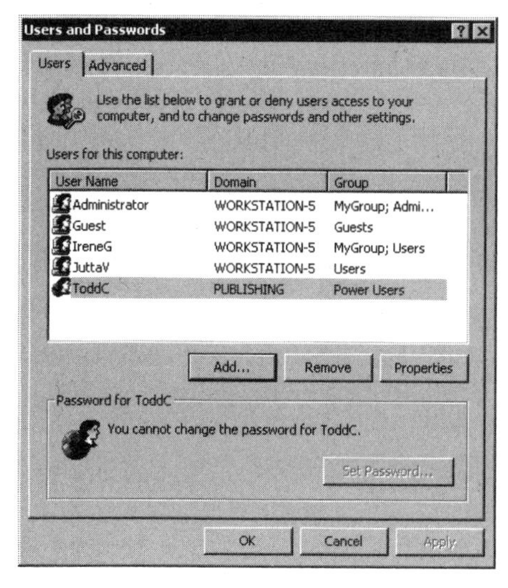


**See Also** Computer Management, Internet Options, Local Users and Groups

# Utility Manager

Utility Manager Program used to manage the Windows 2000 Magnifier, Narrator, and On-Screen Keyboard Accessibility options. Choose Start ➢ Programs ➢ Accessories ➢ Accessibility ➢ Utility Manager to start the Utility Manager.

**TIP** You must have administrative privileges to run Utility Manager and to configure utility options.

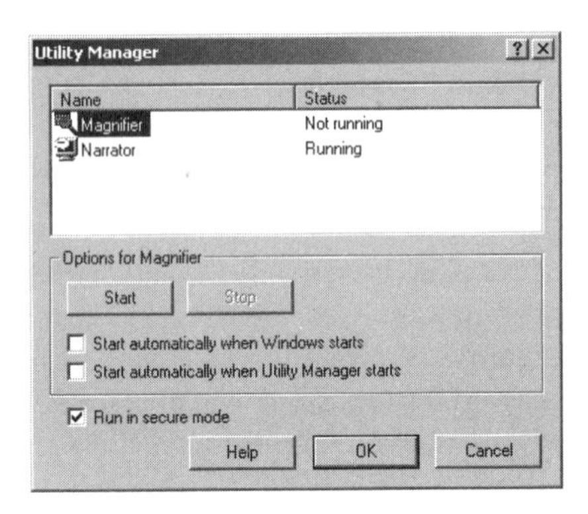


In the Utility Manager list box, all of the Accessibility utilities currently installed in Utility Manager are listed. Narrator and Magnifier are installed automatically. The on-screen keyboard can be added by a user with administrative privileges through the on-screen keyboard's File menu. In the list box, you can see the utilities' name and status. The status column entry will be Running, Not Running, or Not Responding. The Narrator utility is set up by default to run automatically when you open Utility Manager. If you wish, you can sort the list by name or status by clicking the respective column header.

To start a utility, select it in the list and click Start. To stop a utility, select it in the list and click Stop. To start a utility automatically when Windows starts or when Utility Manager starts, select the utility and place a check mark in the appropriate check box. To run Accessibilty options in secure mode, check the option Run In Secure Mode. This setting applies to all utilities added to the Utility Manager.

**TIP** Starting utilities automatically is helpful for users with special needs because they don't have to start the utilities manually.

**See Also** Accessibility Wizard, Accessibility, Magnifier, Narrator, On-Screen Keyboard, Accessibility Options

## Virtual Memory

**See** System

# Volume Control

Lets you control the balance of sound coming from your speakers , as well as control the volume and bass and treble settings of sounds you record and play back through any audio device or multimedia application.

Choose Start ➢ Programs ➢ Accessories ➢ Entertainment ➢ Volume Control to open the Volume Control dialog box.

**TIP** Alternatively, you can double-click the Sound icon in the status area of the taskbar to open the Volume Control dialog box, or you can click Volume under any device on the Audio Devices tab of Sound Recorder's Audio Properties, or the Audio tab of Control Panel's Sounds and Multimedia.

In the Volume Control dialog box, a separate volume control slider, balance slider, and Mute check box is available for each available audio device, and you can change settings independently.

Use the sliders under Volume Control to affect all devices, and click the Mute All check box to mute all devices.

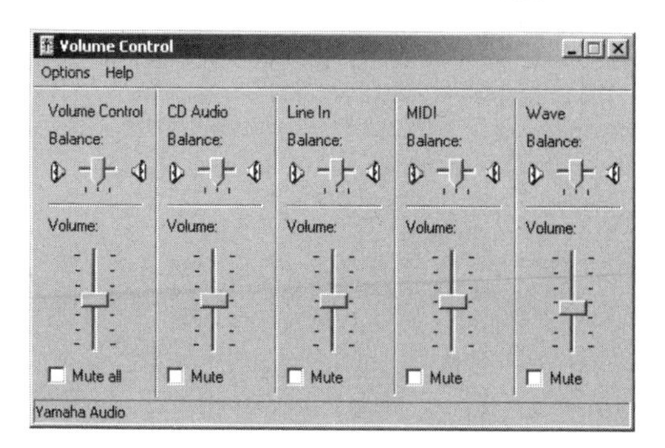


## Options Menu

The Options menu has two choices: Properties and Advanced Controls.

**Properties** Displays the Properties dialog box. Here you can choose the Mixer Device for which you want to change settings (if more than one is installed in the computer), and whether you want to be able to adjust settings for Playback, Recording, or other devices. The default setting is Playback, which means that the corresponding volume controls appear in the Volume Control dialog box. If you change the setting to Recording and click OK, Windows displays the Recording Control dialog box instead.

In the bottom portion of the Properties dialog box, you can select the devices for which you want to display volume controls. The choices change according to your selection under Adjust Volume For.

**Advanced Controls** Lets you configure bass and treble settings. When you choose Advanced Controls from the Options menu, the Advanced button becomes available on the Volume Control dialog box. Click Advanced to open the Advanced Controls for Volume Control dialog box. Adjust bass and treble settings by moving the sliders between Low and High.

Additionally, you may be able to adjust other hardware-related controls in the Advanced Controls dialog box.

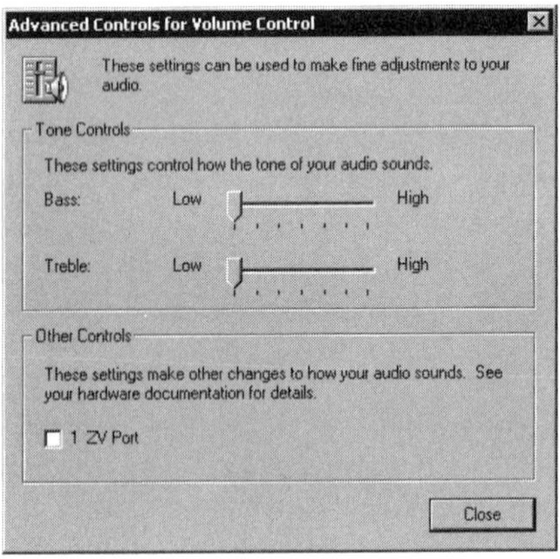

Advanced Controls for Volume Control
These settings can be used to make fine adjustments to your audio.
Tone Controls
These settings control how the tone of your audio sounds.
Bass: Low High
Treble: Low High
Other Controls
These settings make other changes to how your audio sounds. See your hardware documentation for details.
1 ZV Port
Close

**See Also** Sound Recorder, Sounds and Multimedia

# Web Sharing

Tab that lets you share folders on a Web site in the network. Requires that Internet Information Services (IIS) has been installed and that a Web site has been created. A defualt Web Site is created automatically when IIS is installed. To access Web Sharing, right-click a folder or disk in Windows Explorer on a Windows 2000 Server computer and choose Properties, then select the Web Sharing tab. Here you can select the appropriate Web site from the Share On drop-down list and indicate whether you want to share the folder or disk.

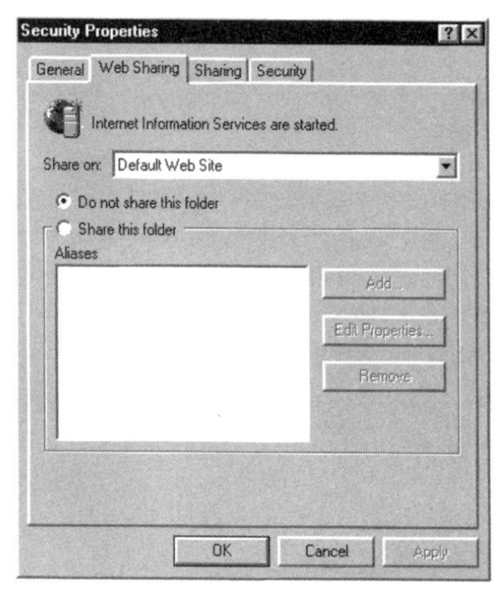


To share the folder or disk, click Share This Folder, which opens the Edit Alias dialog box. Here you need to specify the name for the alias to be used on the Web site, and configure access permissions—Read, Write, Script Source Access, and Directory Browsing—and application permissions—None, Scripts, and Execute (Includes Scripts). Click OK to share the folder or disk.

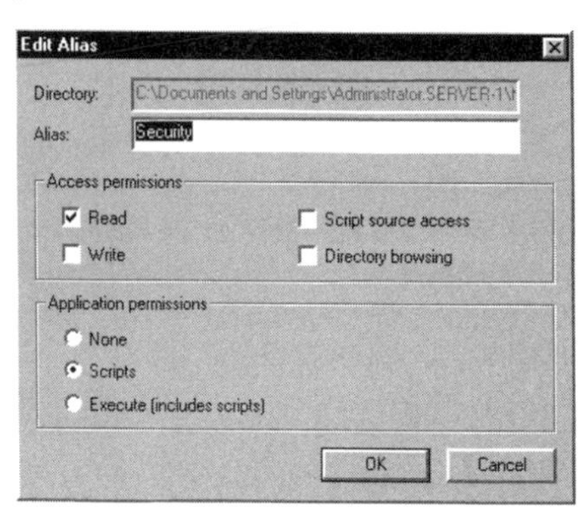

After you create the alias, it appears in the Aliases list box on the Web Sharing tab. To create an additional alias for the folder or disk, click Add and complete the information in the Edit Alias dialog box.

To edit an alias, select it in the list and click Edit Properties; to remove an alias, select it in the list and click Remove.

**See Also** Sharing

# What's This

What's This? Lets you access context-sensitive help. What's This is usually available in dialog boxes. To access What's This, right-click an item in a dialog box. If available, the What's This selection pops up. Click it to read help information about the item.

In some dialog boxes, you can also access the What's This information by selecting the question mark icon in the top-right corner of the dialog box and then placing the cursor (which now has a question mark attached to it) over an item and clicking it.

**See Also** Help

# Windows Explorer

**See** Explorer

# Windows Components

By default, many Windows components are installed on Windows 2000 Professional and Server computers. However, many other components are also available to suit your environment's specific needs. Also, the components available and installed by default are not identical for Windows 2000 Server and Professional.

Examples of Windows Components installed by default include WordPad, Calculator, Hyper Terminal, Phone Dialer,

Media Player, Volume Control, Indexing Service, Internet Information Services (IIS), DNS, DHCP, Microsoft Script Debugger, and so on. Additional Windows Components that are available include Certificate Services, Message Queuing Services, Remote Storage, Terminal Services, QoS Admission Control Services, WINS, and so on.

To add Windows components not installed by default, use Add/Remove Programs (found in Control Panel). For information about each of the available components, use the Windows 2000 Help system.

**See Also** Add/Remove Programs, Control Panel, Help

# Windows Media Player

Windows Media Player

Lets you play audio, video, and mixed-media files in a variety of different formats. For example, you can view video clips of a movie, listen to radio broadcasts (over the Internet), or enjoy a music video. Supports both streaming and non-streaming media files. When you play a streaming media file, playback begins before the entire file is downloaded. Streaming files are received and played using a continuous process of downloading portions of the file, storing those portions in memory, and then playing them back while more of the file is downloaded and stored in memory. This allows users to receive live media content, such as newscasts or live concerts.

Supported media file formats include audio files, such as Wave (.WAV) and Sound (.SND) files, MIDI files (.MID, .MIDI, and .RMI), MP3 files (.MP3, and .M3U), Microsoft streaming media files (.ASF and .ASX), MPEG files (such as .M1V, .MP2, and .MPA), Quick Time files (.MOV and .QT), and Video files (.AVI).

To access Windows Media Player, choose Start ➢ Programs ➢ Accessories ➢ Entertainment ➢ Windows Media Player.

## Windows Media Player Window

The Windows Media Player window consists of several components, which will vary depending on the view you have selected and the type of file you are playing. Components can include the following:

**Menus** Let you use and configure Windows Media Player.

**Navigation Bar** Contains Forward and Back buttons to move through previously played media files. Also contains the Radio, Music, and Media Guide buttons, which let you access different areas of WindowsMedia.com. Radio takes you to the portion of the Web site where you can listen to radio stations that broadcast via the Internet; Music takes you to the portion where you can access music files; and Media Guide takes you to the WindowsMedia.com main page, where you can access a variety of media files as well as other media-related information.

**Video Area** Displays the video content of a playing video media file.

**Captioning Area** Displays closed captioning. Not all media files include closed captioning. You must also choose View ➢ Captions for this function to work.

**Seek Bar** Slider that displays the progress of a playing media file. You can move the slider to skip to a different place in the media file.

**Controls** Lets you issue commands that affect play by clicking the appropriate control. Controls include play, pause, stop, skip forward, skip backward, rewind, fast forward, preview, mute, and volume control.

**Go To Bar** Lets you go to a specific marker in a media file, if markers exist. Think of markers as similar to tracks on a CD.

**Display Area** Displays information about the media file, such as show title, clip title, author, and copyright.

**Status Line** Displays information about the current status of Windows Media Player, such as playing, buffering, connecting, and paused. Also displays information about reception quality, and total and elapsed playing time, as well as closed captioning and sound icons.

## Windows Media Player Menus

Windows Media Player menus contain options that enable you to use and configure Windows Media Player.

### *File Menu*

The File menu contains the following options:

**Open** Lets you open (start playing) a media file.

**Close** Closes the currently open media file.

**Save As** Lets you save the currently open media file under a different name.

**Properties** Lets you access the currently open media file's properties.

**More Information** Provides additional information about the currently open media file, if available.

**Exit** Closes Windows Media Player.

### *View Menu*

The View menu contains these options:

**Standard** Displays the standard Windows Media Player window, including the display area and status line.

**Compact** Displays all Windows Media Player window components except the display area.

**Minimal** Displays only the menus, video area, and controls components of the Windows Media Player window.

**Full Screen** Displays the currently playing media file full screen. Press Alt+Enter to return to normal viewing size.

**Zoom** Lets you change the video area size to 50%, 100%, or 200%.

**Statistics** Provides statistical information about the last played media file. The type of information you'll see depends on the type of file played and whether it was played locally or over a network connection.

**Settings** Available only when you are playing Windows Media content. Lets you configure Windows Media source filter properties, such as buffering options and playback protocol settings. Also lets you configure Microsoft MPEG-4 Video Decompressor options, such as picture quality, brightness, contrast, saturation, and hue.

**Captions** Toggles the display of closed captioning.

**Always on Top** When selected, always displays Windows Media Player on top of other windows.

**Options** Opens the Options dialog box, where you can configure Windows Media Player settings for items such as playback, player, custom views, file formats, and other advanced options.

### *Play Menu*

The Play menu contains options that let you control the playback of media files. The options include:

**Play/Pause** Toggles the selection from playing the media file to pausing play.

**Stop** Stops playing the currently open media file.

**Skip Back** Returns to the beginning of the current clip in a show.

**Skip Forward** Starts playback of the next clip in a show.

**Rewind** Starts rewinding the current clip in a show. Not available with streaming media files.

**Fast Forward** Starts moving forward through the current clip in a show. Not available with streaming media files.

**Preview** Plays a small portion of all clips in a show.

**Go To** Moves directly to a marker in the currently open media file.

**Language** Lets you make a language selection from a submenu, if available.

**Volume** Has a submenu from which you can adjust the volume by selecting up, down, or mute.

### *Favorites Menu*

The Favorites menu lets you add and organize Web sites where you can access media files. Links you add to favorites appear as options on the Favorites menu. Many predefined links are already included in Windows Media Player. The Favorites menu contains these options:

**Add to Favorites** Lets you add new links to your list of favorite links.

**Organize Favorites** Lets you organize your favorite links into folders.

**TIP** For more information on how to use favorites, see the heading Internet Explorer.

### *Go Menu*

The Go menu contains these options:

**Back** Lets you open the previously open media file.

**Forward** Lets you open the media file that was open before using the Back option.

**Media Guide** Opens Internet Explorer and, if you're connected to the Internet, takes you to WindowsMedia.com (on Microsoft's Web site), where you can access a variety of media files as well as links and information about media files.

**Music** Opens Internet Explorer and, if you're connected to the Internet, takes you to the portion of WindowsMedia.com where you can access music media files.

**Radio** Opens Internet Explorer and, if you're connected to the Internet, takes you to the portion of WindowsMedia.com where you can access radio stations that broadcast on the Internet.

**Windows Media Player Home Page** Opens Internet Explorer and, if you're connected to the Internet, takes you to Microsoft's Windows Media Player home page.

### *Help Menu*

The Help menu contains these options:

**Help Topics** Opens the Help system to Windows Media Player topics.

**Check for Player Upgrade** Checks Microsoft's Web site for an updated version of Windows Media Player.

**About Windows Media Player** Displays information about Windows Media Player, such as version and copyright information.

# Windows Report Tool

Windows Report Tool

Lets you create a problem report, including a description of the problem and a snapshot of system settings and system and program files. When troubleshooting a problem, you can give this information to technical support personnel.

To access the Windows Report Tool, choose Start ➢ Settings ➢ Control Panel, double-click Administrative Tools, double-click Computer Management, expand System Tools, and select System Information. Then choose Tools ➢ Windows ➢ Windows Report Tool.

## Windows Report Tool Window

The Windows Report Tool window consists of menus, a link to user information, a description area, a link for selecting system files to be included in the report and the Next and Cancel buttons.

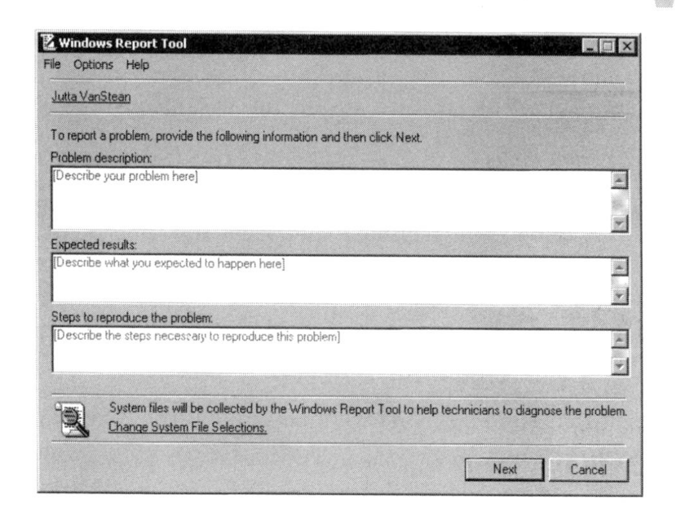


### *File Menu*

The File menu contains these options:

**New** Opens a new report window.

**Open** Lets you open an existing report.

**Save** Lets you save a report.

**Save As** Lets you save a report under a different name or a new report for the first time.

**Print** Collects system information and then lets you print a report.

**History** Displays the history of submitted reports.

### *Options Menu*

The Options menu contains these options:

**Collected Information** Collects system information and lets you decide which files and information to include in this report.

**User Information** Opens the User Information dialog box. Here you can specify user information for the report, such as username, e-mail address, company, postal address, and phone and fax numbers. Also lets you specify that you want to include user information in submitted reports, and lets you configure network settings. Alternatively, on the Windows Report Tool dialog box, you can click the link that shows the Windows 2000 registered user name to access the User Information dialog box. The Windows 2000 registered user name is the name you specified during the Windows 2000 installation as the registered user of the software.

**Auto Save on Submit** When selected, automatically saves the report on submission.

## Creating and Submitting a Report

To create and submit a Windows report, follow these steps:

1. Start Computer Management from Control Panel, select System Information, and start the Windows Report Tool by choosing Tools ➢ Windows ➢ Windows Report Tool.
2. Choose Options ➢ User Information and enter information about yourself. Select the option Include User Information in Submitted Report if you want this information included in the report. Make any necessary choices regarding your network proxy settings. Click OK.
3. In the Problem Description, Expected Results, and Steps to Reproduce the Problem fields respectively, enter descriptive information about the problem, what happens when the problem occurs, and steps for reproducing the problem.
4. If you want to include or exclude specific files from the report, click the Change System File Selections link and make your selections in the list box. To add files, click Add. To select all files, click Select All. When you've finished, click OK.
5. Click Next and enter a filename for the report. Then, click Save to save the report to a file that you can later send to a support technician via e-mail. The Report Tool collects system information and creates the report information file. This process can take some time.

6. When the file is created, you're returned to the Windows Report Tool, where you can create a new report or close the tool. To close the tool, click Cancel or choose File ➢ Exit.

# Windows Update

Connects you to Microsoft's Windows Update home page. Here you can download Windows product updates and obtain additional support information on how to use the Windows Update site. Click the appropriate links to find the information you're looking for, such as critical updates, recommended updates, top picks, device drivers, additional Windows features, and help on using the site.

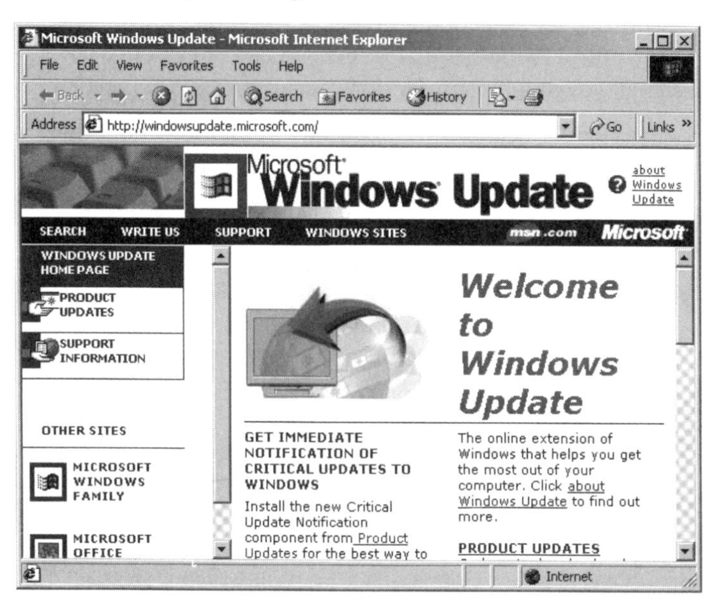

**TIP** Other ways to access Windows Update include clicking the link in Control Panel, opening Add/Remove Programs in Control Panel, clicking Add New Programs and clicking Windows Update, or choosing Tools ➢ Windows Update in Internet Explorer.

**See Also** Add/Remove Programs

# WMI Control

Windows Management Instrumentation MMC console snap-in that lets you manage settings and configuration for Windows Management Instrumentation (WMI), which is designed to let you manage your enterprise over the Internet or an intranet.

To access WMI Control, choose Start ➢ Settings ➢ Control Panel, double-click Administrative Tools, then double-click Computer Management. You'll find the WMI Control snap-in under Services and Applications.

## WMI Control Properties

To work with WMI Control properties, select WMI Control in the console tree and choose Action ➢ Properties. This opens the WMI Control Properties dialog box, which contains five tabs: General, Logging, Backup/Restore, Security, and Advanced.

**General** Lets you view general information about the computer to which you are currently connected (such as processor, operating system, operating system version, WMI version, and WMI location). Also lets you connect to the WMI Control service as a different user by clicking Change, deselecting Log on as Current User, specifying a username and password of a different user, and clicking OK.

**Logging** Lets you specify the logging level and size and location of log files.

**Backup/Restore** Lets you back up the WMI repository to a file, if a change to the repository has occurred since the last time a backup was performed. Also lets you restore from a backup and specify the automatic backup interval. To manually backup or restore the WMI repository, click the Back Up Now or Restore Now buttons, respectively, and follow the prompts.

**Security** Lets you configure permissions for any name space (directory) in the WMI directory structure.

**Advanced** Lets you specify advanced settings, such as the name space WMI Scripting should use by default.

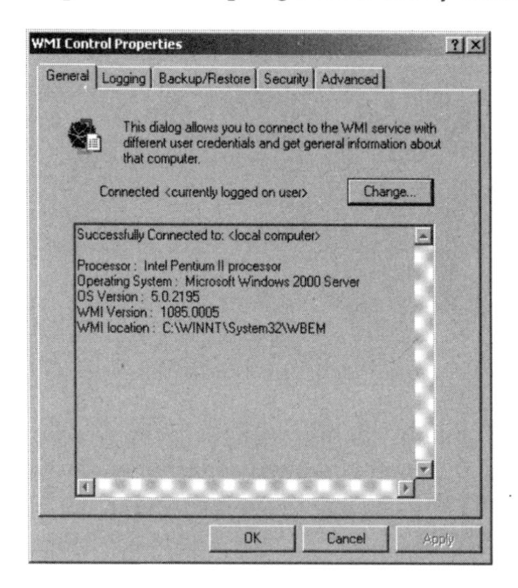

**TIP** For more information about WMI services, see the WMI software development kit (SDK), which is available on the Microsoft Developer Network (MSDN).

**See Also** Microsoft Management Console (MMC), Computer Management

# WordPad

WordPad Basic word processing program included with Windows 2000. Lets you create, edit, and view files using several different formats, including Word for Windows 6.0, Rich Text Format (RTF), text documents (ASCII), and Unicode text documents.

## WordPad Window

Choose Start ➢ Programs ➢ Accessories ➢ WordPad to open WordPad. The WordPad window consists of a menu bar, toolbar, Format bar, ruler, text area, and status bar.

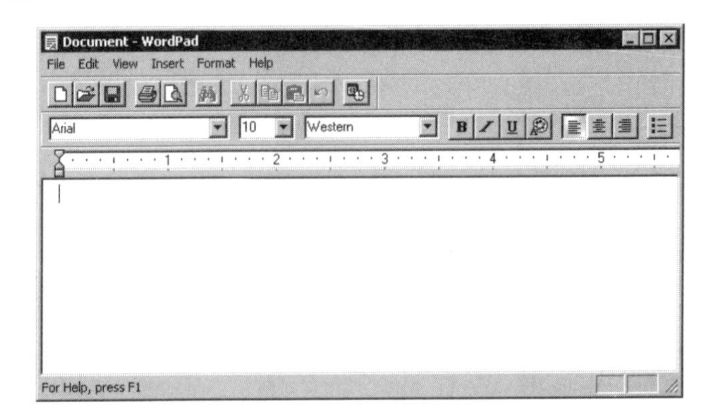


## WordPad Menus

The WordPad menus contain many options you use to work with documents. You'll find many of these options are also used with most other Windows programs.

### *File Menu*

The File menu contains the following options:

**New** Creates a new document.

**Open** Opens an existing document.

**Save** Saves the currently active document.

**Save As** Lets you save the currently active document using a different name.

**Print** Opens the Print dialog box, which lets you print the currently active document. Here, you can specify the printer to use, the pages to print, the number of copies to print, whether you want to collate the print job, and whether you want to print to a file.

**Print Preview** Displays a preview of how the currently active document would look if printed using the current print settings.

**Page Setup** Opens the Page Setup dialog box, where you can choose settings for items such as paper size and source,

orientation, and margins. You can also choose the printer to use and configure printer settings.

**Send** Sends the currently active document via e-mail.

**Exit** Closes WordPad and asks you to save unsaved documents.

### *Edit Menu*

The Edit menu contains these options:

**Undo** Lets you reverse the last action.

**Cut** Lets you cut a selected portion of the document from the document and place it on the Windows 2000 Clipboard.

**Copy** Lets you copy a selected portion of the document and copy it to the Windows 2000 Clipboard.

**Paste** Pastes the contents of the Windows 2000 Clipboard into the document at the insertion point.

**Paste Special** Provides you with paste options before you paste Clipboard contents, such as pasting the Clipboard contents using different formats.

**Clear** Erases the currently selected text.

**Select All** Selects the text of the entire document.

**Find** Lets you find text in the document.

**Find Next** Lets you find the next match for your search defined with Find.

**Replace** Lets you replace text you find with different text.

**Links** Lets you edit linked objects, including updating the object from the original source, opening or changing the source, or breaking the link.

**Object Properties** Opens the Object Properties dialog box for the currently selected object.

**Object** Activates a linked or embedded object.

**TIP** The title of the Object option may change to better reflect the type of object depending on the type of object you have selected. For example, if the selected object is a bitmap, this option reads Bitmap Image Object.

### *View Menu*

The View menu contains the following options:

**Toolbar** Toggles the display of the toolbar.

**Format Bar** Toggles the display of the Format bar.

**Ruler** Toggles the display of the ruler.

**Status Bar** Toggles the display of the status bar.

**Options** Opens the Options dialog box, where you can configure settings to include the units of measurements to use (Inches, Points, Centimeters, or Picas), and configure word wrap and toolbar options for each supported document format (Text, Rich Text, Word, Write, and Embedded). Word wrap options include No Wrap, Wrap to Window, and Wrap to Ruler. Toolbars you can display include Toolbar, Format Bar, Ruler, and Status Bar.

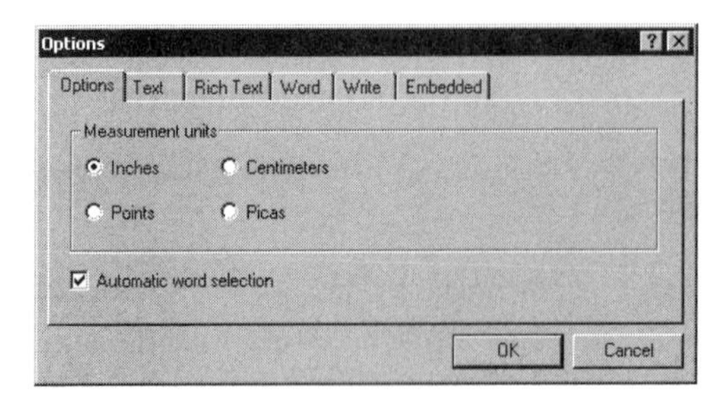


### *Insert Menu*

The Insert menu contains the following options:

**Date and Time** Lets you insert the current date and time in one of several available formats.

**Object** Lets you create and insert objects (such as images, media clips, and wave sounds, to name just a few) into the currently active document.

### *Format Menu*

The Format menu contains the following options:

**Font** Lets you choose a font, font style, size, effect, and script for your entire document or selected portions of the document.

**Bullet Style** Lets you create bulleted lists in your document.

**Paragraph** Lets you specify settings for the current paragraph, such as indentation and alignment.

**Tabs** Lets you specify tab stop positions.

## WordPad Toolbars

WordPad has two toolbars: the Standard toolbar and the Format bar.

### *Standard Toolbar*

The Standard toolbar contains these buttons:

 **New** Creates a new document.

 **Open** Opens an existing document.

 **Save** Saves the currently active document.

 **Print** Prints the currently active document.

 **Print Preview** Lets you preview the currently active document before printing it.

 **Find** Lets you search the active document for specific text.

 **Cut** Cuts the selected portion of the document and places it on the Clipboard.

**Copy** Copies the selected portion of the document and places it on the Clipboard.

**Paste** Pastes the contents of the Clipboard into the currently active document at the insertion point.

**Undo** Reverses the last action.

**Date/Time** Lets you insert the current date and time into the currently active document. You can choose from several date/time formats.

### *Format Bar*

The Format bar contains these buttons:

**Font** Lets you select the font for either the entire document or a selected portion of the document from a drop-down list. The displayed font is the current font.

**Font Size** Lets you select the size for the selected font from a drop-down list. The displayed size is the current size.

**Font Script** Lets you select the font script for the entire document or a selected portion of the document. The displayed font script is the current font script.

**Bold** Toggles bold on and off for the selection.

**Italic** Toggles italic on and off for the selection.

**Underline** Toggles underline on and off for the selection.

**Color** Lets you select a color from a drop-down list to apply to the selection.

**Align Left** Left-justifies the paragraph.

**Center** Centers the paragraph.

 **Align Right** Right-justifies the paragraph.

 **Bullets** Inserts a bullet on the current line. Lets you create bulleted lists.

## Ruler

The ruler lets you see where you are in the current line. Measurements used on the ruler depend on your selection in the dialog box that opens after you select View ➢ Options. You can also set tab stops on the ruler by clicking the desired position in the ruler. Slide the ruler markers to the left of the ruler to adjust indentation.

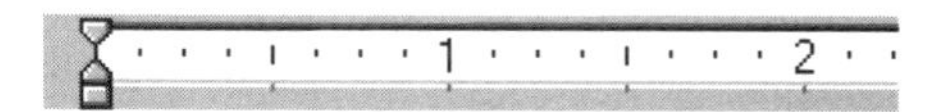


## Creating a Document in WordPad

You can create documents in WordPad in several ways:

To create a new document, follow these steps:

1. Place the cursor in the text area and type your text.
2. Use the menus, Standard toolbar, and Format bar buttons to format your text and adjust settings.
3. Choose File ➢ Save to save your document.

To create a document by pasting the contents of the Windows Clipboard, perform the following steps:

1. In another application, or in another WordPad document, select text or other document contents and choose Edit ➢ Cut.
2. Switch to WordPad (or open it if it's not yet open), place the cursor in the text area where you want to insert the contents of the Clipboard, and click the Paste icon on the toolbar.
3. Add other text and format your document as desired.
4. Click Save to save your document.

To create a document by inserting an object, perform the following steps:

1. Place the cursor where you want to insert the object.
2. Choose Insert ➢ Object.
3. Select Create New and choose an object type or select Create from File and enter or browse to the path to the file.
4. Click OK.
5. Add any other text and format your document as desired.
6. Choose File ➢ Save to save your document.

**See Also** Notepad

# Index

**Note to Reader**: In this index, **boldfaced** page numbers refer to primary discussions of the topic; *italics* page numbers refer to figures.

## Symbols & Numbers



## A

## B

## C

# D

## E

## F

## G

## H

## J



## K



## L

# M

## N

## O

## P

## Q



## R

## S

## T

## U

## V

## W

## Y



## Z